WHAT'S GOING ON IN THERE?

BANTAM BOOKS

New York Toronto London
Sydney Auckland

WHAT'S GOING ON IN THERE?

How the Brain and Mind Develop in the First Five Years of Life

LISE ELIOT, PH.D.

WHAT'S GOING ON IN THERE?

A Bantam Book/September 1999

Book design by Laurie Jewell
Illustrations on pp. 13, 16, 20, 124, 148, 160, 175, 199,
201, 231, 233, and 266 by Deborah Rubenstein.

Library of Congress Cataloging-in-Publication Data
Eliot, Lise.
What's going on in there? : how the brain and mind develop
in the first five years of life/ Lise Eliot.
p.   cm.
ISBN 0-553-10274-5
1. Developmental neurophysiology Popular works.
2. Developmental psychobiology Popular works. I. Title.
QP356.25.E   1999
612.8′2′083—dc21
99-35423
CIP

Published simultaneously in the United States and Canada

Bantam Books are published by Bantam Books, a division of Random House, Inc. Its trademark, consisting of the words "Bantam Books" and the portrayal of a rooster, is Registered in U.S. Patent and Trademark Office and in other countries. Marca Registrada. Bantam Books, 1540 Broadway, New York, New York 10036.

PRINTED IN THE UNITED STATES OF AMERICA

BVG 10 9 8 7 6 5 4 3 2 1

Contents

ACKNOWLEDGMENTS

This book was uniquely inspired by my children: Julia, whose newborn brain presented the first mystery; Samuel, whose gestation, birth, and infancy raised (and answered) some of the most pertinent questions; and Tobias, born in May 1999, who will hopefully benefit from all the revelations inside. I have always been fascinated by the brain, but there is nothing like watching a young child's steadily expanding mind to bring its evolution to vivid life. Writing this book throughout my own experiences of pregnancy, childbirth, and rearing young children has felt complete in every way—merging both the scientific and the maternal halves of my life—and allowed me to feel that I was contributing to their development even during the many hours spent researching and writing it. I dedicate this book to them.

I owe a special debt to Jenny Cox Blum, who critiqued most of the manuscript and always had interesting insights about motherhood to share. My agent, Kim Witherspoon, has been a terrific advocate. Linda Gross Kahn had the initial faith in me and was especially encouraging during the book's early stages. My editor, Ann Harris, served as an expert midwife, with her many wise queries and suggestions for tightening my prose. I could not have delivered it without her.

Several colleagues shared useful discussions, reviewed chapters, or answered my questions, whether in person or on-line. I am indebted to Jocelyne Bachevalier, Jack Crawford, Richard Davidson, Ruth Anne Eatock, Kathleen Gibson, Jeri Janowsky, Martha Johnson, Christine Leonard, Julie Menella, Sarah Pallas, Julie Pollock, and Esther Thelen for their help. Though not directly involved with this book, my mentors, Eric Kandel at Columbia University and Dan Johnston at Baylor College of Medicine, nurtured my earlier career, together instilling a strong critical sense while also giving me the confidence to pursue the larger picture.

Many friends and family members shared their observations about the hectic amazements of child-rearing. Though only a few are named, all contributed to the portrayals of the parents and children depicted in the book. My own parents, Caryl and Allen Eliot, have been especially supportive and I am deeply grateful for all their wisdom about raising children—imparted both directly and indirectly.

Finally, there is my husband and colleague, William Frost. We fell in love on opposite sides of a microscope but never dreamed our mutual interest in neural plasticity would turn out to be so personal. He was the one who first asked of Julia, "What's going on in there?"—planting the seed that grew into this book. I could not have cultivated it without his complete support—emotional, intellectual, and domestic—nor can I imagine a finer man with which to share the wonder, frustrations, and utter joy of raising babies.

WHAT'S GOING ON IN THERE?

Chapter 1

Nature or Nurture?
It's All in the Brain

Wouldn't you know it? Just as I get this beautiful, healthy neuron filled with dye and ready to image, Julia wakes up and starts crying. The experiment takes a long time to set up; I've been at it most of the day and need just ten more uninterrupted minutes. She has been so cooperative—sleeping like a baby (a nine-week-old, to be exact) in her cozy, blanket-lined computer box, safe and secure near my desk in the darkened laboratory. Finally, all the conditions are right: the microscopic neuron, vividly fluorescing down to its tiniest branches, an electrode carefully implanted to measure its electrical activity. I'm about to stimulate the cell's input pathway, to test whether it will "learn" from simulated sensory experience—when of course, Julia wakes up and wants to be fed.

What the heck. I pick her up, hike up my shirt, and start nursing, all the while twiddling dials with my free left hand. "Take off the holding current," I tell myself. "Set the extracellular voltage, configure the data acquisition, and then *go!*" The pulse goes out, the neuron fires a lovely train of electrical potentials, and the cell fills with calcium, color-coded, on the computer screen, with red for the most intense spots, yellow in between, and blue for the "cold" spots—distant branches that don't seem to have many pores for calcium to flow in. It's a great cell, an almost ideal experiment, until Julia suddenly pulls off my breast (curious, no doubt, about the flash of light on the computer screen) and, kicking her right foot into the delicate micromanipulator, knocks my perfect electrode right out of the perfect cell.

"*No!*" I wail, staring in disbelief at the computer screen. I watch as the neuron blows up into a big balloon, its membranes ripped open by the moving electrode. As it ruptures, the image on the computer screen flashes to red, then fades to orange, yellow, green, and blue as the dye dissipates. The cell is dead, a quick demise that is painful only for me.

Nobody ever said it would be easy being a mother and neuroscientist. But the juxtaposition does have its rewards at times. Here I am, trying to figure out how the neurons in a young rat's brain change with experience, and I have my own little experiment brewing right under my nose. Annoyed as I am by Julia's gymnastics, who can blame her baby brain, just trying to get some exercise for its budding motor pathways? Everything I'm trying to study in young rats is going on in her small head, a billion times over, every second of every day.

I spent ten years studying neural plasticity—the ways our brains change with experience—before Julia came along. I always knew I wanted to have children, but I had no idea how much my own research related to parenting until I actually became a mother myself. Like most new parents, I found myself suddenly fascinated by the nature/nurture issue, the degree to which Julia's future talents and weaknesses would be a product of our genes or her experience. The question is as old as humanity itself, but it is more than a mere academic debate. Whether one sides with "nature" or "nurture" makes a tremendous difference in the way we, both as parents and a society, raise our children.

Earlier in this century, the pendulum had swung fully to the "environmental" side. In a famous series of studies in the 1940s, psychiatrist René Spitz compared two groups of disadvantaged babies: one group was raised in what was then considered a perfectly adequate foundling home, and another group was comprised of infants whose mothers were in prison and who were being reared in a nearby nursery. Although both institutions were superficially similar—both were clean and provided the babies with adequate food, clothing, and medical care—they differed enormously in the amount of nurturing and stimulation each provided.

Babies in the prison nursery were fed, nursed, and cared for by their own mothers, who lavished enormous attention and affection on them. These children developed normally, in spite of the institutional setting and the fact that the number of hours of contact with their mothers was limited. Babies in the foundling home, by contrast, had very little stimulation; there was only one nurse for every eight infants, and except for brief feedings and diaper changes, each baby was kept isolated in his or her crib, its sides draped with sheets to prevent the spread of infection. With nothing to look at or play with and, worst of all, a bare minimum of human contact and affection, these babies suffered devastatingly. An enormous number didn't even survive to two years of age. Those who did were physically stunted, highly prone to infection, and severely retarded, both cognitively and emotionally. By three years of age, most couldn't even walk or talk, and in marked contrast to the exuberant nursery-reared children, they were strikingly withdrawn and apathetic.

Spitz's work went a long way toward changing adoption policies—eliminating the waiting periods that were at one time thought necessary to allow babies' "natural" personalities and intellectual talents to unfold. Early adoption is now universally recognized as the best option for orphans and unwanted babies, although the tragic fact is that babies in many parts of the world continue to wither in orphanages even worse than Spitz described.

Spitz showed that early nurturing and stimulation are essential to child development, and he was not alone in this view. At the time, the field of psychology was dominated by the theory of "behaviorism," which proposed that all our actions, from the simplest smile to the most sophisticated chess move, are learned through reward and punishment, trial-and-error interactions with other people and objects in the world. Babies, according to this view, are born as "blank slates," without predispositions, and infinitely malleable through parental feedback and tutoring. John Watson, the founder of modern behaviorism, even went so far as to claim:

> Give me a dozen healthy infants, well-formed, and my own specified world to bring them up in and I'll guarantee to take any one at random and train him to become any kind of specialist I might select—doctor, lawyer, artist, merchant-chief, and yes even beggar-man and thief, regardless of his talents, penchants, abilities, vocations, and race of his ancestors.

No doubt Watson overstated his case, but such emphasis on early environment eventually led to the establishment of important social programs like the welfare safety net and Head Start. If children are so greatly malleable, then the best way to ensure a great society is by improving the environment of its youngest members.

These days, things have swung to the opposite extreme. We are now fully entrenched in the Era of the Gene. Every day, molecular biologists get a little closer to pinpointing which stretch of chromosome is responsible for some dreaded disease or complex behavior—alcoholism, Alzheimer's disease, breast cancer, dyslexia, sexual orientation. The government-sponsored Human Genome Project has made us heady with the potential of "decoding" the blueprint for every individual, figuring out where each of our strengths and weaknesses lies, what troubles may lie ahead, and eventually, how to cure our genetic ills. These fast-paced discoveries are exciting, to be sure, but the renewed emphasis on genes also has its discomfiting side—the tendency, fostered by books such as *The Bell Curve* and *The Nurture Assumption*, to say that parents and society make little difference. A child's fate, according to this view, is largely determined by heredity, leaving little we can do to improve matters.

As a neuroscientist, it's hard to fully accept this position. Of course, genes are important, but anyone who has ever studied nerve cells can tell you how remarkably plastic they are. The brain itself is literally molded by experience: every sight, sound, and thought leaves an imprint on specific neural circuits, modifying the way future sights, sounds, and thoughts will be registered. Brain hardware is not fixed, but living, dynamic tissue that is constantly updating itself to meet the sensory, motor, emotional, and intellectual demands at hand.

My own fascination with neural plasticity was only magnified with newborn Julia in my arms. If ever there was a time for experience to mold her brain, this was it. Although we know from studies of adult learning that the brain remains malleable throughout life, it is massively more so in infancy. Brain surgeons can even remove an entire hemisphere from the cerebral cortex of a young child (which in rare instances is the only treatment for profound epilepsy), and he or she will suffer surprisingly little loss of physical function or intellectual capacity.

I found myself wondering about every interaction: What is this caress, this diaper change, this lullaby doing to Julia's brain? Which circuits are already turned on, and which are still wiring up? What happened, at six weeks, to make her suddenly start smiling, or at eighteen weeks, so that she could finally reach out and grasp her rattle? Can Julia see those computer designs I taped up in her box? Hear the neuron firing away through the audio monitor? Know that I am her mother? Are we, her enraptured parents, in any way responsible for these wiring events, or would they have happened without any particular nurturing on our part, unfolding, like a budding flower, along a programmed trajectory that requires nothing but the most basic food, water, and air?

In other words, I needed to know: What is going on inside that little head, and what difference can I, as a parent, make in her putting it all together?

This book is the result of my own odyssey of discovery—an attempt to chart, from the earliest moment of conception, the way a child's brain is assembled and the implications of this sequence for each of her emerging mental skills: sensation, movement, emotion, memory, language, and "intelligence." I wanted to go beyond the cursory remarks in many pregnancy and parenting tomes to the real data on brain development and the ways it can be influenced by environment and experience. The information here is detailed yet accessible to a reader without a scientific background.

Whether we realize it or not, almost every decision parents make boils down to a matter of our children's brain development: whether to have a glass of wine during pregnancy, whether to use drugs during childbirth, how long to breast-feed, how soon to return to work, whether to treat every ear infection, whether to enroll a child in nursery school, what kind of discipline to use, how much TV they should watch, and on and on. The reason we fret so about these decisions is because we know, at some level, that they may have lasting consequences for the way our children's minds will work. And the way their minds will work—the kind of emotional and intellectual lives they eventually grow into—is wholly a function of how their brains sculpt themselves.

My bias is thus that of a biologist: the conviction that we cannot understand children's minds until we understand the structure and physiology of their brains. But biology also offers another hope, a way of finally resolving the age-old nature/nurture debate. From the first cell division, brain development is a delicate dance between genes and environment, and it is only by understanding each of these subtle interactions that we can grasp, for each fascinating facet of the mind, the degree to which heredity and experience make us who we are.

Neuroscience has made tremendous strides over the last quarter century. Powerful techniques now allow us to visualize every part of the living brain in action, from the largest circuit down to the tiny gap between neurons, the synapse; to record electrical activity from single molecules in the brain; and

FIGURE I.I

One noninvasive method for measuring brain activity in children uses a net of some sixty scalp electrodes, which together give much more precise information about the location of electrical activity than traditional EEG methods. This cheerful three-month-old was a subject in a study of early language perception by Ghislaine Dehaene-Lambertz and Stanislas Dehaene.

Reproduced by permission of photographer Jack Liu.

to pluck out, from the enormous haystack of human DNA, single genes involved in early neural development, mental retardation, and senile dementia, to name just a few neurological phenomena. Babies, alas, are far too uncooperative for the most advanced brain-imaging techniques—they tend to squirm and fuss, cry, kick, or fall asleep at the most inopportune times. Nonetheless, researchers have devised other ingenious ways to probe their emerging sensory, emotional, and cognitive abilities. These often delightful experiments, together with our rapidly expanding knowledge about brain function and development, give us a far better understanding of "what's going on" in an infant's mind than ever before.

Babies, as we'll see, are not "blank slates" at birth. They come into the world with all kinds of mental skills and predispositions, abilities uniquely suited to the critical needs of early life. Their brains are small, to be sure, but they are not miniature versions of an adult's. The nervous system matures in a programmed sequence, from "tail" to head. By birth, the spinal cord and the brain stem—lower-brain structures that control all of our vital bodily func-

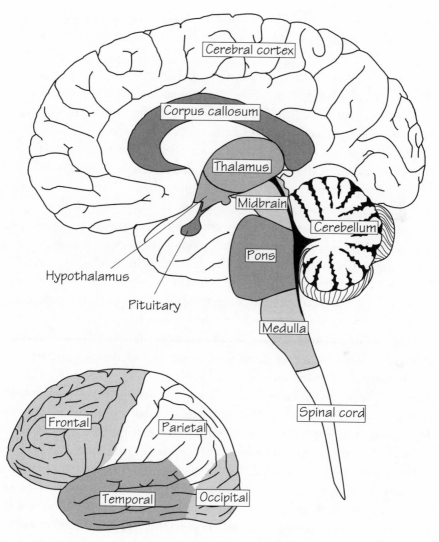

Lobes of the cerebral cortex

FIGURE 1.2

Major components of the central nervous system. The midbrain, pons, and medulla together constitute the brain stem. The spinal cord is shown considerably truncated.

tions—are almost fully developed and are largely responsible for meeting a newborn's essential needs: to survive, grow, and bond with caregivers. (See Figure 1.2.)

This sequence continues after birth, as higher-brain areas progressively take control of a baby's mental life. These areas include the cerebellum and basal ganglia, which are involved in movement; the limbic system (See Figure 12.1), which controls emotion and memory; and finally the cerebral cortex, the seat of all our willed behavior, conscious experience, and rational abilities. Of all parts of the brain, the cerebral cortex remains the most markedly unformed at birth. As the cortex gradually matures during the first months and years of life, a child grows steadily more capable and aware of her own existence.

This sequence of brain development is, by all accounts, genetically programmed. Why else would infants the world over progress through the same endearing milestones on virtually identical schedules? Whether carried as "papooses," in slings, or in high-tech infant seats, all healthy babies manage to walk, talk, and throw food in much the same way, at much the same age, give or take a few weeks. Even Julia, I had to admit, seemed to be developing right along the expected course, in spite of her unusual daytime environment and parents who thought they knew it all about neural plasticity.

But an obvious question is why babies are born with such primitive brains. Why, if development is largely preordained, do they not begin life with full vision and hearing, able to walk, talk, and do long division? According to one line of reasoning, it is our upright posture that is to blame: a bipedal lifestyle sets certain limits on pelvic size, so women can squeeze out babies only with relatively small heads—that is, babies whose brains are only partially developed. There may be some truth to this argument, even though humans are not born any more helpless than many other mammalian species. Rats and cats, for instance, don't even open their eyes for several days after birth. We humans do indeed take longer to complete our cognitive development, but that is because we have more mental functions to add—we have further to go.

A better reason why we, and other intelligent species, are born with such poorly developed brains is so that we can learn. Babies' brains are learning machines. They build themselves, or adapt, to the environment at hand. Although the brain is often appropriately compared to a computer, this is one way in which they differ: The brain actually programs itself. Imagine that you bought a PC, but instead of loading any software, you just plugged it in and the computer did the rest: it assembled its own operating system, and built its own drivers for the CD-ROM, the sound system, the printer, the modem, and whatever other hardware it happened to be equipped with. A little later it decided a word-processing program would be useful, so it made one, in English, Spanish, German, Hebrew—whatever would allow it to best communicate with the outer world. Eventually, it needed to read and calculate, so it set up character-recognition and spreadsheet programs. Children's brains are like this, accessing neural circuits as they're needed, wiring them up and honing them to the task at hand—to walk, talk, read, forage for tubers, play the piano, and so on.

Such adaptability is a property of the brain from its very first emergence. While genes program the *sequence* of neural development, at every turn the *quality* of that development is shaped by environmental factors. In the earliest stages embryonic cells respond to a slight gradient in the concentration of particular molecules, which tell them to become head or tail, spinal cord or cerebellum. Later, it will be a certain pattern of electrical excitation that subtly alters some synapses in a child's cerebral cortex. These innumerable, intricate interactions take place inside the brain, at the molecular level. But because the brain is a chain of communicating cells, it is inescapably linked to the outside world. Every touch, movement, and emotion is translated into electrical and chemical activity that shifts the forward genetic momentum, subtly modifying the way a child's brain is wired together.

Developmental biologists use another analogy: a ball rolling down a steep mountainside. Genes act much like gravity, forcing the ball inevitably downward. But at many points choice or chance intervenes. When the ball runs into different elements in the environment—rocks or holes or trees—it gets diverted in a particular way. Each diversion makes the path more distinctive, but it also limits the possibilities for later encounters, because there's no going back up the mountain to try the other side.

To the extent that most healthy babies develop in similar ways, the underlying genetic programs are tolerant of a wide range of "normal" environments. This resilience should be comforting to those parents who are consumed with worry about properly positioning their babies' Stim-Mobiles or teaching their six-month-olds how to "read." At the same time, there can be little doubt that the quality of early experience does shape children's brain development in critical ways. Genes and environment are both important, but the fact is that we can do very little about our genes, and a great deal about the kind of environment we provide for our children.

In the following chapters, I explain how each important "system" of the brain develops, and the degree to which genes and environment are known to influence that system's formation. This book covers the period from conception until roughly five or six years of age, but it is not strictly chronological. Each chapter begins at the beginning—in the womb, for sensory and motor abilities, and at birth for all of the higher mental functions—in explaining how and why a child's various mental abilities emerge when they do.

Chapter 2 outlines the basic processes of brain development—how the remarkably complex human brain emerges from the mere fusion of egg and sperm and, in particular, how its many crucial circuits become "wired up" through the dual influence of genes and experience. The same biological principles hold for every sensory, motor, and higher system in the brain, so this chapter serves as a foundation for the rest of the book and is relevant from gestation throughout childhood.

Each of the chapters that follow is more narrowly focused. Chapter 3 is devoted to brain development in the womb and all the ways it can be affected by a pregnant woman's lifestyle and exposure to various environmental agents. Chapter 4 describes the effects, both positive and negative, of birth itself on a baby's brain. Chapters 5 through 10 focus on the development of each sensory system in roughly the order in which they mature—touch, balance, smell, taste, vision, and hearing—and include discussions of various related topics, such as why massage is so good for babies, how breast milk promotes brain development, and why congenital vision or hearing problems are dangerous to a child's sensory and cognitive growth. Chapter 11 explains how motor skills improve. Chapters 12 through 17 delve into the higher mental functions—how a child's emotional, memory, language, and other cognitive skills emerge and evolve through the interaction of programmed brain maturation and early experience.

Nowhere is the nature/nurture debate more heated than when it comes to sex differences in the brain. Readers who are interested in this topic will find it addressed in Chapters 5, 7, 9, 10, 12, 14, and 16. Also included is a discussion of how genes and environment, or hormones and socialization, interact to create such differences.

The brain is without doubt our most fascinating organ. Parents, educators, and society as a whole have tremendous power to shape the wrinkly universe inside each child's head, and, with it, the kind of person he or she will turn out to be. We owe it to our children to help them grow the best brains possible.

Chapter 2

The Basic Biology
of Brain Development

It's Thursday morning, and Jessica is barely conscious when she realizes her period is now five days late. Suddenly wide awake, she shakes her husband and blurts out, "Dave! I think we should do the test!" He too is instantly roused, the combination of fear, excitement, and her seismic shaking jolting him out of a pleasant dream. He knows she's talking about the home pregnancy test she's had stashed away in the medicine cabinet for several months. They hadn't dared use it earlier, when she was only a couple of days late. They didn't want to get too hopeful too soon.

Both hold their breath as the little blue line appears. They compare it to the sample result in the package insert. It's a little fainter but obviously a blue line. "Oh, yes! It's definitely positive. The negative result has no line at all." They hold the strip up to the sample once more, to be sure, and the meaning of it all slowly sinks in.

"We did it! We're going to have a baby!" Dave says, hugging Jessica. A new emotion floods over them. Then Jessica suddenly looks at him and says, "Oh wow! There's a whole little life inside me! I wonder what it's like right now?"

Even though home pregnancy tests now give us the news remarkably early, an amazing amount of development has already happened by the time most of us learn we're pregnant. Jessica and Dave think back: "Let's face it," she said, "we were pretty busy a couple of weeks ago. It can only have been that Saturday night, after Joe's party." He smiles and quickly figures, "That means our baby is nineteen days old."

Actually, their baby's age is determined not by the time of intercourse but the time of Jessica's ovulation. That was the moment, about two weeks after the start of her last menstrual period, when one of her ovaries released a ripened egg. Since the egg survives for only about twenty-four hours after its release, fertilization must have taken place during that one day. But sperm are capable of living up to four days inside a woman's reproductive tract, so even if Jessica ovulated a few days after the party, their evening's recreation may have been successful.

Nonetheless, conception is a likelier event on the actual day of ovulation, because Jessica's reproductive tract would have offered a much more hospitable environment—copious, runny mucus in which Dave's sperm could happily swim toward their target. Indeed, as Jessica and Dave were luxuriously sleeping in that following Sunday morning, a single one of the 500 million sperm Dave released around midnight beat all the others in the race to successfully penetrate Jessica's egg, just released from her left ovary. By 3:00 A.M. it had made it through her uterus, and by 7:00 it had swum all the way to the end of her left fallopian tube (a good choice!), where it met the egg, monstrous by comparison but still a mere one-tenth of a millimeter in diameter. Of the few dozen sperm that made it this far, only this single tiny titan managed to fight its way through the egg's sticky outer coat (the *corona radiata*), to dissolve a path, using its powerful enzymes, through the next layer, an entangled fortress of proteins known as the *zona pellucida*, and finally to slip inside the egg's thin lipid membrane. Once penetrated, the egg set up a fast electrochemical defense to prevent other sperm from also making it through, which would compromise its normal development. Finally, at precisely 10:18 A.M., came the true moment of fertilization: the nuclei of both egg and sperm fused, merging twenty-three chromosomes from Jessica and twenty-three from Dave, including his Y chromosome, to form a new individual—a boy!

Monday evening, as they were sitting down to dinner, their future son underwent his first cell division. By Thursday, four days after fertilization, the tiny embryo had divided five times and resembled a ripened blackberry—a clump of thirty-two round cells, altogether no larger than the initial egg, but about to begin the remarkable and fateful process of cellular differentiation: segregation into all the different tissue types of the body.

At this stage, the embryo is called a *blastocyst*, and experiments with mice have shown that any one of these thirty-two cells has the capability of forming an entire individual if it is removed and allowed to divide on its own. Nonetheless, if left intact (and if the entire blastocyst doesn't spontaneously split in two, producing identical twins), only three to five of these cells will actually become their son. These few cells, located well inside the blastocyst, will give rise to every cell of their baby's body, while all the rest, those on the outside, will become the placenta. The momentous decision about whether to become body or not is made entirely on the basis of chance—whatever position a given cell happens to land in. Rather than a cell's genetic information, it is its location that determines its fate. This is one of the earliest instances of how the environment profoundly affects development.

After this point, the blastocyst begins forming a cavity, the inner cells remaining in contact with just one arc of the sphere of outer supporting cells. All this takes place as the embryo travels along Jessica's fallopian tube toward her uterus. Near the end of the journey, the blastocyst "hatches" from the zona pellucida, exposing the outer layer of cells, which are now specialized for implanting in the wall of Jessica's uterus. (See Figure 2.1.)

The following Saturday evening (almost seven days after fertilization), just as she and Dave are heading out to the movies, the tiny embryo comes

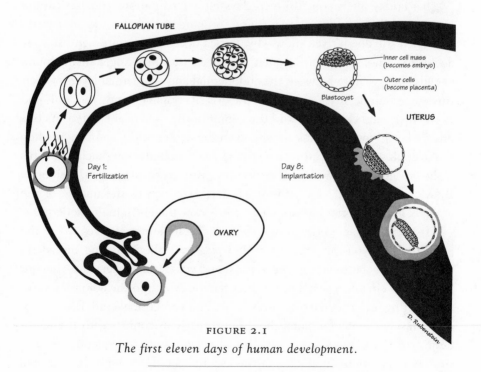

FIGURE 2.1
The first eleven days of human development.

in for its landing: a good spot, along the rear wall of Jessica's uterus, right along the midline of her body. Still less than one-fifth of a millimeter in diameter (less than one-hundredth of an inch), the embryo literally invades her uterine lining. It will take another two weeks before it is completely implanted and fully nourished by Jessica's blood supply. Until then, the embryo grows very little in size, but it nonetheless undergoes some remarkable developmental feats.

By Monday morning, the inner cell clump has flattened out into a disk and undergone its first differentiation into two tissue types. Smaller, cube-shaped cells form a bottom layer, the primary *endoderm*, while larger, columnar cells form a top layer, the *ectoderm*. Endoderm will give rise to most of the internal organs: the gut, lungs, liver, and various glands. Ectoderm will become the outer skin, sensory organs, and after a critical process known as *neurulation*, the entire brain and nervous system. But before neurulation can happen, the third type of primordial tissue must form: *mesoderm* (*meso* means "middle"), which will eventually evolve into all of the bones, muscles, and connective tissues of the body, including the circulatory system and the smooth muscles of the digestive tract.

It's Friday afternoon, thirteen days after fertilization, and Jessica and Dave are talking on the phone, trying to figure out what to do after work. Although she doesn't yet know why, Jessica doesn't feel quite right, so they decide to go home and have a quiet dinner. As they're eating, a small mound of cells emerges from between the endodermal and ectodermal layers of their tiny embryo. It begins at one end of the disk, its origin creating the "tail" end of the body, and extends toward the center of the now-oval embryo. As this middle layer grows, it forms a track down the center of the embryo, molding the overlying ectoderm into a long trench with mounds along each side. This is the *primitive streak*, and it is creating the entire vertical axis of the embryo. By Monday (sixteen days), the streak has extended to the middle of the embryo, and the inner layer producing it is now the emerging mesoderm.

It is the contact between mesoderm and ectoderm that gives rise to the primordial nervous system: the *neural plate*. As the emerging mesoderm threads its way between the endodermal and ectodermal layers, it is thought to release a chemical signal that flips a genetic switch in the adjoining ectoderm, fating it to become the baby's future brain and spinal cord. Ectodermal cells outside the neural plate, those not directly in contact with the mesoderm, are not exposed to this chemical trigger and consequently become skin, hair, and nonneural parts of the eye and ear. Thus, both the skin and the nervous system originate on the outside of the embryo, but the nervous system soon detaches and sinks beneath the surface of the embryo, away from the emerging skin.

Neurulation begins nineteen days after fertilization, the same Thursday morning that Jessica and Dave first learn that she's pregnant—so it is just as they're realizing that there actually will be a baby that his earliest brain tissue is beginning to form. Out of this primordial oval sheet will emerge their child's entire mental universe—all of his thoughts, feelings, actions, and dreams—and his parents-to-be are suddenly very curious about it.

"Our baby will be born in May," Jessica figures. "What a beautiful month!" And they begin to wonder about the person they have just created: Boy or girl? Dark or fair? Fragile or tough? Kind? Smart? Athletic? Musical? To varying degrees, each of these traits has already been determined by his genetic endowment, in the forty-six chromosomes that merged that Sunday morning. But genes alone will not mold this embryo into the person he will become. Before long, Dave and Jessica will also realize the great responsibility they've just assumed. "Nature" has already been set. The rest of the story is "nurture," and it's largely up to them.

How a Brain Is Sculpted

Superficially, embryonic brain development appears quite rapid. By the following Wednesday (twenty-five days), the neural plate has folded up to form a groove, and then fused along its top edges to form a tube running most of the length of the two-millimeter embryo. By twenty-six days, this neural tube will have closed, starting in the middle and finishing first in the head end at around twenty-four days postfertilization, and then at the tail end. (See Figure 2.2.) The closed tube is already enlarged at the top end, where the brain is emerging. The rest of the tube, gradually tapering down toward the tail, will become the spinal cord. The transformation from neural tube to spinal cord is relatively straightforward: the tube's walls thicken and then divide into four primary regions, a sensory and a motor area on both left and right sides. But the transformation of the top end of the neural tube is considerably more complicated. First, the top of the tube enlarges into three primary swellings: the forebrain, midbrain, and hindbrain, each separated by a sharp flex so that all together the entire nervous system looks like an uncomfortable worm, scrunched up in the rapidly growing head. (See Figure 2.3.) The

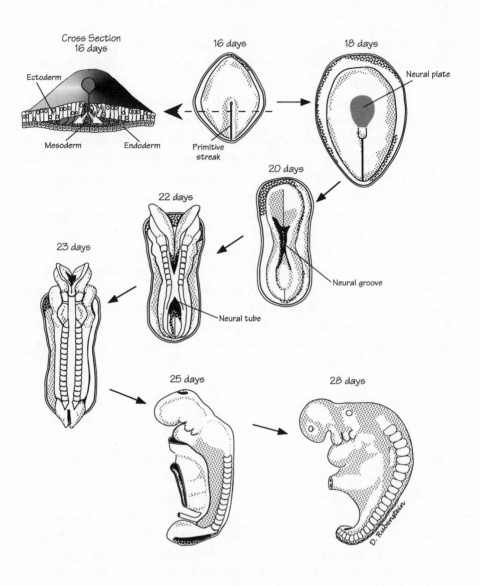

Cross Section
16 days

Ectoderm

Mesoderm   Endoderm

16 days

Primitive
streak

18 days

Neural plate

20 days

Neural groove

22 days

Neural tube

23 days

25 days

28 days

D. Rubenstein

FIGURE 2.2

Formation and closure of the neural tube. The first primordial nervous tissue forms about eighteen days after fertilization from the interaction of mesoderm and ectoderm. The neural plate transforms first into a neural groove, then a neural tube, whose ends close up by twenty-six days. Failure of the tube to close at any point results in a neural tube defect, as discussed in Chapter 3.

three brain swellings have fully formed by Sunday, four weeks after fertilization. By this time, the eyespots appear, the rudimentary heart has begun beating, and all four limb buds that will develop into the arms and legs are about to sprout. Jessica and Dave's little embryo is only three millimeters long (a mere tenth of an inch), and Jessica has begun feeling positively awful.

In the fifth week, as she begins wondering why she ever wanted to get pregnant in the first place, their baby's three brain swellings enlarge and further subdivide so that there are now five of them. The frontmost, or *telencephalon*, begins dividing along its midline to form distinct left and right hemispheres. By six weeks, the swellings have begun differentiating into all the major brain structures, creating the rudiments of the pons, medulla, cerebellum, thalamus, basal ganglia, limbic system, and cerebral cortex. Also by this point, the twelve *cranial nerves* that will transmit sensory and motor information between the brain and the eyes, ears, nose, face, mouth, and other body structures have made their first appearance, although they are not yet connected to the face and other target organs.

Seven weeks after fertilization, Jessica and Dave go in for her first obstetrician's appointment, and they learn that she is nine weeks pregnant. That's a surprise! The timing of prenatal development is always a little confusing because of the difference between "menstrual age"—the time elapsed since the first day of the woman's last menstrual period—and "fertilization age"—the time elapsed since the actual fusion of egg and sperm, which is within twenty-four hours of ovulation. Doctors and midwives have traditionally dated pregnancy from the first day of the last menstrual period, because it is the one date about which there is no uncertainty. Actually, it is now relatively easy to date ovulation, using either an over-the-counter hormone test or ultrasound imaging, but since most women get pregnant without this information, practitioners continue to assume that ovulation occurred two weeks after the onset of the last menstrual period. Since fetal development takes an average of thirty-eight weeks, pregnancy calculated in this way averages forty weeks from the date of that last period. Here, however, we are interested in development from the baby's perspective, so all ages referred to in this chapter are in terms of fertilization age—the thirty-eight-week time frame.

After eight weeks of development, the baby is about two inches long from head to heel and is no longer called an embryo; he is now properly referred to as a fetus. The division between embryonic and fetal periods is not as dramatic as it sounds. While all of the major organ systems are in place, they are far from fully formed and are only minimally functional. The division between

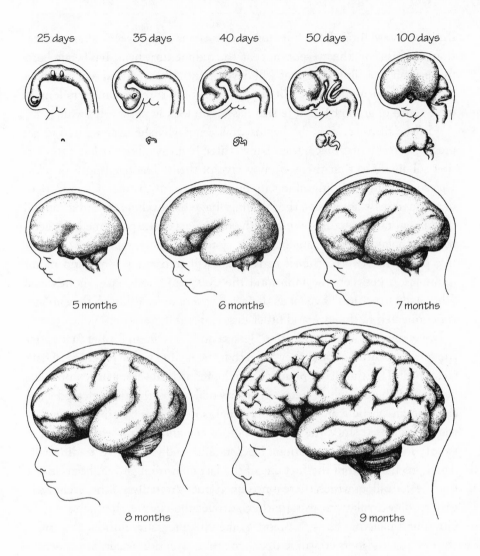

25 days 35 days 40 days 50 days 100 days

5 months 6 months 7 months

8 months 9 months

FIGURE 2.3

Prenatal growth of the brain. Drawings are enlarged to show detail between twenty-five and one hundred days postconception. Actual sizes (proportional to lower drawings) are shown in the second row.

Modified from W.M. Cowan, "The development of the brain," *Scientific American*, September 1979; by permission of Nelson Prentiss.

embryonic and fetal periods is better thought of as the point at which the developing baby takes on a visibly human form. A few weeks earlier Jessica and Dave's baby could have been mistaken for almost any other vertebrate embryo. Now, however, the tiny fetus has long fingers, short toes, and forward-facing eyes, and he has even shed his vestigial tail; it's a baby after all!

Development and Evolution

The similarity between different vertebrate embryos is indeed remarkable. Since the early 1800s, embryologists have been struck by the parallel between early development in various animal species and their evolutionary relationship, a resemblance conveniently abbreviated by the saying "ontogeny recapitulates phylogeny." Of course, each of us does not really pass through a "lizard" stage on our way to a fully developed human form. But it is true that animals who are more closely related in terms of evolution will resemble each other for a longer period of embryonic development. At four weeks, a human embryo is barely distinguishable from any other vertebrate embryo—bird, reptile, or mammal—but by six weeks it resembles only other mammalian embryos, and by seven weeks, only certain primate embryos, such as monkeys. (See Figure 2.4.)

The similarity between ontogeny and phylogeny shows that the strategy of early development has been highly conserved in evolution. This makes sense, if you think about the precise timing and series of events necessary to turn a single fertilized egg into many different complex organ systems; it's simply much easier to add changes at the end of a common developmental sequence than to alter things from the outset. A slight change early in neurulation, for example, could invalidate all kinds of later, subtly timed cues, throwing off the whole process of brain formation. (Just such a problem occurs in *spina bifida*, a relatively frequent condition in which part of the spinal cord is not fully enclosed because of a defect in the early neural tube.) It has been much easier for evolution to take an existing structure, like a forelimb, and turn it into a wing, or a primate cerebral cortex, and enlarge it into the human cortex, than to start with a whole new game plan for each species. Evolution proceeds through the selection of random mutations, and the later in development such a change occurs, the likelier it is to produce a viable offspring than a horrible mistake. Indeed, this is why miscarriages are more common in early pregnancy, a topic that will be discussed more fully in the next chapter.

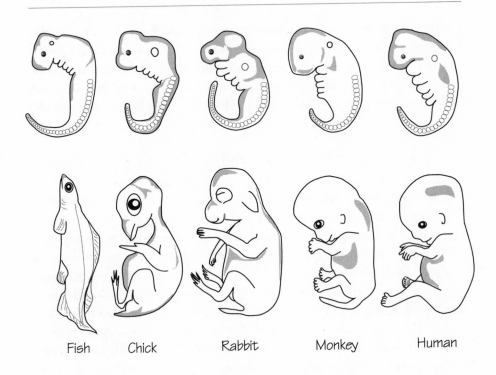

Fish   Chick   Rabbit   Monkey   Human

FIGURE 2.4

*"Ontogeny recapitulates phylogeny." All vertebrate species pass
through comparable stages of early development (top row), reflecting
our common evolutionary heritage. The human embryos depicted here
are approximately four- and eight-weeks postconception.*

The Brain of a Fetus

The ontogeny/phylogeny relationship explains why complete development
of the nervous system takes so long, especially when compared to the development of other organ systems. Our highly complex brain is what most dis-
tinguishes us from other primates, and accordingly takes longer to emerge
from its embryonic form than, say, the circulatory or digestive system. This
relationship also helps explain the regional development of the nervous system—the fact that brain structures that control more rudimentary functions,

such as breathing and feeding, mature earlier than regions that control more sophisticated functions like language and reasoning. At the beginning of the fetal period (week nine), the brain is still assuming its basic shape, whereas the spinal cord is well formed and is even beginning to function. This precocious spinal cord is what controls the first fetal movements, like head and limb flexion and simple reflex responses, although they are still too small and weak for Jessica to feel.

By the end of the first trimester (thirteen weeks), Jessica is starting to feel better, but she still can't keep down her breakfast. As discussed in the next chapter, this early-pregnancy sickness may actually protect her baby's brain, which now consists of a prominent thalamus (a critical sensory relay station), sitting up behind two small, thin cortical hemispheres at the front. Below the thalamus is the cerebellum, which stands out at the back and base of the brain, just above the spinal cord, and has begun forming its *folia*—the many fine grooves and ridges that give it an intricate, almost floral appearance. After three full months in the womb, Dave and Jessica's future son is just over five inches long and has fairly well developed mid- and hindbrain structures, but his cerebral cortex—the seat of all our most distinctly human mental abilities—remains smooth and undifferentiated.

In the next few weeks, the cerebral hemispheres grow dramatically, thickening and expanding toward each other at the top of the head. As they grow, the important bridge that connects them—the *corpus callosum*—begins to form. The hemispheres also expand toward the rear of the head, so that they now cover the thalamus, which will eventually be buried in a central location deep beneath them.

Sixteen weeks after conception, Jessica and Dave go in for an ultrasound and get their first baby picture: a little fetus, now about eight inches long. They're relieved to see ten fingers and toes, four beating chambers in the heart, and a central nervous system that's fully intact. (While not foolproof, ultrasound screening has considerably improved the detection of major neural abnormalities, particularly when combined with maternal blood tests; see Chapter 3.) Routine ultrasound can show the overall shape of the brain and spinal cord, but it is not sensitive enough for finer details, such as the first cerebral groove—the *lateral fissure*—that's just beginning to form on the side of each hemisphere. It is nonetheless sensitive enough to pick up another interesting structure sticking out between the fetus's legs, and Dave's thrilled to discover, "It's a boy!"

About a week later, little Jack lets his presence be known; Jessica feels the first flutter of fetal limbs, an event called *quickening.* These movements actually begin in the sixth week after conception, but it takes ten or twelve more weeks before they're strong enough for the woman to detect (but a little less for women in subsequent pregnancies, who already know what they feel like). Jessica recognizes them now, and it will not be long before she starts thinking there's some kind of Olympic tumbling event going on in her womb.

By twenty-four weeks, the fetus is fourteen inches long and capable, in the direst circumstances, of surviving outside the womb. His lungs can breathe air, if they need to, and the brain stem is capable of directing rhythmic breathing movements. But his cerebral cortex is still not functional, which is reflected in its immature structure: its surface is still mostly smooth, just beginning to form the major *sulci* (the singular is *sulcus*), or invaginations, that give the human cerebral cortex its distinctive, highly convoluted appearance. These fissures allow the growing brain to fold in on itself, massively increasing its surface area, while still fitting inside the skull. The elevated regions between the sulci are called *gyri* (the singular is *gyrus*), and it is within these mounds of gray matter that the most sophisticated processing in our brains takes place.

Cortical sulci come in three sizes: primary, secondary, and tertiary. The large primary sulci, like the central sulcus that separates the frontal and parietal lobes, are present in every person's brain. Secondary sulci show more variation, while the smallest or tertiary sulci vary tremendously among individuals, suggesting that they are not purely genetically determined. Primary sulci first appear on the inner surface of each hemisphere after the twentieth week of fetal development, becoming well defined in the seventh month. (See Figure 2.3.) Tertiary sulci, by contrast, don't even begin forming until the last month or so of gestation and are not fully formed until a baby's first birthday.

The cerebral cortex processes information within columns of neurons that run perpendicular to its surface, each column containing thousands of cells that function as a distinct processing unit, like one chip on a computer circuit board. The larger the surface area of the cortex, the more processing units it can hold. Following the phylogenetic ladder up from, say, rats to cats to monkeys to humans, one sees not only that the cortex gets considerably larger, relative to the rest of the brain; it also has many more and deeper convolutions, so that the surface area and corresponding number of brain "chips" have enlarged manyfold. As occurred in this phylogenetic progression, the number and depth of cortical convolutions also dramatically expands during an infant's development, beginning in the late fetal period and continuing into the first year of life.

Thus, even by the time of birth, as Jack prepares to squeeze out of his warm, wet world, his cortex has only a few of its eventual processing units in place. Brain development, especially of the cerebral cortex, is by no means complete after nine months in the womb. A great deal of further maturation will take place in the first year of Jack's life, as his brain nearly triples in size, growing from about one-quarter to nearly three-quarters of its adult weight. From a functional point of view, these postnatal changes are just as dramatic as the elaborate processes of prenatal brain formation we have followed so far. The difference is that they take place, for the most part, at the microscopic level. Superficially, the brain changes very little after birth, but its outer appearance belies the profound growth of the billions of tiny cells within.

The Birth and Growth of Neurons

What makes a brain develop? How does a neural plate transform itself into a closed tube and eventually into a central nervous system of brain and spinal cord with special circuits for vision, hearing, movement, language, emotion, and all the other complex cognitive functions of which we are capable?

As in most of biology, the answers lie at the level of individual cells. The human brain is built out of billions of nerve cells, or *neurons*, each of which is shaped much like a tree. Thus, a mature neuron has an extensive root system, called the *dendrites*, that receive input from other neurons, and a trunk, or *axon*, that can be extremely long and ultimately branches out to relay information to the next neurons in its circuit. In between these two branched systems lies an enlarged area, the *cell body*, which contains the nucleus and oversees the cells' basic metabolic functions. (See Figure 2.5.) Within each neuron, information is transmitted electrically by brief impulses called *action potentials*; but when the impulse arrives at the end of each axon branch, the information must cross a gap, the *synapse*, in order to be transmitted to the next neuron in the circuit. The gap is traversed by the release of a chemical messenger, or *neurotransmitter*, from the presynaptic terminal of the axon. Neurotransmitter molecules then diffuse the short distance across the synapse, where they bind to special receptors on the postsynaptic neu-

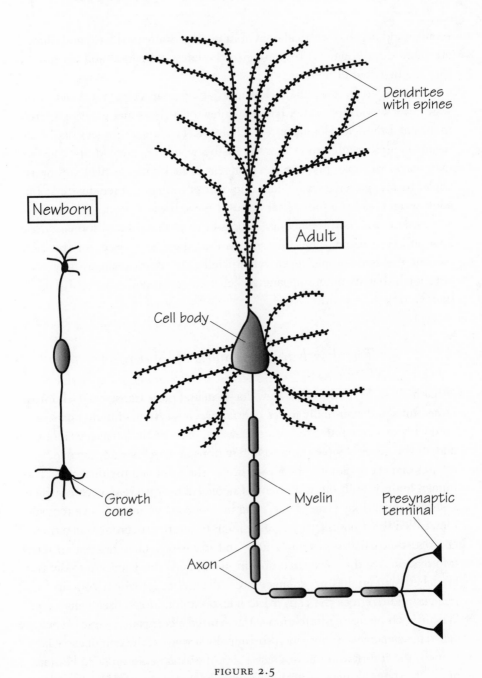

Newborn

Adult

Dendrites
with spines

Cell body

Growth
cone

Myelin

Axon

Presynaptic
terminal

FIGURE 2.5

Structure of cerebral neurons in a newborn and an adult.
Individual brain cells undergo enormous elaboration during
infancy and early childhood.

ron's dendrites, triggering electrical responses in each such receiving neuron. This same sequence of electrical and chemical transmission repeats itself through every cell and synapse of the circuit.

Actually, there are two different types of cells in the nervous system: neurons themselves, which by connecting in the process just described form information-processing circuits, and *glia*, which are supporting cells that provide the structural framework and metabolic sustenance for the neurons. While glia are very important in both the development and functioning of the nervous system (in fact, they outnumber neurons by some ten to fifty times), neurons are where the action is, mentally speaking.

Neurons originate from the division of neuroepithelial cells—neural precursor cells fated to become part of the nervous system by the initial events of neurulation. Like epithelial cells that line the skin and gut, neuroepithelial cells originate at the border between the embryo's body and the outer world—which in this case is the space inside the amniotic sac. But as the neural tube closes up, the neuroepithelia are trapped inside and become its inner wall. By five weeks of development, the space inside this tube has evolved into the five *ventricles* of the central nervous system: four fluid-filled chambers in the forming brain and one that runs along the entire inner length of the spinal cord. (All five ventricles remain continuous with each other, which is why a spinal tap—in which a sample of the fluid is taken from the base of the spinal cord—provides information about infections or chemical imbalances in the brain.) The walls of these ventricles play a special role in early brain development, because this is where the final cell division takes place that converts neuroepithelial cells into neurons and glia, a process called *neurogenesis*.

Neurogenesis begins as soon as the neural tube forms (at three weeks of development), reaches a peak in the seventh week, and is largely completed by eighteen weeks. To a very small extent, some neurons continue to be produced in the latter parts of fetal life and on into the first few postnatal months. (By contrast, glia continue to be produced at a low rate throughout life.) But for the most part, these basic building blocks of our brains are all formed by just four months' gestation—back when Jack was only nine inches long and weighed a mere nine ounces. Even more amazing is the fact that these neurons (most of them, anyway) will survive as long as Jack does—to experience his grandchildren! The brain is unlike other tissues, such as the liver, blood, or even bone, whose cells can continue to divide, generating new cells throughout an individual's life. Neurons are terminally differentiated, meaning that the cell division that produces them is the last they will ever undergo. This fact explains why brain damage is often much more devastating than damage to other tissues: once the cells comprising a particular neural circuit are lost, they can never be replaced. (Fortunately, the brain does have other compensatory mechanisms that can somewhat lessen the impact of brain injury.)

The speed of neurogenesis is mind-boggling. In order to produce the 100 billion neurons in a human brain, they must be born at a rate of 250,000 per minute, averaged over the nine months of gestation. Since the vast majority of neurons are produced by the midpoint of gestation, the actual rate is over half a million per minute.

This massive, unrelenting neural cell division is what fuels the initial formation of different brain regions. But the remaining and most intricate part of brain sculpting is accomplished by neural cell *migration*. After their birth on the ventricle walls, new neurons migrate outward, away from the ventricle, along tracks made by individual glial cells called *radial glia*. Like spokes on a wheel, radial glia are strong, elongated cells that extend outward from the ventricle. New neurons, which consist at this point only of an oblong cell body with two hairlike processes extending from either end, hop onto the radial glia and, following various molecular cues, shimmy their way along to a predestined zone in the thickening brain. In the cerebral cortex, which is composed of six layers of neurons, this migration proceeds in an inside-out sequence: the first cells to migrate stop in a layer closest to the ventricle, while each of five subsequent waves of neurons pass by the earlier cells to settle in progressively higher spots.

Neurons migrate immediately after being born. By the end of neurogenesis, halfway through gestation, most have taken up their final position, and all the major brain structures are in place. But in a sense, this is just the beginning of brain development. The neurons are there, but they are mere saplings. With just a tiny axon, a few short dendritic branches, and virtually no synaptic connections, they cannot *do* anything. It's as if every one of the six billion people on earth each had some twenty telephones, but none of them was yet hooked up. The potential for communication is enormous but still to be realized.

The real business of brain development is in synapse formation. *Synaptogenesis* begins in the spinal cord by the fifth week of embryogenesis and, in the cortex, as early as seven weeks. But unlike neurogenesis and migration, it is a very prolonged process. In the cerebral cortex, whose 10 billion cells form their synapses later than any other part of the brain, synaptogenesis continues all through gestation, through much of the first year, and in some regions well into the second year of postnatal life. At its peak, some 15,000 synapses are produced on every cortical neuron, which corresponds to a rate of 1.8 million new synapses *per second* between two months of gestation and two years after birth!

The synapse is a communication point between two cells, and in order to accommodate this massive synapse formation, neurons must vastly expand their dendritic surfaces. Initially, synapses form directly on the smooth surface of new dendrite branches and branchlets. But before long, this contact coaxes the branch to produce a little nubbin, called a *dendritic spine*. (See Figure 2.5) Dendritic spines measure just one-thousandth of a millimeter in diameter, but they profoundly affect the way electrical signals are processed by the postsynaptic neuron. Spines dot the entire length of mature dendrites, their number closely paralleling the surge (and later pruning) in the number of synapses.

As much as 83 percent of total dendritic growth occurs after birth, to accommodate the enormous influx of new synapses. During this period, brain development is physically analogous to the growth of a new forest, when saplings branch upward and outward in their competition for sunlight. Like a rapidly thickening forest canopy, Jack's cerebral cortex triples in thickness during his first year of life as a result of this enormous dendritic growth. (See Figure 2.6.)

Use It or Lose It:
The Natural Selection of Brain Wiring

With billions of neurons and a quadrillion or so synapses to produce, the sheer numbers involved in brain development make it an awesome feat. But what is even more astounding, and perhaps the most difficult issue in all of neural development to understand, is how all these neurons and synapses get properly hooked together. How, for example, does a neuron in the retina of the eye know to bypass countless other targets in directing its axon to its correct terminus, the visual area of the thalamus? And once there, how does it find the right few hundred neurons to form synapses with—those that respond to the same tiny portion of the baby's visual field? How does a corti-

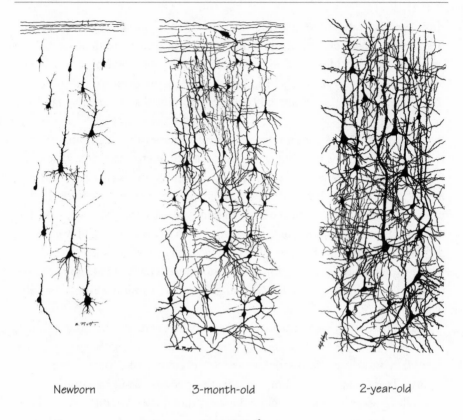

Newborn   3-month-old   2-year-old

FIGURE 2.6

Cellular growth in the cerebral cortex during the first two years. No
new neurons are added after birth, but new dendrites and synapses
sprout furiously during a child's earliest years, causing the cerebral
cortex to thicken and its circuitry to grow massively more complex.
These drawings are from the orbitofrontal zone of the frontal lobe,
a cortical area important for memory and emotion.

Reprinted from J.L. Conel, *The Postnatal Development of the Human Cerebral Cortex*, 8 vols.,
Cambridge, MA: Harvard University Press, 1939–75, by permission of the publisher.

cal auditory neuron know how to find a particular language area of the brain,
configuring its connections to activate only the speech sound /p/? Somehow,
out of seemingly infinite possibilities, each neuron manages to grow both its
axon and dendritic branches to precisely the right positions, aligning its
input and output connections so that we end up with coherent circuits for
vision, language, movement, and so on, and not just a hopeless tangle of
wires and switches. How in the world do they do it?

Neuroscientists have only begun to crack this difficult problem, but what we already know has profound implications for how we raise our children. Brain wiring involves an intricate dance between nature and nurture. Genes direct the growth of axons and dendrites to their correct approximate locations, but once these fibers start linking together and actually functioning, experience takes over, reshaping and refining these crude circuits to customize each child's hardware to his or her unique environment.

Brain wiring begins with the outgrowth of axons. Once a newborn neuron has migrated, planting its cell body in a permanent position, it sends out a fine axon shoot with an enlarged tip known as a *growth cone*. At the end of the growth cone are about a dozen long tentacles that shoot out in all directions and act like radar, picking up all manner of navigational signals. They feel out the best-textured surfaces, sniff around for chemical cues, and even use tiny electrical fields to help the axon find its way to appropriate targets. Axons can grow to very great lengths, so long-distance connections, which pose the greatest challenge, tend to get an early start, at a time when the absolute distance between any two parts of the embryo (say, the spinal cord and the toe) is still comparatively short. Axon guidance also makes use of specific chemical attractants, released, much like insect pheromones, by potential target neurons to attract synaptic mates over relatively long distances. Led by their own genetically coded receptor molecules, these axons can't help but elongate in the direction of an ever-increasing concentration of the attractant molecule until they reach its source, the target neurons with a matching chemical identity.

Once an axon completes its traverse, whether near or far, it branches out extensively, contacting up to hundreds of target neurons that have released the same potent lure. Contact leads to synapse formation, but these initial connections are promiscuous: both far too numerous and highly unselective. During infancy and early childhood, the cerebral cortex actually overproduces synapses, about twice as many as it will eventually need. The initial wiring scheme is thus quite diffuse, with a lot of overlap that makes information transfer both imprecise and inefficient. It's as if all those billions of phones were first connected as party lines; you could dial Grandma at any of thousands of numbers, but it's unlikely she'd be the first to answer.

Why does the brain bother to produce so many excess synapses? Why not save time and energy and simply wire things up precisely from the start? The answers to these questions cut right to the core of the nature/nurture issue.

Up to now, genes have been largely responsible for establishing brain wiring. They prescribe all the early targeting cues—the pheromones that attract one class of axon to a particular class of neuron, the surface receptors that sense these attractants (or in some cases, repellents), as well as the receptors for other chemical, textural, and electrical cues that guide axon growth and synapse formation. But the fact is that there are not nearly enough genes in the entire human genome to accurately specify every one of our quadrillion synapses. There are perhaps 80,000 genes scattered among the miles of DNA in our chromosomes, and even if a generous half of these were allotted to the delicate job of brain wiring (after all, the body does have some other important functions to perform with its genes), we would still be far short of having enough cues to specify an accurate wiring diagram for the entire brain.

This is where "nurture" steps in and finishes the job. By overproducing synapses, the brain forces them to compete, and just as in evolution or the free market, competition allows for selection of the "fittest" or most useful synapses. In neural development, usefulness is defined in terms of electrical activity. Synapses that are highly active—that receive more electrical impulses and release greater amounts of neurotransmitter—more effectively stimulate their postsynaptic targets. This heightened electrical activity triggers molecular changes that stabilize the synapse, essentially cementing it in place. Less active synapses, by contrast, do not evoke enough electrical activity to stabilize themselves and so eventually regress. (See Figure 2.7.) It's "use it or lose it" right from the start; like other forms of Darwinian selection, this synaptic pruning is an extremely efficient way of adapting each organism's neural circuits to the exact demands imposed by its environment.

Our best evidence for how experience guides synaptic selection comes from studies of visual development, which are discussed in Chapter 9. But there's another dramatic demonstration—some classic experiments on laboratory rats that were inspired by something Charles Darwin himself described back in 1868.

Ever the careful observer, Darwin rounded up a bunch of rabbits, measured their head and body sizes, and found that those raised in captivity had far smaller brains, relative to body weight, than those that grew up in the wild. Compared to the wild rabbits, Darwin realized, the domestic rabbits "cannot have exerted their intellect, instincts, senses and voluntary movements, either in escaping from various dangers or in searching for food," so that "their brains will have been feebly exercised, and consequently have suffered in development."

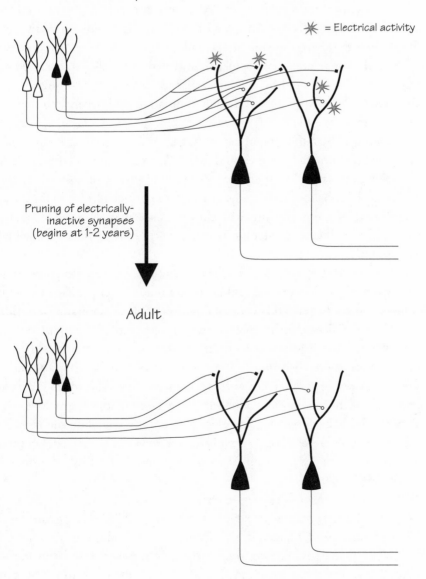

"Exuberant" period (1-8 years)

※ = Electrical activity

Pruning of electrically-
inactive synapses
(begins at 1-2 years)

Adult

FIGURE 2.7

*During the "exuberant" period of brain development, children produce
about twice as many synapses (depicted as small circles and squares)
as they will eventually need. Experience, or electrical activity, determines which synapses will be preserved and which will be eliminated.*

A century later, neurobiologists finally started to figure out how a challenging environment stimulates brain growth. Much like Darwin's rabbits, laboratory rats that have been reared in an "enriched" environment—in a large cage containing several litters and a wide variety of "toys" to see, smell, and manipulate—have larger brains, with a notably thicker cerebral cortex, than those raised in an "impoverished" environment—isolated, in a small empty cage, without any social stimulation and a bare minimum of sensory experience. The reason their cerebral cortex is bigger, researchers have found, is that their neurons are larger, with bigger cell bodies, more dendritic branches, more spines, and more synapses than those in the brains of impoverished rats. In other words, the extra sensory and social stimulation actually enhances the connectivity of the enriched rats' brains, a difference that probably explains why they are also smarter—they learn their way around a baited maze significantly faster—than their impoverished laboratory mates.

It is no great stretch to see the implication of these experiments for human development: A young child's environment directly and permanently influences the structure and eventual function of his or her brain. Everything a child sees, touches, hears, feels, tastes, thinks, and so on translates into electrical activity in just a subset of his or her synapses, tipping the balance for long-term survival in their favor. On the other hand, synapses that are rarely activated—whether because of languages never heard, music never made, sports never played, mountains never seen, love never felt—will wither and die. Lacking adequate electrical activity, they lose the race, and the circuits they were trying to establish—for flawless Russian, perfect pitch, an exquisite backhand, a deep reverence for nature, healthy self-esteem—never come to be.

The magnitude of this synaptic sorting is enormous. Children lose on the order of 20 billion synapses *per day* between early childhood and adolescence. While this may sound harsh, it is generally a very good thing. The elimination of stray synapses and the strengthening of survivors is what makes our mental processes more streamlined and coherent as we mature; the party lines sort themselves out into clear, private, efficient channels for information transfer. On the other hand, it may also explain why our mental processes become less flexible and creative as we mature. Although the brain continues to exhibit certain more subtle forms of plasticity in adulthood (which is, after all, the way we learn or remember anything at all), it is never as malleable as in childhood.

Myelination: Insulating the Wires

Coinciding with the extended period of dendritic growth and synapse refinement is one more critical event in neuronal development, called *myelination*. In adults, the axons of most neurons are coated with a fatty substance, *myelin*, that acts as an electrical insulator and is essential to proper information flow. Fiber bundles in the brain or nerves can contain many thousands of different axons. Since these fibers are packed closely together, they run the risk of electrically interfering with each other. Just as the two wires in an electric power cable are encased in plastic or rubber to prevent shorting, neuronal fibers or axons are sheathed in myelin to prevent cross-talk that would scramble the information each is transmitting.

An even more important function of myelination is to speed the transmission of electrical signals. Neurons transmit electrical signals not by the flow of electrons but by the flow of ions—dissolved salts like sodium, calcium, and potassium (which carry a positive charge) and chloride (which carries a negative charge). But nerve cell membranes are leaky. As electrical signals race along the length of an axon, some of these ions leak out, reducing the efficiency of transmission. Myelination solves this problem by sealing up the leaks. In fact, before they are myelinated, many fibers are incapable of transmitting impulses all the way to their endpoint, the synapse, because they lose too much ionic current along the way. Another by-product of this leakiness is that unmyelinated axons cannot fire successive action potentials fast enough to meaningfully transmit information. So even when neurons have grown their branches and formed the synapses that complete the fundamental brain circuits, these circuits don't work very well until the axons are myelinated.

The importance of myelin is poignantly illustrated in patients with demyelinating diseases. The most common of these is multiple sclerosis (MS), caused when a person's immune system destroys his own myelin. MS sufferers eventually develop severe sensory and motor deficits—such as blindness and paralysis—because their nerves cannot properly conduct action potentials.

Myelination begins in the nerve fibers of the spinal cord at just five months of gestation, but not until the ninth prenatal month in the brain. It is another very slow process, advancing through several stages in which the myelin wrapping gets progressively thicker and is also altered to a more mature composition. Different areas of the brain are markedly uneven in their pace of myelination. Together with the surge in synapse formation, the onset of myelination is critically important for the emergence of a particular region's function, and the rate of myelination controls the speed at which that function progresses. This is particularly evident in the emergence of different motor skills, as we'll see in Chapter 11.

The order of myelination in different regions of the brain is largely genetically controlled and follows a roughly phylogenetic sequence: axonal fibers in older brain regions, controlling basic vegetative and reflexive functions, tend to get myelinated well before fibers in higher areas, which control more sophisticated mental abilities. But while genes control the timing of myelination, environmental factors, such as malnutrition, have been found to adversely affect the degree of myelination, that is, the thickness of the wrapping around individual axons. Whether myelination can also be positively influenced by a child's environment or experience is not yet known but is a fascinating topic for research.

Myelin is composed of about 80 percent lipid (including about 15 percent cholesterol) together with about 20 percent protein. It is produced by special types of glial cells, whose number is sensitive to the quality of nutrition in early life. Myelin production is the primary reason why pediatricians recommend a high level of fat (including whole milk) in children's diets until about age two, in spite of the general trend to lower fat intake in adults and older children. In fact, an extremely high-fat diet is the preferred form of treatment for some forms of epilepsy in young children. Poor myelination may contribute to these seizures by permitting too much electrical cross-talk between neurons.

Regional Brain Development as a Map of the Developing Mind

Neurogenesis, migration, synapse formation, synapse pruning, myelination: the same events are taking place in every part of Jack's nervous system but often at different times. Indeed, one of the more striking features of human brain development is its marked unevenness. Now nearing the end of gestation, some parts of Jack's nervous system are already almost fully mature, while others will still be developing past puberty, a sequence that has enormous implications for his emerging mental abilities.

Generally speaking, the nervous system matures in a gradient, from tail to head. The spinal cord and brain stem are almost fully organized and myelinated by birth; the midbrain and cerebellum begin myelinating just afterward; subcortical parts of the forebrain (including the thalamus, basal ganglia, and parts of the limbic system) follow a little later in the first (and for a few pathways, the second) year. Last of all is the cerebral cortex, which is both the slowest and most uneven of all brain structures to mature. Sensory areas of the cerebral cortex mature relatively quickly, followed by motor areas, but large areas of the parietal, temporal, and frontal lobes, which are known as the higher-order "association" cortices, are still pruning their synapses and myelinating their axons late in the second decade of life. These are the circuits responsible for our most sophisticated mental processing—language, attention, judgment, planning, emotion, and reasoning—so it is little wonder humans take such a long time to reach a truly mature level of thought.

The sequence of brain maturation has been established largely through anatomical methods, using autopsy material and, more recently, MRI scans, which are especially good at detecting myelin. But the same maturation has also been confirmed by actual measures of babies' brain activity. The classic method is electroencephalography (EEG), which uses harmless electrodes, taped to a baby's scalp, to detect tiny electrical signals emanating from the brain. EEG recordings pick up considerable activity in the brain stem of newborns but very little from the cerebral cortex. Beginning around two to three months, the cortex shows its first sign of "alpha" activity—faster, spikier rhythms associated with an alert awake state. (See Figure 2.8.) Except for cortical responses to simple sensory stimuli, however, maturation of the electrical rhythms of the cerebral cortex is markedly slow throughout infancy and most of childhood.

EEG is still widely used for studying neural processing, especially in babies, because it is noninvasive, and they don't have to hold perfectly still to give accurate readings. But it is not very precise at determining *where* activity is coming from in the brain. For this, researchers have turned to several exciting new imaging techniques, such as PET (positron-emission tomography) and functional MRI (magnetic resonance imaging). In PET scanning, subjects are injected with a form of the brain's most important energy source, glucose, that has been enhanced with a short-lived radioactive tracer. Electrically active brain areas use more glucose than inactive areas, so the scanner, which measures the radioactive emissions, allows us to visualize

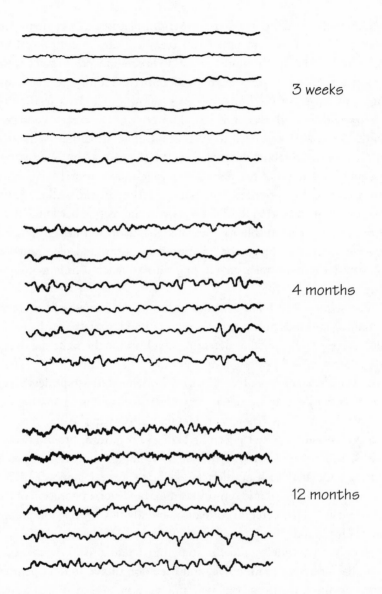

3 weeks

4 months

12 months

FIGURE 2.8

Awake EEG activity recorded from the scalp of the same infant at three different ages. EEGs grow increasingly "spiky," or complex, throughout childhood but undergo their most dramatic changes during the first year.

After I. Hagne, "Development of the waking EEG in normal infants during the first year of life," in P. Kellaway and I. Petersen, eds., *Clinical Electroencephalography of Children*, Stockholm: Almqvist and Wiksell, 1968.

the amount of activity in different parts of the brain. Although the amount of radioactivity involved is relatively harmless, PET can be performed on children only for strict medical reasons—that is, for diagnosing brain injury. Functional MRI does not involve any radioactivity. But both methods require that the subject hold extremely still, so neither unfortunately is ideal for studying babies.

Nonetheless, researchers at the University of California at Los Angeles were able to complete one large series of PET scans on children between the ages of five days and fifteen years of age. Out of more than a hundred pediatric patients, twenty-nine turned out to have no neural impairment, so their PET data serve as a measure of glucose utilization in the normal developing brain. This study revealed a close correspondence between the level of glucose utilization and the synaptic organization of different brain regions at different times in development. In newborns, brain activity is largely confined to subcortical structures such as the brain stem, part of the cerebellum, and the thalamus. These structures are responsible for the characteristic reflexes of newborns—their rooting, grasping, sucking, stepping, and startle responses—all of which disappear when the cortex develops further and comes to actively override them. In the newborn, however, the cortex uses very little glucose, which shows once again that it really isn't doing very much in the first month or so of life.

But the situation changes dramatically during the next several months. Around two or three months after birth, activity levels shoot up in several cortical areas, most notably in the roughly rear half of the brain that controls visual perception. Then after six or eight months, the frontal lobe begins to rise in glucose utilization. Within the frontal cortex, phylogenetically older areas are activated before newer ones, which don't register significant activity until the last few months of the first year. As we will see, frontal activation is responsible for the first inklings of higher cognitive function in babies, a surge in memory, emotion, and general awareness that takes off around eight months after birth.

Glucose use continues to increase through early childhood, reaching a peak between four and seven years of age, depending on brain region. At its height, cortical glucose use is about twice the level of that in the adult brain; it then gradually declines throughout the rest of childhood and adolescence. This pattern of glucose use—low initially, followed by a rapid increase and overshoot, followed by a gradual decline to adult levels—is strikingly similar to the change in numbers of cortical synapses during development. Developing brains thus appear to use the most energy during the pruning period, when they are making all those critical decisions about which synapses to preserve and which to eliminate.

Critical Periods for Enriching Brain Wiring

The sequence of brain development is fascinating for helping us understand what's going on in the minds of babies like little Jack, now a sleepy, hungry newborn. But it is even more important for understanding what Jessica and Dave can do to help that mind fully blossom. That's because this sequence defines the various critical periods for mental development—the windows of opportunity, some narrow, some wide, during which Jack's experience will fatefully and permanently shape each of his mature mental skills.

All of the essential refinements in brain wiring—dendritic growth, spine formation, synapse selection, and even myelination—can be influenced by a child's experience. But once a given brain region has passed the refinement stage, its critical period has ended, and the opportunity to rewire it is significantly limited. Thus the critical periods for basic sensory abilities, like vision and hearing, end much earlier than those for more complex skills, like language and emotion, whose underlying neural circuits prune their synapses and myelinate their axons over most of childhood. Nonetheless, all critical periods probably begin within the first four years of life, when the synaptic tide turns from waxing to waning in all brain areas.

It would be hard to overstate the importance of synaptic refinement to a child's developmental potential. The initial wiring of a particular brain region (the period of synapse overproduction) marks the onset of a particular ability, such as vision in the first few months and language in the second year. But it is the prolonged pruning period that fixes the overall quality of that ability, because this is when experience—translated into neural activity—decides which connections will be preserved and, consequently, how the brain will be permanently wired for certain ways of thinking, perceiving, and acting. As long as an excess number of synapses are present, the brain remains maximally plastic and can develop in a variety of ways. But once those excess synapses are gone, the critical period is over, and it must make do with its existing circuitry; there's no trading up for a faster computer.

In the chapters that follow, we will trace the development of every major circuit of the brain, seeing how its initial wiring takes shape, when it myelinates, when its critical period begins, and how long it remains open for improvement, or atrophy, during a child's life. For many abilities, the critical period is mercifully long, extending throughout childhood and even early adolescence. For others, it closes in just the first months or years of life, often before parents are even aware that their child's mental development is vulnerable in some way. Understanding brain development clarifies these various critical periods and can thereby help us make the most of every child's priceless neural plasticity.

Chapter 3

PRENATAL INFLUENCES
ON THE DEVELOPING BRAIN

"Nausea, headaches, no aspirin, no alcohol, watch the caffeine—pregnancy is tough!" Jessica complains to her sister, who's already been through it twice. "I know," Melanie replies, "but it's all worth it. As soon as you see that little baby, you're going to be really glad you didn't do anything to jeopardize his development."

As long as there have been old wives to tell tales, mothers have known that the way they treat their body during pregnancy can affect the developing fetus. But only in the last few decades has research begun revealing exactly how and when a woman's diet, health, emotional state, and exposure to various environmental agents influence fetal formation. Of all fetal organs, the central nervous system is probably the most sensitive to the wide range of prenatal influences, because its development is so protracted—from three weeks after conception all the way to adolescence.

In a sense, this vulnerability is just the flip side of the necessary and positive influence that experience has on brain development, which depends on the outer world to shape the emerging senses, emotions, actions, capacities, and thoughts of a young child. Later chapters will spell out how and when a fetus begins to sense and respond to its environment, and how these prenatal experiences influence all aspects of development, from basic limb and organ formation to early memory and language abilities.

Prenatal experience is important, to be sure, but if there is one feature that best characterizes life in the womb, it is the relative *lack* of stimulation. The womb, like a sturdy eggshell, is a highly protected environment: dark, warm, confining, and generally quieter than the outside world. This isolation seems to be just the right thing for early brain development, judging by the many problems that result when babies are born prematurely. Despite all the dramatic advances in modern neonatology, babies born eight or more weeks early remain at high risk for many mental and neurological problems, including visual, hearing, and motor deficits, poor emotional regulation, attention problems, and language delays. By grade school, children who weighed less than 1,500 grams at birth (3 pounds, 5 ounces), most of whom were premature, perform more poorly in school and score about six points lower on IQ tests than children born full term. Of course, premature birth poses many challenges beyond an altered sensory environment (including difficulty in breathing, resisting infection, and obtaining nourishment), but there is growing evidence that preterm babies who are treated to a more "womblike" experience—kept in quieter, darker incubators and snugly nested in special buntings and a more fetal, flexed position—stay healthier, develop more rapidly, and score higher on later infant "IQ" tests than those housed in traditional neonatal intensive care units, with their bright lights, loud noises, and all-too-spacious incubators.

The womb is obviously the safest place for a fetus to develop in. Nor is its isolation the womb's sole means of defense. According to one theory, the fatigue and nausea that many women suffer during early pregnancy are another means of protecting the embryo and young fetus. These symptoms peak during the baby's most vulnerable phase, when all of its organs are first forming. Fatigue tends to keep a woman from risky physical activities, while "morning sickness" (a misnomer since it often lasts all day) tends to keep her diet bland, helping her to avoid natural toxins present in spoiled or exotic foods. Our best guess is that these symptoms are caused by the placental hormone human chorionic gonadotropin (HCG). This hormone can be detected in the mother's blood as early as one week after conception (which is why its measurement is the basis of pregnancy testing in home kits). HCG levels rise rapidly during early pregnancy, reach a peak around ten weeks (eight weeks postconception), then rapidly decline until about midgestation, much as the nausea and fatigue of pregnancy wax and wane in many women. Miserable though it can be, morning sickness is actually regarded as a good sign in pregnancy, because it means that the placenta is developing well; several studies have found that women experiencing nausea are less likely to miscarry than those who don't.

By this standard, Jessica is off to a good start: she's now throwing up twice a day and can barely stay awake in afternoon meetings. But while the placenta is trying, in this way, to protect little Jack from harmful influences in the environment, it is unfortunately not foolproof. The womb is isolated but by no means wholly immune from the outside world. Almost every drug, hormone, metabolite, infectious agent, or other chemical that makes its way into Jessica's bloodstream will cross the placenta in some measure.

Ever since the thalidomide disaster in the 1960s, women have become aware that exposure to various agents can harm their developing fetus. Those that have been documented to cause fetal malformations in a statistically significant number of cases are known as *teratogens*. It is surprisingly difficult, however, to prove that a particular agent is a teratogen, because its effect must always be compared to the baseline risk for any birth defect, which is disturbingly high. Overall, two or three of every hundred babies born has some kind of defect that will affect their appearance, development, intellect, or ability to function. Compare that to the risk of thalidomide, one of the worst teratogens ever identified, which causes limb and other malformations in about 20 percent of fetuses exposed during the first trimester. Even with known teratogens, it's a probability game, making it difficult to know for certain whether a particular defect was caused by that specific agent or was simply a result of the generally high odds for any sort of defect.

The fact is that most birth defects—an estimated 65 percent—occur without any identifiable cause. Another 20 to 25 percent can be attributed to recognized defects in chromosomes or genes, but only some of these are inherited; the others occur spontaneously. Known environmental or disease agents are responsible for no more than 10 percent of all defects. Still, the more we know about these causes, the better able we will be to protect parents from the difficult decisions and responsibilities of bearing a defective fetus.

Teratogens are likelier to have more devastating effects on the fetus during the first three to four months of pregnancy, when the different organ systems are all forming. In the case of the brain, however, one must always beware of effects later in gestation and even well after birth, since neural development is such an extended process. These effects tend to be subtler than gross malformations and may not even be evident until later in childhood. They are also more difficult to identify, since the underlying brain damage is caused by doses of teratogens lower than those known to cause gross congenital abnormalities. Such subtle effects can include slower development of sensory, motor, or language abilities; disorders of behavior, attention, or sleep; or sometimes merely poor academic achievement. While less severe than gross malformations or mental retardation, "neurodevelopmental disorders" like these can be equally worrisome to parents.

Since very few drugs and chemicals have actually been tested for these more subtle effects, health care providers have adopted a "better safe than sorry" attitude and generally advise against heavy exposure to anything suspect, regardless of whether its risk has been documented. This approach is clearly warranted from a public health standpoint, because even if a particular agent harms only a fraction of exposed babies, reducing all women's exposure will measurably decrease the total number of defects and developmental disorders in the population. It also makes sense because many teratogens act cumulatively; so even if the risk of any one exposure is quite low, exposure to several agents or risk factors can multiply the overall risk to the fetus. (Smoking, for instance, is known to increase fetal susceptibility to many other teratogens.) Since every woman faces a slightly different combination of risk factors, "better safe than sorry" is, again, a wise way to protect the public at large.

The problem, however, arises among the few women who take this general warning to an extreme and worry themselves sick about a few cocktails or having painted the dining room in the weeks before learning they were pregnant. Nine months is a long time to try to live in a plastic bubble, and (as we'll see later in this chapter) the stress of avoiding hundreds of minute risks may be more hazardous to the fetus than the combination of all these risks themselves. There's also another side effect to the "better safe than sorry" prescription—the fact that a significant minority of parents will choose to terminate otherwise wanted pregnancies because of their exaggerated fears about risk to the fetus. Just such an "epidemic" of induced abortions occurred in certain European countries after the 1986 Chernobyl accident, even though the amount of radiation reaching these areas was not high enough to measurably increase the birth defect rate.

Although women today are fairly well informed about harmful agents, they are often unsure about the precise doses or degrees of exposure that can cause problems. Theoretically, almost anything can be harmful in a high enough dose—peanuts, broccoli, salt, even fresh water! Conversely, even the most dangerous agents—like radioactivity, lead, or PCBs—do not pose a significant threat if their dose is minuscule. So it's important to know what the real risks are.

The purpose of this chapter is to present the actual data on prenatal influences, to tell pregnant women exactly which agents and doses are known to be harmful and which appear, based on solid scientific evidence, to be safe. I wrote much of it while pregnant myself, because I was frustrated with all the standard manuals that simply told me to avoid everything in sight. Of course, every pregnant woman presents a unique set of risk factors, and information about prenatal influences is constantly being updated. Therefore, while this chapter should provide a useful guide for finding that middle ground—somewhere between the plastic bubble and the real world— concerns about specific agents or combinations of risk factors should always be addressed to your obstetrician or midwife.

Neural Tube Defects

One of the most sensitive periods in brain development is during its earliest formation. Between twenty-two and twenty-eight days after conception, the neural tube must fuse along its entire length to create a properly enclosed central nervous system. As we saw in the last chapter, closure begins at the top end, in the area that will become the brain, and proceeds over these few days to the bottom, creating the tail end of the spinal cord. (See Figure 2.2.)

Failure of the tube to close properly can result in a number of defects. If the failure occurs in the area of the spinal cord, the defect is known as *spina bifida*, in which part of the spinal cord develops outside of the vertebral column, often within a large cyst that protrudes out of the back. If the neural tube fails to close at its top end, a defect called *anencephaly* results, in which most of the brain above the brain stem fails to develop at all. Spina bifida can range in severity from totally symptomless to highly debilitating, with problems including paralysis, bowel and bladder incontinence, and sometimes mental deficiency due to secondary infections. Anencephaly, however, is a lethal condition; such babies are often stillborn and, if they are born alive, generally do not survive longer than a few days or weeks.

Neural tube defects (NTDs for short) occur in about one out of a thousand pregnancies in the United States (0.1 percent) and more often in female than in male fetuses. It is possible they are much more common than this, since one study suggests that as many as 2.5 percent of spontaneously aborted embryos show some form of NTD. Because the defect occurs so early in gestation, it may often go undetected among the relatively high number of miscarriages in early pregnancy.

NTDs have several suspected causes and have been linked to genetic, ethnic, nutritional, drug, and environmental factors. It is probably the combination of several of these that produces an abnormality in any particular fetus. A genetic predisposition is suggested by the fact that women who have already given birth to one child with a neural tube defect are twenty to thirty times likelier than most to have an NTD in subsequent pregnancies (that is, their risk is 2 to 3 percent). Neural tube defects are more prevalent in particular ethnic groups and in particular geographical locations. Rates are high in the United Kingdom and are especially low in Finland. Within the United States, rates are higher in certain East Coast locations and much lower in California. Black and Jewish populations have a low incidence of neural tube defects, while Native Americans have a high incidence. There have even been reports of seasonal variations in the occurrence of neural tube defects, with a greater proportion of affected babies born in the winter months—that is, conceived in the spring.

Neural tube defects are more common when mothers suffer from particular illnesses during pregnancy. Women with insulin-dependent diabetes have a considerably higher risk, although the better their diabetes is controlled, the lower is their risk for both NTDs and other types of fetal abnormalities. Mothers with epilepsy also have a higher risk of neural tube defects, but this depends in part on the type of anticonvulsant medication they take during pregnancy. Valproic acid and carbamazepine both raise the risk for neural tube defects about tenfold, but fortunately, other anticonvulsants are available. Other agents suspected of causing them are the anticancer agents methotrexate and aminopterin, if a mother is exposed to them during the fourth week after conception.

Of wider concern is the possibility that a mother's elevated body temperature increases the risk of NTDs. Although not all studies agree, the majority indicate that mothers who either experienced an illness-related fever or who used a hot tub or sauna during early pregnancy were about twice as likely to have a fetus with an NTD than mothers who did not have a temperature-elevating experience in the first trimester. Temperature elevation of more than 1.5°C (2.7°F) is known to perturb early development in both animals and humans; presumably, if this disruption occurs while the neural tube is trying to close, an NTD is more likely.

The good news about NTDs is that most cases can now be detected by early in the second trimester. Prenatal diagnosis involves a combination of two methods: measuring the level of *alpha-fetoprotein* (AFP) in the mother's blood or amniotic fluid (obtained by amniocentesis) and direct observation of the fetus with ultrasound imaging. As its name implies, alpha-fetoprotein is produced by the fetus and is present in a very high concentration in the fetus's cerebrospinal fluid, which is contained inside the ventricles of the brain and spinal cord. It is normally present in a very low concentration in the amniotic fluid. When the neural tube fails to close, however, some of this protein leaks out into the amniotic fluid and crosses the placenta into the mother's blood. Therefore, elevated levels of AFP either in the mother's blood or in the amniotic fluid suggest that the fetus has an open neural tube defect. (In a small proportion of spina bifida cases—about one out of six— the defective spinal cord is enclosed by skin; because alpha-fetoprotein does not escape into the amniotic fluid, it cannot be detected with this measurement. These cases are called "closed" NTDs and tend to be less severe.)

The blood test is best performed between sixteen and eighteen weeks of pregnancy, because that is when the chance of detecting an abnormal level of AFP is the highest. By itself, this test is just a preliminary screening for neural tube defects. It can give a false-positive result when AFP readings are high for other reasons—for example, if the pregnancy is actually further along than thought, or if more than one fetus is present. Therefore, positive results from maternal blood measurements are usually followed up by measurements of AFP and another fetal brain enzyme, *acetylcholinesterase*, which can independently confirm or reject the initial result. Finally, careful ultrasound screening is used to look directly for brain and spinal cord defects. Each of these methods has some degree of error, but by combining more than one screening method, an estimated 93 percent of all NTDs can now be detected before the end of the first half of pregnancy.

Thanks to these sensitive screening methods, the number of babies born with neural tube defects has dramatically declined in the last decade or so. When several tests confirm the diagnosis of a severe neural tube defect, most parents choose to terminate the pregnancy. Fortunately, more and more parents are being spared this difficult decision, because of the breakthrough in NTD *prevention* that recently evolved.

First published in 1981 and widely confirmed by 1992, it was found that women who take the B-complex vitamin folic acid at the time of conception and during the first several weeks of pregnancy are substantially less likely to have a fetus with a neural tube defect than women who do not take folic acid. The initial studies were conducted on women who had already had a pregnancy with a NTD, because their risk of a subsequent NTD is so much higher than for women without such a history. This simple measure—taking a multivitamin pill that includes folic acid—reduced their chance of having a second NTD by an impressive 76 percent. After this finding, studies were extended to a general population of women, and folic acid was found to prevent about 60 percent of first-time NTD occurrences.

This result has been replicated in many different countries. Because the data are so strong, the effect so great, and the solution so simple, public health officials now recommend that all women capable of becoming pregnant consume 0.4 milligram (400 micrograms, abbreviated as *mcg*) of folic acid every day. This is the amount of folic acid present in most standard multivitamin supplements bought over the counter. Prescription prenatal vitamins generally contain a higher dose, 0.8 to 1.0 milligram, which has not been proven more effective but appears to be safe. Folic acid is also naturally present in many foods, particularly in green leafy vegetables, peas, beans, citrus fruits, liver, and whole wheat bread, but natural forms of folate are often only partially available to the body and are also less stable when cooked. Therefore, some experts argue that it may not be possible to get the full 0.4 milligram of folic acid even with an outstanding diet.

A greater problem with ensuring adequate folate intake is that about half of all pregnancies (in the United States and Canada) are not planned. Because neural tube closure begins so early—just eight days after a missed period—many women simply will not get around to taking folic acid at the time it is actually needed. This very early timing is the reason why health agencies in many countries have begun mandating the addition of folic acid to widely consumed foods. In the United States, folic acid fortification has been required since the beginning of 1998 for all enriched grains—flour, cornmeal, bread, pasta, rice, and cereal—in amounts estimated to raise the average woman's consumption by 0.1 milligram per day. While this fortification should reduce the prevalence of neural tube deficits in the population at large, it is modest enough that women are still advised to take a 0.4-to-0.8-milligram folic acid supplement beginning at least one month before conception and continuing through the first trimester of pregnancy.

Effects of Nutrition on the Developing Brain

The role of folic acid in neural tube defects points out just how sensitive brain development is to the nutritional state of the mother. It also illustrates the most important point about prenatal influences of any sort: timing is everything. The impact of a particular drug or deficiency depends entirely on what's going on in neural development at that moment. Generally speaking, prenatal insults have a more drastic effect early in pregnancy, when basic brain structures are still being laid down by the division and migration of neurons. Once these structures are in place, and specifically once all the neurons have formed (by about eighteen weeks postconception), the brain remains sensitive to harmful influences, but they are less devastating.

In the case of a mother's more general nutritional status—her total caloric intake—the brain is actually *less* sensitive during the first three to four months of gestation. In spite of its massive developmental changes, the fetus grows surprisingly little in size during this period, so its growth is not very dependent on the mother's diet. (This is probably no accident, since women are often unable to consume many calories because of first-trimester nausea.) Beginning around midway through gestation, however, and continuing until about two years after birth, the brain's growth is highly sensitive to the quantity and quality of nutrition it receives. This sensitive period coincides with the great spurt in synapse development, dendritic growth, and myelination, which together wire up the brain and also greatly increase its total weight. The quality of nutrition during this period has a profound impact on a child's future cognitive, emotional, and neurological functions.

Because this sensitive period begins before birth, it means that a mother's diet can shape her baby's brain development. And because it continues throughout infancy and toddlerhood, it means that special attention must be paid to a child's diet during these first two years. Nutritional deficits can be very specific, such as insufficient iodine, iron, or vitamin B12 intake, each of which can permanently alter brain and cognitive development if it continues for any substantial portion of the sensitive period. It is more common, however, for young children to suffer from a generalized nutritional deficiency—too few calories during gestation and early life—that can permanently compromise their brain development. Insufficient nutrition threatens the brain if it occurs at any time during the sensitive period, but is more devastating the earlier in this period it occurs and the longer it lasts, and when the lack of calories is compounded by inadequate protein intake.

The effects of malnutrition have been thoroughly studied in experimental animals, where we have achieved a fairly detailed understanding of the timing and type of nutrients needed for optimal brain development. Unfortunately, plenty of data are also available for human populations. A large proportion of children in the world are undernourished because of famine, poverty, war, and other natural or man-made disasters. It is through studies of such children that we have learned the ways in which inadequate early nutrition can permanently impair brain function. Children who were undernourished as fetuses or infants tend to score lower on IQ tests, perform more poorly in school, have slower language development, exhibit more behavioral problems, and even have difficulties with sensory integration and fine motor skills, compared with children from the same culture who were adequately nourished. The earlier the malnourishment begins (starting with midpregnancy) and the longer it lasts, the greater will be the resulting problems and the less likely they can be overcome later on. By comparison, adults who undergo even the most extreme starvation do not suffer any intellectual impairment. Thus the brain has a special sensitive period for nutrition in infancy corresponding to the phase of massive synapse growth and axon myelination, both of which require considerable metabolic energy.

Babies of malnourished mothers are small at birth, with correspondingly smaller head sizes than babies well nourished in the womb. Within the normal range, birth weight and head size are only modestly related to later intelligence. But babies in the lowest tenth percentile, whose birth weight is less than four and a half pounds, do have a higher incidence of neurological impairment and mental deficits than larger infants. And malnourished babies are very likely to be in this smallest group.

Birth weight, unlike many traits, is influenced much more by a mother's nutrition than by heredity. Optimally, a pregnant woman should gain about 20 percent of her ideal prepregnancy weight (for example, twenty-six pounds for a 130-pound woman). Bigger is generally better, but there is a limit. (See Figure 17.3.) Babies who are very large at birth are likelier to cause a difficult delivery, and the brain is the organ most vulnerable to damage during a complicated birth. For optimal development a woman needs to consume about 300 extra calories per day during pregnancy, and 500 to 600 extra calories during lactation. It is recommended that many of these additional calories come from protein, which is especially important for brain development; women are advised to consume an extra 10 to 12 grams of protein per day during pregnancy and 12 to 15 grams during lactation.

When a pregnant mother is undernourished, the placenta fails to develop sufficiently, which further compounds the lack of nutrients available to the fetus. Even in well-nourished mothers, the placenta occasionally fails to develop normally because of other causes, and the babies are affected by a syndrome known as *intrauterine growth retardation* (IUGR). Like malnourished infants, babies with IUGR are at high risk for various mental and neurological problems.

The problems are much the same when a mother carries more than one fetus; they are forced to compete for a single supply of placental nutrients. Studies of rat pups have shown that birth weight is inversely proportional to litter size: animals born into large litters are smaller, with correspondingly smaller brains, than animals from small litters. They are also less intelligent, judging by their performance on mazes and other tests of "rat IQ." Similarly, human twins, whose birth weights are considerably lower than children born as singletons, are known to score an average of seven points lower on IQ tests than singletons. Moreover, when twins differ dramatically in birth weight, the one who was smaller at birth and apparently received less blood flow from the placenta tends to score lower on IQ tests later in life.

Autopsy studies have revealed more about how nutrition affects brain growth. Malnourished children have significantly smaller brains, with less dendritic growth and myelin than well-nourished children. Because neurons are produced largely during the first half of gestation, their number is generally not affected by prenatal malnutrition. But glial cells, which are responsible for producing myelin, are formed throughout gestation and infancy, and their number is dramatically reduced. In rats, undernourishment that extends through both the pre- and postnatal periods results in fewer synapses per neuron, fewer synaptic spines, and considerably less myelin than normal nourishment. These findings together suggest that the brains of malnourished children are both slower and more poorly organized than they could be.

In studying the cognitive effects of postnatal nutrition, it is often difficult to separate the influence of inadequate food intake from other aspects of the baby's environment. Malnourished children almost always grow up in less supportive and stimulating environments than well-nourished ones, compounding the effect of inadequate nutrition on brain development. They may be neglected, sick, abused, or simply so hungry that they have little energy or motivation to learn and practice new skills. On the other hand, an otherwise strong environment can protect an infant from the effects of postnatal malnutrition. For instance, babies who are undernourished because of illnesses in which they cannot absorb food well—cystic fibrosis is one example—do not suffer cognitive deficits if they are raised in a stimulating and

supportive environment. It therefore appears that in terms of brain maturation, an excellent environment can compensate for malnutrition, probably
by stimulating the same synaptic development that would otherwise suffer
from the lack of nutrients.

There is also good news for children who are rescued early in life from
malnourishment. Those who are given excellent nutrition, coupled with
emotional support and intellectual stimulation, can recover most of their
intellectual ability. However, this rehabilitation must begin very early.
After two years of age, a child will have lasting mental deficiencies, even if
he is now adequately nourished and stimulated. Again, this window of
opportunity corresponds to the period of massive synaptic growth and
myelination, suggesting that as long as these cellular processes are ensuing,
the brain has a way to recover. One can't help wondering, though, if a child
ever fully recovers his or her true intellectual potential after suffering starvation during the fetal or infant period. One famous study, for instance,
looked at female Korean War orphans who were adopted by middle-class
American parents before the age of two. Although all the girls achieved IQ
scores in the normal range by grade school, those who had been most
severely malnourished as infants scored significantly lower than those who
had been well nourished.

The importance of early nutrition for later brain function has been recognized for nearly three decades and has figured importantly in government
efforts to feed infants and pregnant women in the United States and other
countries. The more we learn about the role of early nutrition in later cognitive function, the more important it becomes to ensure that every child is
adequately nourished during this sensitive period of brain development.

Maternal Drug and Chemical Exposure

These days, drugs are assumed to be harmful in pregnancy unless proven otherwise, and women are counseled to avoid any kind of medication when possible. There are, however, clearly times when pregnant women need to take
drugs to treat chronic or life-threatening diseases, and the general rule is that
a given drug is acceptable if its benefit to the mother outweighs its risk to the
fetus. Different drugs vary tremendously in this relationship, so to help clarify things, the U.S. Food and Drug Administration set up the following clas-
sification system for drug use in pregnancy:

Pregnancy Category	Consensus of Available Studies on Risk/Benefit
A	Controlled studies in humans have demonstrated no fetal risks in the first trimester, and the risk of fetal harm appears remote.
B	Human and animal data have not demonstrated a significant risk.
C	Existing studies are inadequate, or animal studies have shown adverse fetal effects, but human data is not available.
D	Fetal risk is clearly present, but the benefits outweigh the risk.
X	The risk outweighs the benefit. The drug is contra-indicated in pregnancy.

At the one extreme, Category X, are drugs such as isotretinoin (the brand name is Accutane), a vitamin A derivative taken orally for cases of severe acne. First-trimester use of isotretinoin results in a major malformation in at least 28 percent of all babies exposed as fetuses, especially of the ears, or the cardiovascular or central nervous system. Since acne is never life-threatening, the use of isotretinoin is contraindicated during pregnancy. In fact, the manufacturer recommends that any woman of childbearing years have a negative pregnancy test within two weeks of beginning the drug and agree to use two forms of birth control. Megadoses of vitamin A (more than 20,000 IU) also pose a grave danger to the developing nervous system and other organs. But, a related medicine, tretinoin (Retin-A), which is applied topically and widely used to prevent acne and wrinkles, is absorbed in only negligible amounts through the mother's skin and appears to pose no risk to the fetus with normal use.

Another extreme situation is diseases like cancer, epilepsy, diabetes, clinical depression, high blood pressure, and certain infections that can indeed threaten the life of both mother and fetus unless adequately treated with drugs. While some established treatments for these disorders are known to be dangerous to the fetus, alternatives are often available that can be used much more safely during pregnancy. In the case of epilepsy, for instance, three common anticonvulsant drugs are known to cause birth defects. Valproic acid and carbamazepine, as mentioned earlier, raise the risk of neural tube defects by about tenfold, while phenytoin (Dilantin) causes a syndrome in 5 to 30 percent of fetuses that can include growth retardation, head and limb abnormalities, and varying degrees of mental retardation. Mothers with epilepsy may be able to control their seizures with less risky drugs such as ethosuximide or benzodiazepines. (For such women, it is always better to switch medications before becoming pregnant if possible, since seizures themselves pose some risk to the fetus, and one can't know in advance whether a new drug will adequately control them.) But, even if a woman *must* take a drug during pregnancy with a known risk to the fetus (Category D), careful prenatal screening can detect major malformations like neural tube defects with over 90 percent accuracy.

While over-the-counter drugs are generally safer than prescription medications, they still should be avoided unless a mother is extremely uncomfortable. Acetaminophen (Tylenol) is the recommended drug for pain and fever because the alternatives, aspirin and ibuprofen, have been associated with third-trimester complications. In particular, babies exposed to aspirin in the one week before birth have a higher incidence of intraventricular hemorrhage—bleeding in the brain—because aspirin inhibits blood clotting. Prenatal exposure to aspirin (but not acetaminophen) has also been linked to IQ and attention deficits in four-year-olds, according to one preliminary report, while another study suggests that first-trimester use of aspirin, ibuprofen, or one of several decongestants increases the risk of *gastroschisis*, a failure of the abdominal wall to close during embryonic development. Other nonprescription drugs, including antacids, antihistamines, laxatives, cough suppressants, and many topical agents are considered safe but should be used only if essential. Many over-the-counter remedies contain a mixture of several drugs, so expectant women should always read their labels carefully and, more important, consult their health care provider before taking *any* medication.

Alcohol   Alcohol has been called "the teratogen of choice" in our culture. Most women are now aware that heavy drinking can harm a fetus, but the condition it causes, *fetal alcohol syndrome* (FAS), whose symptoms include face and head defects, growth and mental retardation, and anomalies of the heart and other organs, still afflicts about two in every thousand babies born. In fact, prenatal alcohol exposure is one of the leading causes of mental retardation in the United States. Alcohol also increases the chances of miscarriage, premature delivery, and birth complications. It readily crosses the placenta and reaches a comparable level in fetal blood to that in the mother's bloodstream. If a mother is intoxicated, her fetus is drunk as well.

Studies in both humans and animals indicate that the brain is the organ most vulnerable to developmental disturbance by alcohol. Alcohol directly kills neurons in fetal brains. It also disrupts the migration of neurons and glia, so that particular brain structures may be out of place or even fail to form. While lower doses do not cause gross brain malformations, alcohol still interferes with dendritic growth, dendritic spine development, and the formation of precise synaptic connections. Different brain regions are affected depending on the timing of alcohol exposure. For instance, some of the last neurons to be produced are in the cerebellum, and studies in the rat have shown that alcohol exposure during a period that corresponds to the third trimester in humans permanently reduces the number of neurons and glia that survive in the cerebellum.

The effects of alcohol on the fetus are clearly dose dependent; full-blown FAS occurs in 30 to 50 percent of infants born to mothers who consume at least six drinks per day. ("One drink" is defined as any beverage containing 0.5 ounce of pure alcohol—the amount in a twelve-ounce glass of beer, a five-ounce glass of wine, or 1.5 ounces of liquor.) And even if the baby is not visibly deformed, his or her risk of future cognitive problems is substantially increased. Up to 80 percent of children born to alcoholic mothers have been found to suffer some degree of mental retardation, hyperactivity, or speech deficit.

With moderate levels of prenatal alcohol exposure, the risk of full-blown FAS is minimal, but children may still suffer some mental impairment. For instance, school-aged children whose mothers averaged about three drinks per day throughout pregnancy scored about seven points lower on IQ tests than children unexposed to alcohol as fetuses, even after correcting for factors like the mothers' smoking, diet, education level, and whether the babies were breast-fed. This IQ decrement is not outside the range of normal intelligence, but it is nonetheless significant, indicating that these middle-class children would have been considerably smarter if they had not been exposed to prenatal alcohol.

The effects of modest alcohol consumption are more controversial. Several studies have looked but found no evidence for increased rates of malformation, newborn behavioral abnormalities, or cognitive delay among children whose mothers consumed one or two drinks per day during pregnancy. Other studies, however, report an increased risk of miscarriage with just four or more drinks per week and of *placenta abruptio* (detachment of the placenta from the uterus) with consumption of up to two drinks per day. Yet another reports that as little as one to three drinks *per month* slightly increases the risk of cleft lip, and the risk steadily rises with consumption of four to ten drinks per month, and again with ten or more drinks. Some of the discrepancies undoubtedly arise from the different ways researchers cluster alcohol consumption among pregnant women. ("Four or more drinks per week," for instance, includes everything but the most modest consumption.) There's also a conspicuous divergence between studies conducted in the United States, which tend to find significant effects of modest consumption, and those conducted in Europe or Australia, which tend to find no effects. So the jury is still out on whether modest alcohol consumption—the occasional drink or even a single glass of wine every night with dinner—has any effect on fetal health or cognitive potential.

Another issue is whether "binge drinking" is particularly detrimental to the fetus. Binge drinking is defined as consuming five or more drinks on one occasion, so technically a woman could be considered a "modest" drinker even if she has a binge every week. Bingeing, however, raises a woman's alcohol level many times higher than when the same drinks are spread out over several days. One Seattle study has found a link between one or more binges during pregnancy and deficits in learning, attention, memory, and sensory and motor skills in seven-year-old children, and in reading and writing skills as late as fourteen years of age. A Danish study, however, failed to find any effect of binge drinking on cognitive tests at eighteen and forty-two months.

It's clear that women should avoid heavy (and probably moderate) drinking while pregnant or even trying to conceive a child. Whether they should abstain entirely from alcohol during conception and pregnancy is less clear. Although abstinence is obviously the safest course and is now advised by most doctors and public health officials, the fact is that we still do not know whether modest alcohol consumption has any deleterious effects on the fetus. Like most teratogens, alcohol presumably has some threshold below which it has no effect on fetal development, but no one yet knows what this threshold level is. The wisest strategy, therefore, is to cut out alcohol as early as possible in a pregnancy and preferably before conception. In one regard, however, this uncertainty about modest drinking may be reassuring. Women who consumed up to two drinks per day before learning they were pregnant can take some comfort in the fact that this amount of alcohol has not actually been proven harmful to the fetus.

It is from a public health standpoint, rather than from knowledge of individual risk, that abstinence is now advised during pregnancy. As of 1995, 16 percent of pregnant women in the United States reported drinking alcohol in the month preceding the survey, and 3 percent admitted to at least one binge. (Alcohol consumption is notoriously underreported in this kind of survey.) Prenatal alcohol use is thought to be responsible for at least 4,000 cases of mental retardation in the United States each year and perhaps ten times that number of children with mild learning or behavioral problems. (Because the milder effects of prenatal alcohol generally do not show up until several years after birth, one wonders how often these effects are attributed to other factors.) Society pays a heavy price for alcohol consumption during pregnancy, which is why the U.S. Congress began requiring warnings about FAS on alcohol bottles in 1989. Although alcohol consumption during pregnancy had declined substantially in the 1980s, it actually *increased* between 1991 and 1995.

Cigarettes   Most women also realize that smoking is bad during pregnancy. Unfortunately, it can be a very hard habit to give up, even for the best-intentioned parent. Smoking is not as detrimental to fetal brain development as heavy alcohol drinking, but it acts on many other organ systems, like the heart and lungs, that compromise the baby's health in a lasting way. Babies born to heavy smokers are substantially smaller than babies born to nonsmokers, averaging about half a pound lighter. In fact, smoking is one of the leading preventable causes of low birth weight, since 25 percent of women are estimated to smoke during their pregnancy. (These babies are born smaller, regardless of the amount of weight the mother gained during pregnancy, so their low birth weight is not due simply to the possibility that their mothers ate less than nonsmokers.) Smoking also increases the risk of miscarriage and premature birth caused by problems with the placenta. Both prematurity and low birth weight increase a child's chances of mental or neurological impairment.

When a pregnant mother smokes a cigarette, nicotine rushes into the fetal circulation and dramatically alters the baby's breathing movements, with periods of apnea (cessation of breathing) alternating with periods of extra-rapid breathing. Babies whose mothers smoked during pregnancy have a greater risk of sudden infant death syndrome (SIDS), which may be related to this altered breathing pattern in utero.

Several long-term studies of children born to mothers who smoked during pregnancy have suggested that their brain development and function are compromised. In various reports, prenatal smoking has been linked to deficiencies in newborn sucking ability, in language and motor skills in one- and two-year-olds, in hyperactivity and auditory attention in four-to-seven-year-olds, and in learning ability in seven-to-eleven-year-olds. Two other studies also link it to attention-deficit hyperactivity in six-to-seventeen-year-old boys and to mental retardation of otherwise unknown cause. Some of these results are controversial and may be complicated by the fact that, on average, smokers tend to consume more alcohol and to be of lower socioeconomic status than nonsmokers. Overall, however, the evidence to date does suggest that heavy smoking during pregnancy has long-term effects on cognitive abilities that are probably due to compromised brain development in the womb.

Cigarette smoke contains numerous chemicals that are potentially harmful to the developing brain. Of these, only the effects of nicotine and carbon monoxide are well understood. Both chemicals contribute to the lower birth weight of babies whose mothers smoke. Nicotine constricts blood vessels and thus reduces the blood supply to the fetus. Carbon monoxide displaces oxygen in the circulation of both the mother and fetus. Both chemicals therefore decrease the amount of oxygen available to the fetus, and less oxygen means slower growth of all bodily organs.

Nicotine is particularly suspect as an agent of neural damage. Nicotine binds very specifically to one class of receptors for the neurotransmitter acetylcholine. (In fact, this class of receptor is known as the "nicotinic" type.) In addition to their role in synaptic communication, most neurotransmitters act during development to promote neuronal growth. Exposure to nicotine in utero may therefore interfere with developmental signals normally communicated by acetylcholine. In rats, prenatal nicotine administration has been found to affect neuron structure and biochemistry in areas of the brain that synthesize and store acetylcholine. Like humans, rats that are exposed to nicotine before birth show later behavioral deficits, such as altered arousal, attention, and motor function, which are probably attributable to these neuronal perturbations.

Women are strongly advised to stop smoking during pregnancy. Smoking is most detrimental to fetal growth during the third trimester, but mothers who quit smoking even earlier, by sixteen weeks of pregnancy, have babies of normal birth weight. Quitting even one month before delivery decreases the chance that the baby will suffer a lack of oxygen during birth, which is one of the most common causes of brain damage. It is not known when the other detrimental effects of prenatal smoking occur, but presumably, the earlier a mother quits, the more likely it is that her baby's brain will be unharmed. At the very least, women who can't quit smoking should limit their smoking to as few cigarettes as possible, since the effects of cigarettes, like most harmful agents, are dose dependent.

In this light, even passive smoking has been found to be harmful to intellectual development. In one study, researchers tested six-to-nine-year-old children on their speech, language, visual/spatial, and general intellectual abilities and found that those whose mothers were exposed to secondhand smoke during pregnancy performed midway between children whose mothers smoked and those whose households were smoke-free during their gestation. Thus, mothers aren't the only ones who should quit smoking before or as early as possible during pregnancy. Fathers and other members of the household can also do their baby's brain a favor by kicking their smoking habit.

Illegal Drugs   It is often difficult to estimate the effect of a single illicit drug, since women who abuse one substance during pregnancy are also likely to use other drugs or alcohol, and to smoke, eat poorly, receive little or no prenatal care, and generally have a lifestyle that puts the fetus at greater risk for miscarriage, birth defects, and developmental problems. With this caveat in mind, virtually every drug of abuse has been linked to higher rates of brain defects or developmental delays, in at least some studies. All of the widely abused drugs (including legal alcohol and tobacco) also increase the probability of miscarriage and premature delivery.

Cocaine does not produce any particular pattern of fetal malformation, but it is associated with gestational problems that interfere with normal brain development. Its use can cause the placenta to detach, triggering premature labor. Babies of cocaine-addicted mothers tend to be small, whether or not they were born prematurely, and have an increased risk of microcephaly—an abnormally small head size—which often causes mental retardation. Cocaine use also increases the risk of stroke or hemorrhage in the fetal brain, both of which can produce lasting damage. Cocaine-exposed babies don't respond well to their environment or interact normally with caregivers. Their behavioral problems are evident even in the womb, when maternal cocaine use is known to disrupt fetal movement and sleep patterns.

Heroin has also been linked to long-term growth and behavioral problems. Babies born to heroin-addicted mothers are themselves addicted and can suffer severe withdrawal symptoms at birth, leading to a high rate of neonatal death. They are also at higher risk for SIDS. Even methadone, which is used to treat heroin addiction during pregnancy, can cause serious withdrawal symptoms in babies after birth. However, birth weight and long-term development are considerably better for babies whose mothers used methadone rather than heroin during pregnancy.

Marijuana use offers the double whammy of a drug effect and the oxygen deprivation caused by smoking. The intoxicating chemical in marijuana, THC, crosses the placenta quite easily and is cleared very slowly from the fetal circulation. Like tobacco smoking, marijuana greatly increases carbon monoxide levels in the fetus's circulation, robbing the developing brain of necessary oxygen. Maternal marijuana use has been linked to altered visual and startle responses in newborns, to behavioral deficits in school-aged children, and to verbal and memory deficits in four-year-olds.

Caffeine   Caffeine is naturally present in many beverages and is a common additive in many others. It is a central nervous system stimulant that increases alertness and attentiveness, as well as heart rate and metabolic rate. In high doses (more than 600 milligrams) caffeine can cause heart palpitations, anxiety, sleeplessness, nausea, and even depression. Depending on how it's brewed, one six-ounce cup of coffee contains from 60 to 150 milligrams of caffeine, a one-ounce cup of espresso contains from 30 to 80 milligrams, and a six-ounce cup of tea, from 20 to 100 milligrams. One can of a caffeinated soft drink contains from 32 to 72 milligrams of caffeine, depending on brand, and an ounce of dark chocolate contains 20 milligrams of a caffeine-related compound, theobromine. Caffeine is also present in many over-the-counter medications, such as Excedrin (65 milligrams per tablet), Anacin (32.5), and Dexatrim (200).

Caffeine crosses the placenta and may even concentrate in the fetal circulation. Concern about its effect on fetal development stems from animal studies, where it has been found to be teratogenic when fed to pregnant rats in high doses; a dose equivalent to 150 cups of strong coffee per day causes malformations in rodents such as missing limbs and digits. However, caffeine does not appear to be a teratogen in humans. The average pregnant woman is estimated to consume 144 milligrams per day of caffeine, which presents no danger to a developing fetus. Even women who consume fairly large amounts of caffeine (more than 400 milligrams per day) during pregnancy do not increase their risk of having a baby with a congenital malformation. And despite old wives' warnings, prenatal exposure to caffeine does not stunt fetal growth; nor, according to one study of seven-year-olds whose mothers drank caffeinated beverages during pregnancy, does it have any effect on a child's later IQ.

Nevertheless, while caffeine does not appear to cause birth or cognitive defects, some studies have found that women who consume fairly large amounts during pregnancy take longer to conceive and have a higher rate of miscarriage. Heavy caffeine use can also cause withdrawal symptoms in a baby at birth. Because of these findings, as well as lingering doubts based on the effects of high doses in animals, pregnant women are advised to consume no more than 300 milligrams of caffeine per day (the equivalent of three cups, or two mugs, of medium-strength coffee).

Aspartame   The synthetic sweetener aspartame (NutraSweet, Equal) is composed of two amino acids, aspartate and phenylalanine, that are normally present in every tissue of the body. When consumed, one molecule of aspartame breaks down into one molecule of each of these amino acids and also releases one molecule of methanol. While methanol is quite hazardous when consumed in large quantities (for instance, by accidental ingestion of varnish or antifreeze), the amount released from one can of diet soda is less than the amount naturally present in a banana or a can of fruit juice. Aspartate doesn't cross the placenta. Phenylalanine does, and is even somewhat concentrated on the fetal side of the placenta, but it is not harmful at normal levels. (As with all aspartame use, however, women with the hereditary disorder phenylketonuria—PKU—who cannot utilize phenylalanine and therefore accumulate it in their bodies to dangerous levels, should not consume it.)

Concern about artificial sweeteners probably stems from a preliminary study, published in 1971, linking prenatal exposure to cyclamates and other unnamed sweeteners to behavioral problems like hyperactivity and nervousness. Aspartame is not included in that group, however, since it was not approved for use until 1981. A more recent study looked specifically at the effects of aspartame on children with attention deficit disorder and found no behavioral or cognitive changes, even when consumed at ten times the usual amount. Several animal studies have tested the effect of prenatal aspartame exposure on various aspects of physical and mental function. The vast majority of these have found no alterations in animal development, reflexes, vision, behavior, and memory, even when mothers were given very high doses.

Thus, current evidence indicates that women can safely consume aspartame during pregnancy without posing any risk to the fetus or its later developmental potential. The other commonly used artificial sweetener, saccharine (Sweet 'n Low), is also considered safe during pregnancy, although it has not been as thoroughly tested as aspartame and some health professionals continue to regard it with suspicion since high doses cause bladder tumors in experimental animals.

Monosodium Glutamate (MSG)   MSG is also composed of a common amino acid, glutamate, together with one molecule of sodium. Although we often hear about the health risks of high sodium intake, it's the glutamate in MSG that is more worrisome with regard to brain development. Glutamate is a potent flavor enhancer commonly used in Asian cuisines, but it is also present in many prepared and convenience foods, especially soups, salad dressings, sauces, marinades, luncheon meats, frozen meals, flavored chips and crackers, and flavored mixes for rice and pasta. (In fact, the average American probably consumes much more glutamate from eating at home than from the occasional Chinese dinner out.) In addition to MSG, glutamate is often added to food in the form of "hydrolyzed vegetable protein," which contains from 10 to 30 percent glutamate, and can be referred to on food labels as "HVP," "flavoring," or even "natural flavoring."

Concern about glutamate arises from the fact that high doses are known to kill brain cells, and younger animals are especially susceptible to its toxic effects. As we have seen, neurons communicate across the synaptic gap using neurotransmitters; these chemical messengers come in two types—excitatory and inhibitory. Glutamate is the most prevalent excitatory neurotransmitter in the brain. When neurons are overexcited by glutamate, as happens, for example, in regions of the brain undergoing an epileptic seizure, they can be damaged or even killed, much as an electrical appliance can be damaged if too much current passes through it.

Despite this scary scenario, it's very unlikely that mothers who consume MSG during pregnancy risk damaging their fetus's brain. The main reason to think MSG is safe is that glutamate does not cross the placenta very well. In addition, the total amount of glutamate consumed as a food additive is just a small proportion (on the order of 2 to 3 percent) of the total amount of glutamate consumed in the form of protein in a normal woman's diet. Like aspartate and phenylalanine, glutamate is one of the twenty amino acids present in all types of protein, and it is used by the body to build its own proteins. Even people who avoid MSG and "natural flavoring" eat large quantities of it every day. Finally, there's no evidence that populations consuming large quantities of MSG (in Asia, for example) suffer any greater incidence of brain damage or mental retardation than populations with low consumption. Common sense, together with current epidemiological knowledge, argues that when these amino acids are consumed in modest amounts, they pose no danger to the developing brain in utero.

Aspartate and Glutamate in Infancy and Early Childhood

Unlike the situation in pregnancy, there is more serious basis for concern about glutamate and aspartate exposure after birth. Without the placenta both amino acids have readier access to babies' brains, particularly to the *hypothalamus*, a major regulatory structure that lies largely outside the protective blood-brain barrier. When young rats or mice are fed large doses of glutamate, significant numbers of hypothalamic neurons die, and the rodents later show hormonal disturbances leading to problems like obesity, infertility, or delayed puberty. Aspartate has excitatory actions in the brain very similar to those of glutamate, and it is also known to damage rat hypothalamic neurons.

Although there is no clinical or epidemiological evidence to suggest that children's brains are being damaged by excess glutamate and aspartate, the growing prevalence of these flavoring agents in all kinds of foods is considered by some researchers as potentially quite dangerous. Infants and young children are particularly vulnerable because their neurons are known to be more sensitive than adults' to glutamate, and because the same serving of any particular food, such as a dehydrated noodle soup cup, will deliver a much greater dose of glutamate to say, a thirty-pound toddler than to a 150-pound adult. Manufacturers voluntarily stopped adding MSG to baby food nearly thirty years ago, but thus far the Food and Drug Administration has decided not to regulate glutamate addition to processed food. While the amount of aspartate in sugar-free yogurt, chewing gum, or soda is rather small, it can add to the high levels of glutamate already present in many children's diets, potentially threatening their neuronal health.

Other Chemicals   Many chemicals in addition to drugs, abused substances, and food additives pose potential risks to fetal brain development. In

general, the chance of a problem is much greater when a woman is exposed through her occupation, and strict guidelines usually exist for pregnant women in jobs that require use of known teratogens. As we've noted, however, the vast majority of potential teratogens have barely been studied. Therefore, women who work in factories, farms, hospitals, laboratories, beauty parlors, dry cleaners, and any other job with daily chemical exposure need to be especially careful during pregnancy, to learn as much as possible about the substances in their work environment, and to minimize their exposure to anything suspect.

Based on what is known, exposure to the following chemicals should be avoided during pregnancy: organic solvents (including toluene, benzene, and gases used in anesthesia), oil-based paints (latex and other water-based paints are safe), all types of herbicides and pesticides, PCBs (which were banned in the United States in the 1970s but remain concentrated in many landfills, as well as in lakes and the fish that inhabit them), vinyl chloride (used in plastic manufacturing), carbon monoxide, hydrocarbons (including gasoline), mercury compounds* (particularly methyl mercury, which is used as a fungicide), and other heavy metals including cadmium (present in cigarette smoke), nickel, and lead.

The greatest risk occurs if a teratogen is inhaled or ingested, so volatile compounds, such as solvents and oil-based paints, should be handled in a well-ventilated area, and hand-to-mouth contact should be avoided when using any kind of chemical. Volatile teratogens have most clearly been linked to birth defects in the case of solvent abusers—pregnant women who regularly sniff toluene to get high. The data are less convincing for women exposed to solvents in their jobs, although studies do suggest that hairdressers, operating room doctors and nurses, and certain factory workers are somewhat likelier to miscarry or to have children with birth defects or developmental delays than women without such exposure. As compared to occupational levels, the occasional exposure to volatile teratogens, like pumping your own gas or painting the baby's room with oil-based paint, is highly unlikely to harm the fetus.

---

*Thermometers and dental amalgam contain mercury in its elemental form—not as a molecular compound—which is not absorbed by the gastrointestinal tract to a significant degree, so even if a pregnant woman accidentally swallows some mercury in this form, her fetus will not be unduly jeopardized.

Lead   The dangers of lead merit special discussion, because it is so widely present in our environment. The greatest risk of lead exposure is to women who work in automotive and aircraft painting, in printing, and in smelting and battery-making industries, and for artists who do glass-staining or jewelry-making. In addition to such occupational exposure, lead is a frequently found contaminant in dust and water, is present in some types of pottery and utensils used for food preparation, and prior to the 1970s was a major component of house paint.

Lead interferes with the function of many enzymes in the body. It is particularly troublesome during development because it blocks mineral absorption, energy utilization, and DNA synthesis—all steps that allow cells to grow and divide. Consequently, women exposed to lead have higher rates of infertility, miscarriage, stillbirth, and premature birth and are likelier to give birth to babies with minor defects. Some of these problems have even been seen when only the father is exposed to lead.

Of wider concern are the subtler effects on mental function seen among children exposed to lead before birth. Researchers have now documented small but significant mental deficits among children whose fetal lead level (measured in umbilical cord blood at birth) exceeded 10 micrograms per deciliter, a level once thought to be safe. If the exposure ends at birth, the effect appears to be reversible and children recover normal IQ scores by four or five years of age. But if a child is also exposed to lead after birth (as is often the case) or is raised in an otherwise disadvantaged environment, his intelligence may be permanently compromised. (Lead exposure that begins only after birth is also dangerous, but only when it reaches somewhat higher blood levels.) The effect of lead is thus quite similar to the effect of malnutrition: the earlier it begins and the longer it lasts, the greater the deficits, but modest exposure can be overcome if a child's early environment is stimulating and supportive.

The risk of intellectual deficits in children helped motivate the U.S. Environmental Protection Agency in 1973 to promulgate the manufacture and use of unleaded gasoline. Reducing lead emissions from automobiles has dramatically lowered the lead in air, soil, and dust over the last twenty-five years. This act, together with the removal of lead from the solder used in food cans, lowered the average level of lead in the blood of preschool children by some 80 percent in the years between 1976 and 1991. Despite this improvement, however, large numbers of young children continue to have blood lead concentrations exceeding the Centers for Disease Control's new maximum recommended level—10 micrograms per deciliter. The risk is particularly high for young black children, 21 percent of whom continue to have blood levels greater than the recommended maximum, as compared with 6 percent of white children.

While lead levels in the air and soil have improved considerably, lead in water and in the paint of older homes continues to present a significant hazard for pregnant women and young children. Lead paint poses a risk when young children eat or suck on paint chips, or when pregnant women or children breathe dust from deteriorating painted surfaces. Houses built before 1978 are especially suspect, and under a new law passed by Congress in 1992, owners of targeted housing have been required to reveal any information about known lead-based paint to potential buyers or renters of the property. Lead solder is no longer used in pipes, but drinking water can become contaminated if lead leaches out of old pipes or solder joints in the plumbing. It is a good idea to have your drinking water tested for lead content if you're pregnant or have young children in the house. If levels are unacceptably high (the EPA's maximum allowable level in drinking water is 50 micrograms per liter), lead-removing filters are available for home tap-water systems, or you can purchase water for drinking that is certified lead free.

Ionizing Radiation

The word *radiation* itself is scary to many expectant parents. It connotes atomic bombs and nuclear fallout, now-obvious sources of grave danger to developing fetuses, as well as the rest of us. Radiation is indeed a potent teratogen, but like all harmful agents, the degree of danger is proportional to the dose encountered, and different types of radiation vary tremendously in their harmfulness.

The potent forms fall under the class of *ionizing radiation* and include X-rays, gamma rays, and particles released from radioactive decay. These forms of radiation are very high in energy, high enough to dislodge an electron from a single atom or molecule, a process known as *ionization*. Each of these forms of radiation can therefore directly damage molecules in the body, causing tissue injury or, if important stretches of DNA are altered, permanent mutations in an individual's genetic code. When adults are exposed to excessive doses of ionizing radiation, some of these mutations may result in cancer. If a fetus is exposed, the mutations can alter entire developmental programs, resulting in fetal death or birth defects, particularly those affecting the brain.

The risks of radiation during pregnancy have been learned the hard

way—from Japanese atomic bomb victims and women who received extensive medical irradiation during the early days of X-rays. In both cases, many
babies who survived exposure in utero were born with abnormally small
heads (microcephaly) and some degree of mental retardation. The larger the
dose, the greater the chance of miscarriage, microcephaly, or mental deficit.
Thus, of the fifty-six babies born to mothers who had been within 1.1 miles
of the Hiroshima bomb, twenty-three had microcephaly, which is twenty-
two more than would be predicted in a normal population.

The developing brain is most vulnerable to ionizing radiation between
eight and fifteen weeks following conception. High doses of radiation during
this period, the phase of maximal neuron production in the brain, are very
likely to produce mental retardation. Exposure during the first two weeks after
conception is nearly always lethal to the embryo. Exposure between two and
eight weeks does not cause mental defects but is very likely to damage organs
other than the brain. Between sixteen and twenty-five weeks, ionizing radiation continues to be dangerous to the fetus, but the risk of mental deficit is
four to five times lower than it is during the eight-to-fifteen-week period.

These findings have helped to establish guidelines for the safe use of
radiation during pregnancy. The maximum recommended dose of X-rays or
other medical irradiation in the course of pregnancy is five rem. (*Rem* is a
measured unit of radiation that takes account of absorption by biological tissues.) This dose is ten times lower than the lowest level that has been associated with mental retardation. For radiologists, laboratory technicians,
atomic energy workers, and any other women exposed to ionizing radiation
in their work, the level of acceptable occupational exposure is 0.5 rem, or a
hundred times lower than the apparent threshold for mental retardation.

To put these numbers in perspective, it's useful to know that the average
amount of radiation a mother is exposed to from natural sources in the environment is about 0.18 rem over her entire pregnancy. This *background radiation*
comes from the sun and cosmic sources and from naturally occurring radioactivity in rocks, soil, air, and even building materials. Its level varies in different
geographic regions, with more radiation at higher altitudes and latitudes. For
instance, airline crew members receive the equivalent of an extra 0.08 rem per
year because of their greater exposure to cosmic and solar radiation. Although
the health effects of low levels of radiation are still poorly understood, babies
born in regions receiving levels of background radiation even ten times higher
than average do not show an excess number of birth defects.

Ionizing radiation is used in medicine for two different purposes: diagnosis and treatment. Doses are considerably lower in diagnostic X-rays, CT scans, and angiography than in therapeutic irradiation, where very strong X-rays or gamma rays are focused on a tumor, or radioactive chemicals are injected for the purpose of cancer treatment. Therapeutic irradiation is virtually never advised during pregnancy, and if its use is necessary for the health of the mother, abortion may be counseled.

Diagnostic radiation is another matter. Although the maximum recommended exposure, five rem, is associated with a slightly increased rate of fetal malformations, the medical profession maintains that women should not be denied necessary diagnostic radiation simply because they're pregnant. It can and should be used if the mother's immediate health requires it. On the other hand, given that diagnostic radiation does pose a small but measurable risk to the developing fetus, any elective radiation (like dental X-rays or occupational exams) should be postponed until after pregnancy.

For mothers faced with the need for diagnostic X-rays during pregnancy (as occurs in 15 percent of all pregnancies), or who were already irradiated before learning they were pregnant, several facts are worth keeping in mind. First, the time of exposure is important, so if X-rays can be performed outside the eight-to-fifteen-week window (the tenth to seventeenth weeks of pregnancy), the risk of fetal brain damage is substantially reduced. Second, medical X-rays are highly focused, so the fetus gets very little exposure from X-rays directed away from the uterus. For instance, the fetus receives about 200 times less radiation from X-rays directed to the mother's head than to her pelvis (and the typical pelvic dose is about one twenty-fifth of the maximum recommended amount of radiation during pregnancy). Third, whenever the uterus does not need to be directly exposed to radiation, the fetus can be largely protected by placing a lead apron over the mother's abdomen. Finally, radiation exposures are cumulative, so the recommended maximum dose of five rem represents the sum of *all* exposures a woman should receive during the entire nine months of pregnancy, not the dose for a single exposure.

Nonionizing Radiation

While the risks of ionizing radiation are well understood, much less is known about the effects of *nonionizing radiation*—energy or sound waves that may penetrate tissue but do not break apart biological molecules. *Nonionizing radiation* is something of a grab-bag term, used to describe both mechanical waves—the collision of molecules that creates sound and ultrasound—and energy waves in the middle and low part of the electromagnetic spectrum. In order of decreasing frequency, these electromagnetic sources include all types of light (ultraviolet, visible, and infrared), microwaves (now widely used for telecommunications, cooking, and radar), radio waves (FM, AM, and shortwave radio frequencies, as well as VHF and UHF television frequencies), and very-low-to-zero-frequency (static) emissions and magnetic fields, which emanate from power sources and electrical devices. (See Figure 3.1.)

Unlike ionizing radiation—X-rays, gamma rays, and cosmic rays—at the high end of the electromagnetic spectrum, these lower-frequency, lower-energy waves cannot directly damage molecules. They can, however, damage tissue by indirect means if the exposure is intense enough. The main factor limiting the safety of nonionizing radiation is the degree to which it raises the temperature of the embryo or fetus. Prolonged temperature elevation increases the chances of spontaneous abortion and fetal malformation, particularly of the brain and eyes. (This is why pregnant women are counseled to avoid saunas, hot tubs, and electric blankets, to reduce high fevers, and to limit exercise to levels that don't overheat them.) Microwaves, radio waves, and ultrasound are all capable of raising body temperature if used at high

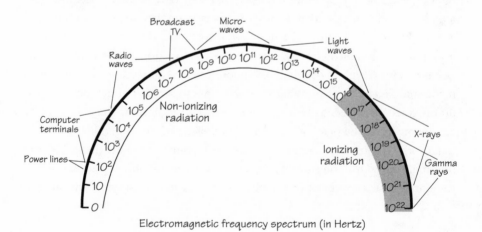

Electromagnetic frequency spectrum (in Hertz)

FIGURE 3.1

Electromagnetic energy spectrum. Only those waves in the ionizing range—above 10^{16} cycles per second—have been proven to alter fetal development.

intensity for relatively long periods. The general consensus about various forms of nonionizing radiation is that they are safe as long as they do not raise the fetus's temperature higher than 39°C (about 102°F), which is unlikely to occur with typical or even with maximum permissible levels of nonionizing radiation exposure, as determined by industrial and government agencies.

However, nonionizing radiation is known to act in other more esoteric ways on biological tissues. Since little is known about these mechanisms, and since our modern world is rapidly adding more and more sources of nonionizing radiation to the environment, some researchers remain suspicious that these invisible, ubiquitous, and seemingly innocuous waves could be responsible for some of that large category of birth defects whose causes are thus far unknown.

Nonionizing Electromagnetic Radiation   A great deal of fear has been generated in recent years about possible health hazards of electromagnetic radiation. Most of this attention has focused on computer monitors and high-voltage power lines—sources of nonionizing radiation in the lowest-frequency portion of the electromagnetic spectrum. At the same time, our society has seen rapid growth in the use of higher electromagnetic frequencies—radio wave, microwave, and infrared bandwidths—which are used for satellite and other telecommunication, broadcast radio and TV, cellular phones, intruder alarms, garage door openers, microwave ovens, and all the ubiquitous "clickers" that make daily life more and more convenient. As our civilization becomes increasingly electronic and remotely connected, we are all being exposed to higher and higher levels of nonionizing radiation. The question is whether this exposure poses any danger during fetal development.

The electromagnetic spectrum spans an enormous range, from cosmic waves, whose frequencies are as high as 10^{22} (10 billion trillion) cycles per second (also known as Hertz, or Hz), to extremely low-frequency waves, which oscillate at less than 30 Hz. As the frequency of a wave decreases, so does its energy. Below the frequency of X-rays (about 10^{17} Hz), electromagnetic waves do not have enough energy to directly ionize biological matter, although they can still damage tissues by heating and other mechanisms.

Within the nonionizing range, ultraviolet light has the highest energy. We're all aware of the damage UV irradiation can do to the eyes and skin, but fortunately, neither UV nor infrared light waves penetrate deeply enough to harm a fetus. Even microwaves, the next group of frequencies below light waves, do not penetrate tissue all that well at the high end of their spectrum (the portion used for satellite, TV, and telephone communication). But lower-frequency microwaves can be quite penetrating and are used in the vast majority of homes precisely because this penetration can heat food.

Microwaves and Radio Waves   Studies with rats, mice, and chicks have shown that intense exposure to radiation in the microwave and radio-frequency range is indeed dangerous during gestation. High-intensity levels can cause fetal death or malformations, especially of the brain and skull. These effects are not surprising, since the exposures also substantially elevate the animals' body temperature. Lower intensities do not cause heating and have generally been found to produce no harmful effects. In any case, the levels of radio- or microwave exposure in these animal experiments are well above those to which most women are normally exposed.

However, there are some occupations that involve exposure to microwaves or radio waves at intensities much higher than the communication frequencies in the air all around us. The power of electromagnetic radiation decreases exponentially with distance, which means that its intensity is considerably higher at the site of generation—on top of a radio tower, for instance—than even a short distance away. People who maintain broadcast towers, work with radar, or operate radio-frequency heating equipment (such as that used to weld plastics together) are exposed to much higher levels of radio- or microwave radiation than the average citizen. Since most of these occupations have been predominantly held by men, there are few data about pregnancy risks associated with intense radio- or microwave irradiation. Other health risks have been noted for such workers, however, including a high degree of infertility among men heavily exposed to microwaves for many years.

Physical therapy is one occupation in which many women are heavily exposed to radio and microwaves. A massage treatment called *diathermy* uses high-intensity microwaves or shortwave-frequency radio waves specifically for the purpose of warming patients' injured muscles. In a number of studies, physical therapists who operated diathermy units early in pregnancy were found to have slightly increased rates of miscarriage, stillbirth, or babies with birth defects. There was also a puzzling finding that they gave birth to many more girls than boys, perhaps because male embryos, who are generally more vulnerable than females, were likelier to be miscarried. When their diathermy units were tested for microwave leakage, some were found to emit levels exceeding the maximum permitted allowance (a voluntary standard for occupational exposure). These findings will presumably lead to improved safety provisions for physical therapists—the easiest remedy is to keep more than a meter away from the unit while it is in operation—but the results do prove that exposure to intense radio and microwaves can have deleterious effects on fetal development. (Obviously, pregnant women should avoid being on the receiving end of diathermy treatment, since the patient's exposure—and risk of overheating the fetus—is many times greater than the physical therapist's.)

And what about that microwave oven in virtually every pregnant woman's kitchen? Although they are certainly *capable* of producing high-intensity exposure, microwave ovens are built with several safety features to avoid this: mesh shielding that prevents microwaves from escaping through the front window, and doors that shut off the microwave generator before opening. Their safety is well regulated in this country by the U.S. Bureau of Radiological Health, which sets the level of allowable leakage both for new ovens and for those that have been in use up to five years. Microwave ovens can get leakier with age, as their door hinges grow loose or the door becomes warped or dented. Because of the rapid decay of electromagnetic power with distance, however, the level of exposure, even from a leaky oven, would be minimal at distances of just a few feet. Microwave ovens are considered safe for use by pregnant women, but it's probably a good idea to stand a few feet away from an older oven while in operation, and to avoid opening the door in the middle of a cooking cycle. (Press the "cancel" button first.)

Video Display Terminals (VDTs)   Televisions and computer monitors produce electrical and magnetic fields that oscillate at frequencies well below the radio and microwave range. (They can also produce ionizing radiation, but this danger has been eliminated since the early 1960s, when manufacturers began constructing picture tubes out of leaded glass.) Most people sit several feet away from their television sets, but computer users tend to sit very close to their monitors, raising some question about the health impact of low-frequency electromagnetic-wave exposure.

Several years ago a number of reports came out describing clusters of miscarriages, prematurity, birth defects, or newborn illness among women who used video display terminals (computer monitors) in their jobs. These findings were alarming, given the growing number of pregnant women who spend several hours a day in front of a computer terminal. But this large number of users has worked to the advantage of epidemiologists, who found in several subsequent, well-designed studies that VDT use by pregnant women does not in fact cause elevated rates of miscarriage or birth defects. One of the largest studies investigated VDT effects on two groups of telephone operators in the southeastern United States. These operators worked for the same companies, and their jobs were virtually identical except that at the time one group, the directory assistance operators, used VDTs, while the other group, the regular telephone operators, did not. Although the directory assistance operators were indeed exposed to larger oscillating magnetic fields emanating from the VDTs, they did not experience any higher rate of miscarriage than the regular operators.

Authorities then reexamined the original reports of birth defect and miscarriage clusters among VDT users and determined that most of them could be explained as simple random occurrences, a statistical by-product of the facts that 10 to 20 percent of all pregnancies end in miscarriage, 2 to 3 percent result in birth defects, and a large population of women use VDTs during pregnancy. Others of the original studies were found to suffer from *recall bias*: women who had suffered miscarriage or had a child with a birth defect were likelier to remember having used a computer terminal than those with normal pregnancies. (Recall bias is a common problem plaguing this type of epidemiological research, since parents who experience an abnormal pregnancy are often desperate to determine the cause so that it won't happen again. And the odds are, it won't.)

Women who use computer monitors during pregnancy can therefore rest easy: they won't harm their unborn baby.

Extra-low-frequency Electromagnetic Radiation: Power Lines and Electric Blankets

In recent years, much concern has focused on electromagnetic radiation at the lowest end of the spectrum. Throughout the world, electricity is supplied to homes and businesses in the form of 50 or 60 Hz alternating current, which produces electrical and magnetic fields that oscillate at the same frequency. Because this frequency is so low, neither VDT nor power-line radiation is energetic enough to heat tissue, the only known cause of damage by higher-frequency electromagnetic radiation. Nonetheless, concerns about electrical exposure were raised by several epidemiological studies in the 1980s, which reported that people who live in the vicinity of high-power transmission lines or who work in "electrical occupations" (such as power and telephone linemen, electronics engineers and technicians, and electric railway workers) were more likely than the general population to develop leukemia and brain tumors. High-voltage power lines do produce large electrical fields from which people are normally shielded by being indoors. Power lines, electric trains, and even some ordinary appliances also produce large magnetic fields, which are not shielded out by buildings or vehicles, so it is primarily magnetic fields that have provoked the greatest concern.

A flurry of more recent research has largely failed to confirm the link between magnetic field exposure and cancer. The risks, if present, appear to be much smaller than originally estimated, and considering the rarity of these types of cancer, they would amount to very few additional cancer cases per year. Nonetheless, the very suggestion that power lines might be linked to malignancy has prompted a search for their possible effects on fetal development. Various studies have produced conflicting results, ranging from an increased incidence of early miscarriages to no effect. Conflicting reports have also come out concerning the effects of electric blankets, which generate about the largest magnetic field exposure of any home appliance. One recent study did find that electric blanket use early in pregnancy modestly increases the risk of miscarriage, but it is not known whether this apparent risk is due to electromagnetic radiation or the effect of heat itself.

The most serious problem with this entire line of research is that no one has yet identified a convincing biological mechanism to explain how extremely low-frequency magnetic fields might alter development or produce malignancies. Animal studies, through which such mechanisms are usually discovered, have provided even less evidence for risk than human studies. In sum, low-frequency electromagnetic radiation does not appear to pose a risk to the developing fetus. But the field is still relatively new, and researchers are currently very busy exploring the possible ways that low-frequency magnetic fields might perturb biological organisms, as well as clarifying what the "safety threshold," if any, is for man-made electromagnetic exposure.

Magnetic Resonance Imaging (MRI)   Magnetic resonance imaging is a diagnostic procedure that uses a very strong magnetic field (25,000 times stronger than the earth's magnetic field), together with radio-frequency energy of approximately 60 megahertz, to construct high-resolution pictures of internal body structures. The magnetic field itself is static (nonoscillating) and acts to align the body's hydrogen atoms, each of which is polarized like a tiny compass needle, so they release a coherent signal in response to the radio-frequency excitation. This signal varies with the particular physical and chemical properties of the tissue in which it lies, so the computerized scanner can use slight differences in signals to produce a very detailed image of a patient's internal anatomy.

Considering that the risks of magnetic fields are still unknown, no one can say for certain whether MRI is safe to perform during pregnancy. Most studies in laboratory animals have not detected any adverse effect of MRI on reproductive outcome. One researcher has found that mice exposed to MRI in utero grow more slowly and have an increased risk of eye malformations, but these mice are genetically prone to these defects, so it is not known whether the findings are applicable to humans. Other evidence suggests that women who operate MRI machines may be at slightly increased risk for miscarriage, but the findings are considered preliminary. MRI is being used increasingly in obstetrics precisely for the purpose of evaluating fetal position, malformations, and other pregnancy complications. Although there is no convincing evidence that MRI poses a risk to the fetus, the National Radiological Protection Board has stated that more studies are needed before it can be declared truly safe, and women are advised to forgo MRI during the first trimester.

Ultrasound   The vast majority of women receive at least one ultrasound examination during pregnancy. Ultrasound imaging works by sending sound waves, whose frequencies are above the range of human hearing, into the uterus and recording the way they bounce back to a special detector. Because different types of tissue absorb ultrasound to different degrees, the computerized scanner can use differences in reflected sound waves to reconstruct an image of the living fetus and its uterine environment. The underlying principle is very similar to sonar, which is used on ships to locate objects under water. Ultrasound waves are also used in portable "Doppler" monitors and external fetal monitors, which are used to measure fetal heart rate during pregnancy and labor.

Ultrasound is not a form of electromagnetic radiation, but like microwaves and radio waves, it can disrupt biological tissues if the exposure is intense enough. Theoretically there are several ways in which large doses of ultrasound could harm a fetus, but the greatest concern is about tissue heating. As long as fetal temperature remains below 39°C (about 102°F), ultrasound does not pose any measurable risk, and normal diagnostic use should keep it well within this range. However, pregnant women suffering from a fever should probably postpone any ultrasound exams until it subsides, to minimize the chance of overheating the fetus.

Epidemiological studies have provided reassuring evidence about ultrasound's safety. While the use of diagnostic ultrasound has steadily increased since 1970, there has been no change in the proportion of babies born with major malformations. Moreover, specific studies have compared the outcomes of pregnancies exposed or not exposed to ultrasound, and they have found no difference in rates of miscarriage, prematurity, birth defects, or cognitive development up to twelve years of age. Considering the tremendous advantages of ultrasound for diagnosing problems in pregnancy, its benefits far outweigh its minimal risk. On the other hand, since there is always a potential with any new technology for some unknown risk to become apparent over time, it is not considered prudent to use ultrasound solely for the purpose of obtaining your first set of baby pictures.

As ultrasound technology continues to advance, particularly in terms of the intensity of ultrasonic waves delivered to the fetus, some practitioners have recommended that safety features be added to the scanners. These could include a shut-off timer to limit the duration of exposure, and special probes to estimate fetal temperature, so that technicians and radiologists cannot inadvertently overexpose the fetus.

Finally, it is important to point out that ultrasound radiation is also used for therapeutic purposes. As with ionizing radiation, therapeutic doses of ultrasound are considerably higher than diagnostic ones. Therapeutic ultrasound uses high-intensity waves, whose specific purpose is to heat tissue as a method of deep massage for physical therapy. Because of the great danger of raising fetal temperature with this method, ultrasound massage is absolutely inadvisable during pregnancy.

Maternal Infections

While many pregnant women are now aware of the dangers that chemicals and radiation pose to their unborn baby, fewer may be familiar with the risks of several seemingly innocuous diseases. In fact, for the majority of pregnant women—those who don't smoke or drink, use drugs, require X-rays, or face occupational exposure to harmful chemicals or radiation—infections are arguably the most significant risk they face. Several viruses and other pathogens are known to cause malformation of the brain or later mental deficits in children exposed prenatally. The dangers are especially great early in gestation, when all the major organ systems are first forming, and before the fetus's own immune system is well enough developed to begin fighting them off.

Medical professionals have a handy mnemonic for keeping track of the most dangerous prenatal infections. They are called the TORCH pathogens: Toxoplasmosis, Rubella, Cytomegalovirus, Herpes (genital), and Others, which include syphilis, chicken pox, and perhaps influenza. While relatively insignificant in children and adults, all these infections can seriously harm an embryo or fetus, and they pose a particular threat to a baby's future mental or neurological health.

Rubella   Rubella is the virus that causes German measles. Infection by the rubella virus early in pregnancy can cause malformations of the brain and special sense organs, leading to mental retardation, cataracts, and hearing loss. The risk to the fetus is greatest if the mother becomes infected during the first month of pregnancy, when the chance of a serious malformation is as high as 50 percent. The risk steadily declines, to 10 percent in the third month and 6 percent in the fourth and fifth months, after which it becomes minimal.

Fortunately, about 85 percent of women in the United States are already immune to rubella by the time they get pregnant, either because they were infected earlier or because they were inoculated with the vaccine that first became available in 1969. A simple antibody test can tell you whether you are immune to rubella and is usually performed at the first prenatal checkup. This is important, since about one-third of pregnant women infected with the virus show no symptoms and therefore may not be aware of contracting the disease. Women who are not immune cannot be inoculated during pregnancy, since there is a theoretical risk of infection from the vaccine, but they are advised to be immunized shortly after their child is born, to prevent the possibility of infection in future pregnancies. Thanks to widespread immunization, congenital rubella infections are now rare. When a case of rubella is confirmed in early pregnancy, many women choose to abort because the risk of severe birth defects is so high.

Cytomegalovirus   Another pathogen that can cause serious brain malformations is cytomegalovirus (CMV), a member of the herpes family that is very prevalent. CMV usually produces almost no symptoms in adults or even in children older than infancy, but it can have devastating effects on a fetus during the first two trimesters. CMV is both the most common and one of the most dangerous infections a fetus can be exposed to before birth. It is the leading infectious cause of congenital deafness and mental retardation in the United States. Prenatal infection can also cause epilepsy and serious disease of the eyes. The good news is that most of the population (50 to 85 percent) has already been infected by the time they are adults. (This is less true, however, of teenage mothers.) Although the disease can resurface in women who were previously infected, such recurrent infections are considerably less dangerous for the fetus than an initial one. The bad news, however, is that CMV is often caught from toddlers, who are not yet immune, so mothers in subsequent pregnancies are especially susceptible to it.

An estimated 1 to 2 percent of women first contract CMV during pregnancy, and about 35 percent of these infections are passed on to the fetus. Of babies infected in utero, about 10 percent will have serious defects that are apparent from birth; another 10 percent will show a neurological, hearing, or IQ deficit later in the first two years. Overall, then, about one out of every thousand babies is born with major brain or sensory damage as a result of prenatal CMV infection.

For women diagnosed with a primary CMV infection during pregnancy, fetal infection can be assessed by amniocentesis. Even if a woman is not known to have been infected, fetal CMV may be suspected on the basis of ultrasound findings, since infected fetuses are often small for their gestational age and show certain brain abnormalities, including microcephaly and a distinct pattern of calcification already indicative of neural damage. Amniocentesis is then used to confirm or reject the diagnosis. Depending on the severity of the ultrasound findings, abortion may be counseled.

The best hope for minimizing the danger of congenital CMV infection will be for women to be routinely vaccinated before pregnancy, but this is not yet possible. A vaccine has been developed, but it has not been fully tested and is not yet available to the public. In the meantime, pregnant women should practice careful hygiene to avoid infection with CMV, which can be transmitted through any bodily fluid—saliva, urine, blood, semen, and even breast milk. This is especially important for women who work in day-care centers or already have small children of their own. Wash your hands after changing diapers, watch out for wet kisses, and no sharing those cups and spoons with young kids!

Toxoplasmosis Many of the same brain defects can occur if a fetus is infected with toxoplasmosis. This comma-shaped parasite can be caught from animal feces, especially those of cats and mice, as well as from raw meat and eggs and unpasteurized milk. As in CMV infection, the mother usually experiences mild symptoms, if any, so toxoplasmosis may very well go unnoticed during pregnancy. Somewhere between one and eight out of a thousand women become infected with the organism during pregnancy. Fortunately the chance of infecting the fetus is low during the first two trimesters (about 20 percent), when it is likely to be more harmful. During the third trimester, the rate of fetal infection rises to 60 to 65 percent, but the consequences are less severe.

About 20 percent of infected infants, or about one or two out of every ten thousand babies born, will be severely impaired due to toxoplasmosis, with problems that include mental retardation, epilepsy, spasticity, blindness, or hearing loss. Another eight out of ten thousand will have less severe central nervous sytstem (CNS) damage; they may show no signs of infection at birth, but milder hearing and IQ deficits become apparent later in childhood. Fortunately antiparasitic drugs are available that can be given to the pregnant mother and greatly reduce the risk of severe damage to the fetus, although they don't completely eliminate it. The problem, however, is in identifying the women who need this treatment. Since the infection rarely produces symptoms in adults, most women who become infected during pregnancy are unaware of it.

Routine testing of pregnant women for immunity to toxoplasmosis has not been judged cost-effective in the United States, although it has been initiated in France, where the disease is more prevalent. If a woman suspects that she may have been infected, blood tests can confirm the diagnosis, and amniocentesis can be used to detect whether the fetus has also been infected. Toxoplasmosis may also be suspected based on ultrasound findings, since it too produces a distinct pattern of brain abnormalities, including calcifications and enlarged ventricles (hydrocephalus).

A better solution to the problem of prenatal toxoplasmosis is prevention. Since only about one-quarter of American women are immune, pregnant women should avoid eating raw or rare eggs and meat (cooked to less than 140°F) and thoroughly wash their hands and all cooking surfaces that have been in contact with these foods. In addition, women with cats should avoid all contact with the cat litter (use gloves, or better yet, get someone else to change it!) and preferably keep cats indoors, where they can avoid becoming infected. All pregnant women should use gloves in the garden (where cats may have left feces), keep children's sandboxes covered when not in use (since outdoor cats like to use these to defecate), and control fleas and cockroaches in the house (since they may spread contaminated soil or cat feces onto food). Such preventive measures have been found to be very effective in reducing the incidence of toxoplasmosis during pregnancy.

Genital Herpes   In rare cases, a woman with genital herpes (herpes simplex type II) can pass the virus on to the fetus during gestation, when it can cause severe abnormalities of the skin, brain, and eyes and often leads to neonatal death. More often, a baby will be infected during a vaginal birth if the mother has an open herpes lesion anywhere that could come in contact with the baby. Newborns infected in this way often get very sick—much sicker than adults with herpes—and are very likely to suffer severe brain damage from the infection unless it is promptly treated. Consequently, pregnant women known to have an active genital herpes infection at term are delivered by cesarean section, avoiding the birth canal and thereby virtually eliminating the chance that the baby will be infected. For babies who are infected at birth because of an undetected herpes lesion in the mother, antiviral drugs have greatly lessened the severity of the infection and the chance that the baby's nervous system will be harmed.

Chicken Pox   A woman infected with chicken pox (varicella-zoster) virus during the first half of pregnancy has about a 2 percent chance of having a baby with major defects, including damage to the eyes and brain. Fortunately, about 90 percent of women are already immune to chicken pox before they become pregnant because they had the disease as children. While the virus can become reactivated, causing the painful condition known as *shingles* or *zoster*, such a recurrence during pregnancy does not cause congenital defects in the fetus. For the 10 percent of women who are not immune to chicken pox, the newly available varicella vaccine offers excellent protection before they become pregnant. (Because the vaccine is still relatively new, however, it is not yet known whether girls who are vaccinated early in life will remain protected through their childbearing years.)

Syphilis   Syphilis, which is caused by a bacterium called a *spirochete*, can cause severe damage to the fetal brain as well as the eyes, bones, skin, and liver if left untreated. The births of babies with congenital syphilis used to be a major public health problem, but women are now routinely screened for syphilis in early pregnancy. If they are found to be infected, treatment with penicillin is quite effective at blocking the spirochete's transmission to the embryo or fetus before it can do any damage. Unfortunately, women who receive no prenatal care will have no such screening, and there has been some resurgence in the number of syphilitic babies born since the early 1980s, in parallel with the rise in cocaine use among pregnant mothers who become infected when trading sex for drugs. This is especially disturbing since the disease is entirely curable.

Influenza   Finally, there have been some suggestions that maternal flu infection can have long-lasting effects on a baby's brain. While influenza is nowhere near as dangerous as the other infections we have considered—it has not been linked to any specific malformations, prematurity, or other obvious adverse outcomes of pregnancy—some researchers suspect that it increases the odds of later-emerging mental deficits. For instance, one line of research has detected a link between prenatal flu and schizophrenia, suggesting that the viral infection, particularly around the sixth month of gestation, may interfere with neuronal migration in such a way as to disturb later cognitive and emotional functioning. Another study suggests that second-trimester influenza infection increases the chances that a child will be dyslexic, perhaps because of similar neuronal perturbations. Yet another hints that influenza in the one month before or three months following conception may increase the chance of neural tube defects, even if the mother did not run a temperature.

All these findings must be regarded as highly speculative at this point. But given the potent effect of other viruses on prenatal brain development, the idea that influenza might significantly perturb neuronal organization is not unreasonable. Further research may clarify these issues soon, so pregnant women will know how vigilantly they need to protect themselves from catching the flu.

Maternal Hormones, Emotion, and Stress

Women have learned about most prenatal influences the hard way: X-rays, drugs, alcohol, and cigarettes were all used indiscriminately during pregnancy until their effects on fetal development were suspected and finally proved. For another class of influences, however, science is only beginning to catch up with an understanding that has been prevalent in virtually every culture throughout history. This is the idea that a mother's well-being—her level of happiness, stress, anxiety, health, activity, and social connectedness—may affect the development and health of her future child. The notion that a mother's emotions and lifestyle influence her growing fetus is as old as history. But it is only in the last few decades that we have begun to understand how these seemingly intangible factors can shape every aspect of fetal development, including a baby's emerging brain and mind.

One 1982 Israeli study offers a fascinating demonstration of how a mother's emotional state affects her fetus. Researchers put headphones on pregnant women and allowed them to listen to various types of music while they measured fetal movements under ultrasound. Remarkably, most of the fetuses became more active when the music was turned on, particularly when their mothers were listening to their favorite type of music, whether pop or classical. Because the music was inaudible to the fetuses, the researchers concluded that they must have been reacting to changes in their mothers' emotional state. The question is: How does an unborn baby know what its mother is feeling?

Like all mental experience, emotions are a function of brain activity. Emotional experience is processed by a part of the brain known as the *limbic system*. As we will see in Chapter 12, the limbic system connects higher areas of the cerebral cortex, particularly in the frontal and temporal lobes, to lower brain structures that coordinate basic bodily functions such as blood flow, metabolism, temperature regulation, fluid balance, appetite, growth, and sex drive, thereby uniting both the mental and physical manifestations of emotion. At the crux of this limbic circuit is the *hypothalamus*, a small but potent regulatory structure located in the dead center of the head, in front of the brain stem and at the base of the rest of the brain. (See Figure 1.2.)

The hypothalamus is responsible for converting neural activity into hormonal signals, and it does this by way of the *pituitary*, the body's master gland, which hangs like a tiny pear just below it. Sometimes the hypothalamus-pituitary combination is activated by purely physiological stimuli, as happens, for instance, when a baby suckles on his mother's breast. Sensory input from the nipple activates the hypothalamus, which then triggers the pituitary to release *oxytocin*, the hormone responsible for the milk ejection or letdown reflex. Sometimes, however, the hypothalamus triggers hormonal responses solely on the basis of emotional stimuli, as when a mother's mere thought of her baby triggers the same letdown reflex.

The hypothalamus-pituitary system oversees the release of most of the body's hormones, including those that control not only lactation but reproduction, metabolism, growth, and the body's response to stress. Most of these hormones have the potential to influence fetal development in one way or another. Some can cross the placenta and enter the baby's circulation, where they directly affect cell division and growth. Thyroid hormone, for instance, is essential for the production and survival of neurons, their synapse formation, dendritic growth, and myelination. Although the fetus begins to secrete its own thyroid hormone midway through gestation, maternal thyroid hormone crosses the placenta as early as the second month. Women who are thyroid-deficient (or have a dietary lack of iodine, an essential component of thyroid hormone) can give birth to children with severe mental and neurological impairments, a condition known as *cretinism*, because this hormone is so essential to neuronal development.*

Maternal hormones can also influence the fetal brain in less direct ways, by altering fetal physiology or behavior. Since the brain's development is strongly influenced by its own electrical activity, changes in behavior, such as a dramatic increase or decrease in fetal movement, can have lasting effects on the way the brain is wired and eventually functions. Maternal hormones can even influence development without themselves entering the fetal circulation. Many hormones, for instance, alter the way in which blood flows to the placenta, which in turn affects the transfer of oxygen and nutrients to the fetus, both of which are critical for fetal growth.

As we learn more about maternal hormones and their influence on the developing brain, scientists are beginning to propose actual biological mechanisms for the kind of folk prophecies that have been around for ages. One recent study, for instance, suggests that a child's shyness is determined, in part, by maternal hormone fluctuations during gestation. Researchers who interviewed several thousand preschoolers in both the United States and New Zealand noted a significant relationship between the incidence of extreme shyness or inhibition (children who seem particularly fearful, anxious, or withdrawn in the presence of a stranger) and the amount of daylight their mothers were exposed to at midpregnancy. Thus, in the United States, only 12 percent of children born in October-November-December were

---

*Even modest reductions in the level of maternal thyroid hormone—in the low-normal range—can subtly impair a child's later cognitive ability, according to one study from a region of Papua New Guinea with a high prevalence of iodine deficiency.

rated as highly inhibited, compared to nearly 18 percent of those born in April-May-June. In New Zealand, where daylight hours are reversed, children showed the opposite pattern, with more shy children born in October-November-December than in April-May-June. Because the production of certain hormones, like melatonin, is known to fluctuate with the amount of daylight in each season, the researchers propose that such substances may subtly alter brain development during a critical period at midgestation, when massive numbers of neurons are migrating to form the basic architecture of the cerebral cortex. (It is also possible that other seasonal differences, like changes in women's diets, physical activity, or exposure to colds and flu, mediate this relationship.)

Effects of Maternal Stress   While there are all kinds of speculations about how maternal emotion and hormones might affect fetal development, the link is most convincing in the case of stress. Fear, stress, and anxiety are all very useful emotions, evolved over millions of years to allow us to respond quickly and efficiently to threatening situations. Whether you've got a predator on your tail, are in intense competition for a mate, or have a deadline looming, the body's response to stress is the same: your heart races, your pupils dilate, blood rushes to your muscles, and you become highly vigilant and aroused, all at the expense of more mundane functions like digestion, growth, and bodily repair.

This *fight-or-flight* stress response is orchestrated by the body's adrenal glands, a pair of pyramid-shaped organs that sit atop each kidney, and by the *sympathetic* nervous system, a division of the *autonomic* or unconscious nervous system that controls virtually every bodily organ. The adrenal glands release adrenaline and noradrenaline (also known as epinephrine and norepinephrine), two hormones from a class of molecules known as *catecholamines*. Sympathetic neurons also release noradrenaline. These hormones are responsible for the sudden rush a person feels in moments of fear, as when you hear a strange noise at night and bolt up in your bed, wondering if you should flee or fight. During stress the adrenals also release another class of hormones, the *corticosteroids*, a group of cholesterol-derived hormones that mobilize energy (glucose) for the brain and muscles. Though they lie outside the central nervous system, both the adrenal glands and the sympathetic neurons are intimately controlled by it, which is how the mere thought or knowledge of a stressful event is translated into major bodily changes.

There is no question that the fetus is sensitive to the ebb and flow of its mother's various hormones, and this isn't necessarily bad. The stress hormones are all normally present in the mother's blood and are capable of crossing the placenta in some measure. The predominant corticosteroid, *cortisol*, even plays a useful role in maintaining fetal circadian rhythms. Blood levels of cortisol are highest in the early morning and lowest in the late afternoon and evening. Babies tend to have more regular rhythms of active and quiet periods before birth than afterward, because their mothers' own circadian hormone fluctuations adapt them in utero to the day-night cycle. Not until several weeks after birth do newborns' brains set up their own circadian rhythms, which is why they tend to alternate between sleep and active periods at all hours of the day and night, as every exhausted new parent knows well.

But like all prenatal influences, problems can arise when hormone levels get too high: mothers who are unduly stressed during pregnancy, or who are very anxious personality types, may "overdose" their fetuses with chronically high amounts of corticosteroids and catecholamines. This is the leading hypothesis to explain many observations—some rigorous, some anecdotal—that link excessive stress to all sorts of problems in pregnancy. In the extreme maternal stress is thought to contribute to malformations such as cleft lip and Down syndrome, to neurological impairment, to newborn health problems including eczema, respiratory difficulty, stomach ulcers, and ear infections, and even to a higher incidence of neonatal death. Many other studies have associated maternal stress or anxiety with higher rates of miscarriage, low birth weight, or premature birth. Finally, there is evidence that prenatal stress interferes with fetal and neonatal brain function, such that babies of more highly stressed or anxious mothers tend to be fussier, more irritable, and perhaps even delayed in their mental and motor development.

Animal experiments provide the strongest proof that maternal stress can affect the developing fetus. It has been known for decades that injecting pregnant mice with large doses of cortisol causes a very high incidence of cleft palate in the offspring. There is a clear critical period for this effect between the ninth and fifteenth days of gestation (a period corresponding to the end of the first trimester in humans), with the most potent teratogenicity on days twelve and thirteen. If, instead of injecting cortisol, pregnant mice are exposed to stressful situations during this period, their offspring also have an increased incidence of cleft palate, although not as high as with the injections. Cleft lip and palate are also more likely in humans following prenatal stress; one recent study noted a doubling in incidence among babies born six months after a severe earthquake in Santiago, Chile. These studies suggest that high maternal cortisol may have the same effect late in the first trimester of human development.

Corticosteroids undoubtedly also contribute to the wide variety of brain and behavioral disturbances animals exhibit in response to prenatal stress. High doses of these hormones can interfere with virtually every step of brain development, from the production of neurons and glia to dendritic growth, synapse formation, myelination, and biochemical specialization. When pregnant rats are stressed during the latter part of pregnancy, by restraining them for about a half hour each day, their offspring show numerous behavioral abnormalities. They explore and vocalize less than control pups, learn more poorly, and are more anxious and emotionally reactive; the males, as we'll see below, are prone to altered sexual behavior. Many of these behavioral effects can be attributed to certain well-documented effects of prenatal stress on brain organization, including impaired growth of the hippocampus (which plays a critical role in learning and memory), disruption of several neurotransmitter systems, and abnormalities in the pups' own stress response system. Human brain development appears similarly vulnerable to prenatal stress. One recent study found that the babies of severely stressed mothers had significantly smaller heads (even after correcting for their lower birth weights) than babies of nonstressed mothers, suggesting that high levels of maternal corticosteroids inhibit nerve cell growth and division.

Corticosteroids are not the only culprits in prenatal stress. Catecholamines also play a role. Ultrasound measurements support the idea that fetuses of highly anxious mothers are exposed to higher levels of catecholamines in the womb than fetuses of calmer mothers; they are more active and show more dramatic heart-rate changes when their mothers are exposed to mild psychological stress (like listening to a recording of a baby crying), both signs of greater sympathetic nervous system activation. Catecholamine levels are also considerably higher in women with high-stress jobs, at least according to one study that compared pregnant intensive-care doctors and nurses to pregnant women in less physically and mentally demanding jobs.

There are several ways in which high levels of catecholamines could interfere with brain development. Catecholamines are known to restrict the mother's blood flow to the uterus, which will tend to reduce the flow of oxygen and nutrients to the fetus, thereby inhibiting brain growth. Moreover, those nutrients that are available will be further expended by all that heightened fetal activity triggered by excess catecholamine stimulation. High levels of adrenaline can also trigger uterine contractions, which may explain the link between stress and preterm birth. Finally, some researchers believe that babies of anxious or highly stressed mothers may become attuned to higher levels of catecholamines in the womb and produce higher levels themselves after birth, which might explain why they tend to be more active, irritable, and temperamental than the newborns of less anxious mothers. Less is known about the effect of prenatal stress on later life, but based on the several effects of catecholamines and corticosteroids on fetal brain development, it has been proposed that such stress contributes to a wide variety of behavioral deficits and mental illnesses in older children.

One problem with evaluating prenatal stress is that it is often associated with other pregnancy risk factors, such as poverty and lack of prenatal care. Women under stress are also more likely to eat poorly, to smoke, and to use alcohol or drugs. While all these factors contribute to the poorer outcome of pregnant women under stress, many studies have controlled for them and continue to find small but real effects of maternal stress on fetal health and development. Of course, every woman is subject to some degree of stress in her daily life, but the risk appears to be elevated for women who (1) experience a very stressful event during pregnancy, such as a divorce or marital separation, loss of a job, rape, or death of a loved one, particularly her husband; (2) have a high degree of chronic stress, whether because of illness, poverty, lack of social support, or a demanding job over which she has little control; or (3) have personalities that are highly stress or anxiety prone.

Prenatal Stress and Sexual Orientation   One of the more controversial proposals about prenatal stress is that it may contribute to male homosexuality. This theory has its origins in some early research on the neural basis of sexual behavior in rats. The hypothalamus, you may recall, plays a critical role in various instinctive behaviors, including sex drive and other reproductive functions. About twenty years ago, researchers discovered a small region near the front of the rat hypothalamus that differs significantly in structure in males and females. This area, which they named the "sexually dimorphic nucleus of the pre-optic area" or SDN-POA, is about twice as large, and contains about twice as many neurons, in male as compared to female rats.

Further research revealed that this sex difference depends on the presence of the male sex hormone, testosterone, during a very brief critical period in development. Beginning in late gestation and continuing for the first few days of postnatal life, male rats' testes release a surge of testosterone that reaches the brain and promotes the survival of neurons in the SDN-POA. Female rats do not experience this testosterone surge, so their brains follow the default developmental pathway, remaining "feminized." Not only does the brief testosterone surge permanently alter male rats' hypothalami, it also shapes their later sexual behavior. For instance, in experiments in which female rats are exposed to testosterone before birth (by injecting it into the pregnant mother), they later act more aggressively, tend to mount other females, and resist mounting attempts by males to a much greater extent than do normal females. Conversely, when male rats are castrated or given drugs that otherwise deprive them of testosterone during the critical period, they behave more like females, presenting themselves to other males in a sexually receptive posture known as *lordosis*.

In humans, too, testosterone is responsible for sexual differentiation of the brain. But unlike rats, in which the testosterone surge straddles both pre- and postnatal periods, the testosterone surge in boys is largely prenatal, reaching its peak around the fourth month of gestation. Researchers have now identified several brain areas in males and females that differ consistently, though no one has yet proved that any of these dimorphisms arise prenatally. Nonetheless, testosterone exposure in utero is known to have profound effects on later gender behaviors that must reflect sex differences in the brain itself.

One striking example is a rare genetic disorder in females known as *congenital adrenal hyperplasia* (CAH). In addition to producing stress hormones, the adrenal glands release all of the major sex hormones, though in smaller quantities than the ovaries and testes. In CAH, however, the adrenal glands produce excessive quantities of androgens (the overall category of male sex hormones, which includes testosterone). This overproduction begins well before birth, so girls with the disorder become masculinized, both in genital appearance and in behavior. CAH girls can be fully treated if their disorder is detected shortly after birth, by altering their adrenal hormone levels and surgically correcting their external genitalia. (CAH does not affect the formation of the internal genitalia, so women treated from an early age are able to bear children.) But even when treated and raised as girls from early in infancy, their behavior suggests that their brains were already somewhat masculinized before birth. They often identify themselves as "tomboys," are very physically active, prefer boys as playmates, and generally show more interest in outdoor play than traditional "girl" games like dolls and dress-up. While the majority of hormonally corrected CAH females end up heterosexual, there is an increased incidence of lesbianism or bisexuality among them.

Similar masculinization has been observed in girls whose mothers were treated during pregnancy with certain drugs, such as DES (diethylstilbestrol), that mimic the actions of testosterone. (DES is no longer prescribed but was once widely used to prevent miscarriages.) Conversely, genetic males with a disorder called *androgen insensitivity syndrome* become feminized because of a congenital lack of testosterone receptors; while they do produce testosterone, the hormone is unable to act on its various target tissues, so males with this disorder are born with female genitalia and typically behave and identify themselves in accordance with female stereotypes. When raised as girls, they usually experience conventionally female heterosexual sexual preferences.

So what does any of this have to do with maternal stress during pregnancy? It turns out that high doses of many of the major stress hormones, including cortisol and adrenaline, interfere with testosterone production. Men, for instance, show a decreased level of circulating testosterone when they are significantly stressed. Because maternal stress hormones can cross the placenta, it has been proposed that pregnant females who are highly stressed may release sufficient quantities of adrenal hormones to interfere with the usual testosterone surge in male fetuses, thereby nudging their brains toward more feminine behavior, including a propensity for homosexuality.

This theory is derived largely from studies with rats. Male rats whose mothers were stressed during pregnancy show some of the same feminized behavioral patterns as those deprived of testosterone. As pups, they engage in less "rough-and-tumble" play like pinning and pouncing on their siblings, and as adults, they exhibit less mounting and ejaculation, and more lordosis, than the male offspring of nonstressed mothers. Moreover, maternal stress has been shown to inhibit the testosterone surge in rat fetuses. Accordingly, males whose mothers were stressed during pregnancy end up with an SDN-POA about half as large as in males of nonstressed mothers, whereas prenatal stress has no effect on this brain structure in females.

But while the evidence in rats is fairly convincing, the link between prenatal stress and sexual orientation in humans is far more tenuous. Researchers have identified three brain structures—the anterior commissure and two distinct hypothalamic nuclei—that differ in size between adult male hetero- and homosexuals, but it is not known whether they are involved in sexual behavior, whether the differences are affected by prenatal stress, nor even how early in life these areas become differentiated. (It is possible that the structural differences are a *consequence* rather than a *cause* of homosexual orientation.) Another missing link is the effect of prenatal stress on testosterone. No researcher has yet attempted to measure how testosterone in human fetuses is influenced by maternal stress or anxiety.

The strongest suggestion that prenatal stress contributes to male homosexuality comes from two German studies published in the 1980s, though the data appear highly questionable. In the first, researchers combed old medical records and noted a striking rise—more than a doubling—in the incidence of homosexuality among men born between 1941 and 1947 compared to the years before and after this war-torn period. In the second study, these researchers interviewed two hundred men—half of them heterosexual and half bi- or homosexual—about stressful events in their mothers' lives and found a dramatic difference: substantially more gay than straight men reported that their mothers had undergone harrowing experiences while pregnant, such as rape, Allied bombings, losing their husbands, becoming a refugee, or carrying an unwanted child.

These studies have been widely criticized on methodological grounds (most importantly, that the subjects were likely aware of the hypothesis being tested). Two more recent American studies have attempted to overcome this problem by querying mothers, rather than their adult children, about their stress levels during pregnancy, and by using questionnaires that did not reveal the purpose of their study. Neither of these studies confirmed the German findings, although one found a modest relationship between male homosexuality and maternal stress during the second trimester only, and the other found that women who are more stress-prone tend to have more effeminate boys than other mothers.

Prenatal stress is just one of several theories for a biological basis of homosexuality. Most researchers now agree that sexual orientation is determined early in a child's life, through a combination of genetic and environmental factors. Although current evidence is very weak, it remains possible that prenatal stress is one factor that biases some boys toward a later homosexual orientation.

Maternal Exercise: Stressful or Beneficial?   While we often think of stress as a mental or emotional experience, the body's reaction is similar whether it is triggered by a fight with the boss, worry about a family member, or a jog around the park. Just as in emotionally trying events, physical exertion releases catecholamines, which elevate heart rate and blood pressure and change blood flow patterns throughout the body.

The fetus clearly responds to its mother's physical exertion. In several studies, researchers have measured fetal movements and heart rate before and then shortly after a pregnant mother performs exercise, such as cycling or treadmill jogging. Generally speaking, the fetus responds well to light or moderate exercise, increasing his or her heart rate in proportion to increased exertion by the mother. At very strenuous levels, however, fetal heart rate and breathing movements actually begin to decline. Other fetal movements also decrease in response to maternal exercise.

There are two main reasons for concern about exercising during pregnancy. One is that it may reduce the baby's oxygen supply, since exercise, like other sources of stress, reduces blood flow to the uterus. Another risk is overheating. As we have already seen, fetal development is highly sensitive to temperature, and elevations of more than 2°C (or above 102°F) can increase the risk of miscarriage and affect the formation of the brain and eyes.

Despite these theoretical concerns, there is little evidence that mothers who exercise or are physically very active have any particular problems with their pregnancies. Most studies have found no difference in prematurity or Apgar scores (measures of newborn health taken one and five minutes after birth) between babies born to mothers who exercise and those who are more sedentary. With regard to birth weight, there are conflicting reports about the effects of exercise; some studies have found that women who exercise have significantly smaller babies, but several recent studies refute these findings, and one actually found that the more women exercised, the larger their babies tended to be. The key factor here appears to be the amount of weight the mother gains. If exercise prevents the mother from gaining adequately, she is likelier to give birth to a low-weight baby, but women who exercise and gain sufficient weight do not appear to compromise their baby's brain and bodily development.

Offsetting its potential harm are the numerous benefits of exercise, many of which can be traced to the fact that it elevates a mother's levels of *beta-endorphin*—a morphinelike substance produced by the body that blocks the transmission of painful stimuli to the brain. In addition, exercise actually lowers the level of another stress hormone, cortisol, in pregnant women. These hormonal changes explain why exercise often counteracts the emotional impact of other sources of stress. Exercise generally increases a woman's sense of well-being, and based on what we know about anxiety and stress, this is likely to have a positive influence on the fetus.

The best-documented benefit of exercise comes in labor and delivery.

Women who exercise regularly fare much better during childbirth compared with women who do not. They perceive it to be less painful, and indeed it may be; one study found that women who exercise spend just twenty-seven minutes in the second stage of labor—pushing—compared with fifty-nine minutes for women who did not exercise during pregnancy. Shorter labor is generally beneficial to the baby, since it reduces the risk of complications, including oxygen deprivation of the brain.

Doctors have traditionally been rather conservative about exercise during pregnancy, but current evidence indicates that it is safe for most women, especially those who were already physically fit before conceiving. Exercise should be kept to a "moderate" level, meaning that it does not elevate the woman's heart rate above 70 percent of its maximum rate (220 beats per minute minus one's age in years)—for example, 133 beats per minute in a thirty-year-old. Because there is evidence that a woman's oxygen reserves are lower in the third trimester, it is a good idea to scale down exercise, particularly weight-bearing types, toward the end of pregnancy, as most women are inclined to do anyway. Other situations to avoid include: (1) exercising at high altitudes (more than 10,000 feet), because the placenta is already having to compensate for lower oxygen levels; (2) exercising in hot weather, because of the risk of overheating the fetus; and (3) scuba and snorkel diving, because of the potential risk of accumulating excess nitrogen and other gases in fetal tissues. But other water immersion sports, like swimming and "aqua-jogging," are among the best forms of exercise for pregnant women, because the water helps dissipate excess heat from the mother's body.

Pregnancy Stress in Perspective   All these findings about prenatal stress are enough to fill any pregnant woman with severe anxiety! But it's just possible that the very fact of being pregnant somewhat overrides the hormonal surges of stressful events. Indeed, to some degree the placenta actually protects the baby from its mother's stress hormones, since it is capable of breaking down moderate concentrations of both corticosteroids and catecholamines. And while pregnancy itself can be a stressful time—whether because a woman is nauseous, uncomfortable, tired, anxious about childbirth, or worried about caring for her baby after birth—it is important to remember that many women actually enjoy it. Perhaps this is because our bodies orchestrate it that way. There may be something to the oft-described "glow" of pregnancy—a way that all those other elevated hormones, particularly endorphins (which steadily rise during pregnancy), modulate the ebb and flow of stress hormones so as to shield the developing fetus from the more momentous events in its mother's life.

On the one hand, it is important to appreciate the profound effects stress may have, particularly compared with all the other minute risks women face at some time or another during pregnancy; you are much better off forgetting about that chest X-ray you had early on than spending nine months dousing your fetus with stress hormones recollecting it. On the other hand, women need to have faith in their bodies and their ability to cope with stress—to realize that pregnancy is a very normal state and that millions of years of evolution have exquisitely molded us to perform our primary biological function, which is, after all, making babies.

SUMMARY OF PRENATAL RISK FACTORS

AGENTS/CONDITIONS KNOWN TO BE HARMFUL TO THE FETUS

Agent/condition	Risk	Recommendation
Folic acid deficiency	Neural tube defects	400-micrograms-per-day supplement from conception through first trimester
Under-nourishment	Smaller brain, cognitive deficit	Gain 20% of ideal prepregnancy weight and consume an extra 10–12 grams of protein daily
Prescription drugs	Varies tremendously, depending on the drug	Avoid Category X drugs. Consult health care provider before using *any* drug during pregnancy
Nonprescription drugs	Varies tremendously, depending on the drug	Consult health care provider before using *any* drug during pregnancy
Alcohol	Mental retardation and malformations at high doses; cognitive delay at moderate doses	Abstinence during conception and pregnancy; however, modest levels of consumption (roughly 1 drink per day) have not been proven harmful
Illegal drugs (cocaine, heroin, marijuana)	Various cognitive and behavioral deficits	Avoid completely during conception and pregnancy
Smoking	Low birth weight, cognitive and behavioral deficits	Stop smoking before or as early as possible in pregnancy; avoid second-hand smoke
Organic solvents, hydrocarbons, and oil-based paints and varnishes	Miscarriage and malformation in solvent abusers and some occupational exposures	Avoid exposure when possible; otherwise use only in well-ventilated areas
Polychlorinated biphenyls (PCBs)	Growth retardation and cognitive delay	Limit consumption of freshwater fish in areas with a history of contamination
Pesticides	Varies with particular agent	Use only local application (no fumigants) always administered by someone other than the pregnant woman

Agents/Conditions Known to Be Harmful to the Fetus
(continued)

Agent/condition	Risk	Recommendation
Ionizing radiation (X-rays, gamma rays, radioactivity)	In high doses, stunted brain growth and mental retardation	Avoid any nonessential X-rays or CT scans. Air travel is safe
Elevated temperature	Neural tube defects	Treat fever with acetaminophen. Avoid saunas, hot tubs, and overheating during exercise, especially in the first trimester
"TORCH" infections: toxoplasmosis, rubella, cytomegalovirus, genital herpes, chicken pox, syphilis	Various birth defects, sensory deficits, and mental retardation	Childbearing-age women should be immunized for rubella and chicken pox *before* becoming pregnant. Avoid cat feces and undercooked meat and eggs. Practice strict hygiene, especially with young children

Possible Risk to the Developing Fetus

Agent	Suggested Risk	Recommendation
Caffeine	Miscarriage and lower fertility at higher doses	Consume no more than 300 milligrams per day while pregnant or trying to conceive
Influenza	Neural tube defects, schizophrenia, dyslexia	Practice careful hygiene during flu season
Severe stress	Miscarriage, prematurity, cleft lip/palate, behavioral problems, cognitive delay, and possibly male homosexuality	Regular exercise, relaxation methods, and a strong network of social support can counteract many effects of stress

NO PROVEN RISK TO THE FETUS

Agent	Comments
Aspartame	Acceptable in pregnancy; limit consumption in young children
Glutamate, including MSG	Acceptable in pregnancy; limit consumption in young children
Video display terminals	Early flawed studies suggested an association with miscarriage; newer evidence indicates no risk
Microwave ovens	Older ovens may leak; microwave intensity negligible one meter away from door
Power lines	Very little data available for women living closer than 25 meters to high-voltage power lines; greater distances appear safe
Electric blankets	Conflicting evidence, some suggesting slightly increased risk of miscarriage and childhood cancers
MRI	Increasingly used for prenatal diagnosis, but not advised during first trimester until more is known
Ultrasound imaging	Newer, higher-intensity scanners may require greater safety precautions; avoid when running a fever

Chapter 4

HOW BIRTH
AFFECTS THE BRAIN

Finally! Jack's big day has arrived. Last night Jessica went to bed feeling a little crampy, and she woke up very early today to find herself in the beginning stages of labor. By midday, her contractions are quite regular and growing more uncomfortable than she's ever imagined. For some crazy reason, she thought it would all be easier to take once they got to the hospital, but having decided to forgo the epidural, she gets to experience the real thing: the unparalleled "My-God-I-think-my-guts-are-ripping-out" joy of childbirth!

Meanwhile, what about Jack? Although we tend to focus on the mother's labor pains, just imagine what her baby is experiencing: hours and hours of crushing contractions, growing steadily stronger, forcing him out through a hole smaller than the diameter of his head, into a birth canal so narrow, it reshapes his skull, distorts his shoulders, and squeezes the very fluid out of his lungs.

Birth itself is possibly the most traumatic event we ever suffer, and it is the baby's brain that bears the brunt of the trauma. Because an infant's head is so large relative to the rest of his body, and is the first thing to be forced through the birth canal, it becomes the battering ram for all of the mother's powerful uterine contractions. The situation is even worse in a breech delivery, when the head is the last thing to emerge, because the baby's chin may get caught by the cervix, stretching the neck too far backward before the head can be dragged out.

A lot of things can go wrong at this momentous point in a baby's life.

Besides the obvious physical trauma, certain situations during labor may compromise the supply of oxygen to the baby's brain, which can produce more serious and long-lasting damage. Fortunately, a baby's brain can tolerate brief periods of oxygen deprivation, or *hypoxia*, much better than an adult's. But in extreme cases, the trial of labor may be too much, and prolonged lack of oxygen is the greatest potential danger a baby faces during birth. Indeed, most of the technological innovations and preventive measures practiced in modern obstetrics are geared toward forestalling brain damage from hypoxia.

Still, it's important to remember that the vast majority of babies manage to survive birth well, and there is growing evidence that the stress of birth may actually play a valuable part in adapting the fetus to life outside the womb. This chapter looks at birth from the point of view of the baby's brain: the several risks as well as benefits of the birth process for brain development and a child's mental future.

Does the Baby's Brain Trigger Birth?

For all of our knowledge of pregnancy and fetal development, birth itself remains remarkably mysterious. We have only just begun to understand what triggers labor in experimental animals. If these findings turn out to be relevant to humans, then it looks as though little Jack's brain is once again where the action is.

In sheep, where this topic has been most thoroughly studied, the birth process is triggered by a complex cascade of hormones that kicks off in the brain of the fetal lamb. First, the lamb's master gland, the pituitary, releases a hormone *adrenocorticotropic hormone* (ACTH) that stimulates the adrenal glands. These glands in turn release the hormone cortisol, which travels through the fetal bloodstream to reach the placenta. Elevated cortisol levels trigger several hormonal changes in the placenta, itself an important endocrine organ, whose net effect is to prepare the ewe for delivery. As we saw in the last chapter, the pituitary gland is activated by the hypothalamus, a critical regulatory brain region. It is really the fetal nervous system, then, that integrates all kinds of sensory and physiological information to judge when it is time to be born.

The buildup to labor is actually a rather slow process. Cortisol levels rise throughout the last three weeks or so of gestation, an increase that also helps prepare the fetal lamb's lungs, liver, gut, kidneys, and other organs for life outside the womb. It is no coincidence that the same hormone is responsible for both the final steps of fetal maturation and for initiating birth itself. By coordinating the fetus's development with the onset of labor, the cortisol surge ensures that the fetus is born at the optimal time for its physiological maturation—neither too early, when it is still dependent on the mother's body, nor too late, when the placenta can no longer adequately support it.

Placental hormones are responsible for maintaining pregnancy, but the rise in cortisol toward the end of the lamb's gestation alters this hormonal mix in several ways. It increases estrogen and decreases progesterone production, which strengthens the uterus's ability to contract. Estrogen, in turn, increases the synthesis of another group of hormones, the *prostaglandins*, that ripen the cervix and further strengthen uterine contractility. Estrogen also increases the number of uterine receptors for *oxytocin*, the hormone that triggers individual contractions.* Together these changes gradually convert the weak, irregular contractions that occur throughout late pregnancy (so-called Braxton-Hicks contractions) into the true, forceful labor contractions capable of expelling the fetus from the womb.

The exact hormonal cascade is somewhat different in primates. Neither humans nor monkeys show the same rise in fetal cortisol or decrease in maternal progesterone late in pregnancy. But late-term fetal monkeys are known to undergo a surge in another adrenal hormone, DHEAS, which acts very much like cortisol to promote estrogen production in the placenta. Like cortisol, the release of DHEAS is controlled by the fetus's hypothalamus-pituitary system. If a similar mechanism operates in humans, it suggests that Jack's brain is ultimately the organ that decides when it is time for him to be born.

The Benefits of Birth for Baby's Brain

Once labor begins, Jack's brain is in for a bumpy ride. There's the physical stress, of course: his entire head and body are increasingly compressed with

---

*Although oxytocin (in its synthetic form *pitocin*) is commonly used to induce labor in women artificially, surprisingly, it is not responsible for triggering natural labor.

every contraction. Each contraction also temporarily reduces his oxygen supply as it constricts blood flow through the placenta and umbilical cord.

Rough as it sounds, the stress of labor may actually be beneficial for babies at the end of a normal, full-term gestation. Much like an adult in a fight-or-flight situation (see Chapter 3), a healthy late-term fetus responds to the stress of labor with a surge in the level of catecholamine hormones, adrenaline and noradrenaline. During birth, compression of the baby's head in the vagina triggers about a twentyfold rise in its catecholamine levels. But Jack's body reacts very differently from the way an adult's would to all the catecholamines circulating in his bloodstream. Whereas catecholamines mobilize an adult for action by increasing heart rate and enhancing blood flow to the muscles, they have an opposite effect on young babies, decreasing their heart rate, slowing breathing activity, and even paralyzing certain movements.* These changes help the baby conserve energy and oxygen during periodic hypoxic episodes, preserving blood flow only to the most important tissues, the brain and the heart. Babies who undergo more severe oxygen deprivation during labor experience even larger increases in catecholamine levels—up to a hundred times the resting level—helping them further compensate for their potentially dangerous situation.

Jack's catecholamine levels remain elevated for about thirty minutes after birth and then rapidly decline, reaching resting levels by the time he is two hours old. Although the most significant danger has passed by birth, the first two hours of life are a critical period of adjustment, and elevated catecholamines appear to promote this adjustment in several ways.

Most of our understanding about stress hormones and birth has been garnered from animal studies, but important corroboration comes from comparisons of human infants born by vaginal versus cesarean delivery. Since it is the actual experience of labor and vaginal compression that triggers the catecholamine surge, babies born by C-section do not experience the same degree of stress or catecholamine surge as babies born vaginally; their levels of adrenaline and noradrenaline are some two to ten times lower, depending on the type of maternal anesthesia. But if cesarean babies are first exposed to labor for several hours—that is, if the C-section was unplanned or deliber-

---

*The reason adults and fetuses respond differently to stress is due in part to differences in the ratio of adrenaline and noradrenaline each secrete; the two hormones have somewhat opposite effects on heart rate and blood flow to peripheral muscles.

ately delayed until after the onset of spontaneous labor—catecholamine levels are much closer to those of the vaginally delivered babies.

Of its several advantages, "birth stress" has been found to be especially beneficial for a newborn's breathing. Compared with babies born by C-section, vaginally delivered babies are quicker to take their first breaths; their blood oxygen levels rise more rapidly after birth; and they are less likely to suffer any of a number of respiratory problems in the first few hours of life. Even among babies delivered by C-section, those who undergo several hours of labor before delivery do much better than those delivered prior to the onset of labor, although not as well as vaginally delivered babies. Higher catecholamine levels explain much of the respiratory advantage of "stressed" babies, because these hormones are known to help absorb some of the excess liquid in the lungs at birth and to promote the release of *lung surfactant*— detergentlike molecules that are necessary for gas exchange through the lung's tiny grapelike air cells, or *alveoli*. Other stress hormones, such as cortisol, probably also contribute to this last-minute lung maturation. Finally, vaginal delivery further aids the onset of breathing in a purely mechanical way: by helping squeeze some of this extra liquid out of the lungs as the baby's chest is compressed during passage through the birth canal.

Higher catecholamines also benefit vaginally delivered babies in other ways. Because catecholamines speed up metabolic rate, vaginally delivered babies are better able to maintain their body temperature, and they have larger reserves of glucose and other energy sources than C-section babies. They are also better adapted neurologically to life outside the womb, judging by their higher scores on tests of reflexes, muscle tone, and sensory responses during the first two days of life. Considering all these benefits of labor stress for the baby, some obstetricians now recommend that women planning to deliver by C-section first undergo at least the early stages of labor before surgery.

Of all the advantages of labor, some of the most intriguing are those that affect the baby's nervous system. There is some evidence that contractions, even of the prelabor Braxton-Hicks type, promote brain development in sheep. Perhaps the additional touch and movement stimulation provided by contractions helps refine synaptic connections or promotes myelination during late gestation. Then, once true labor and delivery ensue, a baby's high catecholamine levels potently stimulate the nervous system. In adults, a large surge of adrenaline is highly arousing and can lead to a feeling of well-being. Catecholamines appear to have the same effect on newborns, who are more alert during the first two hours of life than for many days thereafter.

Is There a Sensitive Period for Parent-Infant Bonding Immediately After Birth?

The fact that babies are highly aroused following a normal delivery has one more important effect on their early health and well-being: promoting parent-infant bonding. As soon as their twelve-hour ordeal has finally come to an end, Jack is placed in Jessica's eager arms. Awake, alert, and fully focused, every one of Jack's senses is oriented, for this brief hour or two, on the most important stimuli in his new environment—Mom, and then Dad— as each takes a turn holding him. His arousal is matched, of course, by their own excitement, but catecholamines add one more twist to increase his irresistibility: they dilate his pupils, a proven attractant that lures his parents even deeper into the miracle of his presence.

Back in the early 1970s, some researchers proposed that this first hour of life marks a very special "sensitive period" for parent-infant bonding: a time in which close, preferably skin-to-skin contact between mother and infant is necessary for optimal development of the mother's attachment to her child. The notion of an early sensitive period for bonding has its roots in studies of animal behavior; several species of mammals (goats and sheep being the most extensively studied) undergo a period of "maternal imprinting" during the first hours and days after birth, when the sight and smell of her infant attaches a mother to her kid in a strong and lasting way. Although there is little evidence for such imprinting among our closer primate relatives, researchers nonetheless became convinced that a similar "gluelike" attachment takes place between a woman and her newborn in the highly charged hour they spend together immediately after birth.

Initial studies offered some compelling evidence that early contact promoted all manner of mothering skills and cognitive abilities in children. Few of these findings, however, held up under later scrutiny, and by the early 1980s the whole notion of a sensitive period for maternal-infant bonding was repudiated. There is no instantaneous gluing between parent and child at birth. Parental love evolves gradually, throughout the first year or more of a child's life. Plenty of parents miss out on this period of early contact—if the baby is adopted, for instance, or requires immediate medical care—and they have not been found to be any less attached to their children than those who had extensive early contact.

Regardless of whether early contact is necessary for parent-infant bonding, however, it is not without benefit. One fact that all bonding studies agree on is that early contact does improve attachment and parenting skills during the period in which it is occurring, that is, during the time in the hospital. This isn't surprising; it's obviously hard for parents to bond with a baby who is not physically present. But it wasn't until these studies raised the issue that standard hospital care was changed to allow parents greater access to their newborns in the first hours of life: to permit skin-to-skin contact and immediate breast-feeding; to postpone routine medical care—cleaning, weighing, shots, and eyedrops—until after the first hour; and to allow rooming-in—keeping the baby with the mother—instead of automatically shipping her off to the nursery for the duration of her hospital stay. In this sense, then, bonding studies have had a positive impact on the first magical moments of many babies' lives.

The Dangers of Birth for the Baby's Brain

While a certain amount of stress is natural and even beneficial to babies during the birth process, there is always the small chance, during any labor and delivery, that the baby may be permanently harmed. Of all of the organs in the body, the baby's brain is the most vulnerable to injury, because of its large size, its massive need for oxygen, and the fact that its neurons, once formed, are irreplaceable.

Modern obstetrics has introduced many advances to reduce the risk of birth for a baby's brain. Prenatal ultrasound, for instance, can detect problems with the placenta, or with the way the baby is positioned, that could lead to an unusually difficult delivery. Another tool is fetal scalp-blood sampling, which helps discern when the baby may be suffering from serious oxygen deprivation. And of course, the high rate of C-sections, which has become so controversial in recent years, is ultimately due to doctors' and parents' desires to avoid even the smallest chance of brain damage during a potentially difficult vaginal delivery—not an unreasonable reaction to a situation with such serious implications.

In spite of all the potential problems, the baby's brain is surprisingly resilient to much of the battering and hypoxia of childbirth. This makes sense, if you think about it, because it's very unlikely that natural selection would go to all the trouble of building our large, sophisticated brains only to damage a large proportion of them on the way out of the womb. Some resiliency is built in, as we've seen, by the baby's release of stress hormones during labor and delivery. And even if they do suffer some kind of neural damage during birth, newborns can recover massively more function than adults with comparable brain injury, thanks to the astounding plasticity of their young brains.

Birth Trauma The first way in which birth can damage a baby's nervous system is by direct physical trauma. When you see the way some babies' heads are bruised and molded during even the smoothest vaginal delivery, it's amazing we're not all brain damaged. Nonetheless, most babies' brains do not suffer during birth, despite the tight fit. Head molding is a normal and very useful way of getting the baby's large brain safely out of the birth canal, and it is permitted by the fact that the skull bones do not fuse until the second year after birth. Both the front and rear *fontanels*—the soft gaps between skull bones—allow the bones to slide together without severely compressing the more delicate neural tissue inside.

Every now and then, however, a baby's nervous system is damaged during a difficult delivery, whether because he is descending in an unfavorable position, is a little too big for the mother's pelvis, or is injured by the forceps or vacuum extractor necessary to rescue him from the birth canal. Such birth trauma has become much less common in the last half century or so, because obstetricians are better able to estimate fetal size and position, have improved the design and use of forceps, and use cesarean deliveries for the most difficult cases. But some injuries do still occasionally occur, so it is reassuring to know that they rarely cause permanent brain damage.

One of the more common results of birth trauma is a swelling on the head known as a *cephalohematoma*. These bumps, which can be quite big, enlarge gradually over the first few days of life, as a result of bleeding in the space between the baby's scalp and skull. They occur in 1 to 2 percent of live births and are caused by trauma to the head as it scrapes over the mother's pelvic bones. They are also considerably more common following forceps or vacuum extraction. As frightening as these bumps may look, they do not pose any threat to the baby's brain (except in the rare case when they are accompanied by an underlying skull fracture) because the bleeding and swelling are segregated outside the protective membranes that cover the brain. (See Figure 4.1.) The head almost always returns to its normal shape within three months after birth.

While the baby's brain is relatively well protected, the nerves that inner-

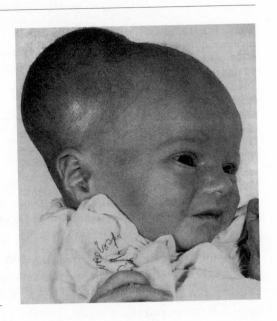

FIGURE 4.1

*Newborn with a cephalo-
hematoma. This type of birth
injury rarely causes any damage
to the baby's brain.*

Reprinted from D.G. Vulliamy and
P.G.B. Johnston, *The Newborn Child*,
7th ed., Edinburgh, Scotland:
Churchill Livingstone, 1994,
by permission of the publisher.

vate the various muscles and organs of the body are more exposed to physical damage. One of the more common types of birth injury is to a group of nerves called the *brachial plexus*, which exit the spinal cord just below the neck and innervate the muscles of the arm. (See Figure 4.2.) In about two of every thousand deliveries, some of these nerves are damaged, resulting in weakness or paralysis of the arm and shoulder, the most common form of which is known as *Erb's palsy*. These kinds of injuries are more apt to occur when the baby is very large (over ten pounds) or is descending the birth canal in an unfavorable position, making his shoulder likelier to get stuck on the way out.

Fortunately, damage to nerves outside of the brain and spinal cord is rarely permanent. Unlike nerve fibers in the central nervous system, peripheral nerves are capable of regrowing to their target after damage, so nearly 90 percent of babies with brachial plexus damage recover within four months after birth.

Another common site of damage is in the face. Injury to the baby's facial nerve causes one-sided paralysis: the newborn can't wrinkle his brow, close one eye firmly, or move his mouth on the damaged side. This type of trauma occurs in about eight of every thousand live births, when the side of the face near the back of the jawbone has been compressed by the mother's tailbone or a forceps blade. It happens more frequently on the left than on the right

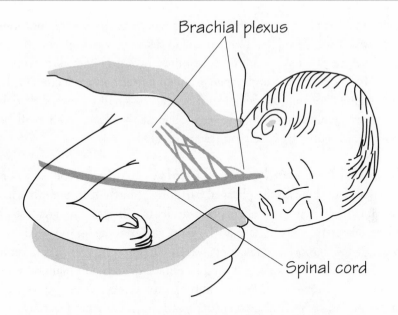

Brachial plexus

Spinal cord

FIGURE 4.2

*Baby emerging from the birth canal, showing the location of
nerves in the brachial plexus that can be damaged during delivery
of the shoulders.*

side, because more babies descend the birth canal with their left ear facing
back, toward the mother's sacral bone. Because the distance between the
nerve root and facial muscles is relatively short, the nerves grow back to their
targets rather quickly, and the paralysis usually disappears within one to three
weeks of birth.

The baby's nervous system is thus remarkably resilient to the mechanical
stress of labor and delivery. There are, however, a few rare events that can lead
to more serious or lasting harm to the brain. One is when the head trauma is
severe enough to tear the thick outer membrane of the brain, the *dura*. Such
tears often lead to bleeding, called a *subdural hemorrhage*. Because this bleeding takes place inside the protective membrane, it can damage neurons in a
way that the more common cephalohematomas do not. Depending on the
location of the tear, a baby with a subdural hemorrhage may die or suffer permanent brain damage, leading to cerebral palsy or mental retardation.

Another very serious type of birth injury is damage to the baby's spinal
cord. Unlike peripheral nerves, axon fibers in the spinal cord cannot grow

back to their proper targets once severed. As in adults, spinal cord injury in newborns is irreversible and may result in death or varying degrees of paralysis. The greatest risk for spinal cord injury is during breech delivery, if the baby's head gets caught and hyperextended more than 90 degrees backward. Although the overall chance of such damage is small in any single delivery, the consequences are severe enough that many obstetricians will deliver breech babies only by C-section (see page 112).

Birth Asphyxia and Cerebral Palsy   Although the baby's brain is remarkably resilient to the physical battering of birth, it is somewhat less tolerant of the biochemical effects of a difficult delivery. The greatest danger during labor and delivery is that the baby will become asphyxiated—unable to exchange carbon dioxide for oxygen. This can happen if the umbilical cord becomes compressed or if the placenta is damaged or malfunctions during labor or delivery. While the brain can tolerate short periods of hypoxia, longer periods of partial oxygen deprivation or even brief periods of total deprivation (known as *anoxia*) can kill neurons, irreversibly destroying certain parts of the brain. Compared to most kinds of physical trauma, oxygen deprivation is a more common cause of permanent mental or neurological handicap.

We've already seen how the baby is equipped to tolerate some degree of hypoxia during labor. Every time the uterus contracts, blood flow to the placenta is temporarily reduced, decreasing the amount of oxygen that passes into the baby's circulation. As noted, healthy babies compensate for this temporary oxygen debt by releasing catecholamines, which restrict blood flow to the peripheral limbs and organs and redirect it to the heart and brain. But if the oxygen deprivation becomes too severe, this compensatory mechanism can be overwhelmed, leading to a variety of problems. As the baby's body struggles to maintain blood flow to the brain, it can actually raise the blood pressure too high in certain capillary beds in the brain, causing bleeding. At the same time, if the asphyxia persists, the heart may eventually fail to maintain adequate circulation to the brain, causing local *ischemia*, or diminished blood flow, and empty blood vessels collapse and become damaged. Both bleeding and ischemia can kill brain cells, so when a hypoxic episode becomes severe, the chances for permanent mental or neurological impairment are fairly high.

The danger with asphyxia is a matter of degree. Experiments with monkey fetuses have shown that total anoxia can be tolerated for up to eight minutes. If it lasts between ten and twenty minutes, brain damage will result. Beyond twenty minutes, the fetus will probably die. Hypoxia can be tolerated for much longer periods of time, between one and three hours, without evidence of harm, but beyond this period, or when the fetus is subjected to repeated hypoxic episodes, brain damage and eventually death will also ensue.

About 2 percent of all babies suffer some asphyxia during delivery, but the vast majority escape without harm. Only one-quarter of these infants show symptoms of birth asphyxia. Among these babies, the most severely affected (about 12 percent) do not survive, and another 15 percent will end up with lasting deficits; the rest will grow up without any obvious mental or neurological problem. Overall, then, fewer than one in every thousand surviving babies suffers significant brain damage as a result of birth asphyxia.

The greatest concern for babies who survive severe birth asphyxia is that they will develop cerebral palsy (CP). Cerebral palsy is actually a group of syndromes, all characterized by disorders of movement or posture caused by brain damage during the fetal or early newborn period. It is nonprogressive, meaning that the area of brain damage and degree of handicap do not worsen as a child grows up. But because newborns are capable of few voluntary movements, the fact that a child is afflicted with CP will not be evident until later in infancy or toddlerhood. The condition varies greatly in severity from child to child, depending on the magnitude and location of the brain lesion. Some show paralysis or spasticity in all four limbs, some only in the legs, and some on one or the other side of the body. About half of all cerebral palsy victims are also mentally retarded, a third have epilepsy, and many have vision or hearing impairments.

This group of deficits can be traced to the most common pattern of ischemia that occurs during asphyxia in full-term infants. Because of the unique developmental state of a baby's cerebral blood vessels at the time of birth, certain capillary beds tend to "dry up" first when blood pressure to the brain falls: those in the primary motor cortex (see Chapter 11), and in particular, motor areas controlling the legs and lower spine, followed by those in cortical areas involved in vision and hearing. If the damage extends over a large enough area of cerebral cortex, mental retardation results.

For many years, it was taken for granted that cerebral palsy is the consequence of a difficult birth. We now know, however, that birth asphyxia is responsible for only 10 or 20 percent of all CP cases. Cerebral palsy occurs in roughly two of every thousand babies born. Most often, it is caused by brain damage that occurs before birth—hypoxic episodes that can occasionally be traced to maternal factors, such as high blood pressure, severe anemia, or seizures, or to congenital problems in the fetus, but that more often are completely unpredictable. CP is also considerably more common in babies who are small for their gestational age, because hypoxia also causes growth retardation, and in babies born prematurely, whose fragile skulls are more vulnerable to cerebral bleeding. In both of these instances, prenatal brain damage may be compounded by damage during labor and delivery, since babies who are already compromised are not able to tolerate the stresses of birth as successfully as healthy fetuses.

The Costs and Benefits of Fetal Monitoring   Despite the fact that cerebral palsy and other forms of brain damage are only occasionally attributable to events that occur during birth, much of modern obstetrics is geared toward detecting and preventing any chance of the baby becoming asphyxiated during delivery. This is certainly a worthwhile goal, and one that has led to many improvements in obstetrical care over the past thirty years or so. Unfortunately, however, there is little evidence that such preventive measures have reduced the number of children born with CP or other neurological disorders. As a result, some researchers are beginning to question whether matters have swung too far, so that millions of women are now subjected to measures that may help fewer than a hundred babies at most.

One procedure that has become particularly contentious is the use of electronic fetal monitoring. Fetal monitors provide an ongoing measure of the baby's heartbeat and are now widely used during labor and delivery to assess the baby's well-being. As of 1992, it was estimated that 74 percent of all deliveries in the United States were monitored electronically. Usually, the recordings are made with an external monitor, using a probe strapped around the mother's belly. Less often, usually when the baby is already judged to be "high risk" or otherwise distressed, an internal probe is inserted under the baby's scalp after the fetal membranes are ruptured, in order to provide a more accurate and versatile measure of the baby's heartbeat. Although the more common external method is basically noninvasive, it is currently highly debatable as to whether this monitoring offers any benefit at all, in view of the primary "side effect" it has produced: substantially increasing the C-section rate.

In principle, monitoring the fetal heart rate can provide valuable information, about both the baby's oxygen supply and its nervous system functioning. Changes in the baby's blood pressure and oxygen–carbon dioxide ratio produce certain predictable changes in fetal heart rate. In addition, since the brain stem and autonomic nervous system control heart rate, certain patterns can also tell something about whether these parts of the brain are functioning normally. But because heart rate is really a very indirect measure of these more important variables, one can never know for sure that a baby with a particular pattern is truly in distress. Even more worrisome is the high degree of subjectivity involved in reading these heart-rate patterns; more often than not, different practitioners come up with different interpretations of the same pattern. Despite the fact that fetal monitoring has been routinely used for at least twenty years, universal agreement as to the significance of different heart-rate patterns is still lacking.

Several studies have now shown that fetal monitoring has not improved a baby's chances of being born healthy; monitored babies are just as likely to die, to be admitted to neonatal intensive-care units, and to develop cerebral palsy as babies who were not electronically monitored during birth. Other studies of children ranging from eighteen months to nine years of age have failed to detect any cognitive advantage for those whose heartbeats were electronically monitored during birth. Several studies have found that monitoring has reduced the incidence of seizures during the newborn period, and such seizures, which are frequently caused by birth asphyxia, can potentially damage the brain. But given that monitored and nonmonitored babies show no difference in CP rates or later cognitive abilities, this finding about seizures appears to be neurologically insignificant.

It turns out that the vast majority of babies with "suspicious" or even "ominous" heart-rate patterns end up being perfectly normal. In one large study, the false-positive rate for predicting cerebral palsy on the basis of fetal heart-rate monitoring was found to be 99.8 percent, meaning that only two out of every thousand babies with abnormal monitor tracings are truly in danger. This fact, by itself, might be acceptable: "Better to be safe than sorry." However, once fetal distress has been diagnosed, doctors are often inclined to terminate labor by emergency C-section. Although as surgery goes, C-sections are generally quite safe, 4 percent of women do suffer serious complications, such as hemorrhaging or bladder injury, and four out of ten thousand actually die when the section is performed under such emergency conditions. When you consider the fact that about one thousand women undergo C-sections for every two babies who might benefit, this risk (not to mention the physical and financial cost) becomes a very important consideration.

As of 1995, 21 percent of all babies in the United States were delivered by C-section, compared with only 5 percent in 1965, and most agree that this increase is related to the increased use of fetal monitoring over the same period. Although perhaps a quarter of these operations are clearly warranted—in cases where the umbilical cord is trapped, the placenta is abnormal, the baby is clearly too large for the mother's pelvis, or the mother has a serious illness—the rest are performed for more controversial reasons, like "abnormal" fetal heart-rate pattern, "failure of labor to progress," or any kind of breech presentation. Yet most studies have found that children delivered by C-section do not show any lower incidence of CP or other neurological problems than those delivered vaginally.

While electronic heart-rate monitoring has yet to prove truly advantageous, it's unlikely that obstetricians will abandon it. Now that most hospitals are equipped for it, electronic monitoring is convenient and much easier than the alternative, which is to have a nurse measure the baby's heartbeat every thirty minutes using a stethoscope or portable Doppler unit. But if electronic monitoring is going to be of real use for reducing the risk of birth asphyxia, most researchers feel that it will need to be improved, particularly in terms of standardizing the way different practitioners interpret it. Computerized methods are currently being developed that may help resolve ambiguity in the interpretation of fetal heart-rate patterns. Nonetheless, heart-rate monitoring will probably live up to its potential only if it is combined with other methods of assessing fetal well-being. There is encouraging news that C-section rates have been slowly declining since the late 1980s, suggesting that electronic monitoring is already being used more wisely.

Childbirth Choices: Obstetrical Drugs and Procedures

It's the strangest feeling at the end of pregnancy: you look down at this huge belly and try to imagine how some little person, whom you haven't even met, is going to emerge from it any day and completely change your lives. First, you wonder how this pregnancy, to which you've grown so accustomed over much of the last year, can, with barely any notice, come to an abrupt end. Then you try to fathom how this baby is ever going to come out; your bowling ball stomach seems misproportioned for what lies between it and the outside world.

And only then do you realize what it all means—that the easy part, pregnancy, is almost over, and it's time to gear up for the tough stuff: childbirth!

Unreal as it all seems, Jessica and Dave are doing their best to prepare for Jack's impending birth. They have finished their childbirth class and read all about contractions, cervical dilatation, breathing, birth positions, and so on. Talking to her mother, Jessica realizes how much birth practices have changed over the years since she was born. Rather than racing to the hospital at the first sign of a contraction and getting knocked out for the duration of labor, she plans to play an active role in her child's birth, with Dave at her side for moral and physical support, hopefully creating the kind of experience that will match the spiritual wonderment of a new life.

Thanks to some much-needed changes, parents are indeed taking a more active role in their own childbirth experiences. Obstetricians and midwives now pay heed to the parents' preferences and consult them to a much greater extent regarding treatment decisions. But with this inclusion comes responsibility, so for parents to contribute meaningfully to the experience of childbirth, they need to be informed about different obstetrical procedures and their relative advantages and disadvantages for both mother and baby. The remainder of this chapter discusses several commonly used obstetrical drugs and procedures from the special standpoint of how they may affect the baby's brain.

What Is the Safest Way to Deliver Breech Babies?

Throughout most of gestation the fetus can move all around in the womb, flexing and extending all her developing muscles and assuming any kind of position. But in the last several weeks, as space gets tight, most babies work themselves into the optimal position for birth: the so-called *cephalic* or *vertex* presentation, with the head pointing downward, where it can help nudge open the dilating cervix and butt its way through when the time is right. *Breech babies* are the small number of fetuses who do not complete this turn and instead wind up at term with a foot, rump, or arm abutting the cervix, which is not ideal for beginning the tricky passage out of the womb. Only three or four out of every hundred full-term babies present in a breech position, but it is much more common in preterm deliveries, when labor begins before the baby has turned herself around. Obstetricians generally agree that preterm breech babies should be delivered by C-section, to reduce the risks of trauma, brain hemorrhage, and hypoxia in these already fragile infants. But there is currently a great deal of debate about how full-term breech babies should best be delivered.

Some of the problems that occur more commonly in breech presentations, and that pose a potential threat to the baby's brain, have already been
alluded to. Breech presentations are associated with an increased risk of brain
damage, both because of trauma—since an after-coming head has a greater
chance of becoming trapped behind the cervix—and because of asphyxia—
since the head doesn't emerge until after the umbilical cord, so that there is
no way for the baby to start breathing should the cord become compressed or
the placenta detach too early. Back in the days when C-sections were more
dangerous, most breech babies were delivered vaginally, and their risk of
death or long-term neurological problems (such as cerebral palsy, intellectual
impairment, or actual mental retardation) was indeed higher than for babies
presenting head first. Beginning in the late 1960s, many obstetricians and
hospitals instituted a policy of delivering all breech babies by C-section.
Today as many as 90 percent of breech babies in the United States are delivered surgically.

There is little question that routine delivery of breech babies by
C-section has reduced the number of incidents of brain damage. Now that
most breech babies are spared vaginal delivery, fewer die or have long-term
neurological problems. But recent studies have shown that this same outcome can be maintained if C-sections are used only for selective breech
deliveries, perhaps no more than a third of such presentations. Breech babies
fare equally well in vaginal and cesarean deliveries if they meet the following conditions: if they are lying in the so-called "frank" breech position (with
their rump down and legs up out of the way, but not if one or both legs are
crossed or extended underneath the rump); if they're of average size (between
about five and a half and eight and a half pounds); if the mother's pelvis has
been measured (using CT or MRI scanning) and determined to be adequately large; and provided that the baby's head is flexed forward and not
hyperextended back, where the risk of spinal cord damage is high. The baby's
size, exact position, and head flexion can be confirmed using ultrasound
shortly before delivery.

Despite these findings, many practitioners remain unwilling to attempt
vaginal breech delivery. Fortunately, there is another procedure that more are
willing to perform and that can reduce the number of C-sections: manually
turning the baby from a breech to a cephalic position in the weeks just before
term. The technique is called *external cephalic version* (ECV), and it is usually
performed under ultrasound, with the aid of drugs that relax the uterus. As
a rule, ECV is attempted at thirty-seven weeks of gestation, when there is

still enough room to move the baby. Ignoring the fact that at least some breech babies will have turned on their own after thirty-seven weeks, ECV has a reported success rate of between 50 and 75 percent. As more practitioners become skilled at ECV, it is conceivable that the overall rate of breech births will decline from 3.5 to just 1.5 per hundred full-term babies.

Even if all breech babies were delivered perfectly, without harm, however, it is important to point out that their rate of neurological and other impairments would still be substantially higher than among babies presenting in a cephalic position. The reason some babies are breech is that they already have some kind of congenital or prenatal abnormality. The rate of major abnormalities is about 6 percent in breech babies, as compared with 2.5 percent in babies who present head first. Babies with motor or neurological impairments are particularly inclined to present in a breech position, because they are less able to maneuver themselves into the proper position for birth.

Forceps   To some people, just the word *forceps* is enough to conjure up images of bruised and battered newborns' heads. Forceps use is linked to a higher incidence of birth trauma, especially cephalohematoma and damage to the facial or brachial nerves. Even more worrisome are reports that associate forceps use with more serious complications, such as birth asphyxia, skull fractures, and brain hemorrhage. Such problems can lead to permanent brain damage, which may explain why some (but by no means all) studies have found slightly lower IQ scores among children delivered by forceps, as compared with spontaneous vaginal delivery. But the research in this area is very difficult to evaluate, because one never knows with certainty whether such problems result from the forceps themselves or from the condition that made forceps use necessary—that is, the baby becoming stalled in the birth canal. A more appropriate protocol is to compare children delivered by forceps with children delivered by C-section after similar kinds of labor difficulty. Studies taking this approach have failed to demonstrate long-lasting neurological or mental deficits attributable to forceps use. (The findings and controversies are much the same for vacuum extractors, an alternative tool for aiding vaginal birth that is used more frequently in Europe.)

Despite the lack of consensus, concern about the safety of forceps has led obstetricians to be considerably more cautious in using them than they were some years ago. Over the past three decades, the number of deliveries in which forceps are used has declined from over 25 percent to less than 5 percent, while the C-section rate has increased in almost exactly inverse proportion. Forceps are no longer used to pull babies out from very high in a woman's pelvis; they are mostly used to extract babies who are well down in the birth canal (so-called *low* or *outlet level* forceps). Given the high C-section rate, however, some obstetricians are asking whether they haven't thrown out the baby with the bathwater (so to speak): traded judicious forceps use for C-sections, even when forceps might be the quickest way to rescue a baby and safeguard the health of the mother.

Obstetrical Drugs: Analgesics and Anesthetics   Despite all the talk about "natural childbirth" in the past few decades, the vast majority of American women receive some kind of medication to reduce the pain of childbirth. These drugs come in two types: anesthetics, which block the transmission of most sensory stimuli to the spinal cord and brain, and analgesics, which specifically lessen the sensation of pain. Whether the various drugs used to relieve a mother's pain affect her baby's brain is a matter of great debate among different medical specialties. Not surprisingly, anesthesiologists tend to argue that the drugs have few effects on the baby, pediatricians tend to be the most concerned, and obstetricians fall somewhere in between.

Obviously, there are certain circumstances in which obstetrical anesthesia is absolutely necessary. Cesarean section, the fail-safe option for ensuring safe delivery of the fetus, would be completely impossible without it, and other procedures, like oxytocin induction, episiotomy, and forceps delivery, would be considerably more difficult. Moreover, in some cases pain relief greatly improves the course of childbirth: some women are so frightened or overtaxed by contraction pain that it actually slows their labor and threatens the baby's oxygen supply. Such labors often pick up after the woman is given some kind of pain relief. Anesthetic drugs may even serve a protective role for the baby's brain in very difficult deliveries. The rationale here is that by slowing the baby's brain metabolism (and impeding the release of potentially damaging neurotransmitters), anesthetics may reduce the chance that a severely hypoxic baby will suffer permanent brain damage.

While anesthesia clearly has a place in some deliveries, the issue is whether the widespread use of obstetrical anesthetics and analgesics is in the best interest of most babies. In general women today are quite careful about what they put in their bodies during pregnancy, so it can seem a little odd that many lose all caution on the last day of gestation, just when the baby is making the difficult transition to surviving on his own and will no longer have the benefit of his mother's circulation to clear drugs out of his system. Certainly, there have been many improvements in obstetrical drugs over the past few decades, with an emphasis on greater safety for the baby. Nonetheless, *all* analgesics and anesthetics used in childbirth are serious controlled substances, in another league entirely from the occasional Tylenol or antihistamine that many women worry about during pregnancy. It only makes sense, then, that parents be advised of the potential effects of these powerful agents on their baby's health and particularly on his brain and behavior.

Most laboring women receive one of three different types of anesthesia/analgesia. The simplest form of pain relief is a systemic drug—one that reaches the entire body—usually an opioid (a derivative of morphine), which is given as a shot in the vein or muscle. These drugs are pure analgesics, meaning that they reduce the experience of pain but do not block all sensation. The next most invasive procedure is epidural block, which numbs a mother's sensation below the waist by infusing analgesics and anesthetic drugs into the space surrounding her spinal cord.* The most extreme form is general anesthesia—total knockout—which is only used for emergency C-sections, when the mother must be prepared as quickly as possible for surgical delivery. For the mother, the risk of complications increases in the same order: systemic analgesia has fewer potential adverse effects than an epidural, which in turn is safer than general anesthesia. For the baby, too, general anesthesia poses the greatest threat, but the risks of epidural and systemic analgesia are less easily compared and depend on the circumstances of the particular labor.

Systemic Analgesia   Systemic drugs are the most commonly employed painkillers in childbirth. Although they sometimes take the form of a sedative (a barbiturate) or a tranquilizer (such as Valium), most often women are given opiate analgesics to reduce the pain of labor. In the old days, this meant morphine, but because this drug can inhibit a newborn's breathing, it has been largely superseded by newer synthetic opiates with more favorable properties. The most common opiate now used in childbirth is *meperidine*, also called *pethidine* (brand name Demerol); other choices include *nalbuphine*

---

*Less common forms of regional anesthesia include *spinal* block (described in the next footnote), *pudendal* block, which numbs only the perineal area, and *paracervical* block, which is still performed in remote hospitals but has fallen out of favor elsewhere because it slows the baby's heart rate.

(Nubain), *butorphanol* (Stadol), and a faster-acting, shorter-lived derivative, *fentanyl* (Sublimaze). These drugs may be given early or late in labor to take the edge off contraction pain, but they do not block the sensation as fully as an epidural block.

From the baby's point of view, the earlier in labor the mother receives the opiate, the better. Although the newer derivatives are better than morphine, all can depress the baby's breathing, especially if the mother delivers between one and four hours after injection. In much the same way as they block transmission through pain fibers, opiates can block the neural centers that control respiration if the dose is high enough. Opiates cross the placenta easily, and the fetus is exposed to nearly the same concentration as that present in the mother's bloodstream. It takes nearly an hour for most opiates to reach their peak concentration in the mother's bloodstream following an intramuscular injection, so if the baby is born in this interval, he will not be exposed to the full dose. After four hours, the mother's circulation will have helped flush the drug from the fetus, so babies born after this time are also less likely to suffer respiratory depression. However, if the baby is born in the intervening interval, when the drug concentration is at its peak, his immature body cannot degrade the opiates nearly as efficiently as his mother's can, and he will remain drugged for several hours after birth. In the case of meperidine, for example, a mother eliminates about half her dose by three hours after injection, but the same reduction takes around twenty hours in her newborn. Moreover, the major breakdown product of meperidine (called normeperidine) takes many *days* to clear from a baby's body, perhaps explaining some of the rather persistent effects of this drug on newborn behavior.

The most dangerous effect of an opiate on the baby is respiratory depression. Fortunately, this life-threatening problem can be rapidly treated by injecting the newborn with another drug, naloxone (Narcan), which blocks opiate receptors. Even when respiratory depression is not observed, however, babies exposed to meperidine may show subtler neurological and behavioral effects for the first few days of life; they tend to be sleepier, less active, and less responsive than unmedicated newborns, and they may have depressed reflexes, difficulty with breast-feeding, and a harder time being comforted by their caregivers.

Whether opiates have any longer-lasting effects on a baby's brain or behavioral development is a matter of controversy. The differences between medicated and unmedicated babies are generally modest and confined to the first few days of life. Some studies, however, have reported behavioral differences up to six weeks after birth, and it is conceivable that small changes in a baby's alertness and behavior during the first few days could make a long-lasting imprint on later development by establishing certain unfavorable patterns of interaction between the parent and infant. For instance, a baby who is difficult to nurse or console in the first week of life may frustrate his mother, or give her a misguided perception of his true temperament, perhaps altering the way she interacts with him in the weeks to come. It is hard to say precisely how important first impressions are for parent-infant relationships, but in some cases it is possible that their effect may be quite persistent.

Epidural Block   In contrast to systemic drugs, which reach the mother's entire body, epidural anesthesia is a regional block, in which only part of her body—roughly the lower half—is numbed to pain. Epidural anesthesia works by infusing the space surrounding the lower spine with drugs that block the transmission of sensory impulses, especially pain information, into the spinal cord. Unlike systemic drugs, this form of pain relief must be administered by an anesthesiologist, who carefully inserts a catheter between two vertebrae in the mother's lower spine, positioning its end just outside the protective membrane surrounding the spinal cord, the *dura*.* Pain-killing drugs are then infused through the catheter, either continuously or as intermittent *boluses*. Anesthesiologists have tested out many different drug combinations in the epidural catheter, but currently the most common cocktail is a mixture of the opiate fentanyl and the anesthetic *bupivacaine*. These two drugs work well together, providing good pain block with very little motor-nerve block, meaning that they do not paralyze the mother's lower limbs. Moreover, by combining both drugs, the anesthesiologist is able to use considerably lower concentrations of each, reducing the overall risks to both mother and baby.

For the mother, epidural anesthesia has a lot of advantages: she is fully alert, but she feels virtually no pain and has surprisingly little loss of mobility in her legs and pelvis. Because of these advantages, the use of epidural anesthesia has grown tremendously over the last decade. At many hospitals,

---

Spinal anesthesia, another form of regional block, is provided by puncturing the dura and injecting similar drugs directly onto the lower spinal cord. It is often used for unplanned cesarean sections, since it provides both more rapid and more complete block of sensation than an epidural, but it poses a greater risk of side effects for the mother, particularly severe headache due to the leakage of cerebrospinal fluid.

the vast majority of laboring women receive an epidural, especially those having their first babies. There is no question that the advent of epidural anesthesia has been a tremendous boon for mothers. The issue here is whether their use in any way compromises babies' health or their rapidly developing brains.

There are two ways in which epidural drugs may affect a baby's brain. They can enter the fetus's bloodstream and directly influence brain function; and they can affect some aspect of the mother's physiology, or the progress of labor, that indirectly influences the baby's well-being. Every drug used for epidural anesthesia can diffuse out of the epidural space and enter the mother's bloodstream, where it travels to the placenta and can cross into the baby's circulation. The good news about epidural administration is that the total amount of drug reaching the baby is considerably lower than in systemic administration. Nonetheless, whatever dose does enter the mother's bloodstream crosses quite efficiently to the baby's circulation: for fentanyl, the fetal concentration is at least two-thirds of that in the maternal circulation, while for bupivacaine, it is about 30 percent. Moreover, studies with guinea pigs have confirmed that bupivacaine reaches the fetal brain when administered epidurally during labor.

Are there any measurable effects of epidural drugs on babies' brain function? The findings are controversial. Although many studies report no effect of epidural bupivacaine on Apgar scores or cursory neurological exams, few of them have used wholly unmedicated mothers as a control group. Using more sensitive indices of infant behavior, some studies have found that newborns whose mothers received epidural bupivacaine are less alert, less able to orient toward stimuli, and less mature in their motor abilities than babies of unmedicated mothers. Greater exposure to bupivacaine also makes babies jumpy and more irritable. The effects are most pronounced on the first day after birth, but some have been found to persist up to six weeks of life. While the drug itself does not stay in the baby's circulation past the first day or two, there is some evidence that bupivacaine alters early parent-infant interactions in a way that might disrupt the baby's longer-term brain and behavioral development.

Epidural drugs can also affect the baby in less direct ways. The most common side effect of epidural administration is hypotension—a reduction in the mother's blood pressure. Maternal hypotension is at least partially responsible for the fact that the baby's heart rate often slows down for a while shortly after an epidural anesthetic is injected. If the mother's blood pressure falls too low for too long, it can seriously compromise blood flow to the placenta, reducing the fetus's supply of oxygen. These serious side effects are prevented by giving the woman fluids through an IV, raising her blood volume and hence her blood pressure before the epidural is inserted. If this countermeasure doesn't work, another drug, *ephedrine*, may be needed to prevent her blood pressure from falling too low and compromising the baby.

Another way in which epidural administration can affect the baby is by altering the course of labor. Many studies have now shown that women who receive epidurals have longer labors, on average, than women receiving systemic analgesia. This is especially the case during the pushing phase, which takes about twice as long in first deliveries if the woman has had an epidural. Women receiving epidurals are more frequently diagnosed with *dystocia*, the failure of labor to progress, four times likelier to require forceps, and two or three times likelier to end up having a C-section, than women receiving systemic analgesia or no pain relief.

Most doctors agree that women who have epidurals tend to have more complicated deliveries. They vehemently disagree, however, about which is the cause and which the effect. That is, one problem with the findings of these studies is that women who receive epidurals may already be having a more difficult time of it—for example, their babies may be less favorably positioned, making labor progress more slowly and also be more painful. Indeed, some studies have found that women who opt for epidurals tend to have larger babies than those who don't, and larger babies are generally more difficult to deliver. It is also possible that obstetricians are more inclined to go ahead with forceps or a C-section if an epidural is already in place, which would tend to inflate the rate of "operative deliveries" compared with the control groups in these studies.

But one could also argue that studies of epidural anesthesia actually *underestimate* its adverse effects, because most use control groups that receive some other kind of analgesia, usually systemic meperidine. (There are simply too few "natural" deliveries to enroll in a clinical study!) Moreover, there is reason to believe that epidural anesthesia really does slow labor directly: Anesthetics relax the pelvic muscles, reduce the mother's urge and ability to push, and may repress the baby's own movements—the head-turns and whole-body writhes that help position him optimally for delivery. Whatever the reason for their slower descent, the fact that babies take longer to be delivered when their mothers receive epidural anesthesia may increase their risk for trauma and hypoxia.

So just how bad are epidurals for the baby? As with systemic opioids, the effects of epidural drugs are subtle and probably insignificant for most babies. There is no evidence, for example, of any permanent effect on children's behavior or mental abilities. It is also important to point out that anesthesiologists now use considerably lower doses of bupivacaine (often with more "break-through" pain for the mother) than were used in many of the studies of newborn behavior.* There is some evidence that the effects of an epidural on the progress of labor can be minimized if the anesthetic is given somewhat late in labor—after about five centimeters of cervical dilatation—and discontinued before the pushing phase. Since many women are frightened of childbirth—not unreasonably—the mere knowledge that effective pain control is available (and not restricted by insurance companies) should reduce their mental and physical stress significantly, which is better both for the baby and the course of labor.

Nonetheless, the conclusion many neonatologists draw from studies of epidural anesthesia is that it probably doesn't need to be used quite as widely as currently practiced. Although most babies are not significantly affected, epidural anesthesia may compromise the health of the small subset of babies already at risk due to illness, prematurity, or a difficult delivery. Encouraging more women to have unmedicated deliveries would be better for babies, and for the women themselves, who would be exposed to fewer side effects, have shorter labors, and might be in better shape to begin breast-feeding and bonding with their babies right after delivery.

General Anesthesia   Although it was common, in our mothers' generation, to be "knocked out" for even the most routine delivery, general anesthesia is now exclusively reserved for surgical delivery—that is, C-section—and then only when there is not enough time for epidural or spinal anesthesia. The fact that general anesthesia has been largely replaced by epidural and other types of regional anesthesia is certainly good from the baby's point of view, since most of the potentially adverse effects that have been attributed to systemic or epidural analgesia apply to general anesthesia, only more so.

At least three different drugs are needed to administer general anesthesia. First, a barbiturate and a muscle-relaxing drug are given by IV, and then the anesthesia is maintained by an inhalant gas. Although the baby is usu-

---

*But this lower dose is permitted only by the addition of opiates to the cocktail, which have effects of their own on the baby.

ally delivered within three minutes of the onset of full anesthesia, both the barbiturate and the inhalant rapidly cross the placenta and begin to affect the fetus even in this short interval. (The longer the interval, the more severe the effects on the baby.) Babies born to mothers under general anesthesia tend to be less active and alert than unmedicated babies or babies born under epidural anesthesia. Their reflexes and sensory responsiveness may be disturbed. They may also have difficulty breast-feeding for several days after birth, long enough to impair their initial weight gain.

It's not surprising that babies born to mothers under general anesthesia should themselves be neurologically depressed. Anesthesiologists regard it as something of a paradox that a sleeping mother could give birth to an awake infant at all. Both mothers and babies are much better off if they can avoid general anesthesia, so the current trend toward performing more C-sections under regional anesthesia is advantageous for all.

Maternal Anesthesia in Perspective   Maternal anesthesia plays an indispensable role in obstetrics and is responsible for the fact that childbirth is no longer a life-threatening event for women. But from the baby's point of view, anesthesia is probably overused, and more would be better off if fewer women were medicated during delivery. At the very least, mothers should be aware of the potential effects of anesthesia on their babies, so that those who do choose to use drugs don't misjudge their newborns in the first hours or days of life and get off to the wrong start in this most important relationship.

Conclusion

Birth is an especially momentous time for the baby's brain. On the one hand, the stresses of labor and delivery pose a very real, if small, threat of brain damage to the baby, in which severe trauma or oxygen deprivation can have a devastating impact on his cognitive future. On the other hand, the normal stress of birth also plays a positive role, helping the baby adapt to life outside the womb and arousing him for that important first encounter with his exhilarated parents. Whether a particular baby is going to benefit or suffer during birth is for the most part unpredictable at the outset of labor, but certain choices the parents make regarding childbirth can help tilt the balance toward a healthier experience.

In spite of all the drama of labor and delivery, one of the most surprising things about birth is how remarkably little it alters a baby's brain function. With the sudden onslaught of new sensations and the demands of an independent life, we might expect profound changes in the way a baby's brain works immediately after birth. On the contrary, newborns' mental activity is strikingly unaltered. As we will see in the next chapters, they retain much the same patterns of behavior and activity that they exhibited as fetuses, and the pace of their sensory and motor development is affected surprisingly little by the momentous event of birth.

Chapter 5

The Importance

of Touch

Who can resist the chance to hold a new baby? Those little limbs, skinny as a broomstick, the small, bulging tummy, barely visible nipples, perfect miniature ears, incredibly tiny hands and fingernails. And that unbelievably smooth, delicate skin, so soft that when you close your eyes, you can scarcely tell you're touching it.

But the tiny newborn can feel your caress. That's because the sense of touch is one of a baby's most advanced abilities at birth. Little Phoebe, who just turned one week old today, can't see very well—the whole room's a big blur—but she loves to be held. She can feel her mother's arm, cradling her comfortably under her head, her hand holding her bottom, and that wonderfully warm breast next to her cheek.

The sense of touch is by no means fully developed at birth. Babies have a long way to go until they can discriminate all different types of tactile sensations and accurately pinpoint the location of a touch on their body. But based on the development of their *somatosensory system*—that portion of the central nervous system responsible for the sense of touch—they can feel at birth a lot better than they see, hear, or even taste. And based on what we know about how the somatosensory system develops, Phoebe's early experiences at touching and being touched are incredibly important—not only for molding later tactile sensitivity, motor skills, and understanding of the physical world but also for her very health and emotional well-being.

The Anatomy of Touch

Touch actually encompasses four different sensory abilities, each with its own distinct neural pathways. There is the obvious sense of touch, or *cutaneous sensation*—the feeling that some part of your skin is contacting another being or object. The somatosensory system also oversees the sensations of temperature, pain, and *proprioception*—the sense of the position and movement of one's body. Touch, temperature, and pain sensations each begin in the skin, where specialized receptors for each modality are located. Proprioception

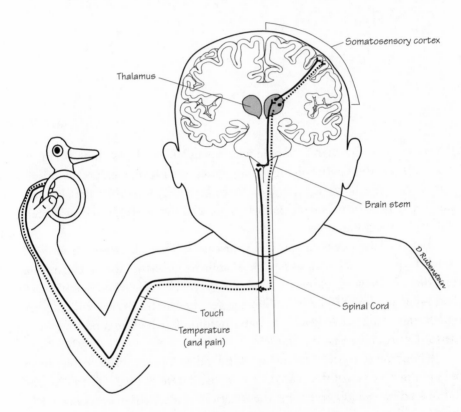

FIGURE 5.1

Neural pathways of touch. The cold teething ring activates both touch and temperature receptors in the fingers, which in turn send electrical excitation through the spinal cord, brain stem, and thalamus to terminate in the somatosensory cortex, where the teething ring is consciously perceived. Gaps in each pathway indicate the location of synapses.

uses information from the skin as well as signals from the muscles and joints to inform the brain about where our limbs are positioned at any given instant. It's this latter sense that allows you to know, for instance, whether your arms are crossed or your legs are moving, even if your eyes are closed.

How do our brains know what our bodies are feeling? Consider eight-month-old Jason, who's just reached out his right hand and grabbed his favorite ice-cold teething ring. The pressure of the plastic ring activates touch receptors in his fingers that are the endpoints of touch-sensitive sensory neurons. These special receptors translate mechanical pressure into long-distance electrical signals—action potentials—that propagate along the sensory neurons' tiny axons all the way from Jason's finger, up his arm, into the right side of his spinal cord, and then on up to his brain stem. When they finally reach the brain stem, these primary-touch neurons synapse on their first set of relay cells, neurons whose axons cross to the other side of the brain stem and terminate up in his left thalamus. (The thalamus is a relay station for nearly all forms of sensory information.) When action potentials in these relay neurons reach the thalamus, they activate a third leg of the relay; touch-communicating neurons, whose axons reach the left somatosensory region of the cerebral cortex, a vertical strip comprising the frontmost portion of the parietal lobe. It's here in the somatosensory cortex that neurons, once activated by this long-distance relay, allow Jason to perceive the feel of that plastic ring.

But that's only half of the process. In parallel with the sensation of pressure, the teething ring stimulates cold receptors in Jason's right hand. These receptors have their own set of sensory and relay neurons, which cross over in the spinal cord, synapse in the thalamus, and then project up to the left somatosensory cortex. It's only when the neural excitation reaches this "touch center" in the cortex that the two sensations—pressure and cold—combine to give Jason the conscious perception of a frozen plastic ring. The only difference between pressure and cold, then, is that they travel up to the brain along different pathways. The same is true for pain and proprioception. While each modality *feels* very different, they're no more distinct than are parallel routes on a subway map. (See Figure 5.1.)

Jason's real ability to feel lies within the two strips of somatosensory cortex, one on each side of his brain. Each strip contains an orderly map of his body's surface: neurons activated by a touch to the forefinger are adjacent to neurons activated by a touch to the thumb, cheek areas are next to lip areas, and so on. When Jason grabs the teething ring, moves it to his face, and then happily chomps down on it, his perceptions of the cold ring, his moving hand, and that delicious soothing of his tender gums are in a sense just illusions produced by the orderly firing of neurons in the maps of his body that reside in his brain.

While Jason's somatosensory map is orderly, it is not a perfect replica of the surface of his body. For one thing, it is divided into halves; because sensory pathways cross the middle of the body on their ascent, sensations on the right side of his body trigger activity in the left strip of somatosensory cortex, and vice versa. So each strip actually contains a map of only half the body—the opposite half. Nor do these maps accurately mimic the surface of the body; they are strikingly distorted. More sensitive regions of his body, like the lips and fingertips, take up a disproportionate share of cortical space, whereas large parts of the body like the back and legs cover comparatively little cortical ground. (See Figure 5.2.)

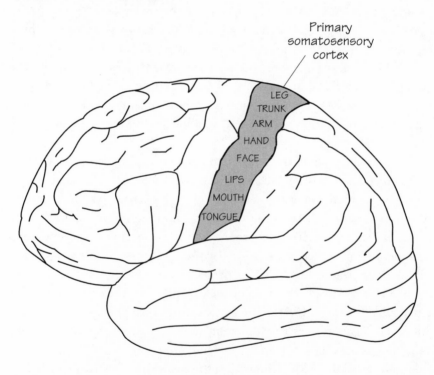

FIGURE 5.2

Location of the primary touch, or somatosensory, region of the cerebral cortex.

Role of Early Experience in
Shaping the Somatosensory Map

How these maps come to be distorted is a topic of great interest to neuroscientists, because it gives us a direct handle on the nature-nurture question: how genes and experience interact to shape our brains. The main source of the distortion is genetic. Our bodies are simply programmed to develop more sensory receptors in regions like the fingertips—parts that need greater sensitivity in order to perform all the delicate manipulations at which we humans (and other primates) are so adept. More sensory receptors mean more relay paths reaching the cortex—thicker cables, if you will. And the more sensory fibers of a particular type that impinge on the cortex, the better they will successfully outcompete rival body parts for cortical territory.

But genes are only part of the equation. Extensive studies in both rodents and primates have shown that the establishment of body maps in the somatosensory cortex also depends on electrical activity in the incoming sensory fibers. The final competition for cortical space is fought out between different body parts based on their relative amount of sensory experience.

Mice, for example, are extremely sensitive to touch or movement of their whiskers, somewhat analogous to our fingertips. A mouse's cerebral cortex contains a very large representation of the whisker region, a map consisting of clusters of neurons ordered in rows much like the rows of whiskers on its face. Each of these neuron clusters extends into the depth of the cortex and is therefore known as a *barrel*. Cortical barrels normally form during the first few days after a mouse's birth. If, however, one of the whisker follicles is removed early in this period, its corresponding cortical barrel fails to develop. Instead, adjacent barrels expand to fill the space it would have held, allowing other whiskers to "conquer" some of the neurons that would have been devoted to the missing whisker. (See Figure 5.3.)

The exact mechanism by which whisker sensory pathways shape the mouse's cortical map is still being debated, but electrical activity is known to play an essential role. Beginning before birth and continuing until about five days afterward, whisker *sensation* is necessary to produce a normal whisker representation in the mouse brain. In humans, whose brains are more mature at birth than rodents', this period corresponds to about the middle of gestation. This implies that all of the touch sensations a fetus feels in the womb are important for establishing his or her later sense of bodily perception.

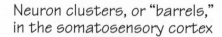

Neuron clusters, or "barrels," in the somatosensory cortex

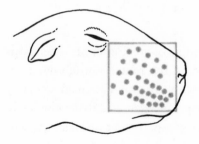

Normal

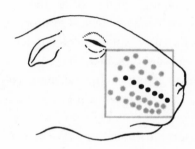

One whisker row removed shortly after birth

FIGURE 5.3

Arrangement of whiskers and neuron clusters, or barrels, in the somatosensory region of the mouse cerebral cortex. Removing a row of whiskers shortly after birth blocks the development of a corresponding row of barrels in the cortex.

Modified from D. Purves and J.W. Lichtman, *Principles of Neural Development,* (Sunderland, MA: Sinauer Associates, 1985), by permission of the publisher; based on research by T.A. Woolsey and colleagues.

Fortunately, this early critical period is not the final chance for plasticity in the somatosensory system. There is now good evidence that experience continues to fine-tune all the different perceptual maps in our brains throughout life. As long as the basic bodily map is intact by birth, it can continue to evolve with a person's changing skills and experiences.

Nonetheless, our early touch experiences determine the extent of *possible* tactile sensitivity. They also play a surprisingly potent role in the overall quality of brain development. We have already seen in Chapter 2 how rats raised in a highly enriched environment develop a thicker cerebral cortex and are actually cleverer than rats raised in a standard laboratory environment. A good share of this enriching experience involves tactile sensation. When young rats are provided with new toys, they excitedly paw, nuzzle, and climb atop them, increasing the electrical activity and ultimately the size of their somatosensory cortexes. If the same toys are left in the cage for several days, the rats grow bored with them, and their cortexes begin to shrink back in size. But if the toys are changed at least twice a week, the increases in cortical size persist.

It is almost frightening, as a parent (though not as a toy manufacturer!), to contemplate the implications of these experiments. Touch experience is essential not only for the development of touch sensitivity but for general cognitive development as well. Fortunately, toys are not the only source of touch stimulation that can elicit these changes. Comparable effects on rats' brains and psychological performance occur when pups receive extra grooming by their mothers or handling by experimenters during the early weeks of life. So we don't necessarily have to break the bank on toys to provide young children with adequate stimulation. Anything that increases a baby's variety of touch stimulation is likely to enhance many aspects of brain and mental development.

How Does Touch Sensitivity Develop?

Janet has known she's pregnant for only three weeks when the three-quarter-inch embryo inside her begins responding to tactile stimuli. Touch is the very first sense to emerge. Embryos of just five and a half weeks postconception can sense touch to the lips or nose. This touch sensitivity then rapidly extends to the rest of the body. By the ninth week, the chin, eyelids, and arms can all sense touch; by the tenth week, the legs; and by the twelfth week, almost the entire surface of the body is responsive to touch. The only exceptions are the top and back of the head, which remain insensitive throughout gestation. This may prove pretty helpful when it comes time for Janet's baby girl to squeeze her head out the birth canal.

But while the fetus can respond to touch from a very early stage, its sensitivity is not at all like an adult's conscious perception of being touched. That's because the initial responses take place only within the lowest levels of the central nervous system—the spinal cord and brain stem. Like the nervous system as a whole, neural circuits mediating the sense of touch develop in a sequence, beginning in those lowest levels and proceeding up to the thalamus and finally, to the cerebral cortex. Simple reflexes, like head or limb withdrawal from a touch, emerge early, because they involve only the sensory neurons and motor circuits within the spinal cord. Somewhat later, sensory fibers reach the brain stem, where touch information gets integrated with other senses like balance and hearing. By the third trimester, this integration permits the emergence of more sophisticated reflexes, such as the *rooting* response, in which the baby turns her head and opens her mouth in the direction of a light stroke on the cheek.

As touch inputs continue their ascent of the nervous system, sensory fibers in the spinal cord align themselves according to the body part they innervate, producing a body map first in the brain stem and then among the next set of relay neurons, in the thalamus. As early as fifteen weeks postconception, thalamic neurons start forming their synapses in the cortex. But these initial connections are, in a sense, just for practice; they arrive early and hold their place on a layer of primitive cortical neurons that will eventually disappear. Finally, at around twenty weeks of development, thalamic axons complete this wait and begin forming synapses onto their mature cortical targets, a process that continues for several weeks into the third trimester. Only after these connections are in place can the fetus possibly begin to have any perception of touch experiences.

These thalamic axons are more than mere wires for transmitting touch information up to the brain. They are actually responsible for turning their cortical targets into the somatosensory cortex. This region of the cortex might have become devoted to any other sense—vision, hearing, taste—but it develops features unique to the somatosensory region largely by virtue of the touch input it receives. During this later half of gestation, as Janet's active baby kicks and flexes, touches her face and legs, and bumps all around in the womb, she is providing herself with a great deal of somatosensory input—electrical activity that allows touch-sensitive thalamic neurons to claim their cortical homestead.

Once the thalamic neurons establish their mature connections in the cortex, the fetus may begin to have some dim awareness of touch experience. We know that premature babies as young as twenty-five weeks postconception exhibit electrical activity in the somatosensory cortex in response to touch stimuli. However, these responses are extremely slow and immature. They speed up dramatically in the last few weeks of gestation and begin to resemble the adult form shortly before term, when they are far more advanced than the electrical signals evoked by visual or auditory stimuli. Indeed, brain-imaging experiments have shown that the primary touch and motor regions are the only areas of the cortex to show any significant activity in newborns. Thus to the extent that anything is going on in a premature or even a newborn infant's mind, it has to do with her awareness of touch.

Nonetheless, the sense of touch is far from mature at birth. Sensory axons entering the spinal cord aren't fully myelinated until six months of age, while thalamic axons entering the cortex begin the process one month before birth and complete it after the baby's first birthday. Electrical responses to touch in the somatosensory cortex grow stronger and faster throughout the first year of life in parallel with this myelination.

By her first birthday, Janet's baby, Alesha, is processing touch information about four times faster than she did at birth. By the time she's six years old, this speed will have doubled once more, reaching a level very close to that of an adult. Her sense of touch will also grow progressively more precise as she develops past infancy. That's because the initial projections to her somatosensory cortex are rather diffuse, with a lot of overlap between different body regions—the map has blurry borders. With time and touch experience, however, it will grow steadily sharper, and she will become more and more accurate at figuring out where a touch is located on her body.

What Can Babies Feel?

It comes as no surprise that babies are best able to feel using their mouths. Touch sensitivity develops in a head-to-toe sequence. The mouth is the first region to become sensitive and, as every parent knows, is used by babies to explore everything, no matter how large or distasteful, small or dangerous. Even at five years of age, children's touch sensitivity remains greater in the face than on their hands.

Nonetheless, some parents might be surprised to learn just how clever young babies are when it comes to using their mouths. In one experiment, newborn babies were found to use different mouth and tongue motions when exploring different-shaped nipples, showing that they can tell objects apart based on feel alone. In another experiment, one-month-olds were able to recognize an object visually that they had previously explored only with their mouths. In this study, babies were allowed to suck on (but not to see) one of two different pacifiers—either a smooth or a nubby sphere. Then they were shown larger versions of both objects. The result was clear: they preferred to look at the type of pacifier they had just sucked on rather than the one they had never felt. So not only can young babies detect different shapes with their mouths, they actually form an abstract perception of an object—a mental image that makes the leap between their tactile and visual senses.

Newborns aren't nearly as talented with their hands. If the same nubby pacifier is placed in Phoebe's hand, without her seeing it, she will not later be able to recognize it visually. Although newborns grasp objects, they don't yet actively explore things with their hands, as they do with their mouths. Phoebe's hands are busy nonetheless. Even before birth, babies begin using their hands to touch all parts of their body, especially the face. At ten weeks of age, Phoebe succeeds in distinguishing different-shaped objects with her hands. By six months, she can also perceive different textures. But not until nearly eighteen months can she distinguish objects that differ subtly, like a regular cube as opposed to a cube with a notch cut out of it.

Hand preference is another aspect of touch that changes dramatically over the first two years. Infants are equally poor at discriminating objects with their left and right hands. But by the time they're two, they are slightly better at identifying objects with their left than with their right hands. This may seem surprising, especially in light of the fact that all of the children in this study were right-handed. But in fact, most people, young and old, discriminate objects better using their left hands; babies are the only age group that shows no preference. So even though most of us use our right hands to write and eat, we tend to use our right hemispheres—that is, our left hands—to process information about shapes and the spatial properties of objects. Apparently, the right hemisphere does not become specialized for this task until somewhat after the first birthday, perhaps because this is when the left hemisphere becomes heavily engaged with language.

A final point about touch sensitivity is that it differs somewhat in boys and girls. Newborn girls tend to be more sensitive to touch than boys, a difference that persists throughout life; the lightest touch that females are capable of perceiving is often below the threshold of detection in males. On the other hand, boys tend to be more lateralized than girls in their touch perception. Beginning in midchildhood (six to eleven years), boys' nondominant side (usually the left) is considerably more sensitive to touch than their dominant side (the right), whereas girls are more symmetrical in their touch sensitivity.

The Development of Pain Sensitivity

Poor Alesha! Only two hours old, and they're already sticking her heel for blood tests and jabbing her thighs with vitamin K and hepatitis B shots. Mommy and Daddy both wince as the needles go in, and then hold their breath . . . a few more seconds . . . until little Alesha screws up her face into a tight grimace, flexes her arms and legs, and lets out a strong wail.

Yes, newborns do feel pain. Along with the other forms of touch, pain is one of the more mature senses a newborn experiences. The sense of pain probably emerges before the beginning of the third trimester. Fetuses are known to react to prenatal procedures that involve sticking them with a needle, like tissue biopsies and blood transfusions. If not sedated, they will attempt to move away from the needle. (But amniocentesis is not painful to the fetus, as long as he is not accidentally poked.)

It's only in recent years that the medical profession has become fully aware of the pain sensitivity of young babies. While it has always been obvious that babies react strongly to painful stimuli, it was thought that they couldn't really *feel* them because their cerebral cortex was too poorly developed. This impression, together with some legitimate concerns about the safety of certain drugs, led doctors to perform all kinds of invasive procedures on neonates, including surgery, without any analgesia or anesthesia.

Now that the somatosensory cortex is known to begin functioning before birth, it is clear that at least some aspects of pain sensation are perceived by newborns and even premature infants. This appreciation has triggered a change in attitude about treating pain in young babies. It is now standard practice to minimize discomfort for babies undergoing surgery and other highly invasive procedures, a task that has been made easier by the advent of safer anesthetic and analgesic drugs.

What do babies feel in response to painful stimuli? Since they can't answer this question directly, we can only guess based on their bodily reactions. They cry, of course, and there's evidence that cries of pain are more intense and higher pitched than cries of hunger and other forms of discomfort. They also show a characteristic facial grimace, body posture, and physiological stress response that includes elevated blood levels of stress hormones, rapid breathing, and accelerated heart rate. These responses are present in even the youngest preterm babies.

There is also some evidence that a newborn grows progressively more sensitive to pain over the first few days of life. This change could be due simply to the gradual wearing off of any anesthesia the mother received during labor. Another intriguing possibility, however, is that the baby produces his own analgesia in response to the stress of birth—that is, his body releases endogenous opiates such as beta-endorphin—and that as these dissipate over the first few days of life, pain sensitivity gradually returns.

Generally speaking, though, Alesha's response to pain will change very little over the course of her first year. It is not a function of the myelination of her peripheral sensory axons, since even in adults, the nerves that carry pain information from the skin to the spinal cord are coated with little or no myelin. But while Alesha's perception of pain intensity changes very little, her ability to localize painful stimuli will improve dramatically during infancy, as the map of bodily sensation becomes more sharply focused in her somatosensory cortex.

Pain perception is unusual in the degree to which it can be modified by circumstances. In certain situations, as when a person is in grave physical danger, even the most terrible injury will not hurt at all, while in others, as when one is emotionally overwrought, even a minor scrape can seem excruciating. The reason pain perception varies so greatly is because the nervous system exerts powerful control over its own flow of pain information. Pain circuits contain special "gates"—points at which emotional, cognitive, or sensory signals from the brain permit or block the flow of input. Not surprisingly, endogenous opiates play a major part in suppressing the flow of pain information. This gating can be quite useful, in that it allows us to ignore pain when it would only get in the way, but to attend to it—that is, to our wounds—when the opportunity presents itself.

In babies, too, pain is not a fixed experience but varies with behavioral state. Infants react more to pain when they are alert, hungry, or fatigued than when they are sleeping, active, or distracted by other stimuli. Moreover, the internal opiate system that modulates pain sensitivity is known to be well developed by birth.

Parents seem to know instinctively how to take advantage of this gating system to soothe babies in pain. Janet, for instance, puts Alesha to her breast immediately after those injections, which quiets her instantly. Holding, swaddling, gentle stroking, rocking, and jiggling are also all effective at reducing babies' reactions to pain. Studies have even shown that allowing babies to suck on pacifiers or sugar-soaked rags reduces their overt distress to heel sticks and circumcision. All these alternative forms of stimulation interfere to some degree with the transmission of painful stimuli. However, sugar and pacifiers do not prevent the physiological stress response—elevated heart and respiratory rates—caused by circumcision. Consequently, the American Academy of Pediatrics now recommends that when parents decide to circumcise their newborn sons, the surgery be carried out using topical (surface) or local anesthesia.

The Psychology of Pain   One of the many nice things about having a girl baby was that Janet did not have to make a decision about circumcision. She and Derek didn't know the sex of their baby before she was born and had really wrestled over what to do in that regard if it was a boy. But now that Alesha was home and they were finally settled into their new family life, Janet realized that she wanted to get Alesha's ears pierced. Again, she wondered, "Will it hurt too much? Will it scar her emotionally?" Janet herself had had her ears pierced as a very young baby, and it hadn't seemed to harm her.

Indeed, it's very unlikely that the inoculations, circumcision, or ear-piercing that many of us experience as young babies have any long-lasting effect on our psyches. While babies can clearly feel pain from a very early age, they lack the so-called "psychological" component of pain, the cognitive perception or knowledge that they're suffering. Even adults, though they can remember the experience of pain, are not capable of conjuring up the actual feeling later on. But young babies also lack conscious memory, for developmental reasons described in Chapter 13, so they will never be able to recall their suffering. This *infantile amnesia* is undoubtedly a major reason why, in cultures throughout the world, so many of these painful procedures are performed early in infancy.

The mind exerts a powerful influence over our perception of pain. That's why Janet, who can anticipate Alesha's reaction, suffers as much or more than her baby when the doctor finally inserts the needle to pierce her ears. Alesha herself won't show this kind of anticipation until her second year of life, when babies begin crying at the sight of an immunization needle. So parents who must witness their baby undergoing painful procedures can take some comfort in the fact that, while he or she does feel the pain, it doesn't penetrate to as deep a mental level as it does in older children and adults.

Still, while it's clear that babies can have no conscious memory of pain, repeated painful experiences may have lasting effects at a more subconscious level. Just as early touch experience shapes the development of the somatosensory cortex, early pain may influence the further development of pain sensitivity and motor reactions to it. We know that while babies don't have conscious memory, they are capable of other forms of learning, like recognizing familiar people or perfecting motor skills with repeated practice (Chapter 13). Painful events may invoke a certain pattern of unconscious emotional responding that might influence mental development in some longer-term way.

There are certainly anecdotal reports linking neonatal pain to all kinds of later psychological difficulties, such as neuroses or psychosomatic illnesses, but little rigorous evidence for any long-term effects of such pain exists. One group of researchers has found that children born very prematurely, who are typically exposed to many painful medical procedures in the first few weeks of life, tended in the late elementary school years to judge various painful events as more unpleasant than children born at term. Another group of researchers has focused on the effects of circumcision and found that circumcised boys react more adversely than uncircumcised boys to routine inoculations at four or six months. These findings have reignited the fires of debate over whether the health benefits of circumcision outweigh the considerable pain it inflicts on newborn boys. At the very least, both studies indicate that greater efforts should be taken to relieve pain during circumcision and other invasive medical procedures early in life.

The Development of Temperature Sensitivity

Grandma is right: newborn Alesha cannot regulate her body temperature as well as you or I. While her tiny body does undergo some changes in response to modest temperature fluctuations (for example, her autonomic nervous system constricts her peripheral blood vessels and increases her metabolic rate in response to cold), it is less able to cope with more extreme conditions. For a variety of reasons—less body fat, higher surface-to-volume ratio, lack of shivering, and inadequate sweating abilities—newborns cannot compensate well in very cool and especially in very warm temperatures.

One way they *can* respond to changes in ambient temperature, however, is to modify their activity level. When it's cool, babies tend to wake up and move their bodies more, as a way of generating internal heat. When it's warm, they sleep more, and favor a "sunbathing" posture—extending their arms and legs—as a way of dissipating heat. In fact, parents can use such postural cues as a way of gauging whether their baby is too hot or too cold, an often mysterious issue.

One-day-old babies can tell the difference between warm and cold stimuli applied to their cheeks: a warm glass tube triggers a rooting response, while a cold one causes the newborn to turn her cheek away. Young infants also withdraw their hands from very hot or cold objects. By six months of age, babies can use temperature information to tell apart two otherwise identical objects; after holding a cylinder that's warm to the touch, they grow bored and prefer to hold another cylinder that feels cool. Thus, from a very early age, babies can feel and use temperature as a way of understanding objects in their world.

Based on the developmental sequence of temperature-sensitive neural pathways, temperature sensation should be capable of reaching the cerebral cortex by birth, if not earlier. Like pain, temperature transmission is not limited by myelination of primary sensory fibers, since even in adults, temperature information is carried between the skin and spinal cord by axons coated with little or no myelin.

On the surface, the perception of temperature would seem to be quite basic, even instinctive—we simply know that something is hot or cold because that's how we're programmed. But in fact, the experience of two unusual children suggests that our sense of temperature may actually be learned. Both children, an abandoned French boy named Victor and an American girl, Genie, spent virtually their entire childhood in the absence of contact with other people, for which they suffered in every way imaginable. Their most notable problem was a permanent deficiency in language, which we will hear more about in Chapter 14. But one other oddity that both children exhibited shortly after they were discovered was a seeming obliviousness to heat and cold. Victor, for instance, was described as pulling potatoes out of a fire with bare hands, and Genie seemed thoroughly unaware of being dressed inappropriately for the weather.

We can only guess at the reason for their undeveloped temperature sense. It is unlikely that their basic pathways of temperature sensation failed to develop. Rather, their reactions—or absence of reactions—suggest that this form of perception, like the perception of pain, has a strong cognitive component; it must be learned by teaching and experience. Since pain and temperature information are carried by closely intermingled pathways, perhaps they become similarly hooked up to conscious and emotional perception only later in development and as a consequence of social experience.

The Benefits of Early Touch

Touch plays a very special role in the life of young babies. Because it is so well developed at birth, it provides these brand-new arrivals more detailed access to their fascinating new world than any other sense. Touch is obviously essential to babies' sensory-motor development, but it also has a surprisingly potent influence over their physical growth, emotional well-being, cognitive potential, and even their overall health, because of some fascinating effects on their immune function.

A now-classic experiment by Harry Harlow at the University of Wisconsin first revealed the critical role of touch in psychological development. He was studying the nature of mother-infant attachment in rhesus monkeys, an advanced primate species that normally lives in extended-family groups of fifteen to a hundred individuals. Harlow raised infant monkeys with two inanimate "surrogate mothers": one was simply a crude face sitting atop a wire mesh body that provided milk from a baby bottle, and the other, which did not provide milk, had the mesh covered up by a soft terrycloth blanket. Contrary to all predictions, the baby monkeys did not prefer the surrogate that fed them. Although they visited the wire "mother" when they wanted milk, they actually grew attached to the cloth-covered surrogate, spending most of the hours of the day hugging their soft "tummies." This, in fact, is the posture rhesus infants normally maintain during their first weeks of life: clinging tightly to their mothers' front, where they are kept warm, can freely nurse, and don't interfere with her movement. (See Figure 5.4.) What Harlow's experiment showed is that it is actual tactile contact, and not the fact of nourishment, that comforts these infant monkeys and bonds them to their mother.

Other experiments with peer-reared monkeys have confirmed the importance of social touch. To some extent, peers can compensate for the absence of a mother in early infancy. When infant monkeys are raised in small groups, without their mothers, they spend much of the day clinging and huddling

FIGURE 5.4

Infant rhesus monkeys spend most of the first months of life clinging tightly to their mother's front side, where they can nurse freely and are easy to protect and carry.

Photo courtesy of Stephen J. Suomi. Reprinted from K.E. Barnard and T.B. Brazelton, eds., *Touch: The Foundation of Experience*, Madison, CT: International Universities Press, 1990, by permission of the publisher.

together. Although such peer-reared monkeys are unusually timid, they otherwise end up much better socially adjusted than monkeys reared in isolation. But if they are prevented from touching each other, by rearing them in individual cages, though all in the same room, they do not reap the same emotional benefits. Even though they can see, hear, and smell one another, the lack of early social touch leaves them markedly disturbed.

Essentially the same finding holds for virtually every mammal; physical contact is vital to infant growth and development. For many species this contact comes in the form of maternal licking. Mother dogs, cats, rodents, sheep, and horses all lick their offspring extensively, cleaning every inch of their bodies in the minutes and hours immediately after birth. So important is this licking that newborn animals often die without it, usually from failure of their urinary or digestive tracts. However, if a newborn domestic animal is given an extensive rubdown by a breeder or veterinarian in lieu of maternal licking, then its health will be preserved.

Scientists have exploited this latter observation to provide some fascinating insights into why early touch is so beneficial. Newborn rats that are handled for just a brief period each day by human experimenters show all kinds of hormonal and behavioral advantages that stay with them throughout life. Handled rats are less fearful, have more brain receptors for benzodiazepines (anxiety-reducing tranquilizers that mimic the action of a natural inhibitory neurotransmitter, GABA), less degeneration in old age of the hippocampus (a critical memory-storing area of the brain), and correspondingly better cognitive performance as they age. All of these improvements can be traced to the fact that neonatal handling permanently reduces the reactivity of rats' stress response systems. Handled animals show the normal hormonal responses to stress (see Chapter 3), but their corticosteroid levels do not rise as high as those of nonhandled animals, and they recover more quickly. Since prolonged elevation of stress hormones can be quite damaging to many organs of the body, including the brain, a better-modulated stress-response system is advantageous to both an animal's health and its mental faculties.

Perhaps the most interesting feature of this handling effect is that it works during only the first ten days or so of a rat pup's life. Pups who are handled only after this critical period do not show the same permanent advantages. Of course, human handling is not a natural stimulus for a rat, but recent research has found many of the same benefits for those rat pups who receive greater tactile stimulation from their mothers. Rat dams, like human mothers, vary in their styles of nursing and contact, and it turns out that those that lick and groom their pups more during nursing induce the same lasting benefits in their offspring. They have a better-modulated stress-response system, including changes in brain neurochemistry that make them less fearful in novel situations.

Other animal studies have focused on the effects of maternal separation on infants' growth and immune function. Infant monkeys become very distressed when their mothers are removed; their stress hormones rise during even brief separations, while longer separations are known to suppress their immune system. This suppression reverses if mother and infant are reunited within ten days, but if they remain separated for longer than that, the effect appears to be permanent; the offspring continue to show reduced immune function as late as six years of age. Rat pups, too, derive an immune benefit from early touch, since handled animals produce higher levels of antibodies in response to an immune challenge than nonhandled rats. As in monkeys, short-term maternal separation raises rat pups' stress hormone levels and is also known to inhibit the release of growth hormone and to suppress cellular growth and differentiation. These effects, which are limited to the first three weeks of a pup's life, can be prevented by firm human stroking, suggesting that it is the mother's actual touch and contact—as opposed to, say, her warmth or nursing—that especially promote infant growth.

Touch as Treatment:
How Early Contact and Massage Can Promote
a Child's Growth and Development

Like other mammals, humans who lack the comfort of touching and holding in infancy suffer dearly. Both Victor and Genie, for instance, were extremely emotionally disturbed (as well as physically and mentally retarded) because of their lack of adequate human contact. Recall also the foundling home babies described in Chapter 1. In spite of adequate nourishment and medical care, their minimal level of sensory and social stimulation left them stunted in every sense—emotionally, physically, cognitively, and judging by their high rate of sickness and death, immunologically as well. Even the occasional well-advantaged baby will fail to thrive for "nonorganic" factors—a lack of adequate nurturing that may alter their growth and stress hormones, much as in experimental animals. When these babies are hospitalized, it's often tender loving care, rather than special feeding or medical intervention, that best promotes their growth and development.

Thankfully, such cases of neglect and malnurturing are rare. But there is one large group of babies for whom the lack of parental touch and contact has traditionally been the norm: those born prematurely. Although infants born as much as sixteen weeks early can now survive, they are often tethered to ventilators, feeding tubes, and other lifesaving devices that preclude the kind of caressing and cradling most newborns enjoy. Many neonatal intensive-care units even have a policy of "minimal touch" to avoid overstimulating these tiny, often fragile infants. However, several lines of research have recently suggested that gentle touch and contact may be just the thing for premature babies, providing further evidence that for humans, as for mammals, touch is an essential ingredient of early nurturing.

Chapter 3 described one way in which the touch experience of preterm babies has been successfully modified. Instead of lying flat in rather roomy incubators, preterm babies are now positioned in a more protected, enclosed environment, their limbs flexed and bodies supported on all sides by soft cloth or lambskin buntings. In some cases, they are placed on tiny waterbeds or hammocks. This "nesting," as it is called, mimics the comforting confinement of the womb and permits critical sensory feedback every time the baby moves against his pliant supports. Nesting techniques have proven very beneficial to preterm babies, who in various studies have been found to gain weight faster, sleep and breathe better, and generally be less restless and irritable than babies cared for in standard incubators.

Another approach is to allow parents to step in and substitute for incubators. In the old days, extensive parental contact was discouraged because of fears about injury or infection. Now, however, some hospitals are encouraging parents to spend up to several hours a day holding their preterm infants, preferably upright and skin-to-skin against their bare chest. This approach has been dubbed "kangaroo care" because of its resemblance to early-life marsupials, which are born prematurely but kept warm and nourished in the maternal pouch.

Studies have shown several advantages of kangaroo care. Babies are better able to maintain their body temperature, so they do not use any excess energy during kangaroo care with either the mother or father. They sleep better, cry less, breathe more regularly, breast-feed longer, gain weight faster, and are discharged from the hospital earlier than comparable preterms who do not have skin-to-skin contact with their parents. Equally important are the benefits to parents, who bond sooner and express greater confidence about parenting when they "kangaroo" their preterm baby. And the greatest advantage of kangaroo care is in promoting breast-feeding, which can be very difficult to establish when babies are born prematurely. Warm, safe, and comforted by the familiar maternal heartbeat, preterm babies nurse more and earlier when held for long stretches close to their mother's bare breasts.

Yet another approach for increasing preterm babies' touch experience is to add a massage to their daily routine. Infant massage has a long tradition in southern Asia, where gentle, systematic stroking and rubbing of the baby's entire body is considered an important part of daily infant care. Even in orphanages, Indian babies are treated to regular massages, and these children grow and develop remarkably well, especially considering their many other disadvantages. In the United States, several controlled studies have now shown that massage improves the health and development of babies compromised by various medical problems, including prematurity, prenatal cocaine exposure, and HIV infection.

For about an hour each day, nurses gently rub or stroke a preterm baby's entire body—face, shoulders, back, chest, arms, and legs—pausing between each region so the baby does not become overstimulated. (If the touch is too light, babies react aversively, as if they're being tickled, and do not experience the same health benefits.) This is often followed with gentle flexion and extension of all four limbs, providing proprioceptive stimulation. Preterm infants who receive these daily massages gain weight faster, perform better on neonatal behavioral tests, and, because of their more rapid progress, are able to leave the hospital earlier than comparable preterms who do not receive this stimulation. Such massaging also improves the development of touch itself; by the time they reached full-term age, preterms given the massages proved to be more responsive to touch than preterms who had not. (But both groups were less sensitive than normal full-term babies.) Most encouraging are later cognitive effects of this early massage therapy; in one study, preterms who had been given the massages performed better on tests of visual recognition at six months of age than comparable control preterms.

Preterm babies are not the only ones who can benefit from daily massage. In one recent study, full-term four-month-olds were given an eight-minute massage shortly before being assessed for "novelty preference," a procedure that tests early memory and sensory discrimination skills. Compared with control babies, who were simply entertained by the experimenters with a red toy for the eight minutes preceding the test, massaged babies were significantly better at detecting when one auditory-visual stimulus changed and a new one appeared. As we will see in Chapter 13, novelty preference actually predicts later IQ better than any other infant skill, suggesting that regular, early massage may have important cognitive benefits for babies of all gestational ages.

Nor do the benefits of massage end in infancy. Massage therapy has been found to improve the clinical course of children with all sorts of medical problems, including asthma, diabetes, cancer, autism, skin problems, juvenile arthritis, eating disorders, and other psychiatric syndromes. In general, children show lower anxiety and stress levels, better mood, improved sleep patterns, and higher levels of attentiveness when treated to a daily massage by their parents. Of particular interest is the finding that massage therapy improves the mood and sociability of children who have been victims of sexual or physical abuse. Given the importance of touch to children's physical and psychological well-being, it is clearly time to rethink the general mandate against social touch by teachers and child-care providers.

The lesson to be learned from all these studies is clear: children thrive on touch and physical contact, particularly in the first few months of life. In many cultures, mothers are almost constantly in contact with their babies, carrying them in slings or pouches by day and sleeping with them by night. Parents in Western societies traditionally do not spend as much time in direct contact with their babies, but there is some evidence that one- to three-month-old babies who are carried in slings or "snugglies" for a couple of extra hours per day spend fewer hours crying.

The amount of touch, whether it is carrying, massaging, patting, cradling, or caressing, is clearly important. But equally important is the emotional significance of that contact, and for most babies, fortunately, loving contact is the norm. It is hard for parents to resist holding, touching, and exploring every inch of their new babies' bodies. These potent parental impulses were doubtless programmed long ago in our evolutionary history, considering how critical they are to the optimal growth and development of our children. Because touch, more than any other sense, has such ready access to young babies' brains, it offers perhaps the best possible opportunity, and one of the easiest, for molding their emotional and mental well-being.

Chapter 6

Why Babies Love to Be Bounced: The Precocious Sense of Balance and Motion

I'll never forget that New Year's Eve over at our friends' house. Paul and Sarah didn't have a babysitter for their six-month-old, so they invited us to supper and to usher in the new year. We didn't have children yet, but I was pregnant with our first, and we were about to learn how a baby could fit surprisingly smoothly into a New Year's Eve celebration.

As we were enjoying our dinner (Thai food and champagne—well, sparkling grape juice for me), little Daniel managed to amuse himself for most of the evening by springing up and down in his Jolly Jumper. There he was, his harness securely fastened to their hallway doorframe, bouncing up and down, up and down, up and down. He could really get the thing going! The higher he jumped, the wider his smile, and he never seemed to tire of it. His parents did eventually put him to bed, but before the new year descended, I added one more resolution to my list: get one of those infant jumpers for our baby.

From the moment of birth, children love the sensation of motion. Whether it's rocking, jiggling, bouncing, or just being carried around the house, babies find great comfort in the feeling of repetitive motion, and older children love to be spun, swung, or flipped upside down. The reason they are so receptive to motion is because they are born with a highly developed *vestibular system*—a "sixth" sense that allows us to perceive our body's movement and degree of balance. The vestibular senses are very old, in evolutionary terms, since all earthly organisms have had to orient themselves with respect to gravity and their own motion. Accordingly, they emerge quite early during embryonic development. Like touch, the vestibular system is precociously poised to transmit sensation that is not only very comforting for babies but also critical to their early brain development.

The Vestibular Senses

Unlike our other senses, we are generally unaware of the senses of balance and motion. That's because the vestibular system functions largely below the level of the cerebral cortex. Every now and then, however, as on a particularly bumpy plane ride, we become acutely aware not only that it exists but that it can be overstimulated, which is why those handy little bags are always within easy reach.

The vestibular system plays an essential role in our abilities to maintain head and body posture, and for accurately moving most parts of our body, especially the eyes. By sensing the direction of gravity and motion, it allows us to adjust our body's position to maintain balance and smoothness of action. The vestibular system is what allows you to go jogging, for example, and not see the world bobbing up and down; it detects the vertical motion of your body and automatically directs the eye muscles to move the eyes in compensation, keeping the visual field in front of you constant.

How does the brain detect motion and balance? The vestibular system is named for the hollow opening in the skull, the *vestibule*, in which it sits. This space houses the *inner ear*, a complicated set of chambers and ducts that includes both the hearing organ, or *cochlea*, and two kinds of vestibular organs: the *semicircular canals*, which detect head turns, and the *otolith* organs, which detect linear movements, head tilts, and the body's position with respect to gravity. There are three semicircular canals, each filled with fluid and oriented in each of the three perpendicular planes of space, so this organ can sense any conceivable rotational movement. Of the two otolith organs, one, the *saccule*, detects linear movements, both side to side and up and down, while the other, the *utricle*, is activated anytime the position of the head changes with respect to gravity, as when you lie down or tilt your head in any direction.

In spite of their differences, each of the vestibular organs converts movement to electrical signals in a similar way. Within each structure lie thousands of tiny receptor cells, called *hair cells* because they are topped by microscopic hairs, or cilia. In the semicircular canals these cilia sit in fluid, but in the otolith organs they are embedded in a gelatinous mass containing tiny crystals. When Daniel jumps up and down, his movement bends the cilia in all his vestibular organs, particularly in the saccule. Depending on whether he's going up or down, this bending either opens or closes tiny ion channels in saccule hair cells' membranes, decreasing or increasing their voltage and thereby translating motion into electrical information.

Hair cells form synapses onto the first neurons in the vestibular pathway, some 20,000 cells whose axons extend from the ear into the brain stem, forming the *vestibular nerve*. In the brain stem these vestibular nerve fibers synapse on several groups of neurons that serve as the hub of vestibular traffic, shuttling information about balance and motion to many places: to the eyes, which automatically move in compensation for a change in head position (allowing Daniel a stable image of our dinner party, even as his whole body is moving up and down); to motor neurons down in his spinal cord that control his overall posture and the position of his arms and legs; to the cerebellum, which integrates vestibular information with vision and touch (proprioceptive) input, thereby coordinating his sense of balance. (Some vestibular fibers also travel directly from the ear to the cerebellum, without stopping in the brain stem, illustrating just how important the role of vestibular input is in the cerebellum's job of coordinating movement.) (See Figure 6.1.)

In general all this activity remains below the level of consciousness. But sometimes when you're out on the dance floor, or racing downhill on skis, or have an inner ear infection, you may become acutely aware of your body's motion and sense of balance. As with the sense of touch, some vestibular fibers travel from the brain stem to the thalamus and thence, via relay cells, on up to the cerebral cortex, where your perception of bodily motion and position becomes conscious.

Development of the Vestibular System

Daniel was a tiny embryo only half an inch long when his vestibular system began to differentiate itself from its surrounding tissue. Both portions of the

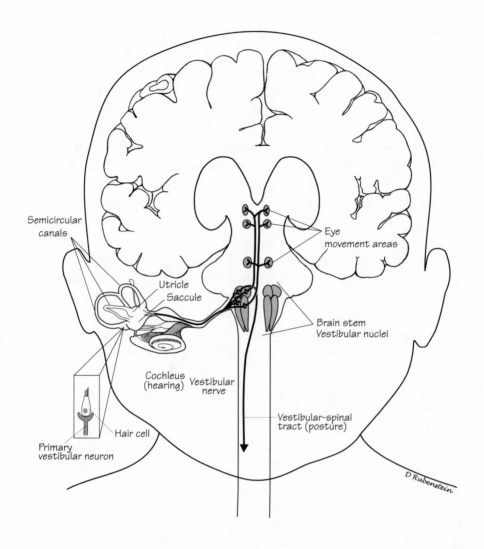

Semicircular canals

Utricle
Saccule

Cochleus (hearing)
Vestibular nerve

Hair cell

Primary vestibular neuron

Eye movement areas

Brain stem
Vestibular nuclei

Vestibular-spinal tract (posture)

D Rubenstein

FIGURE 6.1

Balance and motion are perceived through tiny movements of hair cells located in the three organs of the vestibular apparatus: the semicircular canals, the utricle, and the saccule. The hair cells excite primary vestibular neurons, which in turn send electrical information to various parts of the midbrain, brain stem, and spinal cord, coordinating our many vestibular reflexes.

inner ear, the vestibular apparatus and the cochlea, begin as a common embryonic structure, the *otocyst*. But while the vestibular and auditory systems start their development together, the vestibular system progresses more rapidly than the sense of hearing, perhaps because the early onset of vestibular abilities is so critical for the proper development of other parts of the nervous system.

The differentiation of vestibular and hearing organs is apparent just five weeks after conception, when three ridges that will become the vestibular canals first fold up out of the smooth otocyst wall. (See Figure 6.2.) By seven weeks, these ridges have thinned and then dissolved at their base, transforming themselves into the three semicircular canals. Between seven and fourteen weeks, all the hair cells form, immediately luring the neurons of the vestibular nerve to grow toward them so they can synapse onto them. These primary vestibular neurons also grow in the opposite direction, working their way into the brain stem, where they form their own very precocious synapses. The vestibular nerve is the first fiber tract in the entire brain to begin myelinating, about the last week of the first trimester. By just five months of gestation, the vestibular apparatus has reached its full size and shape, vestibular pathways to the eyes and spinal cord have begun to myelinate, and the entire vestibular system functions in a remarkably mature way. In spite of its precocious start, however, myelination of some other vestibular pathways progresses at a very slow pace, all the way to puberty.

Prenatal Vulnerability of the Vestibular System

Because of its rapid early development, the vestibular system is especially vulnerable during the prenatal period. Back in the 1940s, a new antibiotic, streptomycin, was introduced to treat tuberculosis in young children. The drug was literally a lifesaver, but unfortunately it also turned out to be very toxic to the developing inner ear. It is now known that this entire class of antibiotics, the *aminoglycosides*, specifically damage hair cells in both the vestibular and auditory portions of the inner ear. (They are also highly toxic to the developing kidney.) Early exposure to streptomycin, or to other aminoglycosides (including kanamycin, amikacin, neomycin, gentamicin, and tobramycin), can cause deafness as well as permanent vestibular dysfunction.

These drugs are most damaging during the period when hair cells are undergoing their most rapid maturation. For hearing loss, maximum vulnerability occurs around fifteen weeks of gestation, but it is probably several weeks earlier for vestibular damage. Physicians are therefore now advised to avoid the use of aminoglycosides in infants and especially in pregnant women. For those cases where the health of the mother or infant requires them, newer types of aminoglycosides and safer dosing schedules may reduce the risk of hair cell damage.

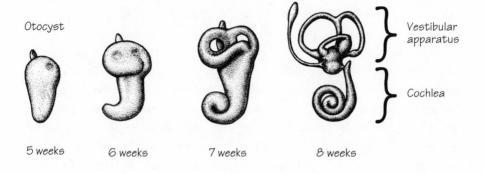

Otocyst

Vestibular apparatus

Cochlea

5 weeks   6 weeks   7 weeks   8 weeks

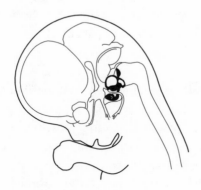

Location of vestibular apparatus in 8-week fetus

FIGURE 6.2

Emergence and development of the vestibular apparatus during the embryonic period.

Because of the structural similarities between the auditory and vestibular systems, many other prenatal factors that are linked to deafness also threaten the developing vestibular senses (see Chapters 3 and 10). In addition to aminoglycosides, these include certain maternal infections (rubella and cytomegalovirus), very low birth weight, hereditary factors, and hypothyroidism.

The Development of Vestibular Function

Fortunately, Anna and Steve's baby is developing a perfectly normal vestibular system. After touch, vestibular sensitivity is the next most precocious sensory skill, permitting their tiny fetus some of his first fetal reflexes. At just ten weeks after conception, when Anna is still managing to squeeze into her blue jeans, their fetus first becomes responsive to movement stimulation. By twelve weeks, it has begun reflexively moving its eyes in response to a change in head position. Anna is now in her eighth month of pregnancy, and often when she stands up or rolls over in bed, her sudden position activates the baby's *Moro reflex*—his arms attempt to fling outward with open hands and legs extended, followed by a slow return to a flexed position. A mature vestibular system is what allows a fetus to sense his orientation with respect to gravity and to turn into the proper position (head down) in the weeks or days before birth. Indeed, babies born with defects in their vestibular system have a much greater chance of being in a breech position, presumably because they can't adequately discern the difference between up and down.

Vestibular function underlies the several postural reflexes that pediatricians commonly test when assessing a newborn's neurological health. One example is the *asymmetrical neck response*, which Dr. Jane tests out on Anna and Steve's baby, Timothy, now one day old. When Dr. Jane turns Timothy's head to the right, he extends his right arm and leg, and he flexes the limbs on his left side. His vestibular system detects the sudden change in head position and commands limb adjustments that would maintain balance if Timothy were standing. Premature babies display this reflex by thirty-five weeks of gestation, and it is well established by one month after birth, but by seven months, it can no longer be elicited by a simple head turn. The reflex never totally disappears, however; even adults spontaneously adopt opposing flexion and extension to stabilize their posture during a sudden position change, as when falling or jumping. (See Figure 6.3.)

FIGURE 6.3

*The asymmetric neck reflex is controlled by the vestibular system
and can be elicited by turning a baby's head to one side. Although this
reflex disappears by seven months, the same postural adjustments
persist into adulthood and are triggered automatically under
certain conditions of imbalance.*

Reprinted from E.R. Kandel et al., eds., *Principles of Neural Science*, 3rd ed.,
1991, by permission of Appleton and Lange, Stamford, CT.

Another vestibular reflex is the *traction response*, in which a newborn
tries (largely in vain) to hold his head up when you pull him from lying to
sitting. The vestibular system senses the forward movement of the head and
triggers contraction of neck flexor muscles, attempting to raise it to a vertical position, even though the neck muscles are not yet strong enough to do
the job. This reflex is present in healthy babies by about thirty-seven weeks
of gestation.

The clearest evidence of a newborn's vestibular function is in his eye movements. When Steve turns Timothy's head to the side, the baby's eyes remain forward, facing his daddy. Stabilizing one's gaze in this manner, a response known as the *doll's eye reflex*, actually requires active eye movements and is one of several vestibular-ocular reflexes that researchers have found useful for tracking the development of the vestibular system.

Another technique is reminiscent of a favorite children's game—spinning a friend around in circles and then watching the way her eyes dart back and forth (fast in one direction and slowly in the other) when she stops. This back-and-forth eye motion, known as *nystagmus*, occurs because the nervous system adapts to the constant rotation and persists in trying to compensate for it. Even though she's not spinning anymore, her vestibular system is temporarily fooled into thinking she is, causing her eyes to try to adjust by moving in the direction opposite the spin.

Even premature babies show this *postrotatory nystagmus*, provided they are awake and alert during testing. To test the response, researchers seat a parent on a swivel chair with the baby on her lap, spin the chair around ten times, and then measure the speed of the baby's eye movements immediately after the spin. Not only do infants show the same nystagmus as older children and adults, their eyes move even faster. In fact, the vestibular system is over-responsive during infancy, reaching peak sensitivity between six and twelve months, then declining rapidly until two and a half years, and more gradually until puberty. This oversensitivity explains, in part, why infants and toddlers are so wobbly on their feet, but it may actually be useful for other aspects of neurological development. The slow maturation of vestibular sensitivity is known to result from gradual modifications in the synaptic strength and dendritic growth of neurons in the brain stem and higher neural centers, as opposed to any changes in the inner ear.

Maturation of the vestibular system is also important for the development of a child's postural abilities. As anyone knows who's ever watched an eleven-month-old trying to stand unassisted, maintaining balance is no easy task. It depends not only on the vestibular system but also on visual, proprioceptive, and motor skills. Nonetheless, researchers have been able to separate these different sources of postural cues and have found that the contribution of the vestibular system to maintaining balance does not fully mature until at least age seven and perhaps not until puberty. This gradual vestibular maturation is necessary to keep up with a child's steadily expanding range of movement, and it may be orchestrated by the very slow myelination of certain vestibular tracts.

Vestibular Development and the Rest of the Brain

Even though we are largely unaware of them, the vestibular senses play a surprisingly important role in mental and neurological development. One study, for instance, found that a large proportion of young children with a deficient nystagmus response were delayed in their motor development; nearly half weren't walking by eighteen months and some walked as late as four years of age. It's easy to see how the sense of balance might influence the development of motor skills, but vestibular deficits are also frequently found among children with emotional problems, perceptual or attention deficits, learning disabilities, language disorders, and autism. Although it is unlikely that vestibular dysfunction is solely responsible for this wide range of disorders, these findings do suggest that the sense of balance and motion is more important than is commonly realized.

Mental development is highly cumulative. As one of the earliest senses to mature, the vestibular system provides a large share of a baby's earliest sensory experiences. These experiences probably play a critical role in organizing other sensory and motor abilities, which in turn influence the development of higher emotional and cognitive abilities.

The Benefits of Vestibular Stimulation

If vestibular deficiency can interfere with other aspects of brain development, some researchers have wondered whether the opposite also holds true: can supplemental vestibular stimulation actually improve a baby's brain and mind? In fact, there is evidence suggesting it can. As we have seen, children, and especially infants, seem to crave vestibular stimulation in the form of repetitive motion like rocking, swinging, bouncing, and spinning. So strong is this impulse that most infants go through a phase when they produce their own vestibular "self-stimulation"—bouncing, swaying, head-shaking, body-rocking, or, in 3 to 15 percent of babies, head-banging. Vestibular self-stimulation typically begins between six and eight months of age, or right when vestibular sensitivity reaches its peak.

One study offers particularly provocative evidence of the benefits of vestibular stimulation. These researchers exposed babies, who ranged in age from three to thirteen months, to sixteen sessions of chair spinning: Four times a week for four weeks, the infants were seated on a researcher's lap and spun around ten times in a swivel chair, each spin followed by an abrupt stop. To maximize stimulation of each of the three semicircular canals, the spinning included one or two rotations in each direction with the babies held in each of three positions: sitting, with the head tilted forward about 30 degrees, and side-lying on both left and right sides. Not surprisingly, the babies loved this treatment. They usually babbled or laughed during the rotation and became fussy during the thirty-second rest period between spins. In addition to this "trained" group, there were two groups of control infants, one that received no treatment, and one that came in for the same sixteen sessions but only sat on the researcher's lap in the swivel chair; they did not get to spin.

The results were striking. Compared with both control groups, the babies who were spun showed more advanced development of both their reflexes and their motor skills. The difference was particularly marked for motor skills like sitting, crawling, standing, and walking. In fact, the study included a set of three-month-old fraternal twins, of whom one received the training and the other did not. By the end of the study, when they were four months old, the twin who had experienced the vestibular stimulation had mastered head control and could even sit independently, while the unstimulated twin had only just begun to hold his head up.

Vestibular stimulation appears to be equally beneficial to very young infants. Newborns cry less when they are being rocked, carried, jiggled, or suddenly changed in position, all actions that activate the vestibular system. In one study, researchers tested several different soothing methods on two-to-four-day-old babies and found that anything that incorporated vestibular stimulation was more effective than methods involving only caregiver touch or contact. Thus, the newborns cried considerably less when they were picked up and held upright over the experimenter's shoulder (providing both contact and vestibular stimulation) than when the experimenter merely leaned over the bed and held them close but did not change their position. Even pure vestibular stimulation—rocking a baby in an infant seat, without any caregiver physical contact—was more effective than contact alone.

Vestibular stimulation can have a profound impact on a baby's overall behavioral state. Young babies tend to go through periods when their behavior is best described as "disorganized"—they flail their limbs, tense up their hands and face, and cry in an insistent, high-pitched way. (Toddlers and preschoolers have similar periods of disorganization, otherwise known as tantrums, but they are fortunately far less frequent.) Parents will do just about anything to try to stop the crying, and when Anna picks Timothy up, holds him over her shoulder, and gently jiggles him, he soon becomes "organized" again; his crying stops, his body relaxes, and for a brief time, he is highly alert—looking intently at the lamp behind Anna's back, then at the bright picture on the wall, and finally, when she moves him to a cradling position, straight into Anna's eyes. Indeed, infants who are comforted through vestibular stimulation show greater visual alertness than babies comforted in other ways. It's during these periods of quiet alertness that babies do their best learning, when they can most effectively absorb information about the world around them.

Continued vestibular stimulation has a very different effect: It decreases a baby's level of arousal. After Anna carries him around for a while, Timothy gets sleepy again and eventually dozes off. This, too, is beneficial to his maturing brain, which does a lot of important growing during the sleeping hours.

The benefits of vestibular stimulation are well known to nurses in neonatal intensive-care units. As with massage and other forms of sensory stimulation, preterm babies thrive much better when they receive additional vestibular stimulation each day. Rocking, swinging, being carried in front-packs, or simply being propped upright in an infant seat are all measures known to quiet distressed preterm babies and help them grow faster. Another good source of vestibular stimulation are those tiny infant waterbeds, where babies virtually rock themselves, every time they move, much as they would if they were still floating around in the womb. With these various improvements, premature babies have been found to gain weight faster, be less irritable, breathe more regularly, move less jerkily, sleep more, and spend more time in the quiet, alert state than preterms not given extra vestibular stimulation.

As one of a baby's most mature senses, the vestibular system provides a fast track into her developing brain. It doesn't take long for most parents to discover the power of this hidden sense, but isn't it nice to know that all that rocking, jiggling, and carrying is not only soothing to your baby, it is actually quite good for her emerging mind?

Chapter 7

The Early World
of Smell

It was a long labor, but when Hannah was finally born, her mother, Rachel, was filled with the most wonderful sense of well-being. Perhaps that was why, as she buried her face into the tiny new body in her arms, she was overwhelmed by the beautiful smell of her baby. Hannah had been dried off but not yet washed, and she carried that unusual, newborn organic scent that Rachel found unspeakably lovely.

As with the vestibular senses, we are often unaware of the powerful role that smell plays in our lives. Of course, odor is an important component of appetite, and to the extent that it helps us select food and avoid potential dangers—like rotten meat and certain toxic chemicals—the sense of smell is quite useful. But smell also plays an essential role in our social interactions, including kin recognition, sexual attraction, and, to a remarkable degree, parent-infant bonding. This latter interaction works both ways; just as Rachel finds Hannah's smell so appealing, so are newborns drawn to their mother's unique odors, thanks to their advanced sense of smell. Indeed, for newborns, whose "long-distance" senses of vision and hearing are still poorly developed, the more immediate senses of smell, taste, and touch are far more important in assuring adequate growth and parental protection.

Smell and taste are known as the "chemical" senses, because both begin with neural excitation in response to specific molecules in the environment. Both are phylogenetically primitive senses; even single-cell organisms can distinguish different chemicals in seeking out those necessary for survival. Smell is unique among the mammalian senses, however, in that its information is transmitted directly from the nose to the cerebral cortex—albeit to more primitive areas of the cortex—without first being relayed through lower brain centers. These primary olfactory areas are better developed by birth than more recently evolved parts of the cortex, so even though smell is one of our less important senses, newborns probably rely on it more heavily than we do at any later time in life.

How Smell Works

Hannah's sense of smell goes to work right away. While still holding her, fresh from the womb, Rachel expresses a little bit of colostrum—the protein-rich fluid secreted by the breasts before true milk comes in. A few molecules escape the drop on her nipple and diffuse through the air to Hannah's nose, where they dissolve into a mucus layer deep inside her nostrils. This watery mucus layer contains the hairlike cilia of *olfactory epithelial cells*, the first neurons in the chain of odor perception. The cilia trap the odorous colostrum molecules, binding them to specific protein receptors that convert their chemical information into electrical signals, or action potentials. Each olfactory epithelial cell is thought to respond to just one or a few specific chemicals, and the strength of an odor is graded by the number of action potentials it generates.

Once activated, olfactory epithelia send their action potentials along short axons that travel straight up through pores in the skull, and they synapse in the *olfactory bulb*, the first relay point within the brain. This oblong structure (there is one for each nostril) lies underneath the frontal lobe, just above the nasal cavity. The olfactory bulb contains a small network of neurons that integrate information from all of the epithelial receptor cells. Its output neurons, the *mitral cells*, send their long axons along the base of the frontal lobe, in a band known as the *olfactory tract*, to several different areas in the *primary olfactory cortex*, which is located at the bottom, innermost bulges of the temporal lobe. Included among the several direct targets of olfactory bulb neurons are portions of the *limbic system*, the part of the brain that controls our emotions, drives, and memories.

So important is the sense of smell to other mammals, such as rodents, that their olfactory and limbic cortex constitutes a single neural system, the *rhinencephalon*, or "smell brain." This older region has a simpler structure, with fewer layers of neurons than the newer six-layered regions of cortex involved in our other senses and higher cognitive abilities. It also takes up a much larger proportion of total brain space in other animals, compared with humans, which is why our sense of smell is comparatively so poor. The sense of smell is thus truly primitive, both in the way it is processed and in the fact that it has such direct access to the neural circuitry that controls our memory and emotions.

Within our "smell brain," different regions use olfactory information for different purposes. For instance, one projection of mitral cells is to a limbic area known as the *entorhinal cortex*, responsible for learning and remembering odors and their associations. Another limbic target, the *amygdala*, uses direct olfactory input to control feeding, as well as certain aspects of social and reproductive behavior in animals. From the primary olfactory cortex, odor information is further shuttled to brain-stem centers that control motor reactions such as salivation, head turning, facial expressions, and sucking. Eventually, olfactory information reaches the higher, or newer, regions of the cerebral cortex. Neurons in the primary olfactory cortex project both directly and via the thalamus to the *orbitofrontal cortex*, also located on the underside of the frontal lobe, not far from the olfactory bulb, where the conscious perception and discrimination of odors takes place. This region may also be responsible for the integration of smell and taste senses, which gives us the perception of flavors. (See Figure 7.1.)

This describes the olfactory system proper, but it is important to point out that we have an additional means of detecting chemicals in our environment. It is called the *common chemical sense*, and it originates in free nerve endings located in all exposed mucous membranes of the body, including the mouth, eyes, nose, and genitalia. This sense is far less specific than true olfaction; the nervous system knows that it's encountered some kind of noxious chemical but can't distinguish with precision what it is. Nonetheless, this type of chemical sensitivity emerges quite early in development, so it probably plays an important role in the ability of fetuses and young infants to detect odors, especially dangerous ones.

Development of the Olfactory System

Though she has only just been born, Hannah's olfactory system is quite mature. It began forming early in the embryonic period, progressing, like all the senses, from the outside in. At just five weeks after fertilization, a nasal

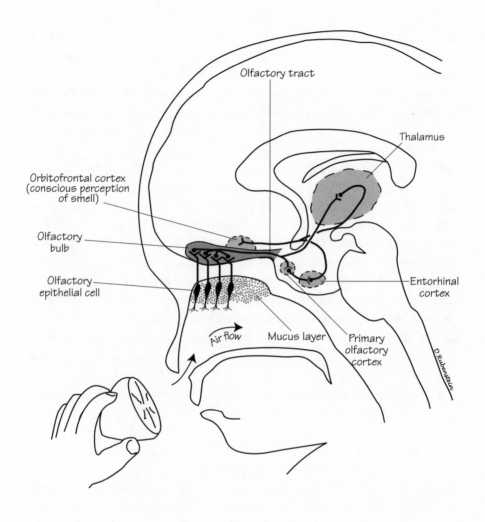

Olfactory tract

Thalamus

Orbitofrontal cortex
(conscious perception
of smell)

Olfactory
bulb

Olfactory
epithelial cell

Entorhinal
cortex

Air flow   Mucus layer   Primary
olfactory
cortex

D. Rubenstein

FIGURE 7.1

*Olfactory pathways of the brain. Odor molecules bind to olfactory
epithelial cells in the nasal cavity, triggering a chain of electrical
excitation that progresses from the olfactory bulb to several cortical
and subcortical areas. (Only some are shown here.) One such target
is the entorhinal cortex, a part of the limbic system that participates
in odor memory. Another target, the orbitofrontal cortex, is
responsible for our conscious olfactory perception.*

pit appeared in the primitive face, gradually deepening and dividing to form true nostrils by seven weeks. At this point the olfactory epithelial cells began to form, taking their place along the lining of the nasal cavity. First, these oval-shaped cells sent a thick dendrite down toward the nasal surface, terminating in the ciliated tuft that would bind odor molecules; then, from their top end, they grew a long, thin axon that pierced the nasal boundary, forming the olfactory nerve, and advanced directly into the brain. By eleven weeks, the olfactory epithelia were abundant and outwardly quite mature. But they did not actually begin to function until several months later, when more subtle aspects of their biochemical development were complete.

The olfactory epithelial cells are truly unique. Among all the neurons in the body, they are the only ones known to be continually generated throughout life. Although the birth of new cells is common for other organs of the body, like the skin, blood, and gut, it is virtually unheard of among neurons. However, olfactory epithelial cells die and are replaced about once every sixty days, progressing through the same sequence of cilia growth, axon projection, and synapse formation in the olfactory bulb. It is not known why olfactory epithelia have this special property; nor does this regeneration mean that the sense of smell cannot be permanently damaged. That's because the generation of new olfactory cells depends on the presence of healthy precursor cells, and these precursors tend to gradually die off (without being replaced) over the years. Thus, adults actually show a considerable amount of degeneration in their olfactory epithelia compared with newborns. This degeneration begins as early as mid-childhood—as a result of the infections, smoking, and exposure to pollutants and toxins—and it explains why the sense of smell typically declines with aging.

As the axons of the olfactory epithelia invade the brain, they initiate the development of neurons in the olfactory bulb. This second relay point begins taking form in the eighth week of prenatal development, with its main output neurons, the mitral cells, first forming in the tenth week. At thirteen weeks, the olfactory bulb becomes walled off from the nasal cavity by an emerging bony plate, perforated with holes through which the various branches of the olfactory nerve pass. The olfactory bulb appears fully mature by midgestation, but it too probably does not begin functioning until the third trimester.

Less is known about the development of the primary olfactory cortex, but because it lies within a phylogenetically older brain region, it probably matures before the newer cortical areas that control senses like vision, hearing, and even touch. Indeed, the primary olfactory tracts are all well myelinated before birth, confirming that the structures underlying smell are comparatively well developed in newborns.

It is interesting to note that fetuses briefly develop another structure, the *vomeronasal organ*, which in other mammals plays an important, parallel role in transmitting olfactory information. Rats, guinea pigs, and other highly olfactory animals use this system specifically to detect pheromones, long-distance chemical cues used for sexual and social signaling. Reflecting our evolutionary relationship, human fetuses also develop vomeronasal organs, but only between seven and twenty-five weeks of gestation. Thereafter they regress and eventually disappear entirely, leaving behind only a bit of vestigial cartilage in the nasal septum. It's possible nonetheless that the vomeronasal system actually works during its brief existence to transmit pheromone-like cues from the mother to the fetus.

Plasticity of the Developing Olfactory System   Just because the olfactory system develops early doesn't mean its development is immune from the effects of experience. When rats, for example, are prohibited from smelling by closing off one of their nostrils just after birth, the olfactory bulb on that side is strikingly stunted, with many fewer neurons and a 25 percent reduction in overall size compared with the unblocked side. Conversely, if newborn rats are treated to an enriched olfactory environment—presenting them with a different odor (such as banana, pineapple, cinnamon, dill, grass, pine) on each of the first twenty-one days of life—their olfactory bulbs form about 20 percent more mitral neurons than rats raised in an unvarying olfactory environment. Since these changes occur at the first relay point in the olfactory system, they likely influence the flow of olfactory information throughout the brain and thereby a rat's very important olfactory abilities.

In humans, the olfactory system develops to a much more mature state before birth than it does in rats. Presuming that our sense of smell is equally influenced by experience, this suggests that its period of sensitivity begins well before birth, with the first emergence of olfactory function.

Smelling in the Womb

Rachel had heard that spicy food can trigger labor, so when it got to be a couple of days past her due date, she and John went for it: dinner at their favorite Indian restaurant, and no sparing the vindaloo sauce. As it turned out, she didn't go into labor for another five days, but while that spicy dinner did nothing to get Rachel's contractions going, it certainly did not escape Hannah's notice.

It may come as a surprise to pregnant mothers, but many of the odors and flavors to which they are exposed are also experienced by their fetuses. The ability to smell begins around twenty-eight weeks of gestation. Although the olfactory neurons develop much earlier, not until this point do they show the final biochemical specializations that make them capable of detecting odors. Moreover, between two and six months of gestation, the nasal cavity is filled with a plug of tissue that prevents chemicals from reaching the receptors inside, perhaps protecting them from premature stimulation. So even if the olfactory neurons were more mature, they wouldn't have any access to odors in the womb until after this point.

Twenty-eight weeks is also the age when premature babies begin to respond to strong odors. In one study, preterm babies younger than that did not show any visible reaction when a tube of peppermint extract was held under their noses, whereas older preterms (twenty-nine to thirty-two weeks' gestational age) clearly responded by sucking, grimacing, or moving their heads.

Olfactory abilities rapidly improve during the third trimester, and fetuses' olfactory life is surprisingly rich. Their sense of smell is not impeded by amniotic fluid, since odor molecules normally enter a liquid phase—the nasal mucus—before binding to their olfactory receptors. In fact, a fluid environment may actually enhance the diffusion of certain odor molecules to their receptors, as do the fetus's own swallowing and breathing movements, which become quite frequent in the third trimester and help circulate odors to the nasal detectors.

Throughout the third trimester, Hannah could smell most everything that Rachel ate or inhaled: perfume on an elevator, truck exhaust on the freeway, the delicious mushroom soup she had for lunch, the vindaloo for dinner. One Israeli report even noted that mothers who ate strongly spiced Middle Eastern food shortly before going into labor gave birth to "peculiar-smelling newborns." Along with the fetus's improving olfactory sense, the placenta becomes increasingly permeable during the third trimester, letting more molecules from the outer world reach the amniotic fluid.

The Impact of Prenatal Smell Given that fetuses can smell and, depending on their mothers' lifestyles, may be exposed to a very rich olfactory environment during the last two or three months before birth, does this prenatal experience have any impact on their brain and behavioral development?

For rats, the evidence is clear that it does. Rat fetuses are seemingly excited when an odorous substance like lemon or mint is injected into the amniotic fluid: they move about much more than fetuses experiencing simple saline injections. If, after exposure to the odor of apple juice, a fetus is injected with a chemical that makes it nauseous, then this pup will show an aversion to the smell of apple juice that lasts for many days after birth.

There is a very good reason why rats are able to learn and remember odors in their amniotic environment. When a mother rat gives birth, she licks her pups all over, picking up amniotic odors that she then licks onto her own nipples. These odors are responsible for leading her blind, newborn pups to the nipple for their first suckling. If the mother's nipples are washed after her licking episode, the newborn pups will not begin to suckle, but if the washed nipples are then painted with a little bit of amniotic fluid, the pups are able to find them and latch on. Or if the entire experience is mimicked by exposing pups to a distinctive odor, say, lemon, both in utero and immediately after birth, these pups prefer to nurse on a lemon-scented nipple, while pups without such olfactory exposure firmly avoid the lemon-scented nipples. (While amniotic scents are critical for initiating pups' first feedings, they find the nipples in later feedings by following the scent of their own leftover saliva.) Rat pups can even discriminate and prefer the smell of their own amniotic fluid to that of another mother, suggesting its odor is used for kin recognition.

Prenatal olfactory experience thus biases a young rat to stay close to its own mother after birth, obviously a useful survival tactic. For humans, olfaction probably does not play as critical a role: a baby will not starve simply because he can't smell. But it is likely that our species exhibits a similar kind of olfactory "labeling," in which the odors from the womb help a newborn recognize his mother after birth. Recent research, for instance, has shown that brand-new babies respond to the smell of their own amniotic fluid; they prefer to nurse on a breast moistened with amniotic fluid, and they cry substantially less when exposed to the odor of amniotic fluid. Women, of course, do not usually paint themselves with amniotic fluid after birth, but back in the days when women assisted in (or even soloed) their own deliveries, their hands were probably covered with amniotic fluid, which was then transferred to the breast as they attempted their first feedings.

All these observations suggest that perhaps we shouldn't be in such a hurry to wash newborns immediately after delivery. Amniotic odors are both appealing and comforting to brand-new babies, and there is evidence that unwashed babies are more successful than washed babies at bringing their hand to their mouth in the first hour after birth, an important method of self-calming. Fortunately, newborns can detect other familiar odors even after they are washed. Their mothers' milk and other bodily secretions like sweat and saliva will contain some of the same odors as her amniotic fluid, since they are colored by the same dietary, environmental, and genetic factors. As long as a newborn stays close to his mother, he will remain in a familiar olfactory environment.

Interestingly, the fetus may not be the only one to imprint on familiar odors during gestation. Recent evidence suggests that mothers may as well. By analogy to other mammals, each person is thought to carry a unique olfactory signature resulting from his or her exact combination of genes. During pregnancy, however, a mother's personal odor tends to become a blend of her own scent and that of her fetus, who differs genetically. Familiarity with this scent is most likely responsible for the fact that most mothers can identify their own newborns based on smell alone, even shortly after birth. To test this hypothesis, mothers of one-day-old babies were asked to choose which of three T-shirts—one worn by her own child and the other two by strangers' newborns—smelled like her child. Mothers who had spent as little as ten minutes with their child were able to correctly identify his or her T-shirt, suggesting that they recognized the odor largely on the basis of their experience during pregnancy.

What Can Newborns Smell?

The sense of smell is quite sophisticated by birth. Hannah is capable of detecting all kinds of different odors, judging by the way she starts kicking when Q-Tips soaked with various scents—vanilla, lemon, coffee—are waved under her nose. Newborns also react to odors by sucking, crying, or changing their rate of breathing. Although not all researchers agree, some reports suggest that newborns even exhibit distinct facial expressions to pleasant or aversive odors—a relaxed face of enjoyment to florals, fruits, and spices, and a wrinkled-nose look of disgust to fish or rotten eggs.

Much as an adult will cease to notice an odor that is constantly present, newborn babies adapt, or habituate, to repeated presentations of the same odor, which provides a very useful way of assessing their olfactory abilities. For instance, to test whether Hannah can discriminate between two closely related odors, we repeatedly present her with one of them, say, spearmint. Initially, this odor makes her suck long and hard on a special electronically monitored pacifier, but with repeated presentations her sucking wanes. If we then switch the scent to wintergreen, she sucks with renewed vigor, showing us that she can indeed tell them apart.

Experiments like this have revealed that newborns are capable of discriminating nearly as many different odors as adults. They can also detect concentration differences of a single odor and localize odors in space. Hannah, for instance, turns her head away from an open bottle of ammonia but toward the smell of Rachel's breast, showing not only that she can tell where these odors are coming from but that she has some sense of which is good and which is bad.

Like pain sensitivity (Chapter 5), olfactory sensitivity may increase steadily over the first few days of life. In one experiment, babies were presented, on each of the first four days after birth, with asafetida (an Asian plant with an unpleasant, garliclike odor); on each successive day, they proved responsive to a somewhat lower concentration. Olfactory sensitivity thus appears to grow increasingly acute, although it is possible that their growing sensitivity was due to the gradual elimination of anesthetics that their mothers had been given during labor.

While Hannah can discriminate different odors, it is unlikely that her appreciation of them is anything like an adult's conscious olfactory perception. Her responses appear to be purely reflexive in nature, since many of them—changes in respiration, heart rate, and limb movements—occur whether she is awake or asleep. Olfactory information apparently makes its way down to the brain stem, where such reflex responses are controlled, but it probably does not yet reach higher olfactory centers in the still-immature frontal lobes, where conscious olfactory perception takes place.

The Smell of Mother's Breast   Among their various olfactory talents, young babies are almost uncannily good at recognizing their mother's breast odor. This makes a lot of sense, given how important her milk is for their growth and survival. But it is fascinating to realize how truly gifted babies are in this regard: They are able to discriminate the breast odor of different women much better than any adult can.

The odor of a lactating female's breast is intrinsically attractive to newborns. Like newborn rats, newborn babies prefer to nurse on their mother's unwashed breast, compared with one that is washed immediately after childbirth. Even two-week-old babies who have never been exposed to breast milk prefer the breast scent of an unfamiliar nursing mother over that of a nonnursing woman; when gauze pads worn overnight by both types of women are placed on either side of a bottle-fed baby's head, she will turn her head in the direction of the nursing mother's pad. It's not yet known what the critical attractants are, but they probably include specific odors in the milk (or colostrum) itself, as well as in the secretion of the areolar glands, which lubricates a nursing mother's nipples.

Not only do young babies instinctively orient to the odor of a lactating woman, they also learn, remarkably quickly, to distinguish their own mother's breast scent from that of another lactating woman. By just six days of age, Hannah reliably turns her head toward Rachel's breast pad and away from that of an age-mate's nursing mother when both are hung on either side of her bassinet. She couldn't do this at two days of age, and her preference steadily increases over the next few weeks. Hannah also prefers Rachel's neck and underarm odor over that of a lactating stranger.

Early olfactory recognition depends on the amount of contact between parent and child. Bottle-fed babies do not recognize their own mother's underarm odor at two weeks of age, and breast-fed babies typically do not recognize their father's scent. Skin-to-nostril contact is what allows a baby to make the pleasant association between milk and a parent's scent, so bottle-feeding parents could presumably enhance their babies' olfactory recognition by holding them bare-chested or under their shirt during feeding. Since young babies can also associate feeding with artificial scents, parents may want to avoid switching their soaps, lotions, or perfumes during a baby's early life or, better yet, use unscented products so as to not mask their intrinsic scent.

Recognizing and turning toward the mother's breast odor is obviously useful for a baby's feeding. It may also help promote the mother's milk production and letdown. In addition, familiarity with their mother's scent seems to provide a lot of comfort to young babies. As early as three days after birth, babies have been observed to slow their often-disorganized body movements in the presence of their mother's scent. Like the feeding advantage, this calming effect aids a newborn in his most important job: growing.

Sex Differences in Olfaction

There is one caveat about the observation that newborns innately respond to the odor of a nursing mother's breast: this effect has been seen only in girls and not in boy babies of the same age. In fact, females of all ages are more sensitive to odors than males. For instance, after being exposed to an unfamiliar odor (cherry or ginger) during their first day of life, two- to three-day-old girls, but not boys, will preferentially turn their heads in its direction. Similarly, nine-month-old girl babies spend more time exploring a scented toy, compared to an unscented one, whereas boys show little preference. Older girls outperform boys on various tests of olfactory discrimination, while women of all ages are known to be more sensitive than men to a variety of odors.

Sex hormones are probably responsible for the differences in male and female olfaction. Testosterone is known to decrease olfactory sensitivity, while estrogen increases it. Thus, women are most sensitive to odors during pregnancy or midway through their menstrual cycle, when their estrogen levels are highest. In rats, sex hormones are known to affect the different size of males' and females' olfactory structures, and a similar differentiation probably begins before birth in humans.

Females' olfactory advantage presumably reflects their greater investment in reproduction. A heightened sense of smell should help women discriminate safe from unsafe food during pregnancy and lactation, when their developing offspring are most vulnerable. Indeed, elevated estrogen levels during pregnancy are thought to contribute to the beneficial "morning sickness" that many women experience during the first trimester. Women's more acute olfactory sense may also play an important role in other aspects of nurturing, like bonding and kin recognition.

Pleasant or Foul:
The Slow Emergence of Hedonics

Considering how advanced the sense of smell is by birth, babies are surprisingly poor at one aspect of olfaction: telling whether a particular odor is good or bad, a distinction known as *hedonic* quality. Although there is some evidence that newborns make different faces or reflexively turn toward pleasant odors and away from unpleasant ones, true hedonic appreciation requires several years before it is fully mature.

For instance, toddlers in the second year of life show very little reaction when odors, even highly unpleasant ones (like simulated feces), are secretly introduced into their play area. They barely look up from their toys! But beginning around the age of three, children demonstrate some awareness of odor hedonics; they are now able to separate good smells (spearmint, wintergreen, strawberry, floral) from bad (spoiled milk, vomit), when instructed to give the good ones to *Sesame Street's* Big Bird and the bad ones to Oscar the Grouch. (This is a better test than simply asking whether they like a particular odor, because young children—despite what their parents might think—have a tendency to answer questions in the affirmative.) Finally, by six or seven years of age, children's olfactory preferences and aversions are comparable to adults'.

Early Olfactory Learning and Its Role in Bonding and Social Development

The sense of smell is especially important in early life. Until a baby's vision and hearing are better developed, her perception is largely restricted to the immediate environment, a universe that is best apprehended by the more proximal senses of touch and smell. Smell is obviously important in helping newborns find the breast and thereby meeting their critical nutritional needs. In addition, olfaction plays a key role in a baby's earliest emotional development, by helping to forge the potent bonds to his parents and other caregivers that are equally essential for his survival.

Once again, rats provide the most striking evidence of the importance of smell. Rat pups don't even open their eyes until days or weeks after birth but rapidly "imprint" on their mother's scent during the first few hours of life. Young rats use olfactory cues to stay close by their mother and can even pick her out of a crowd using scent alone. More impressive still is the duration of their olfactory learning. In one experiment, adult male rats preferred to mate with females carrying the same scent (in this case, lemon) that had been painted on their mother's nipples during nursing. Freudian implications aside, this study offers striking evidence of the powerful influence of early olfactory experience. Neurobiologists have found that this learning involves changes in the olfactory bulb itself—in the number and electrical responsiveness of its neurons. Thus, early olfactory experience, and particularly the association between a mother's scent and the way she licks and touches her offspring, appears to permanently alter a rat's olfactory system, and, with it, the way an animal perceives and responds to odors throughout life.

Olfactory recognition may also be the first step toward human bonding and attachment. As we've seen, newborns quickly learn and prefer the scent of their own mother or other caretaker. Nursing babies clearly have the richest olfactory experience, being bathed several times a day in the odors of their mother's milk and areolar secretions. Nonetheless, bottle-fed babies also can learn their parents' scents rather rapidly, depending on the amount and closeness of their contact. After the breast, a caregiver's neck is probably the most potent source of olfactory input, since it is often uncovered and close to a baby's nose when he is being held upright.

Young children are also known to recognize and prefer the odors of their own siblings, based on some more T-shirt sniffing experiments. Children as young as three years of age can correctly identify the odor of their own sibling, which undoubtedly contributes to the development of this special bond.

In addition to the scents of family members, babies also find comfort in their own bodily odors. Just as rat pups lay claim to a favorite nipple through the smell of their own saliva, babies are probably attracted to their residual salivary odors left on their mother's breast. This process, called *scent-marking,* appears to grow more and more important as a child begins to achieve some independence from his primary caregiver. All those tears, drool, and other secretions provide a rich, familiar olfactory environment as infants and toddlers begin to spend longer and longer periods of time out of immediate contact with their parents. In fact, the comforting smell is probably one important reason why toddlers grow especially attached to their blankets and stuffed animals toward the end of the second year. Toddlers often hold these comfort objects near their nose and mouth, where they can inhale their own familiar scent, and they can become terribly upset if their blanket or favorite stuffed animal is washed. Between their soft touch and their familiar odor, these objects make ideal transitional objects, providing much of the comfort of Mommy but in a way that they can control as they drag it all over the house. In this regard, it is interesting that children in non-Western cultures do not show as much attachment to these kinds of comfort objects as Western children, perhaps because the former continue to have a great deal of touch and olfactory contact with their parents. (They often keep nursing and sleeping with their parents well past infancy.)

A World of Smell

It may be a little hard for us adults, who so rarely take note of our olfactory environment, to appreciate the importance of smell to children and young infants. But I was reminded of it recently when Julia, commenting on her father's absence for several days on a business trip, told me how much she missed "Daddy's good smell."

The sense of smell is truly primordial, both developmentally and in terms of the neural pathways that process it. While largely not conscious, smell provides babies with many of their first impressions about their social and physical surroundings and can be a potent source of sensory stimulation. Given the importance of smell to bonding and emotional security, parents and other caregivers should try to make young children's olfactory environment as pleasant, stable, and comforting as possible.

Chapter 8

TASTE, MILK, AND THE ORIGINS
OF FOOD PREFERENCE

Matthew's getting bored with milk. It's all he's ever tasted in the entire five months of his life. Everyone else in the family gets to eat all this great stuff—mashed potatoes, green beans, and that tantalizing garlic-roasted chicken—but he just has to sit there, inhaling it all. Well, not this time. Suddenly he leans forward, nearly falling out of his reclining seat, and tries to grab a lick at brother Nicky's dinner plate.

"Gee," says his mother, Lorna, rescuing him just before his head sinks into the mashed potatoes, "maybe it's time to start Matty on solid foods."

Along with touch, smell, and the vestibular senses, the ability to taste emerges early in development. This makes sense, given the importance of nutrition to the survival and growth of young children. The sense of taste—*gustation*, as it is known medically—first becomes functional during the third trimester of gestation, and it gets a considerable amount of practice in the womb. By birth, babies already prefer pleasant tastes and dislike unpleasant ones. Their sense of taste is highly attuned to appreciate the sweet flavor of mother's milk, the perfect food that provides them with optimal nourishment as well as considerable pleasure.

Taste is a big part of little babies' lives, both because of its nutritional significance and because their other senses and motor abilities are still rather poorly developed. It is an important route for new sensory experiences and holds potent sway over their mood and emotional well-being.

Taste ability itself changes only slightly during infancy, but taste preference is highly malleable. Matthew, for instance, has already begun to form some preferences based on the wide variety of flavors he began experiencing in the womb and now in Lorna's milk. In this chapter, we'll learn about the extent to which early experience can (and cannot) modify a child's later taste preferences as well as the special benefits of breast milk for a baby's brain and behavioral development.

How Taste Works

Like smell, taste is another one of our "chemical senses," in which the nervous system detects specific molecules in the environment and converts this information into distinct electrical signals. Compared with smell, however, taste is strikingly simple. Instead of the thousands of different chemical detectors in our nose, our taste buds detect only four basic categories—sweet, salty, bitter, and sour.* Full flavor appreciation therefore involves considerable interaction between taste and the sense of smell, which is why foods taste so bland when we have a cold.

How does the brain know what the mouth is eating? Let's say Matthew does manage to get a mouthful of those mashed potatoes. As the various spud-butter-milk-salt molecules wash over his taste buds, they activate taste receptor cells—special elongated epithelial cells that line the pore of each pitlike bud. The taste buds are mostly distributed over the perimeter of the tongue—about 4,500 altogether on its tip, sides, and back—with some also present on the roof, or soft palate area, of the mouth, as well as in the upper throat area. Each taste bud contains some forty taste receptor cells, whose hairlike microvilli wave around in the pore, preferentially binding to one of the four basic types of food stimuli that float by. Some cells, for instance, will be activated by the natural sugar in the potatoes, while others will bind to salt ions. A bad spot in the potatoes might activate bitter-preferring cells. But your typical mashed potato recipe will not significantly activate the last class of taste receptors, sour-preferring cells.

*Some scientists now believe that there is a fifth category of taste, called *umani*, which is sensitive to the amino acid glutamate (as in MSG).

It is within the taste receptor cells that chemical information is converted into neural, or electrical, signals. Each of the four categories of food molecules activates a different kind of molecular receptor located in the microvilli, but the end result is similar: a change in the taste cell's voltage that triggers its release of neurotransmitter, exciting little dendritic buds in the first neurons in the gustatory pathway. These primary taste neurons then transmit their action potentials along axons that run through the base of the skull and into the first relay station for taste in the central nervous system, located in the lower brain stem, or medulla.

Taste input has a big impact on the medulla. It helps trigger several brain-stem reflexes that are necessary for feeding, including salivation, swallowing, and tongue movements. The medulla also shuttles taste information both to the upper brain stem, or pons, and to the thalamus. From the pons, taste input is relayed to several limbic structures—to the amygdala and hypothalamus, which control our motivation to eat and drink, as well as to the limbic cortex, where the hedonic, or pleasurable, aspects of taste are sensed. From the thalamus, taste input is relayed up to the cerebral cortex—the site where tastes are consciously perceived. (See Figure 8.1.)

The conscious awareness of taste is controlled by a relatively small area of the cerebral cortex, tucked in at the border between the frontal and temporal lobes, just underneath the area that receives touch input from the tongue (Chapter 5). This proximity probably makes it easier for information about taste to be integrated with information about food texture, helping us to identify different foods. However, the full appreciation of flavor distinctions, which depends on the integration of both taste and smell, occurs at further relay sites in the cortex, probably in the orbitofrontal region that is responsible for olfactory perception.

The Ability to Taste Begins in Utero

Matthew's first taste buds emerged just eight weeks after his conception. By thirteen weeks, taste buds had formed throughout his mouth, and they were already communicating with their invading nerves. Although taste buds mature remarkably early in gestation, the number of buds continues to increase for some time postnatally, contributing to certain changes in taste sensitivity that occur during infancy.

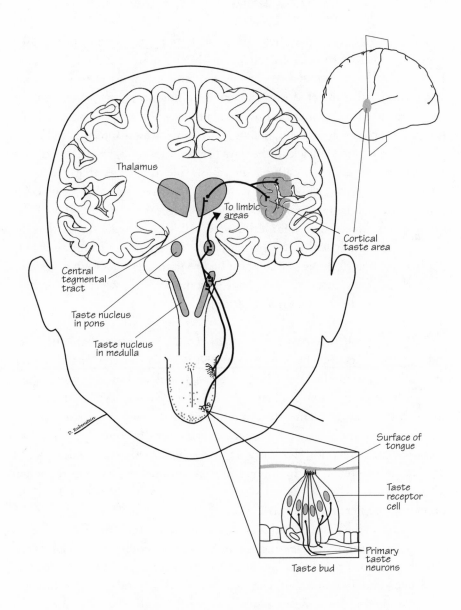

Thalamus

To limbic
areas

Cortical
taste area

Central
tegmental
tract

Taste nucleus
in pons

Taste nucleus
in medulla

D. Rubenstein

Surface of
tongue

Taste
receptor
cell

Primary
taste
neurons

Taste bud

FIGURE 8.1

Neural pathways of taste perception.

There's good evidence that babies can taste even before birth and that they are sensitive to different chemicals in the amniotic fluid. Late-term fetuses have been observed to change their swallowing pattern when a flavored chemical is injected into the amniotic fluid: they swallowed more of the fluid when saccharine was injected, but less when a noxious-tasting substance, an opaque dye for enhancing X-ray contrast, was injected. (This last observation was made back in the days before ultrasound, when X-rays were the primary means of visualizing the fetus.) We also know that premature babies, tested as early as thirty-five weeks' gestation, are able to perceive tastes: they suck more when presented with a sugar solution than they do for plain water. Their response is all the more striking when you realize that the babies in this study had never had any taste experience outside the womb, because all their feedings to that point had been through stomach tubes. It is clear, then, that fetuses can taste at least some flavors—sweet, and perhaps bitter—by the last two months of gestation.

What's the Function of Prenatal Taste?

It is probably no coincidence that the taste buds mature at the very end of the first trimester, which is right around when the fetus begins to suck and swallow. Both these actions increase the flow of chemicals over the taste buds, stimulating them in a way that may influence the formation of their synaptic connections. As for the other senses, early taste function may critically control the development of taste perception. For instance, rats whose mothers were deprived of sodium during pregnancy are forever deficient in their ability to taste sodium salts, suggesting that a normal chemical environment is required for the proper development of taste structures.

Amniotic fluid is rich with chemicals that can excite taste cells: sugars, such as glucose and fructose, that stimulate sweet receptors; acids, such as citrate and lactate, that stimulate sour receptors; and various salts, such as potassium and sodium, that may activate fetal salt receptors. Moreover, amniotic fluid is constantly changing—over the course of pregnancy, with strong flavors in the mother's diet, and (though it may not sound very appealing) with the fetus's own urination—all of which provides an ever-varying mix of stimuli to activate taste receptors and their emerging neural pathways.

Like prenatal smell, a fetus's taste experience in the womb may bias his or her later behavior—in this case, influencing food preferences. This has been clearly demonstrated in animal studies. For instance, baby rabbits whose mothers were fed juniper berries during pregnancy clearly preferred foods containing the aromatic juniper flavor when tested at the age of weaning. In another report, adult rats that had been exposed to apple juice before birth by amniotic injection showed a greater preference for apple juice than rats exposed to control or saline injections. And more worrisomely, adult rats that were exposed to alcohol in utero showed considerably more preference for it than rats that had not been exposed to alcohol before birth. If the same kind of "memory" occurs among the children of alcoholic mothers, it may in part explain why alcoholism tends to run in families.

The fact that babies begin to taste before birth thus has important developmental consequences. Not only does it affect the formation of taste pathways and preferences, it probably also acts, like smell, to help babies recognize and find comfort with their mothers after birth, since many of the same dietary flavors that make their way into a woman's amniotic fluid will also be present in her breast milk.

What Can a Newborn Taste?

While Matthew hungers for new flavors now, he wasn't so interested in them around five months ago. Newborns can discern many different flavors, but they care only for the taste of sweet. From the very beginning, a drop of sugar water or Lorna's milk had a big impact on Matthew; his face would relax, he'd start sucking and drinking, and his heart would even slow a bit.

Based on observations like these, the taste of sweet is thought to be innately pleasurable. Within hours of birth, and even before they've received their first feeding, newborn babies respond positively to sugar. Not only can they detect sweet, they can tell the difference between different types of sugar and even between different concentrations of the same type of sugar. In every case, they prefer the sweeter solution. Their favorite is sucrose, or simple table sugar, which is preferred over fructose, the type found in fruit. Fructose, in turn, is preferred over simple glucose, which is preferred over lactose, the sugar present in milk and formula. And interestingly, female and heavier babies show a stronger preference for sweeter solutions than do males and smaller newborns.

Newborn Matthew reacted very differently when, one night after dinner, Nicky sneaked up and held a wedge of lemon to his new brother's lips. Although the strong smell captured Matty's interest, he became quite upset after opening his mouth and getting his first taste of this intensely sour flavor. Sour and bitter tastes both provoke strong reactions in newborns. They tend to wrinkle their noses, purse their lips, and drool or salivate to sour stimuli, while bitter tastes, like quinine, cause gaping, tongue protrusion, and a generally angry reaction.

Newborns thus have built-in opinions about three of the four basic categories of taste. But they are surprisingly indifferent to the fourth category, salt. Although careful measurements of heart rate, tongue protrusion, and sucking patterns have shown that they can detect salt, they seem neither to like nor to dislike the flavor. They don't show any type of characteristic facial response to salty solutions and will even freely drink a strong salt solution that most adults would find unpleasant. Indeed, a tragic consequence of this indifference occurred back in 1962, when several newborns in an upstate New York hospital died from a formula mistakenly prepared with salt instead of sugar. Unable to fully taste the salt, six of fourteen babies who were given the formula drank enough to become fatally poisoned before the error was discovered.

Do Babies Consciously Perceive Taste?   While young babies can detect most types of taste, it's hard to know whether they are actually aware of their gustatory perceptions. The responses to taste that are measurable in young babies—sucking, swallowing, salivation, and facial gestures—can all be controlled by reflex circuits residing in the brain stem alone. These responses show that taste information is fully integrated at lower brain levels, but they do not tell us whether the information is reaching the cerebral cortex. In fact, the very same facial responses to sweet, sour, and bitter flavors can be seen among anencephalic newborns, who lack most of their cerebral cortex. These instinctive lower-brain reflexes are certainly useful—they help babies ingest milk and reject unpalatable, potentially toxic substances, while also providing a very effective means of communicating their experiences to their caregivers. But they don't provide any information about the baby's conscious taste experience.

Still, it is possible that taste information is making its way up to the cerebral cortex. We do know that the two sequential relays that transmit taste information from the brain stem to the cortex—first, the pathway from the medulla to the thalamus (called the *central tegmental tract*), and second, the thalamus-to-cortex projection—begin myelinating before birth. Moreover, because taste perception is intimately interrelated to touch perception in the area of the mouth and tongue, taste pathways may form their cortical connections as early as the precocious touch system (Chapter 5), allowing early conscious awareness of taste.

Changes in Taste Perception

Although babies are equipped from birth with some useful taste abilities, this sense does continue to evolve during early childhood. The biggest changes are in the perception of salt. Whereas Matthew was relatively indifferent to salt at birth, he now actually prefers the taste of salty solutions over that of pure water. Babies undergo an abrupt change in salt preference around four months of age, because this is when sodium-sensitive receptor proteins first emerge in the membranes of their taste receptor cells. Before these receptors are present, the cells can respond to other salts but not to sodium—the main ion we perceive as salty in our food. While exposure to salt can influence a child's preference for salted foods, this early change in salt acceptance appears to be purely hard-wired—that is, due to the normal maturation of taste cells and pathways, rather than to a baby's early experience.

Why such delayed development of salt sensitivity? It may be related to the development of the kidney. In older infants and adults, the kidneys use sodium to concentrate the urine, but this ability is not present in young infants, who consequently have no real need to consume salt. Moreover, human milk is very low in sodium, so there is no natural need for young babies to taste it.

The response to salty solutions changes again after about two years of age, when children begin to reject salt water, much as an adult would. In this case, experience probably does play an important role: what's changing is not the child's ability to detect salt, but rather his growing sense of what should and should not be salted. For instance, children between two and six years of age generally refuse to drink straight salt water but prefer salted over unsalted versions of foods like carrots or stew.

Children's perception of bitterness also evolves. While newborns clearly perceive some bitter tastes, the variety of bitter compounds they can detect increases during infancy, and children achieve adultlike sensitivity by two years of age. This fact may be useful to researchers who are attempting to develop safe, bitter-tasting compounds to add to household products to prevent young children from ingesting them.

During early childhood, the perception of sweet and sour tastes doesn't appear to change. Children continue to prefer sweetened to unsweetened foods throughout the preschool years. That's not to say that diet and experience don't play any role in sweet preference. As with saltiness, children's expectations of what should and should not be sweet do influence their preferences. But generally speaking, they innately love sweets, and there's little a parent can do to prevent it.

Given that taste abilities and preferences emerge so early in infancy, it can be a little bewildering that youngsters so frequently ingest so many unsuitable things—crayons, coins, pills, paint, small toy parts, household cleansers, and worse. In an attempt to learn more about this problem, children between one and five years of age were specifically tested as to their sense of what should and should not be consumed. All of the children were apt to put inappropriate things in their mouths, such as paper, leaves, Play-Doh, or a sponge. Generally, however, only the youngest (sixteen to twenty-nine months) attempted to put a dangerous substance in their mouth—in this test, a simulated dishwashing detergent. This tendency rapidly declined as children reached three or four years, as did the tendency to mouth repulsive items (a grasshopper, a dried fish, or simulated "doggie doo"). Thus, while taste perception is well developed in infancy, the understanding of what is edible is largely learned. Only gradually, through parental teaching and their own experience, do toddlers and preschoolers acquire the knowledge of what they should and shouldn't eat.

Why Kids (and Adults) Love Sweets

Finally! Matthew's getting a chance to try some solid foods. He loves the rice cereal, especially when it's mixed with a little bit of formula or apple juice. But he's not so keen on pureed vegetables: carrots are okay, but he spits out the green beans and spinach. Fortunately, fruits are another matter. He can't seem to get enough of those pears, peaches, and mashed bananas.

It is obvious to any parent that young kids simply love sweets. We think we can control this craving by giving them lots of fruits and even some of the sweeter vegetables (peas, carrots, sweet potatoes) that offer some vitamins in addition to their carbohydrate load. But eventually, children learn better. A cookie here, a bite of ice cream there—it doesn't take long for youngsters to discover sucrose and to realize that they like it best of all. The struggle between parent and child continues, for good nutritional reasons. But is it really so awful for kids to eat sweets if that's what they want?

In fact, there's a good reason why kids (and many adults) so often crave sweets. Sweets taste good because it literally feels good to eat them—they induce pleasurable sensations in the body. And it's not just because they give us a big energy boost. The pleasurable feeling associated with eating sweets turns on quite quickly; we don't have to wait for the sugar to reach the gut and be digested. Research now indicates that sweet receptors in the mouth are coupled to brain areas that release endogenous opiates—those natural morphinelike chemicals that induce a sense of pleasure and well-being and even block the transmission of painful stimuli to the brain. So the taste of sweet in itself is enough to activate pleasure centers in the brain.

Sweets seem to be especially effective in mood-altering when one is under stress. For babies, this happens a lot of the time. Crying is a stressful state, and researchers have found that drinking sugar water or sucking on a sweetened pacifier has a tremendous calming effect on young infants. Sugar reduces crying, lowers a baby's heart rate, and decreases his or her less-coordinated, energy-wasting body movements. These findings explain why newborn boys undergoing circumcision seem to feel less pain when they're allowed to suck on sugar-soaked rags (see Chapter 5). In addition to its calming effects, sugar is known to make babies more alert and to encourage their hand-to-mouth coordination.

The evidence that sweets activate endogenous opiate pathways comes largely from animal experiments. When rat pups are isolated away from their litter, they tend to cry—to emit ultrasound vocalizations that help their mother locate them. Researchers found that infusing a sugar solution into the mouth of an isolated rat pup reduces these distress vocalizations, as well as the animal's actual sensitivity to physical pain. However, if the pup was previously injected with a drug that blocks endogenous opiate action, both the calming and the analgesic effects of sugar were inhibited.

The same processes appear to operate in human infants. Although we can't inject newborn babies with drugs to block endogenous opiate action, there is one population of newborns that already has markedly reduced levels of opiates: babies born to mothers maintained on methadone during pregnancy. Methadone, which is used to treat heroin addiction, is itself an opiate, and exposure to it before birth strongly suppresses the baby's synthesis of his own endogenous opiates. After birth, the baby suffers from methadone withdrawal, at least until his own endogenous opiates gradually return to normal levels. During this withdrawal period, a baby's experience is much like that of the rats that were injected with opiate blockers; he is very irritable and derives little comfort from sweet solutions or sucking on sugared pacifiers. Without a functioning opiate system, the babies do not experience the usual pleasant rewards of sweet taste, although they do find some comfort in the oral stimulation of pacifier sucking.

Of course, sugar water is not the most nutritious of substances, but it's important to keep in mind that the link between opiates and sweets evolved in the context of nursing. Human milk, which is considerably sweeter than cow's milk, provides young babies with virtually complete nutrition. Since this is the only natural situation in which a newborn experiences sugar, it is logical that our species would evolve to best appreciate the one food we need to survive as infants. Even after weaning, which our ancestors probably delayed until the late toddler years, sweet foods continue to be an important source of energy and vitamins and are generally some of the safest foods to be found in nature. It makes sense, then, that sweets should be innately pleasurable, though it is unfortunate that we have bypassed their natural nutritional value through the invention of refined sugars.

The Many Pleasures of Nursing
Sugar is not the only pleasurable substance to be found in milk. It also contains high levels of fat, which has many of the same calming effects as sweets. Fats, too, trigger the release of endogenous opiates, as well as a hormone from the gut called *cholecystokinin*, which has a similar quieting effect on young laboratory rats.

Humans, like these rats, have a tendency to overeat under stress. In fact, stress may trigger a craving for sugary, fatty foods precisely because of their soothing, opiate-mediated effect. This trait would have been useful during our earlier evolution, when the most significant stressors were physical dangers that required greater energy expenditure. In the modern world, however, most of our stress is psychological, so such overeating often comes at the cost of unhealthy weight gain.

Fortunately, the fats and sugar in milk are very good for infants. Obviously, their high caloric content is critical for a baby's growth. In addition, their calming effect, produced by endogenous opiates, promotes growth and development by helping the baby conserve energy and concentrate on the important task of learning about his environment. In fact, milk itself contains a natural morphinelike substance called *beta-casomorphine*. We don't yet know whether this compound, which is present in both human milk and cow's-milk-based formula, is actually absorbed from the gut and reaches the baby's brain intact. It is known, however, that when beta-casomorphine is injected into the brains of rat pups, it acts just like other opiates to reduce their sensitivity to pain.

Nursing offers a baby many pleasures other than taste. As we saw in Chapter 5, the physical contact of nursing is also very comforting. Between the secure feeling of being cradled, the close skin contact with the mother, and the intense oral stimulation of suckling, nursing provides some of the richest tactile stimulation a young baby can experience. In fact, the act of sucking alone has been shown to produce a genuine calming effect and reduction in pain sensitivity in young infants. Unlike taste, however, the comforting effects of touch and oral stimulation are not mediated by endogenous opiates. Through some as yet unidentified brain mechanism, touch acts in parallel with the opiate-mediated taste system to provide great pleasure, comfort, and pain reduction to babies.

The Special Benefits of Breast Milk for Brain Development

By now, Lorna's heard it a hundred times: "Breast is best. Breast is best. Breast is best." And she does plan to continue nursing Matthew until he's at least a year old. But sometimes she gets so tired, and feels so drained, that she wonders how much longer she can go on.

Ever since the advent of modern formulas, mothers have been presented with a choice about how to feed their babies. Based on everything we know about the advantages of breast milk and the nursing experience, few would argue that bottle-feeding is a superior method. But that's not to say breast-feeding doesn't have its drawbacks: sore nipples, breast infections, fatigue, the baby's teeth, and the fact that it keeps the mother on a very short leash. Breast-feeding also exposes the baby to any drugs, infections, and environmental toxins the mother may have encountered, and in certain circumstances, such as adoption and maternal HIV infection, it is either impossible or actually dangerous to the baby. Prematurity poses another problem, since many preterm babies are too young to suckle, and even if their mothers manage to maintain lactation, the babies may need additional nutritional supplements to grow optimally.

For most babies, however, breast milk is perfectly evolved to their needs, and recent research keeps uncovering new reasons why it is superior to formula. It may seem surprising that in our era of high-power biotechnology, formula manufacturers cannot more closely replicate the composition of human milk. But that's because breast milk is much more than a collection of nutrients, vitamins, and minerals. It also contains enzymes, immune factors, hormones, growth factors, and many other agents that haven't even been identified yet—all of which aid the baby's nutrient absorption, fight off infections, and promote the development of various organ systems. In fact, in many ways, the breast can be thought of as carrying on the function of the placenta. Science is still a long way from constructing an artificial womb, and similarly, attempts to replicate the function of the breast are poor approximations at best.

Most parents now know about the immune benefits of breast milk. It provides the baby with a large array of antibodies, enzymes, and even whole immune cells (macrophages, neutrophils, T-cells, and B-cells) that protect her from most of the infections to which the mother has ever been exposed. Breast-fed infants suffer fewer respiratory, ear, and urinary tract infections than bottle-fed babies, and in particular they are shielded from diarrhea and other gastrointestinal problems, since it is the digestive system that is most generously exposed to the immune factors in breast milk.

In a similar way, many researchers believe that human milk specifically benefits a baby's brain development. This notion originates from a fascinating, although complicated finding: *breast-fed children are actually smarter than bottle-fed children!* In dozens of studies, breast-fed children have been found to hold a significant cognitive advantage over formula-fed children; they score higher on tests of mental development (such as language, social, fine motor, and object response skills) between one and two years of age, on various intelligence tests during the preschool years, and on scholastic achievement tests as late as ten years of age. Many studies, moreover, have looked at the *duration* of breast-feeding and found that the longer babies are breast-fed during the first year, and the less formula supplementation they receive, the higher their IQ or academic achievement tends to be.

No one disputes the association between breast-feeding and intelligence. The problem, however, is in figuring out the reason for it, because breast-fed children differ from bottle-fed children in several other ways known to predict cognitive achievement. Breast-feeding mothers tend to be older, more educated, more affluent, and less likely to smoke and use drugs than bottle-feeding mothers. It is possible, therefore, that breast milk itself has nothing to do with the relationship; breast-fed children may be smarter simply because they come from more advantaged homes, have smarter parents, or—given the difficulty and degree of sacrifice involved in breast-feeding for many women—have "better" parents, on average, than bottle-fed children.

Researchers are well aware of these sociological differences and have attempted to compensate for them in virtually all studies. In most cases, they do so through statistical corrections, adjusting children's test scores to take account of their parents' education, socioeconomic status, the mother's IQ and her cigarette and drug use, the quality of the home environment, parenting style, and so on. Even after factoring out such "covariates," however, most studies find significant cognitive differences between breast- and bottle-fed babies, although the size of the difference is reduced.

One 1992 British study took another approach to circumvent this problem. These researchers studied the cognitive development of two groups of premature babies, whose mothers were of similar educational and socioeconomic standing and all of whom had intended to breast-feed. Because preterm infants are often too weak or undeveloped to nurse when they're born, they must receive their nutrition through a stomach tube. "Breast"-feeding therefore requires that mothers express their milk several times a day, which is a very difficult way to initiate and maintain lactation. In spite of their attempts, not all mothers in this study were successful, so some babies received their mothers' milk while others received formula through the tube. (This feeding method eliminates the possibility that some difference in nursing style between bottle- and breast-feeding, such as the degree of physical contact, could affect cognitive development.)

The results were striking. IQ tests some eight years later showed that children who had received breast milk were significantly smarter, scoring over eight points higher than the children who had been fed formula. It is still possible that these two groups of mothers differed in some other unrecognized way that might underlie the children's cognitive differences. But in another preliminary study, the same researchers found that preterm babies reared entirely on *donor* breast milk—that is, whose own mothers had never even intended to nurse them—were more developmentally advanced at eighteen months than preterm babies reared on a standard infant formula.

All together the data are compelling. Human milk really does seem to improve a child's intellectual prospects. Although on average, breast-feeding mothers do offer their children other advantages, both genetic and environmental, the milk itself is an important part of the package. In this light, it is interesting to note that some of the first studies of breast-feeding and cognition date back to the early twentieth century, when the tables were turned and only the more affluent, educated classes could afford to bottle-feed. Even so, breast-fed babies developed better.

What is it about breast milk that promotes cognitive development? You can be sure that researchers and formula manufacturers are avidly trying to figure it out. Remember that the brain undergoes an enormous growth spurt that begins in the third trimester of gestation and continues until at least eighteen months after birth. All of that massive myelination and synaptic reorganization may be facilitated by specific nutrients, described below, that are present in human milk but missing from cow's milk, which serves as the base for most infant formulas.

Taurine   One component that may contribute to breast-fed babies' advantage is the amino acid *taurine*. Even though this molecule was originally isolated from the bile of an ox (hence its name), it is not found in any appreciable quantity in cow's milk. It is, however, quite abundant in human milk and, perhaps not coincidentally, in the brains and eyes of newborn babies. We don't know precisely what taurine's function is in the brain. (It is not one of the standard twenty amino acids that get incorporated into protein molecules.) There is some evidence that it acts to reduce neural excitability and may prevent the possibility of seizures, a frequent side effect of high fever in newborns. Taurine levels are over twice as high in newborns' brains as in the brains of adults, suggesting that it plays a special role in neural development. Moreover, when cats or primates are deprived of taurine, they can suffer serious degeneration of the retina of the eye, and there are many structural similarities between neurons in the retina and those in the brain.

Humans do not have much capacity to synthesize their own taurine, especially in early infancy. Therefore it must be obtained from the diet. Taurine levels are high in utero and are maintained in breast-fed babies, but they become depleted within two weeks after birth in infants fed formula without added taurine.

Based on these findings, taurine was first added to infant formula in 1984 and is now present in all formulas manufactured in North America. Unfortunately, we don't know whether this supplementation has had any effect on mental development, because almost every study that has compared cognitive achievement in breast- and formula-fed children (including those published in the mid-1990s) was initiated with babies born before 1985. But regardless of its impact on mental development, taurine is known to have many other functions in the body, so that its supplementation in formula is undoubtedly a good idea.

Lipids   More recently, focus has shifted to the role of milk fat in brain development. Brains are composed of a great deal of fat, some 60 percent. Nervous tissue is second only to fat tissue itself in lipid concentration. But the brain is one place in which leaner does not mean fitter. Specific lipid molecules are needed to produce the cell membranes that cover the millions of miles of axons and dendrites in the brain. (Since neurons are so long and skinny, they have an exceptionally large amount of outer membrane compared with other types of cells.) The need for new membranes is largely confined to the brain growth spurt of infancy, when neurons are most busy sprouting new dendrites and forming and reconfiguring their synaptic connections.

In addition, fats are essential to the process of myelination. Myelin is a dense material, composed of 30 percent protein and 70 percent lipid, which together form a thick, greasy coating that prevents water-soluble ions from leaking through the membranes of nerve cell axons (see Chapter 2). All of the massive myelination that takes place during the first two years of life requires several specific types of lipids.

Although the body can produce many of the different lipids it needs for membrane and myelin synthesis, a few types are *essential*—a term meaning they can be obtained only through the diet. Still other types of lipids can be synthesized by the body later in life but are poorly produced in infancy because the necessary enzymes are not yet active. Given how important lipids are for brain development, and how important brain development is in determining cognitive potential, it is not surprising that researchers have begun taking a keen interest in the precise lipid mix of different types of milk.

The good news is that, overall, the amount of fat in breast milk, cow's milk, and all types of commercial infant formula is similar: about 4 percent by weight. This percentage is just an average value for human milk, since the fat level varies during the course of a feeding (becoming richer in the hindmilk), over the course of the day (being highest in late afternoon), and even with the mother's level of body fat. (Heavier women have more fat in their milk, but not until about six months postpartum.) The bad news, however, is that neither cow's milk nor cow's milk– or soy-based formulas supply all the specific *types* of lipids now thought to be essential for brain development.

The dominant form of fat in milk is *triglycerides*, the same form the body uses to store energy. As their name implies, triglycerides are composed of three fatty acid molecules—long chains of carbon and hydrogen atoms that are highly varied in structure. Human milk contains at least 167 different types of fatty acids, the types and proportions of which differ tremendously from cow's milk. For instance, cow's milk is much lower than human milk in one essential unsaturated fatty acid, *linoleic acid*; consequently, the U.S. Food and Drug Administration now requires that a minimum level of it be included in all infant formulas. The most abundant fatty acid in human milk is *oleic acid*, another unsaturated form that is also one of the commonest lipids found in myelin. Many formulas are therefore also supplemented with vegetable oils that contain substantial amounts of oleic acid. Despite these additions, however, babies cannot use the lipids in formula as efficiently as those in breast milk, because human milk also contains an enzyme, *lipase*, that helps break down triglycerides into their component fatty acids, a process necessary for their absorption. (Interestingly, taurine also plays an important role in the absorption of fatty acids by the gut.)

Another lipid that is relatively abundant in breast milk, especially compared with commercial formulas, is *cholesterol*. Although cholesterol has become a dirty word when talking about adult nutrition, there is good reason for its prevalence in breast milk. Cholesterol is the dominant form of lipid found in myelin, comprising over one-quarter of all lipids in this extremely fat-rich substance. (The same properties that make it an artery clogger also make it a great neuronal insulator.) While infants can, like adults, synthesize enough cholesterol to compensate for what's missing in their diet, some researchers have suggested that early exposure to dietary cholesterol may actually help keep its levels in check in later life, by promoting the development of enzymes necessary for its degradation.

The hottest topic in infant milk research concerns two specific fatty acids, *docosahexaenoic acid* (or DHA) and *arachidonic acid* (AA). Both are very long-chain, polyunsaturated fatty acids that are present in breast milk but are notably absent from formulas currently available in the United States. Both accumulate rapidly in the fetus during the last trimester of pregnancy. For babies reared on formula, however, blood levels of DHA decline substantially in the months after birth. Although both AA and DHA can be synthesized by adults and older children (provided that the right precursors, linoleic and linolenic acids, respectively, are present in the diet), babies are limited in their capacity to produce DHA, which probably explains why breast milk evolved to contain it in the first place.

The excitement about DHA and AA stems from the fact that they are particularly abundant in the brain and eyes. Perhaps, some researchers suggest, the better cognitive performance of breast-fed children can be traced to their greater consumption of these long-chain fatty acids in infancy. This proposal is supported by the finding that visual function is permanently impaired in rats or monkeys that have been deprived of DHA and its precursors throughout gestation and infancy.

Many studies have now been conducted to evaluate the effects of DHA on human visual development. Some of them are quite promising, but the data are unfortunately far from consistent. In one Australian study, full-term babies were divided into three groups: those whose mothers chose to breast-feed, those reared on a standard formula, and those reared on the same formula, but which had been supplemented by a mix of fish oil (a rich source of DHA) and evening primrose oil (a source of AA precursor). As expected, babies fed regular formula showed steadily declining levels of DHA, while breast-fed babies and those given the supplemented formula maintained their DHA levels for several months after birth. More importantly, this pattern of DHA accumulation matched the babies' performance on visual acuity tests at both four and seven months of age: breast-fed and supplemented babies both had significantly sharper vision than babies reared on the standard formula. Similar findings have been reported in other studies of both preterm and full-term infants. On the other hand, other studies have failed to find any difference in visual acuity between breast- and formula-fed babies, or between babies reared on standard versus DHA-enriched formulas.

Researchers have focused on vision because it is easy to test. But what about the effects of DHA on brain development? Is it responsible for breast-fed babies' cognitive edge? One group has found that babies' DHA levels correlate with performance on mental development tests at four months of age; babies reared on a DHA-supplemented formula tended to score higher than babies reared on standard formula and comparably with breast-fed infants. Another study of preterm babies found that those who had been fed DHA-enriched formula processed visual information more rapidly than those reared on a standard formula. Yet another preterm study suggests that DHA supplementation increases "baby IQ" scores at twelve months.

Much of this research, then, is quite promising, and we can probably expect to see DHA and AA added to infant formulas in the near future. Indeed, the World Health Organization recently recommended that DHA be added to all infant formulas, and it has already been incorporated into some commercial preterm formulas marketed in Europe. Manipulating fatty acid levels is a tricky business, however, since at least one study has found that preterm babies reared on a fish-oil-enriched formula actually grew less and showed poorer motor development than preterm babies reared on a standard formula. Adding a source of AA should overcome this problem, but manufacturers are still working out the details of how to safely add these important long-chain fatty acids to infant formula.

And finally, what about breast-fed babies? Might they also benefit from further DHA supplementation? Breast milk DHA does vary with a woman's diet, and American women consume some of the lowest levels in the world. DHA levels are also particularly low in the milk of vegetarian mothers. Because babies accumulate DHA and AA so rapidly during the last trimester and early postnatal months, often at the expense of a mother's own stores, women are well advised to increase their consumption of long-chain fatty acids during pregnancy and lactation. Fish, shellfish, egg yolks, liver, and other organ meats are all rich sources of DHA, while two vegetable oils, soybean and rapeseed, are good sources of its precursor. Increased maternal consumption does translate into higher blood levels of DHA for breast-fed babies, and one study even found a slight cognitive advantage for babies whose mothers took DHA supplements during the first twelve weeks of lactation, although the advantage disappeared by the time the children turned two.

Nonnutrient Components of Breast Milk   By and large, researchers have focused on the role of specific nutrients in promoting brain development. But it is important to realize that the difference in cognitive ability between breast- and bottle-fed children may also be due to the many nonnutrient factors present only in breast milk. Certain enzymes, growth factors, or hormones may directly influence the way in which neurons develop, enhancing the intense brain maturation that takes place during infancy. Thyroid hormone, for example, is present in human milk and is known to play a critical role in neuronal survival and maturation (Chapter 3). Another possibility is that the immune factors in breast milk permit better brain development, either by protecting the brain from infections that might compromise its maturation, or simply by keeping a baby in healthier shape for all the important learning that occurs during infancy.

It will be many decades before research fully elucidates all of the components in breast milk that facilitate brain development. In the meantime, women have an ideal solution to the problem of what to feed their babies.

Human milk is clearly the best food on earth for human infants, not only for their health and nutrition but for their emerging minds as well.

Breast Milk and Early Taste Experience

One reason why researchers have had such a hard time replicating the composition of breast milk is that it isn't a fixed commodity. No two women's milk is identical, nor is the composition of any one mother's milk constant at all times; it varies with the amount of time that has elapsed postpartum, gradually changing in composition to match the baby's changing nutritional needs. It also varies with time of day, with the thinnest milk (the lowest fat content) being produced early in the day and the richest produced in the evening. Finally, it varies with the mother's diet, providing breast-fed infants a rich medium for experiencing many different flavors in early life.

Breast-fed babies clearly like this flavor variation. In one experiment, three-to-four-month-old babies were found to suck longer and consume more milk after their mothers had ingested a garlic pill than when they ingested a tasteless placebo tablet. The difference was most pronounced two to three hours after mothers ate the pill, the same period when the garlic odor of their milk was the strongest. Although garlic-flavored milk may not sound very appealing, young babies apparently love it. If the mothers repeatedly consume the garlic tablets, however, their infants no longer suck for extra periods of time. Like adults, they seem to get bored with tasting the same thing over and over and prefer some variety. Fortunately, there are plenty of possibilities. Women's milk is also known to be altered by ingesting vanilla, mint, and cheese, and probably most other distinctive flavorings, herbs, and spices.

Variation in breast milk flavors may play an important role in taste development itself. Even before a baby is exposed to any solid foods at all, he experiences all kinds of new flavors through his mother's breast milk, perhaps biasing his later taste preferences. Indeed, studies of rats, cows, and lambs have shown that when nurslings are exposed to distinctive flavors through their mothers' milk, they tend to prefer that flavor well after weaning.

Most animals, including humans, have a tendency to reject a new flavor when they taste it for the first time. Such rejection of novelty makes sense when you consider that many foods in nature are potentially toxic, and one way to stay healthy is to stick to familiar foods that you already know are safe. By exposing her infant to the various flavors of her diet, a breast-feeding mother essentially communicates which foods are safe, getting around the problem of novelty rejection once the baby begins eating solids. Indeed, one recent study compared the food preferences of breast- and bottle-fed infants at four to six months of age and found that breast-fed babies were more apt to consume certain vegetables—like pureed peas or green beans—when exposed for the first time. Either the breast-fed babies were already familiar with the vegetable flavors through their mothers' diet, or they were more willing to try new foods because of their generally wider taste experience.

Thus, breast milk serves as an important medium for varying a baby's early sensory experience. It may also play a role in a newborn's recognition of his mother. Because dietary flavors find their way into a woman's amniotic fluid during pregnancy, many of the flavors in her milk should already be familiar to her baby, assuming she does not significantly change her eating habits after giving birth. Like odors, the distinctive tastes in mother's milk may thereby help a newborn begin to bond with her.

Alcohol and Breast Milk

One flavor that makes its way into milk may be cause for some concern. Alcohol passes freely from a mother's blood into her milk. When a nursing mother has a drink, alcohol can be detected in her milk after thirty minutes, and it peaks at one hour postingestion. By three hours, it is nearly gone, although levels remain elevated longer if she consumes more than one drink. Alcohol tends to make milk smell sweeter, and babies actually suck and drink more of their mother's milk when it is expressed and a small amount of alcohol is added to it. Similarly, babies nurse more vigorously after their mother has consumed an alcoholic compared to a nonalcoholic drink. But despite this vigor, they actually ingest less milk, possibly because alcohol interferes with the letdown reflex.

The amount of alcohol that actually makes its way into milk after one drink is quite small: even if the baby nursed at the time of peak alcohol content, he would consume only one four-hundredth of the amount of alcohol in one beer (or correcting for body weight, a dose no more than 3 percent of what the mother consumed). Nonetheless, this may be enough to influence an infant's behavior and development. Babies sleep less following such modest alcohol ingestion, and one study found that babies whose mothers drank one or two drinks a day during nursing scored some four points lower on tests of motor skills at one year of age, than did babies of nondrinking nursing mothers. (Mental development scores, however, were not affected by maternal drinking.) We do not know how such small quantities of alcohol might influence neural development, but it is known that young babies' immature livers do not metabolize alcohol as efficiently as those of adults, so it will tend to accumulate more than in an adult's body.

Whether these developmental differences persist beyond the first year of life is still an open question. But prudence dictates that nursing mothers should moderate their drinking. Total abstinence is the safest course, but mothers who do choose to drink can minimize their baby's exposure by consuming no more than one alcoholic drink every other day, by drinking slowly on a full stomach, and by forgoing nursing for several hours after taking a drink.

Does Early Taste Experience Influence Later Preferences?

Once a baby starts on solid foods, the world of taste comes fully to life. Although Matty has had some exposure to different flavors through Lorna's milk, they were pretty subtle compared with what he's experiencing now. Cereal! Strained fruits! Mashed potatoes! While not exactly haute cuisine, all this full-blown taste sensation is pretty exciting. And just as the flavors he's experienced in breast milk are helping to shape his developing taste preferences, these early encounters with food may have a profound impact on the eating habits that he will carry with him through life.

Taste preferences are remarkably malleable. Although we are innately programmed to like sweet and salt, virtually every other aspect of food preference appears to be a product of experience, or an "acquired taste." Genes play very little role in taste preference, based on the observation that identical twins are no more likely to prefer the same flavors than fraternal twins. Nurture, rather than nature, clearly dominates when it comes to our choice of foods and decisions about what we do and don't like to eat.

If food preference is largely a product of experience, it is not surprising that this learning may be most potent in early childhood. Rats who have been exposed at an early age to a variety of flavors in their diet are likelier later in life to ingest a novel flavor—chocolate—than rats reared on a more restricted diet; but this effect is not found in rats whose experience is broadened only in adulthood. Early exposure to a variety of flavors seems to reduce the fear of novel foods that is innate in rats, as in people. This preference for familiar foods is especially strong in young children, but by the same token, even two-year-olds can cultivate a taste for novel flavors, like exotic fruits and cheeses, if repeatedly exposed to them over the course of several weeks. Toddlers may go from actively spitting out a food that they're tasting for the first time to clearly preferring it after several tries.

Recognizing that early food experience can have a lasting effect, many parents are now trying to take a more active role in shaping their children's food preferences. Whether it's reducing their intake of salt or refined sugars, or increasing the variety of vegetables and protein they consume, health-conscious parents believe that by controlling their children's diet in the youngest years, they can pave the way to healthier eating habits throughout their lives. Is there any evidence that this really works? Or are parents fighting a losing battle, for instance, in preventing young kids from eating sweets, by actually making them crave them and seek them out when they get a little older?

When it comes to salt and sweets, there's little a parent can do to alter a child's innate craving, which begins, as we've seen, early in infancy. There is some evidence, however, that early diet can at least modify the circumstances in which children will seek out sweet and salty flavors. As early as six months of age, babies who have been exposed more often to salted food show a stronger preference for salted over unsalted cereal than babies with less salt experience. Similarly, six-month-old babies who have been fed sugar water tend to drink more of it than babies not previously exposed to it. This effect lasts a surprisingly long time, because even if the parents stop giving their baby sugar water by six months of age, she will continue to show a greater preference for it at age two.

This doesn't mean that raising children on a low-salt or no-sweets diet will erase their desire for these tastes. No matter what their experience, young children still prefer most foods in their sweeter or saltier forms. (Indeed, their preferences are stronger than most adults'.) But experience can influence their sense of which foods should be sweet or salty, toning down their cravings somewhat. It may take a little longer for a toddler to accept a new food that's not sweet or salty, but with enough exposure, its familiarity should make it palatable. Fortunately, baby food manufacturers have finally figured this out and no longer add salt or sugar to their simpler jarred foods. (On the other hand, when a child starts getting *really* picky, around the late preschool years, you can sometimes entice them to eat their meat or veggies by adding a little extra salt or sugar.)

There is little danger in putting young ones on a low-salt diet, since the minimum requirement for sodium can easily be obtained from the natural content of foods. However, the current trend toward low-fat eating is entirely another matter, at least as far as young children's brains are concerned. As we have seen, fats are crucial for building and wiring up young neurons, and there is little justification for restricting children's fat intake during the brain growth spurt, which continues until around two years of age. Infants and toddlers need fat from a variety of sources, both animal and vegetable, and they need a larger proportion of total fat in their diet (30 to 54 percent of total calories) than is currently recommended for older children and adults (30 percent or less). Parents aren't doing young children any favor by feeding them low-fat foods. Fortunately, taste preferences remain malleable throughout life, so there is plenty of time to instill adultlike patterns of fat consumption after your toddler's brain has completed its growth spurt.

Little Brains, Big Taste

Taste is a big deal to little kids. For young infants, it is the major source of pleasure. For older babies, it is a realm of great discovery. For toddlers, it is a new route for rebellion. And for preschoolers, it can simply be a lot of fun.

The sense of taste is quite well developed at birth and obviously plays an essential role in growth. But taste is also surprisingly important for children's emotional development. Certain foods—sweets and fats—literally have mood-altering effects that can calm a baby, improve his attention span, and eventually help him to sleep. Moreover, the associations a baby makes between pleasurable tastes and those who feed him serve as an important foundation for the growing bond between them. Familiar flavors in his mother's milk provide a comforting bridge between the womb and the outside world and begin to shape a baby's later food preferences. After weaning, when little brains have hopefully reaped the special benefits of mother's milk, they can begin learning about food tastes and textures directly, and—with the right kind of experience—develop a lifelong palate for a well-balanced, nutritious diet.

Chapter 9

WIRING UP THE
VISUAL BRAIN

Compared with the other senses we've considered so far—touch, smell, taste, and vestibular perception—the sense of vision is still primitive at the time of birth. Newborn babies, like little red-headed Ginna, can't yet adjust their focus and are unable to make out any kind of detail in the visual world. Ginna can see clearly only about eight inches in front of her, and even there the particulars of her mother's face or her crib mobile are lost in a blur. With such a fuzzy, two-dimensional view of the world, how can she even begin to figure out such simple things as what an object is or how to grasp it with her hand?

Thanks to the rapid wiring of neurons in her visual cortex, however, her sense of vision will dramatically improve within a few short months. By six months of age, all her primary visual abilities will have emerged, such as depth perception, color vision, fine acuity, and well-controlled eye movements. And by one year they will be almost fully tuned, revealing to her the rich visual universe in all of its colorful, three-dimensional glory.

Why should a baby's vision be so poor at birth? We've just seen how much young infants benefit from their more mature senses, such as smell and touch. Considering how important vision is to our species, why didn't Nature get the ball rolling with this sense as well?

In fact, it may be precisely because vision is so important that it waits until after birth to undergo its most important developmental advances.

Waiting until postnatal life maximizes the role that experience can play in shaping the visual centers of the brain. Ginna's limited vision is all she needs to begin learning about the key features of her world, like her brother's face, her mother's nipple, and her own tiny hands as she waves them before her face. This rather limited starting point may permit just the right amount of visual experience—not too much, and not too little—for her to gradually construct an internal image of the outside world without becoming over-loaded, all at once, by the incredibly rich experience that our mature visual systems provide.

As we'll see in this chapter, visual experience—the right amount at the right time—is essential for the proper development of the brain circuits underlying vision. Indeed, of all the senses, vision is the only one that receives no stimulation in the womb, so it is not surprising that it is poorly developed at birth. Ginna's eyes have just begun to see, and what passes before them in the next few weeks and months will have a critical and last-ing impact on all the remarkable abilities that will constitute her mature sense of vision.

How Vision Works

On the surface, vision seems so simple: we look out into the world—even onto a totally unfamiliar scene—and instantly know that what we're seeing is a building, a tree, a room, a person. But like most great technology, the pro-cessing that makes vision seem effortless is actually enormously complex. The brain devotes more of its territory to vision than to all the other senses combined. It's because of this massive processing space, and the special ways in which its intricate components are wired together, that our brains can per-form all the very rapid and complicated computations that make everyday visual tasks—like reading, driving, and watching TV—seem so easy. Even today, the most advanced computers fall far short of the mammalian brain when it comes to visual tasks such as recognizing faces or identifying objects in a complicated scene.

How does such a powerful computational system emerge from so simple a mass of neural tissue in a tiny embryo? Thanks to nearly four decades of intensive research, we know more about the development of vision than of any other mental ability. What we have learned has proven enormously valu-able, not only for improving the visual abilities of many children, but also for elucidating important principles of brain development that apply to every aspect of mental growth.

Vision begins, of course, in the eye, when light passes through the *cornea*, the transparent outer coating, is focused by the *lens*, and then strikes the *retina*, a three-layered blanket of neurons that covers the entire back surface of the eyeball. Now begins the journey through the nervous system, whose job is to convert light information into electrical signals that map out color and intensity at each point in the visual field. This is exactly the opposite of what a TV set or computer monitor does, which is to convert electrical signals into images using dots of different colors. Our sense of vision, however, is much more sophisticated than the decoding of a TV monitor. Not only must the brain map out color and intensity, it must also *interpret* what the eyes see, deciding, for instance, which array of dots corresponds to a single object (that is, where one object ends and another begins); what the object is; where it is located in three-dimensional space; the direction and speed in which it may be moving; and a host of other judgments that continue to elude even the most sophisticated computers.

The extraction of visual information begins at the very first level of visual processing, within the retina. When you look at an object—say, this page of text—light reflected from the page strikes the two different types of *photoreceptors* in the retina, *rods* and *cones*. Photoreceptors are specialized nerve cells that contain pigment molecules capable of capturing a single light particle, or photon, and converting its energy into a chemical reaction. (These pigment molecules are derived from vitamin A, which is why eating carrots is good for your vision.) The resulting chemical cascade in turn produces an electrical signal that begins the process of neural transmission in the visual system. (See Figure 9.1.)

Rods contain many more pigment molecules than cones; hence they are much more sensitive to light and are especially useful for seeing in low-light conditions, such as nighttime. Rods also play a dominant role in peripheral vision, because they are mostly located away from the center of the retina. Cones are less sensitive to light overall, but unlike rods, they are able to detect color. They are responsible for our most acute vision, because they are densely packed in the centermost part of the retina, called the *fovea*.

Three different types of cones contain three different types of pigment molecules. One absorbs blue light best; one green light; and one red light. By

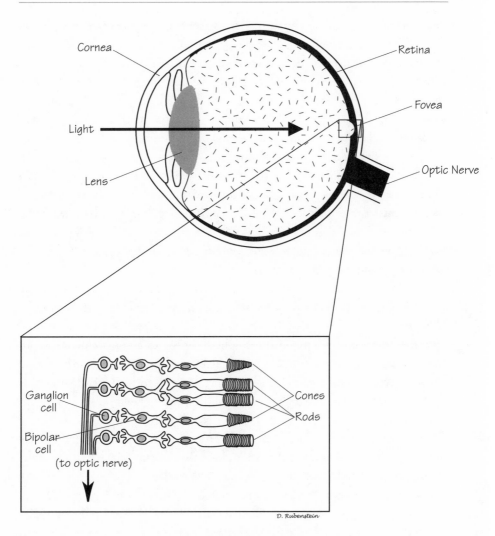

FIGURE 9.1

*Structure of the mature eye. The major neurons
of the retina are shown below.*

comparing the degree of activation of these three classes of cones, the nervous system is able to differentiate all the different colors of the spectrum, much as a computer monitor displays millions of colors simply by blending different proportions of the same three colors.

Both rods and cones synapse on the next layer of retinal neurons, called *bipolar cells.* Bipolar cells, in turn, synapse on the third layer of retinal neurons, the *ganglion cells.* Ganglion cells put out very long axons that constitute the main output fibers from the eye, and they divide themselves up into two different pathways. One pathway goes to the brain stem, where visual information is used to control eye movements and reflexes. The other pathway projects to the visual area of the thalamus, known as the *lateral geniculate nucleus* (LGN), which in turn sends visual information to the cerebral cortex.

Of the two pathways, the brain-stem, or subcortical, route is the older one evolutionarily and also the earlier to mature in a baby's development. Its main target is an area of the midbrain called the *superior colliculus*, which is largely responsible for a baby's vision until about two months after birth. Although capable of some fairly sophisticated visual tasks, this subcortical pathway operates at an entirely subconscious level and is not responsible for what we commonly think of as "seeing."

Rather, it is the second pathway that creates conscious visual perception. A million ganglion cells from each retina send their long axons through each *optic nerve* to form synapses in the LGN. LGN neurons, in turn, send their axons to the occipital lobe of the cerebral cortex, to an area called the primary visual cortex, or V_1. Inside V_1, thalamic axons synapse on the first set of visual cortical neurons, initiating the intense cortical processing that underlies our most sophisticated visual abilities. (See Figure 9.2.)

The Segregation of Left and Right   Like most sensory and motor abilities, visual perception is divided in half: the left side of the brain receives input from the right half of the visual field, and vice versa. This division actually requires some tricky routing on the part of retinal ganglion cells, because each eye takes in some light from both the left and right halves of our full visual field. (You can see this by closing one eye and moving the other all the way toward your nose.) Ganglion cell axons sort themselves out when they reach the crossover point of the two optic nerves, the *optic chiasm*: regardless of which eye they originate in, axons that "see" the right side of your visual field terminate in the left LGN and vice versa. Left LGN neurons then project exclusively to the left visual cortex. Thus, each side of the visual cortex contains a map of the visual field on the opposite side of the body.

The flip side of this routing is that each side of the brain receives input from both eyes. Despite the mixing of left and right ganglion cell axons at the optic chiasm, their synaptic terminals remain carefully segregated; the LGN is composed of several layers of cells, and each layer receives input

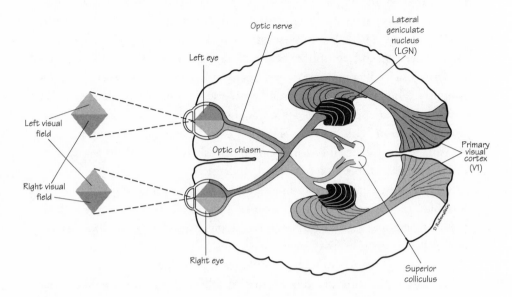

FIGURE 9.2

*Visual pathways from the eyes to the midbrain (superior colliculus)
and to the cerebral cortex. Shadings indicate how information from
each half of the visual field is processed by the opposite half of the
brain throughout this portion of the visual stream.*

from only one eye. Similarly in V1, whole columns of neurons are devoted
exclusively to the input from one or the other eye. Every neuron in the
LGN and in the first stage of the cerebral cortex is thus said to be *monocular,* while in the next stage of cortical processing, neurons receive input
from both left and right monocular neurons and are known as *binocular.* The
initial segregation of left and right eye inputs, as well as their successful
reconvergence onto binocular neurons, are essential for depth perception
and other abilities. Such binocular abilities, however, are not present at
birth, and as we'll see, their development is strongly influenced by a child's
early visual experience.

"What" vs. "Where": The Brain's Division of Visual Labor

When you look out in the street and see a red car speeding by, you don't
notice that your brain is separately processing its color, shape, location, and
direction of motion. Just as the brain segregates information from the left and

right visual worlds, so does it parse visual input according to several other properties, each processed by a distinct region, or module, in the brain's large visual anatomy. At last count, researchers had identified thirty-two distinct visual areas in each hemisphere of the cortex. Each of these areas—V1 plus the thirty-one others not even mentioned yet—appears to be specialized for a slightly different aspect of visual perception. Some areas detect object shape, others are specialized for color, fine detail, motion, location, and depth perception. This division of labor is extremely useful, because it allows us to analyze many visual features simultaneously (also known as *parallel processing*), massively speeding our visual perception.

Fortunately, our understanding of all these modules is simplified by the fact that they are divided into just two basic streams. One route, which appears to mature slightly earlier in development, is known as the "where" stream. It is concerned with visual space and is specialized for detecting an object's speed, direction of motion, and location in three-dimensional space, as well as for directing eye movements to follow visual targets. The other route is the "what" stream, and it houses the circuitry we use to identify objects or familiar features; it is specialized to detect color, shape, and fine detail. These two streams actually begin to separate in the retina, but they don't fully diverge until the cortex, after they reach V1. Then the "where" stream courses up through several visual areas on its way to the parietal lobes, while the "what" stream flows downward, to terminate in the lower temporal lobes. (See Figure 9.3.)

The different functions of the "what" and "where" streams are most dramatically illustrated in patients who have suffered strokes in one or the other region. A person with a lesion in the posterior parietal area has no difficulty identifying an object that she's looking at, but she is very poor at picking it up. Lacking a functional "where" stream, she can't guide her hand to the right place or use the appropriate motion to grasp it. On the other hand, a patient with temporal lobe damage can accurately track a moving object or pick it up off a table but can't identify visually what it is. Temporal lobe visual deficits can be very specific, such as an inability to recognize colors, or animals, or familiar faces. This last symptom was eloquently described by Oliver Sacks in *The Man Who Mistook His Wife for a Hat*, the case of a musician who, though able to discern abstract visual features of objects, like size, shape, and color, had nonetheless lost the ability to identify even the most familiar of objects—including his own wife's face.

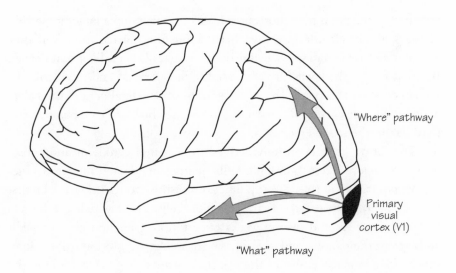

"Where" pathway

Primary
visual
cortex (V1)

"What" pathway

FIGURE 9.3

After its initial processing in cortical area V1, visual information is divided up into two parallel streams: the "what" pathway in the temporal lobe and the "where" pathway in the parietal lobe.

How the Visual System Develops

Considering its great size and complexity, it is not surprising that the visual system takes a while to put itself together during a baby's development. This isn't for lack of an early start, however. Visual development begins in the fourth week of embryonic life, with the initial formation of the eye. It then proceeds in a sequence from outside in: neurons and synapses form first in the retina, followed by subcortical visual areas, followed by V1, followed by the higher visual centers in the temporal and parietal lobes. But in spite of its early start, it's not until many months after birth that the whole system is up and running, and years more before all of its pathways are firmly stabilized.

The first optic tissue emerges a mere twenty-two days after fertilization, with the formation of two large bubbles at the front of the neural tube. By five weeks, these bubbles have collapsed into two cup-shaped structures and differentiated to include both the retina and the lens. Each eye cup is attached to the brain by a short, broad stalk and takes up a large proportion of the space inside the primitive head. From the outside, however, they appear as just two small spots, facing out sideways, like a bird's or lizard's eyes. By eight weeks, the spots have migrated to face forward and now look like human eyes. At this point, the very beginning of the fetal period, the baby's upper and lower eyelid folds form and then fuse shut, not to separate again until late in the second trimester.

The retina itself is entirely derived from neural ectoderm and consequently develops like a "minibrain." Its neurons divide and migrate to successive layers, where they take up functions distinct to their layer. The first layer of neurons to emerge is the ganglion cells, all of which are formed between about six and twenty weeks of gestation. Ganglion cells immediately sprout their axons, and as early as eight weeks of gestation, young fibers can be found emerging out of the eye stalk, where they begin forming the optic nerves.

The retina matures along a second, slower gradient, progressing from the fovea out toward its most peripheral regions. Thus all of the foveal cells are formed by just fourteen weeks of gestation, while some rods and bipolar cells in the most peripheral parts of the retina are still emerging several months after birth. This slow development of the peripheral retina is surprising because, as we shall see, a newborn's vision is actually better toward the edge than in the center of his visual field. But foveal vision improves dramatically in the first several months after birth because of additional, very specialized changes in the cone photoreceptors that are described below.

Neurons begin forming in the next visual relay station, the LGN, later than they do in the retina, but the whole process is much quicker; by just eleven weeks of gestation, all the LGN neurons have formed. By the end of the first trimester, they receive their first synapses from retinal ganglion cells. Synapses continue forming in the LGN until early postnatal life, but these later connections come from the cerebral cortex, and are responsible for establishing cortical control over lower-brain visual functions.

The second trimester marks a period of massive growth in the visual cortex. All of the 100 million neurons in the primary visual cortex are formed between just fourteen and twenty-eight weeks of gestation. In the fifth month, synapses begin forming in V1, but it is only the beginning of a process that continues for nearly another full year, at the astonishing rate of some ten billion new synapses per day!

Recent evidence suggests that the "where" stream develops somewhat earlier than the "what" stream. By birth, far more synapses involved in motion processing have formed than those involved in form perception, and by four months of age, the first relay in the "where" pathway has reached its maximal synaptic density, while the "what" pathway takes until eight months to reach this peak. Precocious development of the "where" stream explains why young babies are better at some visual feats, like detecting motion, than others, like fine visual acuity.

Synaptic density reaches its peak in V1 at around eight months after birth. Then, around age two, it begins a slow decline that lasts until late childhood. This long period of synaptic pruning, in which about 40 percent of visual cortex synapses are eliminated and the remaining circuits grow progressively more efficient, coincides with the gradual refinement of many visual skills. It also corresponds, as we will see, to the outer limit of the critical period for visual development.

Just as the emergence of cells and synapses progresses inward—from the eye, to the LGN, to V1, to higher cortical areas—myelination of visual axons proceed along a similar gradient. Thus the optic nerves begin to myelinate two months before birth, continuing until seven months postnatally. LGN neurons, however, don't begin to myelinate until seven weeks after birth, and they continue until about eight months of age. Within V1, cells from different layers myelinate according to the same sequence in which their synapses formed. Finally, higher visual areas myelinate even later than V1, some of them continuing until mid-childhood.

Getting the Wiring Right: The Roles of Nature and Nurture

It's one thing to describe visual development in terms of numbers of neurons and synapses, but quite another to figure out how the whole system gets wired together properly. Consider V1 alone, where each of the 100 million neurons receives synapses from thousands of others and in turn forms connections onto thousands more. How in the world do these *trillion* synapses manage to form in the right location, forgoing every wrong possibility to end up creating coherent pathways for color, shape, detail, spatial location, depth perception, and the like? Given this enormous complexity, it's amazing that we don't end up with a tangled mass of synaptic knots for a brain.

In spite of its complexity, neurobiologists have made substantial headway in solving the problem of visual wiring. We now know that it occurs in two phases. The first phase, which is controlled by genes, succeeds in establishing a crude wiring diagram. During this period, large groups of neurons use a host of programmed molecular cues to guide their axons to the approximately correct location. If you think about the whole process as a kind of long-distance journey, this phase is analogous to the plane ride; it gets a load of travelers most of the way to where they're going but leaves them off at the airport—not exactly the "final destination" for which they were headed.

At this point, nature leaves off and nurture finishes the trip. The second phase of visual wiring is controlled by experience, specifically, by the electrical activity generated by a baby's actual act of seeing. During this phase, neighboring axons compete for space in the crude map and either lose their synapses or link onto specific targets, depending on the level and timing of their electrical activity. This synaptic pruning—survival of the fittest or most active connections—completes the journey of visual wiring, refining the crude map into a precise representation of visual space.

Visual Deprivation and the Miswired Kitten Cortex   The discovery that visual experience actually directs the wiring of the visual brain was perhaps the most important one in all of developmental neuroscience. It was made in the early 1960s by two neurobiologists, David Hubel and Torsten Wiesel, who won a Nobel Prize for their work. They began with a rather simple experiment, in which they deprived kittens or monkeys of visual experience by sewing their eyes shut shortly after birth. This deprivation had a profound effect on both the structure and function of the visual cortex. More remarkable, however, was what happened to kittens reared with just a *single* eye sutured. Contrary to expectations, these kittens' brains were even more disturbed than those of the kittens who had been deprived of vision in both eyes. From this observation, Hubel and Wiesel concluded that some kind of competitive interaction underlies the process of selective brain wiring. When both eyes are closed, electrical activity in the visual system is substantially reduced, but at least it remains symmetrical. (There is always some background electrical activity, even when the eyes are closed.) In contrast, when only one eye is closed, its minimal electrical input is overwhelmed by that of the open eye, and it ends up losing considerable space in the visual cortex.

Remember that each side of the brain receives visual input from both eyes. During the first phase of development, axons representing each eye grow in, branch out, and tend to form synapses in overlapping areas. During the refinement phase, however, electrical activity causes these pathways to segregate; synapses from, say, the right eye tend to stabilize one another because their electrical activity will be strong and synchronous. On the other hand, the occasional left eye synapse that happens to find itself in a clump of right eye inputs will be forced to retract, because its activity will be out of sync with them.

Eventually, this pruning process results in the complete segregation of left and right inputs. Inputs from each eye end up retracting about half of their axon branches, leaving the primary visual cortex with a striped pattern—one millimeter of tissue representing the left eye, the next millimeter representing the right, and so on throughout area V1. When the pathway from just one eye is visualized with a special dye, one can actually see the alternating areas of left and right visual input appearing as a striking zebra pattern. (See Figure 9.4.)

The cortex looks quite different in animals reared with one eye sutured. In this case, inputs from the open eye win all the activity contests, so that eye ends up conquering a greater share of cortical space; each of its stripes ends up about four times wider than stripes innervated by the closed eye. This difference has important consequences for visual abilities, because with

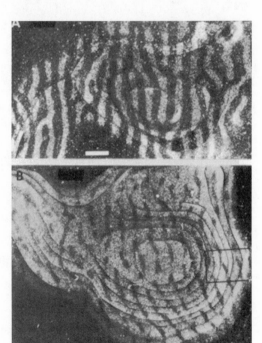

FIGURE 9.4

"Stripes" of synaptic input in a monkey's visual cortex. The top photo shows the visual cortex in a normal monkey. The black stripes, which receive input from the left eye, are the same width as the white stripes, which receive input from the right eye. The bottom photo shows the visual cortex of a monkey reared with the left eye sewn shut. The right eye (white stripes) now dominates the cortical space.

From T.N. Wiesel, "Postnatal development of the visual cortex and the influence of environment," *Nature*, 299:583–91, 1982. Reprinted by permission of Macmillian Magazines Ltd.

very few surviving inputs to the cerebral cortex, the disadvantaged eye has little access to higher visual circuitry. Even after it is reopened, it will remain functionally blind.

Critical Periods for Visual Development   Having shown that visual experience and synaptic competition are essential for normal visual wiring, Hubel and Wiesel next wondered how long this holds true. Once the stripes of visual input have formed in the cortex, can they be undone? We know, for instance, that adults do not lose their vision if they suffer from cataracts or wear an eye patch for an extended period. Is there a critical period for visual experience in early development, and if so, how long does it last?

This time Hubel and Wiesel waited until kittens were three or four months old before suturing one eye shut. Unlike the earlier suturing, this deprivation was no longer devastating; it did not erase the stripes of visual input in the cortex. The brain, then, needs experience to properly wire up, but only at a very specific time—during the pruning period, when the initial, promiscuous synaptic contacts are being refined. Once this pruning period is over, the cortex cannot be drastically rewired, no matter how normal or abnormal the visual experience thereafter.

Understanding how the visual system develops explains why visual problems in babies, such as crossed eyes, can be so harmful to their long-term visual perception. We now know that there are several critical periods during normal visual development. Generally speaking, a particular visual skill first emerges when synapses initially form in its underlying circuit. It then remains plastic, that is, subject to modification by experience, as long the synapses are in their refinement phase. Since different parts of the visual system undergo synaptic refinement at different times, the period during which they are sensitive to visual input also differs, so that various aspects of vision—acuity, binocularity, and the like—are vulnerable to abnormal experience at different times in a baby's life. Fortunately, the critical periods for babies' visual development extend considerably longer than those for kittens. Because synaptic pruning continues so long into childhood, visual abilities are highly malleable until age two and then, somewhat less so, until eight or nine years of age.

Early Experience and the Development of Visual Skills
Neuroscientists now believe that experience, or activity-based competition for synaptic space, underlies the development of every circuit in the visual

cortex. For example, when kittens or monkeys are made artificially cross-eyed shortly after birth, their eyes cannot work cooperatively, so their visual cortex is deprived of the kind of electrical activity normally necessary for the development of binocular neurons, the cells that play a critical role in depth perception and high acuity.

Another example concerns cortical neurons that are responsible for detecting the orientation of lines or objects in space. When kittens are reared under conditions in which they are able to view only one type of orienta-tion—by maintaining their heads upright in a room painted with vertical stripes—a much larger proportion of their orientation-sensitive neurons become responsive to vertical stimuli and an abnormally small number respond to horizontal stimuli. A similar effect may occur in humans, though the range of environments is not nearly so extreme. It turns out that most of us who are reared in houses or apartments—so-called "carpentered" environ-ments—tend to have slightly better acuity for both horizontal and vertical orientations than we do for objects with oblique or diagonal orientations. In contrast, one study found that a group of Canadian Indians, who had been reared in traditional teepee-shaped dwellings, had considerably better acuity for oblique angles than people reared in carpentered environments.

It is very possible, then, that every subtle variation in a child's early visual experience has a long-lasting impact on her visual circuitry and per-ceptual abilities. Though heredity obviously plays an important role in the quality of one's vision, it is likely that early experience also critically shapes a child's skills of observation, spatial perception, hand-eye coordination, and so on. The more a baby sees, and the better that input is suited to her visual ability at that particular stage, the better she is likely to be at the many later tasks that depend on vision. Who knows? It may even make the difference in whether she ends up as an artist, or a naturalist, or an expert tennis player.

How Vision Improves

Considering how much basic visual development takes place after birth, it's amazing that newborns can see at all. But while Ginna's visual cortex is only beginning to wire up, her subcortical visual structures are already well developed and control most of what she is able to do visually during the first two months of her life. Fetuses as young as twenty-four weeks postconception have been observed to move, or alter their heart rate, in response to strong lights directed at the mother's abdomen. The brain-stem pathways that con-trol such reflexes myelinate faster than those leading to the LGN and cortex, beginning about two months before birth and completing the process by three months postnatally. Brain-stem circuits are also responsible for most other newborn visual skills, including simple eye movements, blinking, dila-tion of the pupil, and the ability to track a moving object. These circuits are all up and running by thirty-two weeks of gestation, judging by the fixation and tracking abilities of preterm babies.

With birth comes the visual experience that is critical for the develop-ment of cortical visual centers, the machinery of conscious visual perception. Things starts off a little slowly, but beginning at about two months, a baby's cerebral cortex starts to take over most visual tasks from the subcortical cir-cuits. As the number of synapses in her visual cortex explodes between about two and eight months of age, new visual skills emerge and rapidly improve until finally, by the end of the first year, a baby's vision is nearly as good as an adult's.

What a Newborn Sees   Ginna's father, Alex, is an optometrist, so he's naturally very curious about what his newborn daughter can see. Here she is, just three hours old, and he's already waving a red sock over her bassinet, trying to attract her attention. The bright sock generates no reaction when he waves it straight above her face, but when he moves it over to the side of her bassinet, she suddenly darts her eyes in its direction. He then slowly moves the sock across her visual field, and Ginna's eyes follow, all the way to the right, until she has to turn her head to follow it even further. "Good news," Alex says to his exhausted wife, Sally, "it looks like our baby can see."

Yes, newborns can see, but not all that well. The world for Ginna prob-ably looks the way it would to you or me if we had to stare out of a frosted window all the time. Though light makes it through her eyes unimpeded, neither her retinas nor her brain can process its information in a manner sophisticated enough to detect most of the objects, shapes, and colors in the world. Her acuity is poor, meaning that she can discern two different objects only if they are separated by a large distance; everything closely spaced tends to blur together. Her contrast sensitivity is weak, so that she notices only the boldest patterns; subtle shading is virtually invisible to her. She can focus only over a narrow range of distances, between about seven and thirty inches in front of her, and her eyes prefer to converge on objects at the closest end of this range. She can see some color but hardly the full spectrum; reds and greens are more distinct than blues. Her perception is entirely two-dimensional, since she has yet to develop any of the tools our brains use to perceive spatial depth. And finally, her spatial vision is particularly odd; she actually sees better toward the perimeter of her visual field. Unlike adults, who move their head and eyes to put something they really need to study into the very center of their visual fields, newborns can best detect features on the edge or rim of what they're looking at, and they don't notice the features that are directly in front of them.

But what Ginna *can* see, she is remarkably drawn to look at: bold objects or patterns, black-and-white designs, brightly colored toys, and conspicuous smiling faces, like big brother Brad, excitedly hovering over the side of her bassinet to get a first look at his new baby sister. Movement also catches her attention, like the red sock her father was waving about. Indeed, newborns see motion better than almost any other visual feature, thanks to the more precocious development of neurons in the "where" stream, and they are especially adept at tracking slowly moving objects. Ginna even has the good sense to grow bored with looking at the same pattern or object for a long period of time. After intently fixating on that bright sock for a while, she becomes agitated, looks away, and won't become interested again for several minutes.

Limited though it is, Ginna's vision is good enough to do several important things for her. Almost everything she can see is right within her reach, so her restricted focal distance actually makes it easier for her to begin coordinating vision with the touch and movement of her hands. Her vision is also optimized for seeing and learning what her family members look like. As we shall see, newborns have an innate preference for faces or facelike objects. As Ginna nurses, her eyes are situated at an optimum range for focusing on her mother's face. Mothers seem to instinctively realize the limited focal distance of newborns, since they tend to hold babies just about eight inches from their own eyes.

Ginna's vision is also just sensitive enough to give her rapidly growing brain the kind of stimulation it most needs. Her attraction for bold patterns and colors provides her cortical neurons with distinctive input to help sharpen their abilities to detect edges, contrast, hues, motion, and all the other basic elements of visual perception. These skills, in turn, will provide the right visual stimulation for refining still higher visual areas and their more sophisticated functions like depth perception and superfine acuity.

The Maturation of Eye Movements and Visual Attention

How can we possibly know what babies are able to see? It is not easy, but one way in which researchers have approached the development of vision is by studying their eye movements. Watching *how* a baby's eyes move has taught us a lot about how the visual machinery matures, because different types of eye movements are controlled by different parts of the brain. Watching *where* a baby is looking can tell a surprising amount about what he can see—which patterns, or colors, or shapes are most easily discerned. That's because young babies are little looking-machines. They are virtually compelled to stare at everything they can clearly distinguish, especially if they have never seen it before.

Between birth and six months of age, the control of eye movements shifts from a largely subcortical to a dominantly cortical function, and babies' eye movements mature correspondingly. Newborns are capable of tracking slowly moving objects, but their eyes move only in jerky, fixed steps, known as *saccades*, and they tend to fall behind the object they are trying to follow. Saccades are a reflexive form of eye movement, controlled by the brain stem, and do not require a functioning cerebral cortex. By two months after birth, however, the cortex has become wired to perceive object motion; babies can now track with smooth, as opposed to saccadic, eye movements, and thereby follow a moving object with considerably greater precision. Finally, between three and six months, infants become able to anticipate, as opposed to merely follow, the position of a steadily moving object. Careful measurements have shown that during this period, the eyes begin to focus slightly ahead of where the object is moving. This anticipatory tracking is a function of special eye-movement control regions in the frontal cortex, and it is a major landmark in cognitive development, because it suggests the baby is actually *choosing* where to look.

The Steady Improvement of Visual Acuity

The most striking improvement during visual development is in babies' acuity, the ability to detect detail. It improves markedly throughout the first six months of life, then more gradually until a child is nearly five years old. Babies begin life with an acuity of about 20/600, which is about thirty times poorer than 20/20 vision, or normal adult acuity. But acuity grows rapidly, thanks to changes in both the eye and the cerebral cortex.

It is the center of the eye, or fovea, that we use for all our fine vision, and this is the slowest part of the retina to mature. In a newborn, the foveal cones are short and fat and therefore respond to a wide area of the visual field. Beginning around birth, however, and continuing for a surprisingly long time thereafter, the cones grow dramatically longer and skinnier. As it loses about two-thirds of its girth, each cone responds to a proportionally slimmer segment of the total visual field. This narrowing makes room for additional cones, which are continuously migrating in from more peripheral parts of the retina. Consequently, babies experience a dramatic increase in foveal cone density that improves their visual acuity, much as adding dots per inch (dpi's) to a computer printer enhances its spatial resolution.

The gradual change in cone shape also improves acuity in a second way. As each cone grows longer, it can stack more and more pigment molecules in the direction of incoming light. This increases the chance that a particular cone will be activated by a single photon; each cone thus becomes much more sensitive to lower levels of illumination. For the baby, this translates into improved contrast resolution: while newborns require very high contrast—like black against white—to see much of anything, older babies can begin to discern more subtle gradations of brightness, like grays or the details of a pastel print. Contrast sensitivity improves most dramatically over the first ten weeks of life, and then more gradually until about one year of age.

Changes in the retina are important, but they don't fully account for the dramatic improvement in acuity. Cortical development also plays a major part. At birth, very few neurons in the primary visual cortex fire action potentials in response to visual stimuli, and most cells require very high contrast in order to be activated. Thanks to the rapid growth of cortical synapses and myelin, however, the number of active neurons rises dramatically, and each neuron's responses also grow increasingly specific to particular types of visual input. Like the maturing cones, cortical neurons initially respond to large areas of the visual field, but gradually, through competitive synaptic refinement, limit their responsiveness to smaller, more precise regions.

Beginning about four months of age, the perception of detail takes another leap forward with the emergence of *hyperacuity*: the ability to discriminate features that are up to ten times finer than the size of the photoreceptors should theoretically permit. It is this ultrafine discrimination that allows us, for instance, to see a very slight glitch in an otherwise straight line, even though the size of the glitch is below our eyes' limit of resolution. It is not yet known how our brains perform this remarkable feat, but it is generally agreed that the necessary processing takes place in the cerebral cortex. Babies show rapid improvement on hyperacuity tests between ten and eighteen weeks of age, in accordance with the massive maturation of the visual cortex over the same period.

While changes in both the retina and the cerebral cortex are important for the improvement in babies' acuity, there is one very important difference between the two. Cortical development is influenced by a baby's visual experience, while cone development is not. Changes in cone structure and distribution proceed in much the same way whether or not the baby has normal vision. In contrast, those aspects of acuity that are controlled by the cortex can be seriously perturbed if a baby's vision is obscured in any way. As we saw with the sutured kittens, visual input is essential to achieve normal wiring in the visual cortex, and one way in which this wiring manifests itself is in the improvement of visual acuity during infancy.

In a sense, all babies see "abnormally" at birth, so it is reasonable to wonder how their brains, unable to receive anything other than blurry visual input, ever wire up in the first place. The answer is that experience actually seems to play a more important role in acuity development *after* the first few months of life. Thus it is only after babies can see detail reasonably well, and their visual cortex is fully participating in vision, that they enter a critical period in which further refinement is heavily dependent on normal, balanced visual input. Visual problems—such as cataracts, crossed eyes, or any other constraint that affects image clarity—are therefore most detrimental to a baby's acuity if they occur during the *second* six months of life. Hyperacuity is particularly vulnerable to abnormal visual experience, since it is fully controlled by the cerebral cortex.

Externality　Perhaps the strangest feature of newborn seeing is its emphasis on peripheral vision, as when Ginna darts her eyes to the side to catch a glimpse of the bright red sock but doesn't seem to notice when her father waves it right above her. This odd quality, called *externality*, is another product of slow foveal cone maturation. Because peripheral parts of the retina are more mature at birth than the fovea, they carry much more of the burden of seeing. In addition, information from the peripheral retina is preferentially routed to subcortical visual circuits, so it has greater access to the part of the visual system that is more mature at birth.

Because of this lag in foveal development, newborns rely much more heavily on their peripheral vision than adults or older children. For instance, an eight-by-ten photograph will attract more attention for its frame than for anything in the center of the picture. Similarly, Ginna soon learns to recognize Alex's face, but what she's really detecting is his hairline and thick beard rather than the details of his nose, eyes, and mouth.

This bizarre pattern lasts until about two months of age, when the baby's fovea is more mature and her cerebral cortex begins to take over the job of fine vision. In the meantime, it's probably best to hang those brightly patterned mobiles off to the side of a newborn's crib, rather than straight overhead, if you really want her to notice them.

Obligatory Looking, or "Why Is That Baby Staring at Me?"

In the second month of life, babies exhibit another striking visual behavior that is related to the externality effect. It is called *obligatory looking,* and as the name implies, babies this age may fixate on a single object, sometimes for thirty minutes or more. The reason their gaze gets stuck is because this is when the visual cortex first begins exerting control over brain-stem visual centers, the net effect of which is to inhibit babies' habitual eye movements toward their peripheral visual field. So even though Ginna, now six weeks old, *wants* to look away from that bright lamp in front of her, an awkward struggle between her cortical and subcortical visual centers prevents her from doing so. Poor thing! She's trapped into endlessly staring at it, until Sally finally sees her distress and rescues her.

Of course, there are times when this obligatory looking can be very useful. Every day now, Ginna seems to engage Sally in these intense, mutual gaze-fests that make her mother's heart melt. In fact, many parents describe this as the age when they first fall in love with their babies, and prolonged eye contact probably has a lot to do with it.

Color Vision

Shopped for any newborn toys lately? You've probably noticed that the layette sections are now crowded full of bold black-and-white patterns—stuffed animals, mobiles, crib buntings, blankets, pillows, toys. Manufacturers have finally figured out what newborns can and cannot see. Not only are these sharp designs best for their limited acuity, they also make sense since newborns' color vision is extremely poor during the first few weeks of life.

The earliest age at which babies have been carefully tested for color vision is three weeks, and their performance is not impressive. Most newborns are unable to distinguish colors, judging by the way a single spot of color fails to capture their attention when displayed against a different background color of comparable brightness. Color vision is limited for several reasons, but a major factor is the same retinal immaturity that limits acuity; the cones, which are responsible for detecting color as well as fine detail, are stubby and widely spaced. As they grow longer and pack more closely together in the fovea during the first few months, they become much more efficient at capturing light. So as a young baby's cones mature, so does her ability to see colors.

By just eight weeks of age, Ginna can discriminate many different pairs of colors, provided the samples she's viewing are large and very bright—an apple and an orange, for example. Reds and greens are also fairly distinct. But Ginna is still quite poor at discriminations that depend on her blue cones, which means that purples and yellow-green hues are also hard for her to make out.

As we saw earlier, colors are discriminated based on the degree to which they activate each of three different types of photoreceptors: the red, green, and blue cones. (Yellow is detected by the combination of green and red cones working together.) In addition, the central nervous system sharpens our perception of colors by a principle of "color opponency," in which red and green provide optimum contrast for each other, as do blue and yellow. We don't yet know whether babies younger than two months of age are limited by the function of their blue cones or by the neural circuitry that processes blue/yellow contrasts. Nonetheless, by three months of age, the blue/yellow system catches up with the red/green system, and babies can make nearly all the same color distinctions as adults.

By four months of age, the special areas responsible for processing color information in the primary visual cortex have fully matured. These areas, officially known as *blobs*, begin to form their connections to higher visual areas at this point, which helps explain why babies this age are suddenly quite intelligent in their understanding of colors; they are able to see, categorize, and even briefly remember all the major hues.

One way researchers test babies' color vision is by running habituation experiments. A baby is repeatedly shown one color—say, a big blue circle—until she grows obviously bored with—or "habituated" to—it, judged by the amount of time she spends looking at each presentation. Next, she is shown another colored circle—say, in a slightly longer wavelength. If the new color looks more blue than green to her, she tends to remain bored, but if it is within the range an adult would call "green," then she shows renewed interest. Using experiments like this, researchers have found that babies group colors in much the same way as adults, suggesting that such categories are truly innate to our visual systems.

Habituation experiments also show that young babies are remarkably good at remembering colors. In fact, young babies seem to have an easier time remembering colors than shapes, and the concept of color may be one of the first abstractions they are capable of.

Because of the way our visual systems process color—along red, blue, green, and yellow channels—older babies are strongly attracted to these four colors, especially in their "purest" and brightest versions. Given a choice, they prefer bright red or blue over intermediate colors like yellow-green or purple. (Adults are similarly strongly drawn to look at pure colors, although we may not describe these colors as "preferred.") These preferences may be a simple matter of maximally stimulating each of the four types of color-opponent cells in the LGN or cortex; the truer and brighter a particular color is—for example, a fire-engine red—the more strongly it will excite one of the four types of color-sensitive neurons. This strong electrical excitation may, in turn, directly stimulate neurons that control a baby's attention. Once again, manufacturers have put this information to use, judging by the sea of primary colors in the baby/toddler section of every toy store.

The Sudden Onset of Binocularity and Depth Perception

Binocular vision is any aspect of seeing that requires the coordination of two eyes. Generally speaking, all vision works much better with two eyes functioning instead of one: acuity, contrast sensitivity, color detection, and locating objects in space. But the one ability that most depends on having the two eyes work together is depth perception. Our sense of depth, or stereo vision, is strongly enhanced by the fact that each eye sees a slightly different scene, because it sits at a different position in the head. The difference between these scenes is translated by our brains into stereo vision: the perception of three dimensions. Stereo vision is not the only trick we use to perceive depth. A number of other cues are also involved, which can be detected by a single eye, such as perspective—the way parallel lines appear to converge in the distance—and the relationship between objects—whether one object obscures, appears larger, or is moving faster than another. Nonetheless, full depth perception depends on binocular disparity—the slight difference in spatial view offered by the two eyes—which is the cue that gives us the actual feeling of seeing in three dimensions.

Binocularity is entirely a function of the cerebral cortex. As noted above, once the visual circuits are properly wired up, inputs from each of the two eyes remain strictly segregated throughout the LGN and the first layer of synapses in the primary visual cortex. After this level, however, inputs from each eye begin to converge on single cortical neurons, combining their information to produce binocular sensation. While it may seem paradoxical, binocularity can emerge in babies only after the synaptic inputs from each eye have become segregated in the cortex—that is, once those alternating stripes of synaptic connections have formed—between two and six months of age. Before this time, when inputs from both eyes are competing for the same targets in the newborn's cortex, higher-level cells have no way of knowing which input is from which eye, so binocular comparisons are impossible. In other words, the cortex must first separate inputs from the two eyes before it can knowledgeably recombine them. Because of this relationship between binocularity and synaptic refinement, the onset of true binocular function in babies is thought to be a good marker of when the cerebral cortex is mature enough to take over the bulk of the job of seeing.

Remember those old View-Master story projectors? Babies can be tested for binocular function using 3-D goggles and specially constructed pairs of images that produce an experience similar to looking through one of these projectors. Alone, each image looks just like a row of vertical stripes, but when both are viewed together through the stereo goggles, a person with normal binocular vision will fuse the two images into one and see some of the stripes appearing to project out of the screen. (See Figure 9.5.) Another test frequently used is called a *random-dot stereogram*—two seemingly meaningless arrays of dots that, when fused into a single image, appear to contain a square projecting into or out of the screen.

Experiments like this are easy to perform on adults, who can simply tell you when they see the 3-D effect, but babies must be tested in more laborious ways. They are presented with a choice of image pairs. On one side of a screen is a pair that produces the 3-D effect, while the pair on the other side does not. When Ginna is tested for binocularity at eight weeks of age, she spends equal amounts of time looking at the image pairs on either side of the screen. However, by six weeks later, there is no contest; she can't take her eyes off the 3-D stripes to her right and barely notices those on the left, which appear merely two-dimensional. In that brief interval, her cortex became wired for stereo vision.

Like Ginna, most babies develop binocularity extremely rapidly. Infants tested between two and five months of age go from virtually no binocular function to nearly adult capability in just a few weeks; the average age when this begins happening is three and a half months. This rapid emergence has

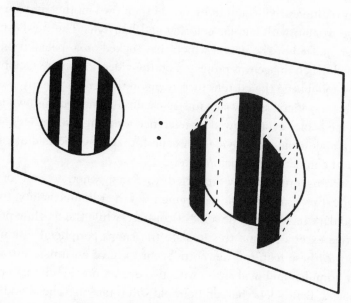

FIGURE 9.5

One type of stimulus used to assess the development of stereo vision in babies. Most babies younger than four months cannot perceive the three-dimensionality of the image on the right.

Reproduced with permission from R. Held et al., "Stereoacuity of human infants," *Proceedings of the National Academy of Sciences* 77:5572-4, 1980.

been confirmed by measuring evoked potentials: an electrical response to random-dot stereograms suddenly appears over the rear part of a baby's skull at exactly the same age.

This rapid improvement in young babies' stereo vision has an unfortunate downside, however. Because normal visual experience is necessary for proper cortical wiring, anything that interferes with the coordinated action of the two eyes in a young baby—such as eye crossing—can permanently compromise her opportunity to develop binocularity. Binocularity has one of the earliest critical periods of any brain function, as noted below, so it's important that young babies with crossed or other eye problems be treated promptly.

Face Recognition   Given how poor a newborn's vision is, one of the more surprising findings is that a baby can recognize his own mother's face within hours of birth. In one study, for instance, babies just one day old were shown two different video pictures, one of their own mother and a second of a strange woman with similar coloring and hairstyle. The newborns' reactions were judged by the rate at which they sucked on a special pacifier that controlled which image was projected on the video screen; by sucking faster, the baby could keep the current picture up on the screen. Nearly every baby tested this way increased his sucking to sustain the image of his own mother's face. Some babies even showed a preference for their own father's face over that of a male stranger, provided, of course, that they had had a reasonable amount of contact with it beforehand.

Newborns are strongly attracted to faces, whether real or merely schematic. Faces satisfy many requirements of their limited acuity; the bright eyes and dark mouth provide a lot of contrast, while the hairline provides a distinctive external frame to stimulate the baby's peripheral vision. But in addition to these features, newborns seem to have an innate attraction to facelike stimuli—any oval shape with two eyes, a nose, and a mouth in the right places. Babies less than an hour old will rotate their head and eyes farther to follow a simple drawing of a face than to follow a similar drawing in which the features have been scrambled. This preference makes sense from an evolutionary point of view, because it means that newborns like Ginna are predisposed to orient toward their parents, enhancing their bonding.

Adult studies have suggested that a special area in the lower temporal lobe is responsible for face recognition; lesions to this area can selectively destroy a person's ability to identify even the most familiar faces. But this cortical center is too immature to be responsible for face recognition in newborns. Rather, a baby's initial ability to recognize faces appears to be a function of subcortical visual areas. Newborns are especially attracted to faces that are slowly moving, as opposed to stationary, a fact that implicates the superior colliculus as the site where early face recognition takes place.

Beginning around two months of age, the cerebral cortex starts taking over the function of face recognition. At this point, babies can begin using the internal features of faces—the unique nose, mouth, and eyes of a particular individual—to discriminate among different faces. They also become much better at recognizing stationary faces. At least part of this improvement can be explained by rapid advances in other basic visual skills, like acuity, binocularity, and color vision. But it may also be that two months marks the age at which specific face recognition areas in the temporal lobe are beginning to function. Indeed, recent brain-scanning experiments have shown that the temporal cortex becomes electrically active when two-month infants are shown faces to look at.

The switch from subcortical to cortical processing produces a strange effect in babies caught just in the middle, at around one month of age; they actually appear to lose their preference for facelike stimuli. At this point, the subcortical process is waning while the cortical one has yet to take off, and babies react similarly to both normal and scrambled-up face drawings. (This neural limbo is similar to what produces "obligatory looking" at the same age.) Still, despite their waning interest in generic faces, one-month-old babies prefer their own mother's face over that of a stranger.

Sex Differences in Visual Development

Like most mental development, vision progresses at different rates for boys and girls. The difference is not obvious in newborns and is virtually gone by six months of age, but between three and six months—right when the visual cortex is undergoing its most rapid surge of synaptic development—girls lead boys in several visual skills. Thus, girls show the first signs of binocularity three or four weeks earlier than boys, and their hyperacuity is also significantly better between the ages of four and six months. There is some evidence that these differences are due to the testosterone surge that boy babies experience between early gestation and the first few months after birth. Testosterone may slow some aspect of cortical-synapse formation or pruning, both of which are at their most intense during early postnatal development.

Another sex difference emerges much later, between about seven and ten years of age. Beginning at this time, and persisting into adulthood, males tend to perform better on tests of visual-spatial skills, such as mentally rotating an object in space, while females perform better on tasks involving perception of the entire visual field, such as remembering the location of items in a large array. There may therefore be sex differences at the highest levels of visual processing that emerge only late in childhood. Whether these differences are purely biological—that is, due to genes or hormones—or are the result of the different skills boys and girls tend to practice as children is a matter of great controversy, but since they really have to do more with cognition than with vision, they are considered further in Chapter 16.

When Something Goes Wrong

Like most babies, Ginna's vision is developing normally. Now six months of age, her acuity is markedly sharper; she can see colors well; she has stereo vision and can focus her eyes well at various distances; she can discriminate faces and can clearly tell the difference between familiar and unfamiliar ones; her eyes can smoothly follow moving objects and even anticipate their position on a millisecond-by-millisecond basis. In short, she's become a true visionary, because of all the remarkable ways in which her eyes and cerebral cortex have matured over the few short months of her life.

Her cousin Jason is not so fortunate. At about six weeks of age, his eyes began to cross; the left eye developed a tendency to drift in toward his nose. Although he is eight months older than Ginna, he has no binocular vision, and the acuity in his left eye is very poor. His parents noticed the crossing early on but only recently sought treatment from a pediatric ophthalmologist. Luckily, it is still early enough for him to recover much of the acuity in his left eye, but his prospects for stereo vision are virtually nil.

Visual problems are unfortunately rather common in children. Up to five percent of infants are born with, or will develop, some kind of visual abnormality in the first few years of life. Because of the critical way in which visual experience shapes the visual cortex, anything that interferes with an infant's vision can potentially miswire it, permanently compromising a child's visual abilities. Fortunately, all aspects of vision are not equally vulnerable to experience. Color and peripheral vision, for instance, are both relatively immune. As we've seen, however, fine acuity and binocularity are both quite sensitive to early experience, because both are dominantly controlled by the cerebral cortex.

The age at which a problem appears also has a lot to do with whether it will affect the development of a child's vision. Since binocularity emerges so rapidly and so early, it is most vulnerable in very young babies, and its critical period begins shortly after birth. Babies whose eyes are misaligned (who have crossed or "walled" eyes, or eyes that deviate in the vertical direction), or whose vision is obscured, will fail to develop binocularity if the problem persists past six to eight months of age. Acuity develops more gradually than binocularity, so babies can tolerate longer periods of abnormal vision without this affecting it. Its critical period begins at about four months, peaks between nine and eleven months, and is largely over by two years of age. Even after they are established, however, binocularity and acuity remain somewhat vulnerable as long as synaptic refinement ensues, up to about eight years of age.

Just about any problem that obscures vision or interferes with the normal coordination of the two eyes can affect a child's visual development. The greater the degree of visual deprivation, and the longer it lasts, the greater will be a child's permanent visual deficits. Fortunately, certain problems, like *myopia* (nearsightedness) and *astigmatism* (blurred vision due to uneven curvature of the eye) do not often affect visual development, because young babies tend to grow out of them before they can cause any harm.* Two other problems do pose a more serious threat, however. The first of these, cataracts, are not very common, but when they occur in infants, they can cause serious deficits, including blindness. The second problem is crossed or lazy eyes—any disorder in which the two eyes look in different directions. The medical term for misaligned eyes is *strabismus,* and while it poses a less serious threat to visual development than cataracts, it is unfortunately much more common.

Congenital Cataract   A cataract is any kind of clouding of the lens of the eye. Cataracts are fairly common in older people, but once they have been removed and replaced with an artificial lens, they do not damage an adult's vision. The situation is entirely different for babies. When significant clouding appears in the lens of a young baby—a condition known as *congenital cataract*—it can have a permanent and devastating effect on the child's vision. Without treatment, a child will lose part or all of the vision in the affected eye, depending on how much of the lens is clouded.

Congenital cataracts have many different causes. About one-third are due to prenatal infections (toxoplasmosis, chicken pox, and especially rubella), another one-quarter reflect a hereditary tendency, 10 percent are associated with certain metabolic disorders and other congenital diseases, and about one-third of cases are of unknown origin. Although rare (between one and four out of ten thousand live births), congenital cataracts are the most common cause of childhood blindness in industrialized nations. Fortunately, they can be detected relatively easily using the *red reflex* test performed by pediatricians at birth and at all well-baby checkups during the first year.

More than any other evidence, the profound effect of congenital cataracts on vision illustrates the long-lasting influence of experience on a

---

*Myopia and astigmatism do frequently crop up in older children, however, and require corrective lenses, or their school performance may suffer.

baby's brain development. Because the cataract blocks the baby's ability to see any kind of form, the visual cortex fails to receive the kind of electrical activity it needs to refine the circuitry underlying fine detail and binocular perception. But like the kittens in Hubel and Wiesel's experiments, a baby's prospects for good vision are actually better if he has cataracts in both eyes, as opposed to just one, because there is no stronger eye to outcompete the affected one for access to cortical circuitry.

Most children have the cataract removed at some point, but the timing is truly critical. If it is removed after six months of age, the baby's chances of achieving reasonable visual acuity are slim, although there is a little more leeway with bilateral cataracts. Pediatric ophthalmologists now remove congenital cataracts as early as possible, often within days of birth and preferably within the first two months.

Removing the cataract actually means removing the lens of the eye, so after surgery the baby must be fitted with a corrective lens, usually a soft contact lens, so that he can begin to focus. (It is now also possible to implant artificial lenses, but not until after the age of two.) If the cataract occurs in only one eye, it is also very important to follow up the surgery with eye patching. The healthy eye is covered for about half of the baby's waking hours, so that the weaker eye does not suffer from competition with it. Patching usually needs to be continued until eight or nine years of age, to avoid loss of visual acuity during the latter part of the critical period. With early surgery, prompt lens fitting, and diligent patching of the good eye, a child can end up with reasonably good acuity in the affected eye. If a baby has cataracts in both eyes, the prognosis is actually somewhat better and no patching is necessary. Even so, children with congenital cataracts rarely achieve any kind of useful binocular vision.

Strabismus   *Strabismus* refers to any condition in which the two eyes are improperly aligned. It is far more common than cataracts; about 2 percent of all full-term babies are afflicted with it, and as many as 10 to 20 percent of all premature infants. We really don't know what causes crossed or wandering eyes. It was once thought that they were due to weak eye muscles, but the problem is now thought to lie in the nervous system. We do know that strabismus can lead to very poor vision if it isn't corrected early. It almost always affects a child's binocular vision and can also degrade fine acuity.

The danger from strabismus is not in the eye, it's in the brain. In order for binocularity to develop, neurons in the visual cortex must receive input from both eyes in corresponding parts of the visual field—that is, both eyes must be focused in the same place. Obviously, when a baby is strabismic, his two eyes do not work together, so the cortical binocular neurons fail to wire up properly. Even after a child has developed binocularity (by five or six months of age), it can be degraded if strabismus emerges at any time during the critical period—up to eighteen months and, to a lesser degree, until eight years of age—because these binocular connections will fail to be adequately maintained.

While the loss of binocular vision is a concern with strabismus, an even greater problem is the loss of visual acuity. Because Jason's eyes are not well aligned, his brain receives simultaneous images from two different parts of the visual world. Anyone who has ever suffered from double vision knows how disconcerting this experience can be, so what our brains tend to do is to suppress the vision in one eye (even when it's open) and pay attention only to the input of the other eye. In the best scenario, a strabismic baby will alternately suppress the input from each eye; only one eye will be working at a time, but each will provide enough electrical activity to properly tune up its cortical acuity circuits. But if, as in Jason's case, one eye is stronger than the other, then the weaker, suppressed eye will fail to provide enough electrical activity to its cortical circuits, and its acuity will be degraded. Because the problem occurs in the cortex, as opposed to the eye, this kind of blurred vision cannot be corrected simply by wearing glasses or contact lenses.

Strabismus is not apparent right at birth. In fact, the eyes of most newborns tend to diverge slightly. If a baby has strabismus, it often shows up between two and four months, the age when normal babies' eyes tend to straighten out. Indeed, it may be the actual experience of seeing a fused binocular image that helps bring the eyes into alignment. Occasionally, crossed eyes will resolve themselves before six months of age, but because even temporary strabismus can harm visual development, some researchers believe that babies with strongly misaligned eyes should be treated even earlier than this.

There are two different goals in treating strabismus: aligning the eyes, so that they can begin to work together, and strengthening the weaker eye, if this is the case, so that its acuity does not become degraded. Sometimes the eyes can be trained into alignment using eyeglasses or eyedrops, which temporarily paralyze the good eye, forcing the baby to use the weaker eye to focus. Most often, however, the only way to straighten them out is through surgery on the eye muscles, and it's not uncommon—about 30 percent of cases—for a child to undergo two operations before the eyes are adequately aligned. Again, the timing of treatment is of utmost importance. Alignment surgery is now routinely performed between six and eighteen months of age, and some ophthalmologists are attempting it even earlier.

The second aspect of treatment is equally important. To prevent a cross-eyed baby from losing acuity in the weaker eye, the stronger eye needs to be patched for several hours each day. With the stronger eye occluded, the weaker eye is no longer inhibited; it now takes over the job of moving and focusing, and its electrical input to the visual cortex is no longer suppressed. Patching should begin as early as possible after a baby is diagnosed with strabismus, and it often needs to be continued even after surgery. However, it is also important not to overdo patching, since the acuity of the good eye may then suffer, and the two eyes must have a chance to work together for several hours a day or binocular vision will not develop.

Ophthalmologists have made great strides in treating strabismus over the last thirty years or so, thanks to our understanding of early visual plasticity. Unfortunately, it is still rare for a strabismic baby to achieve perfect vision. Of the two potential losses, acuity has been easier to preserve than binocularity. With early alignment and conscientious patching, children can achieve excellent acuity in both eyes. But full stereo vision is rare, and most children continue to use only one eye for their most acute, or foveal, vision. The reason acuity fares better than binocularity probably has to do with the difference in their critical periods; because binocularity develops so early and so quickly, it leaves very little time to catch and treat misaligned eyes. Acuity, by contrast, improves more gradually, and so remains malleable for a longer period. In an attempt to improve the stereo vision of strabismic babies, some ophthalmologists are now advocating surgery as early as ten weeks of age. Preliminary results with babies operated on between thirteen and nineteen weeks look promising, but it is still too soon to know for certain whether full binocularity can be routinely preserved.

Fortunately, acuity is much more important for everyday visual tasks than binocularity. A person lacking stereo vision won't be able to fly an airplane or appreciate 3-D movies, but he will have no difficulty perceiving depth, driving a car, or hitting a tennis ball. Stereo vision is really a kind of perceptual luxury, one that many people function perfectly well without.

Visual Development and the Rest of the Brain

Our rich understanding of visual development has not only improved the visual prospects of babies with strabismus or crossed eyes, it has also taught us a great deal about the mechanisms of brain development in general. We now know how something as seemingly intangible as "experience" can permanently change the structure of the brain. If the same principles apply to every other area of the brain—and all evidence suggests that it does—then visual development serves as an invaluable guide for understanding every aspect of mental development, including such "higher" functions as emotion, language, and intelligence.

Then again, vision serves as more than a mere example for these more sophisticated aspects of development. It also critically influences them. Because vision develops so quickly and so dominates human sensory experience, it soon becomes the major means through which children learn about the people and properties of their world. We humans are extraordinarily visual creatures, so the types of visual experience and visual-motor activities a child engages in early in life are profoundly important in shaping his emerging mind.

Chapter 10

HOW HEARING EVOLVES

Young children love music. It constantly amazes me to see our two-year-old amuse herself for twenty minutes or more, just singing her little songs while flipping through a pile of books or rummaging around in her toy box. And it's not only toddlers who feel this way. From the moment of birth, babies find music highly appealing, which is why lullabies and nursery rhymes often work so well in calming a fussy newborn.

The reason music is so appealing is that a baby's sense of hearing is quite advanced in many ways. Like touch, smell, taste, and the vestibular senses, the neural structures underlying hearing form early in utero and begin functioning well before the end of gestation. By birth, babies already have about twelve weeks' worth of actual listening experience, and they have even become somewhat discriminating about what they like to hear. Mother's voice tops the chart, especially when she speaks in the higher-pitched, singsong style known as "motherese." In contrast to vision, where newborns show a distinct preference for simpler stimuli, their hearing preferences tilt toward the more complex, and music or highly intonated speech fills the bill better than pure tones or other simple sounds.

The development of hearing contrasts with vision in other ways as well. Whereas vision emerges late and matures quickly, hearing begins early but matures gradually. Human babies, in particular, hear much better at birth than most young mammals, but their auditory skills continue improving over a very long period, all the way up into school age. It may be no coincidence that hearing evolves gradually, in parallel with a child's eventual mastery of language.

One feature that hearing does share with vision is its ability to be modified by experience. The act of hearing itself influences the quality of auditory development, and all the listening children do, from the third trimester on, importantly shapes the way their brains become wired to process and understand different sounds. Nor is its influence limited to the development of the auditory system. Children's early experience with speech and music are tremendously important in shaping many higher aspects of brain function, including emotion, language, and other cognitive abilities.

How Hearing Works

"Airplane!" Timothy cries as he hears a loud roar overhead. Though only twenty months old now, he's fascinated by anything with an engine, and planes are the latest addition to his transportation vocabulary. How does Timmy's brain detect and then recognize the far-off sound of a jet engine?

Hearing begins in the ear, of course, and auditory information then passes through a number of brain-stem sites before making its way up to Timothy's auditory cortex. Together, all of these structures are known as the *auditory system*, whose job is to receive sound waves, translate them into electrical signals, and then discriminate these different signals according to all the sounds Timothy has grown familiar with thus far.

Sound waves are produced whenever a physically vibrating source, such as a violin string, a person's vocal cords, or a jet engine, creates an alternating pressure change in the surrounding medium (air or water). A sound wave is characterized by its amplitude—the height of its peaks—and its frequency—the number of times the wave crests per second. The amplitude of a sound wave corresponds to its loudness, and the frequency to its pitch. The human ear is sensitive to pressure waves ranging from about 20 to 20,000 vibrations per second, or Hz, lower numbers corresponding to deeper tones. Loudness, or sound pressure, is quantified in units of decibels, which is a logarithmic scale. Thus, a 20-decibel increase in loudness actually corresponds to a tenfold increase in sound intensity; 40 decibels corresponds to a hundredfold increase; and so on. The following is representative of the sound levels, in decibels, of various sources:

Decibels	Type of sound
0	Threshold for human hearing
20	Faint whisper
40	Average home
60	Normal conversation
80	Heavy traffic, ringing telephone
100	Subway train, power mower
120	Loud thunder
140	Jet plane 100 feet overhead (causes pain and damage)

The ear itself is divided into three sections: outer, middle, and inner. When sound waves strike Timothy's outer ear flap, or *pinna*, they are funneled into the ear canal until they strike the *eardrum*. Sound waves set up a vibration in this elastic membrane, which in turn makes the three bones in his middle ear oscillate. These bones—the *malleus, incus,* and *stapes* (Latin for hammer, anvil, and stirrup)—amplify the vibration and transmit it to the *oval window*, a second membrane that marks the border of Timmy's inner ear. Normally, both the outer and middle ears are filled with air, and the inner ear with fluid (except when Timmy had that ear infection last winter, and his middle ear was temporarily filled with fluid).

The auditory organ of the inner ear is known as the *cochlea*, and it is here that vibration is converted into electrical signals. Named for its striking resemblance to a snail's shell, the cochlea is a long, coiled tube that is divided into three lengthwise compartments. In the middle compartment sit hair cells very similar to those in the vestibular system (Chapter 6). Sound-induced vibrations bend the fine cilia that sit atop the hair cells, and these tiny movements (a mere billionth of an inch) stretch open ion pores in the cells' outer membrane. Charged sodium and potassium ions rush in through these briefly opened pores, changing the electrical potential of the hair cells. This depolarization, in turn, sets off a chain of synaptic excitation that transmits auditory information to the brain. (See Figure 10.1.)

This explains how the airplane sound is transformed into an electrical

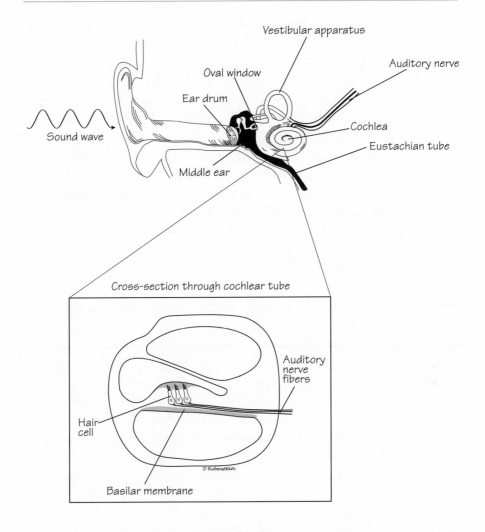

FIGURE 10.1

Structures of the ear. The inset shows the location of hair cells and primary auditory nerve fibers in the cochlea.

signal, but how does Timmy's brain distinguish this sound from every other one? Sound *discrimination* also begins in the cochlea and is attributable to some well-evolved properties of the *basilar membrane*, a long sheet of tissue on which the hair cells sit. The width and flexibility of the basilar membrane change continuously along the length of Timothy's cochlea. Near the oval window, the membrane is narrow and stiff, while at its far end, deep inside the coil, it is wide and very flexible. Just as the strings of a piano resonate at different frequencies based on their length and stiffness, so do various parts of his basilar membrane move, or resonate, better to different-frequency sound waves. High-pitched sounds deform the membrane at its narrow end, while low-pitched sounds, like the airplane, deform it at its wide end. Since it is the movement of the basilar membrane that actually causes hair cell cilia to bend, this gradient means that different sounds are translated into electrical excitement in different portions of the cochlea. To boost this frequency segregation, Timmy's hair cells also differ progressively along the length of his cochlea. Those nearest the oval window have shorter, stiffer cilia, which respond best to higher frequencies, while those at the far end have long, flexible cilia that are more responsive to low-frequency sounds.

The cochlea, then, discriminates different sounds by separating them in space, a transformation known as *tonotopy*. Similar tone maps are repeated at every step of auditory processing in the brain, including the cerebral cortex. It's as if our brains contained a whole string of piano keyboards, linked together so that striking one key played the same note at every relay station.

Here is how sound impulses make their way into Timothy's perception: The cochlear hair cells synapse onto primary auditory neurons—cells whose axons travel from the inner ear, through the auditory nerve, to reach the *cochlear nucleus* in the lower brain stem. Then, from the cochlear nucleus, some auditory fibers travel up to a higher brain-stem site, the *superior olive*, which plays an important role in localizing sounds in space. The next relay station is in the midbrain, an area called the *inferior colliculus*, which is located, as its name implies, just below the visual system's superior colliculus. The last stop before the cortex is the thalamus, in a region called the *medial geniculate nucleus*, or MGN (adjacent to the visual system's lateral geniculate nucleus). Finally, fibers from the MGN travel to the primary auditory region of the cerebral cortex, which is located on the upper ridge of the temporal lobe. Higher-order auditory areas surround this primary auditory cortex, but they are also all located within the upper part of the temporal lobe. (See Figure 10.2.)

Based on their names alone (*colliculus, geniculate*), it is evident that there are many parallels between the pathways of the auditory and visual systems. But auditory processing differs from visual processing in a couple of important ways. First, auditory information passes sequentially through all the brain-stem relay stations before it reaches the cortex, whereas the visual system is divided up into separate subcortical and cortical routes. This arrange-

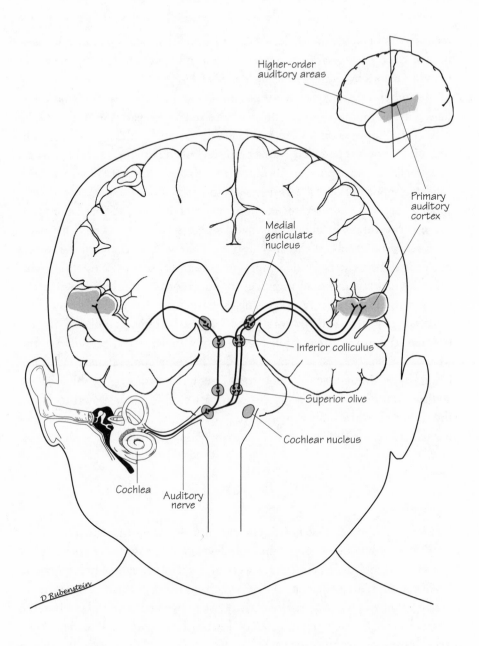

Higher-order
auditory areas

Primary
auditory
cortex

Medial
geniculate
nucleus

Inferior colliculus

Superior olive

Cochlear nucleus

Cochlea

Auditory
nerve

D Rubenstein

FIGURE 10.2

*Neural pathways of hearing. Auditory information is shuttled from
the cochlea through several relays in the brain stem, midbrain, and
thalamus, before reaching the cerebral cortex.*

ment comes in handy for tracking auditory development, as we'll see, because it is possible to measure the electrical transmission through these various relays in babies by using simple scalp electrodes.

Another difference between the auditory and visual systems is that information from the two ears does not remain strictly segregated, as it does in the case of the two eyes. From the moment it leaves the cochlear nucleus, auditory information is parceled out to both sides of the brain stem, where it can be compared or combined with input from the opposite ear. The first point at which input from both ears merges is in the superior olive. Based on very small differences in the timing or intensity of input from each ear, neurons in the superior olive are able to compute where sounds are located in space. Each relay station above the olive also processes sound information entering both ears. Thus, the brain does not segregate the two sides of the body with regard to hearing as it does in processing touch or visual information.

While much auditory processing is carried out by the brain stem and thalamus, it is not until auditory input reaches the temporal lobe of his cortex that Timothy consciously perceives it. By analogy to the visual system, where complex scenes are perceived first by their component elements—color, shape, motion, space—and then assembled into recognizable objects, auditory information is first processed for its pitch, loudness, and location, then interpreted by higher areas of the auditory cortex as a certain piece of music, or a spoken phrase, or a jet airplane flying overhead.

How the Auditory System Develops

Long before Anna had even a glimmer of his fascination with engines, Timothy's sense of hearing was beginning to develop. After just four weeks in her womb, two fireplug-shaped structures emerged on either side of his embryonic head: the primordial *otocysts*, out of which both his cochlea and vestibular organs would evolve (See Figure 6.2). Between five and ten weeks, while the vestibular canals were branching out of the top of the otocysts, his two cochlear tubes were elongated out of their bottoms, coiling as they grew. By eleven weeks, his cochleas had completed all of their turns and looked much like the snail shells they resemble in adults, although they continued to grow in girth until midgestation. Between ten and twenty weeks of development, all of his roughly 16,000 hair cells (in each cochlea) matured, sprouting their characteristic cilia and forming synapses with the first neurons in the auditory system.

Hair cells do not emerge simultaneously along the cochlea but in a gradient, beginning at the base and finishing at the apex, or coiled end. This gradient presents somewhat of a paradox because, as we'll see, fetuses can first hear only in the low-frequency range, the part of the sound spectrum that is normally sensed by hair cells at the apex. But the paradox is explained by the fact that individual hair cells actually change their frequency response during development. Cells near the base, which mature first, initially respond to lower frequencies, but as the properties of the basilar membrane change, these cells become sensitive to higher and higher tones, while hair cells farther out in the cochlea, which are just beginning to mature, take over the job of sensing low frequencies. Thus there is a gradual shift in the tonotopic map during development, with lower tones moving out to progressively more distant cochlear locations.

Well before the cochleas have fully formed, auditory neurons begin emerging in the embryonic brain stem. The earliest auditory neurons appear at just three weeks of development. By six weeks, the auditory nerve, the cochlear nuclei, and the superior olive are all clearly distinguishable. Higher brain-stem auditory centers are apparent by thirteen weeks, and the MGN begins to show its adultlike subdivisions at just seventeen weeks. Cortical neurons emerge somewhat later, but in general, the auditory cortex matures earlier than any other part of the cerebral cortex, with the exception of areas involved in touch perception. In all parts of the auditory system, synapses form shortly after growing axons reach their targets, but there is a prolonged period of synaptic refinement, during which the tonotopic maps become more sharply defined.

The pace of auditory development is perhaps best revealed by its pattern of myelination. Like other tracts in the brain stem, the first several projections in the auditory system start to myelinate quite early in development. By twenty-four weeks of gestation, all of the relays between Timothy's ear and the inferior colliculus had begun myelinating, and by birth, they were nearly fully insulated. By contrast, the higher relay tracts of the auditory system myelinate only gradually. Timothy's thalamic auditory fibers are still undergoing this process and won't be fully myelinated until he is at least two years old.

The Maturation of the Auditory System Can Be Tracked Electrically
Much of what we know about the development of the auditory system has come by directly measuring electrical activity in babies' brains, recordings known as *auditory evoked potentials*. Hearing is especially

amenable to this kind of study because of the way its information travels up sequentially through several brain-stem areas on its way to the cortex.

Anna has some history of deafness in her family, so she was very keen on having Timothy's hearing tested early on. When he was just five weeks old, his parents brought him in for auditory-evoked-potential testing, a simple, painless procedure. A small earphone was placed over his ear, and three scalp electrodes were taped to his head, one on the bump of skull behind each ear, and the third on the very top of his head. When a brief sound—a click—is played into the earphone, the electrodes record the flow of electrical activity through his brain stem. Each click produces a sequence of tiny electrical waves (about one-millionth of a volt in amplitude) that correspond to the transmission of action potentials at each relay point in his auditory system: the first wave represents activity in his auditory nerve, the second wave corresponds to the cochlear nucleus in his medulla, the third is the superior olive, and so on, with seven waves in total before activity even reaches his cerebral cortex. Fortunately, Timothy's hearing checked out fine in both ears; all seven waves were present and of the appropriate amplitude and speed, racing auditory information through his brain stem in a mere one-hundredth of a second. Anna and Steve were much relieved.

The same testing procedure has been used with preterm babies, as a way of estimating how hearing normally develops during the last trimester of gestation. During the period corresponding to the sixth month of pregnancy, babies' brains show very weak electrical responses to sound stimuli. Only loud clicks evoke any kind of activity, and the resulting waves are small and sluggish. But beginning around twenty-seven weeks, these responses grow dramatically in size and especially in speed, because of rapid increases in synaptic efficacy and the myelination of brain-stem auditory pathways.

Evoked potentials illustrate most clearly the low-to-high maturation of the auditory system. Thus wave I, which represents the transmission of impulses between the cochlea and the brain stem, reaches its full speed by just five weeks after birth, while wave V, which corresponds to the firing of neurons in the inferior colliculus, continues accelerating into the preschool years. Waves of activity can also be measured that correspond to auditory activity in the cerebral cortex, although they are usually not recorded in routine testing. Cortical potentials mature much more gradually than those in the brain stem, especially during the prenatal period, and are not fully mature until the *midteen* years.

What Can a Fetus Hear?

Just because preterm babies show electrical activity in response to sounds doesn't necessarily mean that unborn babies of the same age process sound information the same way, or that they have anything to listen to even if they can hear. For one thing, the fetus's ears are filled with fluid, which could impede the transmission of sound impulses. The mother's abdomen also presents something of a barrier, at least for sounds emanating from outside her body.

Researchers therefore set out to test whether fetuses can hear, using several different tactics. In some studies, they have observed fetal movements under ultrasound in response to sound stimuli played toward the mother's abdomen. Fetuses also have a tendency to blink in response to loud or unexpected sounds, much as you or I do, and this blinking response can be measured under ultrasound. Still other studies have used fetal heart rate as a measure of how the fetus is processing sound information.

Based on measures like these, fetuses as young as twenty-three weeks of development respond to sound stimuli. One such precocious fetus is Melanie, whose mother, Carrie, is enjoying watching ultrasounds of her daughter's development as the subject of a prenatal hearing study. Melanie suddenly jerks her head the first time a loud, low tone is played into Carrie's abdomen. Her response is not altogether surprising, given that her cochlea and lower brain-stem auditory areas are well formed by this stage. But not all five-month fetuses tested in this way respond to sounds, and Melanie responds only when they are played very loudly. She is also quite limited in the range of frequencies to which she responds; only mid- to low-pitched tones provoke any response. When the researchers play higher- or very low-pitched tones, she appears oblivious. As each prenatal week passes, however, Melanie requires less and less volume to hear the stimulus, and her frequency range also steadily expands.

Although most fetuses begin hearing by early in the sixth month of gestation, it's not until considerably later that they can actually discern the differences between sounds. To test their discriminative abilities, researchers presented third-trimester fetuses with two different sounds, both known to be within their range of hearing. First, they played one tone, a middle C, repeatedly over the mother's abdomen. Initially, most fetuses responded with vigorous head or arm movements, but gradually their responses to the tone waned, or habituated, until they barely moved to it at all. Then, the researchers switched the stimulus to a high C. Younger fetuses, studied when their mothers were in their twenty-seventh week of pregnancy, did not respond to the new tone, whereas older fetuses, at thirty-five weeks of pregnancy, moved with renewed vigor when the tone was switched, indicating that they could tell the two apart. Sound discrimination improves during the third trimester due to the progressive lengthening of the cochlear "keyboard"—the gradual shifting in hair cells' frequency response, previously described.

Experiments like this prove that fetuses are capable of hearing in the womb, at least throughout the last trimester of gestation. Another issue, however, is figuring out what types of auditory stimuli actually make it into their watery world. To investigate this question, one group of researchers relied on the participation of some very cooperative women, who agreed to have sounds measured from inside the womb while they were undergoing the first stage of labor. After the women's water had broken, the researchers fed a tiny microphone up through the cervix and into the uterus, where it was used to measure how effectively sounds cross the abdominal wall and uterine tissues.

Generally speaking, sounds are transmitted remarkably well from the outside world. But not all of them penetrate a mother's abdomen with equal efficacy. Lower-frequency tones cross better than high tones, much as a bass beat penetrates apartment walls better than the higher, melodic notes from the music at a neighbor's party. Accordingly, the researchers also found that male voices from the outside world tend to penetrate the uterus better than female voices. One important exception is the mother's own voice, which is actually louder to the fetus's ears than to outside listeners, because it travels directly through her body to get there.

In fact, Melanie's auditory environment is largely dominated by the sounds of Carrie's own body: her heartbeat and blood flow, which provide a constant, low-frequency back beat, her occasional stomach gurglings, and of course her voice. At the same time, it is clear that Melanie is exposed to sounds from the outside world—her father's voice, the TV set, a passing train, a night at the opera. Every reasonably loud stimulus makes its way into Carrie's uterus and, beginning in the sixth month of pregnancy, begins introducing Melanie to her future auditory home.

So fetuses can not only hear, they have plenty to listen to in the womb, suggesting that auditory stimulation may actually begin influencing this aspect of brain development well before birth. It may be no coincidence that the first sounds Melanie is able to hear—those in the low-frequency range—are also those that best penetrate Carrie's abdominal wall. The auditory system seems to take advantage of whatever stimuli are present to begin stabilizing its synapses and fine-tuning its tonotopic maps.

Nor is the auditory system the only part of the brain to benefit from pre-natal hearing. Older fetuses can actually discriminate different speech sounds, like *ba* versus *bi*, or *ee* versus *ah*, suggesting that prenatal hearing actually begins shaping the development of language areas of the brain (see Chapter 14). Babies may even benefit emotionally from prenatal exposure to their mother's voice. As we will see, fetuses can not only hear before birth, they can also remember what they're listening to, and their ability to learn about familiar sounds in their environment may, like learning about familiar smells and tastes, help provide a comforting introduction to the world that awaits them at birth.

If any type of prenatal stimulation is going to make a difference to a baby's mental development, it is auditory input. Because hearing begins so early, and because sounds penetrate the womb so well, they are probably the best tool for stimulating a fetus's rapidly developing nervous system. Fortunately, you don't have to buy any kind of special "prenatal tapes" or other current gimmicks to reap the benefits of this precocious sense. Every fetus is naturally immersed in a rich auditory environment, much of which will remain familiar after birth.

Noise Damage in Fetal and Preterm Babies' Ears

There is one cau-tionary note about prenatal hearing. Now that we know fetuses can hear and that sounds reach them through the mother's body, some researchers have raised concerns about the dangers of excessive noise exposure during preg-nancy. Animal experiments have proved that loud noise can damage cochlear hair cells, leading to some degree of permanent hearing loss. The hair cells are especially vulnerable in infant animals just after the onset of hearing. For humans, the period of greatest sensitivity to noise damage begins at six months of gestation and extends through a few months after birth.

The danger of noise-induced hearing loss is thus greatest for premature babies. Not only do preterms lack the modest shielding of their mother's body during this critical period, but they are often housed in noisy incuba-tors (60 to 80 decibels) and subjected to the many alarms and other loud sounds of a neonatal intensive-care unit. Hearing loss is especially prevalent among children born preterm, and while many other factors are involved (see page 252), it is generally agreed that reducing noise exposure in neona-tal intensive-care units should improve their auditory prospects.

But babies don't have to be outside the womb to be affected by excessive noise. There is some evidence that fetuses exposed to high levels of noise within the womb suffer a higher-than-normal rate of permanent hearing loss. One study, for instance, tested the hearing of six-to-ten-year-old children whose mothers had worked in noisy occupations during pregnancy (such as textile workers) and found that the higher their prenatal noise exposure, the greater their chance of hearing loss.

Findings like this have raised questions about the safety of the *fetal acoustic stimulation* test, which is used by obstetricians to assess fetal well-being late in pregnancy. In this "nonstress" test, an auditory stimulus is projected into the mother's abdomen, and fetal heart rate and movements are recorded as a way of determining whether the fetus is healthy and responsive. Although the sound is brief, typically no longer than five seconds, it is often very loud (91 to 129 decibels). It is not yet known whether children tested this way in utero suffer any long-lasting hearing deficits, but the sound level is within a range known to be potentially damaging to young ears.

Hopefully, our new awareness of the noise sensitivity of the young auditory system will lead to improved safety standards for premature babies and pregnant women in the near future. The American Academy of Pediatrics has recently recommended that incubator noise be kept below 45 decibels. Researchers further recommend that pregnant women not be exposed to occupational noise levels higher than 85 decibels.

Learning in the Womb

My friend Andrea swears that her third child, Edgar, learned Seitz's first violin concerto in the womb. His ten-year-old sister, Lucy, had been practicing this piece all summer, during Andrea's third trimester of pregnancy. Then, very shortly after Edgar was born, Andrea brought her sleepy newborn along to Lucy's violin lesson and was amazed at how he suddenly perked up when she began to play the piece. Was this just a coincidence, or did he actually recognize the concerto from his experience in the womb?

Observant parents have long suspected that their newborns were able to recognize familiar sounds heard repeatedly before birth, like a certain song, story, or distinctive voice. The fact that fetuses can hear so well certainly makes such learning plausible, but it also requires them to be able to discriminate different sounds and be able to remember them for rather long periods of time. As much as parents may have wanted to believe their unborn babies are capable of such feats, it wasn't until researchers did properly controlled experiments that we learned how truly impressive babies are in this regard.

One way researchers have tested prenatal auditory learning is by taking advantage of the potent sucking reflex of newborns. While still in the hospital, two-to-three-day-old babies were outfitted with a set of headphones and a special pacifier that measured the strength and frequency of their sucking. The babies were then allowed to hear two different recordings, one of their mother reading a passage from Dr. Seuss's *To Think That I Saw It on Mulberry Street*, and the other of another woman reading the same passage. The pacifier was rigged up so that the baby could actually control which voice was being played into the headphones by adjusting his or her rate of sucking.

The results of the experiment were clear. Nearly all the babies adjusted their sucking rate so that they could spend more time listening to their own mothers and less to the strange woman. Thus, newborns can not only distinguish different women's voices, they already prefer their own mother's. But does this learning really take place in the womb? It is possible that these babies had learned to recognize their mother's voice in the few days after birth, just as they learned to visually recognize her face during the first twenty-four hours (Chapter 9). Brand-new babies may simply be ripe for absorbing as much information as possible about their mothers, in much the same way that baby ducklings instantly imprint on the figure of their mother after hatching.

Another experiment, however, proves that babies really do imprint on auditory experiences while still in the womb. In this case, mothers were asked to read a particular story aloud, twice a day, during the last six weeks of pregnancy. The story was by Dr. Seuss again, this time *The Cat in the Hat*, and it was estimated that the babies spent a total of about five hours listening to it in the womb. Shortly after birth, they were tested to see whether they preferred listening to their mothers read this story or another one, *The King, the Mice, and the Cheese*. These newborns sucked more to hear *The Cat in the Hat*, showing that they both remembered and preferred a story they'd heard only in the womb. Still another study showed that newborns prefer the sound of their mother's voice as it is actually heard in the womb—in the same muffled, deeper tones produced by the sound traversing her body (which researchers were able to mimic by filtering out frequencies above 500 Hz)—to the way it sounds outside the womb.

So fetuses not only begin hearing well before birth, what they hear in the womb has a surprisingly large impact on them. In addition to their mother's voice, newborns recognize and prefer several other kinds of sounds from before birth. One of their favorites is her heartbeat, a steady, comforting companion that they hear from the onset of hearing to the moment of birth. Newborns are known to be calmed by the sound of a maternal heartbeat, and one study even found that repeatedly playing the recording of a mother's heartbeat into the incubators of preterm babies improved their mental development as measured at two years of age.

If babies can remember *The Cat in the Hat* after several repetitions in utero, it is easy to imagine other familiar sounds they develop a liking for— a lullaby sung every night to an older child, a currently popular song on the radio, or (as in the case of my second baby) the fan inside a desktop computer. One British researcher found that newborns whose mothers watched a particular soap opera during pregnancy stopped crying when they heard the show's theme song, whereas babies whose mothers hadn't watched the program showed no reaction to the song. Newborns apparently have a keen memory for their prenatal auditory experiences, and hearing those familiar sounds is yet another way of smoothing their transition to postnatal life.

Unfortunately, one stimulus that doesn't appear to register prenatally is Daddy's voice. When tested, newborns have not been found to be capable of recognizing their own father's voice better than that of a strange male. This result is surprising, because as we have already seen, lower tones penetrate the womb better than high ones. It may be that fetuses can't learn their father's voice because it is masked by all of the other loud, low-frequency tones coming from the mother's own body—her heartbeat, blood flow, and stomach rumblings. This masking, together with newborns' strong familiarity with their mother's voice, means that they generally prefer female over male voices, even a strange woman's voice over that of the father.

But fathers need not despair. Within a few weeks of birth, the baby will know and prefer his voice to that of other men. It is also quite possible that if a father made a special effort to speak loudly to his wife's stomach every day over the last month or two of pregnancy, his child would know his voice from the moment of birth. The experiment simply hasn't been done yet.

What Newborns Can Hear

Birth obviously brings about major changes in a baby's auditory environment. Gone are Carrie's comforting heartbeat and gurgling stomach, but sounds from the outside world take on a new clarity for newborn Melanie, without the filtering effect of her mother's belly and the fluid in her middle and outer ear. Because her vision is still so poor, hearing provides Melanie with her first access to the world outside her immediate reach.

But hearing is far from mature at birth. Newborns' greatest limitation is their insensitivity to quiet sounds. Their hearing threshold is some 40 to 50 decibels higher than that of adults, meaning that Melanie is basically deaf to quiet music and conversation and notices only sounds that an adult would consider rather loud. Fortunately, many parents seem to be intuitively aware of this immaturity; Carrie, for instance, tends to speak more loudly and very close to Melanie's face when she is really trying to communicate with her.

Newborns are also limited in the range of tones they can perceive. As in the womb, they hear and discriminate low frequencies better than high ones. Luckily, human speech is a broad-band stimulus, meaning each of its components contains a mixture of many frequencies, and young babies are far better at discriminating broad-band stimuli than pure tones. So despite her limited frequency sensitivity, Melanie is not restricted in her ability to detect the different components of speech.

In fact, newborns are surprisingly astute when it comes to recognizing language. Not only can Melanie identify familiar voices, but even on the first day of life, she has a subtle way of moving her body in synchrony with the rhythm of an adult's speech, which she doesn't do in response to other rhythmic stimuli. Obviously, she can't yet distinguish individual words, but she is quite sensitive to the overall melody or intonation of spoken language. It is these differences in "prosody" that newborns primarily use to distinguish different voices.

Very young babies can even use prosody to distinguish different spoken languages. In one study, four-day-old French babies sucked more to hear French, as opposed to Russian phrases spoken by the same bilingual woman. When the researchers then filtered the recordings in such a way that individual words were no longer detectable (producing an effect not unlike listening to speech under water), the babies still showed a preference for their native tongue, showing that it is really prosody differences that they are detecting.

One other special skill of newborns is sound localization. Under the right conditions (in a dimmed room, and when lying in a semihorizontal position), Melanie is quite precise at turning her head or eyes in the direction of a loud sound, like a noisy rattle. This works much better for sounds coming from either side than from above or below her head. It also requires that the sound persist for several seconds, because young babies process and react very slowly to auditory stimuli. The ability to localize the source of sounds evolved early among vertebrate species and has obvious survival value (as in detecting predators), but it is most useful for human infants in helping them locate their caregiver and better attend to what she is saying.

How Hearing Improves

While certain aspects of hearing are well advanced in newborns, others are far from mature. Children's hearing grows steadily more acute as first the brain stem, then cortical structures involved in hearing progressively myelinate and complete their synaptic refinement. The following five sections detail several important ways in which children's hearing improves during infancy and early childhood.

Frequency Sensitivity   The first feature of hearing to mature is frequency sensitivity. Although newborns are poor at perceiving high-pitched sounds, this changes rapidly after three months of age. By six months, they actually perceive high frequencies better than low ones, and their ability to distinguish the full range of frequencies is almost fully developed. The same maturation can be seen in babies' auditory evoked potentials; while electrical responses to low tones reach their full capacity during the newborn period, the responses to higher tones continue accelerating until midway through the first year. This improvement results from a shifting in the frequency response of neurons in higher areas of the brain stem and auditory cortex. (It is not caused by any change in the cochlea, which reaches its full adult form before birth.)

Sound Localization   Another ability that improves considerably over the first six months is sound localization. While newborns are reasonably adept at identifying the location of a sound in the horizontal plane, it is not until they are four or five months of age that they can figure out its vertical location. Babies also grow steadily faster and more precise at locating sounds during the first six months. Sound localization then continues to improve, although at a more gradual pace, until the child is about seven years old.

One trick our brains use to figure out the location of a sound is to compare the time it takes to reach each ear. For example, sound waves emanating from a wind chime located to your right will reach your right ear a few milliseconds earlier than they reach your left ear, and the brain uses this small timing difference to compute exactly how far to your right the chime is located. Researchers have capitalized on this timing difference to test sound localization, using a special experimental trick known as the *precedence effect*: by playing the same sound, slightly separated in time, out of two loudspeakers located on either side of a subject, they produce the illusion that it is located to the left or the right. When older children or adults hear such a sound sequence—with, say, the right speaker preceding the left by several milliseconds—they perceive the sound as coming from the right. Newborns, however, fail miserably at the precedence effect. They are unable to use timing differences to calculate the location of a sound until about three or four months of age, when the cerebral cortex becomes fully engaged in the process. (But newborns can detect differences in *loudness* between the two ears, which is the cue they use to localize sounds in the horizontal plane.)

Interestingly, young babies go through a brief period, at around six weeks of age, in which their ability to locate sounds actually deteriorates before it improves. This regression is reminiscent of a similar decline in certain visual skills, like face recognition, at about the same age (Chapter 9). As in the visual system, the auditory system passes through a phase of neural limbo, when sound localization has left the brain stem but is not yet fully developed in the cortex. Once this shift is complete, however, it likely represents a big conceptual leap for babies. Whereas newborns more or less reflexively turn their heads in the direction of a sound, older infants seem to actually understand its spatial location.

Like so many other aspects of cortical functioning, boys and girls show a small sex difference in their ability to localize sounds, judging by their performance on the precedence effect. Between three and five months, girls lead boys slightly in the age at which they first respond to a timing difference between two speakers. As in the visual cortex, testosterone may slightly delay the synaptic refinement and/or myelination of neurons in the auditory cortex.

Threshold   Compared with these other features of hearing, babies' overall hearing sensitivity matures at a rather leisurely pace. As we have seen, newborns are virtually deaf to quiet sounds, and although their sensitivity does improve dramatically during the first few months of life, babies remain somewhat hard-of-hearing at six months, when their auditory threshold is still some 20 to 25 decibels higher than adults. Thereafter, it gradually improves until puberty. Thus, toddlers and preschool-aged children still have hearing thresholds about 10 decibels higher than adults, but teenagers' hearing is actually *more* sensitive than adults' (at least, until the loud music begins to take its toll!).

Hearing sensitivity is very much a function of the frequency of the sounds being tested. While adults have roughly similar thresholds across most of the frequency spectrum, children are much more sensitive to high-pitched sounds, like a whistling teakettle. This is somewhat the reverse of newborns, whose high-frequency hearing has yet to develop at all. But once babies' high-frequency hearing kicks in—between three and six months—it matures much more quickly than their low-frequency hearing. In fact, by seven years of age, children hear the highest tones better than adults. Sadly, they lose this special sensitivity beginning around ten years of age, as hair cells at the base of the cochlea—which respond to high-frequency sounds and are more sensitive to damage than those further along in the coil—begin succumbing to noise and other forms of environmental damage.

Temporal Resolution   Children also gradually improve in their ability to discriminate sounds in time. For instance, while adults can distinguish sounds that differ by as little as one-hundredth of a second in duration, six-month infants require differences twice as long, and six-year-olds fall roughly in the middle. Similarly, children's ability to discriminate closely spaced sounds improves between the ages of three years and puberty. Although we don't yet have any direct evidence for how this works, it seems likely that the gradual acceleration of auditory processing is due to the very protracted myelination and synaptic refinement of the auditory cortex.

Discriminating Sounds in a Noisy Background   One last auditory skill that remains rather poor in infants and young children is their ability to discriminate sounds in a noisy setting. Researchers use the term *masking* to describe the way in which background sounds obscure speech or other sounds of interest if they contain similar frequencies. Infants perform more poorly on masking tests than adults, and while they improve a good deal during the first two years of life, children's ability to distinguish signal from background noise does not fully mature until about the age of ten.

Under normal circumstances, masking doesn't present much of a problem because parents instinctively talk louder to compensate for children's lower hearing sensitivity. Unfortunately, though, the modern world offers plenty of opportunities to overwhelm a child's auditory environment: traffic, television, radio, and electronic toys are all potential sources of excessive background noise that may interfere with the ability to pick up on important auditory cues. Particularly while they are learning the subtleties of speech, young children are much better off listening to one thing at a time than having to sort through a constant cacophony.

Speaking in "Motherese"

I once had a coworker, a fortysomething bachelor scientist, who swore, when I first brought Julia into the lab, that he would never resort to "that stupid baby talk that everyone uses around infants." Well, smart though he is, Rick was dead wrong about this one. Babies really do prefer "motherese," the slower, higher-pitched, and highly intonated way of speaking that caregivers tend to use when talking to infants and small children.

It just so happens that motherese is in many ways ideally suited to stimulate young babies' sense of hearing. Its unhurried cadence is easier for babies to follow, since as we've seen, their nervous systems process auditory information at least twice as slowly as adults. Its louder, more direct style helps babies distinguish it from background sounds and overcomes the fact that their hearing is much less sensitive than adults'. Its simpler words and highly intonated structure—with wide swings in pitch and loudness that enhance the contrast between sequential syllables—make it much easier for babies to distinguish individual parts of speech. And finally, its high pitch corresponds to babies' most sensitive frequency range from the age of about three months onward. In many ways, then, motherese is an optimal auditory stimulus for babies, especially after the immediate newborn period, and it is particularly good for them as they begin to acquire the basics of their native language.

Mothers are not the only ones who speak in "motherese." Fathers, older siblings, and others also tend to talk to infants and small children in this special "baby talk" that my colleague found so objectionable. The same speech pattern has also been observed among infant caregivers across many different cultures. It's hard to say whether we use this speech purely instinctively or because we learned it when we ourselves were children. But whatever the reason parents begin speaking to their babies in motherese, the reason they continue to do so is because the babies respond better to it than to normal speech. For instance, four-month-old babies given a choice between listening to recordings of a strange woman speaking in motherese or in regular adult speech preferred the former, judging by the number of times they turned their heads to activate each recording. The earliest that babies have been shown to be capable of recognizing motherese is about five weeks of age, when they will suck more to hear recordings of their mothers speaking in a highly inflected voice than in a flat monotone.

The preference for motherese probably begins forming in the womb, where the intonation and pitch of the mother's voice are transmitted more faithfully than her specific speech sounds. The preference is then soundly reinforced after birth, since this mode of speech is inevitably accompanied by lots of affection and attention. Given the emotional reinforcement and the auditory features that make it so optimally stimulating to their hearing, motherese is one of the most potent forms of stimulation a young baby receives.

Plasticity and Critical Periods in Auditory Development

Motherese seems to have worked well on little Timothy, now just past his second birthday. He's talking up a storm, and listening well enough to pick up fancy new words—*bagel, escalator, bobcat, ferry*—after a single hearing. All the improvements in his hearing abilities—in his sensitivity, frequency discrimination, sound localization, and speech perception—can be attributed to changes in the way his brain receives and processes sound information, that is, to the gradual improvements in his auditory wiring that make his neurons responsive to finer and finer features of sound. But to what extent is this maturation the inevitable outcome of genetic programming, and to what extent does it result from all of the rich auditory experience he has had in the two-plus years since his hearing first began in utero?

Obviously, Timothy's auditory system did not develop in a vacuum. Although the overall plan of auditory development is coded in the genome, all kinds of external influences affect how this program is carried out. We've already seen how one type of experience—loud noise exposure—can harm the developing inner ear. Later in this chapter, we will learn about other harmful influences—certain drugs, infections, and birth-related traumas—that can permanently damage the sense of hearing during various critical periods in its early development.

Once again, animal studies have provided our most detailed insight into how auditory experience shapes the development of hearing. As in the visual system, just about any manipulation that alters the amount or type of sound input that an animal experiences early in life permanently affects the structure of the auditory system. The most radical manipulation, removing one cochlea shortly after birth, has massive effects, reducing both the number and size of auditory neurons in the brain stem. Smaller but still substantial effects are seen if one or both ears are merely plugged in early life. Not surprisingly, animals raised in such ways show several permanent hearing deficits, such as an inability to discriminate different frequencies and inaccuracy at localizing sounds in space.

One pair of researchers has taken another approach to studying auditory plasticity. Rather than depriving animals of auditory input, they reared them in a highly defined auditory environment. By analogy to the kittens reared in the presence of a single type of visual stimulus (vertical stripes, see page 209), young mice were reared in the presence of a single, constant auditory stimulus—a broad-band clicking sound. After a couple of weeks' exposure to this monotonous input, the mice become rewired in a very specific way. Instead of responding to sounds of a specific frequency, as most mature auditory neurons do, the neurons in these mice remained broadly tuned to respond to a wide range of frequencies—the same broad-band frequencies the clicks provided—thus muddying these animals' ability to discriminate different tones.

If specific experiences can rewire the auditory system in such specific ways, it is not hard to imagine how every subtle aspect of a child's early auditory experience might bias hearing development. We do know, as described in Chapter 14, that a baby's early experience with language profoundly and permanently influences the range of speech sounds he will later be able to perceive and speak. Similarly, the variety of music or natural sounds to which Timothy has already been exposed may make the difference in whether he ends up with perfect pitch or an "ear" for bird calls.

Although auditory development is most plastic during prenatal life and infancy, it remains malleable throughout the preschool and early grade school years—that is, as long as its synaptic wiring is still being refined. By analogy to the visual system, simpler aspects of hearing—like frequency discrimination— pass out of their critical period before more complex features do. For instance, binaural interaction, which plays a critical role in the ability to detect sounds in a noisy background, is one of the later abilities to emerge in children and therefore remains plastic for a relatively long period of childhood.

Plasticity in the Auditory Cortex of Deaf Children   The most dramatic illustration of the auditory system's plasticity comes, ironically, from children who can't hear at all. Studies of the brains of people born deaf show that there is real biological truth to the idea that a disadvantage in one area can turn out to be an advantage in another. Although their auditory cortex is of little use when it comes to hearing, people born profoundly deaf actually use this area of their brains to process visual information. For instance, when a congenitally deaf subject is presented with a flash of light in her peripheral visual field, a surge of electrical activity appears over her auditory cortex. Hearing subjects show no such activity in this location. Like the kittens deprived of vision in one eye, whose other eye ends up conquering a greater share of cortical space, deaf children use their "extra" cortical space to hone their ability in another area; in this case, however, it is an entirely different sensory modality.

What probably happens is that midway through gestation, when thalamic axons are still scoping out the cerebral cortex, an occasional visual fiber "mistakenly" makes its way up to the auditory cortex. Normally, such fibers are outcompeted by auditory fibers, once the fetus begins to hear and electrical activity refines the neural connections between thalamus and cortex. In a deaf child, however, these visual fibers face no competition; their synapses are preserved and refined, to be put to good use once seeing begins. Indeed, congenitally deaf subjects perform better than hearing subjects on tests involving their peripheral vision, and these extra visual connections are probably responsible.

Hearing Impairment

The fact that auditory development is so plastic means that anything that interferes with a child's hearing can potentially perturb their future auditory skills. Moreover, because hearing is the normal route for language learning, early problems in this domain pose a serious threat to many other aspects of a child's development. Unable to understand others or to express their own thoughts, children with hearing deficits are often highly impulsive, physically aggressive, and emotionally demanding, and they tend to fall behind in various cognitive and academic skills.

Congenital hearing loss is the term used to describe any impairment that is caused either before or shortly after birth. About one in a thousand babies is born deaf, and up to 3 percent of all children have some milder form of permanent hearing impairment. Half of these cases are purely hereditary, meaning either that deafness runs in the family or that the baby has another genetic defect—such as Down syndrome—in which deafness is a common attribute. The remaining cases are more or less preventable, and their causes are described in the following three sections.

Prenatal Infections   As we saw in Chapter 3, deafness is one of the most common deficits that can result from certain prenatal infections. The most devastating culprits are rubella (German measles) and cytomegalovirus (CMV) infections in pregnant women. Toxoplasmosis, genital herpes, and syphilis have also been known to cause hearing loss in unborn babies.

The rubella virus attacks both inner and middle portions of the developing ear. Most fetuses infected with rubella during the first half of gestation are likely to be severely hearing-impaired, but the rate drops to about 20 percent for those infected during the second half of pregnancy. When prenatal rubella is the cause, deafness tends to be severe, although it may have a delayed onset. Fortunately, most American women of childbearing years today are already immune to rubella, thanks to childhood immunization.

CMV is a much more common cause of congenital deafness, both because fewer women are immune to it and because, even if a previous infection has subsided, the virus can become reactivated and be passed on to the fetus. Although such recurrences in pregnant women tend to be much less severe for the fetus than an initial infection, hearing deficits are still the most common outcome. All together about 12 percent of congenital deafness can be attributed to prenatal CMV infection. The best way for pregnant women to avoid infection is to practice careful hygiene, especially around young children, who are a major source of the virus's transmission.

Drugs and Chemicals   More than a hundred different drugs and chemicals are known to specifically damage the developing auditory system. These include various medicines (certain classes of antibiotics, anticonvulsants, diuretics, and antithyroid drugs), recreational drugs (nicotine and alcohol), and environmental toxins (mercury and lead). The developing auditory system is most vulnerable to such agents during the prenatal period, so extreme caution is warranted when administering certain drugs, particularly aminoglycosides (a class of antibiotics that includes streptomycin, kanamycin, and amikacin; see Chapter 6) and "loop diuretics" (such as furosemide, used to treat respiratory problems), to pregnant women or preterm babies.

Perinatal Factors   Because it continues to undergo rapid development during the first month or two after birth, the auditory system remains highly vulnerable for some time after the baby leaves the womb. Thus, the same infections and drugs that threaten a baby's hearing before birth continue to pose a problem after birth, though to a lesser degree. Another significant risk factor is birth asphyxia: babies who are severely deprived of oxygen during or shortly after birth (see Chapter 4) are at high risk for hearing impairment. Nearly 5 percent of all newborns suffer some degree of asphyxia, but only the most severe cases—those that develop other neurological disorders, such as mental retardation, epilepsy, motor deficits, or cerebral palsy—are likely to suffer hearing loss.

Two other neonatal conditions are also associated with hearing loss: jaundice and bacterial meningitis. *Jaundice* is a rather common newborn condition that is caused by elevated levels of a substance called *bilirubin*, a breakdown product of blood that can destroy nerve fibers when its concentration gets too high. Fortunately, neonatal jaundice is now highly treatable with light therapy, and few babies in developed countries suffer hearing loss from it anymore. *Bacterial meningitis*, however, is another matter. Somewhere between 5 and 27 percent of congenital deafness has been estimated to be attributable to this disease, an inflammation of the brain's membranes. The infection can damage virtually every site in the auditory system, from the inner ear all the way up to the auditory cortex. The problem is compounded by the need to treat the disease with antibiotics, often of the aminoglycoside class. When hearing loss does result from meningitis, it is usually in both ears and tends to be quite severe.

The last major risk factor for hearing loss is low birth weight, which usually results from premature delivery. It's hard to say precisely how many cases of deafness are attributable to early birth alone, because preterm babies are also more likely to be exposed to all the other factors that can compromise hearing: they are likelier to have suffered from infections in utero, to have elevated bilirubin levels, to develop infections or respiratory problems that require aminoglycoside or furosemide treatment, to experience severe asphyxia, and to be housed in noisy incubators. Each of these problems contributes to the fact that children born prematurely have a much higher rate of hearing impairment than children born at term, and the earlier their birth or the lower their birth weight, the higher their risk.

Screening for Hearing Loss

Emma seemed perfectly healthy at birth. It had been an easy delivery for her mother, Vicky, and their little girl was just beautiful, even for a newborn. Her Apgar score was good, and the pediatrician, after a thorough check of her basic anatomy and reflexes, pronounced her fit. She was an easy baby, too, fussing much less than had her three-year-old brother, Geoff, and smiling and cooing in all the ways that thoroughly enchant parents.

Because she was so good, it would be many months before Ben and Vicky learned that little Emma was almost totally deaf. Yes, Vicky noticed that she didn't respond much to recorded lullabies, as Geoff had, but she was just as easily soothed by swinging or rocking, and she did seem to pay a lot of attention when Vicky held her in her arms and talked or sang to her. So Ben and Vicky just chalked it up to another of the temperamental differences between their two children and didn't give it much thought in the first few months.

By one year, however, they began to grow worried. Unlike Geoff, who had been spitting out "mama" and "dada" by his first birthday, Emma seemed to be babbling less and less with each passing month. By twenty months, when she still didn't say a word, they were positive something was wrong, and finally they asked the pediatrician to have her hearing tested. Sure enough, she did prove to be completely deaf in her left ear, and to be capable of detecting only very loud sounds with her right. Careful testing showed that she had a *sensorineural* hearing loss—a defect in the auditory system itself— and not some kind of ear blockage that could be easily treated. None of the doctors could say with certainty why her auditory system had failed to develop normally, but now that the problem had been identified, it was time to get to work so Emma could get the language stimulation that is so important at her age.

It is not uncommon for deafness to go unnoticed in babies. More observant parents may notice that their baby doesn't react to loud sounds, like a slamming door or a crack of thunder. But in the typical case, deafness is not confirmed until a child is two and a half years old, a great deal of time to be deprived of adequate auditory stimulation. Since the most important function of hearing—perceiving language—begins even before birth, deaf children may go for as long as three years without any meaningful linguistic input, deprivation that can seriously affect their social interactions, emotional health, and intellectual advancement. Because of the critical role that hearing plays in so many aspects of development, it is vitally important to identify deafness as early as possible, so that children can either be treated (using hearing aids or cochlear implants) or else be introduced to sign language so that they don't fall behind.

In the ideal situation, all babies would be screened for hearing impairment by three months of age, as the U.S. National Institutes of Health has recommended. Although there are several practical ways in which this can be done, such universal screening remains an expensive proposition and is unlikely to be implemented in the near future.* A more cost-effective approach is to screen all babies who fall into one or more of the high-risk categories (familial deafness, head or facial deformity, birth asphyxia, infections, prematurity, or time spent in neonatal intensive care), and many states have now instituted programs to identify hearing impairment among such infants. Nonetheless, this approach will still miss about 50 percent of congenitally deaf children—babies like Emma—who may for several years be thought of as quiet, withdrawn, slow, or difficult, simply because they can't hear or respond appropriately to all the important signals that are being communicated to them. In the absence of universal screening, parents and pediatricians must be especially vigilant in searching for hearing problems at a young age, because the earlier they are detected, the lesser the chance a child's overall development will suffer.

Middle Ear Infections

Ear infections pose another potential threat to children's hearing and language development. Although not nearly as serious as congenital deafness, middle ear infection, or *otitis media (OM)*, is far more common. Eighty percent of all children will be diagnosed with at least one bout before the age of three, and the incidence of OM appears to have risen in the last ten or twenty years. Some of this increase is probably due to more vigilant monitoring by pediatricians, but some of it may also be real, fueled by the enroll-

---

*It has been argued, however, that universal screening for deafness would actually be cheaper than existing screening programs for other neonatal disorders, like phenylketonuria, when you divide the total cost by the number of children identified with such problems.

ment of more young children in group care or nursery school, as well as by the emergence of strains of bacteria that are resistant to current antibiotics.

Actually, ear infections themselves are not contagious. They are secondary infections that develop when the middle ear fills up with fluid that permits bacteria or viruses to grow. As we've seen, the middle ear is normally filled with air, and it is the purpose of the *eustachian tubes*, which extend from the middle ear to the back of the throat, to ensure that the bones of the middle ear remain ventilated to the outside world so that they can vibrate normally. But when a child has a cold, or is all stuffed up with allergies, the eustachian tubes may sometimes become blocked, filling the middle ear with fluid. This results in an acute infection, which can cause irritability, pain, and fever in babies and young children.

Unpleasant as these symptoms are, they are not the reason for the great concern about OM. The real worry has to do with what comes after the initial infection clears up. Often the fluid persists in the child's middle ear for several weeks, a condition known as *otitis media with effusion* or *secretory otitis media*. Although this condition is otherwise symptomless, the fluid can interfere with a child's hearing, raising the threshold in the affected ear(s) by somewhere between 10 and 40 decibels. While a loss of 10 decibels is not very significant, a loss of 40 decibels (in both ears) means that only very loud sounds or speech can be heard. Thus, children with middle ear effusion hover right around the point at which their hearing loss could be depriving them of important auditory input.

In about 60 percent of cases, the effusion clears up within four weeks after the initial infection, and the mild-to-moderate hearing loss following an occasional infection is transitory and of no concern. But for about 10 percent of OM sufferers, the effusion persists beyond three months, a long period for a young child to go with impaired hearing. Clinicians worry also about the 15 percent of young children who suffer from recurrent acute infections (more than three bouts in six months, or four in one year). Even if their ears clear up within a few weeks of each infection, these children may accumulate many months all together of hearing impairment.

The good news about chronic middle ear effusion is that it generally doesn't produce any long-term hearing deficits. That's because the age range in which OM is most common—between six months and three years—follows the most intense critical period for hearing development, and because the auditory deprivation produced by OM is relatively mild. However, there is some evidence that children with a history of OM have added difficulty detecting sounds in a noisy environment, an aspect of hearing that depends on binaural interactions and thus emerges somewhat later in development. They may also suffer some loss of hearing for very high frequencies.

Of greater concern is the effect of chronic OM on language acquisition. We've already seen that children who are severely hearing-impaired have tremendous difficulty learning language, a handicap that may also impair their cognitive and emotional development. The issue, then, is whether the more modest hearing loss experienced by OM-prone children during the first three years of life is enough to cause any long-term linguistic or intellectual deficits.

Since this issue was first raised more than forty years ago, an enormous number of studies have been carried out to try to resolve it. Unfortunately, we still don't know the answer. Although some studies have found poorer verbal skills and academic performance among children with a history of chronic OM, a similar number of equally rigorous studies have failed to find such relationships.

While far from conclusive, the data do permit a few tentative conclusions. One is that whatever effect chronic OM has on language development and school achievement, it is relatively minor. Children whose hearing is seriously impaired, particularly in the first three years of life, probably do suffer some delay in learning language and attaining academic skills. But the effects are most pronounced during the preschool years, when otitis-prone children are actually suffering a hearing loss. They generally do not persist into the grade-school years, when hearing has returned to normal.

The issue continues to be hotly debated nonetheless, because its resolution is fundamental to deciding how ear infections should be treated. It was probably an initial wave of reports in the 1970s linking chronic OM to language and academic deficits that led to the "epidemic," as some have called it, of toddlers having ventilation tubes installed in their eardrums. The purpose of these tubes is to drain fluid from the middle to the outer ear, and they do improve a child's hearing and reduce his risk of recurrent infections for the six to twelve months that they remain in place. By 1982 about a million children a year were having these tubes surgically implanted. Now that the developmental consequences of OM are less certain, however, their widespread use has begun to be severely criticized. Ventilation tubes are not without their risks: they are installed under general anesthesia and can cause such complications as infection, eardrum scarring, and persistent eardrum perforation. Moreover, in spite of the large number of toddlers who have had tubes inserted over the last two decades, no study has yet been able to demonstrate that this treatment significantly improves their language development or later school achievement.

In 1994, concern about this "epidemic" of overtreatment led the U.S. Agency for Health Care Policy and Research to establish a set of guidelines for managing chronic ear infections. This panel of pediatricians, family practitioners, and ear specialists has recommended that ventilation tubes be inserted only in cases in which a child has been documented to have fluid in both ears for three or more months and, more importantly, when the child has a demonstrated hearing deficiency in both ears, defined as the inability to detect sounds of 20 decibels. For children with milder hearing loss, or with hearing loss in only one ear, but whose effusion has lasted more than three months, the panel recommends either antibiotic treatment or no treatment at all. (The chances of the ears clearing up spontaneously are 65 percent within three months and 85 percent within six months, respectively.) Children with long-lasting effusion or with recurrent infections should be given at least one course of antibiotics before any decision is made about inserting tubes. And most importantly, the new guidelines emphasize that any decisions about how to treat chronic ear infections be based on actual measurements of hearing loss in both ears, rather than simply the duration of the effusion or the number of infections.

As for the occasional acute infection that nearly every child gets, current practice in the United States still recommends that they be treated with antibiotics. The drugs do prevent the kind of rare complications (like meningitis, or infection of the mastoid bone surrounding the ear) that used to make ear infections life-threatening. But while such treatment is inexpensive and relatively easy for parents to administer, it is not without its own controversy. Antibiotics actually only help one in seven children with acute OM; the vast majority of acute infections (81 percent) would clear up on their own, even without any treatment. Moreover, given the prevalence of these acute infections, such widespread antibiotic use has almost certainly contributed to the emergence of resistant bacterial strains, which are now responsible for a sizable fraction of all ear infections.

Finally, it's important to try to understand why certain children get frequent ear infections, so that we can begin to try to prevent the problem. Infants and toddlers are especially susceptible because their eustachian tubes are shorter, which permits bacteria from the mouth easier access to the ear. Their eustachian tubes are also more pliable, making them likelier to collapse and trap fluid in the middle ear. Highly susceptible children are probably those with less favorably shaped eustachian tubes, a tendency that appears to run in families. Chronic OM is also much more frequent among boys, who account for 60 to 70 percent of all sufferers; whether this reflects structural differences in their ears, hormonal differences, or perhaps slower maturation of their immune systems than girls', we don't yet know.

While there's no escaping a genetic tendency for ear infections, parents can take several steps to improve their children's odds. One is to breast-feed. Breast-fed babies are only half as likely to get multiple ear infections as bottle-fed babies, and their protection may last up to three years. The advantage appears to be related to some factor in the milk, rather than differences in feeding position or the way sucking develops in breast- versus bottle-fed babies. To be effective, breast-feeding should be the exclusive form of nutrition up to four months of age and the only source of milk for six months or longer.

Another risk factor is enrollment in group care. When babies and toddlers are exposed to many other children, they tend to catch more colds and other respiratory infections—the kind of illnesses that foster secondary middle ear infections. Several studies have shown higher rates of otitis media among children enrolled in group care at an early age. In one report, babies eighteen months and younger who attended day care were seven times likelier to have ventilation tubes implanted than babies cared for at home. Similarly, second or later-born children have more ear infections than firstborn or only children, because they tend to pick up more primary infections from their siblings.

One last risk factor is the presence of secondhand cigarette smoke. Children exposed to their parents' or babysitters' smoking suffer about 40 percent more ear infections than unexposed children. Secondhand smoke appears to reduce a child's resistance to colds and other infections that lead to middle ear infections.

While nearly every child seems destined to get at least one ear infection early in life, babies who experience their first infection before six months of age are much likelier to suffer from chronic OM. Such children may be inherently more susceptible, but it is also possible that such early infections leave a child more vulnerable to later recurrence. So anything parents can do to reduce their risk of infections during infancy—longer breast-feeding, stopping smoking, or postponing day care, if possible—may improve their child's chances of remaining otitis free.

Hearing, Language, and Emotion

Hearing is arguably a baby's most important sense. Through it, children experience language and music, both of which stimulate their intellectual and emotional development in ways that no other sense can. As we will see in Chapter 14, babies' brains are primed from before birth to attend to speech, and the simple act of hearing it, over and over during the first few years of life, is enough to refine the neural structures needed to both understand and produce all the intricacies of spoken language. Because language is the primary means we use to teach our children, hearing is probably the most important sense for their intellectual growth.

Hearing is also vital to emotional development. While touch, smell, and vision all play a role in establishing the bond between parent and child, only hearing permits them to fully communicate. Even newborns find comfort in a familiar voice or lullaby. Music is both a source of great pleasure and a particularly effective way of promoting children's cognitive development, as we'll see in Chapter 17, which is perhaps why they love it so.

Chapter 11

MOTOR MILESTONES

It always happens at the playground. You and your little butterball are minding your own business, filling up dump truck loads in the sandbox, when another mother and child show up and spoil the fun.

"What a cute little guy," she says, as her baby starts toddling off to the kiddie slide. "How old is he?"

"Fourteen months," you say, and then obligatorily ask, "How old is yours?"

"Actually, his first birthday is tomorrow. Isn't it amazing how much they change in a year?" she says.

"It sure is," you say, trying to sound enthusiastic, "but we're beginning to wonder if this kid is ever going to walk."

Of course, you know that sooner or later he will take those first steps, but it's hard, as a parent, not to be consumed by your baby's motor development. Motor milestones are the most obvious index of neurological progress in the first year of life, apparent even out on the playground. So it's virtually impossible to talk to another parent without tallying them up and feeling secretly elated or disappointed with your own baby's advancement.

Motor skills come in two forms, gross and fine, according to the types of muscles involved. Gross motor skills require the coordination of large muscles of the trunk and limbs, and they include both postural and locomotor (moving from place to place) activities. Fine motor skills use the smaller muscles of the arms and hand and basically involve manipulative activities. On the gross scale, babies begin with mastering control of the head and then progress to rolling over, sitting, crawling, standing, and finally walking, around the end of the first year. Fine motor skills begin with swatting movements by the whole arm then grow increasingly articulated as babies master first reaching and grasping an object with the whole hand, followed by grasping between the thumb and several fingers, followed by a true *pincer* grasp— holding an object between the thumb and forefinger—also around the end of the first year. Of course, new motor skills continue to emerge thereafter, and the speed and accuracy of all movements continue to increase throughout childhood. But considering the very helpless state from which babies begin, the motor progress they make in the first year is remarkable.

From a researcher's point of view, the most striking thing about motor development is its predictability. Virtually every baby, from virtually every culture, acquires the same fine and gross motor skills in the same consistent sequence. Different babies do vary, of course, in their rate of motor development, so that a more advanced child may lead a slower one by several months in the emergence of each basic skill. Nonetheless, on average, healthy babies of all cultures achieve the same motor milestones at just about the same time, such as reaching and sitting around the middle of the first year, and walking right near its end.

The charts below list babies' major motor milestones and the median age at which they are first mastered. This means that about half of all children achieve the milestone before the indicated period, while the other half achieve it some time later, so it's perfectly normal for any individual child to lead or lag the table by several weeks or months. For instance, it is considered normal for babies to begin successful reaching anywhere between two and seven months, to sit alone between five and nine months, and to walk well between nine and fifteen months.

The good news, if your baby happens to lag behind these medians, is that the rate of motor achievement in infancy has little relevance to a child's overall development. It cannot, for instance, reliably predict later IQ score or any other measure of cognitive performance. Just because a baby can't walk at fifteen months doesn't mean he won't be taking calculus in high school or even play starting forward on the basketball team. As long as he is within the nor-

Typical Month of Onset	Gross Motor Skill
1-2	Holds head erect and steady
2-3	Lifts head and chest with arm support on tummy
2-3	Sits with support
3-4	Rolls tummy to back
6-7	Rolls back to tummy
6-8	Sits alone
8-9	Pulls to stand
9	Crawls
9-10	Walks with handholds ("cruises")
11-12	Stands alone
12-13	Walks alone

Typical Month of Onset	Fine Motor Skill
birth	Reflexive grasp
1-3	Pre-reaching (ineffective)
3	Voluntary grasp
4-5	Successful reach and grasp
6-7	Controlled reach and grasp
9	Pincer grasp (thumb and forefinger)
10	Claps hands
12-14	Releases objects crudely
18	Controlled release

mal range for acquiring motor skills in infancy, there is no reason for concern about his later achievement.*

At the same time, motor skills are not completely unrelated to mental development. Particularly in infancy, before a child understands language, motor skills are a critical tool for learning about her social and physical environment. For instance, once a baby can successfully reach out and grasp an object, she can begin exploring physical properties such as shape, weight, and texture. Crawling allows her to actively seek out new encounters with people and things. Every motor milestone broadens a baby's experience and changes her perspective on the world, creating an ever-changing environment that is essential for emotional and cognitive growth.

Of course, motor development is also important in and of itself. Each new skill builds on previous abilities, as muscles grow progressively stronger and neural circuits more highly coordinated. Babies are obviously delighted as they succeed at new skills, so the progression of abilities contributes to their growing self-esteem and sense of independence.

What underlies this inevitable progression of motor skills? How does the brain produce movement, and how does it change, during infancy, to become capable of new tasks almost weekly? What role does practice play in motor development, and is it possible, or desirable, to further stimulate a baby's motor progress? These are the main issues covered in this chapter, which explores the basis of motor development in infancy.

How the Brain Produces Movement

Ethan's mother, Stephanie, has certainly heard it before, but not until she had a child of her own has she begun to appreciate how truly helpless babies are. She happens to be a physical therapist, and her newborn's almost total lack of muscular and bodily control is disturbingly reminiscent of some of her patients with spinal cord injuries. Unlike these patients, of course, Ethan is not paralyzed; he has feeling throughout his body and is capable of stretching

*It's important to point out, however, that the whole purpose of developmental charts is to identify babies with mental or motor deficits, so if a baby is *especially* slow at acquiring motor skills—that is, among the slowest 5 percent of all children—then he or she is considered at risk for lower cognitive achievement and may require special training to help compensate for the underlying neurological problem.

and contorting it in all sorts of ways. But for the most part, he is incapable of performing any kind of useful, voluntary movement. Why? What is it about motor development that takes so long to come together in human infants?

One reason motor maturation is so slow is because motor circuits are incredibly complex. In contrast to sensory systems, where information basically travels in one direction—from the outside world to the brain—motor circuits involve a lot of feedback: information cycling back and forth continuously between the brain and the world during the execution of even a single motion.

Consider, for example, the simple act of flexing your right biceps muscle. Since this is a voluntary movement, the command is initiated in your cerebral cortex—specifically, in the motor areas of the left frontal lobe. (Like sensory input, the nerves that transmit motor information cross over to the opposite side of the body as they travel from the brain to the spinal cord, so the left brain controls movement on the right side, and vice versa.) There are three motor areas in the cerebral cortex, all located in the back half of the frontal lobes: the *primary motor cortex,* the *supplemental motor area,* and the *premotor cortex.* (See Figure 11.1.) The primary motor cortex directly triggers voluntary movements, while the other two areas work at a higher level, planning and executing more complex sequences of movements.

The primary motor region lies along a vertical strip of tissue located just in front of the cortical strip that receives touch sensation. Like the somatosensory cortex, the motor cortex contains a distorted, upside-down map of the body: the lower end of the strip, located near the temples, controls muscles in the head and face; the upper end, located near the top of the head, controls the legs and feet; and the middle part of the strip controls the arms and hands. The map is distorted because body parts like the hands and face, which contain more muscles and carry out more highly articulated movements, need more processing space than areas like the trunk and legs, which have fewer muscles and engage in coarser movements.

When you decide to flex your biceps, neurons in the "arm" region of your left motor cortex send action potentials directly down to the spinal cord through an important pathway known as the *corticospinal tract.* (Some information is also transmitted through a parallel but indirect pathway, which synapses in the brain stem.) Down in the spinal cord, these corticospinal axons excite *motor neurons* that send their axons out through peripheral nerves to reach muscle fibers in the biceps. This electrical excitation, in turn, causes the biceps to contract. (See Figure 11.2.)

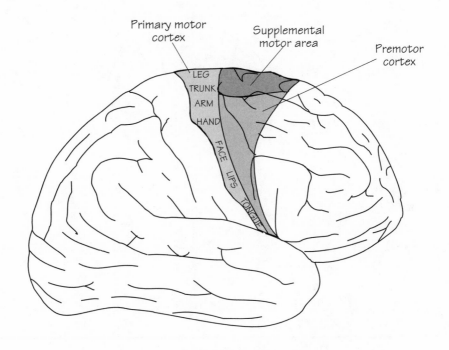

FIGURE 11.1

Major motor areas of the cerebral cortex and the body parts whose movements they control.

This sounds simple, but it is only the beginning. As the muscle begins to contract, it changes in both tension and length. These changes are detected by special sensory neurons, called *proprioceptors*, whose job is to inform the brain about any kind of muscular activity. Proprioceptive information feeds back to the spinal cord, where it influences the firing of the biceps motor neurons, and it also makes its way up to the cerebral cortex, where it gives you the conscious perception of arm position. Proprioceptive feedback thus enables you to sense your flexion and fine-tune its strength on a millisecond-by-millisecond basis.

While all of this is going on to control the biceps, exactly opposite effects are taking place in the antagonist muscle, the triceps. Its motor neurons decrease their firing, causing the muscle to relax, which reduces activation of triceps proprioceptors, which feeds back to the spinal cord and cortex,

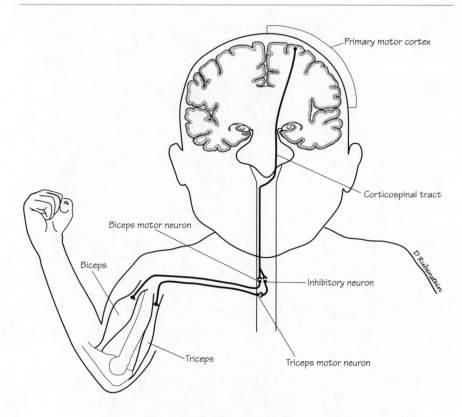

Primary motor cortex

Corticospinal tract

Biceps motor neuron

Biceps

Inhibitory neuron

Triceps

Triceps motor neuron

FIGURE 11.2

*Anatomy of a simple movement. Voluntary movements are initiated
in the motor cortex, which sends electrical signals down the
corticospinal tract to control the appropriate motor neurons,
whose cell bodies are located in the spinal cord. In this case, the cortex
both excites a biceps motor neuron and represses (through an
intermediary inhibitory neuron) a triceps motor neuron, causing
the biceps muscle to contract and the triceps to relax.*

and so on. Depending on how elaborately you're flexing, your nervous system is probably also coordinating all of this activity with similar circuits that control the muscles of the lower arm and hand. Finally, the sense of vision also plays a role, since you're undoubtedly watching your arm, and this visual information is routed to act upon the motor circuitry that coordinates each muscle contraction.

Thus, even a simple movement requires some fairly complex neural processing. Now consider a more elaborate task, such as walking, which involves dozens of muscles as well as postural adjustments throughout the body. The control of movement is clearly a very complicated job, and for the nervous system to accomplish it requires large, complex circuits of neurons that interact in a highly exact fashion.

To keep all of these movements coordinated and precisely timed, the brain relies on one structure in particular, the *cerebellum*. This wrinkled knob sits at the back of the brain, underneath the cerebral cortex and behind the brain stem. The cerebellum is effectively the air traffic control system of the nervous system. It is composed of an incredibly dense network of neurons; though only one-tenth the size of the whole brain, the cerebellum contains half of all its neurons. The cerebellum receives input from both the motor cortex—telling it what kind of movement is being attempted—and from various senses—vision, hearing, balance, and proprioception—telling it what kind of movement is actually taking place. By comparing all these inputs, the cerebellum is able to modify motor commands, while they are being transmitted, to better match the intended movement, and to make sure—much like air traffic controllers—that all of the body's movements are proceeding according to plan and without interfering with one another.

One other part of the brain plays a critical role in producing movements: the *basal ganglia*, which include several distinct clusters, or nuclei, of subcortical neurons. The basal ganglia are located deep inside the brain, under the lobes of the cerebral cortex, atop the brain stem, and adjacent to the thalamus, with which they are closely interconnected. Their role in movement is best revealed when they are damaged, as in Parkinson's or Huntington's diseases. People with basal ganglia disorders have great difficulty initiating voluntary movements; they are either incapable of actions like talking, walking, or shaking hands or very slow at them. But they are not paralyzed. In fact, they move a great deal; it's just that their gestures are largely involuntary—such as tremors, writhing, or flailing movements. The basal ganglia thus exert important control over which motor actions are carried out, suppressing involuntary types while allowing desired movements to proceed.

The elaborate feedback circuitry that links the motor cortex, basal ganglia, cerebellum, brain stem, and spinal cord is shown schematically in Figure 11.3. Given just how much neural hardware has to be up and running in order to carry out even simple voluntary movements, it is not surprising that babies are so strikingly uncoordinated, or that it takes such a long time for their motor actions to become organized during development. Ethan's brain has just begun a long phase of motor wiring and refinement, that will con-

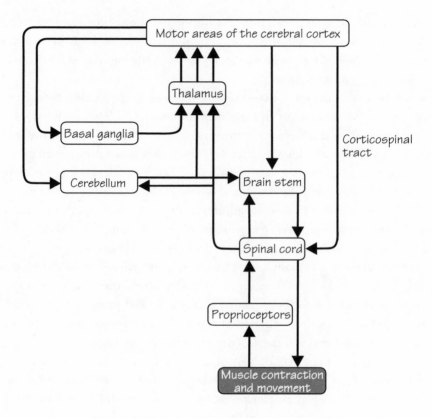

FIGURE 11.3

*Summary of the complex circuits involved in the execution of
a voluntary movement.*

After C. Ghez, "The control of movement," in Kandel et al., *Principles of Neural Science.*

tinue throughout his childhood. No wonder, then, that he is still years away
from even being able to tie his shoe!

Fetal Movements and Their Significance

How *do* all these complicated circuits get wired together? Is it simply a matter of waiting for the right connections to form, or does Ethan's experience—
all that constant, seemingly random motion of his arms and legs—play a role
in hooking them up?

Like all of brain development, motor development involves a delicate dance between nature and nurture—between a programmed sequence of neuronal maturation and the consistent daily exercise a baby puts himself through. But even for newborns like Ethan, this dance is nothing new. It began in the earliest months of gestation, when he was just a tiny embryo and the very first synapses were forming in his microscopic spinal cord.

Thanks to the widespread use of ultrasound imaging, we now have a fairly detailed understanding of fetal movements. They begin in the sixth week after conception, with the first spontaneous arches and curls of the embryo's entire body, still a mere third-of-an-inch long. A week or two later, the limbs themselves begin initiating whole-body "startle" movements. Isolated movements of the arms or legs begin around eight weeks, and of the fingers about two weeks after that. By nine weeks, most fetuses are able to bring a hand slowly into contact with their face, but they don't become expert thumb-suckers until the fifth month in the womb. Other surprisingly coordinated movements that emerge during the first trimester include hiccuping, stretching, yawning, sucking, swallowing, and grasping. Thus, well before most mothers can feel any of it, the young fetus is busy exercising most of the muscles in his tiny body.

The number of fetal movements actually peaks around midgestation, then slows down as space gets a little tighter and some spontaneous movements begin to come under the control of higher brain centers. But the second half of pregnancy also marks the onset of more elaborate movements, many of which will be necessary for survival outside the womb. For instance, babies begin to "breathe" continuously by about twenty-seven weeks of development, meaning that their fluid-filled lungs expand and compress in a regular fashion due to rhythmic contractions of the diaphragm and chest muscles. Sucking and swallowing abilities become coordinated by twenty-eight weeks. But not until about thirty-three weeks can babies integrate sucking and swallowing with breathing; babies born before this time thus cannot feed from a nipple and need to be nourished intravenously or through a tube in the stomach.

This busy fetal activity is not just idle exercise. It is critical for strengthening muscles and refining a baby's developing motor circuits. Experiments with chicks have shown that if one leg is immobilized (by injecting it with a paralytic drug) for as little as one day during embryonic development, it becomes permanently fixed in a posture resembling a human clubfoot. Prenatal practice also influences the structure of tissues other than nerves and muscles. For instance, fetal breathing appears to be necessary for the proper development of lung tissue, and the swallowing of amniotic fluid is thought to promote gastrointestinal development.

By birth, a baby already has accumulated seven or eight months of exercise that are essential for preparing him for life outside the womb. Clinicians are particularly attentive to fetal movements, since they provide an excellent indication of the baby's well-being. Given how neural activity critically shapes developing dendrites and synapses, this steady stream of fetal movement is probably the single most important form of stimulation a fetus's brain receives.

The Nature and Nurture of Motor Development

Believe it or not, it is only relatively recently that scientists have begun to appreciate the importance of babies' earliest motor activity. In the first part of this century, most researchers championed the view that motor development is largely innate, or "hard-wired." Struck by the remarkable consistency of skill acquisition, they argued that motor development depends solely on a fixed process of *neuromuscular maturation* (as their theory came to be called), with little role for practice or experience.

One 1940 study was often cited as supporting the neuromuscular maturation theory: an analysis of walking in Hopi Indian babies. Traditionally, a Hopi baby spends much of her first year as a papoose—strapped to the mother's back in a cradleboard in which she can barely move. Despite this confinement, researchers found that Hopi babies reared in the traditional manner developed no differently from those reared in Western fashion, without the cradleboard: both groups of babies began walking at fifteen months, which is a little late but still within the normal range. Of course, the traditionally reared babies were not swaddled during all hours of the day; in the early months, they were removed for bathing and changing, while in later months, they spent several hours each day outside the cradleboard, and few were cradled at all beyond nine months of age. Nonetheless, this study convinced many early researchers that practice and muscular exercise are relatively unimportant in determining when motor skills emerge.

If motor restrictions have little effect, what about the opposite—intensive exercise in early life? As another way of testing their theory, researchers in the 1930s used identical twins for some remarkable training experiments.

In each study, one twin was extensively helped and encouraged to practice at a particular skill—like rolling over, sitting, standing, stair-climbing, block-building, tricycle-riding, or potty use—while the other twin received no special training. Despite their lengthy workouts, the trained twins were no more advanced in their motor skills than their siblings who spent their infancy in comparative leisure. This was particularly true for more basic abilities, such as walking and standing. So again researchers concluded that it is the fixed pace of neuromuscular maturation that determines a baby's motor progress; all the practice in the world isn't going to accelerate a particular motor skill if the baby's brain and muscles are not developed enough.*

Brain Maturation and Myelination Most babies do, as we've seen, achieve the same motor milestones at very similar ages. The timing is so predictable that one can often guess a baby's age better by looking at what he is doing than by his size. Sitting up but not crawling? Probably around seven months. Cruising but not walking alone? Probably eleven months.

The neuromuscular maturation theory is supported, to some degree, by what we know about the development of motor areas of the brain. There is no question that higher motor areas are poorly developed at birth. Although the motor cortex is one of the first areas to show electrical activity in newborns, it still has a great deal of basic maturation to accomplish in infancy. *Maturation* refers to the genetically coded plan by which neurons are born, migrate to the appropriate spot, sprout their axons and dendrites, form synapses, and myelinate. Since the last process, myelination, is both the slowest and the easiest to observe, it is the chief index scientists have used to relate brain maturation to behavioral development.

There are three major gradients of motor maturation that contribute to the predictable sequence of motor skill acquisition. The first is from lower to higher brain regions; motor circuits in the spinal cord mature first, well before birth, followed by those in the brain stem, followed by the primary motor cortex, followed finally by the higher-order motor areas located farther forward in the frontal lobe. Thus, motor nerves leaving the spinal cord are some of the first fibers in the entire brain to begin myelinating, by midgestation, while motor areas of the brain stem begin myelinating in the third

---

*One problem with these early twin studies was that the two babies were generally not kept apart. Thus, it's possible that the training did have an effect, but the untrained child may have caught up by copying his or her sibling.

trimester. Pathways from the primary motor cortex begin myelinating around birth and continue the process for more than two years. Finally, myelination progresses forward in the frontal lobe at a particularly slow rate; fibers in the premotor and supplemental motor areas don't even begin until midway through the first year and continue for several years thereafter.

As motor circuits mature in progressively higher areas of the brain, the movements they control grow progressively more purposeful and coordinated. Thus, all of a fetus's movements, which are directed exclusively by the spinal cord and brain stem, are either spontaneous or reflexive. Even after birth, lower brain regions continue to dominate a baby's movement repertoire. In fact, most of the neurological tests that a pediatrician performs in a routine newborn exam are to assess lower brain function: the *rooting reflex* (the baby turns his head, opens his mouth, and readies his tongue to feed in response to a light touch on the cheek); the *pupillary reflex* (constriction of both pupils in response to bright light); the *doll's eye reflex* (the baby's eyes remain forward when his head is turned to the side); the *Moro reflex* (the baby flings his arms outward, extends his legs, and opens his hands in response to a slight drop of his head, after which he slowly returns to a flexed position); the *traction response* (the baby holds arms flexed and attempts—usually in vain—to raise his head while being pulled from a lying to a sitting position). Even a newborn's basic sucking and swallowing abilities are largely reflexive, controlled by circuits in the brain stem and spinal cord. As the motor cortex gradually matures over the first year of life, however, it supplants many of these reflexes with the familiar progression of voluntary motor skills.

The earlier maturation of the brain stem also accounts for a second gradient of motor development: from central to peripheral parts of the body. Babies first gain control of their trunk and head muscles—allowing them to maintain posture, as in a sitting position—before mastering movements with their limbs and hands. That's because the neck and torso muscles are largely controlled by motor circuits residing in the brain stem, while limb muscles are influenced more by motor circuits in the cortex.

Finally, within the primary motor strip, a third maturational gradient importantly influences the sequence of motor development. This area develops from bottom to top or, in terms of the muscles it controls, from head to toe. Thus, babies generally master head and facial movements (smiling, mouthing, and neck control) before arm movements (reaching and voluntary grasping), which in turn come before leg movements (crawling and walking).

This cortical gradient can be seen in the structure of neurons along the strip, but it is especially evident among the main output fibers of the motor cortex, the corticospinal tract. This tract is the chief route through which the brain commands the body to perform voluntary movements, especially any kind of fine, fast, or highly skilled movement. The tract on each side of the brain contains about a million nerve fibers—axons from the motor cortex (and other sites) that travel all the way down into the spinal cord and synapse on motor neurons that control specific muscles throughout the body. The corticospinal tract is a new pathway, evolutionarily speaking—it is present only in mammals, has grown progressively larger during primate evolution, and is the largest in humans—and accordingly, is one of the later pathways to mature in children.

The first corticospinal fibers to form synapses are those controlling muscles in the head, followed by the arms and upper body, followed by the legs. Their myelination follows the same sequence, although it is considerably more protracted. As we have seen, the main function of myelination is to increase the speed of neural transmission, and the longer the nerve, the greater the improvement in speed that myelination provides. Since the corticospinal tract houses some of the longest nerve fibers in the body, myelination is especially important for "turning on" the circuits for voluntary motor actions. Direct measurements in children have shown that impulses between the motor cortex and the spinal motor neurons increase rapidly in speed throughout the first two years of life, then more gradually all the way until puberty. This acceleration of corticospinal transmission is responsible for the steady increase in speed at which children can perform simple repetitive movements, like tapping a finger on a table, and probably has a lot to do with the way quickness and agility in general increase throughout childhood.

There is a neat little reflex that one can use to track the early maturation of a baby's corticospinal tract, called the *Babinski sign*. When you stroke the bottom of a young baby's foot with a pointed object (such as a capped pen), his toes will flare or extend up. This response is present for only about the first four months of life; after that, stroking the sole of the foot elicits an opposite reaction, in which the toes curl downward. The switch in this response corresponds to the initial onset of function in the lower corticospinal tract. People who are paralyzed because of disease or damage to this pathway respond like newborns, their toes flaring upward. If the Babinski sign persists beyond about six months of age, it is evidence of a possible neurological delay.

The corticospinal tract is not solely responsible for the emergence of voluntary movements. The maturation rates of the basal ganglia, cerebellum, and higher areas of the motor cortex also set important limits on a baby's motor development. The cerebellum is notable in being one of the last places in the brain in which new neurons form. In fact, much of its basic cellular development takes place postnatally, making it especially vulnerable to environmental insults such as malnutrition. Motor pathways in both the cerebellum and basal ganglia myelinate even more slowly than the corticospinal tract. Slower still are the two higher-order motor centers, the premotor and supplementary motor cortex, which explains, in part, why it takes children so long to master tasks involving more complicated planning strategies, such as fitting shapes into a sorter box, drawing a circle, or simultaneously steering and pedaling a tricycle.

Role of the Environment   Clearly, motor pathways take a lot of time to establish themselves, and there is little question that the pace of neuromuscular maturation sets important limits on when various motor skills emerge. But it is not the whole story. While early researchers were focused on the broad similarities among babies, recent investigators have focused more on their subtle idiosyncrasies and found that motor development is not wholly a matter of waiting for the right neural circuits to wire up according to some genetic blueprint. Many other factors also play a role, including the pace of sensory development, physical growth, strength, nutrition, motivation, emotional well-being, and yes, even consistent daily practice.

We saw in Chapter 1 that babies reared under conditions of extreme neglect are stunted in virtually every aspect of their development, including their motor skills. It's not too surprising that neglected babies would suffer in terms of emotional and cognitive development, but their motor delay—many children could not even sit up by one year or walk by two years—show that factors other than neural maturation are involved. An encouraging, loving, and stimulating environment is also essential.

Another example is blind babies, whose sequence of skill acquisition differs notably from that of sighted infants; they roll over before they can raise their chest from a prone position (reversing the sequence of sighted infants) and are delayed in crawling and walking but not in sitting. Unable to see interesting people or objects, blind babies are simply less motivated to develop their locomotor skills. They are also slower to begin reaching for objects, since they are neither motivated to explore them, nor can they use visual cues to guide their hand movements.

The recent trend of putting young babies to sleep on their backs also appears to be having an effect on their motor skill acquisition. This posture, which has proven advantageous in reducing the number of SIDS fatalities, does not permit babies to exercise their arm and neck muscles as much as tummy-lying, a posture that requires them to push up in order to look around and see the world. In one recent study, pediatricians found that babies who slept on their backs were significantly slower to roll over, sit, crawl, and pull to stand than babies who slept on their stomachs. Fortunately, the delay was modest—still within the normal range for each milestone—and does not justify abandoning back-sleeping as the preferred posture for preventing SIDS. Nonetheless, parents should keep in mind the advantages of upper-body exercise in the early months and attempt to give their babies as much "tummy time" as possible during their waking hours.

Each of these examples shows that the sequence of skill acquisition is not perfectly uniform—not "locked in the genes," as it were, but to a considerable degree dependent on the form of experience in early life. In fact, contrary to the claims of early researchers, who studied a large but fairly homogenous population of babies, there are also small but consistent differences in the developmental schedule of infants from different cultures. The most famous example has been called *African infant precocity*: the finding that babies from various traditional African cultures are several weeks ahead of the norms in industrialized nations when it comes to motor skills like sitting and walking. To some extent, these differences may reflect genetic factors, since African-American babies are also consistently ahead of white Americans in motor skill acquisition. However, the same advancement has been found among babies from preindustrial societies in Latin America and India, so many researchers believe that differences in rearing style are also responsible.

There are several good reasons why babies in preindustrial cultures might develop more rapidly on the motor scale. One is that mothers in such societies often make a great effort to teach their babies specific skills, like sitting and walking, because they are advantageous to her as she attempts to carry out her daily chores. By contrast, parents in industrial societies rely more on equipment to carry their babies and do housework, so they are less in need of establishing their babies' motor independence. The fact that mothers in such cultures tend to carry their babies in slings for the majority of daytime hours may also contribute to their motor advancement; carrying requires more motor activity on the baby's part to maintain balance and head support, and it also provides vestibular and proprioceptive stimulation, which are known to promote motor development (see Chapter 6). Yet another factor is breast-feeding, since babies in the most primitive cultures are unlikely to be reared on formula, and some studies have found that breast-fed babies hold an advantage in their rate of motor skill acquisition (see Chapter 8).

The Role of Practice   Kick, kick, kick, kick, punch, punch, flail, kick, flail . . . little Ethan, now eight weeks old, doesn't seem to know how help-less he is. If he's awake, chances are he's moving something—cranking around his big, round head, searching for his mouth with his busy hands, or rattling his toy bar with his stubby, jerky legs.

Ethan's movements look as if they are purely random. Only occasionally does his hand actually make it to his mouth or his foot successfully rattle the toy bar. Still, it's hard to conceive that all that intense activity could serve no purpose at all. Given how important practice is when adults take up a new motor activity—Rollerblading, for instance—how could it not play an equal role in babies and young children?

In fact, babies do improve their motor skills much as adults do—as a result of diligent practice. New skills, such as walking independently, don't suddenly emerge out of nowhere but gradually build out of prior, simpler abilities—kick-ing, standing, and walking with support—after weeks or months of trying. The only difference between infant and adult motor learning (aside from the fact that infants seem to crave the exercise more than most of us) is that babies can train themselves in a particular skill only when their brains are maturationally ready. In other words, practice *is* essential, provided it's done at the right time. Done too early, the necessary circuits simply aren't there to benefit from it. (Indeed, some researchers believe that premature practice can actually inter-fere with the acquisition of certain skills, either because it ends up training the wrong neural pathways or because the baby grows frustrated with trying to do something he has no hope of mastering at the time.)

Once again, it all comes down to understanding *how* the brain becomes wired up to perform certain tasks. Like each of the sensory systems, motor pathways are initially specified by genes—by innate signals that direct axons from the motor cortex, for instance, to grow down into the spinal cord, then stop at the appropriate level to innervate, say, the cervical motor neurons that control the hand. Though fairly specific, these initial connections are not precise enough to control all the skilled and elaborate movements of which Ethan will eventually be capable. Rather, motor pathways go through another stage of development in which they are refined through use; the more a particular pathway is activated during consistent, purposeful action, the likelier it is to be stabilized.

Even in adults, motor pathways can be modified with training. Recent brain-imaging studies have shown that when a person becomes skilled at a certain motor task, like a set sequence of finger movements, a larger area of the motor cortex is activated during the sequence than before it was well practiced. At the same time, repeated practice is also known to decrease the degree to which the cerebellum is activated during a task; although the cerebellum is critical during motor learning, it drops out once a skill is so well practiced as to require little concentration.

These kinds of imaging studies can't be performed in babies, but there is little doubt that the same sorts of changes take place in Ethan's brain as he masters each new motor skill. Motor learning involves a process of neural selection. The same movement can be accomplished by many different pathways and patterns of activity, but only some of these will be the most efficient. What practice does is to find, by trial and error, the few most efficient patterns and to strengthen and stabilize them, so that each time Ethan attempts a particular movement, he is increasingly likely to use the fastest, smoothest route.

Practice also has another kind of benefit. Remember those early twin studies? Even though deliberate training did not accelerate the mastery of skills like walking or stair-climbing, in the long run it did end up increasing those twins' confidence and interest in motor skills, as compared with their untrained siblings. So while it may not affect the timing of motor milestones, the act of moving itself, especially when encouraged by an enthusiastic adult, does contribute to a child's ultimate success at physical activities.

Motor development is thus a blend of both nature and nurture. Genes set the lower limit on when a skill first becomes possible. But once a baby's nervous system is ready, diligent practice is needed to hone these circuits and turn the initial, awkward attempts at a task into a refined, skilled movement. This intricate blending may be better appreciated by looking at the emergence of babies' two most significant motor milestones: reaching and walking.

The Development of Reaching

He's finally got it! After weeks of trying, four-month-old Ethan is finally able to grab hold of the colorful rattling rings dangling above his bouncy seat.

This is a big step. When he was just a tiny newborn, almost swimming in that seat, he barely seemed to notice them. Then, around ten weeks of age, he began to swat in their direction. By three months, he managed to land a good grasp every now and then, but was noticeably frustrated that he couldn't control them in any reliable way. But now he can follow their movement, extend out his arm, open his hand, and swipe! He grabs them (almost) every time.

Reaching out and grasping an object may not seem like much, but after weeks and weeks of being more or less at the mercy of his environment, it is a major milestone. For the first time, Ethan can exert some small degree of choice about what he is experiencing; he gets to decide whether he will pick up that rattle or pacifier or soft crib toy, and he's clearly thrilled at this new autonomy. The onset of reaching also marks the beginning of a baby's active exploration of the physical world. From studies with adults, we know that simply grasping an object is not enough to discern its various properties; perceiving weight or texture or hardness requires dynamic exploratory movements of the hands, which can begin only after a baby is able to reach out and grasp an object at will.

Reaching is the first in a long succession of manipulative milestones. Successful reaching typically begins in the fourth month, although the normal range of onset is anywhere between two and seven months. These initial reaches are fairly clumsy, but by about six months, reaching grows much smoother, more controlled, and more accurate. After six months, babies grow progressively better at articulating their wrists and fingers, until they master a pincer grasp somewhere between seven and twelve months of age. The next milestone, releasing an object, is surprisingly difficult and doesn't emerge until around thirteen months. On a practical level, this means that children only gradually master some of the most basic self-care skills: use of a spoon at eighteen months, of a fork at twenty-eight months, buttoning by three years, tying shoelaces between four and five years, and knife use only around six years of age.

In a sense, reaching can be said to begin in the womb. All those random arm flails and punches that Ethan performed during Stephanie's midpregnancy ultrasound exam were a first step toward refining the motor systems responsible for reaching. Arm movements appear as early as seven weeks after conception, indicating that motor pathways at the level of the spinal cord have already begun to function. Grasping also begins before birth, though it is purely reflexive. These spontaneous and reflexive movements continue for many months after birth. Through them, Ethan begins to stabilize the synapses and select the motor patterns that will allow him to move his arm in precise ways once his cerebral cortex takes over their voluntary control.

Reaching takes another leap forward at birth, when Ethan is first able to see. Now those random arm movements are no longer as random as they seem. Careful analysis has shown that one-week-old babies extend their arms more when their eyes are fixated on a toy, and that these movements tend to be in the general direction of the toy (although they are rarely close enough to touch it). Researchers refer to this action as *pre-reaching*, and it involves a coordinated extension of the shoulder, elbow, and hand—the hand is open, as if it were going to grasp an object, except that it never does. A newborn will also tend to move her arm more when she is looking at that arm (or its image on a computer screen). All of this indicates that, despite their random appearance, young babies' arm movements may actually be intentional.

Pre-reaching ends around two months of age, when babies enter into a phase known as *fisted extension*: the arms continue to extend, but the hands are flexed tightly closed. Ethan at this stage looked like a tiny boxer working out for a big bout. Then, a few weeks later, he returned to reaching with his hands open. The reason for this flip-flop is that newborns initially master extension of the entire arm, including the hand, and only later become able to differentiate hand from arm extension. It is at this point, around three months of age, that babies can be said to make their first realistic reaching attempts. Grasping has ceased to be purely reflexive and has begun to come under the control of the cerebral cortex.

Finally, at around four or five months, babies execute their first success-ful reaches, where they actually prevail at grasping an object located in front of them. Success at this age is due to the convergence of several factors. One is the initial maturation of corticospinal fibers innervating the arm and hand muscles. Although crude reaching can be accomplished using other motor pathways, any kind of refined hand movement requires the function of the cerebral cortex and corticospinal tract. Motor cortical areas innervating the hand continue maturing until about six months, while further refinement of hand movements—and in particular, the evolution of a pincer grasp—are known to parallel the refinement of corticospinal synapses. Myelination of the corticospinal tract begins at around three months and continues until at least three years of age, contributing to increases in the speed, accuracy, and articulation of children's hand movements during this period.

Another factor contributing to the onset of reaching is vision. Recall that babies develop binocularity—a key component of depth perception—quite suddenly, at around three and a half months. Depth perception is especially important for locating objects at close range. (You can demonstrate this to yourself by trying to reach for an object with one eye closed.) Visual acuity also improves dramatically over the first four to six months, so that babies can now see both their target and arm position much better. Vision continues to be essential for reaching until about nine months, when proprioception takes over and babies become equally accurate at reaching whether or not they are looking at the target.

Other aspects of brain maturation—such as the development of limbic and motor planning areas—undoubtedly also contribute to the onset of reaching. Here too, however, experience plays an important part. A baby has to *want* to reach for an object (recall the blind infants who are delayed at reaching) and to clock many hours of "practice," or pre-reaching, in order to help all those motor circuits wire up appropriately. There is even some evidence that more active infants succeed at reaching a few weeks earlier than babies who use their arms less.

Righty or Lefty? How Handedness Emerges

As Ethan's reaching improves, Stephanie notices that he seems to be favoring his left hand. Now ten months old, he can immediately take hold of almost any object—her finger, his crib bars, a favorite rattle or board book. He can even feed himself, by drinking from his handled juice cup or picking up a fistful of Cheerios, getting most of them, anyway, into his mouth. And though far from consistent, it seems as if he's using his left hand more frequently than his right to perform these various feats.

"Oh, no," Stephanie tells her father, remembering back to her own youth spent struggling with scissors and right-handed school desks. "It looks like we've got another southpaw in the family."

Actually, it is still a little too soon to tell which hand Ethan will prefer in the long run. Although babies generally show some preference for one hand or the other during the first year of life, this preference is notoriously unstable and is often not fixed until late preschool age.

Surprisingly, researchers are still unsure about exactly what causes hand preference. About 85 to 90 percent of people are right-handed. The number varies among different cultures and is about 2 percent higher for women than men. Genes are at least partly responsible, since left-handed parents are far likelier than right-handed parents to have left-handed children. But there is no simple genetic model that can account for the fact that only half of all children who have two left-handed parents will themselves be left-handed—or that a child is likelier to end up left-handed if her mother alone is left-handed, as opposed to her father alone. Nonheritable factors also play a role.

We know, for instance, that despite hereditary tendency, handedness can be switched. This tends to happen in cultures in which left-handedness is considered unacceptable, as in China or certain Muslim societies. While only a small percentage of these populations are left-handed, the figure is considerably higher when children of the same ethnic origin are reared in Western countries, where there is now less bias against it. Indeed, countries like Britain and the United States have seen a steady rise in the proportion of left-handers over the span of the twentieth century, as teachers and parents have stopped trying to "teach it away."

Even if parents aren't deliberately teaching their child which hand to use, kids nonetheless seem to learn it, to some extent, by copying those around them. Such mimicry would explain why children tend to match the handedness of their mothers, with whom they typically spend more time in early life, more than that of their fathers. It may also explain why fewer females end up left-handed, since (as we'll see in the next chapter) girls tend to be more socially attuned at a young age than boys are.

Regardless of whether heredity or learning predominates, the ability to use one hand more skillfully than the other is ultimately a matter of structural differences between the two cerebral hemispheres. Right-handed adults are known to have deeper fissures and a higher ratio of gray to white matter in the left than in the right frontal lobe; both these features favor more localized neural processing, which is the kind needed to execute fine motor tasks. Asymmetry between the hemispheres is known to arise as early as twenty-nine weeks of gestation in language areas of the brain (see Chapter 14), while ultrasound observations suggest that fetuses as young as thirteen weeks postconception prefer to suck their right thumb, a bias that is maintained throughout gestation. Thus, it is possible that primary motor and somatosensory areas begin to diverge on each side of the brain well before birth. Indeed, the electrical processing of touch information already differs in newborns who are destined to become left- or right-handed; future left-handers show cortical activity only in response to stimulation of the left arm, whereas the brains of future right-handers respond equally well to stimulation of either arm.

Because it develops so early, this brain asymmetry appears to be largely innate. It is possible, however, that environmental factors begin operating even before birth. One hypothesis is that the right hand becomes more skillful because it has greater freedom to move in the womb. About three-quarters of all fetuses spend the last several weeks of gestation with their right arm facing out—toward the mother's abdominal wall. This arm has more space in which to move than does the left arm, which keeps running into the mother's spine. This may lead to differential growth and wiring of the hand areas on each side of the motor cortex. However, studies to test this prenatal position hypothesis have thus far proven inconclusive.

Another possibility is that the right hand tends to become more skillful because of an innate preference in head orientation. It turns out that most newborns favor turning their head to the right. Because head-turning triggers the asymmetric neck reflex in newborns—a brain-stem response in which both the arm and leg extend on the same side that the head is facing, while the opposite limbs flex (see Figure 6.3)—babies spend a lot more time looking at their right arms than their left, a posture that will preferentially promote hand-eye coordination on the right side. In fact, studies have shown that babies who have just begun reaching tend to favor the same hand as their head orientation, although they don't necessarily preserve this hand preference later. It's not known why babies favor a right-head orientation, but it may have to do with the fact that most parents hold their babies in their left arm, regardless of their own handedness.

Finally, there is one school of thought (though not a very popular one among left-handers) that states that right-handedness is the "normal" or default developmental pathway and that all left-handedness is the result of some kind of pathology. The logic here is that the brain is genetically destined to be right-handed, but that any kind of prenatal or birth-related damage to the left hemisphere is going to switch hand control to the right hemisphere—the left hand. Left-handedness is indeed much more common among people with disorders related to brain damage, such as epilepsy or mental retardation. Some studies have also found that babies experiencing more difficult deliveries are likelier to have altered patterns of hand use. But it seems very unlikely that all left-handers could have experienced some kind of covert left-hemisphere damage that left them cognitively unaffected in other respects. Rather, most researchers believe that there are two categories of left-handed individuals: the majority, whose handedness is largely inherited, and the minority, whose handedness is due to some kind of pathological event before or during birth.

Whatever cause is ultimately responsible for determining Ethan's hand-edness, it will take several years to become fully expressed in his brain. Typ-ically, a child will switch back and forth several times before finally settling in on a preferred hand. It may be that the two hemispheres undergo alternate growth spurts until the preferred one finally comes to dominate. Such switch-ing is actually quite useful—making sure that both hands master the basic manipulative skills while the brain is still in its most intensive wiring period.

While switching is the rule for any single child, infants as a group do show a gradually increasing preference for the right hand. This bias first shows up in their grasping; from the first days of life, most babies grip longer and tighter when an object is placed in their right hand than in their left. With regard to reaching, a right-hand bias is slower to emerge. Some reports even suggest that babies favor the left arm in their earliest pre-reaching attempts. But by seven months of age, the majority of babies are reaching more with their right hands, a bias that grows stronger and stronger over the remainder of the first year. Also by the end of the first year, babies begin to use their two hands in somewhat different ways: the left hand tends to play the supporting role—for instance, holding a cup of yogurt—while the right hand will be the active partner—trying to spoon it into the mouth.

After the first year, children begin to master the skills that we more typ-ically associate with handedness: eating, pointing, throwing, drawing, and object manipulation. By eighteen months, about half of all children have adopted a stable hand preference. The proportion increases to nearly 90 per-cent by four years of age, but some children take as long as seven years to finally settle in on a preferred hand. Whenever they settle, children do not favor one hand as strongly as adults do; they continue to experiment with both hands, typically alternating between periods of ambidexterity and single-hand preference until fairly late in childhood.

"Learning" to Walk

At last, it happens! Your little butterball has finally taken his first indepen-dent steps. Just when you thought you'd be carrying him around forever, he lets go of the coffee table and . . . step, step, step, step, step . . . down he goes. And up again, with a huge grin and a squeal, to try to repeat one of the most exciting moments in his entire fourteen months of life.

The onset of walking is indeed momentous. Like the onset of reaching, it marks a major change in the way a baby interacts with his environment, multiplying his opportunities for exploration and bolstering his sense of independence and self-confidence. In fact, many studies have noted significant spurts in babies' cognitive and social development following the onset of independent locomotion (both crawling and walking).

Most infants begin walking right around the end of the first year. Compared with other animal species, this is a very late age to finally achieve independent locomotion. But that's because our preferred way of getting around—walking upright, on two legs—is an especially difficult task. Babies must first develop a great deal of strength, and especially stability, before they can manage the tricky maneuver of briefly balancing on just one leg, which is necessary to walk without help.

In fact, while walking proper emerges quite late, its most basic neural mechanism matures very early. Walking is controlled by a neural circuit known as a *central pattern generator* (CPG), a network located in the central nervous system that triggers rhythmical muscular activity, such as that underlying breathing, chewing, or any kind of locomotion. The walking CPG is located in the spinal cord and, like other spinal cord circuits, is phylogenetically quite old. Whether they walk, gallop, or swim, most animals move using a similar spinal circuit, which commands alternate flexion and extension among the limb muscles on either side of the body.

Befitting its long evolutionary history, the walking CPG matures quite early, perhaps no later than twenty-four weeks in utero. As a result, very young babies exhibit a *stepping reflex*: when held up vertically, with feet touching a flat surface such as a table, they will alternately lift each knee up high, as if trying to take some steps. This nifty party trick is exhibited by all newborns, even those born very prematurely, but it disappears by the time a baby reaches a full-term age of six to eight weeks. Although this marching behavior looks quite sophisticated, it is not in any way voluntary: even babies born without a cerebral cortex can perform it, and studies of experimental animals have proven that the cortex is not necessary for this most basic form of locomotor movement.

Why does such "walking" disappear, given that it is the ultimate goal of a baby's gross motor development? For a long time, neurobiologists believed that increasing activity in the cerebral cortex was responsible; after about two months of age, the cortex was thought to begin actively inhibiting the reflexive activation of the walking CPG in preparation for taking over its voluntary control. While it is true, as we will see, that cortical maturation is required for the onset of true walking, it doesn't happen until much later in infancy. The real reason why reflexive walking disappears in early infancy is much more mundane: babies simply get too fat to lift up their legs.

This point was proven by some clever experiments on two-to-six-week-old infants. Researchers divided the babies into two groups by whether or not they still exhibited the walking reflex on a tabletop. The first group, which could no longer do it, proved capable when they were suspended in a torso-deep bath of water. Conversely, the second group, who were still stepping well on the tabletop, were unable to do so if little weights were strapped around their ankles. Because of their rapid increase in body fat during the first few weeks of life, babies' legs grow heavier but not much stronger, so they simply can't pick themselves up. Indeed, young babies with stockier builds—that is, greater weight relative to length—are known to "lose" their stepping reflex earlier than those with slighter builds.

What, then, is the purpose of this stepping reflex, if it's going to disappear long before a baby even attempts to walk voluntarily? As far as we can tell, stepping per se has no real value for newborns. But the same pattern of muscle activation and joint movement is also involved in kicking, a favorite pastime of young babies whenever they're awake and lying on their backs, suggesting that the same CPG is involved. Unlike stepping, kicking does not require a baby to pull up his chubby legs against gravity. Babies begin kicking in earnest in the third month, peak between four and seven months, and then gradually taper off during the rest of the first year, when they begin to take their first "real" steps. Kicking seems to be the more useful expression of this CPG, a bridge between reflexive and true walking that allows babies to practice the same pattern of joint movement without having to support their own weight.

Still, a great deal must happen to convert the spinal CPG into a true agent of independent walking. Real walking requires further maturation of the nervous system—of brain areas controlling leg movement, as well as sensory and motor systems involved in maintaining posture and balance. It also awaits basic changes in bodily proportion; the legs grow longer, the shoulders broaden, and the head becomes smaller, relative to the rest of the body, all of which lowers a baby's center of gravity, making it easier to balance in an erect posture. Finally, walking depends on practice. In spite of what earlier researchers believed, babies must clock many hours of standing, cruising, and walking with some type of support before they can develop the strength and stability to walk independently.

First, let's consider the necessary neural maturation. Unlike reflexive stepping, true walking is a voluntary action, so it requires activation of the cerebral cortex. Even though the spinal cord CPG can put out a stepping pattern, only the cortex can decide when it's time to walk and adjust the CPG to match the exact environment in which a baby is trying to navigate—that is, to avoid that pile of toys on the floor or to change speed depending on how excited she is. It's like having a machine—say, a car or a lawn mower—without someone to operate it; the motor can't do its job unless there's someone there to turn it on and steer it in the right direction.

True walking therefore awaits maturation of the cortical motor areas controlling movement of the legs, and because of the head-to-toe gradient in the motor strip, the leg area is the last to mature. Even at fifteen months of age, this area lags developmentally behind the rest of the primary motor cortex. Similarly, corticospinal fibers innervating the legs myelinate considerably later than those innervating the arms, and continue the process well into the preschool years.

Maturation of the corticospinal tract is especially important for the later refinement of a baby's stride. When they first begin to walk, infants exhibit a pattern of joint flexion and muscle activation that is much like their reflexive walking as newborns; they tend, for instance, to lift their knees up high, and to step by putting the front part of the foot down first. Soon after the onset of independent walking, however, they begin to assume a more adultlike stride, and by two years of age, they have achieved the smooth heel-toe progression and other features of a mature gait. Corticospinal maturation is thought to contribute to this switch by inhibiting certain leg and foot reflexes that cause the jerkier infantile stride. Indeed, children with cerebral palsy, who have damage to the corticospinal tract innervating the legs, can sometimes manage to walk, but they never achieve a prominent heel strike and other features of a mature stride.

To a large extent, then, true walking awaits the programmed maturation of various motor and sensory systems of the brain. At the same time, practice and exercise are also necessary. Before a baby takes her first steps, all of those months of kicking, standing, and walking with support are needed to strengthen leg and torso muscles and to select the optimal neural pathways for maintaining balance and limb position. Then, when true walking begins, those wobbly first steps themselves help stabilize the corticospinal and other pathways needed for the transition to a smooth adultlike gait.

In fact, contrary to all of the early anecdotes claiming that practice has no effect on the onset of walking, one carefully controlled study has shown that special exercise can indeed accelerate it. In this study, a group of newborns were given just ten minutes per day of "practice walking." Every day between one and nine weeks of age, the baby would be held upright by a parent, with his feet on a table, and allowed to exercise his stepping reflex. Two additional groups of babies received, respectively, either no exercise but weekly testing of their walking reflex, or passive exercise, in which a parent would alternately pump the baby's legs and arms while he was lying down. Compared with these two control groups, whose walking reflex declined during the eight weeks, the babies who were actively exercised maintained their walking reflex and even took more steps with each passing week. Moreover, when it came time to walk independently, the actively exercised babies achieved this milestone a full month earlier than the other two groups of babies, and two months earlier than an additional group of babies whose walking reflexes were not even tested during those early weeks.

How does early practice accelerate later walking? Probably not by affecting the corticospinal tracts, which mature too late to benefit from exercise during the newborn period. Rather, it is likely that it strengthens babies' muscles and tunes up their more precocious neural pathways, such as the circuits involved in balancing upright. The fact that the amount of acceleration is modest—babies in this study walked at around ten months of age (still within the normal range) and not at two, or five, or even eight months— shows that motor development is not massively plastic; basic neural and bodily development does set a lower limit on when a child can begin to walk. Nonetheless, learning to walk, like all other motor skills, takes practice, and even in the earliest weeks of life, motor activity influences in a lasting way how a baby's brain and muscles develop.

Infant Walkers Don't Help Infants Walk   While practice is important in learning to walk, one type of exercise does not help and even poses a significant danger for babies: the use of infant walkers. One researcher found that babies who spent about an hour per day in their walkers, beginning around four months of age, did not walk any earlier than babies who had never used walkers, while others found that babies who used walkers for about two and a half hours per day were actually delayed in walking and other gross milestones. The problem with walkers may be that they make it too easy for babies to move around. They can explore and satisfy their curiosity without developing their balance or locomotor skills, so these abilities come more slowly. Another problem is that walkers block babies' view of their feet, and this visual feedback is important when babies take their first independent steps.

Many parents are now aware of the significant safety hazards of infant walkers: they are responsible for an extraordinary number of emergency room visits as children tumble off stairs or into obstacles and end up with broken bones, severe burns, or worse. As much as many babies seem to love cruising around in them, these walkers serve as little more than babysitters, and very inattentive ones at that. They are certainly no substitute for the kind of enthusiastic teaching that an involved caregiver can provide.

How to Encourage a Baby's Motor Development

Obviously the brain does have its own fixed schedule for laying down basic motor pathways, which helps explain why most babies proceed through the same motor skills in a very similar sequence. Genes are also responsible for some of the differences in motor development among infants. Whether a baby is inherently very active, heavy, curious, or simply "fast" in his developmental clock, will influence when he finally succeeds at reaching or sitting or walking. So to some extent, parents can relax—your baby will reach-sit-crawl-stand-walk according to his own timetable, and even if he is a month or two "late," it won't make any difference in his overall development. Babies are always learning something, and if they happen to be a little slow on the motor side, they are probably making up for it through more precocious development of some other skill.

But you may not want to relax too much. Despite the limits of neuromuscular maturation, there can no longer be any doubt that experience plays a key role in motor development. Once the basic neural pathways are in place, their final function depends on practice, on being selected and stabilized by actual motor activity. Only with repeated exercise can these complex motor circuits select the precisely timed patterns of activity that permit smooth, efficient movement. One wonders, too, whether there isn't some kind of critical period for optimizing motor wiring. When you see the perfectly fluid movements of a golfer or violinist who began playing as a toddler, it's hard not to conclude that motor pathways respond best to practice during their most intensive wiring phase of infancy and early childhood.

Fortunately, most babies are already incredibly motivated to practice on their own. When our second baby, Sammy, was first able to reach for a toy, it seemed as if he *had* to be holding something at all times—a cup, a toy, some sunglasses, or the all-time favorite, my car keys. New locomotor skills are similarly reinforcing. What baby who has just mastered crawling is content to sit still for any length of time? More than at any other age, babies are intensely driven to exercise their growing muscles and motor pathways, a compulsion that paves the way for each subsequent motor milestone.

Still, there is a lot that parents and other caregivers can do to help them along. The most important step is to provide a safe, unrestricted environment for exploration. Studies with monkeys have shown that those reared in small cages, with little opportunity for physical activity, end up with smaller, less elaborate cerebellar neurons than monkeys reared with ample opportunity to run and play.

Baby-proof your home early and often, so that your child is free to flex those muscles, find new and interesting objects to play with, or stumble off in any direction without hurting himself or hearing "no" at every turn. Babies undoubtedly also benefit from gentle challenging—to hold up their head, roll over, reach, sit, stand, and so on—when just on the cusp of acquiring each skill. For exercise to be most effective, a baby must be in the right mood—not tired or hungry or fussy—and must be allowed to work for herself, though always with the close attention and enthusiasm of her caregiver. The nice thing about this kind of exercise is that most babies just love it. And while early exercise may not greatly accelerate the rate of her motor progress, it will very likely improve the quality of her movement and especially her interest and confidence in physical activity.

Nor is exercise the only trick for promoting motor development. In several preceding chapters, we've seen various ways in which sensory stimulation is known to enhance the acquisition of motor skills. Vestibular stimulation—like those simple chair-spinning experiments (page 154)—is one example. Another is infant massage (page 142), which seems to work especially well in very young babies. Given the critical role that sensory feedback plays in controlling every kind of movement, sensory systems are at least as important as motor pathways themselves in honing babies' emerging motor skills.

And lastly, don't forget about breast-feeding. Among its many developmental benefits, breast-feeding is associated with the earlier acquisition of both fine and gross motor skills during infancy, as well as a decreased incidence of long-term neurological problems. Once again, breast is best, for both a baby's mind and body.

Chapter 12

SOCIAL-EMOTIONAL
GROWTH

Emotions dominate our early lives more than they ever will again. One minute a baby will be smiling so hugely, his chin triples up, and the next—say, if you're leaving to go to work—he'll burst into tears, his face an arrow of pure anguish that shoots straight into your heart. Babies can go from laughing to fussing to crying to smiling to squealing almost without taking a breath. And toddlers or preschoolers aren't much different, once the tantrums and defiance set in. While children gradually develop longer and longer stretches of self-control, the early years are really one extended emotional roller coaster, with lucky parents along for the ride.

Perhaps because it's so much a part of our daily lives, we tend to take our children's emotional development for granted. Though we may keep careful track of every motor milestone or vocabulary addition, we rarely think about the ways in which their emotional abilities are also rapidly evolving. Yet this aspect of development is in many ways the most important one of all, because it establishes the critical foundation on which every other mental skill can flourish. Well before they master language, babies communicate through emotional expression, and it is through these interactions that they develop the security, confidence, and motivation to master their more obvious motor, verbal, and cognitive achievements.

Indeed, though we often place more emphasis on IQ, it is arguably children's *emotional intelligence*—the ability to recognize and control their own feelings, as well as to read and respond to the feelings of others—that plays a much greater part in determining their later success. Consider an experiment that was begun on a group of four-year-olds. Each child was given a marshmallow and told that he could eat it now, in which case he would get only the one marshmallow, or he could wait until the experimenter returned in fifteen minutes, in which case he would get a second marshmallow and could then eat both. Some of the youngsters downed the marshmallow immediately, the moment the experimenter was out the door. Others squirmed and fidgeted, sang songs or talked to themselves, or even covered their eyes to keep from looking at the marshmallow, but managed to hold out for the greater reward. Remarkably, the children's performance on the marshmallow test forecast their success at the end of high school better than their four-year IQ scores. Thus, the preschoolers with greater impulse control achieved higher grades and better SAT scores than their less-controlled peers. They were also better adapted socially as teenagers, getting along well with their peers and more dependably in their interactions with adults. This experiment illustrates how very important are the skills of emotional regulation— the ability to concentrate, delay gratification, and work within a defined social framework. In other words, all the brain power in the world won't guarantee success if a child lacks the emotional skills and maturity to put it to use.

Of course, emotion is every bit as much a function of the brain as intelligence. Our emotional and social lives are governed by the large set of neural structures known as the *limbic system*. Like every other part of the brain, a child's limbic system is molded through the dual influence of nature and nurture. Each child is born with his or her own unique emotional makeup, what we often refer to as "temperament." But this innate bent is then acted upon by the unique environment in which the child is reared—by his parents, siblings, peers, and other caregivers, his history of tenderness or abuse, cuddling or criticism, attention or neglect, discipline or disorder, and by the forms of emotional display and social interaction he sees modeled by those around him. Out of this great mix of genes and experience, the limbic system becomes wired to produce a singular human personality, the answer to the riddle every parent contemplates: "I wonder what he'll be like when he grows up."

Neuroscientists have recently made great strides in understanding how the brain creates emotion, and how emotional circuits influence everything from communication, intellectual skills, and decision-making to physical health and well-being. Based on their findings, we can begin to unlock the mystery of the emotional life of infants and, more importantly, learn how to best foster the emotional health of our children during the critical years of early limbic development.

How the Limbic System Generates Emotion

The limbic system is named after the Latin word for "border," because its various structures, the source of our rich and tumultuous emotional lives (as well as the ability to store long-term memories; see Chapter 13), sit right on the divide between the cerebral cortex and the brain stem. This positioning makes sense when you consider the two planes on which we experience emotion. So-called "lower" limbic structures—those lying outside of the cerebral cortex—give us the raw, spontaneous manifestations of emotion: the adrenaline rush, racing heart, weak knees, and other bodily reactions during moments of passion or fright, elation or dread. These responses are instinctive, prewired in the nervous system, and therefore universal. People of all cultures exhibit the same facial expressions, such as grimacing in fear or smiling in greeting, and we even share some of these expressions with other species of mammals, such as dogs and monkeys. Because they are programmed at a more basic level of the nervous system, such automatic emotional responses appear in babies from their earliest days.

While the lower limbic system takes care of the bodily manifestations of emotion, the upper tier is devoted to conscious emotional experience. Whether petty or sublime, emotional thoughts occupy a large share of our conscious existence, because a large share of the cerebral cortex participates in producing them. These areas, collectively known as the *limbic cortex*, consist of a ring of gyri that forms the inner core of the frontal, parietal, and temporal lobes. It is here that we become aware of our feelings, and it is also here that we are able to gain some measure of control over them. Thus, while the lower limbic system expresses emotions in their purest, most instinctive form, the limbic cortex modifies these responses according to the culture and training of each individual. As with most cortical functions, this aspect of a baby's emotional life has a long way to go before reaching its full expression.

The Amygdala: Gatekeeper of the Emotional Brain
At the hub of the limbic system, literally lying at the border between the cortex and subcortical parts of the brain, are two small, almond-shaped structures called the *amygdala*. (See Figure 12.1.) There is one amygdala in each hemisphere,

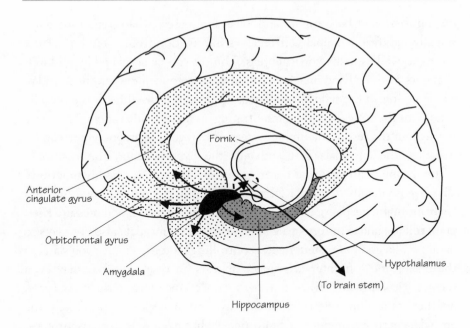

FIGURE 12.1

Structures of the limbic system. Limbic areas of the cerebral cortex are indicated by dots. The amygdala branches out widely in its connections to both higher and lower limbic structures.

nestled at the front and innermost edges of the temporal lobe. Though surrounded by cortex, the amygdala is not a cortical structure. It is derived from an evolutionarily older part of the brain, has a more primitive structure, and accordingly develops earlier than the many-layered cerebral cortex.

People who suffer amygdala damage undergo profound changes in their emotional and social responding. They seem genuinely blind to emotion, both their own and other people's. As a neurologist describes one such patient: "If someone put a gun to [her] head, she would know intellectually to be afraid, but she would not feel afraid as you or I would." Unable to read or understand other people's emotions, they lose all ability to relate normally to friends, family members, or coworkers. Indeed, amygdala damage or dysfunction is one of the leading hypotheses to explain autism, a profound deficit in social responsiveness that can be seen as early as infancy.

Sitting as it does right between the cerebral cortex and various subcortical structures, the amygdala is perfectly poised to track ongoing mental activ-

ity and then alert both higher and lower brain areas when something emotionally significant happens. It receives information from every one of the
senses, as well as many cortical areas. Thus, it can be activated by all kinds
of events, both real and imagined: the sight of an oncoming car, the sound of
a baby crying, or the sudden recall of an approaching deadline. It is especially
active in the case of fear, orchestrating a rapid, wide-ranging response
throughout the rest of the limbic system. When you see an oncoming car, for
instance, the amygdala first activates the hypothalamus, the hormone-
orchestrating brain area that controls so many of our basic bodily functions.
The hypothalamus triggers a large cascade of hormones, culminating in a
"fight-or-flight" response (see page 83); your heart races, blood pressure rises,
pupils dilate, and skin turns pale and sweaty. The amygdala also connects to
basal ganglia and brain-stem nuclei controlling motor reactions; you slam on
the brakes and a frightened grimace appears on your face. You may even
scream, without being aware of it, because of connections to the *central gray*,
another brain-stem region that directs involuntary vocalizations. Finally, the
amygdala activates important brain nuclei that release neurotransmitters—
norepinephrine, dopamine, and acetylcholine—hormones that sharpen your
senses and leave you highly aroused mentally.

The Limbic Cortex: Where Feelings Are Felt   While the amygdala is responsible for generating emotions, it is in the cerebral cortex that we
actually *feel* happy or sad, nervous or calm, vengeful or amorous. From the
amygdala, emotional information reaches most areas of the cortex, where it is
translated into mood, motivation, or social awareness. This wide branching
explains how emotion influences every aspect of thought, in spite of our illusions of "pure" rationality. It biases even simple processes like visual perception, as well as complex reasoning tasks like planning or decision-making.
Without emotion, we couldn't appreciate art, make lasting friendships, or
even be able to choose which box of cereal to buy at the supermarket.

While most of the cortex is influenced by emotion, two specific regions
are especially involved in emotional experience. These are the *orbitofrontal
gyrus* and the *anterior cingulate gyrus*. (See Figure 12.1.) Both regions line the
middle (or *medial*) and underside of the frontal lobes, the orbitofrontal gyrus
running along their bottom edge (immediately above the eye sockets, or
orbits) and the anterior cingulate gyrus forming their rear, innermost curvature. It is through these structures that the amygdala informs the conscious
mind about the emotional state it has generated in the lower brain. Like

amygdala damage, damage to either of these frontal-lobe sites may dramatically change a person's emotional responses and social behavior, so much so that his or her personality may seem entirely altered. Damage to the orbitofrontal site, in particular, affects social judgment; such people become impulsive or rude and generally lose the kinds of inhibitions that keep our behavior in check around other people. Damage to the anterior cingulate tends to dampen motivation; a formerly ambitious person may become placid, apathetic, or physically inactive. (A similar "calming" effect was produced by surgical destruction of the medial frontal lobe—the so-called "frontal lobotomy" used as a radical treatment for mental illness that fortunately fell out of favor in the 1950s.)

Just as important as the connection from the amygdala to the frontal cortex is the reverse flow of information. Cortical fibers feed back to the amygdala and other subcortical limbic structures, their main function being to inhibit lower limbic activity. This is the route we eventually use to hold our feelings in check; it blocks some of those reflexive reactions of fear, anger, jealousy, or greed that wreak havoc with our relationships or thwart our loftiest goals. Negative feedback from the frontal cortex lobes is what permitted those four-year-olds to save their marshmallow until the experimenter returned, or impels an adolescent to do his homework before watching TV. It underlies the kind of self-control that is necessary for any successful social interaction or disciplined achievement. Not surprisingly, this arm of the limbic network is one of the slowest to come on line during development.

Left and Right in the Emotional Brain

There's another interesting twist to the anatomy of emotion. Like most mental functions, emotion is not processed equally by both sides of the brain. Generally speaking, the right cerebral hemisphere plays a more important role in emotion. Limbic structures on the right side have a higher resting metabolic rate than those on the left, and emotional deficits are more common with brain damage to the right than to the left half of the brain. Right-hemisphere structures tend to complement the more analytical abilities of the left hemisphere in interesting ways. For instance, while the ability to understand and produce language is located in the left hemisphere, the right hemisphere is where we appreciate its emotional content. Depending on the area affected, people suffering strokes on the right side can still speak but may lose all intonation in their voice, or be unable to discern another person's facial expression, or fail to appreciate a moving piece of music. And because the right hemisphere controls sensory and motor functions primarily on the left side of the body, most of us discern the emotional tone of speech slightly better with our left ears and show greater expressiveness on the left sides of our faces.

This asymmetry holds true in the frontal lobes as well, where the right orbitofrontal gyrus is considerably larger than the left. But this doesn't mean that the left side lacks feeling entirely. Both sides are essential to social and emotional life, but they play fundamentally opposite roles. Simply put, the left medial frontal cortex is where we feel good, and the right medial frontal cortex is where we feel bad. Normally, these two sides hold each other in check, except for the occasional moment of distress or euphoria when one side breaks through and dominates. But people who suffer damage to the right frontal lobe can become overwhelmingly depressed or worried, while those with damage to the left may become unduly cheerful, unconcerned about their own serious brain disorder. Among healthy people, variations in the amount of left or right frontal-lobe activity appear to explain basic differences in temperament—why some people tend to have negative personalities while others are blessed with sunnier dispositions. This imbalance also spills over into social behaviors, with left-dominated people tending to be shyer and more withdrawn, while right-dominated types are more outgoing and assertive. As we'll see when we get to the subject of infant temperament, such differences emerge quite early in life and are probably largely genetic, although life experiences do help tip the balance in one direction or the other.

Considering the different functions of the two hemispheres, it's intriguing that they do not develop synchronously. Throughout childhood, there is a tendency for the two sides to trade off growth spurts, each taking its turn to hopscotch ahead of the other. Although these growth cycles take a few years for the brain as a whole, my own suspicion is that there are also much shorter oscillations—on the order of weeks to months—in the development of frontal limbic areas. Perhaps such rapidly alternating growth spurts could explain how a three-year-old who was perfectly wonderful a week ago could be so infuriatingly difficult today!

Development of the Emotional Brain

Like most of the brain, the limbic system develops from bottom to top. By birth, a baby is in possession of roughly half of her emotional hardware—the lower half. The amygdala, in particular, is well formed by the end of gestation and its connections to the hypothalamus and numerous brain-stem sites are fully functional. Early maturation of this circuitry means that babies, even the youngest ones, have some form of emotional experience; when faced with painful, pleasurable, or surprising stimuli, they undergo much the same physiological changes—respiration, heart rate, circulation, pupillary dilation, motor activity—and produce the same facial expressions that you or I would.

But this doesn't mean that babies actually *feel* things the way an adult or older child does. Being aware of how one is feeling takes a functioning limbic cortex, and this upper tier of the emotional brain takes considerably longer to develop. In particular, the orbitofrontal gyrus matures quite gradually, since it is located in the evolutionarily new *prefrontal* zone of the frontal cortex. Neurons in the prefrontal cortex are still markedly immature at birth: it takes about two years before their dendrites are fully extended and synapses have reached their maximum density. Although there is a tiny bit of electrical activity in the prefrontal lobes by birth, most evidence suggests that cortical emotion centers do not begin functioning in any meaningful way until six or eight months of life. Beginning in the second six months, the orbitofrontal gyrus steadily assumes more and more control of a baby's emotional life; she can genuinely be said to feel things and to begin exerting some self-control over the lower half of her limbic brain. Then, beginning about two years of age, cells in the prefrontal cortex (including the orbitofrontal gyrus) enter a very long phase of synaptic pruning, which continues well into adolescence. This prolonged phase of synaptic refinement—which is clearly influenced by a child's environment and experiences—underlies the emotional growth that is the very essence of what it means to "mature."

The limbic system is notable for its especially slow pace of myelination. The main fiber tract linking frontal limbic areas to those in the temporal lobes remains poorly myelinated until at least nine months of age. Fibers within the limbic cortex itself are slower still. And slowest of all to myelinate are several fiber tracts that transmit information to and from the hippocampus, another subcortical limbic structure located in the temporal lobe; as we'll see in the next chapter, this helps explain why we have so little conscious memory of events in infancy, even if they did have a profound emotional impact at the time.

Parents may find it disconcerting to learn that their young babies don't *really* feel happy when they're beaming or giggling at your latest antics. The good news is that they're equally unaware of those occasions when you let them "cry it out"—as at bedtime or in lieu of being picked up for the ten thousandth time that day. Though the baby may work himself up into quite a state, it really is true that it won't hurt him, he won't remember it, and as long as these episodes are countered by a predominance of loving attention, the overall effect on his developing limbic brain will be positive.

Emotion and Memory

Emotion is not the only province of the limbic system. Many of the same limbic structures also play a critical role in memory storage. This close anatomical linkage helps explain why emotion and memory are so intimately related on a psychological level: why we are likelier to store memories about events that had a strong emotional impact and, conversely, why strong emotions tend to bring back vivid memories that are not otherwise easily recalled.

Babies, however, are not yet capable of conscious, long-term memory, for reasons described in the next chapter. They are nonetheless capable of simpler forms of memory, such as recognizing familiar faces, learning that they will get attention if they cry, or forming emotional associations with particular people or places. These kinds of memories, habitual behavior patterns that are stored at lower levels of the brain, differ from "real," conscious memories in that they rarely register after a single experience but require many repetitions of stimulus-response pairing to take hold.

This repetitive requirement explains why babies respond so well to consistent, responsive caregiving. Through repetition, a baby learns that his needs will be met, and he grows secure in his ability to control his environment. The occasional bout of crying, even if ignored for fifteen or twenty minutes, will generally have little impact against a reliable background of loving attention. On the other hand, if the care is inconsistent, so that the baby can never predict what will happen to him, he'll fail to develop the confidence and emotional security that are so essential to a healthy psyche. In the worst case, when a baby is abused, the link between emotion and memory can be especially devastating. For even though the child will never remember the specific events at any conscious level, his lower limbic system—and the amygdala in particular—does store powerful associations between an emotional state, like fear or pain, and the person or situation that brought it on, associations that may be indelible.

Limbic Development over the First Six Months

The first six months mark a period dominated by the lower limbic system. Babies are born with a set of innate emotional expressions and an instinctive understanding of other people's emotions. Despite an undeveloped limbic cortex, they have a rich social and emotional life. After all, most of their behavior is directed at satisfying one kind of need or another, and the very purpose of emotion is to drive the rest of the brain to seek food, protection, and comfort. Babies' drive for social interaction is especially strong because satisfying these needs depends almost entirely on other people.

The Social-Emotional Life of a Newborn

Here she is, just minutes out of the womb, and Natalie is already an adept communicator. As soon as the labor nurse takes her out of Eva's arms, she starts to wail, a piercing cry that seems to emanate from her entire tense little body, complete with wracked-up face and quivering lower chin. Poor Eva, a first-time mom, feels her first pains of maternal angst even before her labor pains have fully subsided. The lifelong conversation between mother and daughter has begun.

By birth, a baby's lower limbic system is equipped to express the rudiments of all the basic emotions. Natalie's facial muscles and motor circuits are almost fully developed, and it isn't long before she can display joy, sadness, fear, disgust, interest, surprise, anger, and affection in the appropriate circumstances. Her social life also begins early. Considering all the crying Natalie does, it is obvious that she is quite effective at communicating her needs. Although crying per se doesn't require any circuitry above the brain stem (anencephalic babies can cry), normal babies do emit distinct types of cries for hunger (rhythmic and repetitive), anger (loud and prolonged), and pain (sudden in onset, punctuated by breaks of breath-holding), which require input from the amygdala, hypothalamus, and other lower limbic structures.

Young babies are also surprisingly adept at recognizing emotions in others. We've already seen how each of their senses, no matter how dim, is primed to detect other people; Natalie's vision is tuned to see faces, while her hearing is most acute for the range and intonation of a human voice. Within days of birth, she can recognize Eva by sight, sound, and especially by her familiar, comforting odor. Such sensory priming ensures that Natalie's attention is riveted to the important people in her world—her parents—who are essential not only to nurture and protect her but also to begin teaching her the emotional skills that will be her invaluable guide through life.

Indeed, emotional learning begins immediately, in the form of imitation. Infants just a few hours old are capable of mimicking certain facial expressions or hand gestures. In one report, newborns were found capable of mimicking happy, sad, and surprised expressions modeled by an actress while she held the infants up in front of her. Although they didn't imitate every time, these babies were more likely to widen their lips when the model was happy, pout their lips when she feigned sadness, and open their mouths wide when she looked surprised.

The fact that newborns can imitate different facial expressions means, first of all, that they are able to discriminate different emotional displays in those around them. This is remarkable, given how poor their vision is at birth, and it shows that even at this young age, emotional communication is a two-way street; babies really can sense the mood of those who are caring for them, even if it is at a subconscious level.

Imitation is also important because it serves as the basis for the development of empathy, the ability to experience what another person is feeling. Although true empathy—which requires the conscious recognition of another person—doesn't emerge until months or years later, newborns appear to have the rudiments of this emotion, since they are known to begin crying upon hearing the cry of another baby. It appears, then, that we are wired from birth with a way of matching sensory input about another person's emotional state to the lower limbic mechanisms that generate emotion in ourselves. (Indeed, autistic children, who likely suffer from limbic deficits at birth, are markedly deficient in their tendency to imitate others.)

Between her own facial expressions and her reaction to others, Natalie is obviously very good at the outward manifestations of emotion. But does she actually *feel* anything inside? Are these emotions registering at all in her higher limbic system? One research team has attempted to address this issue by measuring frontal-lobe activity in babies just two or three days old. To elicit both positive and negative emotions, the babies were given small tastes of either sugar water or vinegar. As expected, the sweet flavor triggered facial signs of interest and relaxation (raised eyebrows, open mouth), while vinegar triggered expressions of disgust (squinted eyes, protruded tongue, wrinkled nose). Despite their facial reactions, however, the cortical measurements revealed that very little was going on in newborns' upper limbic systems. Though the babies did exhibit some asymmetry in frontal-lobe function—left activation in response to sugar—they did not show the expected right-hemisphere activation in response to the vinegar, nor were any of their responses restricted to the frontal lobe as they would be in adults. So even though some kind of emotional information appears to be making its way into the limbic cortex, a newborn has a long way to go before she can know the true peaks and valleys of emotional experience.

Social Smiling   The first milestone in Natalie's emotional development comes at six weeks of age, when she begins to smile at other people. These are not her first smiles; she's been flashing brief, mouth-only grins since birth, but up to now, such gestures have been mostly random, the result of spontaneous firing in her brain-stem circuits that is unrelated to any particular emotional state. Indeed, babies begin to smile spontaneously as early as thirty weeks gestation and are especially likely to do so in their sleep, because the motor neurons controlling the necessary facial movements are located quite close to the brain-stem area that directs REM sleep.

But now Natalie is actually smiling in response to specific social cues—her mother's voice, her father's gaze, gentle stroking from her Aunt Louise—and suddenly the whole family delights in provoking her apparent joy. They are not alone. Many parents report this age (which also coincides with the period of "obligatory looking"; see page 215) as the time when they first began to feel deep affection for their babies.

Social smiling is probably the most universal of all developmental milestones. Babies of all cultures begin to smile between four and eight weeks of age, and premature infants begin social smiling right around six weeks after the date when they *should* have been born, as opposed to their real birthday. Indeed, twin studies suggest that what variation there is between babies is largely inborn. Even babies born blind begin smiling to the sound or touch of another person at nearly this age. This is one milestone that appears truly hard-wired.

Why do all babies begin social smiling in the second month of life? One theory holds that its onset is due to myelination of the basal ganglia. These structures, you may recall, are a key part of the motor system. Animal experiments have shown that certain of the basal ganglia are responsible for a particular class of motor behaviors: stereotyped displays that are used to communicate social status, competitive challenge, alliance, and courtship to fellow members of the species. Smiling serves a similar function in humans—as a universal sign of greeting—and is probably triggered by activity in these same basal ganglia. Myelination of these structures begins right around birth and progresses rapidly during the first weeks of life.

Equally interesting is what *doesn't* trigger smiling. Smiling is a motor action, like all of the milestones discussed in the last chapter, so it's a little surprising that its onset is *not* attributable to maturation of the motor cortex. The reason is that smiling is not voluntary. Although you can willfully concoct your face into a smile, this kind of "polite" smile uses only the muscles of your mouth. Genuine smiles, by contrast, also involve a specific muscle that surrounds the eye, the *orbicularis oculi*, and movement of this muscle is entirely involuntary. The orbicularis oculi is controlled solely by the limbic system, as we've learned from patients who have suffered specific lesions; people with motor cortex damage cannot give you a deliberate, polite smile, but will easily smile when provoked by something amusing. Patients with limbic damage, on the other hand, can voluntarily contract their mouths, but they can't smile, even when genuinely moved to do so. The basal ganglia mature somewhat before the motor cortex, so you can be sure that your baby's first social smiles are genuine.

"Protoconversation"

"Protoconversation"   With our first baby, Julia, it was her smile that really hooked us. With our second child, it was his witty conversation. Sammy really came to life for me at about eight or ten weeks of age, when he would suddenly look at me, tilt his head, raise his eyebrows, and launch into a prolonged discourse: *aaaaaaahhhhhhhhhhhhhhhh*. His voice would rise and fall, and his tongue would wiggle all around, experimenting with different ways of letting out the long syllable. He seemed so earnest in his desire to "talk" that I would respond in every possible way to encourage him.

After smiling, the next milestone in babies' social development is this fervent attempt to begin communicating. Researchers use the terms *prespeech* and *protoconversation* to describe the face-to-face verbal interaction that babies enter into beginning around six weeks and continue until about four months of life. This cooing and "oooing," with full intonation, are often accompanied by hand or finger movements, and by a smile or excited facial expression that is maintained as long as the baby keeps her conversational partner in view.

It takes two to hold a conversation, and parents seem to instinctively know how to communicate with their young infants. Close examination of these protoconversations reveals a natural turn-taking, where the mother first listens to her baby's utterances with various signs of agreement, surprise, or praise, then responds during the baby's pauses, so as not to interrupt. Mothers also do a lot of imitating—matching their babies' facial expressions, hand gestures, and the pace and intensity of their "speech." This mirroring completes the emotional exchange and helps the baby develop an awareness of his own movements and expressions. (Fathers are no doubt equally capable but have yet to be studied.) Though important to language acquisition, these conversations are fundamentally an emotional exchange, because it is in emotional centers of the brain that this type of behavior is triggered.

The emergence of prespeech may reflect the onset of significant activity in the anterior cingulate. This gyrus is known to play a role in emotional vocalization—the spontaneous moans, groans, coos, or yelps that people (and monkeys) make in the grip of disgust, rage, tenderness, or jubilation. Though less mature at birth than subcortical limbic structures, the anterior cingulate is further advanced than the orbitofrontal cortex. Its major outflow pathway, the *cingulum*, begins myelinating at around seven weeks of age, although it is a very slow process that takes nearly a year to complete. It's not known why protoconversations subside after three or four months of age, but it may coincide with increased activity of the cortical areas truly designated for language.

Six to Eighteen Months: Attachment, Inhibition, and Emotional Awareness

Socially adept though young babies are, their emotional life takes a giant leap forward around six months of age, when higher limbic centers start entering the picture. We first noticed the change in Sammy at seven months, when he really began to be fun. Those long fussy periods were gone, and he would now beam back every morsel of attention with a huge, squinty smile. Suddenly, too, he seemed like a real member of the family: joyfully sucking on his sister's Duplos, bouncing excitedly at the dinner table, and keenly aware of all our comings and goings, especially mine.

Babies' social and emotional lives pick up in the second six months of life because this is when the frontal lobes begin serious functioning. We know this based on PET scans: metabolic activity in the medial frontal lobe—site of the orbitofrontal gyrus—first becomes detectable around eight months of life, then rises steadily until about four years of age. This increase mirrors the massive growth of dendrites and synapses among frontal-lobe neurons over the same period. Many limbic pathways also begin their prolonged phase of myelination during this time, although the process continues up to years later.

All this maturation means that during the second six months, emotional information finally begins making its way up from the lower limbic system to become part of a baby's emerging consciousness. We can see this in EEG measurements. Whereas a newborn shows only a trickle of frontal-lobe activity in response to emotional stimuli, a ten-month-old, like our next-door neighbor Jessie, shows the mature pattern of electrical responses; a happy stimulus, like watching a videotape of a person laughing, preferentially activates her left frontal lobe, while a disturbing event, watching the same person crying, invokes comparatively more activity on the right.

Once these higher limbic centers get involved, babies' emotions and social interactions really begin to blossom. This is when they genuinely begin to *feel* the emotions that correspond to all of those precocious facial expressions. Frontal-lobe involvement also means that babies can finally begin making sense of their emotions, relating them to what's going on around them and actually putting this knowledge to use. Jessie, for instance, has become quite masterful at capturing her mother's attention and communicating precisely how she feels, whether she is tired, or hungry, or frustrated that she can't reach those intriguing salt and pepper shakers up on the table. At snack time, she not only takes great pleasure in eating her Cheerios, she begins offering them to her mother, Sandy, as though finally understanding that she has feelings too. Jessie's even showing the first signs of behavioral inhibition—the ability, albeit still primitive, to actually control her feelings and actions. It is this inhibitory input that helps her calm down when she's put in her crib at bedtime, and that also makes her stop, after the two-millionth warning, crawling out the front door anytime it's open. Between this new inhibitory control and the greater awareness of their own feelings, babies like Jessie and Sammy generally become a lot happier and great fun to be around in the second six months of life.

Attachment and the Fear of Strangers   Of all the social/emotional advances in infancy, the most important is the emergence of attachment: a baby's potent tie to her primary caregiver, usually the mother.* Whereas parents begin to bond with their babies in the first few days or weeks of life, the process is slower in the reverse direction, because of babies' considerable limbic disadvantage. Once Natalie's frontal lobes are up to speed, though, she's able to feel the initial inklings of genuine affection, and Mom—the one person who has most consistently fed, changed, comforted, and cuddled her—becomes her first true love.

Now eight months old, Natalie can't seem to get enough of Eva. She leans out longingly every time her mother enters the room, or flashes one of those adoring, irresistible smiles. For now, Natalie relies on her communicative skills—cries, smiles, and coos—to keep Eva nearby, but soon she'll be crawling and cruising after her. And her mother is eating it up.

Much as Eva enjoys the attention, though, Natalie's blossoming attachment does have its downside. It means their daily separations have become mutually excruciating. Eva winces every morning after leaving Natalie at day care, images of her daughter's tears and protest all too fresh as she tries to start her day's work. Natalie has also begun exhibiting "stranger anxiety," the fear of unfamiliar people, even a friendly older woman at the supermarket who tries to get a smile out of her. No such luck. Just as she can now single out preferred people, Natalie has become wary of those she's never seen before. She actually starts to cry when this well-intentioned woman comes too close for comfort.

Attachment is regarded by many psychologists as the seminal event in a person's emotional development—the primary source of a child's security, self-esteem, self-control, and social skills. Through this one incredibly intimate relationship, a baby learns how to identify her own feelings and how to read them in others. If the bond is a healthy one, like Natalie and Eva's, she will feel loved and accepted and begin to learn the value of affection and empa-

---

*Whoever is the most consistent caregiver, the one who most reliably fulfills a baby's physical and emotional needs, will become his or her primary attachment figure. Mothers tend to have the advantage here, especially if they're nursing, but babies can certainly grow equally attached to a father, grandmother, or anyone else who fills this role. Furthermore, while babies do seem to be programmed to form a primary attachment to a single, preferred individual, they are clearly capable of forming simultaneous bonds with other family members or caregivers. It's just that they tend to prefer their mothers, especially in any kind of strange or distressing situation, and continue to do so until at least eighteen months of age.

thy. At the same time, this relationship will inevitably provide some dose—hopefully a small one—of frustration, conflict, and shame, which are necessary to round out her emotional education. Particularly toward the end of the first year, when babies begin exploring in earnest, attachment complements their growing independence in an important way. Eva represents a secure emotional base from which Natalie can test her new assertiveness, someone to whom she can periodically return for comfort and reassurance, even as Eva begins to set firm limits on her more dangerous forays.

Attachment and stranger anxiety are strikingly universal among human societies. Whether they're raised in urban America, on an Israeli kibbutz, in a remote Guatemalan village, or in a primitive African society, babies throughout the world show attachment and social fear at the same time: beginning around six months of age, and growing increasingly intense until about eighteen months. Even babies who spend eight hours a day away from their mothers—in day or nanny care—exhibit attachment and stranger anxiety at the same age, although (as we'll see below) there is some controversy about the quality of infants' attachment when both parents work full time. Attachment thus appears to be programmed into limbic development. The only babies who fail to grow attached are those who are seriously neglected, or whose limbic systems—as in certain cases of autism—are incapable of making a connection with another human being.

Attachment bears a lot of similarity to the instinctual imprinting of other young animals, like ducklings, who are compelled to follow whatever parental figure (whether avian or human) they first see after hatching. Indeed, attachment behaviors are prominent in every species of bird or mammal whose survival depends heavily on parental care. Monkeys in particular cling to their mothers through much of infancy and cry when she puts them down—all of which keeps her nearby and creates a bond that is essential for their emotional health and normal social development. So there is a clear precedent for attachment behaviors in vertebrate evolution, suggesting that it is deeply rooted in our genetic heritage.

But if attachment is so important, why does it take half a year before babies even begin to bond with their parents? Wouldn't it have been more advantageous for Natalie to cement herself to Eva immediately after birth—as ducklings do—at her most vulnerable age? In fact, when you look across different species of animals, there is a correspondence between the timing of attachment and one particular developmental milestone: the onset of independent locomotion. It turns out that young animals of various species show attachment or imprinting behaviors right at the age when they begin to walk or waddle. Babies, by this logic, may not *need* to feel attached until they reach the point when they're actually capable of crawling away on their own.

Nonetheless, babies have other means, which emerge much earlier than attachment, to ensure that they'll stay close by their caregivers. Crying, cooing, and smiling are all instinctive tricks that young babies use to signal their needs and maintain proximity to their caregivers. They are also remarkably astute when it comes to recognizing their own mothers. As we have seen, babies can discriminate her voice, face, and odor within the first few days of life, and it's not long before they can recognize other individuals in the family as well. These skills keep the baby's senses focused on her primary caregiver, setting the stage for attachment, but they do not add up to the same deep bond that emerges later. In fact, young babies react positively to any kind of approach, even from a stranger, and though at around five months they may begin to fuss when their mother leaves the room, they can generally still be comforted by almost anyone else.

A likelier reason why attachment takes so long to emerge is that it is limited by the slow development of the frontal lobes. Attachment is related to another cognitive advance, the realization of *object permanence*—that things or people continue to exist even when you can't see them. It's hard to grow attached to something or someone if you can't remember it for any significant length of time. This form of short-term memory is known to require the function of another area of the prefrontal cortex, and it similarly emerges during the second six months of life (see Chapter 15).

Our best evidence that frontal-lobe development is responsible for the onset of attachment comes from actual measurements of babies' brain activity. Just as ten-month-old Jessie experiences a surge of left frontal-lobe activity in response to other happy events, the sight of Sandy, headed toward her from across the room, uniquely activates her left frontal cortex. Tonight, unfortunately, it does not last. When Sandy then passes her to me for a rare evening out, Jessie's right frontal lobe explodes with activity. EEG measurements like this suggest that babies experience attachment only when their frontal lobes are mature enough—when they genuinely *feel* happy around their primary attachment figures and distressed by the presence of strange ones.

Another interesting finding has emerged from these EEG measures of attachment and stranger anxiety. Ten-month-olds do occasionally manage to shoot off a grin at a total stranger. However, researchers have found that these are not genuine limbic smiles; they do not activate that special eye muscle, the orbicularis oculi, nor are they accompanied by activation of the left frontal lobe. So even at this young age, Jessie is capable of those disingenuous "polite" smiles that occasionally mask the unease and wariness she now feels around strangers. Truly happy smiles, by contrast, are saved for her favorite people, especially Mom and Dad, the two who best fire up her left frontal cortex.

When Mothers Work:
How Nonmaternal Care Affects Attachment and Later Emotional Development

If babies are programmed, as a matter of frontal-lobe maturation, to grow attached to their primary caregivers, what happens when they spend a large share of their waking hours away from both their mothers and fathers? Do they fail to develop the primordial bond essential for later psychological health? Now that a majority of mothers are returning to work during the first year of their babies' lives, this issue has come under considerable scrutiny. Are we raising a generation of children at risk for serious behavioral problems, or is all the fuss about day care and babysitters merely another kind of backlash against women, a way of making working mothers feel all the guiltier about the time they spend away from their young children?

The good news, as we've already seen, is that most babies do manage to bond with their mothers, regardless of her employment status. Attachment is a powerful instinct, once the necessary neural hardware is in place, and since most working parents make great efforts to spend the bulk of their nonworking hours with their young children, there actually are enough hours in the day (and evenings, weekends, holidays, and maternity leave) for working mothers to be the most consistent, attentive, and loving caregiver in their baby's life. Nor is it necessarily bad for a young baby to form his primary attachment to someone other than his mother, if the regular caregiver is a loving, responsive, and stable figure in his life. Children can, and generally do, form attachments to several adults over the first few years, and as long as these relationships are a source of security and healthy interaction, they are a positive influence.

But while the *fact* of attachment is not in dispute, there is considerable debate about its *quality* in the children of working mothers. Researchers distinguish several different categories of attachment based on infants' behavior toward their mothers in a laboratory test known as the *Strange Situation*. This twenty-minute assessment, performed in an experimental playroom on babies between about twelve and eighteen months of age, involves eight different episodes of coming and going by both the mother and a friendly female stranger. The quality of attachment is judged by how the child reacts during reunions with the mother. Babies who seek out their mothers, especially when distressed, who protest her leaving, and who seem to be comforted when she returns are judged "securely attached," while babies who avoid proximity or contact with their mothers or who actually cry more during their reunions are judged as various forms of "insecurely" attached.

Using this test as their measure, several studies in the 1980s concluded that babies with working mothers are less likely than babies of nonworking mothers to be securely attached. The numbers vary, but one consensus study puts the figure for insecurely attached infants at 37 percent for infants who experienced regular nonmaternal care in the first year versus 29 percent of infants in exclusive maternal care. It's a small effect, but not insignificant, particularly if maternal attachment is as important to future emotional adjustment as many developmentalists believe. But some critics argue that these findings may be meaningless, because the Strange Situation, which was devised back in the 1960s for children whose mothers did not work, is probably not valid for babies with extensive experience with other caregivers. According to this view, children whose mothers work are obviously going to be less distressed by the Strange Situation, since they are already accustomed to maternal separation on a routine basis.

Researchers therefore began looking for effects of maternal employment in other aspects of children's behavior. Here the findings have been more mixed. While some reported worrisome effects—that children who began nonmaternal child care in the first year were prone to be more aggressive, less obedient, and to develop poorer relationships with peers and teachers during the preschool and grade-school years—others failed to find the same effects, while still others reported significant *advantages* for children who began some form of group care (family- or center-based day care) at an early age: higher social competence, more cooperative play, and greater peer popularity than home-reared children.

Given all the controversy, as well as the great importance of the issue, the U.S. National Institute of Child Health and Human Development (NICHD) in 1991 embarked on a massive nationwide research project to try to settle it. Fifteen sites were established, and more than 1,300 children from all major ethnic groups and socioeconomic strata were enrolled at birth for a long-term study of the impact of early child care on children's emotional and cognitive growth. In addition to its large size, this study has two other noteworthy features. One is that it takes account not only of *whether* infants are enrolled in nonmaternal care but also the quantity and quality of that care, since both factors are known to influence children's emotional development. The other is that it includes elaborate controls for so-called "selection" effects: the fact that working mothers and nonworking mothers tend to differ in certain ways—in personality, parenting style, education, and degree of spousal support—that contribute to differences in their children's development. Selection effects also operate among working families, so this study has also attempted to control for differences in the quality of child care that are attributable to family income, education, parenting style, and similar factors.

The main findings to emerge thus far are encouraging for those who use early child care. In every analysis, family factors have been found to play a much greater role than child-care factors in determining how young children turn out. Thus, in contrast to previous studies, fifteen-month-old infants were equally likely to be securely attached to their mothers regardless of their daily care situation—in exclusive maternal care, paternal care, babysitter care, or in family- or center-based day care. What *did* matter in determining attachment security was mothering style—how sensitive the mother is to her baby's needs during their time together. In other words, insensitive mothers tend to have less securely attached infants, whether or not they work.

Similar findings emerged at two and three years of age. The main factors determining whether toddlers exhibited behavioral problems were all family-related, and in particular the mother's psychological adjustment and sensitivity toward her child. The study found "little evidence that early, extensive, and continuous non-maternal care was related to problematic child behavior, in contrast to results from previous works." But while nonmaternal care per se had little effect, the *quality* of that care was found to exert a small but significant influence over toddlers' behavior. Children in smaller groups, with a higher caregiver:child ratio, and with more positive, responsive caregivers were more compliant and socially competent than those in poorer child-care situations.

The latest research, then, suggests that children do not suffer emotionally when their mothers return to work during their first year of life. In most circumstances, working parents exert as much influence over their young children's development as nonworking parents. There are, however, some important caveats that emerge from the data. One is that the NICHD study is still in progress, and it is possible that adverse effects of child care will emerge later in the preschool and middle-childhood years, as several earlier studies reported. Another finding is that, while child care per se plays a rather small role in children's emotional adjustment, it can interact with poor parenting to put some children at greater risk for emotional problems. For instance, the NICHD study found that insecure attachment was likelier for children with *both* insensitive mothers and poorer quality or long hours in child care. Yet another caveat is that boys and girls do not fare equally well in nonmaternal care. Several studies, including the NICHD project, have found that social-emotional development is more likely to suffer in boys, and to benefit in girls, when their mothers are employed during the first few years. There are all sorts of speculations about why boys might be more vulnerable—greater immaturity, less attention by nonmaternal caregivers, or the possibility that working mothers favor their sons to a lesser degree than more traditional, nonworking mothers—but this finding does give one pause when considering child care for infant sons.

In spite of all the controversy, there is one thing that researchers agree on, and that is the importance of child-care *quality*. High-quality care can ensure children's emotional health, improve their social competence, and in particular, advance their cognitive development, as we will see in Chapter 17. According to recent estimates, however, the vast majority of young American children are in care that does not meet this standard. Most caregiving situations have too many children, with too few adults, a dismal physical environment, a lack of developmentally appropriate play materials, insufficient language stimulation, inadequate caregiver training, and a high rate of caregiver turnover that can be very emotionally unsettling for infants and young children. Parents obviously need to be very careful about choosing child care, and we as a society need to do much more to bring the quality of child care in the United States up to the standards of many European nations, where high-quality day care has been proven beneficial to children's emotional and cognitive development.

Stress, Attachment, and Brain Development

Attachment and brain development are a two-way street. Just as frontal-lobe maturation is a critical antecedent to attachment, so is a baby's stable, secure relationship with his caregiver essential to normal brain development and in particular the development of a healthy limbic system.

In this case, the critical link is stress. A growing body of evidence indicates that elevated stress hormones can be hazardous to the brain, especially to limbic components such as the hippocampus, anterior cingulate gyrus, and amygdala. In adult rats, for instance, excess stress hormones make hippocampal neurons more vulnerable to injury, and the longer they remain elevated, the greater the extent of permanent damage to these important memory-storing cells. Humans appear similarly vulnerable, based on observations of hippocampal atrophy in patients suffering from depression or post-traumatic stress disorder, two syndromes in which the stress hormone cortisol is known to be elevated. One study even found that one-year-old babies with higher cortisol levels showed dampened electrical activity emanating from the hippocampus, suggesting that babies' brains may be similarly vulnerable to the effects of stress.

Though babies don't talk about it, early life can be very stressful. Newborns are especially prone to large cortisol surges, even from events so seemingly minor as being undressed and weighed. Fortunately, however, their stress response systems soon mellow, and it appears that a healthy caregiver relationship is largely responsible. Baby rats, for instance, pass through a period from four to fourteen days when their stress response systems are notably difficult to activate, and this effect is known to be due to maternal contact. Infant monkeys are similarly buffered from large stress hormone surges as long as they remain in contact with their mother or a responsive substitute caregiver.

Babies' stress response declines steadily after two months of age; by fifteen months, their cortisol levels don't even increase following immunization shots (which doesn't mean they don't cry; crying and cortisol don't always go together). As with rats and monkeys, attachment seems to be responsible for modulating the stress system, since babies judged to be securely attached to their mothers show lower stress hormone elevations in response to strange or fearful events (like an approaching clown) than babies judged to be insecurely attached. Fortunately, mothers are not the only caregivers capable of buffering babies' stress response systems. Studies conducted with unfamiliar babysitters have shown that as long as the caregiver is friendly, playful, and sensitive, a baby will not experience a significant cortisol rise, even when left with her for the first time. But if the caregiver is cold, distant, and unengaging, babies do show a significant cortisol rise. (Once again, cortisol levels do not correlate with the amount of crying or protest a baby puts out when his mother leaves.) Again we see that quality child care (and quality parenting) is the key to protecting babies' brain and emotional development.

Do Boys and Girls Differ in Their Social and Emotional Development?

Ask this question of any parent who has both a son and a daughter, and you are sure to get a long list of the "innate" differences between the sexes. That males and females differ, particularly in emotional style and social responsiveness, is little disputed. Women are known to display their emotions more prominently, both verbally and through facial expression, and to more accurately decipher the emotion in another person's face or behavior, which underlies their tendency to be more empathetic. Men, while seemingly less emotional, actually show greater physiological effects of emotion, like sweating and heart-rate changes, and are more expressive with regard to one particular emotion, aggression. Like most gender effects, the actual magnitude of these differences is much smaller than the range of responses within each sex. In other words, there are plenty of women who act more aggressively than many men, and lots of men who are more emotionally sensitive than many women. Nonetheless, gender differences continue to fascinate us, because they strike right at the heart of the nature/nurture question. Are such emotional differences fated in our genes, or are they learned, early on, through the different socialization of boys and girls?

Parents lean toward the "nature" side, probably because few are willing to admit that we may be rearing our children differently. There is, in fact, good evidence that emotional differences are innate, because some are present as early as the first few days of life. For instance, girls just one to three days old respond more than boys to social stimuli, like a human voice or face. They also maintain eye contact longer and are likelier to exhibit the first form of empathy—crying in response to another infant's cry. By four years of age, girls are better at recognizing other people's facial expressions and are likelier to report that they actually *feel* the emotion depicted on another's face.

While baby girls have the advantage in social responsiveness, baby boys are actually the more emotional sex. They really are fussier! Newborn boys grimace more, startle more easily, are more irritable, and are harder to console than girl babies. Greater emotional lability may also explain why boys are more vulnerable than girls to insecure attachment when their mothers work (as previously noted).

One problem with many of these findings, however, is that they are often confounded by observer bias. In one study, for instance, adult raters were found to score babies' facial expressions differently, depending on whether they believed the child to be a girl or a boy; regardless of their actual sex, babies dressed in pink and coded with girls' names were likelier to be described as joyful, while babies dressed in blue and given boys' names were more often rated as angry, sad, or distressed.

Given this finding, it is not surprising to learn that parents do treat boys and girls somewhat differently. Mothers, for instance, have been found to smile more at baby girls than boys, whereas they pay greater heed to expressions of anger in their sons. Fathers reinforce this training by engaging their sons, much more so than their daughters, in the playful aggression known as "rough-and-tumble play." In general, both parents tend to be more actively involved with children of their same sex. This early segregation facilitates the process of *gender identification*, the point between eighteen and thirty months when toddlers figure out whether they are boys or girls. It's not long, then, before they become highly sensitive to gender-typing by the culture at large—that is, by their peers, television, advertisements, and so on—that tells boys that crying is unacceptable but aggression is all right, and girls that aggression is bad but nurturing and empathy are good.

Why do parents—even the most "liberated" among us—continue to treat our sons and daughters differently? There's no doubt that gender stereotyping, plain and simple, is partly responsible; much as we may think we'd accept any kind of emotional traits in our children, we simply expect boys and girls to be different because of our own cultural training—and parental expectations go a long way in child-rearing. But it's important to realize that parents also treat boys and girls differently for the simple reason that they really *are* different. For instance, mothers may smile more at daughters because they are more responsive and less fussy, and fathers may wrestle more with their sons because they tend to be physically larger. In other words, nature *creates* a different kind of nurture for each sex, making it all the more difficult to disentangle their influences.

A better approach may be to look directly at the brain, and particularly at the early development of the limbic system, to try to understand the origin of social-emotional sex differences. Recent PET studies confirm the existence of sex differences in adult limbic system functioning; women exhibit higher resting activity in the orbitofrontal cortex, while men tend to show more asymmetrical activity (right-hemisphere-dominant) throughout limbic portions of the cerebral cortex. It is not possible, for ethical reasons, to perform similar PET experiments on babies. However, work on infant monkeys has uncovered gender gaps in the development of two key limbic regions that find a direct parallel in the limbic development of boys and girls.

In male monkeys, the orbitofrontal gyrus develops earlier than in females, judging by infants' performance on a particular task, *object reversal,* known to depend on this limbic area. Females, by contrast, experience earlier maturation in the medial temporal lobe, an area that includes the amygdala and hippocampus and whose function is assessed by a different task, *concurrent discrimination.* Both the precocity of males' orbitofrontal gyrus development and the delayed development of their medial temporal lobe appear to depend on testosterone, since infant females treated early on with male hormones perform about as well as males on both tasks. Infant monkeys, then, show a double dissociation between the sexes in limbic system development that is hormonally based and most likely genetic in origin.

Recent evidence suggests that the same sexual dissociation occurs in human development. Researchers administered the same two tasks to children, ranging in age from one to four and a half years. Like young female monkeys, toddler-aged girls outperform boys on the concurrent discrimination task, which requires them to learn, for several pairs of items, which of the pair will give them a Froot Loop reward; while they underperform them on the object reversal task, which uses just one pair of items but requires them to learn that the Froot Loop may switch at any time from one item to the other. Although these tasks tap another limbic system function—memory—more than emotional processing, they nonetheless support the idea that two brain areas known to underlie social-emotional experience develop at different rates in the two sexes.

Earlier maturation of the temporal lobe could explain why girls are more socially oriented, since the amygdala and other temporal-lobe structures are known to participate in recognizing faces and emotional expressions. On the other hand, boys' orbitofrontal precocity might explain why they tend to express emotions less dramatically, since one function of the orbitofrontal cortex is to inhibit activity in lower limbic structures. Whatever the relationship between limbic structure and emotional function, it looks as though parents may be right after all: emotional differences between the sexes really do seem to have an innate origin. Socialization does play a role, but it may be more a matter of reinforcing the already diverging development of boys' and girls' limbic systems.

The Neural Basis of Temperament

Much as parents like to dwell on the differences between their sons and daughters, the fact is that all children differ emotionally, regardless of their sex, and these differences are as much a function of genetic fate as whether they're male or female. Psychologists use the term *temperament* to refer to a person's characteristic emotional and social style. Although we tend to use this word interchangeably with *personality*, temperament refers more specifically to those emotional traits that are innate, carried into the world from the moment of birth, if not earlier. Temperament is thus considered a genetic trait,* and though it continues to evolve as a child grows—just as physical traits continue to change—at its core, it remains fundamentally stable over the lives of most people.

Every parent who's had more than one child knows they can differ tremendously, even as young babies. In our case, Julia was the easier one—a good sleeper who cried very little and was always very independent. Sammy, alas, is fussier; he cries more, sleeps lightly and less reliably, and basically needed to be held for most of his first six months. Whereas Julia was a breeze to care for and we could take her anywhere, our lives have gotten a little more confined with Sammy around (although having two kids may have something to do with it!). On the bright side, Sammy, who's less physically active than Julia was, is also the cuddlier of the two; he'll nurse quietly for long stretches at an age when Julia was constantly kicking and tugging on me.

Temperament is not the only factor that determines what type of personality a child will end up having. As psychoanalysts first persuaded us, and as neuroscientists are now beginning to demonstrate, emotional style is also shaped by an individual's life experiences and, in particular, by the values and personalities of the people who rear him. Even here, however, a child's unique temperament has a way of shaping the form these early relationships

---

*Prenatal factors may also account for some aspects of a baby's behavior that we attribute to temperament, since we know that factors like maternal stress and drug use can affect a newborn's irritability or activity level. (See Chapter 3.)

take. Parents handle and respond to different children in different ways, depending on how irritable, sociable, or physically active they are. I know already that I hold Sammy more than I did Julia, and that I nursed him more frequently as a newborn. I've also been more cautious about starting him in day care, since he seems to adapt less well to new people and situations. All of this means that, in spite of our best intentions to treat our children equally, the emotional environment in which each one is raised is different because of the unique emotional style each brings to the relationship.

Why do people vary so much in temperament? What is it about their brains that makes some children cautious and others impulsive? Reactive or easygoing? Adaptable or irritable? Shy or sociable? Active or placid? Emotional or impassive? Happy or sad? Regrettably, we still know very little about the neural basis for most of these interpersonal differences. However, scientists have made great strides in understanding the neurobiology of one dimension of human temperament: the tendency to be inhibited or uninhibited in the face of novelty.

Shy or Bold? Two Extremes on the Temperament Spectrum

Andrew is not having much fun today. His mother, Patricia, signed him up for a study of toddler behavior, but when she brings him up to the laboratory playroom, thinking it might be very stimulating for him, the twenty-one-month-old is patently miserable. He shows no interest in exploring, remains clinging to Patricia's leg, and is completely silent, even when a friendly graduate student comes over and tries to engage him with a colorful jungle puzzle.

To the scientific observers replaying the episode on videotape, it's clear that Andrew is an *inhibited* child. His great reluctance to approach the new person and objects in the room, the close proximity he maintains to his mother, and the absence of verbalization (even though he speaks well at home) are all behaviors that mark a child as highly inhibited, a type of temperament exhibited by about 15 percent of all toddlers. Of course, many toddlers are initially shy in a new environment, even after they've passed the phase of extreme stranger anxiety, but inhibited children like Andrew never seem to warm up, no matter how friendly the stranger or how enticing the toys.

At the other extreme are another 15 percent or so of toddlers who are notably *uninhibited*. These kids act very differently in the lab playroom. For instance, little Allison, who's next on the experimental roster, races into the new room without a glance back at her mom, checks out all the toys in rapid succession, and even initiates a conversation with the unfamiliar graduate student. Whereas inhibited children tend to fear any kind of novelty—whether person, place, or thing—uninhibited children strongly gravitate to it, so researchers can objectively quantify inhibited behavior by looking at the degree of *withdrawal* or *approach* children display in this kind of experimental situation.

Twin studies have shown that a child's position on the inhibition spectrum is largely determined by genes. Although some inhibited toddlers do manage to "grow out of it" by school age, the tendency to approach or withdraw is one of the more stable dimensions of human temperament. By kindergarten, about 60 percent of children who were very inhibited as toddlers continue to be extremely shy or subdued around strange children or adults. They rarely smile at new people, take a long time to relax in new situations, and are generally cautious in all they do. These children are also prone to strong fears or phobias, and when they are a little older, they may worry excessively about taking a trip or losing their parents.

Although this may not sound like a very happy existence, a highly inhibited temperament does not bode poorly for a child's future. Inhibited children are often good students—perhaps because they're more afraid of failure, or possibly because they find solitary schoolwork less threatening and more rewarding than social challenges. If the opportunity is there, many go on to be very successful academically and end up enjoying satisfying careers and family lives.

Uninhibited children are much likelier to remain that way between toddlerhood and kindergarten; only about 10 percent tend to become more reserved over this period. (This reflects the fact that a bold, outgoing style is more highly valued in our culture; in Asian cultures, where social restraint is prized, more children remain inhibited.) While an uninhibited temperament has certain advantages—the children socialize easily and learn a lot through their assertive exploration—it can occasionally prove to be a problem. Highly uninhibited boys, in particular, may end up overly aggressive if they lack a positive channel for their exuberance.

The Physiology of Timidity According to Harvard psychologist Jerome Kagan, inhibited children are genuinely more fearful at the neurological level. Remember that fear, which is often a very useful emotion (and especially so for our more vulnerable ancestors, in whom it was selected), is also a complex physiological state, tightly orchestrated by the amygdala. Kagan proposes that inhibited children are simply those with a more reactive amygdala. Ever on guard for detecting danger, the amygdala in an inhibited child may more easily trigger all the physical manifestations of a fear response, encouraging him to retreat from whatever new situation makes him so uncomfortable. The situation is reversed in an uninhibited child, whose amygdala is only rarely active enough to trigger a fear response. Without this kind of internal, negative reinforcement holding them in check, uninhibited children are driven more by their raw energy and curiosity, occasionally even to the point of breaking bones or violating social rules.

Kagan's theory finds an interesting parallel in studies of house cats, which vary in temperament almost as much as children. It turns out that, like humans, about 15 percent of cats are very timid; they hold back from novelty, are not very exploratory, and won't even attack rats. Their defensive behavior first shows up about a month after birth, when a cat's amygdala is known to take control over its hypothalamus. Electrical recordings from the brains of these shy cats show that it is indeed the amygdala, and not other limbic structures, that is hypersensitive; neurons in the amygdala of timid cats are more easily excited by sensory input than amygdalar neurons in more assertive animals.

One way in which the amygdala translates fear into a bodily reaction is by activating the sympathetic nervous system, the part of our unconscious or autonomic nervous system that coordinates the body's fight-or-flight response. (See pages 83 and 294.) Studies by Kagan and his colleagues have shown that inhibited children do indeed show more signs of sympathetic activation. Although any one child may not exhibit every sign, inhibited children are generally more likely to have a higher resting heart rate, greater dilation of the pupils in a stressful situation, and less variability in the pitch of their voice, giving it a nervous sound. They also have higher levels of two circulating stress hormones, cortisol and norepinephrine. Uninhibited children, by contrast, tend to measure on the low end for all of these sympathetic signs. It does appear, then, that these children differ fundamentally in how their bodies react to mild stress.

Of course, fear is more than just a set of physiological responses. It is also a state of mind that holds powerful sway over the ways in which we choose to act. As we have seen, the conscious appreciation of feelings takes place in the frontal lobes, and the two sides of the brain process fundamentally different types of emotion. Feelings of fear, distress, and anxiety, which serve as the basis of withdrawal, generally involve heavier activity on the right side of the brain. The left frontal lobe, by contrast, is where feelings of joy, interest, and affection take place, emotions that underlie the tendency to approach new people or situations. We don't yet understand the neural basis of this left-right emotional dichotomy, but Kagan speculates that the brain's two amygdalas, whose primary function is to detect and respond to fear, are not equally connected to frontal limbic areas; this connection may be stronger on the right than on the left side of the brain.

Recent studies have confirmed that inhibited children exhibit greater activity on the right side, while highly uninhibited children experience greater left-sided activation. Four-year-olds who seem happy and readily play and talk with their peers show greater activation of the left frontal cortex, whereas those who are very reserved socially, who tend to isolate themselves and look on while others play, show relatively greater activation of the right frontal area.

A child's tendency to be left- or right-dominated appears as early as ten months of age—that is, from the very outset of frontal limbic function. This difference was noted during EEG experiments used to measure frontal-lobe activation during maternal separation. While nearly all the babies were upset to see their mothers leave and had a correspondingly active right frontal lobe, their brains differed during the "resting" period at the beginning of the experiment, recorded while the mother sat quietly smiling in front of her child. Babies whose baseline activity was higher on the left side were much less likely to cry when their mother left the room, while right-dominated babies put up the greatest protest. In other words, it looks as though babies are already wired to be more or less anxious, even at an age when their frontal lobes are only beginning to participate in emotional processing.

Predicting Temperament in Early Infancy   Ten months is early, but it is possible that differences in social inhibition at this age are already a result of rearing, as opposed to true temperamental distinctions. It is not hard to image how certain aspects of parenting style, consistent across the three hundred or so days since birth, could wire up the frontal lobes differently in inhibited and uninhibited children. For instance, it is possible—although completely untested—that extremely protective mothers may foster greater right frontal development in their infants by consistently modeling fearful behavior.

To resolve this issue, researchers have begun to look at babies even younger than ten months for evidence of temperamental markers that may predict where a child will end up on the inhibition spectrum. In early infancy, the cortex is not yet advanced enough to identify inhibited behavior, but Kagan and his colleagues have found two characteristics—both driven by the lower limbic system—that, when they occur in combination, do seem to predict later inhibition. These are *irritability* and *motor activity*, especially in response to novel sensory stimuli. Four-month-olds who cry, fuss, or fret a good deal *and* who show a strong motor response—pumping their limbs or arching their backs—in response to a brightly colored mobile or a whiff of an alcohol swab, are more likely to end up being fearful toddlers. Irritable four-month-olds who aren't very physically reactive to stimuli like these don't turn out to be inhibited children. And four-month-olds who are physically quite reactive but not irritable—that is, who are more prone to smiling or vocalizing—are likelier to end up on the bolder end of the spectrum.

The relationship between early motor reactivity and later fearfulness may seem surprising, but it fits with the idea that an inhibited child is one whose amygdala has an especially low threshold for activation. The amygdala is known to influence neural pathways that control movement, especially in young babies whose motor cortex has yet to take over voluntary control of the limbs and torso. The amygdala also connects to lower brain circuits responsible for crying and distress vocalization. The combination of high motor reactivity and lots of crying may therefore mark babies whose amygdala is especially easily aroused. Then, once the cortex gets involved, this arousal translates into greater fearfulness. Indeed, researchers have found that by nine months of age, babies who exhibited both of these characteristics at four months were already right-frontal dominant, whereas babies who at four months were very active but prone to positive emotions showed greater activity in the left frontal cortex.

The fact that early behavioral patterns can predict later temperament suggests that the basic tendency for approach or withdrawal is genetically based. Though experience can certainly modulate these tendencies, as described in the next section, this neural predisposition to react positively or negatively toward new experiences is rooted early in limbic development.

Harnessing Limbic Plasticity: How Parenting Shapes a Child's Personality

Patricia is well aware of Andrew's timidity. He was inconsolable for weeks when she went back to work, soon after his first birthday. Whenever they go out, he remains glued to her: on the playground, at the doctor's office, and on the few playdates she's managed to drag him to. He'll sit or stand off to one side of the room, watching the other kids but making no movement to join in. He even seems suspicious of the toys an older child hands him to play with.

Patricia confesses that she's worried about Andrew's reticence. Does this mean he's destined to be a wallflower? Is there any way she can help coax him into a more outgoing style? How malleable is a child's personality, especially during the early brain-building years?

There is no question that genes play a large part in determining the kind of people we turn out to be. Each of us begins life with an innate temperament that sets the ball rolling, deciding which side of the personality mountain we'll head down. But while temperament is largely genetically determined, personality is considerably less so. The best estimates, based on comparisons of identical and fraternal twins in adulthood, indicate that heredity accounts for about half of the variance in personality traits such as emotionality, sociability, aggressiveness, cautiousness, and traditionalism. This leaves experience, of course, to shape the rest of Andrew's personality development, and Patricia is determined to make the best of it.

The reason personality is more malleable than temperament is that they are controlled by different parts of the brain. Whereas temperament is largely a product of the lower limbic system—the amygdala in all of its varying degrees of excitability—the rich and nuanced emotional lives we eventually lead are governed more by higher limbic structures, our slowly developing frontal lobes. And like the cortex as a whole, the frontal lobes are remarkably plastic, shaping themselves according to the cumulative emotional experience of the individual. This is particularly so in infancy, when prefrontal synapses are first forming, but it continues on into the early preschool years, when they are remodeling themselves at breakneck speed, and throughout childhood, when they have yet to finish their limbic wiring. Just as Andrew's visual experience has already shaped the way his visual cortex sees, so will all the emotional and social experiences of his childhood critically determine how the limbic areas of his cerebral cortex are put together.

Obviously, a baby's most important limbic tutors are his parents. Every moment of interaction—whether a shared meal, a tickling session, or a stern rebuke—fires off a select group of synapses in his limbic brain, stabilizing them at the expense of others. Parents model one style of emotional responding and social interaction, and their children—even as newborns— mimic that style, rehearsing their parents' behaviors. This activates specific neural pathways, locking in the limbic circuits that will serve them for a lifetime. Such intense limbic entrainment explains why we find ourselves—especially as parents—reacting surprisingly much as our own parents did. For better or worse, the millions of moments parents share with their children create a limbic legacy that may live on for generations.

Social Deprivation and the Miswired Monkey Brain The best evidence that parents actually change the course of limbic development comes from studies carried out in monkeys. Like human babies, infant monkeys are utterly dependent on their mothers, and this dependence extends to more than protection and nourishment. Monkeys that are removed from their mothers at birth, reared in isolation from other monkeys, and have limited human contact become profoundly emotionally disturbed. Rather than playing and exploring, as young monkeys normally love to do, monkeys reared in isolation will remain huddled in a corner, rocking or swaying with sad or vacant looks on their faces. Clearly missing their mothers' contact, these monkeys try to compensate by holding or sucking their own bodies, or else banging themselves against the wall, even to the point of self-injury. Their disturbance is especially marked when they are later introduced to a group of normally reared monkeys. Isolated monkeys are virtually incapable of normal social interactions; they withdraw completely, except for the occasional inappropriate act of aggression. They rarely mate, and even when an isolated female is artificially impregnated, she fails dismally as a mother, neglecting or abusing her own baby, sometimes mortally so.

In many ways, these isolated monkeys resemble orphans and other abandoned children who have been raised in institutions (see Chapter 1), so these studies have been extremely useful for teaching us how social deprivation affects the developing brain. We know, for instance, that monkeys reared in isolation have less dendritic branching among the neurons in the prefrontal cortex and probably a lower level of synaptic communication. They also show disturbances in the brain levels of many neurotransmitters. The most marked effect is a permanent reduction in norepinephrine, which may impair the growth and stabilization of limbic pathways and may explain why these animals (like human infants who are not securely attached to their parents) have a very low capacity for coping with stress. Interestingly, fewer effects have been observed in the amygdala and hypothalamus, suggesting that social experience selectively influences higher limbic structures, as might be expected given that more of the development of these structures occurs postnatally.

It is not surprising that social isolation would warp a baby's brain. Anyone would go a little crazy under the kind of solitary confinement faced by these monkeys. But what is remarkable, as we have learned from further studies, is the limited period over which such permanent distortions are shaped. Monkeys who spend just three months with their mothers and are then isolated show less severe behavioral abnormalities than those isolated from birth, while monkeys isolated for the *second* six months of life show almost no long-term emotional deficits. Thus there is a critical period for emotional tutoring in monkeys, extending over the first six months of life, which corresponds to a phase of rapid development in their higher limbic structures. In humans, the critical period for social nurturing probably extends until about three years of age, with deprivation during the first year being the most devastating.

The Limbic Legacy of Child Abuse   Very few children grow up in anything like the kind of isolation these monkeys have been exposed to. But a great many do suffer lesser degrees of neglect during the critical period for emotional development, and more still are victims of abuse, reared in an environment of violence and fear. It is only in the last decade that we have become fully aware of the frequency of child abuse. Abuse is an underlying factor in many different psychiatric disorders, as well as in such social problems as aggression, drug abuse, and delinquency. There is little doubt that childhood neglect and abuse are major contributors to societal problems, and the reason is that they permanently alter the wiring of a person's emotional brain.

Neuroscientists are just beginning to piece together the ways in which neglect and abuse leave their lasting marks on children's limbic systems. In one recent study, MRI scans of severely neglected children revealed that their brains are as much as 30 percent smaller than those of control children. In another study, researchers compared the brain activity records of two groups of young psychiatric patients, those who had a history of physical, psychological, or sexual abuse versus those who clearly had no such history. Abused children were twice as likely to exhibit abnormal electrical activity, particularly in the frontal and temporal regions where limbic system activity is most pronounced. They were also likely to show disturbances in the left frontal region—the "feel-good" side. Finally, there is some evidence that the hippocampus, the limbic structure whose main function is to store long-term memories, is atrophied in adults who were abused as children. Such hippocampal damage might explain why few people who were severely abused are able to consciously remember these events, even if they occurred rather late in childhood.

These findings demonstrate where the real scars of child abuse and neglect lie: inside children's brains, and especially in the limbic system that defines their personality and governs their emotional future. Not only are abused children raised in a world of pain and fear, they lack the healthy attachment relationship that is known to buffer young brains from such overwhelming stresses. The resulting limbic scars can haunt them throughout life.

Parenting Style   Fortunately, most children are not abused, but these findings inevitably make us wonder about all the other ways in which early experience might shape a child's developing limbic system. Children grow up in all kinds of circumstances, and it is possible that each variation leaves a particular imprint on the emotional brain. How, for instance, is limbic wiring influenced if a child has multiple caregivers, as when both parents work? What is the effect of birth order? What about growing up without a father? Without peer contact? And how do different parents' personalities and caregiving styles influence limbic development? What is the effect of parents who are relaxed versus stressed? Patient or intolerant? Effusive or reserved? Cautious or carefree?

We are still a long way from understanding how each of these factors might mold a child's limbic connections. But neuroscientists have begun to tackle the influence of parental personality by focusing on one particular type of mother—women who are suffering from depression. Depressed mothers were chosen for study because it is known that they treat their babies differently from nondepressed women. They tend to smile at their babies and stimulate them less than control mothers. They are also less in tune with their babies' feelings; rather than adjusting their responses to meet the baby's needs, depressed mothers tend to let their own moods govern these interactions.

Researchers at the University of Washington wondered whether these differences might affect the babies' limbic development, so they compared frontal-lobe EEG measures in the infants of depressed and nondepressed mothers. By about one year of age, babies whose mothers are depressed do indeed exhibit a different pattern of neural responsiveness than control babies. During playful interactions, like a game of peekaboo, they experience less activation of the left hemisphere (the "feel-good" side) than control babies. On the other hand, during an unhappy event, like watching their mothers leave the room, the babies of depressed mothers produce greater left-side activation, while control babies experience greater activity on the right side.

This inverted response may explain why the babies of depressed mothers seem to suffer their own form of depression; they tend to be more irritable and withdrawn and to show very few positive facial expressions compared with babies of nondepressed mothers. Of course, the emotional correspondence between mother and infant could be due to an inherited tendency toward depression; and it could also reflect a prenatal (for example, hormonal) influence on the baby's temperament. But based on everything we know about how experience shapes cortical development, it is likely that these babies' limbic systems are actually being molded by their mothers' example.

Implications for Emotional Parenting   If a mother's depression can alter the wiring of her baby's limbic system, it is easy to imagine how other parental behaviors also leave their mark on a child's developing brain. Every parent has at least a couple of idiosyncrasies that are likely to rub off on the baby's limbic system. This, as much as heredity, is what people mean when they say "He's his father's son," or "She's just like her mother!" With luck, a given child will adopt the good more than the bad in the emotional styles of her parents, siblings, teachers, and peers.

But can parents do more than hope for good luck? Is there a way to deliberately tip the balance, to preserve the "positive synapses" and prune away the negative tendencies in a child's temperament? Undoubtedly there is. Psychologists agree that the key to nurturing a child's healthy psyche lies in sensitive parenting. This means, for starters, being aware of a baby's signals and responding promptly and appropriately to his needs for food, sleep, comfort, or affection. Children need to feel accepted and respected, even if you are correcting or punishing them. No matter how busy you are, they need to feel that you are accessible and not ignoring them (except, of course, for brief "time-outs"). And when they're old enough to begin to understand, somewhere in the third year, it also means talking to them about their feelings and relationships, so you can help them develop the very important frontal-lobe skill of introspection.

As in all things, however, there is a limit to just how sensitive parents should be. Researchers were surprised to learn that babies with the most attentive mothers—those who responded instantly to every gurgle, squawk, or hiccup—were actually *less* securely attached than mothers who responded a little less consistently. In other words, children react poorly to smothering attentiveness, even in infancy. It hampers their drive for independence and their growing ability to regulate their own emotions. Whether you're helping your one-year-old walk across the room or your ten-year-old with her botany project, children need to feel that you are cooperating with rather than interfering in their latest endeavors.

But with the right balance, parents *can* modify even the most difficult side of their children's temperaments. As an example, consider those 15 percent or so of toddlers who are very inhibited—kids like Andrew, whose right frontal lobe explodes with anxiety whenever he's confronted by new people or a new environment. While many of these children don't change, about 40 percent do lose their extreme timidity by kindergarten. Researchers have observed that these are the youngsters whose parents, though sensitive, manage to gently challenge them, encouraging them to face their fears and learn how to cope with minor stresses, thereby coaxing along those connections on the left side of the brain.

Patricia is one parent who's decided to try challenging her child more. She's enrolled Andrew in nursery school, now encourages him to be more adventuresome on the playground, and has begun traveling with him, so he can spend his first nights away from home. So far he's not too happy about it, but he is showing signs of gradually adapting, rising to the challenge his parents are laying out for him. Before long he'll probably actually enjoy school and will undoubtedly even make a few friends. Though it's likely that he will always be a pretty cautious kid, he'll surely have a happier youth than if his parents hadn't stepped in and deliberately helped rewire his limbic system.

Chapter 13

THE EMERGENCE
OF MEMORY

It was the perfect vacation: Mexico in February. We went when Julia was still a baby—eleven months old—and she seemed to have as great a time as her parents. I have vivid memories of her cruising (but not yet walking) around brilliant bougainvilleas, splashing happily in warm tidepools, and delighting in our treks along white sand beaches, riding high up in the backpack, where she could watch the waves crash in and feel the warm breeze on her face.

Too bad, then, that she'll never remember a minute of it. For all her enthusiasm at the time, Julia will have no recollection of this trip or, in all likelihood, any other event in the three years now since her birth. As each of us knows from personal experience, adults cannot remember events from the earliest years of life. Psychologists call this profound lapse *infantile amnesia*, but it lasts well past infancy. A very few adults can remember a dramatic event, such as a sibling's birth or being hospitalized, from around two years of age, but most of us recall nothing before three and a half years. Even then memories remain sketchy until age five or six, when infantile amnesia has fully waned.

Why do we have so little recall of early life? All memories fade over the years, but infantile amnesia is not simply a matter of the passage of time. Seventy-year-olds can recognize high school classmates even if they haven't seen them for fifty years, but ten-year-olds are hard-pressed to identify preschool chums from just six or seven years earlier. The absence of early memory is all the more paradoxical since—as we've seen throughout this book—early experiences have a profound impact on virtually every other aspect of a child's neural and mental development.

Psychologists have put forth all kinds of explanations for infantile amnesia, but they basically boil down to two alternatives: either early memories are never stored in the first place, or else they are stored but remain somehow inaccessible later in life. Sigmund Freud took the latter view, convincing generations of therapists that nothing is ever really forgotten, only repressed by the conscious mind. Early memories are buried especially deeply, according to Freud, but continue to percolate around the subconscious mind in ways that importantly shape our adult personalities. Many contemporary psychologists agree that infantile amnesia is a retrieval problem, but they pin it on the absence of certain cognitive skills in young children, especially language.

There's something very appealing about the notion that memories are never really lost, only hard to access. Unfortunately, it doesn't hold up very well to what we know about the neural mechanisms of memory. We now know that specific circuits in the brain are responsible for storing permanent memories, and there is good reason to think that infantile amnesia is a simple consequence of the fact that these circuits take several years to develop. Infantile amnesia is thus a problem of storage, not retrieval. Early experiences never make it into long-term memory banks because the brain's recording machinery isn't yet functional.

This doesn't mean, however, that very young minds are incapable of storing information. We have already seen that even from their earliest days, babies can perform all kinds of feats that require learning—acquiring information as a result of experience—and memory—storage of that information for some period after the event has ended. Even four-month-old Megan can recognize familiar people and toys, master new motor skills, and adapt in many other ways to predictable features of her environment. By the time she's in preschool, she'll be reciting facts and perhaps even reminiscing about her second birthday. All this in spite of the fact that she won't remember any of it later in life!

Memory is not a single entity but a patchwork of several different forms of information storage that emerge progressively with the maturation of different brain circuits. Babies begin life with a primitive yet very useful set of memory skills; lower parts of the brain can store information, but it is at an automatic level, beneath consciousness, and lasts for relatively short periods of time. Then, starting at eight or nine months of age, they show signs of a more flexible, deliberate type of information storage, the first inklings of memory as we more commonly think of it. Memories then grow longer and increasingly conscious throughout the preschool years until finally, during early elementary school years, children become aware of their own memory skills and begin to use them in a truly mature way—to intentionally study and acquire new information.

The development of memory is both fascinating and fundamental to every other aspect of cognitive growth. It's fascinating because in a very real sense, we are the sum total of what we can remember; memories create the mental continuity that gives each of us a coherent sense of who we are and what we have uniquely experienced. Watching memory dawn in a young child is almost like seeing consciousness gradually emerge out of the fog bank of early experience. Memory development is also critically important, because the brain's enormous capacity to store information is what makes every kind of learning possible. Whether it's bonding with Mother, recognizing Aunt Betsy, mastering crawling, associating words with objects, or figuring out that water is wet, every mental advance depends on the brain's ability to file away experience and then use this stored information to act with greater wisdom and efficiency. Memory is truly the cornerstone of intellectual growth, the brain's sole means of acquiring knowledge, so it is not surprising that even in infancy, it serves as a marker for later intelligence. At the same time, memory is a flexible skill that can improve with practice. By understanding how the brain's various storage systems develop, we may be able to optimize the several mnemonic skills that are essential to intellectual growth.

The Many Types of Memory

To fully appreciate how memory emerges in children, it first helps to understand all of the different kinds of information that our brains are capable of storing. Just as computers use separate memory banks for separate purposes, so does the human brain cache several qualitatively different forms of memory. Most people are familiar with the distinction between short- and long-term memory; you can remember a seven-digit phone number for a few seconds—long enough to close the phone book and dial—but recalling it for longer than that requires serious concentration and mental rehearsal. This short-term recall is analogous to the information stored in a computer's random access memory (RAM), which is used for immediate, ongoing applications but disappears every time the machine is rebooted. Long-term memory refers to any kind of recall outside this immediate time frame (from minutes to decades) and is comparable to a computer's "hard" memory—the kind stored on disk or CD-ROM—which is more or less permanent and can be recalled at any time (except for the unfortunate fact that our memories are far more fallible than the digital variety).

Memories can also be distinguished in another fundamental way: by whether they are conscious. It turns out that Freud was right about one thing; the mind does store a great deal of information at a purely unconscious level. Though the word *memory* usually connotes facts we can recite or events we can recall—our conscious or *explicit* recollections—our brains are also chock-full of another, entirely different type of stored information. These are our *implicit* memories—all the skills, habits, and conditioned or habituated responses that are equally learned through experience but that we are generally quite unaware of. Implicit memories include the kind of emotional conditioning described in the last chapter, as well as the stored neural patterns used to guide any kind of motor, perceptual, or cognitive skill, such as riding a bike, driving, or reading. Unlike conscious memories, which can be stored after a single experience, unconscious memories usually require a lot of practice or repetition to take hold. Once they are stored, however, implicit memories tend to be much less fallible than explicit memories, which is why you probably can't remember the day you learned to ride a bike but have never forgotten how. Returning to our computer analogy, implicit memory is like the programs stored on a computer's hard drive—the knowledge of *how* to do things—while explicit memory is more like the data files—the information that tells us who we are, what we've experienced, and what we know.

Amnesia in Adults and Infants   The most vivid illustration of the difference between explicit and implicit memory is found in amnesia. When certain parts of the brain are extensively damaged, people permanently lose the ability to store new conscious memories. The most famous such case is a man known as H.M., who has been amnesic since he awoke, in 1953, from surgery that was performed to alleviate severe epilepsy. (The procedure, performed when he was twenty-seven years old, worked well to control his seizures, but because of its devastating effect on his memory, the surgeon who performed it subsequently campaigned widely to prevent others from repeating his mistake.) While H.M. can recall the events of his life preceding his surgery, he has not been able to learn or recall any new facts in the nearly half century since. Every day, every hour, is a new existence for him. He cannot recognize famous faces (unless they achieved notoriety before about 1950), recall what he had for breakfast, or describe a single detail about a job he worked at every day for months. But in spite of this profound memory loss, H.M. is capable of learning new skills. He easily mastered a backward drawing task that involves learning, through repeated practice, how to copy objects using an apparatus that permitted him to view his hand only in a mirror. He also improves every time he assembles a particular jigsaw puzzle. Remarkably, though, H.M. never admits to any proficiency at mirror drawing and will claim never to have seen the jigsaw puzzle before!

Recent studies with other brain-damaged patients have uncovered all kinds of unconscious memory skills unaffected by amnesia. These individuals perform perfectly well, for instance, at a kind of perceptual bias known as *priming*. In a typical priming experiment, a subject is shown a list of words and then, after some distraction, is asked to complete a list of three-letter stems with the first word that comes to mind. Amnesics are just as likely as normal subjects to complete the stems with words from the original list, like filling in "organ" when given the stem "org—." They are even capable of mastering new cognitive skills, like abstraction and categorization, provided the training involves lots of repetition and trial-and-error learning. (Such studies are fascinating, not only for what they reveal about amnesics, but also for what they reveal about the rest of us, namely, the surprising degree to which our most sophisticated learning takes place outside of our conscious awareness.)

It is no coincidence that the memory lapse of early childhood is also known as "amnesia." Babies too can learn all kinds of motor, perceptual, and cognitive skills, but they are largely unaware of what they have accomplished and have no explicit memories of these experiences. Young children are even quite proficient at priming, provided, of course, that the tests do not use written language as the stimulus. Babies' memories are thus strikingly similar to those of adult amnesics, suggesting that the same brain structures damaged in amnesia are also the ones slowest to develop in early childhood.

How Does the Brain Store Memories?

H.M. lost his memory when surgeons removed the inner or medial section of both his temporal lobes. We now know that this is one part of the brain essential for storing long-term, conscious memories. The medial temporal lobe forms the hub of the limbic system, the dense network of cortical and subcortical structures that, as we saw in the preceding chapter, is responsible for our rich emotional lives. Memory is the other essential business of the limbic system. But whereas emotion is controlled by the amygdala, the small oval nucleus that sits in front of the temporal lobe, memory is governed by the hippocampus, a larger, elongated structure that lies immediately behind the amygdala, filling the inner curvature of the temporal lobe. (The hippocampus is technically part of the cerebral cortex but is phylogenetically more primitive than most of it.) People suffering damage to the hippocampus and/or surrounding parts of the temporal cortex on both sides of the brain (which provides all of the synaptic input to the hippocampus) will experience permanent memory impairment.

Besides the medial temporal lobe, three other brain regions have been implicated in long-term memory storage, based on the amnesic syndromes that result when they are damaged. One of these, the *medial thalamus*, is known to undergo degeneration in alcoholic patients who exhibit a type of amnesia known as *Korsakoff's syndrome*. Another area is the *basal forebrain*, which serves as the brain's primary source of the neurotransmitter acetylcholine. As its name suggests, the basal forebrain is located toward the front of the brain, ahead of the thalamus, but is buried equally deeply under the cerebral cortex. Degeneration of the basal forebrain contributes to the memory loss in Alzheimer's disease, because it depletes the brain of acetylcholine, a known memory-promoting chemical.

A fourth area critical for conscious, long-term memory is the prefrontal cortex. You may recall from the previous chapter that the prefrontal cortex is intimately interconnected with medial temporal-lobe structures and thus comprises an important part of the limbic system. People who suffer brain damage confined to the frontal lobe suffer memory loss, but it is a very specific kind. Unlike patients with hippocampal damage, frontally damaged patients can remember events, facts, people, and the like, but where they fail is in remembering *when* or *where* something happened or they learned a particular fact. This higher-order skill is called *source memory* by psychologists, and it is one of the slowest types of recall to emerge in development. (It is also one of the first types to deteriorate in older people.) Though young children are good at remembering specific facts and details of events, they are notoriously poor at remembering where they learned something, or when an event occurred, which may be why they can be so easily led astray by suggestive questioning (as in certain recent sex abuse cases) or even their own fantasy.

· · ·

Hippocampus, medial thalamus, basal forebrain, prefrontal cortex: all four of these structures are critical for the storage of long-term, conscious memories. (See Figure 13.1.) But they are not the only parts of the brain involved in storing information. The complicated truth is that the entire nervous system (including the spinal cord and all the peripheral nerves) participates, because information storage is a fundamental property of neurons. All nerve cells are capable of modifying themselves—of remodeling their synapses and dendrites—according to their "experience," or pattern of electrical activity. All memories, whether conscious or not, are stored as patterns of synaptic change somewhere in the brain. Motor skills, like riding a bike or playing the clarinet, are stored as changes in motor circuits, such as the cerebellum, basal ganglia, and motor cortex. Perceptual skills, like mirror-reading or discriminating jigsaw puzzle pieces, are stored in sensory pathways. Emotional memories, like the warm cozy feeling you associate with the smell or sight of Grandma's house, are stored through the actions of the amygdala and its connected circuitry.

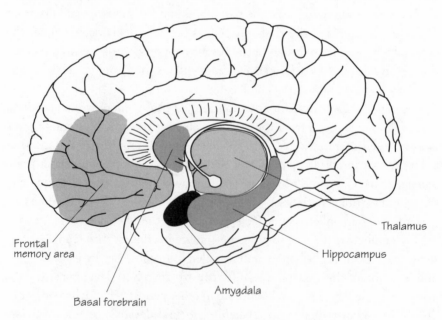

FIGURE 13.1

Brain areas involved in conscious memory.

After M. Mishkin and T. Appenzeller, "The anatomy of memory,"
Scientific American, June 1987.

And of course, our large cerebral cortex also participates in the storage of memories, both implicit and explicit. Those sophisticated but nonetheless unconscious skills like priming and abstraction are filed away as synaptic changes in higher-order sensory areas, while conscious memories for events and facts are probably stored as collections of changes in many cortical regions. The important difference, however, is that only conscious memories depend on the hippocampus–medial thalamus–basal forebrain–prefrontal cortex circuit during the learning and storage phase. In effect, these four structures act as the brain's special recording device; they create conscious memories but then ship them off to the cerebral cortex for long-term warehousing.

While much is still mysterious about the brain's mechanisms of memory storage, one fact should sound familiar: our brains store memories in much the same way that they shape themselves during development. Experience, as we have seen over and over, rewires the brain. Whether early in a baby's life or well into old age, active synapses and pathways continue to be strengthened, and inactive ones weakened, according to the sights, sounds, feelings, and events of daily life. Learning, then, is really just an extension of development, a later manifestation of the remarkable ability of each individual's brain to modify itself according to his or her unique experiences.

Brain and Memory Development

The fact that every part of the brain takes part in some form of information storage helps make sense of the way memory emerges during infancy. Implicit memories dawn first, the kinds of habits and conditioned responses that can be stored in more precocious, lower-brain areas like the spinal cord and brain stem. Babies' repertoire of implicit memory skills then grows broader as structures such as the basal ganglia and cerebellum rapidly mature during early infancy. Memories that depend on the cerebral cortex, including certain implicit and all types of explicit memories, emerge more slowly, since the cortex lags well behind subcortical structures in its maturation. Finally, children's source memory—their awareness of where and when they learned or experienced something—emerges quite late, due to the very protracted maturation of the frontal lobes. This explains why children only gradually

achieve deliberate control over their memories—a skill necessary for studying and which becomes increasingly important in later years of schooling.

Cortical development may not be the only factor limiting conscious memory in babies. Important evidence suggests that the hippocampus is also
responsible for the phenomenon of infantile amnesia. Although in many ways
the hippocampus develops well before most cortical structures (it begins forming earlier in gestation and shows more advanced synaptic and dendritic development), it is notably slow in two respects. First, it is one of the very few brain
areas in which neurons are still being formed after birth; some 20 percent of
cells in the first hippocampal relay, the *dentate gyrus*, are added between birth
and around nine months of age. Second, several of the major input and output
pathways of the hippocampus are among the slowest to myelinate of all fiber
tracts in the brain. One tract in particular, the *fornix*, which carries information from the hippocampus to the thalamus (see Figure 12.1), doesn't even
begin myelinating until the second year after birth and continues the process
into late childhood. To some degree, then, infantile amnesia really is the same
problem faced by adults with amnesia—lack of a functional hippocampus.

Fetal Memory

Lately Julia has gotten very curious about her origin. She keeps asking me to
tell her the story about when she was in my tummy. So I give her the G-rated
version and then ask her if she can remember anything from before she was
born. "I liked to kick your stomach," she replies, repeating a well-rehearsed
fact, something she's heard over and over throughout her three years, but not
actually recalling her prior existence in utero.

Nonetheless, somewhere low down in her nervous system, there probably are a few memories left of prenatal life—some basic motor pattern, or
refinement of sensory feedback that was stored after all that repeated kicking. Long before the hippocampus and cerebral cortex get into the act, babies
and even fetuses are able to store information about their experiences.
Sensory-motor learning is the first type to emerge in development because it
can be supported by some of the simplest neural pathways. Even worms and
sea slugs can "remember" to squirm or retract their gills in a certain way if
experience dictates it. In babies, whose reflex pathways in the spinal cord
and brain stem begin functioning well before birth, such simple forms of
learning have been demonstrated as early as the third trimester of gestation.

The first type of learning to emerge is *habituation*, the progressive decline in responding that psychologists find so useful for probing babies' minds. Almost as soon as they begin to hear, fetuses habituate to a repeated acoustic stimulus, a loud sound or vibration applied close to the mother's abdomen. Initially, the sound triggers a dramatic startle response—large movements of the baby's limbs or torso that can be observed under ultrasound—but if the stimulus is repeated every twenty seconds, a fetus will respond less and less vigorously until finally he ceases altogether. A few babies show habituation as early as twenty-three weeks of gestation, and by twenty-nine weeks, all healthy fetuses can do it.

Habituation may seem trivial, but it is actually a very important form of information storage. It allows you to screen out constant, meaningless stimuli, such as the feel of the clothes on your body or, during prenatal life, the loud sound of the maternal heartbeat. If a fetus startled every time the ventricles of his mother's heart contracted, he would waste terrific amounts of energy needed to grow and develop. Nor is habituation trivial on a neural level. It is not simply a consequence of sensory adaptation or muscular fatigue but involves long-lasting changes in the electrical properties of cells and synapses in the central nervous system. Babies whose brains are compromised in utero because of oxygen deprivation, genetic abnormality (such as Down syndrome), maternal smoking, or other prenatal problems do not habituate normally. Fetal habituation can thus be used clinically to predict a baby's neurological health and mental development.

Habituation is not the only form of learning that babies exhibit before birth. The same fetal reflexes have also been shown to adapt by a process known as *classical conditioning*, a learned association between stimuli. Most of us learned in school about Pavlov's famous discovery—that dogs will begin to salivate to the sound of a bell if they have repeatedly heard it rung with the delivery of food. A human fetus can similarly learn after repeated pairings that a sound will signal a vibratory stimulus or, perhaps more meaningfully, that a brief clip of music will relax its mother. In the latter case, pregnant women were asked to consciously relax whenever they heard a particular piece of music, say, Beethoven's *Moonlight Sonata*. As any pregnant woman knows, fetuses are most active when their mothers are the most relaxed, but the mothers in this experiment soon noticed their babies beginning to move to the music alone, even before they had a chance to relax themselves. Then, after birth, the same music was found to have an especially calming effect on the babies. Classical conditioning has been reported in fetuses as early as five and a half months of gestation and remains an important form of learning throughout life.

All of this proves that babies can form memories before birth. But how long do such memories last? Is it really possible that we retain implicit memories from before we were born?

Thus far, researchers have been able to demonstrate fetal habituation lasting no more than twenty-four hours. But we have already seen in earlier chapters that newborns can recognize many stimuli that they were exposed to extensively before birth. A newborn will suck preferentially to hear his own mother's voice, or *The Cat in the Hat*, if she repeatedly read it out loud over the several weeks before birth; he can also be comforted by the sound of a maternal heartbeat, played as he would remember it sounding in the womb (Chapter 10); he can even recognize his own mother's odor from his time in utero (Chapter 7). So it's clear that babies do carry memories out of the womb with them that last for weeks, if not longer. Though these earliest memories are inaccessible to conscious recall, they undoubtedly influence the way babies perceive and react to the world after birth, and thereby shape much of the important learning that takes place in the early months of life.

Memory in the First Six Months

It is not easy to figure out what babies can remember; obviously, you can't ask them. But fortunately, decades of research on animal learning have established very reliable ways of probing the memories of nonverbal creatures. One type of learning that has proven especially informative is called *operant conditioning*, the association between a subject's own action and some reward or punishment. Like pigeons in the famous Skinner box, who learn that pecking at a light will release some seeds to eat, babies quickly refine their budding skills by learning and remembering that a reward (milk, Mother's smile, a toy, or simply the joy of accomplishment) is associated with a particular motor action (sucking, smiling, reaching, walking).

Infants are really good at operant conditioning, so researchers take advantage of it, whenever possible, to better understand what they can recognize and discriminate. All those tests of newborn sensory preference, for instance, exploited the fact that babies can learn to suck at different rates in order to obtain a particular reward, such as their mother's face or voice. But operant conditioning is also useful, in and of itself, as a way of probing how well and how long babies remember.

The best-studied operant procedure is so simple, and babies enjoy it so much, that you might want to try it with your own child. It is called *mobile conditioning*. A young baby, like bright-eyed three-month-old Robert, is laid in a crib, facing up at an attractive mobile of five dangling, brightly colored blocks. The mobile itself is pretty exciting, but it gets even better after the experimenter ties a ribbon around one of Robert's ankles and attaches the other end to the mobile's crossbar. Suddenly, Robert is kicking two or three times more frequently than before the ribbon was attached (established as the baseline period). He has discovered that he can actually *move* the mobile by moving his leg and is simply delighted at this newfound power.

This is the learning phase of the experiment. Memory-testing comes later, when the mobile is reinstalled in his crib but not connected to his foot. Though he hasn't seen it for three days, Robert starts kicking as soon as he sees the mobile, showing that he remembers, at some level in his nervous system, that this behavior will prove rewarding. (It won't, of course, since there is no ribbon this time, so this phase of the experiment can *extinguish* his increased kicking if allowed to continue more than a couple of minutes.)

Babies as young as two months of age can learn to move the mobile and remember how to do it for a day or two. Between two and six months, they master the task more and more quickly and also remember it for longer and longer periods; three-month-olds remember up to a week and six-month-olds remember up to two weeks after a single training session. They also steadily improve in the amount of detail they can remember. For instance, if the mobile is changed in some way—say, by replacing the blocks with five balls—Robert will still kick to get it moving. By six months of age, though, he is much more particular and won't kick at the accelerated rate to anything but the identical mobile he trained on. He won't even kick if his crib is moved to a different room or if its distinctive bumper is replaced by another pattern. The fact that young babies are sensitive to the exact environment or *context* in which they learn something is quite remarkable and shows that they learn not only *how* to obtain a reward but *where* certain actions will be reinforced, like rooting for milk only in their mothers' arms, or smiling only when making eye contact.

It doesn't take a cerebral cortex, or even a hippocampus, to learn and remember simple forms of conditioning or habituation. The memory for mobile-kicking is thought to be stored in the cerebellum and its steady

improvement, like that of other motor tasks, to reflect the continuing development and myelination of this important motor center. But many other
brain areas, including the visual cortex and hippocampus, are also undergoing rapid maturation during this same period and probably contribute to the
improvements in the specificity and context-sensitivity of mobile conditioning.

Recognition and Novelty Preference   Babies crave novelty. They
quickly grow bored with the same old toys or food or four walls, which is one
reason even the fussiest newborn is calmed by a trip outside or in the car. At
three months, Robert eagerly swats at anything new dangling from his toy
bar, while my ten-month-old, Sammy, now a masterful crawler, races across
the room at the merest glimpse of a toy or kitchen utensil he has yet to play
with. Novelty preference ensures that babies constantly seek out new forms
of stimulation for their growing brains, keeping those nascent synapses hum-
ming with activity.

Novelty detection depends on memory; Robert can't figure out what's
new and different unless he remembers what's old and the same. Known
technically as *recognition*, this is a rather straightforward sort of memory,
because the neural traces are stored and retrieved by precisely the same stimulus—a particular face, toy, smell, sound, and the like. Recognition is not as
difficult as *recall*, which properly defined means the ability to remember
something without any kind of cue. But neither is it trivial. Amnesic patients
like H.M. have great difficulty recognizing even the most familiar faces or
places. Recognition memory depends on the function of the hippocampal
memory circuit and is therefore considered a form of explicit memory. It is
not, however, a conscious act. Even newborns will cease looking at a
repeated stimulus, but it is unlikely that they're actually aware that it is familiar. Because recognition memory uses some of the same circuitry as conscious
memory but is not itself fully conscious, researchers have settled on the term
pre-explicit to describe this ability in babies.

However it is classified, babies are surprisingly good at recognition. We
have already seen that newborns can recognize familiar stimuli such as
Mother's voice, face, or odor. Each of these forms of recognition is contaminated, however, by conditioning, because the baby inevitably associates
them with positive reinforcement, such as milk, comfort, or warmth. To
study the development of recognition memory more rigorously, researchers

have had to design experiments in which a baby is exposed to a brand-new stimulus, something she can't possibly have seen or heard or smelled before. Then, after a delay, she is given a choice between that stimulus and a completely novel one. Whereas a baby will clearly prefer the familiar when Mama is one of the choices, she will usually prefer the *un*familiar when no other reward is involved. Novelty preference is thus an excellent way to assess memory in children who can't yet say whether something is familiar.

Even the youngest babies demonstrate a clear preference for novel stimuli, provided that the choices are sufficiently distinct for their immature senses to tell them apart. Newborns prefer to look at novel over familiar photos of faces, and their auditory recognition is even more impressive. In one study, brand-new babies were found to prefer listening to an unfamiliar word—in this case, *beagle*—twenty-four hours after repeatedly hearing another unusual word, *tinder*. By eight months of age, babies can recognize specific words up to two weeks after hearing them read repeatedly from a storybook—a good reason to start reading to your baby early and often!

Recognition memory improves steadily throughout infancy and childhood. Whereas newborns need to stare at a new visual stimulus for many seconds or minutes to store its representation, five-month-olds can do it in just a few seconds. Babies' memories also grow steadily longer; newborns can recognize a visual stimulus only a few minutes after seeing it, while five-month-olds can remember it up to two weeks later. These improvements in recognition memory are more a function of brain maturation than of experience, since preterm babies tend to perform as well as full-term babies only of the same *conceptional* age. (For instance, a six-month-old who was born three months prematurely remembers visual stimuli about as well as a three-month-old born at term.) Research on monkeys has shown that the critical maturation takes place in the latter part of the visual "what" pathway (page 202), a temporal lobe site that feeds directly into the hippocampus. Children's recognition memory continues improving until at least nine years of age, perhaps reflecting the protracted myelination of the fornix, as well as the cortical synaptic refinement that continues through childhood. Interestingly, one type of recognition—the memory for object locations—seems to mature earlier than others; children as young as five years perform as well (and sometimes even better!) than adults on location tasks, such as the card game Concentration.

Infant Recognition Memory and Later IQ

Recognition is obviously important for cognitive development. A child must be able to remember objects, people, places, colors, words, and numbers before she can categorize, converse, or reason about them. As the basis for novelty preference, recognition keeps babies focused on the newer, more stimulating elements of their environment, feeding their brains with ever-changing sensory experiences.

Of course, parents and other caregivers can do a lot to help this process. Put those toys away when it's obvious your child is no longer interested in them, or at least move them to another room or shelf. Remember that even young babies learn to associate activities with the *context* in which they were experienced, so the same old toy or book may become a lot more interesting if it suddenly appears in the car, or kitchen, or bathroom.

Given the importance of recognition and novelty preference to infant learning, it is perhaps not surprising that they are especially good indicators of later intellectual ability. Almost two dozen studies, performed between 1975 and 1989, have looked at the relationship between early recognition memory and early childhood IQ, and nearly every one found a significant predictive relationship. That is, babies who show strong novelty preferences when tested between two and eight months of age are likelier to score high on IQ tests administered between two and eight years of age. Recognition memory is actually a far better predictor of intelligence (or at least, the type of intelligence measured by IQ tests; see Chapter 15) than "baby IQ" tests, such as the Bayley Scales of Infant Development, which are heavily weighted by motor skill performance.

Why should something as simple as recognition presage a child's later cognitive abilities? Some researchers believe that it all comes down to the speed of processing. Some brains may simply be faster than others—whether because of innate, prenatal, or early postnatal factors—at coding, retrieving, and discriminating information. Babies who recognize familiar stimuli more efficiently may therefore be better at building a vocabulary, solving problems, and using abstract reasoning during the preschool and early elementary school years. Infants with better recognition memory probably also benefit more from their early experiences, learning faster than babies with poorer recognition skill. So if you find yourself run ragged by a baby who seems to grow instantly bored with every new toy or variation on peekaboo, try to look on the bright side—it may mean you've got a budding Einstein on your hands.

Testosterone and Memory Development

Like many other areas of development, memory generally matures more rapidly in girls than boys. Beginning in the womb, female fetuses are known to habituate to auditory stimuli about two weeks earlier than males. After birth, they are more advanced at visual habituation. Toward the end of the first year, girls are about a month ahead in tests of short-term, explicit memory, like remembering, after a few seconds' distraction, where they just saw a toy being hidden. Girls also outperform boys on a test of long-term implicit memory, the "concurrent discrimination" task described in Chapter 12 (page 315), in which they must learn, over many repetitions and for several pairs of objects, which of the pair conceals a tasty Froot Loop. Between one and three years of age, girls make fewer errors on this task than boys; after that, both sexes perform comparably. Finally, females tend to perform better on tests of verbal recall, like remembering details about recent events, a difference that emerges in the fourth year and persists into adulthood.

Studies of infant monkeys have provided some clues to the neural basis for these gender differences. Once again, testosterone appears to be the culprit. Testosterone levels surge in male monkeys early in gestation and remain elevated until three or four months after birth. By six months of age, they are back down to around female levels. (They then surge again at puberty.) Males' performance on the concurrent discrimination task parallels these changes in testosterone, since it is notably poorer than females' at three months but equivalent by six months of age. Even among different three-month-old males, those monkeys with the highest testosterone levels show the poorest memory performance and vice versa. But the most convincing evidence that testosterone influences the development of memory-storage mechanisms in the brain comes from experiments in which hormone levels were manipulated, either by castrating young male monkeys or by injecting testosterone into young females whose ovaries were removed. As predicted, the castrated males remembered which objects were paired with the reward (in this case, a banana pellet) better than normal males and comparably with females of the same age, while the females injected with testosterone performed more poorly than control females.

The testosterone surge in humans lasts somewhat longer than in monkeys, not reaching its nadir until the end of the first year, which may explain why boys are generally slower learners than girls during infancy and early childhood. Testosterone appears to slow cellular development in certain cortical regions, including the inferior temporal cortex, an area of the visual system known to be involved in the concurrent discrimination task and which is both structurally and functionally more mature in female infant monkeys than in males.

Understanding *how* testosterone retards these forms of memory development is somewhat easier than understanding *why*. The assumption is that testosterone has some other, countervailing benefit. It is known that boys excel earlier on another cognitive task, the "object reversal task" (see page 315), which requires learning, for just a single pair of objects, that at any time the Froot Loop can switch so that it is now lying under the previously unrewarded object. While adults and even preschool-aged children master this test of mental flexibility quite rapidly, toddlers have a lot more difficulty with it, especially girls aged fifteen to thirty months, who are slower than boys to figure out that the reward has reversed. Young monkeys can also master this task (and indeed, do so considerably earlier than human infants); studies of their brains provide evidence that the sex difference is due to differential maturation of the orbitofrontal cortex. In this case, testosterone appears to accelerate neural development. So it appears that testosterone has different growth-related effects in different parts of the brain, promoting certain features of boys' mental function at the expense of some of their memory skill.

Eight Months and Beyond: The Emergence of Recall

In spite of their considerable ability at recognition and skill-learning, young babies are not capable of storing the kind of memories that we normally think of as *memory*—conscious recollections of facts or past events. Such "real" or explicit memory emerges only very gradually, beginning in late infancy and progressively improving throughout childhood. Late infancy is when granule neurons in the hippocampal dentate region have all finally formed, when myelination of many important limbic pathways gets under way, and when activity in the frontal lobe—which plays a part in both short- and long-term conscious memory—really takes off. So just as in social-emotional development, eight months of age marks an important watershed in the development of memory.

The big change is the emergence of recall. Unlike recognition, where a baby simply has to look at (or hear, feel, smell, or taste) a stimulus and decide whether he has encountered it before, recall takes place without any such reencounter. Prior events, faces, words, objects, and so on simply come to mind—triggered no doubt by associated stimuli but not as a result of exactly the same experience. Whereas recognition is automatic or reflexive, recall is by definition conscious, so it is exciting to see when a baby first demonstrates it.

Eight months is when babies are first able to retrieve a hidden toy, a feat that eludes most six-month-olds. It is also when separation anxiety emerges—the way Natalie begins fussing whenever her mother leaves her sight. At this age, babies can finally retain some kind of mental image of Mom, a toy, or an event, for a few moments after it is gone from view—the ability known as *object permanence*, which is essential for attachment. (See page 307.) This kind of conscious, short-term memory is thought to emerge as a result of a developmental spurt in the prefrontal cortex at around this age.

But do infants have any kind of long-term recall? Once I've left Sammy at day care and he's gotten over his separation distress, does he reenvision my departing minutes or hours later? What about more distant events, like yesterday's trip to the pool or last month's vacation? We know babies don't retain these memories in any permanent sense, but how long can they remember events during infancy itself?

This is not an easy question to answer. But researchers have made considerable progress in understanding the development of recall by using a procedure called *deferred imitation*. By exploiting the virtual compulsion that children this age show for imitating other people's actions, they have shown that babies *can* remember unique events in their lives, and that they can do so for surprisingly long periods of time.

Deferred Imitation   The basic idea behind deferred imitation experiments is to demonstrate some unusual action or, better yet, a sequence of several actions, to a young child and, after some delay, to test whether he reproduces the sequence. If he does imitate it, especially if he repeats the same actions without having practiced or seen them a number of times, then, researchers argue, he must be consciously recalling the actual event of the demonstration and not merely aping it through some kind of implicit memory.

For instance, a fourteen-month-old observes an experimenter lean over from the waist and touch his head to the top of a flat box. Or an older toddler watches the experimenter construct a gong from a set of three metal pieces.

Days or even months later, each child is brought back to the lab, given the props, and observed to see if she reproduces the sequence. Experiments like this have shown that babies just nine months old can remember an event and reproduce it up to twenty-four hours later. By thirteen months, they can remember up to a week later. Fifteen-month-olds imitate after a *four-month* delay—that is, when they are nineteen months old—and more importantly, they perform equally well whether or not they were given a chance to practice the actions immediately after viewing them.

Deferred imitation involves some kind of genuine recall. But researchers disagree in their opinion of just how conscious or deliberate it is. The fact that young toddlers can imitate actions like these, even months later, and *without any practice*, shows that it is not a simple matter of implicit memory. So does the fact that amnesic patients fail at this; people suffering amnesia due to hippocampal damage or Korsakoff's syndrome are unable to imitate a significant number of demonstrated actions, even when specifically asked to. This task therefore shares many properties, including the same brain hardware, with "real" memory, leading many investigators to posit that babies really are consciously performing it.

On the other hand, deferred imitation falls short of pure recall in other ways. For one thing, deferred imitation depends on the presence of specific toys or props. Although the babies must do more than simply recognize them, these props provide strong hints for recall. Psychologists call this kind of memory task *cued recall*, and it is considerably easier than pure or *free recall*. For instance, you may have trouble digging up the state capitals you memorized in fourth grade, but if given a hint that the capital of Wyoming rhymes with *Diane*, the word *Cheyenne* springs to mind. Another problem is that imitation itself is usually not a conscious act. Recall that newborns are able to imitate facial expressions well before their cerebral cortex has begun to significantly participate in vision (page 300), and even as adults, we unknowingly copy each other's gestures, expressions, and accents all the time. Like other highly social primates, humans seem to be programmed at a very basic level to "ape" the actions of those around us. Indeed, it is only with great effort, and especially during the teen years, that children begin to overcome this tendency in order to exert their own individuality.

The Danger of Deferred Imitation   Regardless of whether babies are aware of what they are imitating, the fact that these memories last so long is truly remarkable—and a little bit frightening. It goes a long way toward explaining why children, even decades later, are so prone to replicating their parents' behavior. If toddlers can repeat, even several months later, actions they've seen only once or twice, just imagine how watching their parents' daily activities must affect them. Everything they see and hear over time—work, play, fighting, smoking, drinking, reading, hitting, laughing, words, phrases, and gestures—is stored in ways that shape their later actions, and the more they see of a particular behavior, the likelier it is to reappear in their own conduct.

Obviously, parents are not the only source of influence for young children. Peers, siblings, babysitters, grandparents, and other caregivers all add to the arsenal of behaviors children copy. As does television. Children as young as fourteen months are known to imitate actions that they have observed only on TV. Deferred imitation is also evident in the well-known link between television violence and aggressive behavior in children. Considering that the *average* two- to five-year-old in America watches some four hours of television and videos per day, it clearly makes a big difference whether this time is spent in front of *Barney* or *Pulp Fiction*. The potent memory embodied in long-term imitation is truly a force for good or bad, depending on what we let our youngsters watch.

Language, Recall, and Infantile Amnesia Reconsidered

The last memory milestone is verbal recall, when children can finally *say* what they remember. Unlike deferred imitation, where we may never know for certain whether toddlers are consciously recalling earlier events, verbal recall is conscious by definition. It is the gold standard when it comes to assessing recall, *the* basis for determining whether a child is truly aware of past events in his life.

Children begin referring to events from memory almost as soon as they begin to talk, early in the second year. Verbal recall then improves dramatically during the toddler and preschool years, in close parallel with language itself. By three years of age, when most children are speaking in complete sentences, they can rattle off all kinds of facts and recollections about past events, even ones that happened up to a year before (although as we have seen, they will not recall them a few years later). Just the other day, for instance, Julia was poking through our recycling bin and amazed me with her detailed recollection of the recycling depot we used more than eight months ago, in another state! More amazing (although I can't boast such feats for my own child) is the occasional anecdote showing that some three-year-olds can refer to events all the way back in infancy.

Indeed, this is perhaps the most remarkable fact about toddlers' recall: that they can talk about events that happened even before they began to speak. Researchers found in deferred imitation experiments that toddlers frequently asked about props that they hadn't seen since they were thirteen months old—well before most could talk. So language is not, as psychologists once believed, a prerequisite for storing conscious memories. On the contrary, it's now thought that children remember much more than they can talk about, at least until about six years of age, when their language skills finally catch up with their various memory abilities.

While language is not required for children to store conscious memories, it does play an important part in making memories last—in overcoming the hurdle of infantile amnesia. Even after the basic hippocampal and cortical circuitry is in place, verbal recall is still not fully developed until children evolve a special kind of linguistic skill: the art of narrative. Only when children begin to see the relationship between events, when they can place their own personal recollections into a framework of time, place, and causality, can their memories survive the transition from childhood to later life.

In one study, for example, children were interviewed seven years after a notable event: a minor fire at their day-care center. Only those who could describe the event in terms of its cause (popcorn catching fire) and sequence ("I was the last one out, because I wouldn't leave until I stapled [something]") could correctly answer a series of specific questions about the incident, such as the name of their teacher at the time, where they were when the fire alarm sounded, and which playground they were evacuated to. All such children were among the older preschoolers, averaging four and a half years of age at the time of the fire (and eleven and a half at the time of interview). Those who had been younger preschoolers (three and a half years then, ten and a half at the interview) showed very little recollection; they were unable to answer specific questions and, when asked to elaborate on what they did recall, could not supply any kind of meaningful narrative about the event.

Training Memory Skills— Is There a Critical Period?

Memory skills vary widely between individuals. Some people never need to make lists or keep calendars, never forget a name or face, and seem effortlessly to recall everything they've ever read or experienced. Others aren't so lucky. Much of this variation, of course, is genetic; some people are simply born with a faster, more efficient way of coding and retrieving information, differences that are apparent even in early infancy, judging by the predictive value of early recognition memory. (See page 342.) Twin studies indicate that some 40 percent of the variation in different people's memory skills is attributable to genes. While this is a considerable contribution, genes play a lesser role in memory skills than they do in other cognitive abilities, such as visual-spatial skills and perceptual speed. This leaves the majority of one's memory skills to be shaped by something other than genes, namely experience. Like any other skill, memory improves with practice—with repeated, deliberate efforts to acquire and hold on to new information.

The most obvious place this happens is in school. Psychologists have tested memory performance in people all over the world and found that those who have completed at least a few years of formal education score higher than those from the same culture and economic status who did not attend school; and the more years completed, the better the performance. Where formal schooling especially helps is in learning memory strategies, deliberate tricks like verbal rehearsal, information clustering, and note-taking that children use to make it through years of quizzes and final exams.

But what about the years before formal schooling begins, when the basic neural circuitry underlying conscious memory storage is still being laid down? Is there a critical period for memory development during these earlier years? We know that children begin using their memory in a deliberate fashion as early as three years of age. In one study, three-year-olds (but not two-year-olds) proved better at retrieving a hidden toy dog if the experimenter explicitly asked them, at the time of hiding, to "*remember* where the dog is" than if he simply instructed them to "*wait* here with the dog" while the experimenter briefly left the room. By three years, kids already figure out tricks like keeping their hand on the hiding place or forcing themselves to stare at it throughout the forty-second waiting period, to help prod their memories.

That children are aware of their memories at such an early age suggests that it may be possible to improve such strategies, if not memory itself, well before they enter elementary school. Indeed, there's good evidence from laboratory studies that children as young as four can learn strategies like sorting and naming that improve their ability to recall words or objects. Even more intriguing is the role parents can play. It is known, for instance, that three-year-olds whose mothers place greater demands on their memories—who more frequently question them about past events or probe their growing body of general knowledge—perform better on tests of recall than children whose mothers place fewer such demands on them. By focusing children on the important facts—the who, what, when, where, how, and why issues—parents can teach their children the requisite narrative skills—how to think about events in terms of time and causality—which is ultimately how we recall facts and events later on. Perhaps this is why young children love to be told stories; it's as if they instinctively crave examples by which to hone their own narrative skills.

Thus it does appear that memory development can be influenced by practice. The more a child is challenged to use her memory, even early on, the better it is likely to serve her later in life. The fact that memory skills can be molded by experience—even at an age when the basic neural pathways for information storage are still being laid down—suggests that the early years may indeed constitute a critical period for establishing a lifelong arsenal of memory skills.

Chapter 14

LANGUAGE AND THE
DEVELOPING BRAIN

"Jia! . . . Jia!" I have to hear it twice in a row to finally convince myself that this is Sammy's first word, his best try at saying his sister's name. He's been blurting it out for a couple of months now, clear and often enough that it's become Julia's latest nickname—a source of great pride for her, the big sister, and for me, a typical anxious parent, of relief that my child really can talk— at least one word!—before his first birthday.

If parents spend the first year of their child's life worrying mostly about motor development, we devote the second to language. We eagerly await each new word, delighting in even the sloppiest pronunciation. Or if the utterances are not all that forthcoming, we begin nervously reading up on language delays and disorders. By the third year, we're either bursting with pride over our toddler's obvious gift for gab (how often have you heard a parent boast, "She's very verbal"?) or silently fretting over every inevitable bout of stuttering or grammatical lapse.

There's really no need to worry. The vast majority of children learn language without a hitch. Indeed, when you think of how difficult it is to master a new language yourself, the fact that children just three or four years old, who can't even add or tie their shoes, can understand and speak in full, complex grammatical sentences *without any training*, then you become convinced, as most linguists now are, that human language is an instinct, a behavior as innate and inevitable as sleeping or eating. Humans can't help but talk; it is our fundamental means of social interaction. Children will even invent a language, like the secret communication between some twins, or spontaneous signing by deaf children, if they are for some reason unable to pick up the ambient one. And the reason language is instinctive is because it is, to a large extent, hard-wired in the brain. Just as we evolved neural circuits for eating and seeing, so has our brain, together with a sophisticated vocal apparatus, evolved a complex neural circuit for rapidly perceiving, analyzing, composing, and producing language.

Children learn language in a remarkably regular way, just as most of them progress through motor milestones in the same consistent sequence. Although there are some differences between languages, children throughout the world follow virtually identical schedules for speaking single words, then two-word phrases, then sentences of ever-greater complexity—all between one and four years of age. Even deaf children abide by this same sequence, effortlessly picking up formal sign language, provided they are immersed in it from birth (that is, if their parents are also deaf). The fact that language acquisition is so strikingly universal, despite what seem to be great differences among the world's many tongues, is one piece of evidence that language is a special component of our mental apparatus and not merely a by-product of our big human brains.

Other evidence comes from the brain itself. Language has its own neural apparatus, like an extra chip that evolution has inserted into the human computer. It can be specifically impaired by certain types of brain injury or disease without affecting a person's general intelligence. But it can also be specially preserved, as in a particular type of mental retardation known as *Williams syndrome*. Adults with this rare genetic deficit have IQs down in the 50s but are surprisingly skilled when it comes to language. They have large and interesting vocabularies (rattling off words like *ibex* and *koala* when asked to name a few animals) and astutely recognize many slight grammatical errors. Although the brains of people with Williams syndrome show many abnormalities, the areas that control language production and comprehension—the same areas damaged in patients with language loss—are mysteriously intact.

Even if we ignore all evidence from the brain itself, there's good reason to believe that language is innate to the human species. Noam Chomsky set off a linguistics revolution in the late 1950s with his discovery that all of the world's languages share the same fundamental structure, what he termed "Universal Grammar." All natural languages are composed of sentences and use the same parts of speech (nouns, verbs, adjectives, adverbs, prepositions, conjunctions, and so on), whose order and agreement are clearly specified by rules. Because the structure of language is so universal, Chomsky argued, it must be inherent in the human mind. His theory put to rest the argument of learning theorists, notably B.F. Skinner, that children learn language through behavioral feedback—by having their proper utterances rewarded (like getting a bottle when they say "milk") and their improper ones ignored (because "mug" will be misunderstood) until they eventually build a useful vocabulary and grammar. As Chomsky pointed out, even young children are constantly coming up with brand-new phrases and sentences that can't possibly have been shaped by prior experience (like Julia's recent *yesternight*, which is clearly different in meaning from *yesterday*). Rather, he argued, language is constructed through grammatical rules that every human brain is programmed to discover, given just a few brief years of exposure.

Grammar, in particular, is what sets our language apart from other forms of animal communication. Many other species communicate, whether through calls, coos, barks, croaks, hoots, songs, cries, or gestures to convey important and specific information—"Predator alert!" "Looking for sex!" "Kids, come home!"—but only human language has the sophistication to combine purely abstract signals (words) in new ways to produce new meanings. Grammar is what makes language infinitely creative. There is truly no limit to the way words can be combined to express new ideas. And grammar, in this sense, does not refer to the stuffy set of rules you had to memorize in high school English class. It is the intuitive and yet complex understanding needed to make sense of sentences like: "The ball I gave you rolled off the deck." Even a two-year-old can figure out which verb goes with which noun in this sentence, but it would baffle any animal, even the few famous apes alleged to have learned language by their human trainers.

But as instinctive as language is to our species, we are obviously not born speaking. The capacity for language may be genetic, and our grammatical rules may be limited by universal features of human brain hardware, but the particular language a child masters, and the way he ends up speaking it, are largely a function of experience. Linguistic experience is important enough that any baby, of any racial or cultural origin, can be adopted into any other country or culture and end up sounding indistinguishable from native-born speakers. This is because the very act of learning language is what directs the specialization of the linguistic brain. Early language immersion and practice is necessary for mastering not only that particular tongue but any tongue at all. Children who are deprived of all language exposure can, if the deprivation lasts long enough, end up permanently incapable of learning and using language, and the feature that is most vulnerable to deprivation turns out to be their grammar.

So language, like vision and most other brain functions, is bounded by a critical period, an early phase in which a child must experience language, or else its special hardware won't wire up right. Fortunately, most children receive this essential language exposure; indeed, only a bare minimum is needed to communicate effectively. Nonetheless, the quality of language experienced during this critical period varies tremendously from child to child, and we now know that differences in the richness and sheer volume of a child's early language exposure do influence the level of language skill he will eventually achieve.

Learning to talk is probably the greatest intellectual leap of an individual's life: it opens up a new universe of questions, reasoning, social communication, and opinions (for better or worse!) that punch all other types of learning into warp speed and make a child finally seem like a full-fledged person. While language is in many ways a distinct module of the human mind and brain, it is also the critical foundation for much of what we consider to be intelligent behavior. The more we understand about how the language organ of the brain develops, the better we can foster this most important basis of our children's intellectual development.

How Language Works

One reason to suspect that language is a distinct mental organ is that it is physically localized in the brain. At some point, you've probably heard the left hemisphere described as our more verbal side. In fact, it is the dominant location of language for more than 95 percent of people, including a sizable majority of left-handers. We literally speak with half a brain. (This doesn't mean, however, that the right hemisphere has no role at all in language. Befitting its more emotional character, the right hemisphere is responsible for *prosody*, the inflection and overall musical quality that lend important emphasis to verbal communication.) Language is further localized to a broad central wedge of the left hemisphere known as the *perisylvian cortex* (for the way it surrounds the *Sylvian fissure*, the deep horizontal canyon that separates the temporal from the frontal and parietal lobes). (See Figure 14.1.)

Much of what we know about the brain mechanisms of language comes

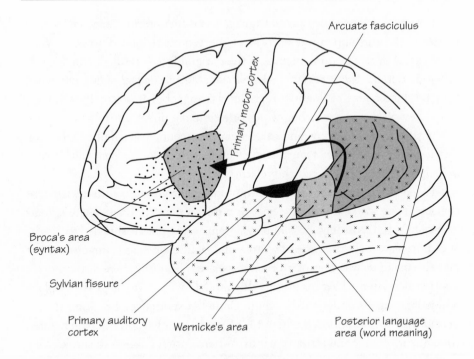

Arcuate fasciculus

Primary motor cortex

Broca's area
(syntax)

Sylvian fissure

Primary auditory
cortex

Wernicke's area

Posterior language
area (word meaning)

FIGURE 14.1

*Language centers of the brain. Dots and X's show brain areas
activated during verb and noun use, respectively.*

After A.R. Damasio and H. Damasio, "Brain and language," *Scientific American*, September 1992.

from people with *aphasia,* the clinical term for any kind of language loss. For well over a century, neurologists have been charting all the various ways that brain damage impairs linguistic skills. In the early days, they had to wait until autopsy to decipher exactly what brain region produces which specific kind of aphasia, but such studies continue today in living patients, enhanced by the latest computerized imaging techniques.

The most striking distinction is between patients with damage to anterior versus posterior portions of the perisylvian cortex. Generally speaking, people with damage to the lower left frontal lobe, and particularly to a lateral zone located just above the Sylvian fissure known as *Broca's area* (for the neurologist who first described it), show great difficulty in *producing* language: they . . . speak . . . ah . . . slow . . . halting . . . ah . . . single . . .

ah . . . words . . . and no sentences. Damage to more posterior language areas—to the back- and uppermost portion of the temporal lobe (known as *Wernicke's area*) or to adjoining regions of the parietal lobe—results in an entirely different deficit. Such patients seem incapable of *comprehending* language; they produce reams of fluent speech (or writing), but it is largely meaningless. They often use the wrong word, or else make up an entirely new word, but if you try to interrupt and ask what they mean, you'll fail . . . *because they'll think what they're saying is stuff or whatever because sleeping's not so good or bad and more or less there's no problem.* . . .

Faced with these very different symptoms, neurolinguists initially thought that language works as follows. Speech enters a person's brain, such as four-year-old Daniel's, through his auditory system and is quickly shuttled to nearby Wernicke's area. (In the cases of written and Braille languages, linguistic input can also make its way to posterior language areas from the more distant visual and tactile systems.) According to this model, Wernicke's area is the place where language is understood—where Daniel's experience of hearing is converted into words, and also where he converts his own internally generated thoughts into a mental script of words. When Daniel chooses to speak, Wernicke's area ships his composition forward to Broca's area, by way of a fiber bundle known as the *arcuate fasciculus.* Broca's area immediately abuts the primary motor cortex and in particular the cortical areas that control movement of the face, tongue, jaw, and throat. This area is a good location for what was presumed to be its basic job of producing language, that is, translating it from the mental script into a motor scheme for speaking, writing, typing, or signing.

This classical model of language held sway for decades, and for good reason. It simply and elegantly accounted for the two fundamentally different types of aphasia, and it also made a lot of sense in terms of the basic sensory-motor design of the cerebral cortex. As so often happens in science, however, the latest research has modified it substantially. Though we still abide by the fundamental distinction between Wernicke's and Broca's areas, we no longer consider comprehension and production to be their primary functions. Rather, recent data suggest that these two areas divide up language by semantics and syntax; left posterior areas are activated during tasks involving the meaning of words, while the left frontal cortex is more specifically activated during tasks involving grammatical processing. For instance, Broca's area lights up when subjects compare two sentences whose meaning is identical but that differ in the order of their words—that is, in syntactic structure. On the other hand, the left temporal-parietal area (including Wernicke's area as well as a large area above and behind it) is turned on more by tasks that tax one's understanding of individual words, like hearing the anomalous sentence *We bake cookies in the zoo*. In other words, the posterior language center is the place where the meanings of words are stored, rather like a mental dictionary, whereas the frontal center functions more like a grammar textbook, the place where we figure out the significance and appropriateness of word order, the classic syntactic problem of who is doing what to whom.

This division of labor is simply astounding. It's as if some high school English teacher were around when the language functions of the brain were parceled out: "Vocabulary goes in back, and grammar up front." What's more, because of the way different parts of speech work, this segregation ends up dividing different classes of words in an equally simplistic way—verbs in the front and nouns in the rear. More than any other part of speech, verbs are the central components in grammar; they determine the relationship between subject and object and are the part of speech most often modified (such as by adding *-ed, -ing, -s*) to convey tense, person, and other conditional features of a sentence. Imaging and electrical measurements support the notion that nouns are retrieved in the left temporal-parietal region, while verbs are processed in the frontal lobe.

According to this new theory, people with damage to Broca's area are impaired not in producing language but in using grammar. Their broken, telegraphic speech is notably lacking in verbs, as well as most of the small connectors (*of, to, and, in, the*) that glue sentences together. But they are able to understand language because verbs are much less essential for inferring meaning. Just about any English speaker, for instance, can comprehend the string of nouns: *I . . . lunch . . . noon . . . McDonald's . . . Big Mac, fries . . . Coke*. Wernicke's aphasics are much worse off. Although they retain the rules for connecting words—the verb tenses, prepositions, and conjunctions that make sentences adhere—they simply don't have enough words left in their damaged mental dictionaries to say (or understand) anything of substance.

The segregation of grammar and meaning also makes sense in terms of the brain's division of other mental functions. Wernicke's area is located near the junction of three important senses—hearing, vision, and touch—so it is a good place for the brain to store the associations between the sound of words and the physical entities—the persons, places, and things—they represent. Grammar, on the other hand, is much more at home in the frontal lobe, where other mental skills involving planning, sequencing, logic, and rule-learning are housed.

Brain Anatomy and the
Development of Language

The neural segregation between meaning and grammar has important implications for language development. After babbling, true language begins with
babies' ability to understand and speak single words, and their first words are
almost always nouns: *cup, ball, Mama, Dada, shoe.* Toddlers then progress to
two-word phrases, which are rudimentarily grammatical but lack all the little function words and special verb endings of mature grammar. Speech at
this stage is often called *telegraphic,* just like that of Broca's aphasics. (It's also
about the best that apes can do, at least those who have been taught sign language or some other symbolic system from an early age.) Only after their
third birthday do children produce the full range of grammatical constructions, including verbs and function words in mostly correct combinations.

The gradual progression from word-learning to grammatical speech
agrees well with what we know about the relative maturation of the two language centers. Several measures indicate that Wernicke's area and the rest of
the posterior language center develop in advance of Broca's area. Whereas
the number of synapses peaks between eight and twenty months in the left
temporal-parietal zone, it tops out between fifteen and twenty-four months
in left frontal areas. Broca's area does not establish its mature pattern of cell
layers until four years of age. It also myelinates considerably later than Wernicke's area; myelin is detectable in all cortical layers by two years of age for
Wernicke's area, as compared to four to six years for Broca's. Especially slow
to myelinate is the arcuate fasciculus, which connects Wernicke's to Broca's
areas and thereby limits the speed with which young children can put meaningful utterances into grammatical context.

The Critical Period for Language Experience

To some extent, then, language development is a simple product of brain maturation, of the different schedules for hooking up Wernicke's and Broca's areas
and greasing the wires between them. This progression is part of the overall
genetic program, beginning early in embryonic development, that directs brain
growth along a rear-to-front gradient. But of course, genes are not the sole influence. Kids don't learn to talk simply by waiting for their synapses to form and

axons to myelinate. Just like each of the sensory and motor skills on which it depends, language development is also critically shaped by experience.

Perhaps even more so. After all, language is fundamentally a social act. To ensure that two people in the same community speak the same language, the very capacity for language has evolved to be intimately dependent on the precise linguistic environment in which a child finds himself. That is, the brain's language network properly and permanently wires up only when it is exposed to the coherent combination of sound, meaning, and grammar in any single human language.* Just as the act of seeing completes the circuitry for visual perception, so do hearing and using language in early life help hone every element in the large language network, from the circuits that analyze word sounds, to those that interpret their meaning and syntax, to those controlling their quick and precise vocal production. And as for vision, language exposure must come at a specific time, during the relatively brief "critical period" of early life.

For most children, language immersion is automatic. They are born into a community of speakers, and it isn't long—indeed, well within the first year—before their dendrites and synapses are being molded to fit a specific linguistic style. However, there are certain situations, some more common than others, in which children's early language exposure is severely hampered, and it is from these cases that we have come to understand what the critical period for language is, and how language exposure during this period shapes the developing brain.

Early Isolation and the Loss of Language   Tales of child abuse seem to be increasingly common, but it's still almost impossible to fathom the way Genie, the girl we learned about in Chapter 5, was mistreated by her own paranoid, psychotic father. Beginning when she was twenty months old, Genie was harnessed to an infant potty seat in a small bare room at the back of the family's suburban Los Angeles house. Her father forbade anyone to talk to her (he himself merely barked or growled in her presence), and except for being fed and moved at night to an equally restraining sleeping arrangement (a straitjacketlike bag inside a crib covered with wire mesh), Genie's social isolation was complete. She had virtually no toys or objects to play with, little of interest to look at, and nothing to listen to (not even a muffled television or radio) because of her father's extreme intolerance of noise. If Genie

*Of course, children in bilingual homes can also acquire language perfectly well, but they are often a little slower to begin talking.

herself dared to make any kind of sound, her father beat her with a large wooden plank that was kept, menacingly, in the corner of her room. As Susan Curtiss, the linguist who would eventually study her, later wrote, "Caged by night, harnessed by day, Genie was left to somehow endure the hours and years of her life."

When Genie's mother, blind and equally a psychological captive of her husband, finally managed to escape with her *twelve years later*, it was in a multitude of ways too late. Genie could barely walk, couldn't focus her eyes beyond twelve feet or chew or swallow food, and was incapable of speaking or understanding language. Though she received intensive rehabilitation (and was intensively studied) for several years after her discovery, her language never progressed much beyond that of a two-year-old.

Genie is not the only child in history to grow up without exposure to language. Similar tales have popped up throughout the centuries, of children imprisoned or left out to die and purportedly raised by wild animals. Among these was Victor, the so-called "Wild Child of Aveyron," in France, who was found in 1800, when he was twelve years old. Despite great interest in his case by some of the leading intellectuals of the day, Victor never did manage to learn how to speak. Another child, Kaspar Hauser, rumored to have been heir to a German grand duke, was drugged and held captive in a tiny dark room from the age of three or four until he was a teenager. He survived only five years after his discovery, in 1828, and while he made great intellectual progress, his speech was never more than "a mere chopping of words."

A last case, Chelsea, turned up in the late 1980s and offers an important contrast to these socially isolated children. Chelsea was not reared by wolves or in a cellar but by a normal family in a remote northern California town whose only mistake—albeit a profound one—was failing to realize that she was deaf. Although her mother suspected shortly after her birth that she couldn't hear, Chelsea was misdiagnosed and mishandled through all of her childhood and early adult years. Not until she was thirty-two years old was her deafness properly diagnosed, and she was fitted with hearing aids that, for the first time, permitted her exposure to real language. But again it was too late. In spite of her relatively normal upbringing, Chelsea has not been able to master many of the simplest rules of spoken English. She has great difficulty in comprehension and herself utters sentences such as: *The boat sits water on. Combing hair the boy. The girl is cone the ice cream shopping buying the man.*

Each of these unfortunate individuals bears testimony to the importance of experience, not only for learning a particular language but for mastering any language at all. The one element common to the rearing of Genie, Victor, Kaspar, and Chelsea was the absence of language during most or all of their childhood, and the one handicap common to all was the severe and permanent loss of language capacity.

It is interesting to note, however, that not every aspect of language is equally sensitive to early experience. Each of these individuals (with the possible exception of Victor) did eventually acquire a useful vocabulary. Chelsea, for instance, could produce words at a better-than-high-school level, while Kaspar Hauser's lexicon was supposedly quite sophisticated. Rather, early isolation took its greatest toll on their ability to use and understand grammar; all failed to master some of the simplest rules, like putting an "s" at the end of a plural noun, adjusting verb tense, or using pronouns properly. Linguistic deprivation would also seem to affect the ability to isolate and produce the individual sounds of speech, since both Genie and Chelsea were noted to enunciate very poorly.

How Long Is the Critical Period for Language? Clearly, early language exposure is essential for full linguistic development. But Genie, Victor, Kaspar, and Chelsea were each isolated for a decade or more. Might they have recovered their linguistic skills if they had been discovered sooner? When, exactly, does the critical period end? To address this issue more precisely, researchers have moved from single case studies to focus on language acquisition in two different groups of children: congenitally deaf children learning their first language, American Sign Language, and immigrant children learning their second language, English.

Like Chelsea, any child born deaf is at risk for losing her full potential for language. Fortunately, most cases of congenital deafness are detected much earlier than hers, but what matters is not so much the age of detection as the age at which a deaf child is immersed in language. For deaf children in the United States, American Sign Language (ASL) is the language of choice. Far more than just a collection of gestures, ASL is a complete language, with the same grammatical complexity as any spoken language. Fluent signers use subtle differences in hand-shape, as well as the spatial location and movement of individual signs, to denote the same logical relations that spoken languages achieve with word endings, word order, articles, prepositions, pronouns, and so on.

Because it is especially sensitive to early experience, grammar has been the focus of studies on language acquisition in deaf children. Researchers at the University of Rochester compared the grammatical skills of two groups of deaf subjects, all of whom had attended the same Pennsylvania School for the Deaf as children but differed in the age at which they were first immersed in ASL. A few of the subjects (*native* signers) were born to deaf parents and thus were exposed to ASL from birth. But most of the others did not encounter fluent ASL until they entered the boarding school at age four or older. (Remarkably enough, signing was forbidden in the classrooms—in an effort to encourage lip-reading—during the years when these subjects attended the school; but students fully immersed themselves in ASL in the dormitories.) At the time of testing, all the subjects had been signing for at least thirty years, so they were at a stable level of competence. Nonetheless, only the native signers—those who had learned ASL from their parents before entering the school—made full use of all the grammatical capabilities of ASL. Those who learned it somewhat later, between four and six years of age, performed well but not as competently as native signers, while those who entered the school after age twelve, and therefore learned ASL late, consistently signed in certain ungrammatical ways. To the fluent signers who evaluated their abilities for the study, these late learners communicated about as effectively as a foreigner, not fluent in English, would sound to you or me.

The same researchers found much the same result when they looked at second-language learning, in this case, English competence in a group of Chinese and Korean immigrants to the United States. Again their study focused on grammar. Adult subjects were asked to listen to a few hundred sentences and then say, for each one, whether it sounded correct. About half of the sentences were ungrammatical, such as:

> The farmer bought two pig at the market.
> The little boy is speak to a policeman.
> Yesterday the hunter shoots a deer.
> Tom is reading book in the bathtub.
> The man climbed the ladder up carefully.

The results of this test were quite clear; command of English grammar was exclusively a function of each immigrant's age upon arrival and not his or her amount of formal training, motivation, attitude, or even the total number of years lived in the United States. Only those who had immigrated by the age of seven performed as well as native speakers, which is to say nearly flawlessly. (The test is easy enough that native six-year-olds score almost perfectly.) Among the rest of the subjects, performance steadily declined as a function of the age at which they arrived: the youngest arrivals performed better than those who arrived between eight and ten years of age, who in turn performed better than those who arrived between ages eleven and fifteen. Subjects who emigrated any time after seventeen years of age performed the worst of all, but within this group, their age at arrival did not make a difference in their grammatical fluency.

These two studies finally give us a clear view of the critical window for language acquisition. A child's brain is maximally capable of absorbing language, particularly the rules and logic of grammar, until six or seven years of age. After this age, the ability to master syntax declines steadily until the end of puberty. By early adulthood, the critical period is completely over. A person who is isolated from any kind of language exposure, such as a deaf child whose hearing loss remains undetected, will never master a single tongue. Because of studies like this, parents who suspect any kind of hearing problem are now encouraged to have their child's hearing tested as early as possible, so that deaf children can be identified and immersed in fluent sign language while they are still within the optimal part of the critical period—that is, before the age of four.

The implications are somewhat different for second-language learning. Obviously, it is not impossible to learn a new language after puberty. Though adults require a lot more effort and concentration than young children, we generally do much better at learning foreign languages than Genie, Victor, Kaspar, and Chelsea did at learning their first. Nonetheless, learning a second language after the critical period does leave certain telltale signs. No matter how hard they try, most adults who learn a foreign language inevitably have certain problems in pronunciation (giving them a distinctive accent) as well as in grammatical usage—like using the wrong pronoun or leaving out an article—that clearly mark them as nonnative speakers. Though with one language under its belt, the brain is better equipped to master new languages later in life, it can never do the job as perfectly or completely as in the early years. If you really want your child to master a foreign language, you should ideally start them out as early as possible, and certainly before the high school years, as is traditionally the time they are taught in the United States.

The Brain and the Critical Period   What is it about young children's brains that makes them so good at absorbing language? Why is a newer, immature brain so immensely better at learning grammar and mastering pronunciation than an older, smarter one? Once again, the answer is in the remarkable plasticity of the young nervous system. Brains learn by resculpting their synapses and dendrites, and early life, when the number of synapses in a child's brain is at its peak, presents the greatest opportunity for selecting the optimal neural pathways for mediating language.

In fact, language offers the most dramatic illustration we have of early brain plasticity. Unlike adults, in whom damage to the left perisylvian area can cause irreparable aphasia, children with comparable brain damage can show fantastic language recovery. A child can even have his *entire left hemisphere removed* (which is occasionally the only treatment for certain intractable brain disorders) and still learn to talk, read, and write, provided of course that the surgery takes place early in the critical period. Children whose hemispheres are removed before four or five years of age recover almost completely, while those who are not operated on until the time of puberty lose all language ability.

Such cases prove that the language circuits of the brain, though genetically biased for the left hemisphere, can put themselves together remarkably well in the right hemisphere, as long as such circuits begin forming fairly early in life. But not all linguistic circuits are equally plastic. In every case of severe language deprivation—social isolation, early brain damage, congenital deafness—the capacity for grammar has been found to be much more vulnerable than the ability to learn word meaning. Recent research confirms that the development of Broca's area is much more sensitive to experience during the critical period than Wernicke's; people who learn a second language later in life (in this case, English for deaf individuals already fluent in ASL) show deviant frontal-lobe activity during grammatical processing, while their posterior brain responses to English words are comparatively normal. This differential sensitivity is reminiscent of the visual system, in which some features, like acuity and stereo vision, are much more influenced by early experience than others, such as color and peripheral vision. Luckily for language, the less stringent critical period for Wernicke's area means that we can continue expanding our vocabularies throughout life.

Language in a Newborn?
How the Brain Is Innately Biased for Language

How does language begin? Obviously, children can't learn it in a vacuum. But as much as language acquisition depends on experience, there's no escaping the fact that only humans do it; in spite of comparable early immersion, no family pet ever managed to speak or to understand more than the rudiments of human language. Experience is critical, but all the language exposure in the world wouldn't do us any good if our brains weren't naturally designed for the task.

This specialization actually begins well before birth. As early as the sixth month of gestation, a brain area known as the *planum temporale*—a thick triangle at the border of the temporal and parietal lobes that includes Wernicke's area—begins to grow larger on the left side of the brain. (See Figure 14.2.) By thirty weeks after conception, the two hemispheres have begun

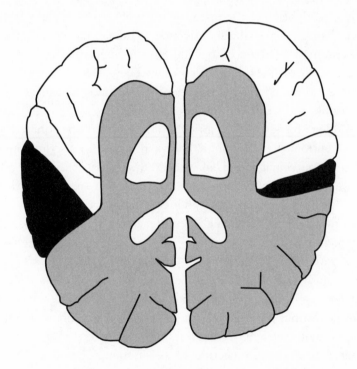

FIGURE 14.2

Cross-section through the brain revealing the upper surface of the temporal lobes (white and black areas). The planum temporale (black) is considerably larger on the left side of the brain, where it contains Wernicke's language region. This asymmetry appears as early as twenty-nine weeks of gestation and is more pronounced in males.

After N. Geschwind and W. Levitsky, "Human brain: Left-right asymmetries in temporal speech region," *Science,* 161:186–87, 1968.

responding differently to speech sounds, judging by EEG measurements in preterm babies. The fact that the left hemisphere is already specialized for language as early as the end of the second trimester argues strongly that it is genetically fated.

This innate asymmetry has important implications for the way each of a baby's ears responds to language. Because the majority of auditory fibers cross over as they ascend to the cerebral cortex, newborns are actually slightly better at perceiving speech with their right ears, while they can distinguish musical tones (a right-hemisphere function) somewhat better with their left ears. (You may want to whisper those sweet nothings into your baby's right ear and save the lullabies for his left.)

Early specialization of the linguistic brain also helps explain other newborn feats, like their special responsiveness to human speech, and their ability to discriminate between native and foreign languages (see Chapter 10). One recent study suggests that newborns are even able to detect the boundaries between words, a remarkable feat given how foreign languages generally sound to us like a river of uninterrupted syllables.

Researchers have focused particular attention on one innate aspect of speech perception: the way babies' brains are biased to discriminate among the different individual sounds of speech, known as *phonemes*. It turns out that no one—neither adult nor newborn—perceives speech exactly as it is spoken. That's because the same phoneme can have an entirely different acoustic structure depending on all sorts of factors—who the speaker is, what sort of mood he is in, what language he's speaking, and even the particular word or phrase in which the sound is embedded. But whether it's spoken by Barney or Cindy Lou Who, we still perceive a /b/ as /b/, because our brains automatically categorize speech sounds, slotting each spoken piece of language into a distinct pigeonhole. Just as we look at a rainbow, a perfect distribution of light wavelengths, but tend to see only a few bands of color, so do our ears pick up the full spectrum of speech sounds, but hear them as only a small number of different phonemes.

Young infants are capable of discriminating and categorizing nearly every type of phoneme—vowels, most consonants, and even foreign speech sounds. To prove this, researchers habituated young babies by repeatedly presenting them with a single, synthetically produced syllable, /pa/. When they then adjusted a single acoustic parameter, producing a sound adults recognize as /ba/, the babies' sucking rate increased, showing that they too distinguish the two phonemes. But when the researchers then tuned the synthesizer in the opposite direction, producing a syllable that, in purely physical terms, differs as much from /pa/ as the /ba/ did, but that adults would nonetheless perceive as /pa/, the babies remained habituated; they acted, in other words, as though they were still hearing /pa/. This experiment and many more like it have shown that even the youngest babies categorize speech sounds, funneling each piece into the relatively few phonemic types we are programmed to detect.

To anyone who's ever attempted to teach phonics to a young child, it will probably seem surprising that our appreciation of different speech sounds is essentially instinctive. In fact, phonemic categorization is not even unique to our species; many other primates and even some nonprimate mammals are also capable of it. It turns out that the mammalian nervous system is exquisitely sensitive to small variations in the timing of speech components, which is the basis of most phoneme distinction. Human languages probably evolved to take maximum advantage of the sounds our brains already knew how to distinguish.

Language in the First Eighteen Months

Babies, then, are born primed for language. They come into the world with a specialized brain that can already recognize human speech, word boundaries, and different phonemic categories. But in spite of this promising beginning, real language is still a long way off. By definition, infants don't talk; the Latin *infans* means "incapable of speech." Though babies are innately predisposed for it, getting a handle on any single, real language requires a lot more work, neurally speaking. Whole circuits must be tuned before they can even begin to make sense of single words. And building this foundation depends on experience, on hearing millions of individual words and phonemes in just the first year alone.

Speech is without doubt the most important form of stimulation a baby receives. When parents talk to their babies, they are activating hearing, social, emotional, and linguistic centers of the brain all at once, but their influence on language development is especially profound. Even before birth, the speech that babies hear biases their later language perception, as described in Chapter 10; newborns prefer their own mother's voice, their native language, and perhaps even a Dr. Seuss story, all because of a few weeks' of muffled language exposure in the womb. But while prenatal experience is concerned with the more global, musical quality of speech—the pitch, intonation, and stress patterns of mother's voice or *The Cat in the Hat*—language has a much more specific effect after birth. Now every vowel and consonant is critical for honing the neural systems that will eventually understand and produce language.

Language lies quietly in wait during the first twelve to eighteen months of a child's life. Though you can see only the merest hints of it in infancy, it grows like an air bubble submerged deep in the sea, rising and expanding until finally, somewhere in the middle of the second year, it explodes at the surface for all to hear.

Tuning In and Turning On (the Circuits for Perceiving One's Native Language)   One of the covert ways in which experience molds early language development is through phoneme perception. Babies, as we've seen, are strikingly good at categorizing speech sounds. In fact, they are better—*much* better—than adults in one respect: they can detect far more speech sounds than we can. Japanese babies, for instance, can tell the difference between /r/ and /l/ sounds, a distinction adult Japanese are famously poor at making. Similarly, English-learning babies can distinguish certain Hindi and Czech phonemes that their parents cannot discriminate. Babies are thus "citizens of the world" when it comes to phoneme perception. Their breadth accounts for the fact that any baby, regardless of ethnicity or country of origin, will grow up to speak the language of his adopted nation as well as any native.

But this remarkable facility doesn't last long. Infants' ability to discriminate foreign speech sounds begins to wane as early as six months of age. By this age, English-learning babies have already lost some of their ability, still present at four months, to discriminate certain German or Swedish vowels. Foreign vowels are the first sort of phoneme to go. Then, by ten or twelve months, out goes the ability to discriminate foreign consonants, like /r/'s and /l/'s for Japanese babies or Hindi consonants for English-learning infants.

Why should we lose something so potentially useful as the ability to discriminate the sounds of other languages? Such losses go hand in hand with a baby's growing sensitivity to her native language. Every time she hears a particular phoneme—each piece of each word spoken within earshot—that experience broadens her perceptual category for that sound, at the expense of neighboring sounds (that is, those with similar physical properties) not a part of her native language. So even though babies are born with the ability to discriminate among all of the world's speech sounds, most of these tiny categories eventually become subsumed by the few phoneme categories needed to interpret their native language. (English, for example, has just forty phonemes in all.) As each category broadens, moreover, the boundaries between them grow sharper. The end result is that babies can more rapidly identify each speech sound they hear (no matter how sloppy the pronunciation) as one of the few types that everyone around them seems to be using. Eliminating all of these extra categories therefore helps babies focus on the few needed to master their native language.

Phoneme perception is thus another example of "use it or lose it" in the developing brain. Our perception of speech sounds gets warped by experience—in this case, very early exposure to a single native language. Although neuroscientists have yet to discover exactly where in the brain this occurs, you can be certain that specific auditory circuits—those responsible for categorizing native speech sounds—are being selected and stabilized at the expense of others—the categories for foreign phonemes.

This very early shaping of phoneme perception has important implications for foreign language learning. Obviously, the better you can hear the sounds of a foreign language, the easier time you will have learning it. Even though babies begin to lose this ability very early on, their brains remain flexible enough during the early critical period for them to be able to recover foreign phoneme perception should they suddenly find themselves immersed in a new language. Adults, by contrast, literally tune out when they hear a foreign language being spoken; our left hemispheres are not even activated when we listen to speech in an unfamiliar language. Although we can, with intensive effort, learn to distinguish some of the more difficult foreign speech sounds, we can never do it as easily, naturally, and completely as children, nor can we come anywhere near matching children's ability to pronounce foreign phonemes properly. This is why adults speak newly acquired languages with an obvious accent.

Nor are *foreign* accents the only consequence of this early phonemic shaping. As babies begin to babble and then talk, they inevitably strive to pronounce phonemes as they have most frequently encountered them—that is, in their local dialect. A child who grows up in Boston will thus store a much different prototype for the sound /a/—open and throaty—than a child born in the Midwest, where the /a/'s are more closed and nasal. Though pronunciation can change during childhood or early adolescence (especially under the influence of one's peer group), those /a/'s are going to be pretty well fixed by the time a young person enters college. As cases like Genie's and

Chelsea's demonstrate, pronunciation is one of the features of language that is most sensitive to experience during the critical period, and the reason is that it directly hinges on early phonemic shaping.

Babbling   Phoneme learning is a two-way street. Babies learn as much about speech sounds by practicing them as they do by hearing. And practice, for babies, means babbling. Well before language means anything to them, babies begin babbling away, experimenting with various ways of making sounds and engaging in conversation. Talking may seem easy, especially if you've ever found yourself stuck with a gabby four-year-old, but it is actually an intricate motor task, requiring the rapid coordination of dozens of muscles controlling the lips, tongue, palate, and larynx. So while babbling may seem to be just an enchanting way for babies to get attention, it also serves as a very important rehearsal for the complex gymnastics of speaking.

Babbling begins at around two months of age, perhaps reflecting myelination of the various motor nerves that innervate the throat, mouth, and tongue muscles involved in speech. Babies throughout the world coo in much the same way at this age, even those who are born profoundly deaf. Most young infants serenade their parents with long melodies of *ooooh*'s and *aaaah*'s, sounds that require the least amount of oral acrobatics and are also common to all languages. Then, beginning around five months of age, they begin to add a few consonants to their repertoire: /b/, /d/, /m/, /n/, /w/, and /j/ are quite common, because they are formed using the well-practiced sucking muscles of the lips and tip of the tongue. In this phase, which lasts until about ten months of age, babies combine consonants and vowels into long, repetitive strings, like *bababababa, nenenenene,* or *mamamama,* also known as *canonical babbling,* which is not unlike the rhythmical kick-kick-kicking and bang-bang-banging infants this age are also using to get their leg and arm circuits up to speed.

By the end of the first year, babbling gets more complex; babies begin mixing syllables and belting out long, highly intonated utterances. Such *variegated babbling* continues well into the second year, even after they start mixing real words into the mash. By twelve months, English-speaking babies can produce most of the vowels and about half of all the consonant sounds in the language. It can take many more years, however, before they finally master the most difficult consonant sounds, which is why you may still hear a second-grader say something like: *I fink dat doze tree bwankies are lellow.* (I think that those three blankies are yellow.)

To some extent, the development of babbling is a simple consequence of the way infants' vocal machinery matures. At birth, the vocal tract has a shape more apelike than human; it is disproportionately shorter, with a broader oral cavity, higher-placed larynx, and more forward-placed tongue than in adults. This shape explains young babies' propensity for certain vowels (those in the words *head, hat, hut,* and *hot*) as well as the consonants /g/, /k/, and /h/. By six months of age, the throat, mouth, and tongue have evolved to a shape much more closely resembling the adult vocal tract, and the speech sounds babies can produce evolve correspondingly.

But anatomy alone does not explain all the changes in babbling that take place during the first year. The evolution of babies' talk is equally affected by learning. For one thing, the sheer quantity of babbling is affected by the amount of attention adults pay to it. Parents who imitate and respond in other ways to their infants' vocalizations will hear more of them, while those who ignore them end up inhibiting their children's utterances, with potentially long-lasting ramifications (see page 383). But even without adult reinforcement, babies take great pleasure in the sound of their own voices, as evidenced by the fact that deaf infants give it up after just a few months. (Deaf babies will, however, begin to "babble" with their fingers at just six or seven months of age if they're exposed to sign language during the first few months.)

The quality of babbling is also influenced by early experience with language. While the youngest babies all sound pretty much the same, cross-cultural studies have shown that ten-month-olds babble in distinctive ways, reflecting the dominant language of their country of origin, in these cases, English, French, Chinese, or Arabic. Following as little as fifteen minutes of "training" by a female speaker, twelve-week-old babies are known to modify their vowel pronunciation to match her examples. Just as early experience shapes the way babies *hear* speech sounds, so does it affect the kinds of sounds they *produce*, and indeed, for precisely the same reason—because it rewires the way their brains categorize phonemes.

First Words   Babbling is great: nothing sounds cuter or more innocent than a baby earnestly chattering away in long strings of nonsense syllables. Sooner or later, though, you can't help but want to hear something interpretable come out of that small sweet mouth. How better to figure out what's going on in his little mind? Fourteen-month-old Nathan, for instance, grows more fervent every day as he points to things and grunts until Mom finally figures out what he wants. Before long, this frustration will drive him beyond mere sound play to actually linking sounds with objects, people, actions, and concepts.

This is no small leap. Just imagine all the possibilities that could be going on in Nathan's mind when his mother responds to his pointing with the word *bottle*. It could refer to the vessel's contents, *milk*; to some piece of it, like the *nipple*; to one of its properties, like its *purple* color or its long *cylindrical* shape; to that specific *long, cylindrical purple bottle with the silicone nipple containing milk*; or finally to the generalized object that we all know as a *baby bottle*. In spite of endless possibilities, babies only a year old manage to make the right level of generalization, to realize that there are many different styles of baby bottles, with different kinds of nipples, containing milk or juice or nothing, but that they are all referred to by the word *bottle*. They do so, scientists believe, because their brains are innately biased to assume three things about words: (1) that they refer to whole objects, as opposed to their parts or properties; (2) that they designate classes of items, rather than individual members of the class (the purple bottle, the clear bottle, the small bottle, and so on); and (3) that objects have only one name. Thanks to these naming assumptions, children quickly figure out a single word to call most objects and then, when faced with a new label for a known item, like *nipple* or *purple*, are able to deduce that it applies to just a part or property of it.

Babies first bridge the gap between sounds and meaning as early as nine or ten months of age. They learn the names of family members and pets, the meaning of *no!* and perhaps a few general labels like *shoe* and *cookie*. By his first birthday, the average child understands around seventy words, mostly nouns like people's names and terms for objects, but also certain social expressions, like *hi* and *bye-bye*. Of course, he cannot say nearly that many. The median number of words spoken by a one-year-old is six, but many say none at all, and a few speak up to fifty. There's typically about a five-month lag between the time a toddler can understand a certain number of words and when he can actually speak that many.

New words accrue slowly between twelve and eighteen months. Nathan picks up a few nouns and expressions each month—*spoon, blankie, nose, milk, up, allgone*—trying each out for several days and often dropping them as he moves on to the next. But then, all of a sudden, his vocabulary hits critical mass: he starts saying new words every single day—*car, cup, kitty, flower, plane, birdie, teeth, keys, hair, light, foot, let's go, ball, kiss, cracker, doggie, peek-aboo, book, dance, water, Gramma, down, night-night, bath-time, eyes, ears, block, phone, bunny, hug, (com)puter, chair, tree, crib* . . . so many his mother can't keep up with the log she had begun keeping. Fifty is the magic number. Most toddlers' vocabulary explodes once they can say about four dozen words. Now they start adding one, two, or three new words to their speech every day, and their receptive vocabulary—the number of words a child understands—grows even more quickly. Between two and six, children are estimated to learn the meaning of a staggering eight words a day. That comes out to more than one new word every two hours they're awake, and they continue at this rate into the elementary school years. By the time a child is six, it's been estimated that he understands some 13,000 words, although he doesn't speak nearly that many.

Seeing this in your own child is one of the more astounding marvels of parenthood. I swear my jaw dropped the other day when Julia named "foxglove" in her grandma's garden. I know where she learned it—from a beautifully illustrated book about flowers we had gotten just two days earlier. But to me—someone who can barely tell a rose from a geranium—the fact that she had not only memorized the name but also figured out which of dozens of flower types it belonged to was simply mind-boggling.

The vocabulary explosion typically begins around eighteen months, but it can be as early as twelve or as late as twenty-four. A twenty-month-old, for instance, may speak as few as three words or more than five hundred, with the median at 169. Of course, it doesn't take long to catch up, once a child begins adding two hundred words a month to her vocabulary. But what is it that happens, right around the eighteen-month point, to suddenly accelerate word-learning to such a massive pace? How does a toddler's brain so rapidly turn into a veritable sponge for new words?

Not surprisingly, the vocabulary explosion is associated with a spurt in brain development. Between thirteen and twenty months, children's brains grow increasingly specialized in the way they respond to words. Toddlers in the early part of this range use a larger area of their cerebral cortex to detect the differences between words that are known and unknown to them, whereas twenty-month-olds show more specialized activation of the left temporal-parietal zone. Moreover, twenty-month-olds who were early talkers (who could already say several hundred words) show more focal electrical responses in the left parietal lobe than late talkers (those who were still speaking fewer than a hundred words). It thus appears that the left temporal-parietal area, which in adults participates in the storage and retrieval of word meanings (especially for nouns), kicks into gear right when a child starts massively learning and producing new words, especially nouns. Of course, it's hard to say which comes first: whether brain growth is what triggers the vocabulary spurt or, conversely, whether early experience, including a child's own first spoken words, sets off a growth spurt in the linguistic brain. In spite of the few months' difference between children, all normal toddlers enter this explosive phase of vocabulary growth sometime during the second year, a period when synapse formation and metabolic activity are at their all-time high in the cerebral cortex.

Eighteen Months On: The Grammar Explosion

The vocabulary spurt is only the first link in the massive chain reaction of language development. It is followed within just a few months by an explosion in grammar: a child's rapid acquisition of all the basic rules of syntax that culminates, by four years of life, in the ability to say virtually anything her little mind can think of.

There are really just two basic tricks of grammar used by all the languages of the world. You can create meaning either by adjusting the order of words or by changing the little pieces (known as *inflections*) that are tacked onto the ends of words (or beginnings, in some languages). For instance, the difference between "Big Bird is tickling Cookie Monster" and "Cookie Monster is tickling Big Bird" is conveyed both by the sequence of words—which proper noun is on which side of the verb—and by the form of the verb, since changing "tickling" to "tickled by" would exactly reverse the meaning of each sentence.

Toddlers begin to appreciate differences in word order before they begin combining words in their own speech. When sixteen-to-eighteen-month-olds were seated in front of a pair of television sets, each showing Sesame Street puppets acting out one of these two sentences, they looked more at the video corresponding to whichever sentence was playing on voice-over. Children thus appreciate the meaning embedded in word order at a very young age, an understanding that becomes quite useful when they begin speaking two-word phrases themselves, usually between eighteen and twenty-four months. Indeed, the vast majority of toddlers' first word pairs are in the proper order, minisentences such as: *All dry. I shut. See baby. More cereal. Mail come. Our car.*

There is no three-word stage in language development. Toddlers hang for several months in the two-word phase, still rapidly building their vocabularies. Then, beginning early in the third year, they swim into another linguistic vortex, this time the rapid accumulation of grammatical skills. It begins, of course, with the stringing together of more and more words, but the number can be three, four, or even more: *I drive car-car. Plane go fast. That big doggie nice. Now go outside. What the man doing on roof?* Though correct in word order, these early sentences tend to lack most of the inflections and little function words—*of, to, the, am, do, in,* etc.—which is why they are called *telegraphic,* as if each word were at a premium. Before long, however, two-year-olds start adding little bits of grammar, and this too happens in a strikingly predictable way. English-learning children usually begin with the present participle (*-ing*) verb ending, as in, *Where Mommy going?* Then come prepositions such as *in* and *on,* followed by plural *-s* endings (*cats*), possessive *-s* endings (*hers*), articles (*the, a*), regular past tense endings (*-ed*), and third person present tense *-s* endings (*walks*), to mention just a few.

What's most fascinating about the way children learn grammar is that they are not simply doing it by trial and error; they are figuring out the actual *rules* for how different classes of words are combined. This means, first of all, that they intuitively grasp the distinctions between different parts of speech—nouns, verbs, adjectives, and so on. Before long, they figure out how to adjust and assemble these various parts to produce the precise meaning they intend. Say, for instance, that four-year-old Daniel is presented with a word he has never seen before: someone shows him a drawing of a birdlike animal and tells him that it is a "wug." If he is next shown a drawing of two such creatures and asked what they are called, Daniel will inevitably say "wugs." He already knows, without ever being taught, how to recognize a noun and make it plural. In fact, there are three different situations in which English grammar requires the use of *-s* endings, and children master all of them before the age of four, but in a distinct sequence: first, they figure out how to make plurals (*dogs, cats, Elmo dolls*); then, to use *-s* to indicate possession (*dog's bone, Fluffy's yarn, Elmo's doll*); and last, to make present tense verbs to agree with a third person singular subject (*The dog barks. Fluffy plays with yarn. Elmo pees!*). That children start adding these different *-s*'s at different times proves that they can distinguish these separate parts of speech and the rules that apply to them; they are not simply imitating individual words or phrases from Mommy and Daddy.

Even more revealing are the mistakes young children make. Though parents may bristle at the sound of them, there's a good reason why older twos,

threes, and fours come up with constructions such as: *He gots a purple truck;*
She beed happy; Katie comed over; We swimmed at the pool. Each error is one
of overgeneralization; the child takes an irregular verb—one of the roughly
180 in the English language whose past tense is not formed simply by adding
-*ed* to the end—and tries to treat it like a regular verb. Children persist in
these mistakes for several years, but the amazing thing is that they tend *not*
to appear in the speech of very young children. In other words, young toddlers will often get a few of these irregular verbs right—like *came, was,* or
has—before they figure out that a rule exists and begin substituting *comed,*
beed, and *gots.* These errors continue, in spite of adults' correction, until children finally manage to memorize, one by one, all the irregular verb past
tenses and override the more convenient rule for regular verbs. Irregular plurals and comparators are a similar source of confusion, which is why you may
hear a preschooler describe a trip to the circus thus: *The goodest part was those*
mans with the funny feets!

Children learn language in a very predictable way. Although there are a few
notable differences between languages, kids throughout the world follow
remarkably similar paths on their rapid journey to fluency. Even deaf children, who must learn language in an entirely different (that is, visual)
medium, abide by a virtually identical schedule, provided they are immersed
in sign language from birth: They "babble" with their fingers in the first year,
produce single signs shortly after that, begin combining signs at around seventeen months, progress to longer, telegraphic sentences, and finally master
most grammatical inflections by about three years of age. Along the way, they
also make mistakes much like those of children learning spoken language.
They overregularize verb forms, producing signs that are in every way analogous to speaking children's *goed* or *holded.* They even get mixed up, as hearing children do, when first learning the meaning of the pronouns *you* and *me.*
This is certainly understandable for spoken language, since the meaning of
each word shifts depending on the speaker. But in sign language, each word
is represented by simple pointing. Although deaf babies initially point appropriately, they begin to confuse the two gestures toward the end of the second
year, the same age as hearing kids do.

   The fact that all children learn language in a very similar way and on a
very similar schedule shows just how deeply rooted it is in our biological
makeup. We are born with a brain primed for language-learning. As long as
it is exposed at the right time, a child's linguistic skills will inevitably flower

on schedule; she will learn to talk (or sign) fluently, memorizing an astonishing number of words and mastering every rule of spoken grammar, all
before the age of four. Children don't really need to be taught language; just
talk to them, and you will see their linguistic brain grow and blossom.

Individual Differences in Language: The Nature and Nurture of Verbal Skills

So far, we've considered just the universal features of language-learning—the
milestones that every normal child passes on the route to fluency. The fact
that children all learn language in more or less the same way is a great asset
if you happen to be a psycholinguist searching to understand its neural basis.
Parents, however, are generally preoccupied with something else: the seemingly great differences between children in the early stages of learning language. Sure, now that Nathan is twenty months old, he can say dozens of
words, but Kelsey, his peer next door, is already speaking in sentences. Even
as our children are speeding through new words and grammatical constructions more rapidly than we ever could, most parents can't help but focus on
their comparative rate of development. Why does he babble so little? Is she
a late talker? When will he start combining words?

More importantly, does it really make any difference, in the long run,
whether a child begins talking a few months earlier or later? Surprisingly, we
still don't know the answer to this question. On the one hand, there is plenty
of evidence that children who are language-delayed in one way or another
(for reasons other than brain damage or retardation) can catch up completely. A striking example is babies who are tracheotomized early in life—
who, as a lifesaving measure, have a breathing hole cut in their windpipe.
Though they cannot practice any kind of babbling or speaking, such children
quickly progress to full fluency once their airways are restored. A more frequent problem is chronic ear infections; in spite of early language delays,
children suffering temporary periods of bilateral hearing loss generally catch
up by early elementary school (see page 256). And think about a child like
Helen Keller who, though deaf and blind from eighteen months of age,
nonetheless learned how to read, write, and even speak eloquently before
public gatherings. Obviously, the capacity for language is incredibly resilient,
at least during the first six or seven years of life.

On the other hand, it's hard to imagine that more linguistically precocious children wouldn't have a great advantage over their slower peers.
Because language-learning is so cumulative, children who start speaking earlier generally move on to phrases, sentences, and grammatical milestones at
a more rapid clip. Indeed, the number of words a child can say at twenty
months is known to predict later language skills, such as grammatical usage
and understanding in the third year. Early talkers are obviously better able to
communicate their needs, initiate interactions with others, and understand
what's going on around them. So an earlier start at language seemingly can't
help but accelerate all aspects of a child's emotional, social, and cognitive
development.

What determines whether a child talks early or late? Why are some
three-year-olds prone to long soliloquies while others can barely put short
sentences together? Is it simply a matter of genes, or can parents do something special to accelerate their children's language-learning?

The Role of Genes   The answer, as always, lies somewhere between
nature and nurture. To some extent, verbal skills are a fact of heredity, like
height and hair color, so they inevitably vary across the population. Twin
studies inform us that verbal ability is roughly 50 percent heritable, although
scholastic skills like reading and spelling are considerably less so. (Only about
20 percent of the variance for such skills is attributable to genes.) Other evidence for the genetic basis of language comes from language deficits, like certain forms of dyslexia and a much rarer disorder known as *Specific Language
Impairment*, which are demonstrably heritable. Adults with the latter condition have tremendous difficulty speaking and/or understanding language;
they tend to talk very slowly and, in spite of great mental exertion, make
obvious grammatical errors, saying such things as: *The boy eat four cookies.*
But they are not retarded, deaf, or otherwise mentally impaired. Their afflic-
tion is thought to stem from a single mutant gene that specifically affects language areas of the brain. (This doesn't mean that language per se is the
function of a single gene; any sophisticated apparatus, such as a computer or
space shuttle, can be disabled by a single aberrant part.) If language ability
can be compromised by a single gene or unfortunate combination of genes,
then it seems inescapable that individuals at the other end of the spectrum—
those with an unusual gift for poetry, public oratory, foreign languages, or in
the case of Helen Keller, overcoming extreme adversity—are the lucky, but
equally rare winners of the genetic lottery for language skills.

The role of genes is probably easiest to detect early in life, before differ-ences in education and language exposure can have much influence. Studies of adopted babies have shown that their language skills at twelve months—how well they understand spoken directions, name objects, gesture, jabber, and imitate verbally—match more closely the cognitive skills of their bio-logical parents than those of their adoptive ones. So early on, at least, genes appear to play the more important role in determining a child's verbal abili-ties. It may even be possible to measure this genetic potential at birth, since researchers have found that a child's earliest neural responses to speech sounds—that is, the exact pattern of electrical activity in a newborn's brain resulting from the presentation of simple syllables—can predict differences in their language skills as late as five years of age.

Given that children come into the world with varying potentials for lan-guage, it's not hard to imagine how an early genetic advantage could snow-ball into a more precocious course of overall language-learning. But genes don't stop working at the moment of birth. Later genetic expression proba-bly contributes to the "grammar explosion" that begins around two years of age, as well perhaps for the occasional "late bloomer," whose verbal talent suddenly flowers much later in childhood. Though it is more difficult to dis-entangle the roles of nature and nurture later in life, genetic factors probably continue to shape the way the linguistic brain wires itself during the entire course of language development.

Sex Differences in Language and the Brain   Another kind of evidence for the role of genes comes from sex differences in language skills. It really is true, as most parents already believe, that girls are more verbal than boys. One recent study found that as early as midgestation, female fetuses move their mouths significantly more than male fetuses, as if already practicing for a lifetime of speech. Girl babies start talking a month or two earlier than boys, and their phrases and sentences tend to be longer. (See Fig-ure 14.3.) Girls' grammar is more varied and contains fewer errors than boys', and their vocabularies tend to be larger, at least in the early years. Boys catch up in most of these areas by around four or five years of age. But in certain respects, they never quite make it. Elementary school-aged girls continue to outperform boys on tests of spelling, capitalization, punctuation, language usage, and reading comprehension tests. And even as adults, women tend to do better on tests of verbal fluency and other tasks, like thinking up words that all begin with a particular letter.

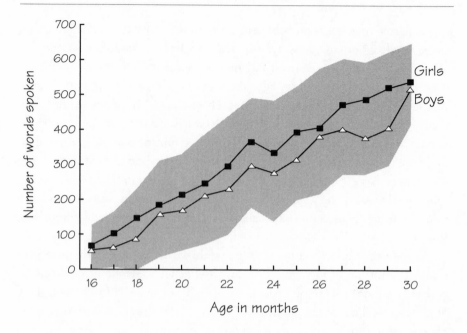

FIGURE 14.3

Girls lead boys by about two months in the number of words they can say, but the average difference between sexes is much smaller than the normal range for all children, two-thirds of whom fall within the shaded area.

Modified from L. Fenson et al., "Variability in early communicative development," *Monographs of the Society for Research in Child Development* 59(5), 1994, by permission of the publisher.

Of course, these data describe only the *average* abilities of males and females as groups. There are plenty of boys who excel at verbal skills, and girls who are slow to begin talking or combining words. (Indeed, my own kids have bucked this trend, at least so far; Sammy started saying words several months earlier than Julia, although I suspect having a chatty big sister around may have had something to do with it.) Overall, the difference between the sexes is much smaller than the range of abilities for either sex alone. Moreover, there are several verbal skills, like vocabulary size and verbal reasoning, in which men and women perform indistinguishably.

We are only just beginning to get a handle on the neural basis for sex differences in language, but one striking observation is the degree to which each sex favors the left hemisphere: by several measures, men are more lateralized, using the left hemisphere more exclusively, whereas women tend to divide language functions more equally between left and right hemispheres. In one recent study, researchers imaged brain activity in the lower frontal lobes while subjects had to make a judgment about the rhyming of pairs of written nonsense words. Only the left hemisphere (that is, Broca's area) lit up in the men, while women tended to show activation of both Broca's area and its homologous region in the right frontal lobe. In another study, researchers used MRI to measure the size of the planum temporale—a part of the posterior language center—in both hemispheres. Contrary to earlier reports, these images of the living brain showed that the planum is asymmetrical only in males; men have a larger planum on the left side, whereas they tend to be identical in size on both sides of women's brains. All of these findings help explain a long-standing neurological observation, that women are considerably less likely than men to lose language function when they suffer strokes or other kinds of damage to the left hemisphere, because their right hemispheres are already doing part of the job. (While greater lateralization may be a liability for language skills, it is probably advantageous for visual-spatial skills, an area in which males excel over females; see Chapter 16.)

In addition to lateralization, several other differences have been found in the basic structure of men's and women's linguistic brains. It has been recently established, for instance, that both Wernicke's and Broca's areas are proportionally larger in women's brains than in men's. Moreover, close analysis of Wernicke's area has revealed that women's neurons are more densely packed and have longer dendrites than men's. We don't yet know how these differences in brain structure translate into specific differences in verbal skill, but it stands to reason that the sex with larger neurons and more brain area devoted to language would tend to have greater expertise in the verbal arena.

Of course, the important issue is not whether sex differences exist but why? How do we know that they are genetic? Perhaps the linguistic brain develops differently in males and females because of consistent differences in language experience. For example, the fact that girls tend to be more social, even very early on (Chapter 12), may mean that parents find it more rewarding to talk to them, so that it is actually greater language exposure that makes their dendrites grow longer and broadens their right hemisphere's involvement in language.

Plausible as this may sound, several lines of evidence argue that sex differences in language are truly inborn. For one thing, in painstaking studies, social psychologists have actually measured the amount of time parents talk to young girls and boys, and they have found that it does not differ. (It's nice to know that parents, at least in this regard, turn out to be so egalitarian.) At the same time, neuroscientists have documented several differences in the way boys' and girls' brains process language. Even on the first day of life, the two sexes differ in their neural responses to simple speech sounds, and by three months of age, girls show greater electrical activity in the left hemisphere to verbal stimuli, while boys show greater activity in the right. Although this result is somewhat contrary to the findings in adults, it suggests that the dominant language areas of the brain—those located in the left hemisphere—actually mature earlier in girls, which would explain their linguistic precocity.

The Role of Experience   Considering all of this evidence—genetic language deficits, twin studies, adoption studies, early neural correlates of language skill, and early sex differences—it is clear that genes play a major role in determining a child's relative skill at language. But as we've already seen, the linguistic brain is also profoundly shaped by a child's experience with language. Cases such as Genie and Chelsea illustrate this point most vividly, but it is equally apparent in every one of us—by the way every person is marked with the particular language and accent of our upbringing. Genes notwithstanding, there can be little doubt that the *quality* of children's language exposure also permanently shapes the structure and function of their linguistic brains.

Children grow up in all kinds of language environments. Some are immersed in a veritable verbal soup, bathed most of their waking hours in the constant conversation of chatty parents, siblings, or caregivers. Others are raised in comparative silence, by shy or quiet parents who, even if very affectionate, simply aren't comfortable talking to children. And a great number are exposed to language continuously, but it is all on television.

What about these many variations on language exposure? How do differences in early language experience contribute to children's later verbal skills? What is the best environment for the linguistic brain to grow in? How, in other words, can we optimize our children's language skills, no matter what their genetic potential?

How Parenting Style Affects Language-Learning   After decades of speculation, experts have finally done the tough research to answer these questions. The most extensive study to date was performed by Betty Hart and Todd Risley, psychologists who followed forty different Kansas City families throughout the first three years of their children's lives. Every month a member of the research team would go into each family's home and record every aspect of how the parents talked to their young children. The children's verbal development was also studied by keeping track of the size and growth rate of their vocabularies as well as their IQ scores at age three (largely a measure of verbal skill at this age). Through their exhaustive analysis, Hart and Risley were able to uncover the several features of parenting style that seem to make the greatest difference in determining children's language skills.

Remarkably enough, the most obvious influence over children's language development turned out to be the mere *amount* of parents' talking; children whose parents addressed or responded to them more in early life had larger, faster-growing vocabularies and scored higher on IQ tests than children whose parents spoke fewer words to them overall. Parents who talk more inevitably expose their children to a greater variety of words and sentences, so a correlation also turned up between the diversity of parents' language—the number of different nouns and adjectives they used, and the length of their phrases and sentences—and their children's linguistic progress.

In addition to these quantitative features, Hart and Risley discovered a particular qualitative aspect of parental language that seems to especially influence children's language: the amount of positive versus negative feedback children hear. Youngsters who heard a larger proportion of *no, don't, stop it,* and similar prohibitions had poorer language skills than three-year-olds who had received less negative feedback. Of course, no parent of toddler-aged children can avoid all prohibitions, but those who kept their negative responses to a minimum, emphasizing instead positive responses, such as repeating their children's vocalizations or following them with questions or affirmations, fostered better language development.

A follow-up study on the same group of children reveals that these differences in verbal skills persisted well into the grade-school years; by third grade, children whose parents spoke more to them during the first three years continued to excel at various language skills, including reading, spelling, speaking, and listening abilities. So even after children enter school, when their parents cease to be the sole influence over their cognitive development, their early language exposure has created a lasting legacy in their language achievement.

There is another, very disturbing side to Hart and Risley's report. In selecting the forty families for their study, they deliberately chose a cross-section of American socioeconomic classes. When the researchers factored in these differences, it became blatantly clear that virtually every feature of parenting style improved substantially as families ascended the ladder of educational and financial advantage. Even something as simple as the number of words addressed to young children tended to increase dramatically, with children on welfare hearing an average of 600 words per hour addressed to them, as compared with 1,200 for children of working-class families and 2,100 for children with professional parents. Socioeconomic level also correlated strongly with the type of feedback parents tended to give their children. On average, professional parents were heard to praise or otherwise respond positively to their children seven times more often than welfare parents, and they doled out negative feedback—those particularly toxic prohibitions and imperatives—only half as frequently. With such enormous differences in both the quantity and quality of interaction with their parents, it's not hard to see how children from different socioeconomic groups are propelled onto wildly different trajectories of language-learning.

The social and political implications of these findings are staggering. Obviously, it would take a massive effort to overcome these extreme differences in children's early language experience. But it's important to realize that socioeconomic class per se is not the primary factor determining children's language achievement. For while children's fate may seem to be sealed by their level of economic advantage, what really matters is their parents' style of interacting with them. In other words, if we look just within a single socioeconomic group, like the twenty-three families that made up the "working-class" rank in Hart and Risley's study, parenting style turns out to be a much better predictor of each child's language skills than the parents' precise financial and educational attainment. Within this group, parents who talked more to their children, who used a greater variety of words and sentences, who asked rather than told their children what to do, and who consistently responded in positive rather than negative ways to their children's speech and behavior, tended to raise more verbally gifted children than those who were poorer at these parenting skills. Similar findings have been reported in a study of professional-class children in Chicago: those whose mothers addressed more words to them in the second year of life had the fastest-growing vocabularies. So even in higher socioeconomic ranks, there is enough variety in parenting styles to significantly affect the quality of children's language development, exploding, as some call it, "the myth of the educated parent."

Accelerating Language-Learning   The obvious implication of these findings is that parents can improve their children's language skills, and perhaps even raise their IQs, simply by altering the way they talk to them. But is there really any evidence that this works? Have any parents actually succeeded in accelerating their children's language development through deliberate changes in their interaction style?

One educational psychologist, William Fowler, reports impressive gains with his attempts to teach parents special methods for enriching their babies' early language exposure. His program begins very early in infancy, and though it doesn't specifically emphasize the *amount* of talk, it instructs parents in *how* to talk to their babies and young children, using several brief sessions per day that undoubtedly do increase the overall amount of verbal interaction.

Fowler's basic strategy is to have parents preview each stage of language development *before* the baby himself has actually entered it. Parents thus begin with *vocalization play*—introducing various phonemes, syllables, and syllable combinations—even before the baby has begun babbling. Next comes *labeling play*, beginning as early as three months, in which parents first encourage noun and verb use by naming any object, person, or action that has drawn the baby's attention, and then move on to more complex parts of speech like prepositions (*on, off, in, out*), adjectives (*big, red, wet, soft*), adverbs (*fast, slowly, quietly, loudly*), and pronouns (*me, you, him, her*). This is followed, as early as nine months of age, by *phrase and sentence play*, in which parents use various tricks like word substitution (*the red/blue/little/fast car*) and expansion (*that balloon; that big balloon; that big yellow balloon; that big yellow balloon is flying away!*) to demonstrate how words can be put together. And finally, the program moves on to *theme play* as early as fourteen months, in which parents are taught how to engage their children in progressively more complex conversations about the events and experiences in their lives.

According to Fowler and his colleagues, all of the thirty or so children exposed to their accelerated training passed the basic milestones of language-learning several months ahead of the norm. Stimulated children spoke their first words between seven and nine months and started combining words around their first birthdays; some began speaking sentences at a mere ten months of age. By two years, most of the stimulated children had mastered the basic rules of grammar, a milestone that is not normally achieved until age four. Moreover, the majority maintained their verbal advantage throughout childhood; most learned to read before first grade, and performed very well in school (even in such "nonverbal" areas as math and science), and by high school, 62 percent were enrolled in some kind of gifted or accelerated academic program.

Fowler's studies must be more rigorously replicated before they are fully convincing. But whether or not his specific program proves effective with larger numbers of children, his prescriptions make sense in terms of what we know about the development of the linguistic brain and its exquisite sensitivity to language exposure in the first months and years of life.

How to Provide Early Language Enrichment

Putting all this research together, we now have a pretty clear picture of how language develops, and what parents and other caregivers can do to best promote this essential mental skill. The following points should be kept in mind by anyone charged with the wonderful task of nurturing a young child's language through the critical, brain-building years.

First of all, language stimulation should begin very *early*: by just three years of age, children are already headed down vastly different paths of verbal achievement as a result of their cumulative experience with language. Ideally, language stimulation should begin at birth, since we know that newborns' brains are already attuned to human speech and immediately start learning the sounds of their mother tongue. In fact, Fowler's group found that babies who entered their program between six and eight months of age were not as successful as those who began at the earliest age, three months, so clearly earlier is better.

Secondly, the *quantity* of language is critical: the more words a child hears, the larger her vocabulary will be, and the faster it will continue to grow. But it cannot be overemphasized that this quantity means the number of words addressed *to the child*. Mothers aren't doing their kids any favors by talking on the phone all day; day-care workers don't help by conversing only with other workers; nor is television an adequate way to increase young children's language exposure. (Indeed, at one point deaf parents were advised to leave the TV on for their hearing babies, but it never succeeded in teaching them spoken language.) A baby can begin to make sense of language only when it refers to something she can directly relate to. Parents and other caregivers should thus talk frequently to their babies and try, whenever possible, to focus on the here and now: pointing out and labeling the objects, people, and events in their immediate environment, especially the babies' own actions, feelings, and attempts at speech.

Which brings us to the *quality* of language to which a child is exposed. Language addressed to young children needs to be *simple, clear,* and *positive* in tone in order to be of maximum value. Fortunately, most caregivers already use a special style when speaking to infants and young children. As noted in Chapter 10, babies clearly prefer the higher pitch, highly intonated style, and slower pace of "motherese," and recent evidence suggests that it even helps them in the earliest stages of phoneme-learning. But it's important to avoid the kind of muddled baby-talk that turns a sentence like "Is she the cutest little baby in the world?" into "Uz see da cooest wiwo baby inna wowud?" Caregivers should try to enunciate clearly when speaking to babies and young children, giving them the cleanest, simplest model of speech possible.

Of course, it's easy to say that speech should be at a level your child can understand, but it's not always easy to figure out what that level is. For instance, older babies understand much more than they can say, so you need not limit your speech to single syllables or words. On the other hand, there's evidence that even *Sesame Street* does more harm than good for children under eighteen months, probably because it comes at the expense of more direct, positive parental interaction. (But it is great for preschoolers.) At every age, parents need to seek out that happy medium of speaking to their child in a way that is largely within his reach of understanding but also stretches him just a bit beyond it.

One trick for keeping speech simple is to use lots and lots of *repetition*. Perhaps because they otherwise have so little control over their world, children simply love the predictability that comes from hearing the same story, song, or nursery rhyme over and over again. By repeating the same words or phrases, you rapidly reinforce specific neural pathways that link sound and meaning in a child's brain. But don't treat it like a drill. Nobody learns when they're bored (and you'll lose your enthusiasm even sooner). Make a game out of repetition by using the substitution and expansion tricks illustrated in the previous section.

No matter what the age, the best way to approach language lessons is as a *conversation* between you and your child. Conversation requires turn-taking, so sticking to this mode will ensure not only that your child hears you but that she also gets her own chance to practice speaking. For young infants, it's important to do this through face-to-face contact, where the baby knows both that he is being addressed and that he is being heard. (It doesn't hurt that young babies are fascinated by human faces; see Chapter 9.) Moreover, face-to-face contact gives them a chance to *see* as well as hear how words are pronounced. It's known that babies just four months old have already begun figuring out which mouth movements go with which sounds, so allowing them to watch you as you speak will aid their own efforts at forming speech sounds.

As in any conversation, *listening* is just as important as speaking. Researchers find that many parents actually miss their baby's very first words, like Nathan's *ba* for *bottle* and *gee* for the family's cat, Chia, because they are inevitably mispronounced and hard to decipher from the rest of their babble. But without positive feedback, many babies actually stop using words for a few months, attempting few new ones or else regressing entirely back to pure babbling for several more months. The best way to ensure that you don't miss those first few words is to pay close attention very early on, when your baby first starts babbling. Try to figure out which consonants and vowel sounds he can say and which he still omits. Once you're in the habit of good listening, you stand a much better chance of catching that first *ba* and being able to reply, "Yes, that's your bottle."

Conversations also offer you your best chance to emphasize the positive and avoid those prohibitions and criticisms that seem to be especially damaging. Responding to your child's utterances with questions (especially the *who, what,* and *why* kind, as opposed to simple *yes-no* queries), affirmations, repetitions, or elaborations will encourage him to keep talking, practicing those brand-new words or phrases or sentences. With young babies, focus on repeating or imitating their attempts at words and syllables. Babies love the sense of control they get from being imitated, and it also gives them very useful feedback about both the sound and the look of their own vocal exercises. In fact, studies of adoptive mothers have shown that imitation is the one type of interaction that best predicts their babies' verbal development at one year of age.

One type of feedback that is surprisingly bad for young children is correcting their speech. Particularly early on, when babies are eagerly trying to spit out their first words, speech development may actually be inhibited if parents spend too much effort correcting or questioning their faulty pronunciation, as in the following exchange:

Baby: Gah.
Mother: What?
Baby: Gah.
Mother: Oh, car! Say "car."
Baby: Gah.

Nor are corrections any more useful later on, when children make the inevitable grammatical errors, like: *Sammy gots a spot on his nose;* or *Ice cream is the bestest food!* Part of the problem is that we are simply too inconsistent; parents let far too many mistakes slip through to make much of a difference. But even if we were much more vigilant, corrections pose the same problem as prohibitions: they send a negative message, in effect saying, "You're really not very good at talking, so why bother trying." Young children are generally much better off if we focus on *what* they're trying to say instead of *how* they're saying it. So don't worry about the mistakes. Luckily, little children are expert at rooting out their own errors and matching their language to the model of those around them. The best route to good grammar is simply to set a good example in your own speech.

Above all, language lessons should be *fun.* Young children learn best through play, and for babies, this means happy social interactions, like games of peekaboo and "This little piggy." Preschoolers love word games, like making up rhymes or alliterations: *The big . . . brown . . . buffalo . . . that built a . . . brand-new . . . boat . . . in the bayou!* And of course, all children love music. Start with the lullabies, but don't forget the playful songs, like "If you're happy and you know it . . ." and "Head, shoulders, knees and toes (knees and toes)." If you've forgotten the words to some of these classics, or desperately need to expand your repertoire, children's tapes and CDs will get you started. But don't rely too heavily on recorded music. Remember that young children learn best when they can hear *and* see how words are made, so your own singing, no matter how off-key, is the best way to use music as a teaching tool.

Last, but by no means least, don't forget the books. There's nothing like cuddling up together with a story to create the perfect, cozy opportunity for language-learning. Simple, bright picture books captivate babies and guarantee that they are focused on precisely the items your words are referring to. Illustrated storybooks help toddlers and young preschoolers understand longer phrases and sentences. For older preschoolers and grade-schoolers, pictureless books teach that words alone can create imagery and entice them to want to read on their own. And try, if you can, to keep up your own reading, especially in front of the kids, since this sets a powerful example they will want to imitate.

Studies show that parents do their best teaching while reading to their young children, and it really pays off. Two-year-olds whose parents read to them early and often show more advanced language skills than children read to less frequently, an advantage that seems to last well into the grade-school years. Books tend to broaden the vocabulary parents use with young children, and also offer a great way to stimulate a child's own speaking, provided you use them as a stepping-off point for conversation. Indeed, one method known as *dialogic reading,* which especially encourages children's comments, responses, elaborations, and so on during story time, has been reported to accelerate two-year-olds' language development by as much as nine months. Books are without doubt the most effective tool for teaching language, and the great thing about them is that they are available to all, free of charge, from your public library.

In sum, there is a great deal that parents can do to nurture their children's language skills. No matter what their innate potential, every child can benefit from a more positive language environment—from less TV and more reading and conversation. And this is true for children of all ages. Remember that the critical period for language is most intense until six or seven years, but it declines only gradually, all the way through puberty. Indeed, recent research has shown that the more years a person completes of high school and college, the longer their dendrites in Wernicke's area. We know that when language enrichment ends, as when disadvantaged children finish Head Start programs and enter poor public schools, their verbal skills and IQ gains invariably slip back. Language enrichment is best if it begins early, but it also must continue well beyond infancy and the preschool years if it is going to have lasting value.

Fortunately, it is all so easy: Just talk to your kids!

Chapter 15

How Intelligence Grows
in the Brain

"Okay Jack," says Dave, "time for your bedtime stories," and into the living room bounds a three-and-a-half-year-old towhead, teeth brushed, face washed, and clad in his favorite Pooh pajamas that already look two sizes too small.

"I want these," he says, digging out three books from the stack on the cluttered coffee table. Father and son then snuggle in for the nicest half hour of the day.

"Wait, wait, Daddy," Jack declares, as Dave is about to begin. "I can read it myself."

"The . . . cat . . . in . . . the . . . hat . . . comes . . . back," he feigns, pointing at each word as he slowly pronounces it.

"Wow! That's great," says Dave, looking up at his wife across the room, who's staring back in amazement. "I didn't know you could read!"

Jack breaks into a big, proud grin but becomes unaccountably shy when Dave turns the page and waits for him to continue.

"I think you should read it now, Daddy."

"Sure, Jackie. But you sure are learning fast!"

What parent hasn't thought, at some point or another, that his own child may be some kind of a genius? It can strike you as early as the first year, if you

have one of those precocious babies who starts walking and talking at nine
months. It's hard to avoid by the second year, when new words start popping
up daily, and your avid explorer insists on doing everything himself—brush-
ing his teeth, using a fork, putting on (or at least trying to) his own shoes.
And it's inevitable by two or three years, when kids amaze us every day with
their complicated sentences, memory of distant events, or sophisticated revelations: "A butterfly isn't really a fly, is it?"

Cognitive development is, after all, the growth of intelligence. Children
get smarter as they get older. They know more, reason better, have longer
attention spans and a better grasp of abstract concepts, and can therefore
solve harder problems as time passes. They also grow steadily more aware of
their own mental capabilities—their consciousness dawns—which means
they can actually begin applying their emerging intellectual powers in a
deliberate and fruitful way.

The change is most dramatic during the early years, because babies begin
with so little, intellectually speaking. Except for a few cognitive instincts (see
below), newborns pretty much just perceive and react, and even these simple input-output processes are markedly immature in the youngest infants.
But what can you expect, with a brain that is only one-quarter of its adult size
and has had little exposure to anything but a warm, watery womb? Cognitive
development is the product of two interacting influences—brain growth and
experience—both of which exert their greatest impact during the first few
years of life. Remember that the brain triples in size in the first year alone and
is virtually fully grown by the time a child enters kindergarten. Experience,
of course, accrues throughout life, but it is infinitely more potent in the earliest months and years, when the synapses are still forming and the brain is
at the height of its plasticity. So we shouldn't be amazed (though it's hard not
to be) when we see kids race through cognitive milestones. Jack really *is* a
genius compared to where he was three years earlier.

Then again, "genius" is a relative term. It's impossible to talk about the
growth of intelligence without admitting that some kids are smarter than
others. This is the uglier side of parenting, the one that has us looking over
our neighbors' fence to see how early their kids are walking, talking, reading,
or composing their first symphony. In our saner moments, most of us realize
that these seeming flashes of brilliance are not all that unusual. Your child is
probably developing quickly in some ways but more slowly in others and will
eventually be talented in some areas but not others. (If nothing else has burst

your bubble, that first parent-teacher conference will probably do the trick.) But even when you realize your child is not perfect, it doesn't lessen the magic of watching her mind grow and her own particular intellectual talents emerge and flourish.

What is the biological basis of intelligence? What properties make a brain "smart," and how do these emerge during infancy and childhood?

Intelligence is notoriously hard to define. Is it a single, overarching capacity or a collection of distinct mental skills? By now, it should be evident that rather than being a uniform pink blob, the brain is a collection of many separate circuits—for perception, movement, emotion, language, memory, and so on. Though all of these circuits interact closely with one another, they remain fundamentally distinct. But can we go so far as to say that the brain is not a single organ at all but a network of separate, powerful machines, each operating on its own and merely wired together to give an illusion of unity?

The logical conclusion, if you take this view, is that there is no single type of intelligence but many different ones, and the concept "intelligence" becomes a synonym for excellence in any single area. Howard Gardner, the educational psychologist who coined just such a theory of "multiple intelligences," posits seven fundamentally different realms of mental excellence: verbal, spatial, mathematical-scientific, musical, bodily-kinesthetic, and "personal," which includes both self- and social understanding. The existence of *idiot savants*—real people who are mentally retarded but nonetheless possess extraordinary powers in a single area, such as language, arithmetic, drawing, or music—supports just such a modular view of intelligence. Recent brain imaging also shows that people with exceptional skills in, say, music, math, languages, or art do use certain parts of their brain differently from people of merely average ability. It is likely, then, that the difference between great poets and the rest of us is an especially well-functioning left hemisphere. Artists and navigators may be especially well ordered in the right hemisphere; dancers and athletes may have a more perfect organization in their motor cortex, cerebellum, and basal ganglia; psychologists and politicians, with their greater insight into human emotion and motivation, may have a more highly tuned limbic system. (Thus far, the location of mathematical and musical skills has been harder to pin down.)

Obviously, different people do have different mental talents, and any theory of intelligence must take account of a variety of skills. But most psychologists maintain that there is also such a thing as "general intelligence"—some overall efficiency or accuracy of processing that influences every mental effort. Intelligence in this sense is thought to involve the more basic elements of cognition—perception, categorization, abstraction, memory, attention, and the like—that are essential for excellence in any pursuit. General intelligence is no substitute for talent, but it's hard to imagine anyone ever becoming a great writer, architect, physicist, pianist, statesman, or even athlete without a good measure of it. (And this is why idiot savants remain mere curiosities.)

The problem comes in figuring out how to measure intelligence. The standard method is the IQ test, a pen-and-pencil exam (except for young children, who are examined using oral questions and tasks) that uses verbal, spatial, and quantitative problems to measure general skills of reasoning and abstraction. IQ tests also tap many nonreasoning traits, such as motivation, discipline, and concentration, that are important for success in any area. Those who believe most strongly in the value of IQ tests point to their high reproducibility and predictive value. The same person is likely to receive a very similar score on a wide battery of different tests, suggesting that they all are tapping a single type of general ability. IQ scores also predict school performance and occupational status with fairly good accuracy.

However, IQ tests are certainly not perfect and have been rightly criticized for racial and cultural bias. The fact that anyone from a preliterate culture would score in the "retarded" range, no matter what his or her skill as a hunter, forager, or peacemaker, illustrates most vividly their limited value. IQ tests obviously do not tap some of the more specific realms of intelligence—such as musical, bodily, or interpersonal skills—nor do they measure other general forms of intelligence, such as wisdom, creativity, and common sense. Psychologists have proven that people can and do perform very wisely in certain real-life situations, regardless of their scores on IQ tests. Experienced shoppers, for instance, can rapidly determine the best value on a supermarket shelf, and devoted horse-racing buffs can astutely handicap a quick succession of races; but neither of these forms of expertise is related to an individual's IQ score, even though both require surprisingly complex calculations. In other words, it may be only a minority of academic types who shine in the context of formal IQ tests or their more widely used surrogates, the SATs, GREs, and the like. For those who don't "test well," IQ tests can pose a danger, as when teachers typecast children based on their scores, or individuals perform below their potential simply because they're aware of how their racial or gender group usually scores.*

Still, for all of their limitations, IQ tests are generally regarded as a valid, highly reproducible way of comparing cognitive function between individuals within a single cultural group. Much of the research discussed in this chapter does focus on IQ, not because it is the "best" gauge of intelligence but because it is the easiest to measure, as well as the primary one that scientists have used to investigate the neural basis of intelligence. Another advantage of IQ measures is that they grow in a reliably steady way through childhood. In this sense, most nine-year-olds really are "smarter" than most six-year-olds, and we can get a fairly accurate picture of an individual's cognitive ability by referring to his or her *mental age*—the average age at which a large population of children attains the same IQ score. For better or worse, IQ tests tend to tap the skills needed for success in school, and the scores are also known to correlate with later financial achievement. However, the basis of this relationship is as complicated as the basis of IQ itself—that is, the degree to which it is determined by nature versus nurture, the subject of the next chapter.

The Neural Basis of Intelligence, and How It Develops

What makes a brain intelligent? Scientists have been trying to answer this question for centuries, searching for some simple measure of head shape or neural activity that might explain why some brains work better than others. To be sure, much of this work has been marred by ideological motivation, such as the "mismeasure" of head size and brain weight that Stephen Jay Gould exposed among early anatomists who were already convinced of their own racial and sexual superiority. While one must remain skeptical about these data, however, certain biological features do seem to be reliably, if

---

*For instance, one recent study found that black college students scored lower than whites on a difficult verbal exam when they had to check off their race on a form beforehand, whereas they scored indistinguishably when they did not have to indicate their race or when they were previously told that the test showed no black-white difference. Similarly, college women scored lower than men on a difficult math test when they were primed with the belief that the test usually shows a gender difference, but indistinguishably when they were told the test showed no gender difference.

weakly, related to individuals' performance on IQ tests. And what is most interesting, for our purposes, is the way these same measures change during the development of every child, suggesting sound biological reasons why children get smarter as they grow.

If you think of intelligence as an index of overall mental ability, it comes as no surprise that there is no single "intelligence center" in the brain. Unlike vision, movement, language, memory, emotion, and the other mental abilities we have considered thus far, no single neural system has been implicated in reasoning, abstraction, problem-solving, and the like. In a classic set of experiments back in the 1920s, psychologist Karl Lashley found that rats with small cortical lesions learn their way around a baited maze quite well, regardless of where in the cortex they are damaged. Rather, Lashley found, it is the *size* of the brain lesion in rats that largely determines the extent of intellectual deficit. Similarly, humans lose remarkably little in the way of IQ when they suffer small lesions in various brain regions. The most extensive of these studies have been performed on American veterans who suffered penetrating head wounds in the Vietnam War. Since all members of the military undergo cognitive testing at the beginning of their service (the Armed Forces Qualification Test, or AFQT), researchers were able to analyze with precision the relationship between brain injury and intelligence in this unfortunately large population of soldiers. Their findings are similar to Lashley's; many veterans showed no significant loss of intelligence, but among those with relatively large brain injuries, the more extensive the damaged area, the greater the decline in AFQT score.

Brain Size   The larger the lesion, the smaller the amount of functional brain tissue left, so an obvious corollary to these findings is that bigger brains should be smarter. This is an old hypothesis, of course, the same one that was so thoroughly "mismeasured" by eighteenth- and nineteenth-century anatomists. But there is a popular presumption (as evinced by Jay Leno's "Mr. Brain" routine) that there is some kind of relationship between brain size and intelligence, and recent evidence, which appears to be free from the kind of bias that plagued that earlier work, indicates that it holds some truth. Several studies have found a small but statistically significant correlation between adults' IQ and head circumference; on a scale of zero to one, where one would be a perfect correspondence between head size and IQ and zero would indicate no relationship whatsoever, head size correlates 0.14 with IQ. Of course, head size is an indirect way of estimating brain size, because skull thickness can vary a lot from person to person. Better data come from CAT and MRI scans, where brain volume can be measured directly and shows about a 0.35 correlation with adult IQ score. A similar correlation holds for children between the ages of five and seventeen. This relationship shows that, generally speaking, bigger brains are better, but its modest value means that head size is of little value in predicting the IQ of any particular individual.*

It is tempting, nonetheless, to try to pin many of the great cognitive advances of early childhood on the simple accretion of brain mass. Babies' brains grow incredibly quickly, from about 250 grams (roughly half a pound) at birth to 750 grams (one and a half pounds) by the end of the first year alone, and then up to some 1,300 grams (nearly three pounds), or full adult size, by just five years of age. Obviously, this pace far outstrips the growth of the rest of the body. None of this brain growth is attributable to the birth of new neurons; as we've seen, young children's gray matter expands rapidly with the explosion of synapses and dendrites, while white matter grows with the rapid myelination of infancy and early childhood (Chapter 2).

More synapses translate into larger, more complex neural circuits, and there is no question that such growth dramatically increases a child's mental capacity. That is why pediatricians keep such close tabs on children's head size during the first months and years of life. (See Figure 15.1.) But children continue to leap ahead intellectually even as their rate of myelination subsides and the number of synapses actually begins to decline. Reading, writing, arithmetic, and computer programming are only a few of the intellectual feats children manage to master after their brains have reached maximum size. Obviously, brain volume cannot fully account for the intellectual growth of a child. We need to look elsewhere—to measures more subtle than the overall weight or volume of the brain—to find the neural basis of intelligence.

Mental Speed One way to think about human intelligence is by analogy to computers: the bigger they are and the faster they go, the smarter they will be. So if brain size alone is not enough to account for differences in intelligence, then another obvious place to look is at the relative speed at which

---

*Indeed, as Gould points out, the early anatomists often found themselves in the awkward position of explaining how certain extraordinary men, such as Walt Whitman or their own Franz Josef Gall, could have achieved so much with their decidedly below-average-size brains.

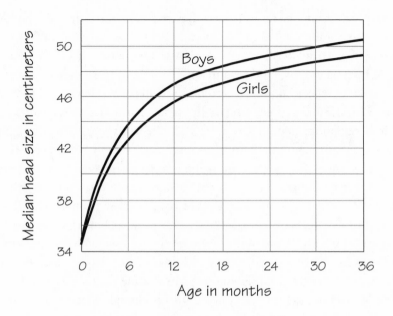

FIGURE 15.1

Head growth during the first three years.

different people's brains perform. Psychologists have been doing this for several decades and have uncovered several measures of mental and neural speed that correlate with IQ. Brighter people react faster at simple tasks like pressing one button in an array when the light above it flashes. They can also make more rapid perceptual judgments, like deciding which of a pair of vertical lines is shorter. This latter task, known as a measure of *inspection time*, is thought to give an especially pure estimate of mental processing speed because it eliminates the movement element inherent in reaction time tasks such as button-pressing; the vertical pair is flashed on a computer screen for just a fraction of a second, but the subject can take as long as he likes to state his response. Subjects with higher IQs can make accurate judgments with stimulus presentations as brief as 50 milliseconds (five-hundredths of a second), while lower-IQ subjects may begin making mistakes when the stimulus duration is still around 100 milliseconds. Overall, inspection time shows about a 0.5 correlation with IQ scores.

Some scientists cut right to the chase in their attempts to estimate processing speed. Using a reasonably large group of subjects, they directly measure electrical transmission within the brain and then compare each individual's rate to his or her score on IQ tests. One way of measuring neural conduction is by using event-related potentials (ERPs)—the characteristic voltage changes triggered by simple visual or auditory stimuli that can be picked up with EEG electrodes pasted to the surface of the scalp. Subjects with higher IQs do tend to have faster ERPs. This relationship is strongest during the first 200 milliseconds (two-tenths of a second) following a stimulus, when the correlation between different individuals' IQ and the speed of their ERPs runs as high as 0.5. This early part of the response is primarily a measure of sensory processing time. But it is too early to tap the decision-making component of a task, which some argue is where real "intelligence" takes place.

In addition to their greater speed, ERP waveforms differ in another way between higher and lower IQ subjects. Brighter people tend to show more complex or "squiggly" ERPs than duller people, as illustrated in Figure 15.2. Such differences in detail are thought to reflect differences in the degree to

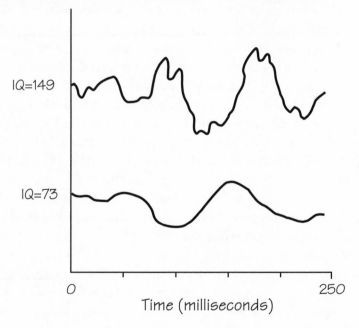

FIGURE 15.2

ERP waveforms in high- and low-IQ children.

After M. Anderson, *Intelligence and Development: A Cognitive Theory*, Cambridge MA: Blackwell, 1992; based on the data of H.J. Eysenck.

which different brains can faithfully follow a sensory stimulus. Just as more sophisticated audio systems play music with higher fidelity to the original recording, so, according to this theory, do more intelligent brains better track every detail of a particular stimulus, resulting in ERPs of higher complexity.

Speed Gains in Childhood   There is little doubt that increasing neural speed plays an important role in children's intellectual growth. By virtually every measure of brain or cognitive processing, children's brains perform faster as they get older. Their reaction and inspection times grow steadily shorter, and they perform consistently faster at simple cognitive tests, like matching letters or mentally rotating objects. Most such studies have been conducted on children aged five and older, and they show the largest gains during middle childhood, between about five and eleven years of age. But even at twelve years, children function at about half the speed of adults on most cognitive tasks. Only around age fifteen does performance speed approach its maximum.

Speed gains are probably even more rapid during infancy and early childhood, although it is impossible to test subjects this young on any of these tasks. But you may recall from Chapter 13 that even the youngest babies rapidly improve at storing the memory for a particular visual stimulus; newborns need to "study" a bull's-eye or other distinctive picture for several minutes in order to recognize it later, while five-month-olds apparently store the memory after only a few seconds. Most adults appreciate the long processing time of babies and young children, which is why we tend to talk more slowly to them, give them extra time to respond to questions, and try to be patient when they attempt new cognitive challenges, like putting a puzzle together or sounding out words. Then again, there are inevitably those times—like when you're trying to get everyone out of the door in the morning—when you can hardly believe how long it takes *to put on a darned pair of sneakers*!

Electrical measurements confirm that children's brains speed up dramatically as they mature. When a newborn is presented with a simple stimulus— say, a touch on the arm—it triggers a wave of electrical changes in her cerebral cortex, but this signal takes nearly three times longer to make it there than it would in an adult. Taking bodily growth into account (which tends to shorten the conduction time for smaller—that is, younger—subjects), this translates into a nearly *sixteenfold* increase in the speed at which her neurons will conduct information between birth and adolescence. The vast majority of this gain will take place during her first year, when myelination is at its most rapid. Nonetheless, neural transmission accelerates another two- to threefold between one and ten years of age, a change that undoubt-edly contributes to children's increasing speed at various cognitive tasks.

Speed is not the only ERP feature that changes with brain maturation. Children's EEG activity also grows increasingly complex during the first months and years of life (as illustrated on page 36), which is again reminiscent of a difference between lower- and higher-IQ adults. Another striking change is the absence, in babies and young children, of a fascinating component known as the *P300 wave*. The P300 (whose name derives from the fact that it is a positive wave that occurs, in adults, about 300 milliseconds after the onset of a stimulus) is perhaps the closest thing we have to an index of conscious mental experience. Unlike the earlier waves in an ERP (those that peak before 300 milliseconds), which reflect sensory processing in the brain stem and early cortical centers, P300s are a measure of higher cortical activity.

By most accounts, P300 waves are simply not present in infants and tod-dlers. The earliest age at which they have been unambiguously identified is four years. Although one recent study describes a candidate P300 in five- to ten-month-old babies in response to an unexpected musical tone, this electri-cal response is considerably smaller and slower than in adults. (P600 would be a more appropriate name.) Other studies describe positive waves in babies that occur at even greater intervals, as much as 1,400 milliseconds after the stimulus. The jury is still out on whether babies do or do not exhibit true P300 responses, but even if they do, it's clear that they are very immature: P300 waves do not reach their full amplitude and speed until late adolescence.

"Efficiency"   It is easy to see why faster brains would be smarter brains; the more information you can process, store, retrieve from memory, and ana-lyze in a given period of time, the greater your mental capacity, in much the same way that a faster-moving stretch of freeway can transport more cars in a given hour than one choked with rubberneckers. In effect, speed is the equivalent of increasing brain size, and an easier one than growing a larger head. But there is also another benefit of speed; faster processing means that any given bit of information is going to be processed more *efficiently*—that each driver will get home sooner, wasting less gasoline and generating less pollution while idling on the freeway.

Recent evidence supports the idea that intelligence is reflected in the relative efficiency of different people's brains. Imaging experiments reveal that smarter subjects actually burn less brain energy (glucose) than those with lower IQs while performing the same mental tasks. In another study, scientists ran PET scans on a group of college students before and after they mastered the computer game Tetris, a visual-spatial task. They found, first, that all subjects used less brain energy as they improved at the game, and secondly, that higher-IQ subjects showed the largest decline in brain metabolism with learning. In other words, mental problems really are easier for brighter subjects; they don't have to flex nearly as much intellectual muscle to solve them as less intelligent subjects.

These findings are particularly interesting when we consider the energy expenditure of children's brains. In spite of their slower processing speed, children's brains actually use *more* energy than adults do. Glucose use rises rapidly from birth to age four, at which point it is about twice as great as in adults; it then gradually declines throughout middle childhood and adolescence. (See also Chapter 2.) This pattern of energy consumption closely parallels the overproduction and pruning of synapses in children's brains, suggesting a simple reason for children's inefficiency: they simply have too many possible routes for information to flow through—freeways, surface roads, back alleys—and not all are equally direct. While this overproduction is certainly useful—it is what permits children's fantastic learning capacity—it comes at the cost of lower overall efficiency.

Here, then, is another neural correlate of IQ in adults—brain efficiency—that contributes to the steady growth of intelligence in children. In fact, we have encountered this relationship before, in the earliest stage of language-learning. Young toddlers use a larger area of the brain to detect words than older toddlers, whose vocabularies are considerably larger (page 373). In another recent study, children aged seven to twelve were found to activate a larger brain area than adults while carrying out a simple letter discrimination task. In cognitive development, as on a factory assembly line, efficiency makes all the difference.

Intelligence and the Frontal Cortex   Size, speed, and efficiency: each of these properties pertains to the brain as a whole and suggests that intelligence, unlike most mental functions, is not localized to a particular region but is a global attribute of the brain. It is impossible, however, to discuss the neural basis of intelligence without mentioning one part of the brain in particular: the frontal lobes, and specifically, the large "prefrontal" zone that lies forward of the motor areas. The prefrontal cortex is comparatively new in evolutionary terms; it is barely evident in older mammalian species but has achieved great prominence among higher primates and especially in

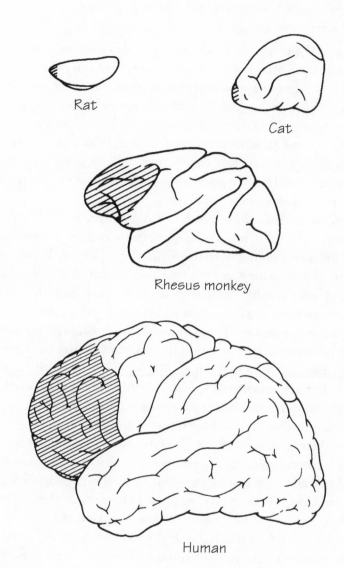

Rat

Cat

Rhesus monkey

Human

FIGURE 15.3

Hatched areas show the location of the prefrontal cortex in four mammalian species. Drawings are not to scale.

Modified from Kandel et al., *Principles of Neural Science*, by permission of the publisher.

humans. (See Figure 15.3.) It participates in all of our most sophisticated mental activities—attention, memory, language, creativity, planning, and self-awareness. As we saw in Chapter 12, people who suffer damage to the frontal lobes may be completely devastated—severely altered in personality and unable to carry out any kind of intellectually demanding work. Yet amazingly, their IQs are often little affected. This is because the frontal lobes engage in a different kind of intelligence from the "quickness" or "cleverness" assessed by IQ tests. They are responsible for the kind of judgment and flexible thinking better known as "wisdom."

Another term that's often used to describe the prefrontal lobes is *executive* function. Like the CEO of a large corporation, the prefrontal cortex tracks information from all over the brain—from each of the senses, from limbic structures mediating memory and emotion, and from subcortical systems that control mood, arousal, and all of our more basic drives. It then weighs this input, makes a decision, and executes it—through speech, movement, or any other action—by way of adjacent motor areas of the frontal lobe. The prefrontal cortex is especially important for integrating information over time, both past and future. People with frontal lobe lesions can have great difficulty remembering when something happened, even though they may recall the details of the event quite clearly. They are also notoriously poor at planning and working toward a goal.

Part of their problem has to do with inhibition, another essential frontal-lobe task; successful planning requires not only that you take action toward your goal but also that you suppress any conflicting actions. People with frontal-lobe damage exhibit poor response inhibition, as evinced by something called the *Stroop test*. A subject is shown the name of a color, say, green, written in ink of a different color, such as pink. It's a little tricky, but normal adults can manage to ignore the written word and correctly state that they see the color pink. Frontal-lobe patients, by contrast, simply can't stop themselves from saying "green." They lack the inhibition that is primarily a function of the "orbital" zone of the prefrontal cortex, the lower portion that also plays a key role in social and emotional regulation (Chapter 12).

Two other frontal-lobe functions that are critical to intellectual development are working memory and *attention*. As its name implies, *working memory* is the kind of conscious, short-term recall that allows you to hold information—like a phone number or the name of someone to whom you have just been introduced—actively in mind. Although it doesn't last long, this kind of memory is essential to most mental tasks. Working memory is mediated by the upper portion of the frontal lobes, an area known as the *dorsolateral* prefrontal cortex.

Attention is controlled by several different parts of the brain. Only one of these, however, mediates the kind of conscious awareness we usually think about when we use the term. This is the anterior cingulate, the frontmost half of the cingulate gyrus, which also plays a critical role in emotional experience.* (See Figure 12.1.) Imaging studies show anterior cingulate activation whenever a person is paying careful attention to a stimulus or task, and the more difficult the task, the greater this activation. On the other hand, anterior cingulate activity tends to decline when a task becomes very well learned or automatic. Depending on its exact location, damage to the anterior cingulate may result in judgment problems, attention deficits, neglect of one's own body and surrounding environment, and other signs of diminished self-awareness. The anterior cingulate is probably the closest thing we have to a seat of consciousness, so it is fascinating to see when it first becomes active in children.

Development of the Frontal Lobes

Young children bear a striking resemblance to adults with frontal-lobe damage; both have a very poor sense of time, a brief attention span, and a pronounced lack of self-control or behavioral inhibition, and they are generally less self-conscious than normal adults and older children. Since the frontal lobes are the slowest part of the brain to mature, this delay poses perhaps the greatest limitation to children's cognitive abilities.

The frontal lobes lag behind all other areas of the brain from the very beginning of their development. In utero, this is the last area to form fissures, the deep cracks that give the cerebral cortex its cauliflowerlike appearance and permit its specialization into different functions. After birth, the frontal lobes form and prune their synapses more slowly than any other brain area. Synaptic density peaks as late as seven years of age (compared with one year in the visual cortex) and then declines very gradually, not reaching a stable level until late in adolescence. Another factor limiting children's cognitive advancement is dopamine, a neurotransmitter that affects many brain circuits and whose levels rise quite gradually in the frontal lobes. Myelination

*The anterior cingulate can be further subdivided into a lower region that is involved in emotion and an upper region that is involved in attention.

of the frontal lobes is especially slow, continuing as late as the midtwenties. Both electrical and metabolic measurements confirm that the frontal lobes lag behind all other brain regions in the onset and evolution of their neural activity. Thus, there is good reason to believe that frontal-lobe immaturity places severe limits on children's intellectual abilities and in particular explains why they are incapable of the kind of judgment, flexible thinking, and mental control that are the hallmarks of wisdom and maturity.

Are Both Hemispheres Equally Intelligent?

Finally, to fully understand how the brain creates intelligence, we must consider the very different functions of the two cerebral hemispheres. In the preceding chapter we saw that language is primarily a function of the left hemisphere. The right hemisphere, for its part, plays a dominant role in visual-spatial skills, such as perceiving patterns, mentally rotating objects, and finding one's way in a new environment. In fact, the differences run deeper than this. The left hemisphere predominates in any task involving sequential processing and symbol manipulation—not just language but mathematics and music as well—and is generally the more analytical of the two halves. The right side is more heavily involved in emotion (as described in Chapter 12) and tends to process information more holistically and simultaneously. One way to think about these differences is that the left is our more rational side and the right our more intuitive side. But the two hemispheres do not complement each other all that perfectly. In most people, the left side actually tends to dominate the right to such an extent that it is actually the more consciously aware of the two!

Interestingly, babies appear to be born with a slight right-hemisphere advantage, given that this side of the cerebral cortex begins forming its surface convolutions earlier in utero than the left. This developmental gradient may be especially useful in infancy, since visual-spatial skills figure so heavily in learning how to reach, crawl, or toddle after a favorite toy. The left hemisphere apparently catches up by the second year, when language skills take off and children rapidly grow more aware of themselves and their own motives. Later still—around four years of age—communication *between* the two hemispheres improves dramatically, integrating a child's analytical and intuitive sides in ways that possibly produce a full blooming of consciousness.

Brain Development and Cognitive Milestones

As the brain develops, so does the mind. Obviously, all these massive hardware changes—growth, increased speed and efficiency, frontal-lobe emergence, and interhemispheric communication—are going to dramatically improve children's intellectual functioning. But we can also go further, beyond these general changes, to actually link certain cognitive milestones to specific events in brain development.

Amazing Baby Tricks: Recent Discoveries About the Cognitive Instincts of Very Young Infants   What can you do with a tiny brain that has few connections and runs very slowly? The answer, of course, is not much. Very young babies have little in the way of actual intelligence; they don't understand language, can't remember all that well, have virtually no control over their actions or emotions, and indeed, can do very little—not even hold a bottle—to promote their own survival. With regard to this last point, however, researchers have learned not to be misled by the severe motor limitations of young infants. If, instead of requiring babies to *do* something, you set up the experiment so that all they have to do is *look at* something, it turns out that even the youngest babies are capable of some fairly sophisticated cognitive feats. Not only can they recognize faces, voices, and other familiar stimuli, as we've already seen; babies under six months engage in certain forms of reasoning, categorization, and abstraction—many of the hallmarks of general intelligence—that are all the more remarkable given the primitive hardware with which they must be doing it.

Babies just four weeks old are already capable of storing a kind of abstract mental representation of objects, as illustrated by the "nubby pacifier" test described in Chapter 5: they prefer to look at whichever one of two pacifiers (smooth or nubby) that they had previously been allowed to suck on but not see. That young babies can infer an object's appearance based on oral experience alone indicates that their senses are already meaningfully coordinated with each other. Another example of this "cross-modal" awareness is in young babies' ability to imitate facial expressions (Chapter 12), which requires rather precise correspondence between a baby's visual perception and her motor output.

Categorization is another example of abstract thinking by infants. Recall that even newborns can judge that certain types of speech sounds, or phonemes, are more similar than others, and cluster them into distinct categories corresponding to the actual categories of human languages (Chapter 14). By four months of age, babies can also categorize objects according to their shape, color (Chapter 9), or number. In fact, even newborns can look at an array of dots and appreciate that "three" is different from "two" (although "four" versus "six" is tougher for them). And perhaps the most amazing "amazing baby trick" is the ability of five-month-olds to do simple addition and subtraction; after witnessing individual dolls added or removed from behind a screen, babies this age appear surprised (that is, they look longer) when the screen is lifted to reveal the wrong number of dolls remaining.

Another line of research has focused on the physical reasoning of young infants. By three months of age, babies can discriminate possible from impossible physical events. They seem surprised to see a tall carrot disappear behind a shorter screen, whereas a short carrot disappearing behind the screen barely fazes them. They also stare longer at a block suspended in midair than one lying on the ground. All of this tells us that they are capable of putting cause and effect together and can predict with surprising accuracy how objects and gravity will affect each other.

Babies, then, are born with some surprisingly sophisticated cognitive skills. That they understand so much, with still so little in the way of experience, tells us that these cognitive building blocks are probably innate to our brains. Intelligence begins as a collection of cognitive instincts—the presumption that certain sensory properties go together, that objects come in types, effects have causes, and quantities add up—preprogrammed to run with a minimal level of cerebral maturity yet importantly shaping the way that early experience is perceived.

Eight Months: The Frontal Lobes Turn On!   Emilie sits on her father's lap and excitedly stares at the shiny brass bell that the research assistant across the table is holding. Making sure Emilie is watching, the assistant places the bell into one of two matching wells in the table and then quickly covers both wells with identical cloths. Emilie is eager to grab the bell, as any eight-month-old would, but her father gently holds back her arms while the researcher distracts her with a funny face. After five seconds, Dad is signaled to release her arms, and Emilie uncovers the right-hand well and happily grabs the bell.

Now Emilie watches the researcher hide the bell in the other well, the one on the left. Again, Dad restrains her arms, both wells are covered, and her gaze is diverted to the experimenter's face. But this time, after another five-second delay, Emilie reaches back to the right-hand well and seems surprised not to find the brass bell in it.

Why didn't she reach to the left-hand well where she clearly saw the bell placed this time? The reason is simple; her frontal lobes aren't up to speed. Neither her working memory nor her inhibitory power are great enough to override the potent urge—or, more precisely, her procedural memory—to reach right back to the well where she had already successfully retrieved the bell.

This classic experiment was originally designed by Jean Piaget and is known as his "A not B" task, because virtually all babies Emilie's age reach for the toy correctly when it is first hidden in well "A," but err when the toy is moved to well "B." Though Piaget would attribute Emilie's mistake to the lack of "object permanence"—the memory that objects continue to exist even when you can't see them—we now know that he underestimated babies in this regard. Emilie remembers the bell's location in well B; she keeps her eyes there even as her hand is reaching to the wrong spot. Her problem is keeping this information in mind while simultaneously blocking her impulse to reach back to well A. She can do it if the interval between hiding and retrieval is short enough, no more than two or three seconds, but keeping track of everything—remembering that the bell is in well B, that she has to remove a cloth in order to retrieve it, and that she must not reach to well A—for five full seconds is simply more than she can manage.

"A not B" is harder than it seems; it requires planning, inhibition, working memory, and at least a minimal attention span—all frontal-lobe functions that are still rudimentary in babies Emilie's age. Each of these skills, however, will come to life over the next few months, as her frontal lobe kicks into action. By nine months, she can remember for as long as six seconds that the hiding place was switched, and by twelve months, she can remember it for a whopping ten seconds.

To prove that memory is not the only frontal-lobe skill improving between seven and twelve months of age, researchers have used another seemingly simple task. Now Emilie is seated in front of a clear Plexiglas box and watches while a red Duplo block is placed inside it. The box is open on the top, but its front end presents a barrier between Emilie and the toy—which, at eight months, simply proves too much for her. Emilie keeps banging on the Plexiglas, trying to reach through it, but she cannot figure out how to reach over it to grab the toy. If the barrier is removed, or if the Duplo is moved several inches, beyond the back of the box, so that she can reach directly along her line of sight, she does fine. She can even retrieve it if the barrier is made opaque so that the toy is fully hidden. The problem comes only when she can see the toy but cannot reach directly for it. At this tender age, she cannot overcome her urge to reach directly at a visible target.

In this task, memory is not an issue. Planning and inhibition are what's missing, but they will come on line very soon. By nine months, she reaches behind the barrier about half the time, and by eleven months, it poses no problem at all.

Eight to nine months is a major landmark in cognitive development. EEG measurements reveal a striking parallel between frontal-lobe activity and babies' improvement on the "A not B" task between seven and twelve months of age. Thanks to this burgeoning frontal activity, babies can for the first time integrate their understanding of the world into a meaningful, if simple, plan of action. No longer does Emilie reach reflexively at anything that crosses her path; now she formulates a goal and can to some degree actually inhibit other impulses while carrying it out.

Recall that eight months also marks an important emotional milestone that is equally dependent on frontal-lobe development: the emergence of attachment. Just as babies this age can now keep track of where a toy is and act in a very directed way to retrieve it, so have they become acutely aware of their primary caregiver and do everything in their power—fussing, crying, clinging—to try to keep her nearby. Attachment is vital to cognitive development, because it provides the baby with a secure base from which to explore his world. But it is not the only way in which emotional and intellectual development are linked. Frontal-lobe maturation also improves babies' motivation, attention, and inhibition during the second six months—all of which helps them to concentrate, however briefly, on the exhilarating new challenges at hand.

Eight months marks the beginning of a wonderful year of exuberant exploration and unchecked affection. Everything is intense and exciting at this age, yet parents still have a cuddly and compliant baby to enjoy.

Eighteen Months: Language and a Sense of Self   The next big cognitive leap occurs midway through the second year. By this point, children's sensory and motor maturation are largely complete, and they can focus in earnest on higher mental skills. This is the point when many parents lament, "He's not a baby anymore!"—when surer feet and nimbler fingers start making it past all your earlier baby-proofing, and you suddenly have a willful, skillful, and insatiably curious toddler on your hands.

Language, of course, is the most obvious change. At twenty months, Jason now seems to understand everything—"Sit at your table." "Where are your shoes?" "Let's make popcorn!"—and his own vocabulary is exploding into two- and three-word minisentences. As we saw in the last chapter, these advances are a product of left-hemisphere maturation, first in the parietal, then in the frontal lobe. With the advent of true language, toddlers cross an important threshold into symbolic thought, where memories and concepts can take shape even without immediate sensory input. This is the age when children finally surpass baby chimps in cognitive ability, and language has a lot to do with it.

However, language is not the only intellectual leap toddlers make midway through the second year. Other striking changes also ensue, thanks to the burgeoning activity in their frontal lobes. One is the emergence of self-control, a more advanced form of the frontal inhibition that first emerges about a year earlier. Though younger babies can manage to block certain reflexes or automatic tendencies if it serves another immediate purpose, such as retrieving a much-desired toy, Jason can actually restrain himself—for a moment, at least—in the face of the desired object itself. For instance, when asked, he manages to wait a full twenty seconds before ripping into a brightly wrapped package or snatching a raisin from under a cup. Self-control is key to any kind of disciplined learning, and though he has a long way to go before it is fully developed, he has at least begun the journey.

Watching Jason stare at the raisin cup, you might even say that he is *consciously* or *deliberately* restraining himself in the brief interval before he succumbs and grabs the treat underneath it. Indeed, eighteen months is thought to mark the beginning of a new phase in children's self-awareness, the dawning, perhaps, of true consciousness. The classic test for self-awareness is to mark an experimental subject in a distinguishing way—say, with a dab of paint on the nose—and then place him in front of a mirror to see if he recognizes the change. Among our primate relatives, only the great apes, such as chimpanzees and orangutans, pass this test of self-recognition. Among children, a few fifteen-month-olds will seem to recognize themselves, but it is not until the second half of the second year that the majority of toddlers try wiping off the paint. (Children with Down syndrome are notably delayed in passing the mirror test, and the age at which they finally recognize themselves corresponds to the degree of their mental impairment.) Another sign of growing self-awareness is the use of words such as *I*, *me*, *my*, or *mine*, which begins close to two years of age. This dawning self-awareness may reflect the recent ascendancy of the left hemisphere, which, as we have seen in adults, tends to dominate our conscious mental lives. It may also be a product of the anterior cingulate, the limbic core of the frontal lobe, which, as noted, acts in many ways as the seat of conscious awareness. Whatever the neural basis of this newfound sense of self, it is a sign of healthy ego development, even as it steals away the perfect innocence of babyhood.

Three to Four Years: Discovering the Mind   Another transition takes place between three and four years of age, perhaps influenced by improved communication between the right and left halves of the brain. Four-year-olds are strikingly wise, compared with children just one year younger. They are much more aware of their own perceptions and have begun to realize that appearance and reality are not necessarily the same. A three-year-old, for instance, has a hard time understanding that a white cloud, viewed through a piece of red cellophane, can still be white; not only does it look red, she'll report, "it *really is* red." On the other hand, if you hand her a sponge that has been shaped and painted to look just like a solid piece of granite, and tell her exactly what it is, she will accept it as a sponge; moreover, she will insist that it actually *looks* like a sponge, not a rock. In other words, when it comes to the *properties* of ambiguous objects, three-year-olds tend to err on the side of appearance, while when it comes to an object's *identity*, they err on the side of reality.

By four, and especially at five years, children are much better at the appearance/reality distinction. They know that a sponge may look like a rock, and that clouds are white, regardless of the color of the sunglasses through which they view them. They are also much better at distinguishing real from imaginary events (although the thought of monsters in the closet remains pretty scary), and appreciating that a single object or person can have different characteristics at different points in time. (Three-year-olds prefer to think of Batman and Bruce Wayne as different people.) As Julia closes in on her fourth birthday, I've noticed her starting to ask whether certain storybook creatures are "real" or not and, sadly, even if Santa Claus is fact or fiction.

One interesting point about this appearance/reality distinction is that it cannot be taught. Researchers have tried, by repeatedly showing three-year-olds objects that look like something else (an apple-shaped candle, silk flowers, a rubber pencil) or that are altered in size or color (a grain of salt through a magnifier glass, milk in a transparent blue glass) and carefully explaining to them how it is that things may look different "to your eyes" than they "really, really" are. But none of this teaching helps. For most objects, people, and events, a three-year-old will persist in believing that appearance and reality are identical. Only age, it seems, can teach children when to doubt their senses, or that the same object can look different at different times. Perhaps the better communication between brain hemispheres at this age is what finally unites a child's perceptual skills (a right-brain product) with her burgeoning analytical skills (a left-brain product), thus raising reality-testing to a new level.

Outward appearance is not the only thing children learn to doubt during the later preschool years. It is also marks the first point at which they appreciate the inner thoughts and motives of other people and realize that these may be different from their own. This change is illustrated by the *false belief test*, a simple exercise that works like this. Two children, say, three-year-old Conor and his four-year-old brother, Max, both watch while an adult blatantly hides a candy-covered cupcake inside a wicker basket. Then Max is asked to leave the room, and while he is gone, the adult moves the cupcake to a new hiding place inside a wooden box, while Conor watches attentively. Before Max returns, Conor is asked, "Where will Max look for the cupcake?" His answer is striking. Conor, like most three-year-olds, says that Max will look in the wooden box, even though he wasn't there to witness the shift. Conor simply doesn't understand that different people are privy to different information and may have beliefs different from his own. Max, on the other hand, has no problem with the test; when their roles are reversed, he quickly realizes that Conor will be unaware of the switch and even takes some delight in knowing that his brother will be unable to find the treat. The fact that Max is aware of Conor's belief is an important step in his social development. Realizing that other people have thoughts and minds of their own helps children move beyond the pure egoism of early childhood and into a stage of greater empathy and sociability.

Both of these advances—the appearance/reality distinction and the appreciation of others' beliefs—reflect a more general trend in cognitive development during the preschool years. Between about three and five years of age, children actually begin to understand what thinking is. They develop a *theory of mind*, as psychologists call it—not a formal epistemological canon, but a basic awareness of mental life and the distinction between perception, memory, dreams, desires, beliefs, and imagination. You can see this in their play, when they adopt the perspective of different roles—mother, child, doctor, patient, teacher, friend—and begin assigning people's actions to internal motives, wishes, secrets, and the like. This is a big step, both in their own self-awareness and in their ability to relate to other people. It's an important milestone for parents too—finally there's a chance that when you talk to your child about other people's feelings, she will actually understand what you're saying.

Six Years: The Dawn of Reason!

Early childhood ends, by definition, when children enter grade school, but this age is more than a mere legal landmark. Six years marks another notable point, when most children, regardless of their cultural experience, reach a new level of intellectual functioning. The change extends both to specific skills—drawing, memorization, and language comprehension—and to the more general powers of attention, control, and self-awareness. None of these advances takes place overnight, of course; most of them improve steadily throughout the toddler and preschool years. But there does seem to be something special about six years, when all the individual pieces of cognition come together and children can start applying themselves toward true, directed learning. Throughout the world, children begin their formal schooling, or are otherwise expected to start contributing to the family's welfare (tending animals, working in the fields, or caring for a younger sibling), at around six years of age.

That this change is found so universally suggests it is a product of brain maturation, and the period around six years does indeed mark a turning point for the cerebral cortex. Recall that the brain's energy consumption—a surrogate for its overall activity level—reaches an all-time high between four and eight years, after which it gradually declines to adult levels. This change parallels the rise and pruning of the brain's quadrillion or so synapses, which in the frontal lobe reverse their tide of production at around seven years of age, and now begin eliminating their least useful members. This is also an important phase in the development of the P300 potential—those slow, positive waves of electrical activity in the cortex that seem to reflect conscious, attentive mental processing. P300 responses undergo their most dramatic acceleration between four and eight years of age, after which they more gradually approach adult rates.

Piaget had his own way of assessing brain maturation during this period, using his now-famous "conservation" tasks. Try this one out on your four-to-eight-year-old: fill two identical short, squat glasses with equal volumes of water, and ask your child, "Do the two glasses contain the same amount of water, or does one have more?" Now, pour all the water from one of these glasses into a tall, narrow glass, and ask your child the same question.

Four-year-olds almost invariably say that the tall glass has more water in it; the difference in the level of the water is simply too great for them to believe that the amount could be the same, even if you pour it back into the smaller glass and show them that it hasn't changed. Eight-year-olds, by contrast, know that the amount cannot have changed. If you press them on why the two look so different, they will tell you that the difference in height is made up for by width, and they will probably even pour the water from the taller glass back into the short one to prove their point.

The difference between four and eight years is the birth of reason, when children finally begin to trust their own thought processes, even over what their senses may be telling them. Piaget called it the emergence of "operational" thinking, when children actually begin applying logic to solve problems. Though younger children can often add a few numbers or recognize some written words, it is only in the latter half of this period—from six on—that most of them click into the rules of thought and realize, for instance, that addition is the opposite of subtraction or that letter sounds flow together into words. Drill them though you may, most four- and young five-year-olds simply can't make these kinds of conceptual connections.

Neurologists know this period in another way: as the age when children first master tasks involving the frontal lobe, particularly those requiring attention and inhibition. At six years, for instance, children achieve adult-level performance on a special version of the Stroop test, in which they are instructed to say "day" when shown a black card with white stars, and "night" when shown a white card with a bright sun. Another test of inhibition is a simple tapping task, where the child is told to tap twice when the examiner taps once, and vice versa. By six or seven years, children largely overcome their temptation to imitate the examiner, and manage to concentrate on tapping a different number of times than his example. On a more practical level, this inhibitory control means that six-year-olds are actually able to delay gratification in a way that three- or four-year-olds find excruciatingly difficult. Remember the marshmallow test from Chapter 12? When three- or four-year-olds are presented with a choice of getting one marshmallow now or two after a twenty-minute delay, they rarely resist the immediate treat, whereas five- and six-year-olds are generally quite good at holding out for the double reward. Inhibition is critical to even the simplest cognitive tasks, and the fact that it improves so dramatically during the latter preschool years accounts in large measure for the new level of discipline and mental control children achieve by age six.

Six years, of course, is not the end of cognitive growth. First-graders have a long way to go before they can reason, concentrate, solve problems, manipulate abstract concepts, and plan for the future—not to mention read, write, and calculate—at an adult level. Helping them along is the fact that they still have plenty of excess synapses to prune, and myelin to add, over the remaining years of childhood. These hardware improvements explain why children, for all their lack of cognitive sophistication, are so much better at learning than most adults. What grown-up can catch on to the latest computer game or memorize the words to a new song after just a few tries? Children's brains are programmed to learn, and when you add this plasticity to their steady improvement in neural speed and efficiency, it's a little less surprising (though no less wonderful) to discover that your twelve- or fifteen-year-old can suddenly speak a foreign language, do calculus, or solve the Sunday crossword puzzle.

Such feats may seem miles away in a first-grader struggling to learn how to read. But in reality, all her remaining hurdles are nothing compared with what she has already achieved intellectually. With a full-grown brain and a fully engaged frontal lobe, a six-year-old actually thinks much more like an adult than like the helpless newborn she so recently sprouted from. By this point, all the basic tools of cognition are in place, and it is simply a matter of sharpening them before your child's intelligence also reaches its full-grown proportions.

Predicting IQ in Early Infancy

What will that full size be? How intelligent will any particular child end up? This is the holy grail of parenting. Of course, we all want our children to be happy, healthy, well adjusted, and all those other good things, but the one trait parents seem to obsess about most is intelligence. Is my child smart? Will he do well in school? What can I do to best promote his intellectual development?

The speculation begins immediately, as soon as the first positive pregnancy test: "I'm glad I married Dave, instead of that dope I dated in high school," Jessica mused back then, even as she worried about the couple of glasses of wine she drank before learning she was pregnant. Speculations run even higher once the baby is actually born, as parents scour their newborn's behavior for signs of genius: "The doctor says he controls his head as well as a four-month-old," Jessica boasted after Jack's eight-week well-baby visit. Even the grandparents make grand predictions about the future brilliance of their latest descendant.

How smart is Jack? Is there a "baby IQ" test we can all run out and buy to predict our children's later intelligence? Psychologists have looked long and hard to try to find such a measure. There are, to be sure, plenty of tools for assessing an infant's developmental progress: the Denver Development tables, the Gesell scales, and the Bayley Scales of Infant Development are a few of the familiar ones. The Bayley scales, for instance, test a wide range of skills, such as whether a four-month-old will reach for a rattle, or a twelve-month-old will respond to a simple command, "Put the block in the cup." They are very useful for uncovering serious problems, such as cerebral palsy or mental retardation, but they are notoriously poor at predicting later IQ in a population of healthy infants. There is no relationship whatsoever between a baby's Bayley score at six or even twelve months and his or her adult IQ. By two or three years, you can begin to see some correlation between a child's score on various development tests and his later IQ, but it's not until five or six years that the correlation is really good, approaching 0.7, meaning that you have a pretty good sense of which kids are smarter than others. In other words, it's still possible that you have a genius on your hands, even if your two-year-old can't talk or stack three blocks into a tower.

The reason such "baby IQ" tests are poor predictors of adult IQ is that they tend to be heavily weighted by motor and perceptual skills. Whether a six-month-old can deftly pick up a cube or a ten-month-old attempts to scribble with a Magic Marker may seem remarkable at the time, but such accomplishments do not tap the same sorts of verbal and spatial skills that we associate with intelligence later in life. Consequently, researchers have turned to tasks that are less dependent on a baby's motor development, but that do seem to tap the same types of information processing that underlie all cognitive abilities.

One such task is visual recognition memory. Recall from Chapter 13 that young babies, even in the first month of life, are surprisingly good at detecting novel visual stimuli. If you habituate a baby to one picture—say, a bold checkerboard print—and then show her another display with an equally bold bull's-eye, she will stare at the new stimulus with renewed interest. This seemingly simple task, which even newborn monkeys can master (indeed, better than human newborns), involves all the basic steps of information processing: motivation, attention, perception, representation, memory storage and retrieval, discrimination, and recognition. Our brains go through much the same sequence when searching for a word or comparing two mathematical quantities, although the number of stored representations will be many times greater.

The best age to test visual recognition memory is between two and eight months. (Younger infants can't see well enough, while older infants can't sit still long enough.) If you test a reasonably large group of babies for visual habituation or novelty preference, then test their IQs later in childhood or even in adolescence, you're likely to see that those babies who spent less time looking at a familiar stimulus (that is, who habituated more rapidly) or, conversely, who spent more time looking at a novel stimulus, show higher IQ scores. Dozens of studies like this have been performed to date, with the typical result that infant recognition memory correlates by a factor of 0.4 with IQ score between two and eight years of age. In one recent report, children were followed all the way to adulthood, and it turned out that the amount of time they spent staring at a checkerboard as tiny babies (all of these subjects were born prematurely) predicted their IQ score as late as age eighteen. These findings tell us that differences in information-processing are relatively stable all the way from infancy to adulthood; babies who process and remember stimuli more effectively are likely to retain these strengths as adults.

Recognition memory is not the only infant skill that predicts later intelligence. Another is cross-modal transfer, the ability to generalize from one sensory or motor modality to another. One-year-olds who can visually recognize a toy that they were previously allowed only to touch but not actually see (it was inside a box) tend to score higher on later IQ tests (at two, three, four, five, six, and even eleven years of age) than babies who can't seem to make this mental transfer. Yet another marker of later intelligence is object permanence. One-year-olds who remember the location of a hidden object, as in the "A not B" experiment, also tend to have higher IQs throughout childhood than babies who are poorer at keeping track of where it is hidden. Another intriguing though less well-documented index of later intelligence is a young baby's ability to discriminate his own mother from an unfamiliar woman; babies who vocalize more in the presence of their own mothers than in the presence of strangers tend to score higher on IQ tests, given as late as twelve years of age, than those who do not show as strong a preference.

A note of caution about these infant measures of later intelligence: none of these correlations, though statistically significant, is very high. Although one can say generally that babies who habituate more rapidly or perform better on the "A not B" task will tend to have higher-than-average IQs, such tasks cannot predict an individual child's later IQ with any great degree of accuracy.

Children's Brains: Smart or Not?

What makes one child better than another at processing information, even early in infancy? Once again, researchers suspect speed as a primary difference separating "brighter" from "duller" individuals. Though infants in general process information many times more slowly than adults, it seems that some babies are already a little faster than others, and that this difference persists all the way to adulthood. Speed is an obvious factor in visual habituation, where babies who more rapidly process and memorize stimuli will tend to become bored more rapidly (that is, to look at a familiar picture for a shorter period of time). For other tasks, like cross-modal transfer, speed probably translates into greater efficiency at processing, storing, and discriminating different stimuli.

There is little doubt that the speed-IQ relationship holds just as well for children as for adults. It's known that between six and twelve years of age, smarter children perform faster than children with lower IQs on a special version of an inspection-time task that is designed to look like a Space Invaders video game. Gifted children between four and seven years of age also show faster P300 potentials than normal-IQ children. In one recent study, researchers confirmed the idea that speed differences persist all the way from infancy by showing that babies who habituated faster at seven months of age tend to perform faster on tests of perceptual speed at age eleven. So even though all children show massive gains in processing speed between infancy and adolescence, the difference between "faster" and "slower" brains tends to persist throughout development.

Speed, however, is not the only factor that makes one brain more intelligent than another. Another difference is memory capacity, the amount of new information a child is able to store and recall. And as we've already seen, IQ is also modestly correlated with children's brain size. Newborns with a head circumference larger than fourteen inches will, on average, score about seven points higher on IQ tests at age four than babies born with a head smaller than twelve and three-quarters inches. (See Figure 15.4.) By mid- to

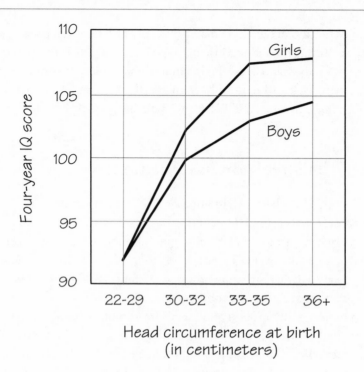

FIGURE 15.4

Preschool IQ as a function of head circumference at birth.

Data from S.H. Broman et al., *Preschool IQ: Prenatal and Early Developmental Correlates,*
Hillsdale, NJ: Lawrence Erlbaum, 1975.

late childhood, brain volume predicts about 20 percent of the variance in children's IQ scores, with the prefrontal cortex, in particular, being the one region whose gray-matter volume best predicts intelligence scores.

Before you get caught up measuring your child's head circumference or clocking her reaction time on the latest computer game, it's important to remember that there are many different kinds of intelligence, not all of which are reflected in a child's IQ score. As we learn more about the neural basis of specific intellectual skills—verbal, spatial, mathematical, musical, kinesthetic, interpersonal, and so on—we will undoubtedly find more specific neural measures that correspond to each child's unique mental strengths. Evidence is already mounting linking verbal skill to the development of specific brain areas. For instance, children who grasp phonics better than their peers (and accordingly read better) tend to have more asymmetry in the planum temporale (left larger than right), an important language area of the cortex described in Chapter 14, while children with reverse asymmetry (right planum larger than left) tend to do better on tests of spatial intelligence. Language skill has also recently been linked to the size of children's corpus callosum, the massive band of fibers that connects the two hemispheres of the brain. As we learn more about how the brain mediates intelligence, we may one day be able to predict a child's particular intellectual skills at an early enough age to optimally promote his or her strengths, as well as compensate for any weaknesses.

Chapter 16

NATURE, NURTURE,
AND SEX DIFFERENCES
IN INTELLECTUAL
DEVELOPMENT

Intelligence, like every other trait, varies tremendously between children, and these differences are a product of the ways their brains work. The real question, though, is not *whether* children's brains differ, but *why*. Are some children predestined, because of luck of the genetic draw, to have faster neural transmission or a larger left planum temporale? Or are these differences a product of experience—of the myriad factors, other than genes, that we know influence brain development from its earliest formation in the womb?

We've just seen that one can predict (to a degree) a child's later IQ even early in infancy. Indeed, one recent study has pushed the forecast all the way back to birth, showing that certain features of newborns' electrical responses to speech sounds presage their verbal skills at five years of age. These findings seem to suggest a strong innate factor to intelligence. It's important to remember, however, that none of these relationships is absolute. Even the most predictive infant tasks can explain only about 20 percent of the variance in children's later IQ,* meaning that plenty of other factors also determine how "smart" a child will end up being. To cite just one example, identified in some of the same studies that linked early habituation to later

*The square of the correlation coefficient determines the amount of variance accounted for, so if the correlation is 0.4 for infant habituation/childhood IQ comparisons, then habituation predicts $(0.4)^2$, or 16 percent of IQ variance in the population.

IQ, researchers found that "maternal encouragement of attention"—that is, the degree to which different mothers direct their babies, through talk and gestures, to focus on particular objects, people, or events in their environment—is also predictive of later intelligence. In fact, one recent study showed a nearly *twenty-point* IQ advantage for eighteen-year-olds who as infants both habituated rapidly and had more interactive mothers, over adolescents who fell short on both measures in infancy. Predicting IQ from infancy is never very precise, but it is certainly a lot better if you take both innate and environmental factors into account.

Then again, how do we know for sure that these early infant skills—habituation, novelty preference, and so on—really do reflect a child's *genetic* potential? This is the second caveat about early predictors of later IQ. Just because a trait shows up early doesn't necessarily mean it is genetic. Habituation differences might just as easily reflect different babies' experiences to date, that is, their lives in the womb. It is known, for instance, that babies born prematurely perform more poorly than full-term babies on visual habituation and cross-modal transfer tasks, even after correcting their chronological age for the number of weeks they were born early. They also tend to have lower IQs later in childhood. There is little doubt that prenatal experience (or in this case, an abbreviated amount of it) can have an enduring effect on children's cognitive performance. In fact, we now know that intelligence is actually *more* attributable to environmental factors in early infancy than at any later time in life. We'll return to this paradox below; but meanwhile it turns out that there are better ways of estimating a child's intellectual potential than depending on the subtle nuances of infant behavior.

The Role of Genes

Everyone agrees that heredity and environment both play a part in determining how smart a child will be, so the real debate is over quantity. How *much* will Dave's and Jessica's genes contribute to Jack's intelligence, and to what extent will it be shaped by his upbringing? Opinions on this issue range all over the map, from strict "environmentalists" who believe that early rearing, education, and culture explain everything, to strong hereditarians, such as the authors of *The Bell Curve*, who believe that genes are more or less our destiny. Resolving this debate, though, is not a matter of opinion, but of science, in particular a branch of psychology known as *behavioral genetics*.

What behavioral geneticists do seems quite simple on the surface. They compare the IQ scores of people with known genetic relationships, plug the results into an appropriate statistical model, and then come up with an estimate of the degree to which intelligence is hereditary. The most obvious choice of subjects is identical twins, who share 100 percent of their genes, but the same goal can be reached by studying ordinary siblings, fraternal twins, or parent-child pairings—who each share 50 percent of their genes— or even grandparent-grandchild, aunt/uncle-niece/nephew, or half-sibling pairings, who share 25 percent.

As you'd expect, people who share more genes tend to have more similar IQs. The highest correlation is for identical twins reared together—a whopping 0.86 correlation between their IQ scores. The correlation between a parent and child is considerably lower, 0.42.* Siblings' IQs correlate by a similar factor, 0.47, which fits with the fact that both pairings share 50 percent of their genes.

Of course, most close relatives share more than the same genes; they are also likely to share the same home, community, religion, culture, education, and socioeconomic status, for at least part of their lives. Consequently, behavioral geneticists must always control for the influence of shared environment. One way to do this is simply to limit their study to relatives who have never lived together—such as adopted children and their biological parents, or identical twins who were raised in different homes. The IQs of adopted children and their biological mothers correlate by a factor of 0.22, or about half as much as when they are reared by them. Similarly, biological siblings adopted into different homes show a 0.24 correlation in their IQ scores. Doubling these numbers, to correct for the fact that siblings or parent-child pairings share only half of the same genes, allows us to estimate that genes account for 40 to 50 percent of a person's intelligence.

The estimate is considerably higher, 0.72, for identical twins reared apart, the seemingly ideal subjects for this kind of study. But there are a couple of problems with this group. One is that they are extremely rare; only about one hundred sets of identical twins reared apart have ever been studied. The other problem is that they actually do share the same environment for a very important part of their lives: while in the womb. Even if they are separated on the day of birth (which most of those studied were not), identical twins have

*If you average both parents' IQ scores, then the correlation rises to 0.72, indicating that children tend toward the average intelligence of their two parents.

already shared some nine months of intimate contact, perhaps the most important months of their entire lives as far as their brains are concerned. It is known, for instance, that fraternal twins show considerably higher IQ correlations than ordinary siblings, even though both pairings have the same proportion of genes (50 percent) in common, presumably because of their shared experience in the womb. Researchers now believe that prenatal experience accounts for up to 20 percent of IQ variance. Subtracting this effect from the IQ correlation of identical twins reared apart (0.72) leaves genes once again accounting for about 50 percent of a person's IQ.

One other type of study confirms this 50 percent figure. In this design, researchers use fraternal twins of the same sex as a control group for identical twins, with both pairings reared by their own biological parents. Both types of twins have shared virtually identical experiences—the same womb, gender, home, parents, schools, siblings, and even the fact of being twins. They differ only in the number of genes they share (100 versus 50 percent). Therefore any differences in the degree to which their IQs correlate should give us a fairly accurate estimate of the contribution of that remaining 50 percent of genes. As we just saw, identical twins reared together show the highest IQ correlation of any group, 0.86. But the IQs of fraternal twins reared together also correlate highly, with a coefficient of 0.60. The difference between these numbers, 0.26, represents the additional IQ correlation that identical twins share because of their extra 50 percent of shared genes, so doubling this number gives us 52 percent heritability, probably the most accurate estimate available.

The consensus, then, is that genes account for about half of one's IQ. But remember that IQ is only one measure of intelligence; not all measures are equally heritable. IQ is actually on the high end in terms of genetic influence. These tests emphasize spatial skills, like map-reading and mental rotation, which show the greatest dependence on genes, and verbal skills, which are not far behind. By contrast, mental speed appears somewhat less heritable, and memory skills are the least heritable of the specific mental abilities that behavioral geneticists have assessed.

Even more important is the divergence between IQ scores and school achievement. Although IQ is a good predictor of how well children will do in school, this does not mean that IQ and school performance are equally heritable. Comparisons of identical and fraternal twins have shown that only about 20 percent of the variance in their scholastic achievement scores can be accounted for by genes. The rest is due to environment and in particular their shared family experience. In other words, while "smart genes" are one important ingredient in the recipe for success in grade school, the bulk of scholastic achievement is influenced by the quality of a child's family life—such factors as the degree of nurturing, encouragement, attention, discipline, opportunity, and several others discussed below.

What is less certain is whether this strong environmental effect holds throughout high school and college. That's because of the surprising finding that intelligence actually grows *more* heritable with age. Only about 15 percent of the variance in babies' IQs can be explained by genes. The figure climbs to 40 percent by the early school years, 50 percent by adolescence, and a few additional points by adulthood. These numbers are based in part on adopted children, who tend to resemble the cognitive level of their adoptive parents and siblings much more in early life than later on. By adolescence, adoptees' IQs come to resemble that of their biological parents much more than their adoptive parents'.*

This is the opposite of what people generally think about genes and environment—that an individual's genetic potential is all laid out by birth, while experience accumulates throughout life. In fact, it works the other way around, and the reason has to do with children's growing independence, which increasingly allows them to select their own experiences. A baby's environment is largely determined by whatever home and family he happened to land in. Later, children begin to make some choices about the peers they associate with and the activities they participate in. Adolescents often go out of their way to find people and experiences unlike those at home. Finally, as adults, most people are free to do and live as they please, choices that presumably reflect their innate drives and interests, as opposed to those of their parents or teachers. In other words, genes increasingly determine environment as children grow older, so that the net genetic effect becomes greater.

Even the youngest babies, however, shape their own environment to an important extent. Babies vary enormously in innate temperament—in their fussiness, alertness, activity level, sociability, and so on—and these genetic characteristics influence the kinds of activities they engage in and the way their caregivers interact with them. While we may delude ourselves into

---

*It is not known, however, whether this change is temporary or permanent, and whether it has anything to do with the particular kind of identity crisis adoptees often face during adolescence.

thinking that we are in control of our children's environment, in fact, they are almost certainly shaping us as much as we are shaping them. Even within the same family, two children can have vastly different experiences because of the different genetic hand each was dealt.

The Role of Environment

If genes account for about half of the variance in different individuals' intelligence (or more precisely, IQ score), this leaves the other half to the environment. By this point, you are familiar with much of the evidence that early experience is critical to a child's later intellectual potential. Earlier chapters detailed how social isolation and lack of stimulation can stunt a child's sensory, motor, emotional, and linguistic development. Orphan babies left to languish in bare cribs do no better cognitively, falling even to the retarded level if their deprivation continues much past the second year. Brain wiring *needs* stimulation. Synapses wither and dendrites will fail to sprout without the steady buzz of neural activity that comes from new and varied experiences. Genes create the blueprint, but actually growing the neural networks inside each child's head requires a steady stream of vigorous interactions with other people, objects, places, and events in the world.

The evidence is less dramatic but equally important on the positive side; disadvantaged children can benefit from a concerted attempt to improve their early environment. The best-known program is Head Start, which provides educational, nutritional, and medical support to needy preschool-aged children. Most studies of Head Start children show that they make substantial IQ gains, some ten points on average, while enrolled in the program. Unfortunately, these gains tend to fade away within just a few years after the children enter public grade schools, although other advantages, like a lower dropout rate and less need for remedial education, do persist.

Head Start begins rather late, at about three years of age, which is well after the brain has gone through its most intensive phase of synaptogenesis and myelination. A few experimental programs have tried to intervene much earlier, and these show more promising results. One is the North Carolina Abcedarian project, which provided forty hours of enriched care per week to about fifty poor children, beginning early in infancy and continuing until they were five years old. By three years of age, these youngsters scored a dramatic fifteen points higher on IQ tests than a matched group of children not enrolled in the program. This difference shrank to seven points by five years of age, the end of the preschool program; nonetheless, the enriched children continued to outperform the nonenriched children as late as twelve and fifteen years of age, scoring significantly higher on academic achievement tests and about five points higher on IQ tests.

These effects are modest, but then again, so is the total amount of time disadvantaged children spend in enrichment programs, relative to their immersion the rest of the time in a culture with little opportunity or emphasis on education. To get a better sense of the degree to which intelligence can be modified by environment, we return to adoption studies and in particular to cases where children from one socioeconomic group are adopted into an entirely different one, as when poor children are adopted into comfortable, highly educated families. Adoptions of this type are really the ultimate intervention: total immersion in a more enriching culture, with greater opportunity both at home and school, and where the values and example set by parents and teachers are likely to be more congruent. Several studies of this type of adoption have been conducted over the years, and most have shown significant IQ gains for children adopted into more fortunate circumstances, ranging from ten to sixteen points.

Perhaps the best data come from a French "cross-fostering" study, published in 1989. These researchers combed through adoption records to find four distinct groups of children: (1) children born to low-socioeconomic-status (SES) parents who were adopted by other low-SES parents, (2) low-SES children adopted by high-SES parents, (3) high-SES children adopted by high-SES parents, and (4) high-SES children adopted by low-SES parents, a very rare group, but the one that makes this study so powerful. Results of their study are as follows:

IQ at Age 16

	Low-SES adoptive parents	High-SES adoptive parents
Low-SES biological parents	92	104
High-SES biological parents	108	120

A couple of points jump out from these numbers. One is that biology does matter or, more precisely, the combination of biology and prenatal experience. Looking down each column, you can see a sixteen-point advantage for being born to more advantaged parents, no matter what kind of environment a child is adopted into. Rearing, however, also makes a substantial difference; comparing across either row reveals a consistent twelve-point effect of being raised in a high- as compared to a low-SES household. These results confirm that nature and nurture exert about equal effects on intelligence, especially when we keep in mind that some of the sixteen-point difference between biological groups is actually due to prenatal environment.

A twelve-point advantage may not sound like much, but this is actually a substantial improvement—the difference between being at the 50th versus the 80th percentile of the whole population. And IQ is probably even more malleable than these adoption studies portray, because of the additional influence of prenatal factors, which are described in more detail in the following chapter.

The "Flynn Effect"   There is one more compelling piece of evidence that dramatically illustrates the importance of environment in determining intelligence. This is a striking fact, one that flies in the face of all we keep hearing about the deplorable state of education and the general "dumbing down" of our culture: We're all *getting smarter!* Ever since the beginning of IQ testing, almost a century ago, each generation has consistently scored higher than the generation that preceded it, a steady rise that has been documented in virtually every industrialized nation studied. The gains appear largest in Western Europe and Japan, where each generation is scoring some twenty points higher than the generation that preceded it. In the United States, the rise has been considerably slower but nonetheless highly significant: Americans' IQs are rising by about 0.3 point every year, or about eight points per generation. This means that the average citizen today scores as well as just the top 2 percent of people back at the turn of the century.*

This steady rise in IQ scores is known as the "Flynn effect," after the New Zealand psychologist James Flynn, who has most thoroughly docu-

---

*Of course, that average person does not actually achieve an IQ score of 130, the cut-off for the top 2 percent, because IQ scores are more normalized. By convention, the average score in any given era is set at 100, and the curve is adjusted so that the middle two-thirds of all scores lie between 85 and 115.

mented it. Researchers argue over whether the increase is due to a genuine improvement in intelligence or merely craftier test-taking. People today are certainly more practiced at taking standardized tests than during the first half of the century; but most psychologists agree that the effect is too dramatic to be a simple matter of testing proficiency. It is also much too rapid to be accounted for by genetic change, which would require high-IQ individuals to reproduce at an impossibly high rate, relative to low-IQ individuals.

This leaves environment, then—the idea that people throughout the world are genuinely getting smarter, thanks to a whole host of significant lifestyle improvements. As we will see in the next chapter, there is fairly good evidence that improvements in nutrition, health, education, and even parenting skills are contributing to the steady IQ rise in industrialized nations. In addition, some researchers point to another less obvious trend as having a substantial impact on our collective intelligence. Noting that IQ gains are considerably greater for visual-spatial skills than for verbal ones, they suggest that the increase may be largely attributable to the explosion of visual media during this century. From photography to film, television, video, and now graphical computer interfaces, each generation has been exposed to increasingly more complex visual displays than the generation that preceded it. The old joke that children can program the VCR better than their parents is only one example of how early exposure to visual technology dramatically improves a person's ability to solve visual-spatial kinds of problems.

Sex Differences in Intelligence

Nowhere is the nature/nurture debate more heated than when it comes to sex differences in intelligence. There is little doubt that, on average, males and females think a little differently, judging by scores on standardized tests. As we saw in Chapter 14, girls are generally more gifted with language; they tend to score higher on verbal IQ tests as well as on specific measures of reading, writing, associative memory, and perceptual speed. Boys, on the other hand, excel at visual-spatial analysis; they tend to score higher on non-verbal IQ tests, on specific spatial tasks (such as mental rotation, detecting embedded geometric figures, direction sense), and on tests of math, science, and mechanical ability. Generally speaking, the size of these differences is quite small, equivalent to just a few IQ points. Moreover, there are several exceptions to the verbal/spatial division; males actually perform better on certain language tasks, such as verbal analogies, while females are better at certain mathematical/spatial tasks, such as numerical calculations and location memory. As always, these group differences make no predictions about the ability of any particular individual; plenty of men (poets, playwrights, clergy, lawyers) are more verbally gifted than the "average" woman, and there are lots of women (artists, engineers, architects, scientists) with better mathematical/spatial skills than the "average" man.

There is, however, a more striking difference between male and female populations that does affect certain patterns of achievement. For most mental abilities, the range of performance is considerably wider for males than for females, at both the upper and lower ends of the distribution. The "normal curve," in other words, is a little "more normal" for girls than for boys, and it is because of their greater variance that boys vastly outnumber girls, both among the top achievers in mathematics as well as among populations identified as "learning disabled."

Researchers agree about these basic differences between males and females, but there is far less consensus about their root cause. Yes, men's and women's minds seem to work a little differently, but is this a reflection of hormones and chromosomes or of experience and socialization? Evolutionary psychologists argue that the differences are indeed innate, a result of the different adaptive pressures on each sex in traditional hunter-gatherer societies. Men, according to this logic, were evolutionarily selected for their spatial, navigational, and large motor skills, which would have enabled them to hunt animals more successfully over a broad territory. Women probably stayed closer to home, because they would have spent much of their adult lives either pregnant, nursing, or caring for children; successful child-rearing could have been the basis for their verbal skill selection, and food-gathering would have depended on perceptual speed and fine motor skills.

This is an appealing theory, not least because it can never be tested. It's a little hard to conceive why navigational skills wouldn't also have been highly useful to females—who probably had to roam fairly far to gather enough food for themselves and their children to survive—and why verbal skills wouldn't have come in handy among bands of male hunters. Nonetheless, several other lines of evidence support the view that sex differences in kinds of intelligence are largely innate.

One finding that is hard to attribute to experience is a difference in brain size. Males really do have larger brains than females, from birth all the way to adulthood. Of course, some of this extra brain tissue is needed simply to innervate their larger muscles and body surface area. (Elephants, for instance, have brains about three and a half times larger than ours, but nobody is arguing that they're smarter.) Even after you factor in differences in height or surface area, however, men still have an extra hundred grams of brain mass, some 8 percent more than women. It's possible that this extra mass is needed to compensate for some other physiological difference between the sexes, such as metabolic rate or body fat ratio (there are no nerves in fat tissue, and women have a lot more of it). Then again, those extra hundred grams may actually be the reason why men are better at spatial skills. Anyone with a personal computer knows that graphical processing requires a lot more disk space than word processing; perhaps spatial skills, which involve integrating information over three or more dimensions, really do require a lot more "brain space" than verbal skills, which involve stringing information (words) together along a single dimension. In fact, it is known that the cerebral cortex in male rats' brains is thicker on the right, or spatial side, while females' hemispheres are more symmetrical. If men similarly carry their extra hundred grams on the right side, as is suggested for infant brains (see page 433), it could very well contribute to their superiority at spatial skills.

What men have in size, women make up for in organization. In Chapter 14 we saw several cerebral differences that could account for females' verbal superiority: larger neurons and a higher density of them in Wernicke's area, and greater symmetry of the planum temporale. Women generally engage both hemispheres more equally than men for all kinds of tasks, and anatomical studies suggest one reason why this is so. There is a single bridging structure, the *corpus callosum*, responsible for the vast majority of information flow between our two hemispheres. When this elongated band of 200 million fibers is severed, as neurosurgeons occasionally must do to treat severe epilepsy, a person's brain is truly spit in two—each half is literally ignorant of what the other side is experiencing.

It turns out that one part of this information superhighway—the posterior portion, or *splenium*, of the corpus callosum—is significantly larger in females than in males. Moreover, the size of the splenium is correlated—in women, at least—with a particular measure of language skill—verbal fluency. Thus it appears that women use their brains more symmetrically because they have more efficient communication between the hemispheres. Such bilateral organization seems to be better for language but worse for spatial skills, perhaps because it diverts the right hemisphere from a more dedicated role in visual-spatial processing. Putting all of these observations together, there is fairly good evidence that women are better equipped biologically for language.

So: men have larger brains, especially on the right, where spatial information is processed, but women's brains are better organized for language. All this says is that different forms of intelligence are meted out by different types of brain organization. It still proves nothing about the causes of these differences. It's possible that these neural differences are, along with the intellectual differences themselves, merely a product of the different experience of boys and girls. It is known, for instance, that the fibers of the corpus callosum are particularly plastic—they grow or retract according to their level of electrical activity. Perhaps the play style of girls better promotes callosal fiber growth, while boys' style promotes right-hemisphere development at the expense of these callosal connections, leading to a difference in callosal size between adult men and women.

In fact, it is known that children of both sexes improve at spatial tasks when they play with spatial kinds of toys—building blocks, Tinkertoys, geometric shapes, and the like—and such toys are often preferred by boys. Pushing a truck around, hitting a baseball, or kicking a soccer ball probably all hone visual-spatial coordination better than does playing dolls or dress-up. Add to the list the latest computer games—also preferred by boys—with their fancy, interactive 3-D graphics, and you can see why boys might get a leg up in the spatial domain. Girls, by contrast, gravitate more toward drawing, painting, and socially imitative types of play, all of which favor verbal and preliteracy skills.

This, of course, brings us to the touchy topic of children's play choices. Boys and girls do seem to gravitate toward different types of activities, and many parents are quick to claim that these choices are purely inborn (though I've yet to hear a good reason why there would be a "wheel gene"). No doubt they do reflect some kind of innate difference between the sexes; boys may prefer spatial play because their energy levels are higher, and girls may prefer dolls because they are more socially attuned. On the other hand, parents often fool themselves when they claim to treat their sons and daughters perfectly equally. While we are surprisingly democratic in many ways—in the amount of interaction, communication, praise, and warmth we show boys and girls—dozens of studies, both old and recent, confirm a significant tendency for both moms and dads to encourage "sex-appropriate" play. Though often unaware of it, most of us simply pay less attention to our sons when they pick up dolls and our daughters when they start pushing trucks around, or we lavishly praise a son's throwing and a daughter's drawing—patterns of reinforcement that will inevitably magnify whatever innate differences already exist in their mental skills.

Play choices are influenced even more by pressures from outside the family. Just turn on any commercial TV station on Saturday morning, and you will see these sex-role stereotypes magnified to a horrendous degree: a few minutes of cartoons, showing active boys and passive girls, sandwiched between endless sex-coded commercials, pink for the latest Barbie getup, and black for the latest Nintendo game. Of course, kids love this stuff, because it plays right into their potent desire for peer acceptance. In fact, children are often a lot worse than parents when it comes to pressuring each other for sex-role conformity, a form of peer influence that begins shaping children's play choices during the early preschool years.

Clearly, "nurture" plays some role in shaping intellectual sex differences. Nonetheless, most evidence suggests that boys and girls do begin with somewhat different strengths, and that social pressures and play styles merely reinforce these differences. For one thing, certain gender differences emerge very early, before socialization and gender-specific play are likely to have much influence. Girls, as we saw in Chapter 14, speak their first words earlier, and continue on a more rapid course of verbal development throughout childhood. Boys show signs of visual-spatial superiority as early as it can be tested, by age three. Moreover, there is evidence that male and female brains differ even before birth in ways that may set them out on slightly different courses of cognitive development. Recall that boys' and girls' brains respond differently to speech sounds, even in the first days of life, and that by three months, girls' left hemispheres are more responsive to language than boys' (Chapter 14). Boys, on the other hand, appear to begin life with a slight right-brain advantage; male fetuses tend to have a thicker right hemisphere, particularly in the higher visual areas that would be involved in spatial analysis, while the hemispheres of female fetuses do not differ in thickness.

Sex hormones are another piece of the puzzle. Recent evidence confirms what people have suspected for ages—that estrogen and testosterone actually affect the way we think. Although both hormones are produced by both sexes in some measure, estrogen levels are considerably higher in women and testosterone levels in men. Estrogen, not surprisingly, tends to promote "female" mental skills, such as verbal articulation, fine motor control, and perceptual speed, while it depresses "male" skills, such as spatial analysis and

deductive reasoning. These findings are based on studies of women at different points of the menstrual cycle, as well as comparisons of postmenopausal
women who either do or do not take estrogen replacement therapy. Estrogen
is highest just before ovulation and lowest in the first few days of menstrua-
tion, so it turns out (contrary to all the flak) that women actually think in
slightly more male ways while they're menstruating and slightly more female
ways toward the middle of their cycles.

The effects of testosterone are more complex. Higher testosterone levels
are associated with better spatial skills, as might be expected, but the relationship is not a linear one. Men as a group obviously have more testosterone
than women (about seventeen times more, on average), and among women,
those with higher testosterone levels outperform those with lower levels on
specific spatial tasks. Among men, however, it's actually those with *lower*
testosterone levels who show the superior spatial skills. (Maybe this is why
MIT and Caltech are not known as football powerhouses.) One exception is
older men, whose testosterone levels tend to be much lower than in earlier
life; in this case, supplemental testosterone has been shown to improve spatial skill performance. Putting all these findings together, *moderate* levels of
testosterone are thought to be optimal for spatial intelligence—levels that
are on the high end of testosterone production in women, but the low end
for young and middle-aged men.

Sex hormones begin exerting themselves well before birth. Male fetuses
experience a surge of testosterone almost as soon as the testes first form, at
just seven weeks' gestation. Boys who are testosterone-deficient from birth
show poorer spatial skills throughout life, even compared with males who
become testosterone-deficient as adults. On the other hand, girl fetuses who
produce high levels of male hormones (caused by a disorder known as *congenital adrenal hyperplasia;* see page 87) end up with superior spatial skills,
even when they are treated with normal female hormones from birth and are
raised as girls. (They are also born with masculinized external genitalia, tend
to prefer traditionally "boy toys" and rough play, and have an increased incidence of lesbianism.) Even the slightly greater prenatal testosterone exposure
of females with a twin male brother is enough to enhance their spatial skills
later in life. There can be little doubt, then, that prenatal sex hormones exert
significant effects on children's specific cognitive abilities.

Sex differences in intelligence become more pronounced after puberty,
but researchers disagree about the exact reason. Hormones obviously have
something to do with it, but other biological and social factors probably also

play a role. There's intriguing evidence, for instance, that sex differences in cognition are influenced by maturational rate. Adolescents who go through puberty earlier tend to be more verbally gifted, while those who mature later tend to excel at spatial skills, and this timing effect holds for both boys and girls. Perhaps the hormonal surges of puberty shut down right-hemisphere development in some way, or else promote the left hemisphere. Since boys generally go through puberty about a year later than girls, their spatial skills benefit and verbal skills suffer accordingly.

Then again, puberty is associated with so many other changes in children's psychological makeup that it is impossible to attribute the cognitive changes solely to biological factors. Adolescents feel intense pressure to conform to adult sex-role stereotypes, probably more than any other age. This pressure may be especially problematic for girls' intellectual development; whereas boys' IQs typically grow by one or two (age-adjusted) points between the seventh and twelfth grades, girls' IQs go the opposite way—down a little over a point, on average. It's possible, of course, that this shift reflects the differential effects of estrogen and testosterone on cognitive functions. But when you factor in the dramatically different ways in which teenage boys and girls spend their time, it is hard to imagine that experience and socialization aren't also responsible. While boys keep on playing sports and video games after puberty—activities that promote spatial skills and probably translate to their achievement in math and science—eleven-year-old girls typically become highly focused on their appearance and social interactions. Even when parents try to de-emphasize this side of their daughters' lives, peer preoccupation with appearance and feminine identity can be so overwhelming that girls' self-esteem often takes a nosedive that carries over to their intellectual performance.

Of course, puberty is no picnic for boys either. Sex hormones undoubtedly contribute in some measure to the intellectual transitions of puberty. But until society fully embraces women as equal (though not necessarily identical) cognitive partners, girls are going to have the greater struggle with their intellectual identity during the difficult but critical adolescent years.

Chapter 17

How to Raise
a Smarter Child

That genes and environment each contribute about 50 percent to a child's intellectual development is rather convenient, whether you're a "half full" or "half empty" kind of parent. On the one hand, it offers parents some breathing room; you don't have to kick yourself *too hard* for not yet buying those preschool computer programs or starting to teach your four-year-old how to read. Of course, we all want to do as much as we can for our children, but the 50 percent ratio can help us keep it within reason. When it comes to our children's intelligence, half of the job was already complete on the night of conception.

On the other hand, 50 percent does mean there is still plenty a parent *can* do to improve a child's intellectual prospects. Early on, in particular, when *you* still exert the deciding influence over your child's environment, is the best time to start cultivating his or her intelligence, as well as all of the other traits—attention, motivation, persistence, curiosity—that determine whether it will be put to good use. It is certainly no coincidence that environment has its greatest effect at an age when the brain is at its most malleable. Evolution seems to have ensured that children will be most receptive to their parents' teaching at a time when they are also wholly dependent on them for all their physical and emotional needs.

But what exactly is "environment"? Is it simply everything that is not genetic? Every physical, sensory, motor, social, emotional, intellectual interaction that a growing child encounters, beginning as a zygote? Obviously, every experience is not equally potent in shaping a child's intelligence. Environmental influences are also complicated by the fact that they change with time. Certain medications, for instance, can be very dangerous during embryogenesis but pose no threat to a full-term fetus. Similarly, certain educational experiences are useless if given at the wrong time, either too early or too late.

In spite of the complexity, researchers have managed to identify several specific aspects of children's environment that clearly do affect intellectual development. Although not every factor is amenable to change for every child, many are, suggesting several concrete steps parents can take to improve their children's brain development and cognitive potential.

Family Characteristics: Socioeconomic Status, Birth Order, and Maternal Employment

Even before a child is born, you can predict a surprising amount about his or her intelligence based solely on certain facts about the family. One of the most potent predictors is socioeconomic status (SES), which shows between a 0.4 and a 0.6 correlation with IQ. SES is a broad construct, and certain characteristics, like parents' education level, correlate better than others, like family income, with a child's IQ and academic performance. Children from higher-SES homes tend to have higher IQs, and neurological studies suggest that their brains function in a more mature and left-dominated manner.

Of course, a good share of this relationship has to do with genes, and the fact that on average, higher-SES parents are themselves endowed with better-functioning brains. At the same time, higher SES is associated with many purely environmental factors that obviously contribute to such children's neural and intellectual advantage—greater opportunity, better health, more educational toys, better parenting skills, higher-quality child care, better schooling, and greater emphasis on education—which are considered in more detail below. While most parents have limited ability to change their basic economic or educational status, they do have some control over these more specific environmental variables, as does our society at large.

Another familial factor is birth order. While we often tend to think of each family as exerting a uniform influence over their children's lives, in fact, the experience of each child varies significantly with his or her unique position in the family. Birth order works to the advantage of older children. Firstborns score an average of three and a half points higher than later-born children on IQ and school achievement tests, and scores steadily decline for each additional child in a family. (See Figure 17.1.) IQ is also affected by birth spacing, at least according to one large-scale study; children born within one year of an older sibling lose about four IQ points, on average, compared with children born two or more years apart. (See Figure 17.2.)

The basis for these relationships seems fairly obvious: the more children there are in a family, or the more closely they are spaced, the less attention there is available for any single child, especially during the demanding early years. Oldest children clearly benefit from their parents' full attention as infants, and there is evidence that they continue to interact more with parents even after other siblings come along. Younger siblings, by contrast, grow up in a world filled with children, and while this may cost them a few IQ points, they generally make up for it with a slight edge in their social-emotional adjustment.

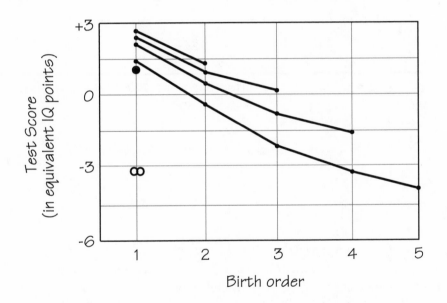

FIGURE 17.1

Intelligence test scores decline with birth order and family size. Scores are based on the National Merit Scholarship Qualification Test given at age seventeen. Each line shows families of a different size. Scores of only children are indicated by the single large dot and twins by the double circle.

Data from R.B. Zajonc, "Family configuration and intelligence," *Science* 192:227–36, 1976.

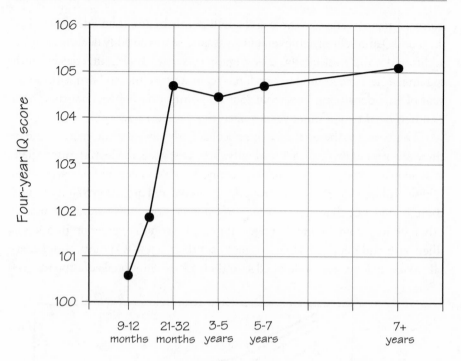

FIGURE 17.2

Preschool IQ as a function of birth spacing.

Data from Broman et al., *Preschool IQ.*

Finally, one unexpected finding to come out of studies of family configuration is that children without any siblings actually fare somewhat *worse* than firstborns from larger families; an only child typically scores about two or three points lower than an oldest child with one or two younger sibs. This observation seems to contradict the "parental attention" theory, since only children should benefit from more attention than children with younger siblings. It suggests, however, that oldest children benefit from another type of experience—the opportunity to teach their younger brothers and sisters, which is often an especially effective way of reinforcing one's own knowledge and self-confidence.

Probably the most controversial aspect of family life is the impact of working mothers. Are young children harmed or helped intellectually by receiving a large part of their care from adults other than their parents? This is a complicated issue, influenced by many factors—the number of hours both parents work, quality and type of child care (babysitter, relative, family day care, or day-care center), quality of parental care, family income, mother's educational level, and even the sex of the child. But it is also a critically important one. According to the U.S. Bureau of Labor Statistics, 62 percent of mothers with children under the age of six worked outside the home in 1995, and the majority of these returned to work within their child's first three to five months of life.

The evidence is fairly strong that economically disadvantaged children can benefit intellectually from enrollment in high-quality preschool or day care, even at a very young age. For middle- and upper-class children, however, the results are decidedly more mixed (as they are for emotional development; see pages 308–311). Two Swedish studies have found a significant advantage for children in full-time day care over those reared at home in their later academic and cognitive performance. In the United States, too, several studies report advanced intellectual development among children enrolled in high-quality day-care centers. Other studies, however, find no cognitive differences between the children of working and nonworking mothers, while still others suggest that cognitive development suffers, particularly in boys, when mothers return to work before the child's first birthday.

The type of child care clearly has a lot to do with the variability, and it may explain why results in the United States are not as positive as in Sweden, where day care is publicly supported and of consistent high quality. Obviously, day care or babysitter care can be enriching only if it provides an environment at least as good (safe, nurturing, attentive, stimulating) as the child would be experiencing with his mother, plus something extra (social, educational, physical, and creative opportunities).

A large, ongoing study by the National Institute for Child Health and Human Development is attempting to sort out the many variables of child-care use, and it thus far supports this view. Overall, this study has found few differences in cognitive or language ability between toddlers who have been exclusively cared for by their mothers and those who have received regular nonparental care. As is the case for emotional development, family characteristics—such as income, education, maternal personality, and parenting style—are much more important than the amount or quality of child care in determining a child's intellectual progress. But the study has found a few developmental differences between children reared exclusively by their mothers and those who received regular nonmaternal care; and these confirm the importance of child-care quality. Compared with children in exclusive maternal care, children in high-quality child care showed more advanced cognitive and language skills, while those in low-quality care showed lower ability in these areas. Of the various types of nonparental care, day-care centers tended to promote young children's cognitive and language development better than day-care home settings or babysitters.

Prenatal Influences

Of all the environmental influences on a child's intelligence, prenatal experience is perhaps the most potent. The most recent estimate pins up to 20 percent of IQ variance on prenatal factors, a reasonable figure given the many ways in which fetal brain development is known to be influenced by a mother's health, nutrition, environmental exposure, and even emotional well-being, as we have seen in Chapter 3.

There's little question that improvements in prenatal care and childbirth have made a substantial contribution to the "Flynn effect"—the steady rise in IQ during this century. More and more pregnant women are abstaining from alcohol and cigarettes, both of which are known to affect brain development and the subsequent cognitive abilities of a fetus. More are also taking vitamins and getting regular prenatal checkups. Improved medical care means that women today are immunized against more potentially threatening pathogens than in earlier generations, that neural defects can be detected at a very early stage, that fewer pregnant women suffer from anemia (which is linked to lower IQ in preschoolers), and that many other problems of pregnancy and childbirth (premature labor, a misplaced placenta, breech presentation, fetal distress) are now considerably less likely to compromise a baby's brain. Last but not least, babies' brains have undoubtedly benefited from improved environmental protection during this century. Pregnant women are breathing in less lead since the elimination of leaded gasoline, are consuming safer and more vitamin-enriched foods, and are increasingly protected from occupational exposure to a variety of harmful agents.

The best evidence that improved prenatal experience is raising IQs is the decline in the percentage of low-birth-weight babies—those weighing less than five and a half pounds—from 16 to 6 percent of all single births in the United States between 1970 and 1988. Since IQ is a function of brain size, and brain size is related to birth weight, larger babies mean smarter babies—at least up to a point. As the graph in Figure 17.3 shows, a child's IQ rises steadily with increases in birth weight (or head size; see Figure 15.4, on page 420) up to about four kilograms, or 8 pounds, 13 ounces. The differences are not large: about one IQ point difference, on average, between a six-and-a-half and a seven-and-a-half-pound baby. For babies nine pounds or greater, IQ actually falls off slightly, perhaps because they are somewhat more vulnerable to injury and hypoxia during birth.

As we saw in Chapter 3, a baby's birth weight depends on the amount of weight the mother gains during pregnancy. For instance, a woman who puts on thirty pounds during pregnancy will tend to produce a baby about one pound heavier than a woman who puts on only fifteen pounds. Most doctors now advise women to gain between twenty and thirty pounds during pregnancy. (The range varies somewhat with height and with prepregnancy weight; taller or thinner women should gain a little more and shorter or heavier women somewhat less.) This range is close to the optimal one for children's later IQs—fifteen to thirty pounds—which is based on one large study completed in the 1970s. Above about thirty pounds maternal weight gain, children's IQs actually begin declining, just as they do at the high end of the birth-weight curve.

Another prenatal factor that may affect children's IQ is maternal stress. As we saw in Chapter 3, high levels of stress hormones interfere with optimal brain development both directly by acting on developing neurons, and indirectly, by altering the course of pregnancy. One recent study found that prenatal stress decreases a baby's head circumference over and above its effect on birth weight, supporting the idea that it acts directly on the developing brain. Most people are now aware of the importance of stress management for their own physical well-being, but pregnancy is a particularly important time for women to try to simplify their schedules, get regular exercise, and to use relaxation or other methods to keep their stress levels down.

One thing expectant mothers *don't* have to worry about is "stimulating" their unborn child. Throughout this book, we have seen how fetuses experience and respond to all kinds of sensory input—touch, taste, light, and especially sound and vibration, beginning midway through gestation. These stimuli undoubtedly play an important role in honing sensory and motor pathways in the brain. This doesn't mean, however, that you need to stay up late playing "prenatal tapes" through headphones against your growing abdomen, reading Dr. Seuss, or tapping out Morse code to your unborn child.

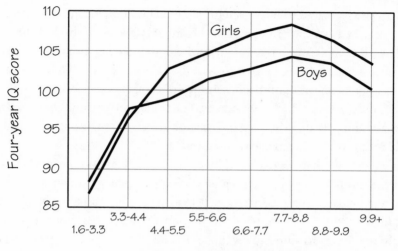

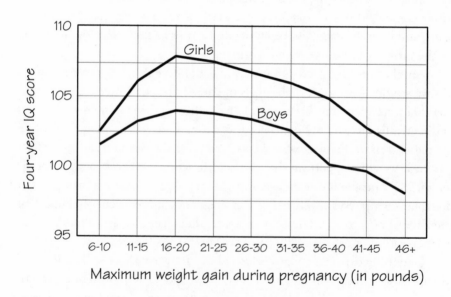

FIGURE 17.3

*Preschool IQ as a function of birth weight and maternal weight gain
during pregnancy.*

Data from Broman et al., *Preschool IQ.*

In spite of all the latest marketing ploys, there is absolutely no evidence that this kind of "stimulation" does anything for a child's later intellectual or emotional development. The reason it is unlikely to make a difference is that the fetus is already bombarded by a constant stream of touch, motion, taste, and sound. By the time he is born, your child will have already spent hundreds of hours listening to your voice (transmitted, most efficiently, right through your body) and thousands of hours listening to your heartbeat. He'll know what kinds of foods you like to eat and what it feels like to move with your gait. Any deliberate "stimulation" you provide cannot make a dent compared to this overwhelming background of sensory input.

Nutrition

Between about four months in utero and two years after birth, babies' brains are exquisitely sensitive to the quantity and quality of nutrients consumed. Children who are malnourished during this period often show substantial IQ deficits, slower language development, behavioral problems, and even sensory-motor deficits because their brains are smaller, with fewer neurons and synapses, shorter dendrites, and less myelin than normally nourished children (see Chapter 3).

While malnutrition continues to be a serious problem in undeveloped countries, few children in industrialized nations suffer from it anymore. Indeed, improved nutrition has probably contributed to the steady rise in IQ test performance in developed countries, because it strikingly parallels similar increases in the average height and head size of these populations. Although it often seems that our kids eat horrible diets, they are actually consuming much better "brain-building" foods than children in the first half of this century: more protein, dairy products, fresh fruits and vegetables, and vitamin-fortified milk and grains. In recent years, improvement has come largely in the realm of infant feeding, thanks to the steady refinement of commercial infant formulas, the addition of iron to formula and cereals, and especially the resurgence in breast-feeding. Another factor, of course, is government programs to feed needy women and children, which have largely eliminated the devastating malnutrition that remains endemic in poorer countries.

Nonetheless, there is still ample room for improvement. Although most children are now consuming all the protein and calories they need, there is evidence that large numbers remain deficient in specific nutrients—vitamins, minerals, and trace elements—many of which are essential to brain development and function. One of these is iron, a deficiency of which can result in anemia, an inadequate number of oxygen-carrying red cells in the blood. Prolonged anemia at any point during childhood can significantly stunt cognitive development. It often begins in the second six months of life, when much of the iron stored in a baby's body during gestation is largely depleted. This is why pediatricians recommend iron-containing formulas for bottle-fed babies, and why breast-fed babies should be started on iron-fortified cereals beginning between four and six months of age. Older children can get their iron from egg yolks, green and yellow vegetables, red meat, potatoes, tomatoes, and raisins. Iron absorption is increased by vitamin C, so it's a good idea to serve a glass of orange juice or other vitamin C–rich food with an iron source.

Iron is not the only nutrient that has been linked to cognitive function in children. In fact, of the forty-five nutrients essential for bodily growth and maintenance, thirty-eight are known to be necessary for neurological development. A few of these, including zinc, iodine, and several B vitamins (thiamin, niacin, B6, and riboflavin) have already been shown to affect children's cognitive abilities. But rather than look at each nutrient individually, some researchers have taken a more global approach and asked simply whether children's intellectual performance can be improved by regularly taking a multivitamin/multimineral supplement that includes most of the specific nutrients known to influence brain development.

Their results are provocative, though far from conclusive at this point. In one British study, children who took daily supplements for four weeks showed no improvement in IQ scores compared with control children, who were given a placebo. In two other British studies, vitamin supplements were administered for four or seven months, and these children showed marginal improvement compared with controls, but the effects were not statistically significant. Two other studies, however, one British and one American, have shown substantial IQ gains in adolescents taking a daily multivitamin/multimineral pill. The British students, who were twelve and thirteen years old, gained an average of nine points in their nonverbal IQ scores (but no gain in verbal IQ) over a matched group of students who took a daily placebo for the eight months of the experiment. The American study followed a smaller group of adolescents and found similar improvement in nonverbal IQ, as well as a pronounced decrease in brain-wave abnormalities, among those taking a vitamin/mineral supplement. Not surprisingly, the children who seem to gain the most from these pills are those whose diets are more deficient to begin with.

Obviously, children are best off getting their vitamins and minerals from a healthy, well-balanced diet, which benefits the rest of the body as well as the brain. Exercise is also a factor, since children who are more physically active will tend to eat more, increasing their nutrient intake directly. But because there is no harm in giving children a regular vitamin/mineral supplement, it certainly seems like a wise way to ensure that their brains are getting all the specific nutrients they need. Note, however, that larger supplements—"megadoses"—of many vitamins, that is, above the Recommended Daily Allowance, or RDA, for the child's age, are potentially dangerous.

Finally, I cannot leave this topic without emphasizing the single most important nutritional choice mothers can make to increase their children's IQ: breast-feeding. Recall from Chapter 8 that children reared on breast milk score some eight points higher on IQ tests at eight years of age than those reared on formula, even after correcting for socioeconomic differences in the mothers. The longer a mother breast-feeds during the first year of her baby's life, the higher the child's IQ. The American Academy of Pediatrics now recommends breast-feeding for a full year after birth, but according to a large 1995 survey, only 59 percent of American women nurse their newborns, and the number falls to 22 percent (many of whom supplement with formula) by six months after birth. Breast-feeding is especially uncommon among poor women (although it has recently been on the rise), which may explain in part the link between lower socioeconomic status and lower IQ.

Activities and Physical Environment

Brain development requires stimulation, so it is hardly surprising to learn that smarter children come from homes that provide a greater opportunity to explore and a greater variety of playthings. Just like young rats, whose dendrites and synapses flourish when they are reared in an enriched environment, children's brains benefit directly from variety in their daily experience. This means, first of all, that they are not heavily restricted—not locked behind gates, left for long periods in a playpen or high chair, or told "no" all the time. The home should be well organized, so that the child can find play materials, and safe enough that he or she can explore freely. But it need not be spic-and-span. The one exception is older homes, in which lead paint is likely to be present. These should be frequently vacuumed and cleaned, especially around windows, where older layers of paint get ground into dust.

Although airborne lead levels have declined substantially in the past two decades, lead paint remains the most prevalent environmental threat to young children's brains and cognitive development (see pages 64–65).

Toys are important, but sheer number matters much less than variety. The trick to effectively stimulating a child is to stay one step ahead of his or her habituation, which is incredibly potent, even early in infancy. It's a good idea, therefore, to rotate different toys and play materials every week or so. Put them away if you can, or at the very least, move them from one room to another; that old Duplo set takes on new life when it suddenly appears on the kitchen table. An even better trick is to trade toys with friends or neighbors. With just a little creativity, parents can find plenty of ways to stimulate their children without breaking the bank on new toys.

Variety also applies to the range of experiences young children are exposed to. Children need to get out of the house—for walks, to the park, the library, a store, or other people's homes. They need to see other children and interact with adults other than their mothers. Indeed, one study of adopted babies found that the single factor that best predicted infant IQ score was the baby's exposure to other places and to other people both in and outside the home. Trips to the zoo, a museum, or a children's concert are great if you can afford them, but anything that provides a change of people, scenery, or experience will do.

There is, however, a limit to how much stimulation a young child should have. Too many toys, activities, and outings can create confusion and actually work to a child's detriment, hampering his ability to focus. Whether a room contains three toys or thirty makes little difference in a young child's play, but an enormous difference in the level of confusion he has to sort through. Noise—from a TV, stereo, or too many other children—can also raise the chaos level and interfere especially with language-learning. While outings and other structured activities are important, young kids also need time to play and explore at their own leisure. Children are usually pretty good at telling us when they're bored but not when they're being overstimulated. Their behavior, such as fussiness or acting-out, is often the only sign.

Of course, all these factors apply equally whether a young child spends most of her time at home or in some kind of day-care situation. Group care obviously adds variety to a child's life: different materials to play with, projects to try, kids and teachers to interact with, and places to play. Working parents need to weigh the quality of all of these factors, balanced against the "confusion" level of a given facility, when deciding which child care to use.

Can Mozart Really Mold the Mind?   One of the more startling findings about early enrichment is the effect of music. You can hardly pick up a newspaper without seeing some kind of reference to how Mozart makes people smarter. The governor of Georgia recently proposed spending $105,000 of state money to provide every newborn baby with a compact disc of classical music, citing its positive effects on brain development and spatial and mathematical skills. What is it about classical music that is so good for mental function, and are children particularly susceptible to its magic?

Almost all the research on this subject has been performed by one group of neuroscientists from the University of California at Irvine. They were struck by the observation that people who are musically talented are often also talented at skills involving spatial-temporal integration, such as mathematics, chess, and engineering. Perhaps, they argued, music directly activates the same patterns of spatial-temporal activity in the brain areas involved in these forms of reasoning. Of course, music itself has no spatial component, but recall that pitch is converted into a spatial map by the inner ear (Chapter 10). Our brains, then, experience music as simultaneous patterns in both space and time, perhaps not unlike the kind of mental patterning required to plot a chess strategy, a geometry proof, or a building's construction. According to this view, certain types of music should be better than others at promoting spatial-temporal reasoning, which is the hypothesis these researchers set out to test.

They began with a bunch of willing college students. One group of undergraduates spent ten minutes listening to a Mozart piano sonata, a second group listened to a relaxation tape, and a third group sat in silence for the ten minutes. Immediately afterward, all three groups were tested using a series of spatial reasoning tasks, such as figuring out the pattern in a series of figures, or what a piece of paper would look like after going through a sequence of mental folding and cutting. The results were quite striking; the Mozart group scored some nine points higher in spatial IQ than the relaxation and silence groups. In a follow-up study, the researchers added the repetitive, minimalist music of Philip Glass to the comparison. Again, only the group who listened to Mozart showed significant improvement on the folding-and-cutting task, and none of the groups differed on a test of short-term memory. So it does look as though certain fairly complex types of music do specifically enhance spatial-temporal reasoning, perhaps by exercising optimal patterns of neural activity in the right hemisphere.

The researchers chose Mozart because he was composing at the age of four. Perhaps, they reasoned, young children's brains are even more sensitive to musical "exercise" than college-aged subjects, and Mozart's music may come closest to replicating the innate patterns of spatial-temporal activity in the cortex. To test this hypothesis, they enlisted the support of several local preschools. Children between the ages of three and five were divided into four different groups, but instead of just listening to music, some of them were given at least six months of instruction in actually *making* music. For one group, these consisted of private piano keyboard lessons. The children were taught basic fingering techniques, pitch intervals, two-hand coordination, musical notation, and playing from memory; and by the end of six months, all were able to play basic melodies, including some simple tunes by Mozart and Beethoven. The other three groups served as controls. One group of children was given private computer lessons, to provide keyboard training without musical experience. Another group was given daily singing sessions, led by a music instructor, and the last group was given no special lessons. All children were tested both before and after the six-month period on two different types of tasks: spatial-temporal problems, like assembling a jigsaw puzzle (which has to go together in a certain order), or more purely spatial problems, like matching or copying geometric designs.

Again, the results were striking. After correcting for the extra six months of age (which invariably raises children's scores), only those preschoolers who had been given piano lessons showed significant improvement on the spatial-temporal task. None of the three control groups excelled in that task, and none of the four groups, including the piano-trained group, showed any age-adjusted advantage on the tests of pure spatial intelligence. In other words, musical keyboard training specifically improved the preschoolers' spatial-temporal reasoning. The reason piano training works so well is presumably that it adds an extra spatial dimension to a child's musical experience; unlike singing, which taxes only the temporal component, and computer training, which in this case emphasized spatial but very little temporal reasoning, piano playing puts it all together—finger movements, location, pitch, timing, and aesthetic feedback—in a way that may be ideal for right-hemisphere development.

It is still too soon to know for sure whether early musical training is beneficial. This study needs to be replicated, and children need to be followed for a longer period of time to see how long the improvement lasts. It is also important to find out whether other abilities, like mathematics, are similarly affected. (The researchers predict that early keyboard training will be especially useful for teaching proportionality, a concept that grade-schoolers often find very difficult.) Another issue is whether there is a critical period for this effect. Music may be, as some suggest, a kind of "pre-language" that directly activates fundamental firing patterns in young children's brains and does so much more effectively than real language. It is known that the vast majority of musicians with perfect pitch began their training at an early age (before seven), suggesting that the young brain is especially ripe for this kind of spatial-temporal honing. On the other hand, the study with college students suggests that musical experience improves spatial-temporal reasoning at any age.

(I'd say more about spatial-temporal patterns of neural network activity, but I have to go sign up Julia for piano lessons. . . .)

Parent/Caregiver Style

A child's activities and physical environment are obviously only part of the equation for early enrichment. What's even more important is the quality of the interactions between parents or other caregivers and their children. Young children learn in many different ways from even the simplest interactions with adults—a diaper change, a walk to the car, a bedtime story. They learn about words, feelings, and how to treat other people, observe details, remember events, solve problems. We teach directly when we deliberately show them how something works, explain what we're doing, or reinforce their own explorations with positive attention or negative feedback. And we teach indirectly, through the example we are continually setting. Intellectual success depends on much more than "raw intelligence." Smarter children are inevitably more curious about the world, more motivated to explore and ask questions, and more persistent in finding answers, and all these qualities can be shaped to an important degree by parent/caregiver modeling.

Which aspects of parenting style are most important? Through detailed home observations, psychologists have uncovered several features that most consistently relate to children's intellectual and academic success. The best parents, by these standards, are those who are more *nurturing* (physically affectionate, emotionally supportive), very *involved* with their children (consistently spend time in shared activities), highly *responsive* to their needs (accept their individuality, serve as consultants to help them solve problems), but also rather *demanding* (expect mature behavior and independence, set clear standards and rules and see that they are followed). The balance of these qualities varies as children grow, but each is important in some way at every stage of a child's life.

It goes without saying that babies need a lot of *nurturing*: holding, cuddling, cooing, and all that other good stuff. Babies thrive on physical contact, and those who consistently experience a lot of warmth, affection, and positive feedback from their caregivers tend toward better cognitive outcomes. Physical contact is not only comforting to infants, it also puts them in the best possible situation for learning, since their vision and hearing remain limited through much of the first year. Warmth, affection, and praise continue to be very important during the toddler and preschool years, when such parental qualities are significantly associated with higher childhood IQ. For older children, nurturing primarily takes the form of emotional support and encouragement; one study of gifted teenagers found that parental support is the single family characteristic that best determined whether they would make the most of their talents.

Responsiveness is closely related to nurturing. For infants, responsive caregiving means not only prompt responding to a baby's physical needs—feeding, changing, sleeping—but also to his or her need for stimulation and interaction. Babies do cry out of boredom, and their verbalization—all that enchanting cooing and babbling—is not just idle practice. They want and expect you to reply, to engage them in "protoconversation," and to light up their day with your interesting facial expressions, their innately preferred stimulus. Verbal responsiveness is essential to language development, but it also critically shapes children's emotional reactions and self-awareness. No matter what a child's age, responsive parenting means really *listening* to your child, taking the time to understand what he or she is trying to say, and engaging in lots of verbal give-and-take. Sensitive, responsive caregivers also appreciate that every child is different. They respect each child's individual needs and, equally important, teach that parent's own needs should be respected in return.

Involvement is another obvious feature of good parenting, but it may not always be clear what the best way is to go about it. "Involved parenting" doesn't mean driving your child around to lessons or arranging play dates where you sit and talk with other adults. It means direct, one-on-one interactions, in which all of your attention is focused on a joint activity with your child—reading a story, making up a song, building a sand castle, taking a nature walk, helping with homework. Several studies have found a relationship between children's IQ or academic achievement and the amount of time they spend in shared activities with their parents, also known by the familiar phrase "quality time."

What kind of shared activities are best for promoting children's cognitive development? Not, as some parents think, those involving a lot of academic instruction. Parents don't need to drill their preschoolers in phonics or hold flash-card sessions with their young infants to maximize their intellectual potential. Although some kids can benefit, in the short run, from early tutoring in reading or arithmetic, what works best in the long run are measures that foster children's enthusiasm, industry, perseverance, and motivation to learn. For babies, this means playful interactions that focus their interest on specific objects, concepts, and feelings. Recall that babies whose mothers (and presumably fathers) do a better job of encouraging their attention actually end up smarter than those whose mothers make less effort in this regard. Their vocabularies grow faster, they are more exploratory, and they even score higher on IQ tests as early as age four and as late as eighteen years. The best way to sustain babies' interest, given their rapid habituation, is to present variations on a theme—move their arms in different ways, or focus on different body parts, colors, shapes, or sounds. Encouraging children's attention, even very early in infancy, helps foster the persistence and motivation they need to master ever more difficult challenges.

For toddlers and preschoolers, choose something *you* enjoy—catching butterflies, putting a train set together, baking cookies, gardening, drawing on the computer, folding laundry, and of course, reading. Kids this age *want* to learn from their parents. They seek us out, following us around the house saying, "*I* see," and "*I* do it." By including them, you can teach that there's pleasure in accomplishment, experimentation, and creativity. Working side by side, parents can usually coax their children to do a little more, try a little harder, than they would on their own, giving them a sense of mastery that bolsters their confidence for future endeavors. Working together also gives children a close-up view of mature thinking in action, a model of how to observe, organize, and remember details, and also, ideally, of how to find joy in intellectual discovery.

Shared activities remain important as children get older, although now these are likelier to involve something of *their* choosing. No matter if you're cheering them on at soccer, helping with their homework, or taking them on a much-awaited camping trip, children obviously benefit by having parents who actively participate in their lives. Parental involvement is especially useful for countering the negative aspects of peer influence and keeping a child focused on school and other positive activities.

The final attribute of more successful parents—that they *demand* a lot of their children—may seem a bit at odds with these other prescriptions. These days, we tend to place a great deal of weight on building children's self-esteem. But this sometimes comes at the expense of teaching them discipline and self-control. Yes, we know we're supposed to set limits and expect rules to be obeyed, but actually *enforcing* these rules requires punishment—and what will all those time-outs and groundings do to a child's self-image? A lot of good, judging by the data. It turns out that children whose parents hold high expectations *and* are highly sensitive to their needs (known as an *authoritative* parenting style) actually have fewer behavioral problems and perform better academically than those with more permissive parents or with demanding parents who are not very responsive (*authoritarian* parenting), and this pattern holds true whether the children are preschool-aged or adolescents. Authoritative parents expect mature behavior, but they help their children figure out how to achieve it; they consistently challenge them, but in a warm, supportive way.

One study conducted during the 1980s is particularly revealing on the subject of parental expectations. It compared a large number of elementary school students in three different countries: the United States, Japan, and Taiwan. By the fifth grade, American children fall far below Japanese and Chinese students in mathematics achievement, a trend that is exacerbated in the high school years and has continued well into the 1990s. The gap cannot be explained by differences in "raw" intelligence, since scores on basic cognitive tests do not differ significantly. Some of the gap is explained by a fundamental difference in schooling: American elementary teachers typically devote a lot less time teaching math and science than do Japanese and Chinese teachers. An important part of the difference, however, results from differences in parenting style. American parents are simply much less demanding of their children and their schools. Compared with Japanese and Chinese mothers, American mothers are much likelier to express satisfaction with their children's performance and the quality of instruction in the schools. The difference is most striking when it comes to homework: American mothers were satisfied with the amount of homework their children were given, even though it is less than half as much as Japanese students are given and less than *one-fifth* as much as Chinese students. (American parents also spend considerably less time each day helping their children with their homework.) The problem, it seems, is that American parents simply do not value hard work in school as much as these Asian parents do, and the result is that most kids in the United States don't learn as much.

Parents' expectations do make a difference in their children's intellectual achievement. However, there is a fine line between "demanding" and "pressuring" that makes this aspect of parenting a difficult one to gauge. Parents can expect hard work and mature behavior, but not a particular level of achievement. No child benefits from undue pressure or unrealistic parental expectations, which are likely to backfire when children get a little bit older. Excess pressure can also come from overscheduling; too many lessons, play dates, and other structured activities can be very stressful and deprive children of the important opportunity to play alone, read, daydream, and simply be kids.

Mothers, Fathers, and the "Flynn Effect"   Hard as it is to find the right balance, there is actually some good news about our parenting skills. Most researchers agree that at least some of the "Flynn effect"—the steady IQ rise during this century—is due to improvements in the typical environment and caretaking of young children. More and more parents are exposed to information about child development and are aware of the importance of being responsive and involved. Women, in particular, are more educated now than at any time in history, a change that we know makes a substantial difference in their children's cognitive development. And even those parents who are not particularly involved with their children seem to understand the importance of early stimulation, judging by the explosion in the number of toys, books, videos, musical tapes, and computer games geared specifically toward young children.

Of particular interest is the role of fathers. It's been known for some time that children reared without fathers do not, on average, achieve as well academically as children reared in two-parent families, even after correcting for socioeconomic differences between the two types of families. At the same time, there is growing evidence that children in two-parent homes benefit significantly from having fathers who are actively involved in their lives; they score higher on IQ tests, perform better in school, and show higher self-esteem, self-control, and social competence than children with less involved, traditional fathers. While these findings raise a lot of concern about the increasing number of single-parent families, they suggest that matters are actually improving for the majority of children, those whose mothers *and* fathers now play a substantial role in caring for and teaching them.

Schooling

The last factor that influences a child's intelligence is schooling. IQ and education are obviously related to each other, but researchers have fervently debated about which causes what. Do people with higher IQs simply stay in school longer because they find it more rewarding, or does increased schooling actually raise a person's IQ—"raw intelligence," if you will—over what it would have been without continuing formal education?

The answer is both. It is certainly true that people with higher IQs tend to do better in school, so they are more motivated to stick with it. On the other hand, there is plenty of evidence that school itself makes children smarter; not only academic abilities but IQ itself actually rises with each year of formal education. For instance, when the public schools in Prince Edward County, Virginia, were closed during the early 1960s to avoid racial integration, black children lost an average of six IQ points per year, compared with a similar population of children in a neighboring county whose schools remained open. Similar deficits have been documented among Dutch children during the Nazi occupation, London gypsies, and Appalachian "hollows" children, all of whose education was interrupted for several years or more. The effect of schooling is so powerful and so cumulative that children who receive no formal education at all (like some of the Appalachian children) can fall into the retarded range by the time they reach adolescence.

At this point, the vast majority of children in industrialized nations *do* attend school for most of childhood, and the steady increase in mandatory schooling during this century is probably responsible for a good share of the Flynn effect. Even today, however, differences in quantity of schooling show up in children's relative IQ scores. Both truancy and early dropout are associated with lower IQs, and even summer vacations produce a small but statistically significant decline in IQ scores.

Most controversial of all is the effect of delayed entry into formal schooling. In recent years, there has been a trend for parents to hold their children back a year before beginning them in kindergarten or in first grade. Boys seem to be a particular target of this delay, because of the perception that their cognitive maturation is slower (which is true only for verbal skills; see Chapter 16), and perhaps because some parents are still more concerned that their sons (rather than their daughters) have a competitive edge. There is some evidence, it's true, that the younger children in a class are more likely to have academic problems than the older children. However, when researchers compared the cognitive achievement of younger first-graders, children whose birthdays fell just before the admissions cut-off date, with that of older kindergartners, whose birthdays fell just a few weeks later, the first-graders were actually far ahead. Moreover, when researchers compared the cognitive growth of young first-graders to that of the oldest children in the class, who were nearly a full year older, there was no difference. Both groups learned at an equivalent rate, and far faster than the oldest members of the kindergarten class. In other words, "school readiness" was not a problem for these younger students.

By the middle school years (grades four, five, and six), age becomes even less of a factor in children's cognitive performance. In one large study, Israeli researchers showed that schooling exerts about twice as much influence as age over a child's IQ; that is, a young fifth-grader will score within a point or two of his older classmates, but some five points higher than his age-mates in fourth grade.

The implication of these studies is fairly obvious: parents who think they are giving their child an advantage by delaying his entry into school are actually stunting his cognitive development. The little bit a child gains by being oldest in his kindergarten class is more than offset by how much he loses from missing a full year of school. (Most children will, of course, eventually get that extra year of schooling, but not until they're eighteen and most of their peers have headed off to work or college. For better or worse, our society does tend to judge people's accomplishments by their age.)

Of course, every child is different, and there will always be a few with late birthdays who can benefit from an extra year at home or in preschool. But the trend in some communities of permitting parents to hold their children back, even when their birthdays fall many months before the class cut-off, seems ill-founded. Not only can this practice backfire for the individual children involved, it also expands the age spread in any given class, making it all the more difficult for teachers to present material that is appropriate for every child.

Does Preschool Increase a Child's Intelligence?   If delaying school hampers a child's intellectual development, then an obvious question is whether early schooling has the opposite effect: does preschool attendance make children smarter? Considering the rapid growth in early childhood programs over the past two decades, both for children with working and with nonworking mothers, you'd think we'd know the answer to this question.

There is solid evidence, as we've seen, that high-quality day care improves the cognitive and academic performance of disadvantaged children. For middle-class children, the data are less consistent, although a few recent studies have found a significant academic advantage for those elementary-aged children who received some kind of formal schooling before kindergarten.

My own view, which seems to be shared by the growing number of parents who are electing to send their children to preschool, is that a good program can be very advantageous to a child's intellectual development. High-quality day care or preschool offers an excellent way to increase a child's social and cognitive stimulation. Few parents (or babysitters) can match the variety of activities, play materials, and social interaction that such preschools or day care provide. Moreover, a good preschool teacher understands young children in a way few parents can and can be a fine role model, both for the child and the parent. By "good," I am of course referring to all of the same ingredients that make for good parenting—warm, nurturing, supportive, responsive, stimulating, yet demanding. But no teacher can do all of this if she is responsible for a dozen preschoolers, so a low teacher-student ratio (at least 1:5 for two-year-olds, 1:7 for three-year-olds, and 1:10 for four-year-olds) is an important part of the equation.

There is, however, one note of caution to sound about early childhood education. This is not a time for heavy academic instruction. Although parents may think they're giving their child a head start by enrolling them in academically focused preschools, there is no evidence that children benefit in the long run from early formal instruction in school subjects. In fact, it may even do some harm. In one study, researchers compared kindergartners who had attended strongly academic and less academically oriented preschools, and they found no difference in their cognitive ability or school performance. They did, however, find that the children from the more academic preschools tended to have greater anxiety about testing and to view school less positively than those from the less academic preschools. In other words, there may be a real danger in pushing academic achievement too early. You don't want kids to burn out on school even before they've entered the real thing, or stifle their imagination and creativity while these are still at their peak.

Preschool should be an enticement—a way to ease children into a school setting and foster a deep love for learning. It is a time for exploration, to exploit children's natural curiosity and to build their sense of initiative and self-esteem. It is not the time to emphasize achievement, to compare different children's performance, or to insist they get things "right." Activities should be "child-centered," not "teacher-centered," meaning that children are largely free to choose how they spend their time and to pursue their chosen activities as long as they like. Teachers should play the role of facilitator rather than instructor—helping each child find interesting and challenging projects, answering questions, suggesting new approaches, and fostering a sense of mastery. Children this age learn by doing, using all five senses and their evolving motor skills, not by being regimented or lectured to in large groups.

There's a reason why education at this age is still referred to as *preschool*. Children under five simply aren't ready, either emotionally or cognitively, for a heavy dose of formal instruction. Recall that it is not until about six years of age that the frontal lobes really kick into gear, when children can follow an adult's reasoning, use their memory in a deliberate fashion, begin to grasp abstract concepts, and have the self-control to sit still and really absorb what's being taught. This isn't to say that younger children can't learn to read, subtract, and recognize the planets. Preschoolers should certainly have the opportunity to flex every one of their mental muscles. But they also need to climb, paint, build, sing, plant, pretend, hammer, pour, clap, laugh, and socialize. Academic subjects should be broached only if the *child* (as opposed to the parent) is highly motivated, and if they are presented in a very concrete, "hands-on" fashion. Psychologists describe this type of preschool experience as "developmentally appropriate," and not only is it better for kids than lectures and workbooks, it's a lot more fun.

The "Perfect" Parent

Putting it all together, there's obviously a lot parents can do to improve their children's intellectual prospects. Perhaps too much. The perfect parent, if she (or he) existed, would devote herself full time to the care and teaching of her child. She would begin, even before conception, by shoring up her folic acid reserves and purging her body of any chemical remotely suspect. Once pregnant, she would never touch a drop of alcohol, pump her own gasoline, get less than eight hours sleep, or allow herself to be stressed in any way. She would have an ideal, unmedicated, and uncomplicated delivery, and breast-feed from the moment of birth until the child was potty-trained. She would know precisely how to stimulate her baby, but also how to avoid overstimulation. She would spend hours every day playing with him—singing, cuddling, talking, massaging, exercising, reading, showing him how all kinds of toys and other fascinating objects work—and never have to leave him in his swing for half an hour while trying to make supper or balance the checkbook. Her house would be perfectly baby-proofed, so he could explore every corner and rarely hear "No!" She'd take him on all kinds of different outings, always giving him her full attention, and never grow annoyed when he pulled all the vitamins off the shelf at the pharmacy or whined for cookies at the grocery store. She'd introduce him to other children, all with similarly perfect parents, and gladly clean up after the messiest play dates. She'd start him on piano/tennis/dance/French/swimming/art/violin/computer/Spanish/tumbling lessons at age three (practicing herself, to provide a good role model) but, if he showed no interest, would happily forfeit the ten weeks' tuition. She'd send him to the perfect preschool, using their time apart to brush up on the latest child-rearing information and prepare all sorts of new and interesting educational activities for him. And of course, she wouldn't do it alone. She'd have the "perfect spouse" right alongside, equally loving/stimulating/nurturing/teaching their child every step of the way.

There may actually be one or two parents in the world like this. And perhaps their kids will turn out to be the most brilliant, talented people ever. Then again, you have to wonder what children learn from parents whose only focus in life is their offspring. The fact is that children pick up much more than mere cognitive skills from their parents and other caregivers. They also learn how to work, share, love, nurture, juggle, and enjoy life. Once again, it is the model we set, rather than the specific teaching we attempt, that is going to have the biggest impact on a child's cognitive abilities and success in life.

Parenting is hard, hard work. Most of us try the best we can, given the limits on our time, stamina, and resources. Of course, we'd all like to do more for our children, to be a little more perfect in the parenting department. I've yet to meet a mother or father who doesn't feel guilty at times, wishing she or he had more time, patience, or money to devote to each child. These are the moments when it's reassuring to remember the other half of the equation: heredity. Given that even the perfect parent doesn't have "perfect genes," maybe we can relax just a little bit and enjoy our kids for who they are.

NOTES

Page   Chapter 1: Nature or Nuture? It's All in the Brain

2   René Spitz: *Dialogues from Infancy: Selected Papers*, edited by R. N. Emde
        (New York: International Universities Press, 1983).

3   John Watson: Quote from his 1924 book, *Behaviourism*, appears in
        L. Stevenson, *Seven Theories of Human Nature* (New York: Oxford University
        Press, 1974), p. 93.

4   *The Bell Curve: Intelligence and Class Structure in American Life:* by R. J.
        Herrnstein and C. Murray (New York: Free Press, 1994).

4   *The Nurture Assumption: Why Children Turn Out the Way They Do:* by J. R.
        Harris (New York: Free Press, 1998).

        Chapter 2: The Basic Biology of Brain Development

11   Primary sources for this chaper: R. O'Rahilly and F. Müller, *Human Embryology
        and Teratology*, 2nd ed. (New York: Wiley-Liss, 1996); B. M. Carlson, *Human
        Embryology and Developmental Biology* (St. Louis: Mosby, 1994); W.J. Larsen,
        Human Embryology (New York: Churchill Livingstone, 1993); M. Jacobson,
        Developmental Neurobiology, 3rd ed. (New York: Plenum, 1991); K. L. Moore
        and T. V. N. Persaud, *The Developing Human: Clinically Oriented Embryology*,
        5th ed. (Philadelphia: W. B. Saunders, 1993); D. Purves and J. W. Lichtman,
        Principles of Neural Development (Sunderland, MA: Sinauer, 1985).

25   Timing of neurogenesis: P. Rakic, "Corticogenesis in human and nonhuman
        primates," in M. S. Gazzaniga, ed., *The Cognitive Neurosciences* (Cambridge,
        MA: MIT Press, 1995), pp. 127–45.

25   Postnatal neurogenesis: One recent study has found surprising evidence that
        new neurons are produced throughout adulthood, but such late neurogenesis is
        probably restricted to only a few small areas of the brain. See P. S. Eriksson et
        al., "Neurogenesis in the adult human hippocampus," *Nature Medicine* 4
        (1998): 1313–17.

27   15,000 synapses per neuron: Data from the visual cortex; P. R. Huttenlocher,
        "Morphometric study of human cerebral cortex development,"
        Neuropsychologia 28 (1990): 517–27.

27   Spine development: L. J. Garey, "Structural development of the visual system of man," *Human Neurobiology* 3 (1984): 75–80.

27   Dendritic growth: J. Dobbing and J. Sands, "Quantitative growth and development of the human brain," *Archives of Disease in Childhood* 48 (1973): 757–67.

30   Wild vs. domestic rabbits: C. Darwin, *The Variations of Animals and Plants Under Domestication* (London: John Murray, 1868), vol. 1, pp. 124–30.

32   Larger neurons in enriched environment: W. T. Greenough et al., "Experience and brain development," *Child Development* 58 (1987): 539–59.

32   Smarter rats: M. C. Diamond, "Environmental influences on the young brain," in K. R. Gibson and A. C. Petersen, eds., *Brain Maturation and Cognitive Development: Comparative and Cross-cultural Perspectives* (New York: Aldine de Gruyter, 1991), pp. 107–24.

32   Rate of synapse loss: Assuming each of ten billion cortical cells loses seven thousand synapses over ten years; data from Huttenlocher, "Morphometic study."

34   Epilepsy: S. L. Kinsman et al., "Efficacy of the ketogenic diet for intractable seizure disorders: Review of 58 cases," *Epilepsia* 33 (1992): 1132–36.

35   Myelination timing: B. A. Brody et al., "Sequence of central nervous system myelination in human infancy. I. An autopsy study of myelination," *Journal of Neuropathology and Experimental Neurology* 46 (1987): 283–301; P. I. Yakovlev and A.-R. Lecours, "The myelogenetic cycles of regional maturation of the brain," in A. Minkowski, ed., *Regional Development of the Brain in Early Life* (Philadelphia: F. A. Davis, 1967), pp. 3–65.

35   PET scans: H. T. Chugani et al., "Positron emission tomography study of human brain functional development," *Annals of Neurology* 22 (1987): 487–97.

Chapter 3: Prenatal Influences on the Developing Brain

41   Cognitive outcome of preterm infants: C. M. Drillien et al., "Low birthweight children at early school-age: A longitudinal study," *Developmental Medicine and Child Neurology* 22 (1980): 26–47; N. K. Klein et al., "Children who were very low birth weight: Development and academic achievement at nine years of age," *Developmental and Behavioral Pediatrics* 10 (1989): 32–37.

41   Womblike care: H. Als et al., "Individualized developmental care for the very low-birth-weight preterm infant. Medical and neurofunctional effects," *JAMA* 272 (1994): 853–58.

41   Morning sickness: M. Profet, "The evolution of pregnancy sickness as protection to the embryo against Pleistocene teratogens," *Evolutionary Theory* 8 (1988): 177–90.

41   Nausea and miscarriage: R. M. Weigel and M. M. Weigel, "Nausea and vomiting in early pregnancy and pregnancy outcome. A meta-analytical review," *British Journal of Obstetrics and Gynecology* 96 (1989): 1312–18.

42 Causes of birth defects: R. L. Brent and D. A. Beckman, "Environmental teratogens," *Bulletin of the New York Academy of Medicine* 66 (1990): 123–63.

42 Low teratogen doses have subtle neurobehavioral effects: C. V. Vorhees, "Principles of behavioral teratology," in E. P. Riley and C. V. Vorhees, eds., *Handbook of Behavioral Teratology* (New York: Plenum, 1986) pp. 23–48.

43 Chernobyl: J. Little, "The Chernobyl accident, congenital abnormalities and other reproductive outcomes," *Paediatric and Perinatal Epidemiology* 7 (1993): 121–51.

44 NTDs in spontaneous abortion: R. O'Rahilly and F. Müller, "Neurulation in the normal human embryo," in G. Bock and J. Marsh, eds., *Neural Tube Defects*, CIBA Foundation, Symposium 181 (Chichester, Eng.: John Wiley, 1994), pp. 70–89.

45 Epilepsy and NTDs: L. B. Holmes, "Spina bifida: Anticonvulsants and other maternal influences," in Bock and Marsh, *Neural Tube Defects*, pp. 232–44; J. Smith et al., "Drugs of choice for pregnant women," in G. Koren, ed., *Maternal-Fetal Toxicology: A Clinician's Guide*, 2nd ed. (New York: Marcel Dekker, 1994), pp. 115–27.

45 Maternal temperature and NTDs: A. Milunsky et al., "Maternal heat exposure and neural tube defects," *JAMA* 268 (1992): 882–85.

46 NTD detection rate: H.S. Cuckle, "Screening for neural tube defects," in Bock and Marsh, *Neural Tube Defects*, pp. 253–69.

46 Folic acid prevents NTDs: N. J. Wald, "Folic acid and neural tube defects: The current evidence and implications for prevention," in Bock and Marsh, *Neural Tube Defects*, pp. 192–211. Interestingly, Wald notes that the one study that failed to show an effect of folic acid was based largely on women from California, where dietary intake of folic acid is normally rather high and the rate of NTDs comparatively low.

47 Public health officials: "Centers for Disease Control recommendations for the use of folic acid to reduce the numbers of cases of spina bifida and other neural tube defects," *Morbidity and Mortality Weekly Report* 41 (1992): RR-14.

47 Dietary folic acid is not sufficient: J. M. Scott, in Bock and Marsh, *Neural Tube Defects*, p. 211.

47 Folic acid fortification does not mitigate the need for supplements: G. J. Locksmith and P. Duff, "Preventing neural tube defects: The importance of periconceptional folic acid supplements," *Obstetrics and Gynecology* 91 (1998): 1027–34.

49 Adult vs. infant starvation: H. K. M. Yusuf, *Understanding the Brain and Its Development: A Chemical Approach* (Singapore: World Scientific, 1992).

49 Malnourishment and mental impairment: B. Morgan and K. R. Gibson, "Nutritional and environmental interactions in brain development," in Gibson and Petersen, *Brain Maturation and Cognitive Development*, pp. 91–105 (see full citation on page 462).

49　　Optimal nutrition in pregnancy: B. Worthington-Roberts and S. R. Williams, *Nutrition in Pregnancy and Lactation*, 5th ed. (St. Louis: Mosby, 1993).

50　　Twins' IQ: Jacobson, *Developmental Neurobiology*, p. 286 (see full citation on page 461).

51　　Korean War orphans: M. Winick et al., "Malnutrition and environmental enrichment by early adoption," *Science* 190 (1975): 1173–75.

52　　Isotretinoin: W. S. Dai et al., "Epidemiology of isotretinoin exposure during pregnancy," *Journal of the American Academy of Dermatology* 26 (1992): 599–606.

52　　Retin-A: S. S. Jick et al., "First trimester topical tretinoin and congenital disorders," *Lancet* 341 (1993): 1181–82.

53　　Screening for drug-induced defects: G. Koren and I. Nulman, "Teratogenic drugs and chemicals in humans," in Koren, *Maternal-Fetal Toxicology*, pp. 33–47 (see full citation on page 463).

53　　Prenatal aspirin and later IQ: A. P. Streissguth et al., "Aspirin and acetaminophen use by pregnant women and subsequent child IQ and attention decrements," *Teratology* 35 (1987): 211–18.

53　　Gastroschisis: C. P. Torfs et al., "Maternal medications and environmental exposures as risk factors for gastroschisis," *Teratology* 54 (1996): 84–92.

53　　Safety of nonprescription drugs: M. Bologa et al., "Drugs and chemicals most commonly used by pregnant women," in Koren, *Maternal-Fetal Toxicology*, pp. 89–113 (see full citation on page 463).

54　　Brain most vulnerable to prenatal alcohol: A. P. Streissguth et al., "The effects of prenatal exposure to alcohol and tobacco: Contributions from the Seattle Longitudinal Prospective Study and implications for public policy," in H. L. Needleman and D. Bellinger, eds., *Prenatal Exposure to Toxicants: Developmental Consequences* (Baltimore: Johns Hopkins University, 1994), pp. 148–83.

54　　Effects of alcohol on dendrites and synapses: J. R. West et al., "Fetal alcohol syndrome: The vulnerability of the developing brain and possible mechanisms of damage," *Metabolic Brain Disease* 9 (1994), 291–322.

54　　Effect of alcohol on cerebellum: J. R. West et al., "Cell population depletion associated with fetal alcohol brain damage: Mechanisms of BAC-dependent cell loss," *Alcoholism: Clinical and Experimental Research* 14 (1990): 813–18.

54　　Children of alcoholic mothers: C. D. Coles, "Prenatal alcohol exposure and human development," in M. W. Miller, ed., *Development of the Central Nervous System: Effects of Alcohol and Opiates* (New York: Wiley-Liss, 1992), pp. 9–36.

54　　Moderate alcohol and later IQ: A. P. Streissguth et al., "Moderate prenatal alcohol exposure: Effects on child IQ and learning problems at age 7-$^1/_2$ years," *Alcoholism: Clinical and Experimental Research* 14 (1990): 662-69.

54 Studies finding no effect of modest maternal alcohol consumption: J. L. Mills and B. I. Graubard, "Is moderate drinking during pregnancy associated with an increased risk for malformations?" *Pediatrics* 80 (1987): 309–14; D. Polygenis et al., "Moderate alcohol consumption during pregnancy and the incidence of fetal malformations: A meta-analysis," *Neurotoxicology and Teratology* 20 (1998): 61–67; I. Walpole et al., "Low to moderate maternal alcohol use before and during pregnancy, and neurobehavioral outcome in the newborn infant," *Developmental Medicine and Child Neurology* 33 (1991): 875–83; J. Olsen, Effects of moderate alcohol consumption during pregnancy on child development at 18 and 42 months," *Alcoholism: Clinical and Experimental Research* 18 (1994): 1109–13.

55 Higher miscarriage risk: G. C. Windham et al., "Moderate maternal alcohol consumption and risk of spontaneous abortion," *Epidemiology* 8 (1997): 509–14; "Alcohol and the fetus—Is zero the only option?" *Lancet* i (1983): 682–83.

55 Placenta abruptio: M.C. Marbury et al., "The association of alcohol consumption with outcome of pregnancy," *American Journal of Public Health* 73 (1983): 1165–68.

55 Cleft lip: R. G. Munger et al., "Maternal alcohol use and risk of orofacial cleft birth defects," *Teratology* 54 (1996): 27–33.

55 Binge drinking: Streissguth et al., "Moderate prenatal alcohol exposure"; A. P. Streissguth et al., "Drinking during pregnancy decreases word attack and arithmetic scores on standardized tests: Adolescent data from a population-based prospective study," *Alcoholism: Clinical and Experimental Research* 18 (1994): 248–54; Olsen, "Effects of moderate alcohol."

56 Maternal drinking patterns: "Alcohol consumption among pregnant and childbearing-aged women—United States, 1991 and 1995," *Morbidity and Mortality Weekly Report* 46 (1997): 346–50; M. Serdula et al., "Trends in alcohol consumption by pregnant women: 1985 through 1988," *JAMA* 265 (1991): 876–79.

56 Maternal smoking patterns: R. L. Floyd et al., "Smoking during pregnancy: Prevalence, effects, and intervention strategies," *Birth* 18 (1991): 48–53.

56 Effect of cigarettes on fetus: P. S. Eriksen et al., "Acute effects of maternal smoking on fetal breathing and movements," *Obstetrics and Gynecology* 61 (1983): 367–72.

57 Neurobehavioral effects of prenatal cigarette exposure: Z. Annau and L. D. Fechter, "The effects of prenatal exposure to carbon monoxide," in Needleman and Bellinger, *Prenatal Exposure to Toxicants*, pp. 249–67 (see full citation on page 464); S. Milberger et al., "Is maternal smoking during pregnancy a risk factor for attention deficit hyperactivity disorder in children?" *American Journal of Psychiatry* 153 (1996): 1138–42; C. D. Drews et al., "The relationship between idiopathic mental retardation and maternal smoking during pregnancy," *Pediatrics* 97 (1996): 547–53.

57   Nicotine: H. A. Navarro et al., "Effects of prenatal nicotine exposure on development of central and cholinergic neurotransmitter systems. Evidence for cholinergic influences in developing brain," *Journal of Pharmacology and Experimental Therapeutics* 251 (1989): 894–900.

57   Smoking effects by trimester: E. Lieberman et al., "Low birthweight at term and the timing of fetal exposure to maternal smoking," *American Journal of Public Health* 84 (1994): 1127–31; C. MacArthur and E. G. Knox, "Smoking in pregnancy: Effects of stopping at different stages," *British Journal of Obstetrics and Gynecology* 95 (1988): 551–55.

58   Passive smoke: J. Makin et al., "A comparison of active and passive smoking during pregnancy: Long-term effects," *Neurotoxicology and Teratology* 13 (1991): 5–12.

58   Cocaine: D. F. Swaab et al., "Functional teratogenic effects of chemicals on the developing brain," in M. I. Levene and R. J. Lilford, eds., *Fetal and Neonatal Neurology and Neurosurgery*, 2nd ed. (Edinburgh: Churchill Livingstone, 1995), pp. 263–77.

59   Heroin: J. M. Davis and C. E. Mercier, "The effects of drugs and other substances on the fetus," in R. A. Hoekelman et al., eds., *Primary Pediatric Care*, 2nd ed. (St. Louis: Mosby, 1992), pp. 412–18.

59   Marijuana: Swaab et al., "Functional teratogenic effects"; P. A. Fried and B. Watkinson, "36- and 48-month neurobehavioral follow-up of children prenatally exposed to marijuana, cigarettes, and alcohol," *Journal of Developmental and Behavioral Pediatrics* 11 (1990): 49–58.

59   Caffeine effects on fetal rats: A. Nehlig and G. Debry, "Potential teratogenic and neurodevelopmental consequences of coffee and caffeine exposure: A review of human and animal data," *Neurotoxicology and Teratology* 16 (1994): 531–43.

60   Caffeine does not cause birth defects or behavioral deficits: L. Rosenberg et al., "Selected birth defects in relation to caffeine-containing beverages," *JAMA* 247 (1982): 1429–32; H. M. Barr and A. P. Streissguth, "Caffeine use during pregnancy and child outcome: A 7-year prospective study," *Neurotoxicology and Teratology* 13 (1991): 441–48.

60   Caffeine effects on conception and miscarriage: J. Golding, "Reproduction and caffeine consumption—A literature review," *Early Human Development* 43 (1995): 1–14.

60   Aspartame: R. S. London, "Saccharin and aspartame: Are they safe to consume during pregnancy?" *Journal of Reproductive Medicine* 33 (1988): 17–21; B. A. Shaywitz et al., "Aspartame, behavior, and cognitive function in children with attention deficit disorder," *Pediatrics* 93 (1994): 70–75.

60   Cyclamates: D. Stone et al., "Do artificial sweeteners ingested in pregnancy affect the offspring?" *Nature* 231 (1971): 53.

61   MSG in pregnancy: L. J. Filer and L. D. Stegin, "A report of the proceedings of an MSG workshop held August 1991," *Critical Reviews in Food Science and*

Nutrition 34 (1994): 159–74; M. Barinaga, "MSG: A 20-year debate continues," *Science* 247 (1990): 21.

62   Aspartate and glutamate in young children: J. W. Olney, "Excitotoxins in foods," *NeuroToxicology* 15 (1994): 535–44; J. W. Olney, "Excitotoxic food additives—Relevance of animal studies to human safety," *Neurobehavioral Toxicology and Teratology* 6 (1984): 455–62.

63   Occupational exposure to solvents: W. M. Kersemaekers et al., "Neurodevelopment in offspring of hairdressers," *Developmental Medicine and Child Neurology* 39 (1997): 358–62; J. A. Valciukas, "The effects of exposure to industrial and commercial solvents on the developing brain and behavior of children," in Needleman and Bellinger, *Prenatal Exposure to Toxicants*, pp. 213–32 (see full citation on page 464); Y. Bentur and G. Koren, "The common occupational exposures encountered by pregnant women," in Koren, *Maternal-Fetal Toxicology*, pp. 425–45 (see full citation on page 463).

64   Sources of lead: A. Oskarsson, *Exposure of Infants and Children to Lead* (Rome: Food and Agriculture Organization of the United Nations, 1989); V. M. Coluccio, ed., *Lead-Based Paint Hazards: Assessment and Management* (New York: Van Nostrand Reinhold, 1994).

64   Mental deficits attributable to lead: D. Bellinger et al., "Longitudinal analyses of prenatal and postnatal lead exposure and early cognitive development," *New England Journal of Medicine* 316 (1987): 1037–43.

64   Number of children with excessive lead levels: J. L. Pirkle et al., "The decline in blood lead levels in the United States. The National Health and Nutrition Examination Surveys (NHANES)," *JAMA* 272 (1994): 284–91.

66   Hiroshima: R. W. Miller, "Delayed radiation effects in atomic-bomb survivors," *Science* 166 (1969): 569–74.

66   Sensitive period for radiation exposure: Y. Bentur, "Ionizing and nonionizing radiation in pregnancy," in Koren, *Maternal-Fetal Toxicology*, pp. 515–72 (see full citation on page 463).

66   Background radiation: F. A. Mettler et al., "The 1986 and 1988 UNSCEAR reports: Findings and implications," *Health Physics* 58 (1990): 241–50.

70   Effects of microwaves and radiowaves on animal development: Bentur, "Ionizing and nonionizing radiation."

70   Male infertility: M. G. Yost, "Occupational health effects of nonionizing radiation," *Occupational Medicine* 7 (1992): 543–66.

70   Diathermy: R. Ouellet-Hellstrom and W. F. Stewart, "Miscarriages among female physical therapists who report using radio- and microwave-frequency electromagnetic radiation," *American Journal of Epidemiology* 138 (1993): 775–86; A. I. Larsen et al., "Gender-specific reproductive outcome and exposure to high-frequency electromagnetic radiation among physiotherapists," *Scandinavian Journal of Work, Environment and Health* 17 (1991): 324–29.

71   Microwave ovens: K. H. Mild and K. G. Lövstrand, "Environmental and pro-
     fessionally encountered electromagnetic fields," in O. P. Ghandi, ed., *Biological
     Effects and Medical Applications of Electromagnetic Energy* (Englewood Cliffs,
     NJ: Prentice-Hall, 1990), pp. 48–74.

72   VDTs are safe: Council on Scientific Affairs, "Health effects of video display
     terminals," *JAMA* 257 (1987): 1508–12.

72   Telephone operators: T. M. Schnorr et al., "Video display terminals and the
     risk of spontaneous abortion," *New England Journal of Medicine* 324 (1991):
     727–33.

72   Leukemia and brain tumors: B. Knave, "Electric and magnetic fields and
     health outcomes," *Scandinavian Journal of Work, Environment and Health* 20
     (1994 special): 78–89.

73   Power lines increase the risk of miscarriage: J. Juutilainen et al., "Early preg-
     nancy loss and exposure to 50-Hz magnetic fields," *Bioelectromagnetics* 14
     (1993): 229–36.

73   Power lines do not affect reproductive outcome: E. Robert, "Teratogen update:
     Electromagnetic fields," *Teratology* 54 (1996): 305–13.

73   Electric blankets increase the risk of miscarriage: K. Belanger et al.,
     "Spotaneous abortion and exposure to electric blankets and heated water
     beds," *Epidemiology* 9 (1998): 36–42.

74   MRI effects on fetal mice: D. A. Tyndall, "MRI effects on craniofacial size and
     crown-rump length in C57BL/6J mice in 1.5T fields," *Oral Surgery, Oral
     Medicine, Oral Pathology* 76 (1993): 655–60.

74   Miscarriage among MRI operators: J. A. Evans et al., "Infertility and pregnan-
     cy outcome among magnetic resonance imaging workers," *Journal of
     Occupational Medicine* 35 (1993): 1191–95.

75   Ultrasound safety: R. L. Brent et al., "Medical sonography: Reproductive
     effects and risks," in F. A. Chervenak et al., eds., *Ultrasound in Obstetrics and
     Gynecology*, vol. 1 (Boston: Little, Brown, 1993), pp. 111–32.

76   Cytomegalovirus: K. B. Fowler et al., "The outcome of congenital
     cytomegalovirus infection in relation to maternal antibody status," *New
     England Journal of Medicine* 326 (1992): 663–67; D. B. Raynor,
     "Cytomegalovirus infection in pregnancy," *Seminars in Perinatology* 17 (1993):
     394–402; M. D. Yow and G. J. Demmler, "Congenital cytomegalovirus dis-
     ease—20 years is long enough" (editorial), *New England Journal of Medicine*
     326 (1992): 702–703.

77   Toxoplasmosis: F. R. Bakht and L. O. Gentry, "Toxoplasmosis in pregnancy:
     An emerging concern for family physicians," *American Family Physician* 45
     (1992) 1683–89; W. Foulon et al., "Evaluation of the possibilities for prevent-
     ing congenital toxoplasmosis," *American Journal of Perinatology* 11 (1994):
     57–62.

79   Chicken pox: A. L. Pastuszak et al., "Outcome after maternal varicella infection in the first 20 weeks of pregnancy," *New England Journal of Medicine* 330 (1994): 901–905; G. Enders et al., "Consequences of varicella and herpes zoster in pregnancy: Prospective study of 1739 cases," *Lancet* 343 (1994): 1548–51.

80   Resurgence of prenatal syphilis: J. J. Volpe, *Neurology of the Newborn*, 3rd ed. (Philadelphia: W. B. Saunders, 1995), p. 705.

80   Maternal influenza and schizophrenia: E. O'Callaghan et al., "Schizophrenia after prenatal exposure to 1957 A2 influenza epidemic," *Lancet* 337 (1991): 1248–50; W. Adams et al., "Epidemiological evidence that maternal influenza contributes to the aetiology of schizophrenia. An analysis of Scottish, English, and Danish data," *British Journal of Psychiatry* 163 (1993): 522–34.

80   Maternal influenza and dyslexia: R. Livingston et al., "Season of birth and neurodevelopmental disorders: Summer birth is associated with dyslexia," *Journal of the American Academy of Child and Adolescent Psychiatry* 32 (1993): 612–16.

80   Maternal influenza and NTDs: M. C. Lynberg et al., "Maternal flu, fever, and the risk of neural tube defects: A population-based case-control study," *American Journal of Epidemiology* 140 (1994): 244–55.

81   Israeli study: E. Z. Zimmer et al., "Maternal exposure to music and fetal activity," *European Journal of Obstetrics, Gynecology and Reproductive Biology* 13 (1982): 209–13.

82   Thyroid hormone: Jacobson, *Developmental Neurobiology*, pp. 293–96 (see full citation on page 461); B. Contempré et al., "Detection of thyroid hormones in human embryonic cavities during the first trimester of pregnancy," *Journal of Clinical Endocrinology and Metabolism* 77 (1993): 1719–22.

82   Shyness: S. L. Gortmaker et al., "Daylength during pregnancy and shyness in children: Results from northern and southern hemispheres," *Developmental Psychobiology* 31 (1997): 107–14.

82   Footnote: P. O. D. Pharoah and K. J. Connolly, "Relationship between maternal thyroxine level during pregnancy and memory function in childhood," *Early Human Development* 25 (1991): 43–51.

84   Maternal cortisol regulates fetal circadian rhythms: B. R. H. van den Bergh, "Maternal emotions during pregnancy and fetal neonatal behavior," in J. G. Nijhuis, ed., *Fetal Behavior: Developmental and Perinatal Aspects* (New York: Oxford University Press, 1992), pp. 157–78.

84   Effects of maternal stress: M. F. A. Montagu, *Prenatal Influences* (Springfield, IL: Charles C. Thomas, 1962); D. H. Stott, "Follow-up study from birth of the effects of prenatal stresses," *Developmental Medicine and Child Neurology* 15 (1973): 770–87; J. Istvan, "Stress, anxiety, and birth outcomes: A critical review of the evidence," *Psychological Bulletin* 100 (1986): 331–48; van den Bergh, "Maternal emotions during pregnancy."

85   Santiago, Chile: M. A. Montenegro et al., "The influence of earthquake-
      induced stress on human facial clefting and its simulation in mice," *Archives of
      Oral Biology* 40 (1995): 33–37.

85   Corticosteroid effects on brain development: Jacobson, *Developmental
      Neurobiology*, p. 300 (see full citation on page 461).

85   Head size: H. C. Lou et al., "Prenatal stressors of human life affect fetal brain
      development," *Developmental Medicine and Child Neurology* 36 (1994): 826–32.

85   Catecholamines, fetal movement, and newborn irritability: van den Bergh,
      "Maternal emotions during pregnancy."

85   High-stress jobs: V. L. Katz et al., "Catecholamine levels in pregnant physi-
      cians and nurses: A pilot study of stress and pregnancy," *Obstetrics and
      Gynecology* 77 (1991): 338–42.

87   CAH: A. A. Ehrhardt and H. F. L. Meyer-Bahlburn, "Effect of prenatal sex
      hormones on gender-related behavior," *Science* 211 (1981): 1312–18.

88   DES and androgen insensitivity syndrome: L. Ellis and M. A. Ames,
      "Neurohormonal functioning and sexual orientation: A theory of
      homosexuality-heterosexuality," *Psychological Bulletin* 101 (1987): 233–58.

88   Prenatal stress feminizes male rats: I. L. Ward and K. E. Stehm, "Prenatal
      stress feminizes juvenile play patterns in male rats," *Physiology and Behavior* 50
      (1991): 601–605; I. L. Ward, "Prenatal stress feminizes and demasculinizes the
      behavior of rats," *Science* 175 (1972): 82–84; I. L. Ward and J. Weisz,
      "Maternal stress alters plasma testosterone in fetal males," *Science* 207 (1980):
      328–29; D. K. Anderson et al., "Effects of prenatal stress on differentiation of
      the sexually dimorphic nucleus of the preoptic area (SDN-POA) of the rat
      brain," *Brain Research* 332 (1985): 113–18.

88   Anterior commissure: L. S. Allen and R. A. Gorski, "Sexual orientation and
      the size of the anterior commissure in the human brain," *Proceedings of the
      National Academy of Sciences* 89 (1992): 7199–202.

88   Hypothalamic nuclei: S. LeVay, "A difference in hypothalamic structure
      between heterosexual and homosexual men," *Science* 253 (1991): 1034–37;
      M. A. Hofman and D. F. Swaab, "Sexual dimorphism of the human brain:
      Myth and reality," *Experimental and Clinical Endocrinology* 98 (1991): 161–70.

89   German studies: G. Dörner et al., "Prenatal stress as possible etiogenic factor
      of homosexuality in human males," *Endokrinologie* 75 (1980): 365–68; G.
      Dörner et al., "Stressful events in prenatal life of bi- and homosexual men,"
      Experimental and Clinical Endocrinology 81 (1983): 83–87.

89   American studies: L. Ellis et al., "Sexual orientation of human offspring may
      be altered by severe maternal stress during pregnancy," *Journal of Sex Research*
      25 (1988): 152–57; J. M. Bailey et al., "A test of the maternal stress theory of
      human male homosexuality," *Archives of Sexual Behavior* 20 (1991): 277–93.

89   Genetic and environmental determinants of homosexuality: S. LeVay, *The
      Sexual Brain* (Cambridge, MA: MIT Press, 1994).

90   Effect of maternal exercise on the fetus: M. A. M. Manders et al., "The effects of maternal exercise on fetal heart rate and movement patterns," *Early Human Development* 48 (1997): 237–47; R. A. Mittelmark et al., eds. *Exercise in Pregnancy*, 2nd ed. (Baltimore: Williams & Wilkins, 1991), pp. 225–29; M. C. Hatch et al., "Maternal exercise during pregnancy, physical fitness, and fetal growth," *American Journal of Epidemiology* 137 (1993): 1105–14.

90   Benefits of exercise: G. Varrassi et al., "Effects of physical activity on maternal plasma beta-endorphin levels and perception of labor pain," *American Journal of Obstetrics and Gynecology* 160 (1989): 707–12; C. Botkin and C. E. Driscoll, "Maternal aerobic exercise: Newborn effects," *Family Practice Research Journal* 11 (1991): 387–93.

91   Recommendations for exercise: R. W. Jarski and D. L. Trippett, "The risks and benefits of exercise during pregnancy," *Journal of Family Practice* 30 (1990): 185–89.

Chapter 4: How Birth Affects the Brain

97   Labor in sheep: P. W. Nathanielsz, "A time to be born: Implications of animal studies in maternal-fetal medicine," *Birth* 21 (1994): 163–69; G. C. Liggins, "The role of cortisol in preparing the fetus for birth," *Reproduction, Fertility and Development* 6 (1994): 141–50.

98   Labor in primates: Nathanielsz, "A time to be born"; D. M. Olson et al., "Control of human parturition," *Seminars in Perinatology* 19 (1995): 52–63.

98   Footnote: M. L. Casey and P. C. MacDonald, "Biomolecular processes in the initiation of parturition: decidual activation," *Clinical Obstetrics and Gynecology* 31 (1988): 533–52.

99   Benefits of birth stress: H. Lagercrantz and T. A. Slotkin, "The 'stress' of being born," *Scientific American* 254 (1986): 100–107.

99   Catecholamine levels in vaginal vs. cesarean delivery: L. Irestedt et al., "Fetal and maternal plasma catecholamine levels at elective cesarean section under general or epidural anesthesia versus vaginal delivery," *American Journal of Obstetrics and Gynecology* 142 (1982): 1004–10.

100   Respiratory problems following C-section: K. A. Hales et al., "Influence of labor and route of delivery on the frequency of respiratory morbidity in term neonates," *International Journal of Gynecology and Obstetrics* 43 (1993): 35–40; J. J. Morrison et al., "Neonatal respiratory morbidity and mode of delivery at term: Influence of timing of elective cesarean section," *British Journal of Obstetrics and Gynecology* 102 (1995): 101–106.

100   Other health advantages of vaginal delivery: K. Christensson et al., "Lower body temperatures in infants delivered by cesarean section than in vaginally delivered infants," *Acta Paediatrica* 82 (1993): 128–31; K. Hägnevik et al., "Catecholamine surge and metabolic adaptation in the newborn after vaginal delivery," *Acta Paediatrica Scandinavica* 73 (1984): 602–609; G. Otamiri et al., "Delayed neurological adaptation in infants delivered by elective cesarean sec-

tion and the relation to catecholamine levels," *Early Human Development* 26
(1991): 51–60.

100   Contractions may promote brain development: D. W. Sadowsky et al.,
        "Pulsatile oxytocin administered to ewes at 120 to 140 days gestational age
        increases the rate of maturation of the fetal electrocorticogram and nuchal
        activity," *Journal of Developmental Physiology* 17 (1992): 175–81.

100   Catecholamines arouse the newborn: H. Lagercrantz, "Neurochemical modu-
        lation of fetal behavior and excitation at birth," in C. von Euler et al., eds.,
        Neurobiology of Early Infant Behavior (New York: Stockton, 1989), pp. 19–29.

101   Parent-infant bonding: W. Sluckin, "Human mother-to-infant bonds," in
        Sluckin and M. Herbert, eds., *Parental Behaviour* (Oxford: Basil Blackwell,
        1986), pp. 208–27; M. E. Lamb, "Early contact and maternal-infant bonding:
        One decade later," *Pediatrics* 70 (1982): 763–68; M. J. Svejda et al., "Mother-
        infant 'bonding': Failure to generalize," *Child Development* 51 (1980): 775–79.

103   Birth trauma: Volpe, *Neurology of the Newborn*, pp. 769–92 (see full citation
        on page 469); P. G. B. Johnston, *Vulliamy's The Newborn Child*, 7th ed.
        (Edinburgh: Churchill Livingstone, 1994), pp. 113–24; M. G. Levine et al.,
        "Birth trauma: Incidence and predisposing factors," *Obstetrics and Gynecology*
        63 (1984): 792–95.

106   Brain damage caused by anoxia/hypoxia: J. A. Low, "The significance of fetal
        asphyxia in regard to motor and cognitive deficits in infancy and children," in
        N. Tejani, ed., *Obstetrical Events and Developmental Sequelae*, 2nd ed. (Boca
        Raton, FL: CRC Press, 1994), pp. 37–48.

107   Overall risk of birth asphyxia: J. Hull and K. L. Dodd, "Falling incidence of
        hypoxic-ischaemic encephalopathy in term infants," *British Journal of
        Obstetrics and Gynecology* 99 (1992): 386–91; C. M. T. Robertson and N. N.
        Finer, "Long-term follow-up of term neonates with perinatal asphyxia," *Clinics
        in Perinatology* 20 (1993): 483–99.

107   Cerebral palsy: K. B. Nelson, "Epidemiology of cerebral palsy," in Levene and
        Lilford, *Fetal and Neonatal Neurology*, pp. 681–88 (see full citation on page
        466); Volpe, *Neurology of the Newborn*, pp. 287–91; K. B. Nelson and J. H.
        Ellenberg, "Antecedents of cerebral palsy: Multivariate risk analysis," *New
        England Journal of Medicine* 315 (1986): 81–86; F. J. Stanley and E. Blair,
        "Cerebral palsy," in I. B. Pless, ed., *The Epidemiology of Childhood Disorders*
        (New York: Oxford University Press, 1994), pp. 473–97.

108   74 percent monitoring rate: S. B. Thacker et al., "Efficacy and safety of intra-
        partum electronic fetal monitoring: An update," *Obstetrics and Gynecology* 86
        (1995): 613–20.

109   Subjectivity in reading fetal monitors: N. Paneth et al., "Electronic fetal mon-
        itoring and later outcome," *Clinical and Investigative Medicine* 16 (1993):
        159–65.

109 Monitoring does not improve birth outcome: Thacker, "Efficacy and safety"; M. J. Painter et al., "Fetal heart rate patterns during labor: Is their place in obstetrics overemphasized?" in Tejani, *Obstetrical Events*, pp. 141–49.

109 False positives: K. B. Nelson et al., "Uncertain value of electronic fetal monitoring in predicting cerebral palsy," *New England Journal of Medicine* 334 (1996): 613–18.

109 Mortality rate of C-sections: M. G. Rosen, *Management of Labor: Physician Judgement and Patient Care* (New York: Elsevier, 1990), p. 3.

110 C-section rate: S. C. Curtin and L. J. Kozak, "Cesarean delivery rates in 1995 continue to decline in the United States," *Birth* 24 (1997): 194–96.

110 C-sections do not lower CP risk: J. M. Scheller and K. B. Nelson, "Does cesarean delivery prevent cerebral palsy or other neurological problems in childhood?" *Obstetrics and Gynecology* 83 (1994): 624–30.

111 Breech presentation: W. E. Scorza, "Intrapartum management of breech presentation," *Clinics in Perinatology* 23 (1996): 31–49; I. Ingemarsson et al., "Breech delivery—Management and long-term outcome," in Tejani, *Obstetrical Events*, pp. 151–65; H. Manzke, "Breech delivery in the term fetus—Relation to neuromotor dysfunction and mental handicap," in F. Kubli et al., eds., *Perinatal Events and Brain Damage in Surviving Children* (Berlin: Springer-Verlag, 1988), pp. 192–201.

113 Forceps: U. L. Verma, "A critical analysis of the long-term sequelae of midcavity forceps and vacuum-assisted delivery," in Tejani, *Obstetrical Events*, pp. 167–85; R. J. Sokol et al., "Practical diagnosis and management of abnormal labor," in J. R. Scott et al., eds., *Danforth's Obstetrics and Gynecology*, 7th ed. (Philadelphia: J.B. Lippincott, 1994), pp. 521–61; Rosen, *Management of Labor* (see full citation above); L. J. Dierker et al., "Midforceps deliveries: Long-term outcome of infants," *American Journal of Obstetrics* 154 (1986): 764–68.

114 Anesthesia may protect the baby: D. H. Penning, "Fetal and neonatal neurologic injury," in D. H. Chestnut, ed., *Obstetric Anesthesia: Principles and Practice* (St. Louis: Mosby, 1994), pp. 160–78.

116 Meperidine clearance: M. L. Wakefield, "Systemic analgesia: Opioids, ketamine, and inhalational agents," in Chestnut, *Obstetric Anesthesia*, pp. 340–52.

116 Neurobehavioral effects of meperidine: C. M. Sepkoski, "Maternal obstetric medication and newborn behavior," in J. W. Scanlon, ed., *Perinatal Anesthesia* (Boston: Blackwell, 1985), pp. 131–73.

118 Epidural drugs reach the fetus: R. Scherer and W. Holzgreve, "Influence of epidural analgesia on fetal and neonatal well-being," *European Journal of Obstetrics and Gynecology* 59 (1995 suppl.): S17–29; M. S. Golub, "Labor analgesia and infant brain development," *Pharmacology, Biochemistry and Behavior* 55 (1996): 619–28.

118 Effects of bupivacaine on the fetus: D. M. Avard, "Risks and benefits of obstetric epidural analgesia: A review," *Birth* 12 (1985): 215–25; C. M. Sepkoski et

al., "The effects of maternal epidural anesthesia on neonatal behavior during the first month," *Developmental Medicine and Child Neurology* 34 (1992): 1072–80; D. B. Rosenblatt et al., "The influence of maternal analgesia on neonatal behaviour: II. Epidural bupivacaine," *British Journal of Obstetrics and Gynecology* 88 (1981): 407–13; Golub, "Labor analgesia."

119   Longer labor with epidurals: Chestnut, *Obstetric Anesthesia*, pp. 403–19; J. A. Thorp et al., "Epidural analgesia and cesarean section for dystocia: Risk factors in nulliparas," *American Journal of Perinatology* 8 (1991): 402–10; J. A. Thorp et al., "The effect of intrapartum epidural analgesia on nulliparous labor: A randomized, controlled, prospective trial," *American Journal of Obstetrics and Gynecology* 169 (1993): 851–58.

119   Epidurals and forceps use: Chestnut, *Obstetric Anesthesia*, p. 409.

119   Epidurals and C-section rate: J. A. Thorp and G. Breedlove, "Epidural analgesia in labor: An evaluation of risks and benefits," *Birth* 23 (1996): 63–83.

119   Larger babies: T. T. Thompson et al., "Does epidural analgesia cause dystocia?" *Journal of Clinical Anesthesia* 10 (1998): 58–65; J. E. Dickinson et al., "Factors influencing the selection of analgesia in spontaneously labouring nulliparous women at term," *Australian and New Zealand Journal of Obstetrics and Gynaecology* 37 (1997): 289–93.

119   Anesthetics may interfere with pushing: Thorp et al., "Epidural analgesia and cesarean section."

120   Delaying epidural until five centimeters: Thorp and Breedlove, "Epidural analgesia in labor."

120   Avoiding epidurals for babies at risk: G. B. Merenstein and S. L. Gardner, *Handbook of Neonatal Intensive Care*, 3rd ed. (St. Louis: Mosby, 1993), pp. 33–34.

121   Effect of general anesthesia on the newborn: Sepkoski, "Maternal obstetric medication."

Chapter 5: The Importance of Touch

127   Whisker barrel plasticity: Jacobson, *Developmental Neurobiology*, pp. 483–88 (see full citation on page 461); D. M. O'Leary et al., "Development, critical period plasticity, and adult reorganizations of mammalian somatosensory systems," *Current Opinion in Neurobiology* 4 (1994): 535–44.

129   Rat toys: M. C. Diamond, "Evidence for tactile stimulation improving CNS function," in K. E. Barnard and T. B. Brazelton, eds., *Touch: The Foundation of Experience* (Madison, CT: International Universities, 1990), pp. 73–96.

129   Fetal touch sensitivity: A. W. Gottfried, "Touch as an organizer of development and learning," in Barnard and Brazelton, *Touch*, pp. 349–61.

130 Simple reflexes: N. Okado et al., "Synaptogenesis in the cervical cord of the human embryo: Sequence of synapse formation in a reflex pathway," *Journal of Comparative Neurology* 184 (1979): 491–518.

130 Emergence of body maps: H. P. Killackey et al., "The formation of a cortical somatosensory map," *Trends in Neuroscience* 18 (1995): 402–407.

130 "Practice" connections in the cortex: I. Kostovíc and P. Rakic, "Developmental history of the transient subplate zone in the visual and somatosensory cortex of the Macaque monkey and human brain," *Journal of Comparative Neurology* 297 (1990): 441–70; I. Kostovíc and M. Judas, "Prenatal and perinatal development of the human cerebral cortex," in A. Kurjak and F. A. Chervenak, eds., *The Fetus as a Patient* (New York: Parthenon, 1994), pp. 35–55.

131 Somatosensory evoked potentials: M. J. Taylor, "Evoked potentials in the neonatal period," in Levene and Lilford, *Fetal and Neonatal Neurology*, pp. 179–89 (see full citation on page 466); G. W. Bronson, "Structure, status, and characteristics of the nervous system at birth," in P. Stratton, ed., *Psychobiology of the Human Newborn* (Chichester, Eng.: John Wiley, 1982), pp. 99–118.

131 Brain imaging experiments: Chugani et al., "Positron emission tomography" (see full citation on page 462).

131 Myelination of touch pathways: Yakovlev and Lecours, "Myelogenetic cycles" (see full citation on page 462).

131 Speed of touch processing: W. Görke, "Somatosensory evoked cortical potentials indicating impaired motor development in infancy," *Developmental Medicine and Child Neurology* 28 (1986): 633–41; K. Müller et al., "Maturation of fastest afferent and efferent central and peripheral pathways: No evidence for a constancy of central conduction delays," *Neuroscience Letters* 166 (1994): 9–12.

131 Blurry borders: M. Armstrong-James, "The functional status and columnar organization of single cells responding to cutaneous stimulation in neonatal rat somatosensory cortex SI," *Journal of Physiology* 246 (1975): 501–38.

131 Five years: T. Moreau and P. Milner, "Lateral differences in the detection of touched body parts by young children," *Developmental Psychology* 17 (1981): 351–56.

131 Newborn oral discrimination: P. Rochat, "Oral touch in young infants: Responses to variations of nipple characteristics in the first months of life," *International Journal of Behavioral Development* 6 (1983): 123–33.

132 Smooth vs. nubby pacifier: A. N. Meltzoff and R. W. Borton, "Intermodal matching by human neonates," *Nature* 282 (1979): 403–404.

132 Eighteen months' discrimination: E. W. Bushnell and J. P. Boudreau, "The development of haptic perception during infancy," in M. A. Heller and W. Schiff, eds., *The Psychology of Touch* (Hillsdale, NJ: Lawrence Erlbaum, 1991), pp. 139–61.

132   Right vs. left hands: S. A. Rose, "Developmental changes in hemispheric specialization for tactual processing in very young children: Evidence from cross-modal transfer," *Developmental Psychology* 20 (1984): 568–74.

132   Sex differences in touch sensitivity: M. Hisock, "Behavioral asymmetries in normal children," in D. L. Molfese and S. J. Segalowitz, eds., *Brain Lateralization in Children: Developmental Implications* (New York: Guilford, 1988), pp. 85–169.

133   Pain sensitivity in fetuses: J. A. Rushforth, "Pain perception," in Levene and Lilford, *Fetal and Neonatal Neurology,* pp. 601–10 (see full citation on page 466).

133   Change in pain treatment for neonates: K. J. S. Anand and P. J. McGrath, "An overview of current issues and their historical background," in K. J. S. Anand and P. J. McGrath, eds., *Pain in Neonates* (Amsterdam: Elsevier, 1993), pp. 1–18.

133   Signs of pain in young babies: K. D. Craig and R.V. E. Grunau, "Neonatal pain perception and behavioral measurement," in Anand and McGrath, *Pain in Neonates,* pp. 66–105.

134   Pain in preterms: K. J. S. Anand and P. R. Hickey, "Pain and its effects in the human neonate and fetus," *New England Journal of Medicine* 317 (1987): 1321–29.

134   Increasing pain sensitivity over first days of life: K. D. Craig and R.V. E. Grunau, "Developmental issues: Infants and toddlers," in J. P. Bush and S. W. Harkins, eds., *Children in Pain: Clinical and Research Issues from a Developmental Perspective* (New York: Springer-Verlag, 1991), pp. 171–93; Rushforth, "Pain perception."

134   Opiate system well developed by birth: M. Fitzgerald, "Development of pain pathways and mechanisms," in Anand and McGrath, *Pain in Neonates,* pp. 19–37.

135   Pacifiers or sugar-soaked rags: Rushforth, "Pain perception."

135   Anesthesia for circumcision: American Academy of Pediatrics Task Force on Circumcision, "Circumcision policy statement," *Pediatrics* 103 (1999): 686–93.

135   Crying before immunization: J. E. Reisman, "Touch, motion, and proprioception," in P. Salapatek and L. Cohen, eds., *Handbook of Infant Perception,* vol. 1 (Orlando, FL: Academic Press, 1987), pp. 265–303.

136   Pain perception of children born prematurely: R. E. Grunau et al., "Children's judgments about pain at 8–10 years: Do extremely low birthweight (≤ 1000 g) children differ from full birthweight peers?" *Journal of Child Psychology and Psychiatry* 39 (1998): 587–94.

136   Circumcised vs. uncircumcised boys: A. Taddio et al., "Effect of neonatal circumcision on pain response during subsequent routine vaccination," *Lancet* 349 (1997): 599–603.

137   Newborn temperature regulation: W. Breipohl and R. Necker, "Ontogeny of thermoreception," in E. Meisami and P. S. Timiras, eds., *Handbook of Human*

Growth and Developmental Biology, vol. 1, part B (Boca Raton, FL: CRC Press, 1988), pp. 85–94.

137   Temperature discrimination in young babies: Reisman, "Touch, motion, and proprioception"; Bushnell and Boudreau, "The development of haptic perception" (see full citation on page 475).

137   Victor: R. Rymer, "A silent childhood," part I, *New Yorker* (April 13, 1992): 43–77.

137   Genie: S. Curtiss, *Genie: A Psycholinguistic Study of a Modern-Day "Wild Child"* (New York: Academic Press, 1977), p. 9.

138   Surrogate mothers: H. F. Harlow and R. R. Zimmerman, "Affectional responses in the infant monkey," *Science* 130 (1959): 421–32.

138   Peer-reared and individually housed monkeys: S. J. Suomi, "The role of tactile contact in rhesus monkey social development," in Barnard and Brazelton, *Touch*, pp. 129–64 (see full citation on page 474).

139   Rubdown or maternal licking: A. Montagu, *Touching: The Human Significance of the Skin* (New York: Columbia University Press, 1971).

139   Handled rats: R. M. Sapolsky, "The importance of a well-groomed child," *Science* 277 (1997): 1620–21.

140   Benefits of "better" mothering in rats: D. Liu et al., "Maternal care, hippocampal glucocorticoid receptors, and hypothalamic-pituitary-adrenal responses to stress," *Science* 277 (1997): 1659–62; C. Caldji et al., "Maternal care during infancy regulates the development of neural systems mediating the expression of fearfulness in the rat," *Proceedings of the National Academy of Sciences* 95 (1998): 5335–40.

140   Effect of maternal separation in infant animals: S. Levine and M. E. Stanton, "The hormonal consequences of mother-infant contact," in Barnard and Brazelton, *Touch*, pp. 165–93 (see full citation on page 474); M. Reite, "Effects of touch on the immune system," in N. Gunzenhauser, ed., *Advances in Touch: New Implications in Human Development* (Johnson & Johnson, 1990), pp. 22–31; M. Laudenslager et al., "Possible effects of early separation experiences on subsequent immune function in adult macaque monkeys," *American Journal of Psychiatry* 142 (1985): 862–64.

141   Touch promotes growth: S. M. Schanberg et al., "Maternal deprivation and growth suppression," in Gunzenhauser, *Advances in Touch*, pp. 3–10.

142   Nesting: A. F. Korner, "The many faces of touch," in Barnard and Brazelton, *Touch*, pp. 269–97 (see full citation on page 474).

142   Kangaroo care: S. M. Ludington-Hoe and S. K. Golant, *Kangaroo Care: The Best You Can Do to Help Your Preterm Infant* (New York: Bantam, 1993); A. Whitelaw, "Kangaroo baby care: Just a nice experience or an important advance for preterm infants?" *Pediatrics* 85 (1990): 604–605.

142   Indian orphans: L. Evans, "Impact of infant massage on the neonate and the parent-infant relationship," in Gunzenhauser, *Advances in Touch*, pp. 71–80.

142   Review of infant massage studies: T. Field, "Massage therapy for infants and children," *Journal of Developmental and Behavioral Pediatrics* 16 (1995): 105–11.

143   Massage benefits for preterm infants: T. M. Field et al., "Tactile/kinesthetic stimulation effects on preterm neonates," *Pediatrics* 77 (1986): 654–58; S. A. Rose et al., "Effects of prematurity and early intervention on responsivity to tactual stimuli: A comparison of preterm and full-term infants," *Child Development* 51 (1980): 416–25; S. A. Rose, "Enhancing visual recognition memory in preterm infants," *Developmental Psychology* 16 (1980): 85–92.

143   Novelty preference: M. Cigales et al., "Massage enhances recovery from habituation in normal infants," *Infant Behavior and Development* 20 (1997): 29–34.

144   Slings or snugglies: U. A. Hunziker and R. G. Barr, "Increased carrying reduces infant crying: A randomized control trial," *Pediatrics* 77 (1986): 641–48.

Chapter 6: Why Babies Love to Be Bounced:
The Precocious Sense of Balance and Motion

149   Myelination: Reisman, "Touch, motion and proprioception" (see full citation on page 476); J. Lannou et al., "Neural development of the vestibular system," in Meisami and Timiras, *Handbook of Human Growth*, pp. 1–9 (see full citation on page 476).

149   Aminoglycosides: K. R. Henry, "Abnormal auditory development resulting from exposure to ototoxic chemicals, noise, and auditory restriction," in R. Romand, ed., *Development of Auditory and Vestibular Systems*, vol. 1 (New York: Academic Press, 1983), pp. 273–308; B. A. Prieve and J. L. Yanz, "Age-dependent changes in susceptibility to ototoxic hearing loss, *Acta Oto-laryngologica* 98 (1984): 428–38; C. J. Dechesne, "The development of vestibular sensory organs in humans," in R. Romand, ed., *Development of Auditory and Vestibular Systems*, vol. 2 (New York: Elsevier, 1992), pp. 419–47.

151   Other prenatal causes of vestibular damage: Dechesne, "Development of vestibular sensory organs"; S. Snashall, "Vestibular disorders," in J. N. G. Evans, ed., *Paediatric Otolaryngology* (London: Butterworths, 1987), pp. 194–217.

151   Second most precocious sensory skill: G. Gottlieb, "Ontogenesis of sensory function in birds and mammals," in E. Tobach and L. R. Aronson, eds., *The Biopsychology of Development* (New York: Academic Press, 1971), pp. 67–128.

151   Breech position: Reisman, "Touch, motion, and proprioception" (see full citation on page 476).

153   Synaptic strength and dendritic growth: E. M. Ornitz, "Development of the vestibular system," in Meisami and Timiras, *Handbook of Human Growth*, pp. 11–32 (see full citation on page 476).

153   Vestibular contribution to posture: H. Forssberg and L. M. Nashner, "Ontogenetic development of postural control in man: Adaptation to altered support and visual conditions during stance," *Journal of Neuroscience* 2 (1988):

545–52; S. Hirabayashi and Y. Iwasaki, "Developmental perspective of sensory organization on postural control," *Brain and Development* 17 (1995): 111–13.

154   Delayed walking: I. Rapin, "Hypoactive labyrinths and motor development," *Clinical Pediatrics* 13 (1974): 922–37.

154   Vestibular problems associated with emotional and cognitive disorders: E. M. Ornitz, "Normal and pathological maturation of vestibular function in the human child," in Romand, *Development of Auditory and Vestibular Systems*, vol. 1, pp. 479–536.

154   Self-stimulation: Ibid.

155   Chair-spinning experiment: D. L. Clark et al., "Vestibular stimulation influence on motor development in infants," *Science* 196 (1977): 1228–29.

155   Contact vs. vestibular stimulation: A. F. Korner and E. B. Thoman, "The relative efficacy of contact and vestibular-proprioceptive stimulation in soothing neonates," *Child Development* 43 (1972): 443–53.

156   Visual alertness: A. F. Korner and E. B. Thoman, "Visual alertness in neonates as evoked by maternal care," *Journal of Experimental and Child Psychology* 10 (1970): 67–78.

156   Vestibular stimulation and preterm health: J. Anderson, "Sensory intervention with the preterm infant in the neonatal intensive care unit," *American Journal of Occupational Therapy* 40 (1986): 19–26; J. Provasi and P. Lequien, "Effects of nonrigid reclining infant seat on preterm behavioral states and motor activity," *Early Human Development* 35 (1993): 129–40; Korner, "The many faces of touch" (see citation on page 477).

Chapter 7: The Early World of Smell

159   Perception of flavor: J. H. McLean and M. T. Shipley, "Neuroanatomical substrates of olfaction," in M. J. Serby and K. L. Chobor, eds. *Science of Olfaction* (New York: Springer-Verlag, 1992), pp. 126–71.

159   Common chemical sense: W. L. Silver, "The common chemical sense," in T. E. Finger and W. L. Silver, eds., *Neurobiology of Taste and Smell* (New York: John Wiley, 1987), pp. 65–87.

161   Olfactory aging: Meisami, "Olfactory development in the human," in Meisami and Timiras, *Handbook of Human Growth*, pp. 33–61 (see full citation on page 476).

161   Third trimester: B. Schaal, "Olfaction in infants and children: Developmental and functional perspectives," *Chemical Senses* 13 (1988): 145–90.

162   Vomeronasal organ: C. J. Wysocki and M. Meredith, "The vomeronasal system," in Finger and Silver, *Neurobiology of Taste and Smell*, pp. 125–50; Moore and Persaud, *The Developing Human*, p. 215 (see full citation on page 461).

162   Olfactory deprivation: Meisami, "Olfactory development in the human."

162   Enriched olfactory rearing: L. Rosselli-Austin and J. Williams, "Enriched neonatal odor exposure leads to increased numbers of olfactory bulb mitral and granule cells," *Developmental Brain Research* 51 (1990): 135–37.

163   Biochemical specializations: H. J. Schmidt and G. K. Beauchamp, "Human olfaction in infancy and early childhood," in Serby and Chobor, *Science of Olfaction*, pp. 378–95.

163   Nasal plug: Meisami, "Olfactory development in the human."

163   Preterm babies: H. B. Sarnat, "Olfactory reflexes in the newborn infant," *Journal of Pediatrics* 92 (1978): 624–26.

163   Peculiar-smelling newborns: G. J. Hauser, "Peculiar odours in newborns and maternal prenatal ingestion of spicy food," *European Journal of Pediatrics* 144 (1985): 403.

164   Prenatal olfaction in rats: W. P. Smotherman and S. R. Robinson, "Behavior of rat fetuses following chemical or tactile stimulation," *Behavioral Neuroscience* 102 (1988): 24–34; W. P. Smotherman, "Odor aversion learning by the rat fetus," *Physiology and Behavior* 29 (1982): 769–71; P. E. Pedersen and E. M. Blass, "Prenatal and postnatal determinants of the first suckling episode in albino rats," *Developmental Psychobiology* 15 (1982): 349–55; P. G. Hepper, "The amniotic fluid: An important priming role in kin recognition," *Animal Behavior* 35 (1987): 1343–46.

164   Amniotic fluid and olfactory labeling: Schaal, "Olfaction in infants and children"; H. Varendi et al., "Attractiveness of amniotic fluid odor: Evidence of prenatal olfactory learning?" *Acta Paediatrica* 85 (1996): 1223–27; H. Varendi et al., "Soothing effect of amniotic fluid smell in newborn infants," *Early Human Development* 51 (1998): 47–55.

165   Mother's scent during pregnancy: G. K. Beauchamp et al., "Evidence suggesting that the odortypes of pregnant women are a compound of maternal and fetal odortypes," *Proceedings of the National Academy of Science* 92 (1995): 2617–21.

165   T-shirt experiment: M. Kaitz et al., "Mothers' recognition of their newborns by olfactory cues," *Developmental Psychology* 20 (1987): 587–91.

165   Newborn facial expressions: G. K. Beauchamp et al., "Development of chemosensory sensitivity and preference," in T. V. Getchell et al., eds., *Smell and Taste in Health and Disease* (New York: Raven Press, 1991), pp. 405–16.

166   Asafetida: L. P. Lipsitt et al., "Developmental changes in the olfactory threshold of the neonate," *Child Development* 34 (1963): 371–76.

166   Recognizing maternal breast odor: L. M. Bartoshuk and G. K. Beauchamp, "Chemical senses," *Annual Review of Psychology* 45 (1994): 419–49; H. Varendi et al., "Does the newborn baby find the nipple by smell?" *Lancet* 344 (1994): 989–90; J. W. Makin and R. H. Porter, "Attractiveness of lactating females' breast odors to neonates," *Child Development* 60 (1989): 803–10; R. H. Porter, "Human reproduction and the mother-infant relationship," in Getchell et al., *Smell and Taste*, pp. 429–42; J. M. Cernoch and R. H. Porter,

"Recognition of maternal axillary odors by infants," *Child Development* 56 (1985): 1593–98; Meisami, "Olfactory development in the human," Schaal, "Olfaction in infants and children"; (see citation on page 479).

168   Sex differences: R. D. Balogh and R. H. Porter, "Olfactory preferences resulting from mere exposure in human neonates," *Infant Behavior and Development* 9 (1986): 395–401; Schmidt and Beauchamp, "Human olfaction in infancy"; R. L. Doty et al., "Smell identification ability: Changes with age," *Science* 226 (1984): 1441–43; K. M. Dorries, "Sex differences in olfaction in mammals," in Serby and Chobor, *Science of Olfaction*, pp. 245–75 (see full citation on page 479); M. Profet, *Protecting Your Baby-to-Be: Preventing Birth Defects in the First Trimester* (Reading, MA: Addison-Wesley, 1995).

168   Hedonics: H. J. Schmidt and G. K. Beauchamp, "Adultlike odor preferences and aversions in three-year-old children," *Child Development* 59 (1988): 1136–43; Schaal, "Olfaction in infants and children" (see full citation on page 479).

169   Male rat mating preference: T. J. Fillion and E. M. Blass, "Infantile experience with suckling odors determines adult sexual behavior in male rats," *Science* 231 (1986): 729–31.

170   Olfactory bulb changes: D. A. Wilson et al., "Single-unit analysis of postnatal olfactory learning: Modified olfactory bulb output response patterns to learned attractive odors," *Journal of Neuroscience* 7 (1987): 3154–62.

170   Siblings: R. H. Porter and J. D. Moore, "Human kin recognition by olfactory cues," *Physiology and Behavior* 27 (1981): 493–95.

170   Comfort objects: Schaal, "Olfaction in infants and children" (see full citation on page 479).

Chapter 8: Taste, Milk, and the Origins of Food Preference

173   Taste buds: C. M. Mistretta, "Developmental neurobiology of the taste system," in Getchell et al., *Smell and Taste*, pp. 35–64 (see full citation on page 480).

174   Medulla: T. E. Finger, "Gustatory nuclei and pathways in the central nervous system," in Finger and Silver, *Neurobiology of Taste and Smell*, pp. 331–53 (see full citation on page 479).

174   Taste bud development: R. M. Bradley and C. M. Mistretta, "Development of taste," in Meisami and Timiras, *Handbook of Human Growth*, pp. 63–78 (see full citation on page 476).

176   Fetal swallowing: C. M. Mistretta and R. M. Bradley, "Taste and swallowing in utero: A discussion of fetal sensory function," *British Medical Bulletin* 31 (1975): 80–84.

176   Premature babies: E. Tatzer et al., "Discrimination of taste and preference for sweet in premature babies," *Early Human Development* 12 (1985): 23–30.

176 Prenatal sodium deprivation: D. L. Hill and P. R. Przekop, "Influences of dietary sodium on functional taste receptor development: A critical period," *Science* 241 (1988): 1826–28.

176 Taste stimuli in amniotic fluid: Beauchamp et al., "Development of chemosensory sensitivity" (see full citation on page 480).

176 Juniper berries: Á. Bilkó et al., "Transmission of food preference in the rabbit: The means of information transfer," *Physiology and Behavior* 56 (1994): 907–12.

177 Apple juice: W. P. Smotherman, "In utero chemosensory experience alters taste preferences and corticosterone responsiveness," *Behavioral and Neural Biology* 36 (1982): 61–68.

177 Alcohol: S. M. Nash et al., "Taste preference of the adult rat as a function of prenatal exposure to ethanol," *Journal of General Psychology* 110 (1984): 129–35.

177 Sugar preference in newborns: J. E. Steiner, "Innate, discriminative human facial expressions to taste and smell stimulation," *Annals of the New York Academy of Sciences* 237 (1974): 229–33; C. Crook, "Taste and olfaction," in Salapatek and Cohen, *Handbook of Infant Perception*, pp. 237–64 (see full citation on page 476).

178 Newborn taste reactions: D. Rosenstein and H. Oster, "Differential facial responses to four basic tastes in newborns," *Child Development* 59 (1988): 1555–68.

178 Salt poisoning: L. Finberg et al., "Mass accidental salt poisoning in infancy," *JAMA* 184 (1963): 187–90.

178 Anencephalic newborns: J. E. Steiner, "The gustofacial response: Observation on normal and anencephalic newborn infants," in J. F. Bosma, ed., *Fourth Symposium on Oral Sensation and Perception: Development in the Fetus and Infant* (Bethesda, MD: U.S. Department of Health, Education and Welfare, 1973), pp. 254–78.

178 Myelination: Brody et al., "Sequence of central nervous system myelination" (see full citation on page 462).

179 Salt perception: D. L. Hill and C. M. Mistretta, "Developmental neurobiology of salt taste sensation," *Trends in Neuroscience* 13 (1990): 188–95; G. K. Beauchamp et al., "Infant salt taste: Developmental, methodological, and contextual factors," *Developmental Psychobiology* 27 (1994): 353–65; G. K. Beauchamp and B. J. Cowart, "Congenital and experiential factors in the development of human flavor preferences," *Appetite* 6 (1985): 357–72.

179 Bitter perception: H. Lawless, "Sensory development in children: Research in taste and olfaction," *Journal of the American Dietetic Association* 85 (1985): 577–82.

180 Edible vs. inedible: P. Rozin et al., "The child's conception of food: Differentiation of categories of rejected substances in the 16 months to 5 year age range," *Appetite* 7 (1986): 141–51.

181 Why sweets and nursing are pleasurable: E. M. Blass and V. Ciaramitaro, "A new look at some old mechanisms in human newborns: Taste and tactile determinants of state, affect, and action," *Monographs of the Society for Research in Child Development*, serial no. 239, vol. 59, no. 1 (1994).

184 Cognitive advantages of breast-feeding: M. Morrow-Tlucak et al., "Breastfeeding and cognitive development in the first 2 years of life," *Social Science and Medicine* 26 (1988): 635–39; W. J. Rogan and B. C. Gladen, "Breast-feeding and cognitive development," *Early Human Development* 31 (1993): 181–93; J. I. Pollock, "Long-term associations with infant feeding in a clinically advantaged population of babies," *Developmental Medicine and Child Neurology* 36 (1994): 429–40.

184 Sociological differences: B. Taylor and J. Wadsworth, "Breast feeding and child development at five years," *Developmental Medicine and Child Neurology* 26 (1984): 73–80.

185 Eight IQ points: A. Lucas et al., "Breast milk and subsequent intelligence quotient in children born preterm," *Lancet* 339 (1992): 261–64.

185 Donor breast milk: A. Lucas et al., "A randomised multicentre study of human milk versus formula and later development in preterm infants," *Archives of Disease in Childhood* 70 (1994): F141–46.

185 Early twentieth century: C. Hoefer and M. C. Hardy, "Later development of breast fed and artificially fed infants: Comparison of physical and mental growth," *JAMA* 92 (1929): 615–19. More recently, C. R. Gale and C. N. Martyn (*Lancet* 347 [1996]: 1072–75) found higher IQ scores among elderly subjects who were born and breast-fed during the 1920s, than among those who were bottle-fed. In this era, bottle-feeding mothers tended to be of higher social standing—fewer of their husbands were employed as manual laborers than the husbands of breast-feeding women. However, the relationship between feeding method and IQ disappeared in this study when other variables (notably, pacifier use!) were factored in.

186 Taurine: R. W. Chesney, "Taurine: Its biological role and clinical implications," *Advances in Pediatrics* 32 (1985): 1–42; W. C. MacLean and J. D. Benson, "Theory into practice: The incorporation of new knowledge into infant formula," *Seminars in Perinatology* 13 (1989): 104–11; A.-L. Järvenpää et al., "Milk protein quantity and quality in the term infant. II. Effects on acidic and neutral amino acids," *Pediatrics* 70 (1982): 221–30.

188 Oleic acid: J. W. Dewille and L. A. Horrocks, "Synthesis and turnover of myelin phospholipids and cholesterol," in R. E. Martenson, ed., *Myelin: Biology and Chemistry* (Boca Raton, FL: CRC Press, 1992), pp. 213–34.

188 Benefits of infant dietary cholesterol: Worthington-Roberts and Williams, *Nutrition in Pregnancy and Lactation*, p. 357 (see full citation on page 464).

188 DHA and AA accumulation during third trimester: R. Uauy-Dagach and P. Mena, "Nutritional role of omega-3 fatty acids during the perinatal period," *Clinics in Perinatology* 22 (1995): 157–75.

188   DHA decline with formula: J. Farquharson et al., "Infant cerebral cortex phospholipid fatty-acid composition and diet," *Lancet* 340 (1992): 810–13.

188   Babies produce little DHA on their own: N. Salem et al., "Arachidonic and docosahexaenoic acids are biosynthesized from their 18-carbon precursors in human infants," *Proceedings of the National Academy of Sciences* 93 (1996): 49–54.

189   Effect of DHA deprivation on animal vision: M. Neuringer et al., "The essentiality of n-3 fatty acids for the development and function of the retina and brain," *Annual Review of Nutrition* 8 (1988): 517–41.

189   Australian study: M. Makrides et al., "Are long-chain polyunsaturated fatty acids essential nutrients in infancy?" *Lancet* 345 (1995): 1463–68.

189   No visual differences between breast- and bottle-feeding: S. M. Innis et al., "Feeding formula without arachidonic acid and docosahexaenoic acid has no effect on preferential looking acuity or recognition memory in healthy full-term infants at 9 months of age," *American Journal of Clinical Nutrition* 64 (1996): 40–46; S. M. Innis et al., "Visual acuity and blood lipids in term infants fed human milk or formulae," *Lipids* 32 (1997): 63–72.

189   No effect of DHA-enriched formula on vision: N. Auestad et al., "Visual acuity, erythrocyte fatty acid composition, and growth in term infants fed formulas with long chain polyunsaturated fatty acids for one year. Ross Pediatric Lipid Study," *Pediatric Research* 41 (1997): 1–10.

189   DHA promotes mental development: C. Agostoni et al., "Docosahexaenoic acid status and developmental quotient of health term infants," *Lancet* 346 (1995): 638; S. H. Werkman and S. E. Carlson, "A randomized trial of visual attention of preterm infants fed docosahexaenoic acid until nine months," *Lipids* 31 (1996): 91–97; S. E. Carlson et al., "Long-chain fatty acids and early visual and cognitive development of preterm infants," *European Journal of Clinical Nutrition* 48 (1994 suppl. 2): S27–30.

190   Manipulating fatty acid levels in formula: M. Neuringer, "Cerebral cortex docosahexaenoic acid is lower in formula-fed than in breast-fed infants," *Nutrition Reviews* 51 (1993): 238–41.

190   Vegetarian mothers: T. A. B. Sanders and S. Reddy, "Infant brain lipids and diet," *Lancet* 340 (1992): 1093–94.

190   Cognitive advantage for babies whose mothers took DHA supplements during lactation: R. A. Gibson et al., "Effect of increasing breast milk docosahexaenoic acid on plasma and erythrocyte phospholipid fatty acids and neural indices of exclusively breast fed infants," *European Journal of Clinical Nutrition* 51 (1997): 578–84.

191   Dietary flavors in breast milk: J. A. Mennella and G. K. Beauchamp, "Maternal diet alters the sensory qualities of human milk and the nursling's behavior," *Pediatrics* 88 (1991): 737–44; J. A. Mennella and G. K. Beauchamp, "The effects of repeated exposure to garlic-flavored milk on the nursling's behavior," *Pediatric Research* 34 (1993): 805–808; J. A.

Mennella, "Mother's milk: A medium for early flavor experiences," *Journal of Human Lactation* 11 (1995): 39–45.

192   Food preferences of bottle- vs. breast-fed infants: S. A. Sullivan and L. L. Birch, "Infant dietary experience and acceptance of solid foods," *Pediatrics* 93 (1994): 271–77.

192   Alcohol in breast milk: J. A. Mennella, "Infants' suckling responses to the flavor of alcohol in mothers' milk," *Alcoholism: Clinical and Experimental Research* 21 (1997): 581–85; J. A. Mennella and G. K. Beauchamp, "The transfer of alcohol to human milk: Effects on flavor and the infant's behavior," *New England Journal of Medicine* 325 (1991): 981–85; J. A. Mennella and C. J. Gerrish, "Effects of exposure to alcohol in mother's milk on infant sleep," *Pediatrics* 101 (1998): 915; R. E. Little et al., "Maternal alcohol use during breast-feeding and infant mental and motor development at one year," *New England Journal of Medicine* 321 (1989): 425–30; P. Schulte, "Minimizing alcohol exposure of the breastfeeding infant," *Journal of Human Lactation* 11 (1995): 317–23.

193   Taste preference in twins: L. S. Greene et al., "Heredity and experience: Their relative importance in the development of taste preference in man," *Journal of Comparative and Physiological Psychology* 89 (1975): 279–84.

193   Early dietary experience in rats: P. J. Capretta et al., "Acceptance of novel flavours is increased after early experience of diverse tastes," *Nature* 254 (1975): 689–91.

194   Two-year-olds: L. L. Birch and D. W. Marlin, "I don't like it; I never tried it: Effects of exposure on two-year-old children's food preferences," *Appetite* 3 (1982): 353–60.

194   Sugar-water preference: Beauchamp et al., "Development of chemosensory sensitivity" (see full citation on page 480).

195   Fat intake for infants and toddlers: Based on nutrient specifications for standard infant formula required by the Infant Formula Act, as cited in MacLean and Benson, "Theory into practice" (see full citation on page 483).

Chapter 9: Wiring Up the Visual Brain

196   Benefits of limited newborn vision: G. Turkewitz and P. A. Kenny, "Limitations on input as a basis for neural organization and perceptual development: A preliminary theoretical statement," *Developmental Psychobiology* 15 (1982): 357–68.

202   Thirty-two visual areas: D. C. van Essen and J. L. Gallant, "Neural mechanisms of form and motion processing in the primate visual system," *Neuron* 13 (1994): 1–10.

202   Two streams: L. G. Ungerleider and J. V. Haxby, "'What' and 'where' in the human brain," *Current Opinion in Neurobiology* 4 (1994): 157–65; M. L. Livingstone and D. Hubel, "Segregation of form, color, movement, and depth: Anatomy, physiology, and perception," *Science* 240 (1988): 740–49.

202 Strokes: M. A. Goodale and A. D. Milner, "Separate visual pathways for perception and actions," *Trends in Neuroscience* 15 (1992): 20–25.

202 *The Man Who Mistook His Wife for a Hat:* by O. Sacks (New York: Harper & Row, 1985).

204 Ganglion cells: Larsen, *Human Embryology,* pp. 341–51 (see full citation on page 461).

204 Foveal-peripheral gradient: A. E. Hendrickson, "Morphological development of the primate retina," in K. Simons, ed., *Early Visual Development: Normal and Abnormal* (New York: Oxford University, 1993), pp. 287–95.

204 LGN: R. G. Boothe, "Visual development: Central neural aspects," in Meisami and Timiras, *Handbook of Human Growth,* pp. 179–91 (see full citation on page 476); A. A. Khan et al., "Development of human lateral geniculate nucleus: An electron microscopic study," *International Journal of Developmental Neuroscience* 12 (1994): 661–72.

204 V1: Huttenlocher, "Morphometric study" (see full citation on page 461); P. R. Huttenlocher and C. de Courten, "The development of synapses in striate cortex of man," *Human Neurobiology* 6 (1987): 1–9.

204 "What" vs. "where" development: A. Burkhalter et al., "Development of local circuits in human visual cortex," *Journal of Neuroscience* 13 (1993): 1916–31.

205 Motion vs. acuity: L. Tychsen, "Vision in infants: Development and testing," in S. J. Isenberg, ed., *The Eye in Infancy,* 2nd ed. (St. Louis: Mosby, 1994), pp. 121–30.

205 Myelination: E. H. Magoon and R. M. Robb, "Development of myelin in human optic nerve and tract," *Archives of Ophthalmology* 99 (1981): 655–59; Brody et al., "Sequence of central nervous system myelination" (see full citation on page 462); A. Burkhalter et al., "Development of local circuits"; J. Atkinson, "Human visual development over the first 6 months of life: A review and a hypothesis," *Human Neurobiology* 3 (1984): 61–74.

206 Visual deprivation: T. N. Wiesel, "Postnatal development of the visual cortex and the influence of environment," *Nature* 299 (1982): 583–91.

208 Crossed eyes: M. L. J. Crawford et al., "Keeping an eye on the brain: The role of visual experience in monkeys and children," *Journal of General Psychology* 120 (1993): 7–19.

209 Orientation-rearing: C. Blakemore and G. F. Cooper, "Development of the brain depends on the visual environment," *Nature* 228 (1970): 477–78; H. V. B. Hirsch and D. N. Spinelli, "Visual experience modifies distribution of horizontally and vertically oriented receptive fields in cats," *Science* 168 (1970): 869–71.

209 Houses vs. teepees: R. C. Annis and B. Frost, "Human visual ecology and orientation anisotropies in acuity," *Science* 182 (1973): 729–31.

209 Fetuses: P. G. Hepper, "Fetal psychology: An embryonic science," in Nijhuis, *Fetal Behavior,* pp. 129–55 (see full citation on page 469).

210 Subcortical visual circuits: M. H. Johnson, "Cortical maturation and the development of visual attention in early infancy," *Journal of Cognitive Neuroscience* 2 (1990): 81–95; L. M. S. Dubowitz et al., "Visual function in the preterm and fullterm newborn infant," *Developmental Medicine and Child Neurology* 22 (1980): 465–75.

211 Eight inches: Turkewitz and Kenny, "Limitations on input" (see full citation on page 485).

212 Maturation of eye movements: Johnson, "Cortical maturation"; G. Bronson, "The postnatal growth of visual capacity," *Child Development* 45 (1974): 873–90.

213 Foveal cone density: Hendrickson, "Morphological development."

213 Contrast sensitivity: N. W. Daw, *Visual Development* (New York: Plenum, 1995), p. 37.

213 Hyperacuity: R. Held, "Development of cortically mediated visual processes in human infants," in von Euler et al., *Neurobiology of Early Infant Behavior*, pp. 155–64 (see full citation on page 472).

214 Critical period for acuity: R. Aslin, "Effects of experience on sensory and perceptual development: Implications for infant cognition," in J. Mehler and R. Fox, eds., *Neonate Cognition: Beyond the Blooming, Buzzing Confusion* (Hillsdale, NJ: Lawrence Erlbaum, 1985), pp. 157–83.

214 Externality: Bronson, "Postnatal growth."

215 Obligatory looking: Johnson, "Cortical maturation."

215 Color vision: J. E. Clavadetscher et al., "Spectral sensitivity and chromatic discriminations in 3- and 7-week-old human infants," *Journal of the Optical Society of America A, Optics and Image Science* 5 (1988): 2093–105; E. Pulos et al., "Infant color vision: A search for short-wavelength-sensitive mechanisms by means of chromatic adaptation," *Vision Research* 20 (1980): 485–93; M. S. Banks and E. Shannon, "Spatial and chromatic visual efficiency in human neonates," in C. Granrud, ed., *Visual Perception and Cognition in Infancy* (Hillsdale, NJ: Lawrence Erlbaum, 1993), pp. 1–46; Burkhalter et al., "Development of local circuits" (see full citation on page 486); D. Y. Teller and M. H. Bornstein, "Infant color vision and color perception," in Salapatek and Cohen, *Handbook of Infant Perception*, pp. 185–235 (see full citation on page 476).

217 Binocularity: R. Held, "Two stages in the development of binocular vision and eye alignment," in Simons, *Early Visual Development*, pp. 250–57; R. C. Van Sluyters et al., "The development of vision and visual perception," in L. Spillman and J. S. Werner, eds., *Visual Perception: The Neurophysiological Foundations* (San Diego: Academic Press, 1990), pp. 349–79.

219 Face recognition: G. E. Walton et al., "Recognition of familiar faces by newborns," *Infant Behavior and Development* 15 (1992): 265–69; J. Morton and M. H. Johnson, "CONSPEC and CONLERN: A two-process theory of infant face recognition," *Psychological Review* 98 (1991): 164–81; M. H. Johnson,

"Brain and cognitive development in infancy," *Current Opinion in Neurobiology* 4 (1994): 218–25.

221   Sex differences: Held, "Development of cortically mediated visual processes" (see full citation on page 487); D. F. Halpern, *Sex Differences in Cognitive Abilities*, 2nd ed. (Hillsdale, NJ: Lawrence Erlbaum, 1992), pp. 71–72: D. F. Bjorklund, *Children's Thinking: Developmental Function and Individual Differences*, 2nd ed. (Pacific Grove, CA: Brooks/Cole, 1995), p. 185.

222   Five percent: Crawford et al., "Keeping an eye on the brain" (see full citation on page 486).

222   Critical period for binocularity: E. E. Birch, "Stereopsis in infants and its developmental relation to visual acuity," in Simons, *Early Visual Development*, pp. 224–36 (see full citation on page 486); Daw, *Visual Development*, pp. 146–50.

222   Congenital cataract: W. S. Potter, "Pediatric cataracts," *Pediatric Clinics of North America* 40 (1993): 841–53; K. W. Wright et al., "Lens abnormalities," in K. W. Wright, ed., *Pediatric Ophthalmology and Strabismus* (St. Louis: Mosby, 1995), pp. 367–89.

224   Strabismus: G. K. von Noorden, *Binocular Vision and Ocular Motility: Theory and Management of Strabismus*, 5th ed. (St. Louis: Mosby, 1996); S. M. Archer, "Detection and treatment of congenital esotropia," in Simons, *Early Visual Development*, pp. 349–63 (see full citation on page 486); Wright, *Pediatric Ophthalmology and Strabismus*, pp. 179–94; K. W. Wright et al., "High-grade stereo acuity after early surgery for congenital esotropia," *Archives of Ophthalmology* 112 (1994): 913–19.

Chapter 10: How Hearing Evolves

230   Decibel table: D. S. Richards et al., "Sound levels in the human uterus," *Obstetrics and Gynecology* 80 (1992): 186–90; American Academy of Pediatrics Policy Statement, "Noise: A hazard for the fetus and newborn (RE9728)," *Pediatrics* 100 (October 1997).

234   Cochlear development: G. Bredberg, "The anatomy of the developing ear," in S. E. Trehub and B. Schneider, eds., *Auditory Development in Infancy* (New York: Plenum, 1985), pp. 3–20.

235   Hair cell development: R. Pujol et al., "Physiological correlates of development of the human cochlea," *Seminars in Perinatology* 14 (1990): 275–80.

235   Tonotopic shift: E. W. Rubel, "Ontogeny of auditory system function," *Annual Review of Physiology* 46 (1984): 213–29.

235   Early maturation of the auditory cortex: Bronson, "Structure, status, and characteristics of the nervous sytem at birth" (see full citation on page 475).

235   Synaptic refinement: D. R. Moore, "Auditory development: Central nervous aspects," in Meisami and Timiras, *Handbook of Human Growth*, pp. 131–37 (see full citation on page 476).

235   Myelination: F. H. Gilles et al., "Myelinated tracts: Growth patterns," in F. H. Gilles et al., eds., *The Developing Human Brain: Growth and Epidemiologic Neuropathology* (Boston: John Wright, 1983), pp. 117–83; Brody et al., "Sequence of central nervous system myelination" (see full citation on page 462).

236   Preterm babies: A. Starr et al., "Development of auditory function in newborn infants revealed by auditory brainstem potentials," *Pediatrics* 60 (1977): 831–39.

236   Auditory evoked potential maturation: J. J. Eggermont, "Development of auditory evoked potentials," *Acta Otolaryngology* 112 (1992): 197–200; Moore, "Auditory development."

237   Prenatal hearing: P. G. Hepper and B. S. Shahidullah, "Development of fetal hearing," *Archives of Disease in Childhood* 71 (1994): F81–87; B. S. Shahidullah and P. G. Hepper, "Frequency discrimination by the fetus," *Early Human Development* 36 (1994): 13–26; Richards et al., "Sound levels in the human uterus"; Rubel, "Ontogeny of auditory system function."

239   Noise damage: Pujol et al., "Physiological correlates"; K. J. Gerhardt, "Prenatal and perinatal risks of hearing loss," *Seminars in Perinatology* 14 (1990): 299–304; M. Nyman et al., "Vibroacoustic stimulation and intrauterine sound pressure levels," *Obstetrics and Gynecology* 78 (1991): 803–806; American Academy of Pediatrics, "Noise: A hazard for the fetus and newborn."

241   Dr. Seuss experiments: A. J. DeCasper and W. P. Fifer, "Of human bonding: Newborns prefer their mothers' voices," *Science* 208 (1980): 1174–76; G. Kolata, "Studying learning in the womb," *Science* 225 (1984): 302–303.

241   Babies prefer muffled maternal voice: W. P. Fifer and C. Moon, "Psychobiology of newborn auditory preferences," *Seminars in Perinatology* 13 (1989): 430–33.

242   Maternal heartbeat: K. E. Barnard and H. L. Bee, "The impact of temporally patterned stimulation on the development of preterm infants," *Child Development* 54 (1983): 1156–67.

242   Soap opera theme: P. G. Hepper, "Fetal 'soap' addiction," *Lancet* (June 11, 1988), pp. 1347–48.

242   Father's voice: A. J. DeCasper and P. A. Prescott, "Human newborns' perception of male voices: Preference, discrimination, and reinforcing value," *Developmental Psychobiology* 17 (1984): 481–91.

243   Newborn hearing threshold: R. N. Aslin et al., "Auditory development and speech perception in infancy," in P. H. Mussen, ed., *Handbook of Child Psychology*, 4th ed., vol. 2: *Infancy and Developmental Psychobiology* (New York: John Wiley, 1983), pp. 573–687.

243   Moving to adult speech: W. S. Condon and L. W. Sander, "Neonate move-
      ment is synchronized with adult speech: Interactional participation and lan-
      guage acquisition," *Science* 183 (1974): 99–101.

243   Preference for native tongue: J. Mehler et al., "A precursor of language acqui-
      sition in young infants," *Cognition* 29 (1988): 143–78.

243   Sound localization: D. W. Muir, "The development of infants' auditory spatial
      sense," in Trehub and Schneider, *Auditory Development in Infancy*, pp. 51–83
      (see full citation on page 488).

244   Frequency sensitivity: L. A. Werner and G. R. VandenBos, "Developmental
      psychoacoustics: What infants and children hear," *Hospital and Community
      Psychiatry* 44 (1993): 624–26; D. C. Teas et al., "An analysis of auditory brain-
      stem responses in infants," *Hearing Research* 7 (1982): 19–54.

244   Sound localization: G. Ehret, "Auditory development: Psychophysical and
      behavioral aspects," in Meisami and Timiras, *Handbook of Human Growth*, pp.
      141–54 (see full citation on page 476); D. W. Muir et al, "The development of
      a human auditory localization response: A U-shaped function," *Canadian
      Journal of Psychology* 43 (1989): 199–216.

245   Threshold: J. E. Peck, "Development of hearing. Part III. Postnatal develop-
      ment," *Journal of the American Academy of Audiology* 6 (1995): 113–23.

246   Temporal resolution: B. A. Morrongiello and S. E. Trehub, "Age-related
      changes in auditory temporal perception," *Journal of Experimental Child
      Psychology* 44 (1987): 413–26.

246   Sounds in a noisy background: Ehret, "Auditory development"; Werner and
      VandenBos, "Developmental psychoacoustics."

247   Motherese: A. Fernald, "Four-month-old infants prefer to listen to motherese,"
      Infant Behavior and Development 8 (1985): 181–95; J. Mehler et al., "Infant
      recognition of mother's voice," *Perception* 7 (1978): 491–97.

249   Early auditory deprivation: E. W. Rubel, "Auditory system development," in
      G. Gottlieb and N. A. Krasnegor, eds., *Measurement of Audition and Vision in
      the First Year of Postnatal Life: A Methodological Overveiw* (Norwood, NJ:
      Ablex, 1985), pp. 53–90; A. J. King and D. R. Moore, "Plasticity of auditory
      maps in the brain," *Trends in Neuroscience* 14 (1991): 31–37.

249   Click-rearing: D. H. Sanes and M. Constantine-Paton, "The sharpening of
      frequency turning curves requires patterned activity during development in
      the mouse, *Mus musculus*," *Journal of Neuroscience* 5 (1985): 1152–66.

249   Plasticity in binaural interaction: D. R. Moore, "Effects of early auditory expe-
      rience on development of binaural pathways in the brain," *Seminars in
      Perinatology* 14 (1990): 294–98.

250   Plasticity in the congenitally deaf: H. J. Neville, "Neurobiology of cognitive
      and language processing: Effects of early experience," in Gibson and Petersen,
      Brain Maturation and Cognitive Development, pp. 355–80 (see full citation on
      page 462).

250   Congenital hearing loss: S. Bellman, "Disorders of hearing," in Levene and
        Lilford, *Fetal and Neonatal Neurology*, pp. 591–99 (see full citation on page
        466).

251   Rubella: J. B. Hardy, "Clinical and developmental aspects of congenital rubel-
        la," *Archives of Otolaryngology* 98 (1973): 230–36.

251   CMV: Fowler et al., "Outcome of congenital cytomegalovirus infection" (see
        full citation on page 468).

251   Ototoxic drugs and chemicals: Henry, "Abnormal auditory development" (see
        full citation on page 478); C. M. Henley and L. P. Rybak, "Ototoxicity in
        developing mammals," *Brain Research Reviews* 20 (1995): 68–90.

252   Perinatal factors: G. T. Mencher and L. S. Mencher, "Auditory pathologies in
        infancy," in Trehub and Schneider, *Auditory Development in Infancy*, pp.
        133–56 (see full citation on page 488).

254   Auditory screening recommendations: NIH Consensus Development Panel,
        Early Indentification of Hearing Impairment in Infants and Young Children
        (Bethesda, MD: National Institutes of Health, 1993).

254   Incidence of OM: A. M. Shapiro and C. D. Bluestone, "Otitis media
        reassessed: Up-to-date answers to some basic questions," *Postgraduate Medicine*
        97 (1995): 73–82.

254   Footnote: K. R. White, in *Early Identification of Hearing Impairment*, pp. 115–18.

255   10 to 40 dB hearing loss: T. J. Fria et al., "Hearing acuity of children with oti-
        tis media with effusion," *Archives of Otolaryngology* 111 (1985): 10–16; D. J.
        Messer, *The Development of Communication: From Social Interaction to Language*
        (Chichester, Eng.: John Wiley, 1994), p. 240.

255   Persistent effusion: C. D. Bluestone and J. O. Klein, *Otitis Media in Infants and
        Children*, 2nd ed. (Philadelphia: W. B. Saunders, 1995), pp. 41–43.

256   Detecting sounds in a noisy environment: Moore, "Effects of early auditory
        experience."

256   High-frequency hearing loss: R. H. Margolis et al., "Effects of otitis media on
        extended high-frequency hearing in children," *Annals of Otology, Rhinology,
        and Laryngology* 102 (1993): 1–5.

256   Effect of chronic OM on verbal/academic performance: P. A. Silva et al.,
        "Some audiological, psychological, educational and behavioral characteristics
        of children with bilateral otitis media with effusion: A longitudinal study,"
        Journal of Learning Disabilities 19 (1986): 165–69; D. W. Teele et al., "Otitis
        media in infancy and intellectual ability, school achievement, speech, and
        language at age 7 years," *Journal of Infectious Diseases* 162 (1990): 685–94;
        S. A. F. Peters et al., "The effects of early bilateral otitis media with effusion
        on educational attainment: A prospective cohort study," *Journal of Learning
        Disabilities* 27 (1994): 111–21; J. Lous, "Otitis media and reading achievement:
        A review," *International Journal of Pediatric Otorhinolaryngology* 32 (1995):

105–21; J. E. Roberts et al., "Otitis media in early childhood and later language," *Journal of Speech and Hearing Research* 34 (1991): 1158–68.

257   Guidelines for treating chronic OM: S. E. Stool et al., "Otitis media with effusion in young children," *Clinical Practice Guideline* 12 (Rockville, MD: Department of Health and Human Services, Agency for Health Care Policy and Research, 1994), Pub. #94-0622.

257   Spontaneous healing of chronic and acute OM: R. M. Rosenfeld, "What to expect from medical treatment of otitis media," *Pediatric Infectious Disease Journal* 14 (1995): 731–38.

258   Breast-feeding prevents OM: D. A. Randall et al., "Management of recurrent otitis media," *American Family Physician* 45 (1992): 2117–223; J. O. Klein, "Otitis media," *Clinical Infectious Diseases* 19 (1994): 823–32; B. Duncan et al., "Exclusive breast-feeding for at least 4 months protects against otitis media," *Pediatrics* 91 (1993): 867–72.

258   OM in day care: E. R. Wald et al., "Frequency and severity of infections in day care," *Journal of Pediatrics* 112 (1988): 540–46.

258   Secondhand smoke: R. A. Etzel et al., "Passive smoking and middle ear effusion among children in day care," *Pediatrics* 90 (1992): 228–32.

Chapter 11: Motor Milestones

261   Motor development does not predict IQ: A. J. Capute et al., "Cognitive-motor interactions: The relationship of infant gross motor attainment to IQ at 3 years," *Clinical Pediatrics* 24 (1985): 671–75.

261   Developmental tables are a consensus from the following sources: N. Bayley, *Bayley Scales of Infant Development* (New York: Psychological Corp., 1969); W. K. Frankenburg and J. B. Dodds, "The Denver developmental screening test," *Journal of Pediatrics* 71 (1967): 181–91; A.J. Capute et al., "Normal gross motor development: The influences of race, sex and socioeconomic status," *Developmental Medicine and Child Neurology* 27 (1985): 635–43; M. C. Piper and J. Darrah, *Motor Assessment of the Developing Infant* (Philadelphia: W. B. Saunders, 1994); D. L. Gallahue and J. C. Ozmun, *Understanding Motor Development: Infants, Children, Adolescents, Adults*, 3rd ed. (Madison, WI: Brown & Benchmark, 1995).

269   First trimester movements: H. F. R. Prechtl, "Ultrasound studies of human fetal behavior," *Early Human Development* 12 (1985): 91–98.

269   Movements peak in midgestation: G. H. A. Visser, "The second trimester," in Nijhuis, *Fetal Behavior* (see full citation on page 469).

269   Immobilized chick leg: D. B. Drachman and A. J. Coulombre, "Experimental clubfoot and arthrogryposis multiplex congenita," *Lancet* ii (1962): 523–26.

270   Fetal breathing and lung development: G. C. Liggins et al., "The effect of spinal cord transection on lung development in the fetal sheep," *Journal of Developmental Psychology* 3 (1981): 267–74.

270   Hopi babies: W. Dennis and M. G. Dennis, "The effect of cradling practices upon the onset of walking in Hopi children," *Journal of Genetic Psychology* 56 (1940): 77–86.

270   Twin studies: M. B. McGraw, *The Neuromuscular Maturation of the Human Infant* (London: MacKeith Press, 1989, originally published in 1945); Gallahue and Ozmun, *Understanding Motor Development*, p. 60 (see full citation on page 492).

271   Footnote: B. J. Cratty, *Perceptual and Motor Development in Infants and Children*, 3rd ed. (Englewood Cliffs, NJ: Prentice-Hall, 1986), pp. 83–84.

273   Speed of motor transmission: J. A. Eyre et al., "Constancy of central conduction delays during development in man: Investigation of motor and somatosensory pathways," *Journal of Physiology* 434 (1991): 441–52.

273   Faster movements: K. Müller and V. Hömberg, "Development of speed of repetitive movements in children is determined by structural changes in corticospinal efferents," *Neuroscience Letters* 144 (1992): 57–60.

274   Blind babies: L. Smolak, *Infancy* (Englewood Cliffs, NJ: Prentice-Hall, 1986), p. 101.

275   Sleeping on back: B. E. Davis et al., "Effects of sleep position on infant motor development," *Pediatrics* 102 (1998): 1135–40.

275   African infant precosity: R. M. Malina, "Racial/ethnic variation in the motor development and performance of American children," *Canadian Journal of Sport Sciences* 13 (1988): 136–43; Cratty, *Perceptual and Motor Development*, pp. 80–83; C. M. Super, "Environmental effects on motor development: The case of 'African infant precocity,'" *Developmental Medicine and Child Neurology* 18 (1976): 561–67.

277   Cerebellum in motor learning: L. G. Ungerleider, "Functional brain imaging studies of cortical mechanisms for memory," *Science* 270 (1995): 769–75.

277   Neural selection in motor learning: E. Thelen, "Motor development: A new synthesis," *American Psychologist* 50 (1995): 79–95.

278   Dynamic exploratory movements: E. W. Bushnell and J. P. Boudreau, "Motor development and the mind: The potential role of motor abilities as a determinant of aspects of perceptual development," *Child Development* 64 (1993): 1005–21.

278   Self-care skills: R. P. Erhardt, "Eye-hand coordination," in J. Case-Smith and C. Pehoski, eds., *Development of Hand Skills in the Child* (Rockville, MD: American Occupational Therapy Association, 1992), pp. 13–27.

279   Pre-reaching: C. von Hofsten, "The organization of arm and hand movements in the neonate," in von Euler et al., *Neurobiology of Early Infant Behavior*, pp. 129–42 (see full citation on page 472).

279   Moving an arm while looking at it: A. L. H. van der Meer et al., "The functional significance of arm movements in neonates," *Science* 267 (1995): 693–95.

279   Differentiating hand from arm extension: C. von Hofsten, "Developmental changes in the organization of prereaching movements," *Child Development* 20 (1984): 378–88.

279   Corticospinal myelination: C. Pehoski, "Central nervous system control of precision movements of the hand," in Case-Smith and Pehoski, *Development of Hand Skills*, pp. 1–12.

280   Reaching may begin earlier in more active infants: E. Thelen and D. Corbetta, "Exploration and selection in the early acquisition of skill," *International Review of Neurobiology* 37 (1994): 75–102.

280   Handedness incidence: H. E. Fitzgerald et al., "The organization of lateralized behavior during infancy," in H. E. Fitzgerald et al., eds, *Theory and Research in Behavioral Pediatrics* (New York: Plenum, 1991), pp. 155–84.

281   Left-handed mothers vs. fathers: Cratty, *Perceptual and Motor Development*, p. 244.

281   Deeper fissures: R. C. Gur et al., "Differences in the distribution of gray and white matter in human cerebral hemispheres," *Science* 207 (1980): 1226–28.

281   Fetal thumb-sucking: P. G. Hepper et al., "Handedness in the human fetus," *Neuropsychologia* 29 (1991): 1107–11.

281   Newborn touch processing: A. Majnemer and B. Rosenblatt, "Functional interhemispheric asymmetries at birth as demonstrated by somatosensory evoked potentials," *Journal of Child Neurology* 7 (1992): 408–12.

282   Prenatal position: J. A. Churchill et al., "The association of position at birth and handedness," *Pediatrics* 29 (1962): 307–309; J. S. H. Vles et al., "Handedness not related to fetal position," *Neuropsychologia* 27 (1989): 1017–18.

282   Early reaching matches favored head orientation: G. F. Michel and D. A. Harkins, "Postural and lateral asymmetries in the ontogeny of handedness during infancy," *Developmental Psychobiology* 19 (1986): 247–58.

282   Parents hold babies on the left: Fitzgerald et al., "The organization of lateralized behavior."

282   Pathological left-handedness: L. J. Harris and D. F. Carlson, "Pathological left-handedness: An analysis of theories and evidence," in Molfese and Segalowitz, *Brain Lateralization in Children*, pp. 289–372 (see full citation on page 476).

284   Walking and cognitive/social spurts: Smolak, *Infancy*, pp. 89–91.

285   Experiments on two-to-six-week-olds: E. Thelen et al., "The relationship between physical growth and a newborn reflex," *Infant Behavior and Development* 7 (1984): 479–93.

285   Kicking: E. Thelen et al., "An 'outside-in' approach to the development of leg movement patterns," in von Euler et al., *Neurobiology of Early Infant Behavior*, pp. 107–18 (see full citation on page 472).

285   Changes in bodily proportion: E. Thelen and N. S. Bradley, "Motor development: Posture and locomotion," in Meisami and Timiras, *Handbook of Human
Growth*, pp. 221–35 (see full citation on page 476).

286   Gradient in motor cortex: M. Konner, "Universals of behavioral development
in relation to brain myelination," in Gibson and Petersen, *Brain Maturation
and Cognitive Development*, pp. 181–223 (see full citation on page 462).

286   Corticospinal myelination: Brody et al., "Sequence of central nervous system
myelination" (see full citation on page 462).

286   Mature stride: H. Forssberg, "Infant stepping and development of plantigrade
gait," in von Euler et al, *Neurobiology of Early Infant Behavior*, pp. 119–28 (see
full citation on page 472).

287   Practicing the walking reflex: P. R. Zelazo et al., "'Walking' in the newborn,"
Science 176 (1972): 314–15.

287   Infant walkers: M. V. Ridenour, "Infant walkers: Developmental tool or inherent danger," *Perceptual and Motor Skills* 55 (1982): 1201–2; A. C. Siegel and
R. V. Burton, as reported by J. E. Brody, "Baby walkers may slow infants'
development," *New York Times* (October 14, 1997).

289   Cerebellar neurons: M. K. Floeter and W. T. Greenough, "Cerebellar plasticity: Modification of Purkinje cell structure by differential rearing in monkeys,"
Science 206 (1979): 227–29.

289   Breast-feeding and motor development: Taylor and Wadsworth, "Breast feeding and child development" (see full citation on page 483); C. I. Lanting et
al., "Neurological differences between 9-year-old children fed breast-milk or
formula-milk as babies," *Lancet* 344 (1994): 1319–22.

Chapter 12: Social-Emotional Growth

291   Marshmallow experiment: Y. Shoda et al., "Predicting adolescent cognitive
and self-regulatory competencies from preschool delay of gratification:
Identifying diagnostic conditions," *Developmental Psychology* 26 (1990):
978–86. This experiment is also described by Daniel Goleman, who popular-
ized the term *emotional intelligence* in his recent book of that title (New York:
Bantam, 1995), pp. 80–83.

293   Neurologist: Quoted in Goleman, *Emotional Intelligence*, p. 297.

293   Austism: J. Bachevalier, "Medial temporal lobe structures and autism: A
review of clinical and experimental findings," *Neuropsychologia* 32 (1994):
627–48.

293   Role of the amygdala: J. E. LeDoux, "Emotion: Clues from the brain," *Annual
Review of Psychology* 46 (1995): 209–35; J. Kagan, *Galen's Prophecy:
Temperament in Human Nature* (New York: Basic Books, 1994), pp. 102–104;
Goleman, *Emotional Intelligence*, pp. 297–300.

294   Emotion and reason: A. R. Damasio, *Descartes' Error: Emotion, Reason, and the Human Brain* (New York: Putnam, 1995).

295   Anterior cingulate damage: D. M. Tucker et al., "Social and emotional self-regulation," *Annals of the New York Academy of Sciences* 769 (1995): 213–39.

295   Inhibitory cortical feedback: J. L. Cummings, "Anatomic and behavioral aspects of frontal-subcortical circuits," *Annals of the New York Academy of Sciences* 769 (1995): 1–13; R. J. Davidson and S. K. Sutton, "Affective neuroscience: The emergence of a discipline," *Current Opinion in Neurobiology* 5 (1995): 217–24.

295   Left vs. right metabolic rate: R. C. Gur et al., "Sex differences in regional cerebral glucose metabolism during a resting state," *Science* 267 (1995): 528–31.

295   Emotional content of language: R. Mayeux and E. R. Kandel, "Disorders of language: The aphasias," in E. R. Kandel et al., eds, *Principles of Neural Science*, 3rd ed. (New York: Elsevier, 1991), pp. 848–49.

296   Greater emotional sensitivity on left side of body: Tucker et al., "Social and emotional self-regulation."

296   Temperamental differences: Davidson and Sutton, "Affective neuroscience"; N. A. Fox, "Dynamic cerebral processes underlying emotion regulation," *Monographs of the Society for Research on Child Development*, 59, nos. 2–3 (1994): 152–66.

296   Alternating growth spurts: R. W. Thatcher, "Cyclic cortical reorganization: Origins of human cognitive development," in G. Dawson and K. W. Fischer, eds., *Human Behavior and the Developing Brain* (New York: Guilford, 1994), pp. 232–66.

297   Prenatal amygdala maturation: J. Bachevalier et al., "Regional distribution of [^{3}H]naloxone binding in the brain of a newborn rhesus monkey," *Developmental Brain Research* 25 (1986): 302–308.

297   Prefrontal synaptic and dendritic development: P. R. Huttenlocher, "Synaptic density in human frontal cortex—Developmental changes and effects of aging," *Brain Research* 163 (1979): 195–205.

297   Limbic myelination: K. R. Gibson, "Myelination and behavioral development: A comparative perspective on questions of neoteny, altriciality, and intelligence," in Gibson and Petersen, *Brain Maturation and Cognitive Development*, pp. 29–63 (see full citation on page 462).

299   Distinct cries: J. J. Campos et al., "Socioemotional development," in Mussen, *Handbook of Child Psychology*, pp. 783–915 (see full citation on page 489).

300   Imitation in newborns: T. M. Field et al., "Discrimination and imitation of facial expressions by neonates," *Science* 218 (1982): 179–81.

300   Crying in response to another infant's cries: L. Brothers, "A biological perspective on empathy," *American Journal of Psychiatry* 146 (1989): 10–19.

300   Autistic children do not imitate: T. Charman et al., "Infants with autism: An investigation of empathy, pretend play, joint attention, and imitation," *Developmental Psychology* 33 (1997): 781–89.

300   Newborn frontal EEGs: N. A. Fox and R. J. Davidson, "Taste-elicited changes in facial signs of emotion and the asymmetry of brain electrical activity in human newborns," *Neuropsychologia* 24 (1986): 417–22.

301   Neural mechanisms of smiling: Konner, "Universals of behavioral development" (see citation on page 495).

302   Spontaneous vs. voluntary smiles: Damasio, *Descartes' Error*, pp. 140–42 (see full citation on page 495).

302   Protoconversation: C. Trevarthen, "Development of early social interactions and the affective regulation of brain growth," in von Euler et al., *Neurobiology of Early Infant Behavior*, pp. 191–215 (see full citation on page 472).

303   Anterior cingulate: U. Jürgens and D. von Cramon, "On the role of the anterior cingulate cortex in phonation: A case report," *Brain and Language* 15 (1982): 234–48.

304   Ten-month-olds' frontal EEGs: R. J. Davidson and N. A. Fox, "Asymmetrical brain activity discriminates between positive and negative affective stimuli in human infants," *Science* 218 (1982): 1235–37.

305   Attachment and stranger anxiety: Konner, "Universals of behavioral development" (see citation on page 495).

306   Independent locomotion: Ibid.

307   Object permanence: N. A. Fox and M. A. Bell, "Electrophysiological indices of frontal lobe development: Relations to cognitive and affective behavior in human infants over the first year of life," *Annals of the New York Academy of Sciences* 608 (1990): 677–98.

307   Attachment and frontal-lobe EEGs: N. A. Fox and R. J. Davidson, "Patterns of brain electrical activity during facial signs of emotion in 10-month-old infants," *Developmental Psychology* 24 (1988): 230–36.

308   Work and attachment: For a more expanded discussion of this issue and its political ramifications see R. Karen, *Becoming Attached: Unfolding the Mystery of the Infant-Mother Bond and Its Impact on Later Life* (New York: Warner Books, 1994).

308   Strange Situation: Campos et al., "Socioemotional development."

309   Consensus study: M. E. Lamb et al., "Nonmaternal care and the security of infant-mother attachment: A reanalysis of the data," *Infant Behavior and Development* 15 (1992): 71–83.

309   Critique of the Strange Situation: K. A. Clarke-Stewart, "Infant day care: Maligned or malignant?" *American Psychologist* 44 (1989): 266–73.

309   Negative effects of nonmaternal care: D. L. Vandell and M. A. Corasaniti, "Variations in early child care: Do they predict subsequent social, emotional, and cognitive differences?" *Early Childhood Research Quarterly* 5 (1990): 555–72; N. Baydar and J. Brooks-Gunn, "Effects of maternal employment and child-care arrangements on preschoolers' cognitive and behavioral outcomes: Evidence from the children of the National Longitudinal Survey of Youth," *Developmental Psychology* 27 (1991): 932–45; J. Belsky and D. Eggebeen, "Early and extensive maternal employment and young children's socioemotional development: Children of the National Longitudinal Survey of Youth," *Journal of Marriage and the Family* 53 (1991): 1083–98; J. E. Bates et al., "Child-care history and kindergarten adjustment," *Developmental Psychology* 30 (1994): 690–700.

309   Positive effects of nonmaternal care: S. Scarr and M. Eisenberg, "Child care research: Issues, perspectives, and results," *Annual Review of Psychology* 44 (1993): 613–44; B.-E. Andersson, "Effects of public day-care: A longitudinal study," *Child Development* 60 (1989): 857–66.

310   Attachment, nonmaternal care, and mothering style: NICHD Early Child Care Research Network, "The effects of infant child care on infant-mother attachment security: Results of the NICHD study of early child care," *Child Development* 68 (1997): 860–79.

310   Effect of nonmaternal care at two to three years of age: NICHD Early Child Care Research Network, "Early child care and self-control, compliance, and problem behavior at twenty-four and thirty-six months," *Child Development* 69 (1998): 1145–70.

310   Influence of working vs. nonworking parents: NICHD Early Child Care Research Network, "Relations between family predictors and child outcomes: Are they weaker for children in child care?" *Developmental Psychology* 34 (1998): 1119–28.

311   Later emotional effects of maternal employment: Vandell and Corasaniti, "Variations in early child care"; Baydar and Brooks-Gunn, "Effects of maternal employment"; Belsky and Eggebeen, "Early and extensive maternal employment"; Bates et al., "Child-care history."

311   Boys fare worse, girls better, when their mothers work: NICHD Early Child Care Research Network, "The effects of infant child care"; S. Desai et al., "Mother or market? Effects of maternal employment on the intellectual ability of 4-year-old children," *Demography* 26 (1989): 545–61; Scarr and Eisenberg, "Child care research"; Baydar and Brookes-Gunn, "Effects of maternal employment."

311   Most American children receive substandard care: A. B. Barnet and R. J. Barnet, *The Youngest Minds* (New York: Simon & Schuster, 1998), p. 252.

312   Hippocampal atrophy: R. M. Sapolsky, "Why stress is bad for your brain," *Science* 273 (1996): 749–50.

312   Effect of stress on babies' brain activity: M. R. Gunnar and C. A. Nelson, "Event-related potentials in year-old infants: Relations with emotionality and cortisol," *Child Development* 65 (1994): 80–94.

312   Responsive caregiving buffers infants' stress response: M. R. Gunnar, "Quality
      of early care and buffering of neuroendocrine stress reactions: Potential effects
      on the developing human brain," *Preventative Medicine* 27 (1998): 208–11;
      M. R. Gunnar et al., "The stressfulness of separation among nine-month-old
      infants: Effects of social context variables and infant temperament," *Child
      Development* 63 (1992): 290–303.

313   Emotional differences between men and women: A. S. R. Manstead, "Gender
      differences in emotion," in A. Gale and M. W. Eysenck, eds., *Handbook of
      Individual Differences: Biological Perspectives* (Chichester, Eng.: John Wiley,
      1992), pp. 355–87.

313   Differences between girls and boys: J. J. Haviland and C. Z. Malatesta, "The
      development of sex differences in nonverbal signals: Fallacies, facts, and fan-
      tasies," in C. Mayo and N. M. Henley, eds., *Gender and Nonverbal Behavior*
      (New York: Springer-Verlag, 1981), pp. 183–208.

314   Differential parental treatment: Manstead, "Gender differences in emotion";
      Campos et al., "Socioemotional development" (see citation on page 496);
      C. Z. Malatesta and J. J. Haviland, "Learning display rules: The socialization
      of emotion expression in infancy," *Child Development* 53 (1982): 991–1003.

314   PET studies: P. J. Andreason et al., "Gender-related differences in regional
      cerebral glucose metabolism in normal volunteers," *Psychiatry Research* 51
      (1993): 175–83; R. C. Gur et al., "Sex differences in regional cerebral glucose
      metabolism" (see full citation on page 496).

315   Sex differences in monkeys' brains: P. S. Goldman et al., "Sex-dependent
      behavioral effects of cerebral cortical lesions in the developing rhesus mon-
      key," *Science* 186 (1974): 540–42; J. Bachevalier et al., "Gender differences in
      visual habit formation in 3-month-old rhesus monkeys," *Developmental
      Psychobiology* 22 (1989): 585–99; W. H. Overman et al., "Sexually dimorphic
      brain-behavior development: A comparative perspective," in N. A. Krasnegor
      et al., eds, *Development of the Prefrontal Cortex: Evolution, Neurobiology, and
      Behavior* (Baltimore: Paul H. Brookes, 1997), pp. 337–57.

315   Limbic development in boys vs. girls, W. H. Overman et al., "Cognitive gen-
      der differences in very young children parallel biologically based cognitive
      gender differences in monkeys," *Behavioral Neuroscience* 110 (1996): 673–84.

317   Inhibited temperament: J. Kagan et al., "Temperamental variation in response
      to the unfamiliar," in N. A Krasnegor et al., eds., *Perinatal Development: A
      Psychobiological Perspective* (Orlando, FL: Academic Press, 1987), pp. 421–40.

318   Inhibition in Asian cultures: X. Chen et al., "Child-rearing attitudes and
      behavioral inhibition in Chinese and Canadian toddlers: A cross-cultural
      study," *Developmental Psychology* 34 (1998): 677–86.

318   Physiology of timidity: Kagan, *Galen's Prophecy* (see full citation on page 495).

320   Inhibition and frontal lobe activation: N. A. Fox et al., "Frontal activation
      asymmetry and social competence at four years of age," *Child Development* 66
      (1995): 1770–84.

320 EEG measurements during maternal separation: N. A. Fox, "If it's not left, it's right: Electroencephalograph asymmetry and the development of emotion," *American Psychologist* 46 (1991): 863–72.

320 Predicting temperament in early infancy: Kagan, *Galen's Prophecy*, pp. 170–207 (see full citation on page 495); S. D. Calkins et al., "Behavioral and physiological antecedents of inhibited and uninhibited behavior," *Child Development* 67 (1996): 523–40.

322 Heritability of personality traits: R. Plomin, *Nature and Nurture: An Introduction to Human Behavioral Genetics* (Pacific Grove, CA: Brooks/Cole, 1990), pp. 90–96.

323 Effect of early isolation on the monkey brain: G. W. Kraemer, "A psychobiological theory of attachment," *Behavioral and Brain Sciences* 15 (1992): 493–541; L. J. Martin et al., "Social deprivation of infant rhesus monkeys alters the chemoarchitecture of the brain: I. Subcortical regions," *Journal of Neuroscience* 11 (1991): 3344–58; G. W. Kraemer, "Effects of differences in early social experience on primate neurobiological-behavioral development," in M. Reite and T. Field, eds., *The Psychobiology of Attachment and Separation* (Orlando, FL: Academic Press, 1985), pp. 135–61; Suomi, "The role of tactile contact" (see citation on page 477).

324 Effect of abuse and neglect on the brain: M. H. Teicher et al., "Neurophysiological mechanisms of stress response in children," in C. R. Pfeffer, ed., *Severe Stress and Mental Disturbance in Children* (Washington, DC: American Psychiatric Press, 1996), pp. 59–84.

324 MRI and severe neglect: B. D. Perry, as reported by M. Gladwell, "Damaged," *New Yorker* (February 24/March 3, 1997).

324 Left frontal disturbances: Y. Ito et al., "Increased prevalence of electrophysiological abnormalities in children with psychological, physical, and sexual abuse," *Journal of Neuropsychiatry and Clinical Neuroscience* 5 (1993): 401–408.

324 Hippocampal damage: J. D. Bremner et al., "Neural mechanisms in dissociative amnesia for childhood abuse: Relevance to the current controversy surrounding the 'false memory syndrome,'" *American Journal of Psychiatry* 153 (1996 suppl.7): 71–82.

325 Babies of depressed mothers: G. Dawson et al., "Frontal lobe activity and affective behavior of infants of mothers with depressive symptoms," *Child Development* 63 (1992): 725–37.

326 Smothering: C. Z. Malatesta et al., "The development of emotion expression during the first two years of life," *Monographs of the Society for Research in Child Development* 54, nos. 1-2 (1989).

327 Reducing inhibition: Kagan, *Galen's Prophecy*, pp. 204–206 (see full citation on page 495); Goleman, *Emotional Intelligence*, pp. 221–24 (see full citation on page 495); S.-Y. Park et al., "Infant emotionality, parenting, and 3-year inhibition: Exploring stability and lawful discontinuity in a male sample," *Developmental Psychology* 33 (1997): 218–27.

Chapter 13: The Emergence of Memory

328   Remembering classmates: N. Newcombe and N. A. Fox, "Infantile amnesia: Through a glass darkly," *Child Development* 65 (1994): 31–40.

331   H. M.: Y. Dudai, *The Neurobiology of Memory: Concepts, Findings, Trends* (Oxford University Press, 1989), pp. 254–56.

332   Amnesics can learn new cognitive skills: L. R. Squire and S. M. Zola, "Structure and function of declarative and nondeclarative memory systems," *Proceedings of the National Academy of Sciences* 93 (1996): 13515–22.

332   Priming in young children: D. L. Schacter, *Searching for Memory: The Brain, the Mind, and the Past* (New York: Basic Books, 1996), p. 175.

332   Memory structures of the brain: M. Mishkin and T. Appenzeller, "The anatomy of memory," *Scientific American* 256 (June 1987): 80–89.

333   Children's source memory: Schacter, *Searching for Memory*, pp. 124–29.

334   How memories are stored: Squire and Zola, "Structure and function"; L. R. Squire et al., "The structure and organization of memory," *Annual Review of Psychology* 44 (1993): 453–95.

336   Delayed hippocampal maturation: A. Diamond, "Rate of maturation of the hippocampus and the developmental progression of children's performance on the delayed non-matching to sample and visual paired comparison tasks," *Annals of the New York Academy of Sciences* 608 (1990): 394–426; Brody et al., "Sequence of central nervous system myelination" (see full citation on page 462); Yakovlev and Lecours, "Myelogenetic cycles" (see full citation on page 462).

337   Fetal habituation: L. R. Leader et al., "The assessment and significance of habituation to a repeated stimulus by the human fetus," *Early Human Development* 7 (1982): 211–19.

337   Long-lasting neural changes: I. Kupfermann et al., "Neuronal correlates of habituation and dishabituation of the gill-withdrawal reflex in *Aplysia*," *Science* 167 (1970): 1743–45.

337   Compromised fetuses: L. R. Leader and M. J. Bennett, "Fetal habituation and its clinical applications," in Levene and Lilford, *Fetal and Neonatal Neurology*, pp. 45–60 (see full citation on page 466).

337   Classical conditioning: Hepper, "Fetal psychology: An embryonic science" (see citation on page 486).

339   Mobile conditioning: C. Rovee-Collier, "The 'memory system' of prelinguistic infants," *Annals of the New York Academy of Sciences* 608 (1990): 517–42.

339   The cerebellum and mobile conditioning: C. A. Nelson, "The ontogeny of human memory: A cognitive neuroscience perspective," *Developmental Psychology* 31 (1995): 723–38.

340   Recognition depends on hippocampus: R. D. McKee and L. R. Squire, "On the development of declarative memory," *Journal of Experimental Psychology: Learning, Memory, and Cognition* 19 (1993): 397–404.

340   "Pre-explicit" memory: Nelson, "Ontogeny of human memory."

341   Newborns prefer novel faces: O. Pascalis and S. de Schonen, "Recognition memory in 3- to 4-day-old human neonates," *NeuroReport* 5 (1994): 1721–24.

341   Newborns' memory for words: I. U. Swain et al., "Newborn infants' memory for speech sounds retained over 24 hours," *Developmental Psychology* 29 (1993): 312–23.

341   Words in stories: P. W. Jusczyk and E. A. Hohne, "Infants' memory for spoken words," *Science* 277 (1997): 1984–86.

341   Preterm babies: J. F. Fagan, "The paired-comparison paradigm and infant intelligence," *Annals of the New York Academy of Sciences* 608 (1990): 337–64.

341   Brain maturation in monkeys: J. Bachevalier, "Ontogenetic development of habit and memory formation in primates," *Annals of the New York Academy of Sciences* 608 (1990): 457–84.

341   Recognition memory improves until age nine: N. Newcombe et al., "Developmental changes in recognition memory for pictures of objects and scenes," *Developmental Psychology* 13 (1977): 337–41.

341   Memory for object locations: Bjorklund, *Children's Thinking,* p. 238 (see full citation on page 488).

342   Recognition memory and later IQ: R. B. McCall and M. S. Carriger, "A meta-analysis of infant habituation and recognition memory performance as predictors of later IQ," *Child Development* 64 (1993): 57–79.

343   Sex difference in fetal habituation: Leader et al., "The assessment and significance of habituation."

343   Visual habituation: D. E. Creighton, "Sex differences in the visual habituation of 4-, 6- and 8-month-old infants," *Infant Behavior and Development* 7 (1984): 237–49.

343   Sex difference in infants' short-term memory: A. Diamond, "Development of the ability to use recall to guide action, as indicated by infants' performance on A$\overline{\text{B}}$," *Child Development* 56 (1985): 868–83.

343   Sex difference in verbal recall: Bjorklund, *Children's Thinking,* pp. 244, 260 (see full citation on page 488).

343   Testosterone-manipulated monkeys: J. Bachevalier and C. Hagger, "Sex differences in the development of learning abilities in primates," *Psychoneuroendocrinology* 16 (1991): 177–88.

344   Testosterone effects in frontal vs. temporal lobe: Overman et al., "Cognitive gender differences" (see full citation on page 499).

345   Object permanence: A. Diamond, "Frontal lobe involvement in cognitive changes during the first year of life," in Gibson and Petersen, *Brain Maturation and Cognitive Development*, pp. 127–80 (see full citation on page 462).

345   Deferred imitation: A. N. Meltzoff, "Infant imitation and memory: Nine-month-olds in immediate and deferred tests," *Child Development* 59 (1988): 217–25; A. N. Meltzoff, "What infant memory tells us about infantile amnesia: Long-term recall and deferred imitation," *Journal of Experimental Child Psychology* 59 (1995): 497–515; L. McDonough et al., "The deferred imitation task as a nonverbal measure of declarative memory," *Proceedings of the National Academy of Sciences* 92 (1995): 7580–84.

347   Imitating TV: A. N. Meltzoff, "Imitation of televised models by infants," *Child Development* 59 (1988): 1221–29.

347   TV violence: W. Wood et al., "Effects of media violence on viewers' aggression in unconstrained social interaction," *Psychological Bulletin* 109 (1991) 371–83.

347   Memory for infancy: N. A. Myers et al., "When they were very young: Almost-threes remember two years ago," *Infant Behavior and Development* 10 (1987): 123–32.

348   Memories from thirteen months: P. J. Bauer and S. S. Wawerka, "One- to two-year-olds' recall of events: The more expressed, the more impressed," *Journal of Experimental Child Psychology* 59 (1995): 475–96.

348   Day-care fire: D. B. Pillemer et al., "Very long-term memories of a salient preschool event," *Applied Cognitive Psychology* 8 (1994): 95–106.

349   Heritability of memory skill: L. A. Thompson, "Genetic contributions to intellectual development in infancy and childhood," in P. A. Vernon, ed., *Biological Approaches to the Study of Human Intelligence* (Norwood, NJ: Ablex, 1993), pp. 95–138.

349   Schooling improves memory: R. Kail, *The Development of Memory in Children*, 3rd ed. (New York: W. H. Freeman, 1990).

349   Memory strategies of preschoolers: H. M. Wellman, "Deliberate memory behavior in the delayed reaction of very young children," *Developmental Psychology* 11 (1975): 780–87; S. Pierce and G. Lange, "Instructing young children in the use of memorizing strategies: Effects at study and recall," *Journal of General Psychology* 120 (1993): 473–87.

349   Parental encouragement of memory skills: H. H. Ratner, "Memory demands and the development of young children's memory," *Child Development* 55 (1984): 2173–91.

Chapter 14: Language and the Developing Brain

351   Language is an instinct: S. Pinker, *The Language Instinct* (New York: HarperPerennial, 1995).

352   Secret twin language: Messer, *The Development of Communication*, p. 69 (see full citation on page 491).

352   Spontaneous signing: S. Goldin-Meadow and C. Mylander, "Gestural communication in deaf children: Noneffect of parental input on language development," *Science* 221 (1983): 372–74.

352   Deaf children of deaf parents: E. L. Newport and R. P. Meier, "The acquisition of American Sign Language," in D. I. Slobin, ed., *The Crosslinguistic Study of Language Acquisition*, vol. 1 (Hillsdale, NJ: Lawrence Erlbaum, 1985), pp. 881–938.

352   Williams syndrome: U. Bellugi et al., "Cognitive and neural development: Clues from genetically based syndromes," in D. Magnusson, ed., *The Lifespan Development of Individuals: Behavioral, Neurobiological, and Psychosocial Aspects* (Cambridge University Press, 1996), pp. 223–43.

356   Semantics and syntax in the brain: Pinker, *Language Instinct*, pp. 307–17.

356   Broca's area responds to word order: K. Stromswold et al., "Localization of syntactic comprehension by positron emission tomography," *Brain and Language* 52 (1996): 452–73; H. J. Neville, "Developmental specificity in neurocognitive development in humans," in Gazzaniga, *Cognitive Neurosciences*, pp. 219–31 (see full citation on page 461).

357   Nouns and verbs: A. R. Damasio and H. Damasio, "Brain and language," *Scientific American* 267 (March 1992): 89–95.

358   Number of synapses: J. F. Werker and R. C. Tees, "The organization and reorganization of human speech perception," *Annual Review of Neuroscience* 15 (1992): 377–402.

358   Mature cell layers: I. Kostović, "Structural and histochemical reorganization of the human prefrontal cortex during perinatal and postnatal life," *Progress in Brain Research* 85 (1990): 223–40.

358   Myelination of Broca's vs. Wernicke's areas: Gibson, "Myelination and behavioral development" (see citation on page 496).

358   Arcuate fasciculus: A. R. Lecours, "Myelogenetic correlates of the development of speech and language," in E. H. Lenneberg and E. Lenneberg, eds., *Foundations of Language Development: A Multidisciplinary Approach*, vol. 1 (New York: Academic, 1975), pp. 121–35.

359   Genie: Curtiss, *Genie*, p. 5 (see full citation on page 477).

360   Kaspar Hauser: A. von Fuerbach, *Example of a Crime on the Intellectual Life of Man* (Ansbach, 1832, translated by Simpkin and Marshall). As quoted by S. Curtiss, "The independence and task-specificity of language," in M. H. Bornstein and J. S. Bruner, eds., *Interaction in Human Development* (Hillsdale, NJ: Lawrence Erlbaum, 1989), pp. 105–37.

360   Chelsea: Curtiss, "Independence and task-specificity."

361   ASL: U. Bellugi et al., "Linguistic and spatial development: Dissociations between cognitive domains," in N. A. Krasnegor et al., eds., *Biological and*

Behavioral Determinants of Language Development (Hillsdale, NJ: Lawrence Erlbaum, 1991), pp. 363–93.

363   Critical period for language: E. L. Newport, "Maturational constraints on language learning," *Cognitive Science* 14 (1990): 11–28.

364   Age of hemispherectomy: K. Stromswold, "The cognitive and neural bases of language acquisition," in Gazzaniga, *Cognitive Neurosciences*, pp. 855–70 (see full citation on page 461).

364   Grammar more vulnerable than vocabulary: Curtiss, "Independence and task-specificity."

364   Late second-language learners: H. J. Neville et al., "Neural systems mediating American Sign Language: Effects of sensory experience and age of acquisition," *Brain and Language* 57 (1997): 285–308.

365   Planum temporale: J. A. Wada et al., "Cerebral hemispheric asymmetry in humans: Cortical speech zones in 100 adult and 100 infant brains," *Archives of Neurology* 32 (1975): 239–46.

366   EEG of preterm babies: M. Cheour-Luhtanen et al., "The ontogenetically earliest discriminative response of the human brain," *Psychobiology* 33 (1996): 478–81.

366   Left vs. right ears: J. Mehler and A. Christophe, "Maturation and learning of language in the first year of life," in Gazzaniga, *Cognitive Neurosciences*, pp. 943–54 (see full citation on page 461).

366   Word boundaries: A. Christophe et al., "Do infants perceive word boundaries? An empirical study of the bootstrapping of lexical acquisition," *Journal of the Acoustical Society of America* 95 (1994): 1570–80.

366   Phoneme categorization: P. D. Eimas et al., "Speech perception in infants," *Science* 171 (1971): 303–306.

367   Evolution of human languages: R. H. Fitch, "Neurobiology of speech perception," *Annual Review of Neuroscience* 20 (1997): 331–53.

368   "Citizens of the world": P. K. Kuhl, "Developmental speech perception: Implications for models of language impairment," *Annals of the New York Academy of Sciences* 682 (1993): 248–63.

368   Loss of phonetic perception: P. K. Kuhl, "Learning and representation in speech and language," *Current Opinion in Neurobiology* 4 (1994): 812–22; Werker and Tees, "Organization and reorganization."

369   Adults tune out: Mehler and Christophe, "Maturation and learning of language."

370   Myelination of motor nerves: Lecours, "Myelogenetic correlates."

370   Sucking muscles: M. Studdert-Kennedy, "The early development of phonological form," in von Euler et al., *Neurobiology of Early Infant Behavior*, pp. 287–301 (see full citation on page 472).

370   English-speaking one-year-olds: M. I. S. Huettner, "Neuropsychology of language and reading development," in P. A. Vernon, ed., *The Neuropsychology of Individual Differences* (San Diego: Academic, 1994), pp. 9–34.

371   Vocal machinery: R. D. Kent, "Psychobiology of speech development: Coemergence of language and a movement system," *American Journal of Physiology* 246 (1984): R888–94.

371   Deaf babies: L. A. Petitto and P. F. Marentette, "Babbling in the manual mode: Evidence for the ontogeny of language," *Science* 251 (1991): 1493–96.

371   Language-specific babbling: B. de Boysson-Bardies et al., "A crosslinguistic investigation of vowel formants in babbling," *Journal of Child Language* 16 (1989): 1–17.

371   Modifying pronunciation in twelve-week-olds: P. K. Kuhl and A. N. Meltzoff, "Infant vocalizations in response to speech: Vocal imitation and developmental change," *Journal of the Acoustical Society of America* 100 (1996): 2425–38.

372   Naming assumptions: E. M. Markman, "Constraints children place on word meaning," *Cognitive Science* 14 (1990): 57–77.

373   13,000 words: Pinker, *Language Instinct*, p. 151 (see full citation on page 503).

373   Vocabulary explosion: V. A. Marchman, "The acquisition of language in normally developing children: Some basic strategies and approaches," in I. P. Martins et al., eds., *Acquired Aphasia in Children: Acquisition and Breakdown of Language in the Developing Brain* (Drodrecht: Kluwer, 1990), pp. 15–23.

373   How toddlers' brains process words: D. L. Mills et al., "Variability in cerebral organization during primary language acquisition," in Dawson and Fischer, *Human Behavior and the Developing Brain*, pp. 427–55 (see full citation on page 496); D. L. Mills et al., "Language acquisition and cerebral specialization in 20-month-old infants," *Journal of Cognitive Neuroscience* 5 (1993): 317–34.

374   Big Bird and Cookie Monster: K. Hirsh-Pasek and R. M. Golinkoff, "Language comprehension: A new look at some old themes," in Krasnegor et al., *Biological and Behavioral Determinants*, pp. 301–20 (see full citation on page 504).

374   Toddler's first word pairs: Pinker, *Language Instinct*, p. 268 (see full citation on page 503).

375   First grammatical constructions: Messer, *Development of Communication*, p. 154 (see full citation on page 491).

375   Wugs: Pinker, *Language Instinct*, pp. 49–50 (see full citation on page 503).

376   Pointing by deaf children: L. A. Petitto, "On the autonomy of language and gesture: Evidence from the acquisition of personal pronouns in American Sign Language," *Cognition* 27 (1987): 1–52.

377   Tracheotomy: Messer, *Development of Communication*, p. 85 (see full citation on page 491).

378   Toddler vocabulary predicts later language skills: I. Bretherton et al.,
      "Individual differences at 20 months: Analytic and holistic strategies in lan-
      guage acquisition," *Journal of Child Language* 10 (1983): 293–313.

378   Twin studies: L. A. Thompson et al., "Associations between cognitive abilities
      and scholastic achievement: genetic overlap but environmental differences,"
      Psychological Science 2 (1991): 158–65.

378   Specific language impairment: Pinker, *Language Instinct*, pp. 48–50, 322–25
      (see full citation on page 503).

379   Adopted babies: K. Hardy-Brown et al., "Genetic and environmental influ-
      ences on the rate of communicative development in the first year of life,"
      Developmental Psychology 17 (1981): 704–17.

379   Predicting language skill from newborns' neural responses: D. L. Molfese and
      V. J. Molfese, "Discrimination of language skills at five years of age using
      event-related potentials recorded at birth," *Developmental Neuropsychology* 13
      (1997): 135–56.

379   Females are more verbal: Halpern, *Sex Differences in Cognitive Abilities*, pp.
      66–67 (see full citation on page 488); D. Kimura, "Sex differences in the
      brain," *Scientific American* 267 (March 1992): 119–25.

379   Fetal mouth movements: P. G. Hepper et al., "Sex differences in fetal mouth
      movements," *Lancet* 350 (1997): 1820.

381   Frontal lobe activation: B. A. Shaywitz et al., "Sex differences in the function-
      al organization of the brain for language," *Nature* 373 (1995): 607–609.

381   Planum temporale: J. J. Kulynych et al., "Gender differences in the normal lat-
      eralization of the supratemporal cortex: MRI surface-rendering morphometry
      of Heschl's gyrus and the planum temporale," *Cerebral Cortex* 4 (1994):
      107–18.

381   Language areas of brain larger in women: T. E. Schlaepfer et al., "Structural
      differences in the cerebral cortex of healthy female and male subjects: A mag-
      netic resonance imaging study," *Psychiatry Research: Neuroimaging* 61 (1995):
      129–35; J. Harasty et al., "Language-associated cortical regions are proportion-
      ally larger in the female brain," *Archives of Neurology* 54 (1997): 171–76.

381   Neuronal density in Wernicke's area: S. F. Witelson et al., "Women have
      greater density of neurons in posterior temporal cortex," *Journal of
      Neuroscience* 15 (1995): 3418–28.

381   Women have longer dendrites: B. Jacobs et al., "A quantitative dendritic
      analysis of Wernicke's area in humans. II. Gender, hemispheric, and environ-
      mental factors," *Journal of Comparative Neurology* 327 (1993): 97–111.

381   Parents speak the same amount to boys and girls: J. Huttenlocher et al., "Early
      vocabulary growth: Relation to language input and gender," *Developmental
      Psychology* 27 (1991): 236–48; B. Hart and T. R. Risley, "American parenting
      of language-learning children: Persisting differences in family-child interac-

tions observed in natural home environments," *Developmental Psychology* 28 (1992): 1096–105.

382   Newborns' neural responses to speech sounds: D. L. Molfese and V. J. Molfese, "Hemisphere and stimulus differences as reflected in the cortical responses of newborn infants to speech stimuli," *Developmental Psychology* 15 (1979): 505–11.

382   Three-month-olds: J. L. Shucard et al., "Auditory evoked potentials and sex-related differences in brain development," *Brain and Language* 13 (1981): 91–102.

382   Kansas City study: Hart and Risley, "American parenting."

383   Follow-up study: D. Walker et al., "Prediction of school outcomes based on early language production and socioeconomic factors," *Child Development* 65 (1994): 606–21.

384   Within-class predictors of language achievement: B. Hart and T. R. Risley, *Meaningful Differences in the Everyday Experience of Young American Children* (Baltimore: Paul H. Brooks, 1995), p. 168.

384   Chicago study: Huttenlocher et al., "Early vocabulary growth."

385   William Fowler's program is described in detail in his book *Talking from Infancy: How to Nurture and Cultivate Early Language Development* (Cambridge, MA: Brookline Books, 1990).

385   Results of Fowler's program: W. Fowler et al., "Accelerating language acquisition," in *The Origins and Development of High Ability*, CIBA Foundation Symposium #178 (Chichester, Eng.: John Wiley, 1993), pp. 207–21.

386   TV for the children of deaf parents: Pinker, *Language Instinct*, p. 278 (see full citation on page 503).

387   Motherese facilitates phoneme-learning: P. K. Kuhl et al., "Cross-language analysis of phonetic units in language addressed to infants," *Science* 277 (1997): 684–86.

387   Muddled baby-talk: J. E. Andruski, as quoted by R. L. Hill, "There's rhyme and reason in our baby talk," *Oregonian* (August 1, 1997).

387   *Sesame Street* inappropriate for eighteen-month-olds: K. Nelson, "Structure and strategy in learning to talk," *Monographs of the Society for Research in Child Development* 38, nos. 1–2 (1973): 1–137.

388   Babies know which mouth movements correspond to which speech sounds: P. K. Kuhl and A. N. Meltzoff, "The bimodal perception of speech in infancy," *Science* 218 (1982): 1138–40.

388   Imitation promotes verbal development: K. Hardy-Brown and R. Plomin, "Infant communicative development: Evidence from adoptive and biological families for genetic and environmental influences on rate differences," *Developmental Psychology* 21 (1985): 378–85.

388   Example of too much parental correction: Nelson, "Structure and strategy."

389   Reading to young children: J. Dunn et al., "Mothers' speech to young children: Variation in context," *Developmental Medicine and Child Neurology* 19 (1977): 629–38; B. D. Debaryshe, "Joint picture-book reading correlates of early oral language skill," *Journal of Child Language* 20 (1993): 455–61; G. J. Whitehurst et al., "Accelerating language development through picture book reading," *Developmental Psychology* 24 (1988): 552–59.

390   Education and Wernicke's area: Jacobs et al., "A quantitative dendritic analysis" (see full citation on page 507).

390   Loss of Head Start gains: R. Haskins, "Beyond metaphor: The efficacy of early childhood education," *American Psychologist* 44 (1989): 274–82; V. E. Lee et al., "Are Head Start effects sustained? A longitudinal follow-up comparison of disadvantaged children attending Head Start, no preschool, and other preschool programs," *Child Development* 61 (1990): 495–507.

Chapter 15: How Intelligence Grows in the Brain

393   H. Gardner: *Frames of Mind: The Theory of Multiple Intelligences* (New York: Basic Books, 1983).

394   IQ scores predict academic and financial achievement: N. Brody, "Intelligence, schooling, and society," *American Psychologist* 52 (1997): 1045–50.

394   Preliterate culture, experienced shoppers, racing buffs: S. J. Ceci, *On Intelligence: A Bioecological Treatise on Intellectual Development* (Cambridge, MA: Harvard University Press, 1996).

395   Stephen Jay Gould: *The Mismeasure of Man* (New York: W. W. Norton, 1981).

395   Footnote: C. M. Steele, "A threat in the air: How stereotypes shape intellectual identity and performance," *American Psychologist* 52 (1997): 613–29.

396   Brain lesions and IQ: J. Grafman et al., "Intellectual function following penetrating head injury in Vietnam veterans," *Brain* 111 (1988): 169–84; D. K. Detterman, "Intelligence and the brain," in Vernon, *Neuropsychology of Individual Differences*, pp. 35–57 (see full citation on page 506).

396   Head size–IQ correlation: A. R. Jensen and S. N. Sinha, "Physical correlates of human intelligence," in Vernon, *Biological Approaches to the Study of Human Intelligence*, pp. 139–242 (see full citation on page 503).

397   Brain volume–IQ correlation: E. D. Bigler, "Brain morphology and intelligence," *Developmental Neuropsychology* 11 (1995): 377–403.

397   Children's brain volume: A. L. Reiss et al., "Brain development, gender and IQ in children: A volumetric imaging study," *Brain* 119 (1996): 1763–74.

397   Brain growth: M. D. Mann, "The growth of the brain and skull in children," *Brain Research* 13 (1984): 169–78; A. Pfefferbaum et al., "A quantitative magnetic resonance imaging study of changes in brain morphology from infancy to late adulthood," *Archives of Neurology* 51 (1994): 874–87.

398 Inspection time: I. J. Deary and C. Stough, "Intelligence and inspection time: Achievements, prospects, and problems," *American Psychologist* 51 (1996): 599–608.

399 ERPs and IQ: I. J. Deary and P. G. Caryl, "Neuroscience and human intelligence differences," *Trends in Neuroscience* 20 (1997): 365–71.

400 Mental speed in childhood: S. Hale, "A global developmental trend in cognitive processing speed," *Child Development* 61 (1990): 653–63.

400 Accelerating neural conduction through childhood: K. Müller et al., "Maturation of fastest afferent and efferent central and peripheral pathways: No evidence for a constancy of central conduction delays," *Neuroscience Letters* 166 (1994): 9–12.

401 "P300" in young children: J. S. Buchwald, "Comparison of plasticity in sensory and cognitive processing systems," *Clinics in Perinatology* 17 (1990): 57–66; H. McIsaac and J. Polich, "Comparison of infant and adult P300 from auditory stimuli," *Journal of Experimental Child Psychology* 53 (1992): 115–28; C. A. Nelson, "Neural correlates of recognition memory in the first postnatal year," in Dawson and Fischer, *Human Behavior and the Developing Brain*, pp. 269–313 (see full citation on page 496).

401 P300 matures throughout childhood and adolescence: E. Courchesne, "Neurophysiological correlates of cognitive development: Changes in long-latency event-related potentials from childhood to adulthood," *Electroencephalography and Clinical Neurophysiology* 45 (1978): 468–82; J. Polich et al., "Normal variation of P300 in children: Age, memory span, and head size," *International Journal of Psychophysiology* 9 (1990): 237–48; T. Fuchigami et al, "Auditory event-related potentials and reaction time in children: Evaluation of cognitive development," *Developmental Medicine and Child Neurology* 35 (1993): 203–37.

401 IQ and brain glucose use: J. Haier, "Cerebral glucose metabolism and intelligence," in Vernon, *Biological Approaches to the Study of Human Intelligence*, pp. 317–32 (see full citation on page 503); J. Haier et al., "Intelligence and changes in regional cerebral glucose metabolic rate following learning," *Intelligence* 16 (1992): 415–26.

402 Children's brain glucose use: Chugani et al., "Positron emission tomography" (see full citation on page 462).

402 Letter discrimination task: B. J. Casey et al., "A developmental functional MRI study of prefrontal activation during performance of a Go-No-Go task," *Journal of Cognitive Neuroscience* 9 (1997): 835–47.

402 Frontal-lobe intelligence: S. J. Segalowitz et al., "Cleverness and wisdom in 12-year-olds: Electrophysiological evidence for late maturation of the frontal lobe," *Developmental Neuropsychology* 8 (1992): 279–98.

404 Orbitofrontal cortex and inhibition: J. M. Fuster, "Prefrontal cortex and the bridging of temporal gaps in the perception-action cycle," *Annals of the New York Academy of Sciences* 608 (1990): 318–36.

405   Anterior cingulate gyrus and attention: O. Devinsky et al., "Contributions of anterior cingulate cortex to behavior," *Brain* 118 (1995): 279–306.

405   Dopamine: A. Diamond, "Evidence for the importance of dopamine for pre-frontal cortex functions early in life," *Philosophical Transactions of the Royal Society of London, Series B* 351 (1996): 1483–94.

405   Frontal lobe immaturity: M. L. Smith et al., "The development of frontal-lobe functions," in S. J. Segalowitz and I. Rapin eds., *Handbook of Neuropsychology*, vol. 7: *Child Neuropsychology* (Amsterdam: Elsevier, 1992), pp. 309–30.

406   Left hemisphere more fully conscious: M. S. Gazzaniga, "Consciousness and the cerebral hemispheres," in Gazzaniga, *Cognitive Neurosciences*, pp. 1391–1400 (see full citation on page 461).

406   Interhemispheric communication at age four: K. W. Fischer and S. P. Rose, "Dynamic development of coordination of components in brain and behav-ior," in Dawson and Fischer, *Human Behavior and the Developing Brain*, pp. 3–66 (see full citation on page 496).

408   Newborns can discriminate two from three: S. E. Antell and D. P. Keating, "Perception of numerical invariance in neonates," *Child Development* 54 (1983): 695–701.

408   Arithmetic in five-month-olds: K. Wynn, "Addition and subtraction by human infants," *Nature* 358 (1992): 749–50.

408   Possible vs. impossible events: R. Baillargeon, "Physical reasoning in infancy," in Gazzaniga, *Cognitive Neurosciences*, pp. 181–204 (see full citation on page 461).

409   "A not B": A. Diamond, "The development and neural bases of memory func-tions as indexed by the $A\overline{B}$, and delayed response tasks in human infants and infant monkeys," *Annals of the New York Academy of Sciences* 608 (1990): 267–317.

409   Retrieving an object from behind a clear barrier: A. Diamond, "Developmental time course in human infants and infant monkeys, and the neural bases of, inhibitory control in reaching," *Annals of the New York Academy of Sciences* 608 (1990): 637–76.

410   EEG measurements: M. A. Bell and N. A. Fox, "Brain development over the first year of life: Relations between electroencephalographic frequency and coherence and cognitive and affective behaviors," in Dawson and Fischer, *Human Behavior and the Developing Brain*, pp. 314–45 (see full citation on page 496).

411   Self-control: B. E. Vaughn et al., "The emergence and consolidation of self-control from eighteen to thirty months of age: Normative trends and individ-ual differences," *Child Development* 55 (1984): 990–1004.

411   Self-awareness: Bjorklund, *Children's Thinking*, p. 311 (see full citation on page 488).

412   Appearance/reality distinction: J. H. Flavell et al., "Development of the appearance-reality distinction," *Cognitive Psychology* 15 (1983): 95–120.

412   Appearance/reality distinction cannot be taught: J. H. Flavell, "The development of children's knowledge about the appearance-reality distinction," *American Psychologist* 41 (1985): 418–25.

413   Theory of mind: Bjorklund, *Children's Thinking*, pp. 204–14 (see full citation on page 488).

414   Responsibilities at age six: C. M. Super, "Developmental transitions of cognitive functioning in rural Kenya and metropolitan America," in Gibson and Petersen, *Brain Maturation and Cognitive Development*, pp. 225–51 (see full citation on page 462).

414   P300: Polich et al., "Normal variation of P300" (see full citation on page 510).

414   Piaget's conservation task: Bjorklund, *Children's Thinking*, p. 74 (see full citation on page 488).

415   Attention and inhibition: A. Diamond and C. Taylor, "Development of an aspect of executive control: Development of the abilities to remember what I said and to 'Do as I say, not as I do,'" *Developmental Psychobiology* 29 (1996): 315–34.

418   Visual recognition in infant monkeys: Diamond, "Rate of maturation" (see full citation on page 501).

418   Infant recognition and later IQ: McCall and Carriger, "A meta-analysis of infant habituation" (see full citation on page 502).

418   Age eighteen: M. Sigman et al., "Why does infant attention predict adolescent intelligence?" *Infant Behavior and Development* 20 (1997): 133–40.

418   Cross-modal transfer and object permanence: S. A. Rose and J. F. Feldman, "Prediction of IQ and specific cognitive abilities at 11 years from infancy measures," *Developmental Psychology* 31 (1995): 685–96; S. A. Rose et al., "Infant information processing in relation to six-year cognitive outcomes," *Child Development* 63 (1992): 1126–41; S. A. Rose et al., "Information processing at 1 year: Relation to birth status and developmental outcome during the first 5 years," *Developmental Psychology* 27 (1991): 723–37.

418   Discriminating own mother: K. V. Roe, "Infants' mother-stranger discrimination at 3 months as a predictor of cognitive development at 3 and 5 years," *Developmental Psychology* 14 (1978): 191–92; K. V. Roe et al., "Vocal interaction at 3 months and cognitive skills at 12 years," *Developmental Psychology* 18 (1982): 15–16.

419   Space Invaders test: M. Anderson, *Intelligence and Development: A Cognitive Theory* (Cambridge, MA: Blackwell, 1992), pp. 162–64.

419   P300s: F. Martin et al., "Long latency event-related potentials (P300) in gifted children," *Brain and Development* 15 (1993): 173–77.

419 Speed differences and memory capacity: S. A. Rose and J. F. Feldman, "Memory and speed: Their role in the relation of infant information processing to later IQ," *Child Development* 68 (1997): 630–41.

419 Newborn head size: S. H. Broman et al., *Preschool IQ: Prenatal and Early Developmental Correlates* (Hillsdale, NJ: Lawrence Erlbaum, 1975), p. 247.

420 Brain and prefrontal cortex volume: Reiss et al., "Brain development, gender and IQ" (see full citation on page 509).

420 Phonics and planum temporale asymmetry: C. M. Leonard et al., "Cerebral asymmetry and cognitive development in children: A magnetic resonance imaging study," *Psychological Science* 7 (1996): 89–95.

421 Children's corpus callosum: L. A. Rowe et al., "Corpus callosum morphology and cognitive functioning in normal children," *Society for Neuroscience Abstracts* 23 (1997): 212.

Chapter 16: Nature, Nurture, and Sex Differences
in Intellectual Development

422 Predicting IQ from newborn EEG measures: Molfese and Molfese, "Discrimination of language skills at five years" (see full citation on page 507).

423 Maternal encouragement of attention: C. S. Tamis-LeMonda and M. H. Bornstein, "Habituation and maternal encouragement of attention in infancy as predictors of toddler language, play, and representational competence," *Child Development* 60 (1989): 738–51.

423 Twenty-point IQ advantage: Sigman et al., "Why does infant attention predict adolescent intelligence?" (see full citation on page 512).

423 Preterm babies: Rose et al., "Information processing at 1 year" (see full citation on page 512).

424 Familial IQ correlations: Plomin, *Nature and Nurture*, pp. 68–72 (see full citation on page 500).

425 Prenatal experience and twin IQ correlations: B. Devlin et al., "The heritability of IQ," *Nature* 388 (1997): 468–71.

425 Heritability of specific mental skills: L. A. Thompson, "Genetic contributions to intellectual development" (see full citation on page 503).

425 Twins' scholastic achievement: L. A. Thompson et al., "Associations between cognitive abilities and scholastic achievement" (see full citation on page 507).

426 IQ heritability increases with age: Plomin, *Nature and Nurture*, pp. 73–76 (see full citation on page 500).

426 Adoptees' IQ at adolescence: S. Scarr and R. A. Weinberg, "The Minnesota adoption studies: Genetic differences and malleability," *Child Development* 54 (1983): 260–67.

426 Footnote: J. F. Jackson, "Human behavioral genetics, Scarr's theory, and her views on interventions: A critical review and commentary on their implications for African American children," *Child Development* 64 (1993): 1318–32.

427 Head Start: A. M. Clarke and A. D. B. Clarke, "The later cognitive effects of early intervention," *Intelligence* 13 (1989): 289–97; Haskins, "Beyond metaphor"; Lee et al., "Are Head Start effects sustained?" (see full citations on page 509).

427 Abcedarian project: F. A. Campbell and C. T. Ramey, "Effects of early intervention on intellectual and academic achievement: A follow-up study of children from low-income families," *Child Development* 65 (1994): 684–98.

428 Ten to sixteen points: C. Locurto, "The malleability of IQ as judged from adoption studies," *Intelligence* 14 (1990): 275–92.

428 French adoption study: C. Capron and M. Duyme, "Assessment of effects of socioeconomic status on IQ in a full cross-fostering study," *Nature* 340 (1989): 552–54.

429 Flynn effect: J. R. Flynn, "Massive IQ gains in 14 nations: What IQ tests really measure," *Psychological Bulletin* 101 (1987): 171–91.

430 Visual-spatial IQ gains: U. Neisser, "Rising scores on intelligence tests," *American Scientist* 85 (1997): 440–47.

431 Sex differences in intelligence and performance range: L. V. Hedges and A. Nowell, "Sex differences in mental test scores, variability, and numbers of high-scoring individuals," *Science* 269 (1995): 41–45.

432 Elephant brains: H. Kuhlenbeck, *The Central Nervous System of Vertebrates*, vol. 3 (Basel: S. Karger, 1973), p. 731.

432 Men's brains are 8 percent larger: C. D. Ankney, "Sex differences in relative brain size: The mismeasure of woman, too?" *Intelligence* 16 (1992): 329–36.

432 Corpus callosum: M. Hines et al., "Cognition and the corpus callosum: Verbal fluency, visuospatial ability, and language lateralization related to midsagittal surface areas of callosal subregions," *Behavioral Neuroscience* 106 (1992): 3–14.

433 Neural sex differences as a consequence of early experience: J. S. Janowsky, "Sexual dimorphism in the human brain: Dispelling the myths," *Developmental Medicine and Child Neurology* 31 (1989): 257–63.

433 Spatial toys improve spatial skills: Halpern, *Sex Differences in Cognitive Abilities*, pp. 214–15 (see full citation on page 488).

433 Parents encourage sex-appropriate play: H. Lytton and D. M. Romney, "Parents' differential socialization of boys and girls: A meta-analysis," *Psychological Bulletin* 109 (1991): 267–96.

434 Visual-spatial differences at age three: D. F. Halpern, "Sex differences in intelligence: Implications for education," *American Psychologist* 52 (1997): 1091–102.

434   Male fetuses have thicker right hemispheres: M.-C. deLacoste et al., "Possible sex differences in the developing human fetal brain," *Journal of Clinical and Experimental Neuropsychology* 13 (1991): 831–46.

434   Estrogen effects on mental skills: D. Kimura and E. Hampson, "Neural and hormonal mechanisms mediating sex differences in cognition," in Vernon, *Biological Approaches to the Study of Human Intelligence*, pp. 375–97 (see full citation on page 503).

435   Testosterone: Ibid.; H. Nyborg, "The neuropsychology of sex-related differences in brain and specific abilities: Hormones, developmental dynamics, and new paradigm," in Vernon, *Neuropsychology of Individual Differences*, pp. 59–113 (see full citation on page 506); J. S. Janowsky et al., "Testosterone influences spatial cognition in older men," *Behavior Neuroscience* 108 (1994): 325–32.

436   Maturation rate: Halpern, *Sex Differences in Cognitive Abilities*, pp. 153–54 (see full citation on page 488).

436   IQ changes between seventh and twelfth grades: Ibid., p. 200.

Chapter 17: How to Raise a Smarter Child

438   SES-IQ correlation: McCall and Carriger, "A meta-analysis of infant habituation (see full citation on page 502).

438   Parents' education a better predictor than income: Ceci, *On Intelligence*, p. 46 (see full citation on page 509); D. Walker et al., "Prediction of school outcomes based on early language production and socioeconomic factors," *Child Development* 65 (1994): 606–21.

438   Neurological differences between high- and low-SES children: G. A. Otero, "Poverty, cultural disadvantage and brain development: A study of pre-school children in Mexico," *Electroencephalography and Clinical Neurophysiology* 102 (1997): 512–16; D. P. Waber et al., "SES-related aspects of neuropsychological performance," *Child Development* 55 (1984): 1878–86.

438   Birth order: M. Rutter, "Family and school influences on cognitive development," *Journal of Child Psychology and Psychiatry* 26 (1985): 683–704; Broman et al., *Preschool IQ*, pp. 63–65 (see full citation on page 513); M. Lewis and J. Jaskir, "Infant intelligence and its relation to birth order and birth spacing," *Infant Behavior and Development* 6 (1983): 117–20.

439   Birth spacing: Broman et al., *Preschool IQ*, p. 68 (see full citation on page 513).

439   Social-emotional adjustment: Rutter, "Family and school influences."

440   Only children: R. B. Zajonc, "Family configuration and intelligence," *Science* 192 (1976): 227–36.

441   Number of working mothers: *NICHD Study of Early Child Care*, NIH Pub. #98-4318 (April 1998).

441   Middle- and upper-class children: Scarr and Eisenberg, "Child care research" (see full citation on page 498).

441   Swedish studies: A. G. Broberg et al., "Effects of day care on the development of cognitive abilities in 8-year-olds: A longitudinal study," *Developmental Psychology* 33 (1997): 62–69; B.-E. Andersson, "Effects of day care on cognitive and socioemotional competence of 13-year-old Swedish schoolchildren," *Child Development* 63 (1992): 20–36.

441   High-quality day care in the United States: J. L. Rubenstein et al., "A two-year follow-up of infants in community-based day care," *Journal of Child Psychology and Psychiatry* 22 (1981): 209–18; Clarke-Stewart, "Infant day care" (see full citation on page 497).

441   No cognitive differences between children of working and nonworking mothers: T. N. Greenstein, "Are the 'most advantaged' children truly disadvantaged by early maternal employment? Effects on child cognitive outcomes," *Journal of Family Issues* 16 (1995): 149–69.

441   Cognitive development suffers in the sons of working mothers: Desai et al., "Mother or market?" Baydar and Brooks-Gunn, "Effects of maternal employment" (see full citations on pages 497 and 498).

441   Family characteristics more important than child care for cognitive development: NICHD Early Child Care Research Network, "Relations between family predictors and child outcomes" (see full citation on page 498).

442   Effect of quality and type of child care on cognitive development: *NICHD Study of Early Child Care.*

442   Twenty percent of IQ variance: Devlin et al., "The heritability of IQ" (see full citation on page 513).

442   Decline in rate of low birth weight: U.S. Dept. of Health and Human Services, *Health Aspects of Pregnancy and Childbirth: United States, 1982–1988* (August 1995).

443   Maternal weight gain, birth weight, and four-year IQ: Broman et al., *Preschool IQ*, p. 243 (see full citation on page 513).

443   Maternal stress and newborn head circumference: Lou et al., "Prenatal stressors of human life" (see full citation on page 470).

445   Nutrition, IQ, and physical stature: R. Lynn, "Nutrition and intelligence," in Vernon, *Biological Approaches to the Study of Human Intelligence*, pp. 243–58 (see full citation on page 503).

446   Anemia and cognitive development: E. Pollitt et al., "Iron deficiency and behavior: Constructs, methods, and validity of the findings," in R. J. Wurtman and J. J. Wurtman, eds., *Nutrition and the Brain*, vol. 8 (New York: Raven Press, 1990), pp. 101–46.

446   Thirty-eight essential nutrients: Lynn, "Nutrition and intelligence."

446 Four-week British study: M. Nelson et al., "Nutrient intakes, vitamin-mineral supplementation, and intelligence in British schoolchildren," *British Journal of Nutrition* 64 (1990): 13–22.

446 Studies showing marginal effects of vitamins: S. Southon et al., "Dietary intake and micronutrient status of adolescents: Effect of vitamin and trace element supplementation on indices of status and performance in tests of verbal and non-verbal intelligence," *British Journal of Nutrition* 71 (1994): 897–918; I. K. Crombie et al., "Effect of vitamin and mineral supplementation on verbal and non-verbal reasoning of schoolchildren," *Lancet* 335 (1990): 744–47.

446 British finding of nine-point IQ gain: D. Benton and G. Roberts, "Effect of vitamin and mineral supplementation on intelligence of a sample of schoolchildren," *Lancet* i (1988): 140–43.

446 American study: S. J. Schoenthaler et al., "Controlled trial of vitamin-mineral supplementation on intelligence and brain function," *Personality and Individual Differences* 12 (1991): 343–50.

446 Children with most deficient diets benefit most: D. Benton and J.-P. Buts, "Vitamin/mineral supplementation and intelligence," *Lancet* 335 (1990): 1158–60.

447 Eight-point IQ advantage from breast milk: Lucas et al., "Breast milk and subsequent intelligence quotient" (see full citation on page 483).

447 Duration of breast-feeding: Rogan and Gladen, "Breast-feeding and cognitive development" (see full citation on page 483).

447 Breast-feeding rates: A. S. Ryan, "The resurgence of breastfeeding in the United States," *Pediatrics* 99 (April 1997), http://www.pediatrics.org/cgi/content/full/99/4/e12.

447 Opportunity to play and explore: R. H. Bradley and B. M. Caldwell, "The relation of infants' home environments to mental test performance at fifty-four months: A follow-up study," *Child Development* 47 (1976): 1172–74.

448 Study of adopted babies: L. Beckwith, "Relationships between attributes of mothers and their infants' IQ scores," *Child Development* 42 (1971): 1083–97.

449 Music for Georgian newborns: K. Sack, "Georgia's governor seeks music start for babies," *New York Times* (January 15, 1998).

449 College students: F. H. Rauscher et al., "Music and spatial task performance," *Nature* 365 (1993): 611; F. H. Rauscher et al., "Listening to Mozart enhances spatial-temporal reasoning: Towards a neurophysiological basis," *Neuroscience Letters* 185 (1995): 44–47.

450 Preschoolers: F. H. Rauscher et al., "Music training causes long-term enhancement of preschool children's spatial-temporal reasoning," *Neurological Research* 19 (1997): 2–8.

451 Early musical training: R. Nowak, "Brain center linked to perfect pitch," *Science* 267 (1995): 616.

452   Nurturing: M. H. Bornstein, "Mothers, infants, and the development of cognitive competence," in H. E. Fitzgerald et al., eds., *Theory and Research in Behavioral Pediatrics*, vol. 4 (New York: Plenum, 1988), pp. 67–99; Bradley and Caldwell, "The relation of infants' home environments."

452   Gifted teenagers: M. Csikszentmihalyi and I. S. Csikszentmihalyi, "Family influences on the development of giftedness," in *Origins and Development of High Ability*, CIBA Foundation, pp. 187–206 (see full citation on page 508).

453   Quality time: M. J. Moorehouse, "Linking maternal employment patterns to mother-child activities and children's school competence," *Developmental Psychology* 27 (1991): 295–303. Surprisingly, Moorehouse and others find that the amount of quality time does not differ significantly between working and nonworking mothers.

453   Fostering attention, persistence, and motivation: Rutter, "Family and school influences" (see full citation on page 515); Bornstein, "Mothers, infants, and the development of cognitive competence"; D. J. Messer, "Mastery, attention, IQ and parent-infant social interaction," in D. J. Messer, ed., *Mastery Motivation in Early Childhood: Development, Measurement and Social Processes* (London: Routledge, 1993), pp. 19–35.

454   Authoritative parenting: S. M. Dornbusch et al., "The relation of parenting style to adolescent school performance," *Child Development* 58 (1987): 1244–57.

454   Parental expectations in three nations: H. W. Stevenson et al., "Mathematics achievement of Chinese, Japanese, and American children," *Science* 231 (1986): 693–99.

454   Mathematics achievement in the 1990s: G. Vogel, "School achievement: Asia and Europe top in world, but reasons are hard to find," *Science* 274 (1996): 1296.

455   Role of fathers: J. H. Pleck, "Paternal involvement: Levels, sources, and consequences," in M. E. Lamb, ed., *The Role of the Father in Child Development*, 3rd ed. (New York: John Wiley, 1997), pp. 66–103.

456   Schooling raises IQ: S. J. Ceci, "How much does schooling influence general intelligence and its cognitive components? A reassessment of the evidence," *Developmental Psychology* 27 (1991): 703–22.

456   Older kindergartners vs. younger first-graders: F. J. Morrison et al., "Nature-nurture in the classroom: Entrance age, school readiness, and learning in children," *Developmental Psychology* 33 (1997): 254–62.

457   Israeli study: S. Cahan and N. Cohen, "Age versus schooling effects on intelligence development," *Child Development* 60 (1989): 1239–49.

457   Advantage of preschool: R. Sheehan et al., "Factors contributing to success in elementary schools: Research findings for early childhood educators," *Journal of Research on Childhood Education* 6 (1991): 66–75.

458   Disadvantage of academic preschools: L. Rescorla et al., eds., *Academic Instruction in Early Childhood: Challenge or Pressure?* (San Francisco: Jossey-Bass, 1991).

Index

Note: Page numbers in *italics* refer to illustrations.

About the Author

LISE ELIOT, a graduate of Harvard, received her Ph.D. in neuroscience from Columbia University. She has published numerous papers in the field in professional journals, and is an assistant professor at the Chicago Medical School. She lives outside Chicago with her husband and three young children.